Blow the Candle Out

"Unprintable" Ozark Folksongs and Folklore

VOLUME II

Folk Rhymes and Other Lore

Blow the Candle Out

"Unprintable" Ozark Folksongs and Folklore

VOLUME II

Folk Rhymes and Other Lore

VANCE RANDOLPH

Edited with an Introduction by

G. LEGMAN

THE UNIVERSITY OF ARKANSAS PRESS
FAYETTEVILLE   1992

96 95 94 93 92   5 4 3 2 1

The paper used in this publication meets the minimum requirements of the American National Standard for Permanence of Paper for Printed Library Materials Z39.48-1984. ∞

Library of Congress Cataloging-in-Publication Data

Randolph, Vance, 1892–1980
    Unprintable Ozark folksongs and folklore/Vance Randolph; edited with an introduction by G. Legman.
      p. cm.
    Includes bibliographical references and index.
    Contents: v. 1. Roll me in your arms — v. 2. Blow the candle out.
    ISBN 1-55728-231-5 (v.1). — ISBN 1-55728-237-4 (v.2)
    1. Folk poetry, American—Ozark Mountains Region. 2. Folk songs, English—Ozark Mountains Region—Texts. 3. Bawdy songs—Ozark Mountains Region—Texts. 4. Ozark Mountains Region—Popular culture. I. Legman, G. (Gershon), 1917– . II. Title.
    PS477.5.B37R36 1992
    782.42162'1307671—dc20
                                         91-17685
                                           CIP

To
Herbert Halpert

CONTENTS

INTRODUCTION

This collection of unexpurgated contributions to American folklore, and specifically to sexual folklore, most of which has never before been seriously handled in English, forms the second and final volume, *Blow the Candle Out,* of this set or series. The first volume, matchingly entitled *Roll Me in Your Arms,* covers the presumably unprintable folksongs and ballads collected with music by Vance Randolph in the Ozark highlands of Arkansas and Missouri over the forty years from 1917 through 1957. None of this material has ever been published before. Almost all of it was refused and rejected by the original publishers of Randolph's earlier folksong and folklore volumes strictly because of his refusal to modify or expurgate it for publication.

The first main division of Randolph's so-called "Unprintable" collection: section A (*Roll Me in Your Arms,* and the first part of *Blow the Candle Out*), comprising the Ozark Folksongs and Ballads with or without tunes simultaneously collected, does show more or less the same logical arrangement as his larger work, *Ozark Folksongs* (1946–50) in four volumes, from which these materials had been editorially reserved. But the further sections in the present volume seem to have been brought together strictly in the order of their collection "in the field." They were intended then only for repository purposes in manuscript, at that point, in the Library of Congress and Kinsey Institute for Sex Research, Indiana University, and in microfilm copies in a few other university libraries of folklore orientation.

This also probably explains the curious and often hasty and infelicitous choice and position given to some of the items, particularly at the opening of section B, "Vulgar Rhymes from the Ozarks," the titles of which the present editor has not often considered himself authorized to change. It is clear that Randolph's purpose was simply to make sure that his important collectanea would not be lost and could be consulted eventually by interested folklorists. Thus the titles of all the following sections speak for themselves: C, "Bawdy Lore from Ozark Children"; D, "Ribaldry at Ozark Dances"; E, "Bawdy Elements in Ozark Speech"; F, "Obscenity in Ozark Riddles"; G, "Folk Graffiti from the Ozarks"; ending with H, "Unprintable Ozark Folk-Beliefs."

This last title in particular shows the development of Randolph's thought and tolerances, over the years and decades of his collecting folksong and folklore among the Ozark highlanders, whose lore he often spoke of in his earlier writing as "survivals of a primitive society." Referring to the British and Scottish rural areas from which the principal Ozark population originated, via the Appalachian mountain-range settlers and those in Canada, since the late-seventeenth and eighteenth centuries, and from whose folk-traditions those of the Ozarks so largely derive.

What are now tolerantly and politely called "folk-beliefs" in the title of section H here were in the first drafts of Randolph's collections, and his earlier books, just plainly superstitions: a hard word to define. The folklorist Wayland Hand once instantly lost all hope of further contact with a good friend and valuable informant for having used that word unguardedly, in reference to the still enormously popular Levantine nonsense of astrology, of Pharaoh's magicians in *Exodus,* 7:11. Even though the same Bible threatens with death exactly such "wizards" in *Leviticus,* 20:6–27, or even one "that hath a familiar spirit (of divining)," like the Witch of Endor in 1 *Samuel,* 28. Vance Randolph's Ozark witch-women go much further than that, and boast of midnight sex-orgies with the Devil himself on Sowcoon Mountain in southwest Missouri, including fabulous details concerning the Devil's (ice cold) penis, which is exactitude indeed.

Where does superstition end, and mere "error" begin? When all the world's folk believed that the earth was flat, and the proud center of the universe, was that a "superstition," a "folk-belief," or just a pre-scientific mistake? Most people nowadays have given up the flatland belief, though we certainly still cling tenaciously to the haughty Ptolemaic notion that our world is surely the essential hub and center of the universe. And accordingly, we send out well-swaddled astronauts and electronic sounds and spy-camera satellites, like twenty-first-century buccaneers and conquistadores, to scout out new and more salubrious colonies in "our" imperial heavens, for us overcrowded former flatlanders to inhabit and pollute inevitably in their turn. Error?—superstition?—neurosis?—scientific and humanistic blunder?—or, more politely, just a "folk-belief"?

It is unfortunate, yet perhaps significant, that Vance Randolph's unstudied organization of his collected material has resulted in the present "Vulgar Rhymes from the Ozarks" (section B) opening not with the humorous animal-and-bird items begun at Nos. 3 to 5, but with an exceptional group of what can at best only be called anti-gallant and anti-woman toasts and "sardonics," and could be called worse. One of the first of these, "Lady Lil," usually known as "Our Lil" in mock pride, was also by some equally significant happenstance the very first bawdy ballad ever published—twice!—in any folklore journal in the English language; the first time, I should admit, by myself. (See the endnote to rhyme No. 2*E*.)

Songs and recitations like these strike every facet of the male-supremacist *macho* "mucker pose," and with evident pride and relish. They glory in the lethal fantasy of sexual intercourse as a primeval or prototypical symbolic battle for personal and social dominance between the sexes, acted out with the sexual organs as the weapons of choice. Some even go so far, unchallenged ever by the appreciative audience, as to fantasize the actual killing of the sexual partner by means of that intercourse, "sickly" gloating on repellent murderous and cadaverous details, and of course glorifying the rampant male penis as the heroic ordnance-symbolic fatal weapon. Or, on occasion, the presumably equally dangerous and dominant *vagina dentata* or Gorgon Medusa, destructively toothed and out for castratory revenge. This is the male-ordeal legend of "Sir Gawain and the Hag" (Child Ballads Nos. 33–34, "Kempy Kay"), also Puccini's ugly modern opera, *Turandot* (1924), and the even more fearful legend of "The Serpent Bride," Oliver Wendell Holmes' *Elsie Venner* (1861).

Although songs and recitations of this kind are, in fact, sometimes delivered by women, and to male or mixed audiences, it should be observed that practically all such sado-masochistic materials are essentially male, and not female fantasy projections. See further on this very important question of male-female folk stereotypes, of status, dominance, and fantasy danger or revenge during sexual acts, the remarkable and now wrongly forgotten historical collaboration, *The Dominant Sex* (1923) by Mathilde and Matthias Vaerting, which first and best exposed the social origins and psychological structuring of these struggles for competitive sexual status in human history. In the end-notes to the folksongs and recitations in the present volume, special attention has been given, almost for the first time, to these naïvely *macho*—and *machista*—elements, as well as in the broader discussion of women's use of bawdy language and forthright folksongs, in the introduction to volume I, *Roll Me in Your Arms*.

The bibliography with which this volume closes includes almost all of the works cited in Randolph's own field-notes, and many of those used by the present editor in preparing the end-notes here. The brief and sometimes truculent prefaces to the various sections are by Vance Randolph, as signed, to whom the pronouns "I" and "my" also refer, *except* in sections A and B (Folksongs, and Rhymes) where reference is to the present editor.

G. Legman
La Clé des Champs
Valbonne (A. M.) France

SECTION A

Songs Collected without Tunes

---

181. THE LORD MADE THE SUN

The Lord made the sun, and then he made the wind,
Then he made a possum a-settin' on a limb;
The possum et persimmons till he couldn't see,
Then he up and farted and blowed down the tree.

Sung as above by Mr. G. P., Reeds Spring, Missouri, March 4, 1947. He had it from an old man at Garber, Missouri. This is part of a blackface minstrel song, "The History of the World," also called "Walk in the Parlor," from the opening line of the chorus, popular in the 1870s and earlier. Randolph gives a full version of this in 5 stanzas (but without this one) in *Ozark Folksongs*, No. 288, collected at Cane Hill, Arkansas, on Christmas Day, 1941, with tune and chorus, the singer calling it "The Creation" and including the following:

> Oh lightnin' is a yaller gal, she lives in de clouds,
> Thunder is a black man, 'cause he holler loud;
> When he kiss de lightnin' she dodge an' wonder,
> Run away an' tear her clothes, an' dat makes de thunder.

See: Jordan and Kessler, *Songs of Yesterday* (1941) pp. 231–33, who give the text and tune from "the Popular Extravaganza of the Buffalo Gals at the Adelphi" theatre, copyright 1847 by C. H. Keith. Also, *Trifet's Budget of Music,* No. 15 (March 1892) p. 123; Cox (1925) pp. 501–03; Brown, vol. III: pp. 399–403; Hubbard (1961) pp. 335–38; and Ira Ford, pp. 278–80. In Randolph's *Ozark Folksongs* (1948) vol. II: p. 373, No. 288, ed. Cohen (1982) pp. 246–47, further reference is made to a version in the Gordon manuscripts, No. 1113, and ten other texts in the Western Kentucky Folklore Archive (now at the University of California, Los Angeles). The present song is similar but superior to another such minstrel set of "Just-So" rhymes entitled "The Darkies' Sunday-School," on Biblical stories rather than natural history mock-explications: in Brown, vol. III: p. 400, with a naughty stanza on Salomé's "hootchy-kootch," and vol. III: pp. 512–14, the related "I Was Born About Ten Thousand Years Ago."

182. PETER AND BALLYX

Oh, Cunt it was a mill-pond, Peter couldn't swim,
Ballyx was a bad man, (he) pushed Peter in.

A. Sung by Mr. A. P., Ozark, Arkansas, October 23, 1948. He said it was common in the early 1890s. The song typifies the sexual organs (*Peter,* the penis; *Ballyx,* the testicles, "ballocks") as human beings, and their instinctive impulsions as partaking of human "free will," and therefore of shame and blame, and right and wrong, or good and evil. This liberates the possessor of these organs from oppressive feelings of responsibility or wrongdoing, as to the actions of these presumably autonomous sexual organs.

This idea is typical of Protestant religious background, with ideals of personal worth and unforgivable sin, as distinct from Catholic cultural latitudinarianism, owing to the possibility of confession and weekly forgiveness, as well as irresponsible sexual holidays at Carnival, often with masks and costume disguises, to reduce feelings of responsibility (as identifiable individuals) to fairly close to zero. This is also the secret of *audiences,* of all religions, being willing to accept and enjoy real or media spectacles (usually sadistic, but also sexual), of which they refer to themselves as *never* partaking "personally." Their eye-pleasure, heart palpitation, and enormous emotional identification with and at the spectacles watched are thus denied and refused as "not personal," even if they experience some visible and palpable physical reaction. "Nothing personal!"

B. From Mr. J. C., Eureka Springs, Arkansas, August 24, 1951. He heard it in Moberly, Missouri, about 1912:

> Prick and Ballyx run a race
> Up and down a hairy place,
> Prick fell down and skinned his face,
> Ballyx says, It is no race.

C. From Mr. J. E., Webster Groves, Missouri, October 13, 1951. Country boys sang it as early as 1895, he said:

> Peter slipped in a place
> Where Ballyx couldn't foller,
> Peter says, Don't get sore,
> It only cost a dollar.

D. From *The Merry Muses of Caledonia* (edited by Robert Burns, 1799–1800) pp. 117–18, as "Madgie Cam' to My Bed-Stock," probably the original song of which the texts preceding form part, though not present in this version:

> Madgie cam' to my bed-stock,
> To see gif I was waukin';
> I pat my han' atweesh her feet,
> An' fand her wee bit maukin.
> *Fal, lal, &c.*
>
> Cunt it was the sowen-pat,
> An' pintle was the ladle;
> Ballocks were the serving-men
> That waited on the table.

The sexual terms in stanza 2 are printed as only their first and last letters, with a dash between, in *The Merry Muses*; these letter-expurgations are extended and restored here. In 1:2, *gif*, if; *waukin'*, waking. 1:3, *atweesh*, between. 1:4, *fand*, found; *maukin*, literally "pussy" or "bunny." 2:1 *sowen-pat*, gruel-pot. 2:2, *pintle*, penis. In 1:1, a *bed-stock* is the wooden bar across the end of an oldstyle wooden bedstead. Tune: "Clout the Cauldron," in Johnson, *Scots Musical Museum* (1787) vol. I, No. 23, as "The Turnimspike."

In 1:3, *atweesh* (between) *her feet,* where a modern speaker would say "between her legs"; compare the additions to *Leviticus* (chapter 26) by the prophet Ezekiel (his 5:10) and to *Deuteronomy* by the prophet Jeremiah (his chapter 19:9, etc.) concerning the "vision" of the siege of Jerusalem half a thousand years later, *Deuteronomy* 28:56–57: "The tender and delicate woman among you, which would not adventure to set the sole of her foot upon the ground for delicateness and tenderness, her eye shall be evil toward the husband of her bosom, and toward her son, and toward her daughter. And toward her young one *that cometh out from between her feet,* and toward her children which she shall bear: for she shall eat them for want of all things, secretly in the siege." (King James translation, London, 1611.)

183. THE JOHNSTOWN GIRLS

... We rode and we rode all down the lane,
And such a sight it never was seen,
But four and twenty Johnstown girls
A-dancing naked on the green.

Such a gettin' upstairs I never did see,
Such a gettin' upstairs it don't suit me.

We romped and wrastled all that day,
And fucked her well all through the night,
. . . .
The Johnstown girls don't need no light.

When I woke up my love was gone,
And she had took her fill of me.
I rode a many-un down the lane,
But the Johnstown girls I never did see.

A. Sung as above by Mr. L. J., Farmington, Arkansas, February 5, 1942. It is part of a longer piece he heard about 1910. We owe to the flair and acumen of Professor Henry M. Belden of the University of Missouri, who was the main author of the research notes for Vance Randolph's *Ozark Folksongs,* the identification of this, probably Randolph's most interesting recovery in the Ozarks, as being "somehow suggestive of 'The Wee, Wee Man'" (Child Ballad No. 38). This has never been collected anywhere, in modern tradition, but one other time since 1828, by the marvelously spirited Mrs. Maude Minish Sutton, as below, giving the whole story as modernized from the eight most identical Scottish dialect versions, all from the late eighteenth or early nineteenth centuries, given by Child. The "Johnstown" girls here may refer to Johnson County in northwest Arkansas. Randolph notes: "The 'getting upstairs' refrain occurs in several play-party jingles" (no references).

B. Sung by Mr. Saunders, Salem, Forsyth County, North Carolina, for Mrs. Maude Minish Sutton (not named, but identified by her note, below, on the stanza expurgated by the singer), about 1920; in Brown, vol. II: pp. 47–48. The singer did not state where he learned the song, but at Brown, vol. II: p. 361, concerning the ugly, anti-gallant "I Wish My Love Was in a Ditch," the same singer "said that his grandfather had known more stanzas but that he himself had forgotten them." We are beholden to Mr. Saunders, to Mrs. Sutton, to the editors of the Frank C. Brown *Collection of North Carolina Folklore,* and to the publisher, the Duke University Press, for the possibility of including this crucial and almost-complete text, on which see further Child-Bronson No. 38, where it is given as part of the "True Thomas the Rhymer of Erceldoune" song-legends dating from the thirteenth century.

Though for some reason Child does not anywhere allude to this in his headnotes to No. 37 ("Thomas Rhymer"); No. 38, the present song; or No. 39 ("Tam Lin" or "Young Tamlane"), the present story is of the protagonist-singer kidnapped by the "Wee Wee Man" to make love to the dancing, naked supernatural young women. Overlooked in Child's sources, it is in essence the legend of Tannhäuser and his one magical night of love—which in reality is a hundred years long—in the symbolic Venusburg cavern with the Queen of Love, after which he forever speaks only the (prophetic) truth: her *Morgengabe* of gratitude to him. As Child well remarks, however (vol. I: p. 322-note): "How the lover escaped in this instance is not explained. Such things happen sometimes, but not often enough to encourage one to take the risk."

> Oh, I went walking one fine day upon the Gomont pier O,
> I saw a little fairy man, no bigger than my ear O.
>
> He wore a coat all gold and green, no bigger than a thimble,
> But he was strong as any buck, like a gandy dancer nimble.
>
> I took him up and I set him down, and I put him on my knee,
> And there he threw a mitchèd stone as far as I could see.
>
> I told him he was a fine, brave man, and as strong as he could be,
> And he said to me, My bucko lad, come you along with me.
>
> So I went his way along the lane, and soon we found a castle,
> And a fine naked lad(y) came out, to see if I would rassle.
>
> *("One stanza Mr. S. censored here, a description of the girl's physical qualities. He didn't know me well enough."* —Mrs. Sutton's note on the manuscript.*)*
>
> She was the gayest wench for bed I ever saw in all my life,
> If Elder Thomson had been there, she could have been his wife.
>
> We lay in a bed all covered with pearl, and I did often kiss her,
> And now at night alone in my bunk I surely do (often?) miss her.
>
> When I woke up and found her gone, I knew I could not stay,
> So I spied around for my little man, but he had gone away.

In 2.2, *buck,* a young Negro; *gandy-dancer,* a railroad track-walker, owing to the odd step required by the close-set ties. 3:2, *mitchèd,* misheard or misunderstood for the original Scottish *mickle,* large. 4:1, *brave,* tall, fine, valiant (not "courageous"), now obsolescent except in French. 4:2, *My bucko lad,* "my bully boy," a term of approval. 5:2, *rassle,* wrestle, a common form of rough sexual testing or preliminary body contact, similar to couple dancing, especially among country people. 7:1, *gay, gayest,* pleasure-loving, wanton (not "blithe or merry"); this is the Scottish sense of the word from which nineteenth-century "gay girl," a prostitute, and mid-twentieth century "gay," homosexual, is derived. In 7:2, *Elder Thomson* replaces "the King of Scotland" in the older Child Ballad versions. On the identification of ministers, parsons, bishops, priests, and monks such as Rasputin, as sexual supermen (so also the Devil at Black Masses, or his human surrogate there, the unfrocked "Black Priest"), see G. Legman, *Rationale of the Dirty Joke* (vol. II: *No Laughing Matter,* 1975) pp. 481–83 and 764–72.

184. SALLY MACWHORTER

Did you ever see Sally MacWhorter?
Sure, she pisses a hell of a stream;
She flings it a mile an' a quarter,
An' you can't see her ass for the steam!

A. Sung by Mr. L. K., Cyclone, Missouri, September 10, 1930. Mr. K., who is of Irish origin, learned it near Pineville, Missouri, in the 1890s. The title is a pun on "make water." The tune is "My Bonnie Lies over the Ocean," but here without the chorus. It has also been collected with the chorus, or refrain, as an echoic repeat of the last line (New York, 1947):

Ass-hole, ass-hole,
You can't see her ass-hole for steam,
For steam!—Ass-hole, ass-hole,
You can't see her ass-hole for steam!

B. Mr. R. S., Galena, Missouri, February 24, 1947, heard this fragment about 1899, near Hurley, Missouri:

She can make water a mile an' a quarter,
Out of her shaggin' machine.

C. Mr. J. E., Webster Groves, Missouri, April 8, 1948, recalled this from the 1880s:

Did you ever see Bridget make water?
She could piss an elegant stream.
She could piss two yards an' a quarter,
And you couldn't see Bridget for steam.

Contests in urination, as to distance or height of the stream ("pissing against the moon") are common among young boys. Note that it is the woman's sexual quality that is here really being assimilated to her urinary powers. In *The Stag Party* (edited by Eugene Field, Chicago, 1888–89), there is a poem about a girl who, on a challenge, "pisses higher than all the boys" by turning around, bending forward, and urinating retromingently like a lioness, thus topping their mark.

185. AFORE DAYLIGHT

Wife sings:
Oh, ye dirty old blackguard,
How dare ye presume
To piss on the floor
With a pot in the room?
Oh, I'll wallop your arse
With the braw of the broom,
Afore daylight in the mornin'!

Husband sings:
My first wife, God rest her
Sweet soul, she is dead,

> But were she alive
> I could shit in the bed,
> And wipe me old arse
> On the hair of her head,
> Afore daylight in the mornin'!

Sung by Mr. J. C., Eureka Springs, Arkansas, August 14, 1951, to the tune of "The Auld Irish Washerwoman" or "The Wild Irishman," No. 140 here. He heard it at Moberly, Missouri, about 1912. In 1:3, *piss on the floor,* a dirt-floored room is to be understood; 1:4, *pot,* chamberpot. Note the Gaelic *braw,* meaning "brave," in stanza 1:6, for the largest or heaviest part of the broom. European country women in the centuries before this one, and as recently as World War I, would beat their husbands in the morning (especially for being drunk the night before) with the twig-end of a besom broom. This is still used in the permitted flagellation of adolescent students on the buttocks in British and Japanese private schools. In a sex-reversal of the rôles, compare the equally scatological No. 26 here, "The Old Woman Pf-fft."

It is unfortunate that the singer gave no details as to the method of performance of the song. This is typically a *controverse* for two voices, both often taken by the same singer, as in "Bollocky Bill the Sailor," or in the non-bawdy recitation, "Pay the Rent!" in which one performer takes *three parts,* using a bowtie held in different positions to help the audience distinguish the parts: Susie Sweetheart, the girl (falsetto voice, bowtie held at head level as a hair-bow); John Strongheart, her lover (bowtie held daintily at neck level); and Rudolph Rassendale, the Villain (Boo!! *Boo-oo-oo!!*—bowtie held at upper lip level as a moustache, the sign of an "evil seducer"). Dialogue: *R: "Pay the rent!"*—*S:* "I *can't* pay the rent!"— *R:* (evil laugh): "Then fork over your Pale Pink Body!"—*John* (arriving just in the nick of time, and Punching the Villain in the Nose): *"I'll* pay the rent!" (The bowtie meanwhile in continuous motion.) Sometimes Rudolph Rassendale also waves the bowtie in the air, representing The Muggidge (on the family homestead), and threatens to foreclose, with line: "I. have. the. *pypers!*"

In homey entertainments of song form of this kind, in Ireland, the singers sometimes do a matching soft-shoe dance while singing. This is also a tradition in the Shakespearean theatre, still today, as in *Henry V,* where one male character surprises another climbing out of his lady-love's window, and twits him on it. G. Legman was once astonishingly favored with a slightly improper "song and dance" of this kind by a strikingly beautiful young Irishwoman, of about thirty-five, waiting for her plane with her fiancé at the airport at Nice, France, at Christmas 1964. She danced lightly and well, and sang even better, but would not sing anymore after I made a terrible *gaffe.* Just as she was about to begin another song, she asked archly, "Who would you say are the most beautiful women in the world?" And I to answer flatfooted: "My mother is Roumanian, so I guess Roumanian women are the most beautiful." "Well!" said the Irishwoman, visibly miffed, "I don't care *how* long you've lived in France. You're certainly not very gallant!" And she would not sing another note. The dance-song she had sung was a fast anapestic jig dating from the seventeenth century, about which more will be learned in Opie, *Oxford Dictionary of Nursery Rhymes,* No. 544, p. 433:

> There was an auld woman, and what do you think?
> She lived upon nothing but vittles and ink.
> Yes! Vittles and ink were the main of her diet,
> But this dorty auld crayture would nivver be quiet!

186. SWEET EVALINO

Evalino an' I, one evenin' in June,
Went fishin' all alone by the light of the moon.
She fished for suckers an' I fished for bass,
Evalino she fell in, right up to her a——

Ask me no questions an' I'll tell you no lies,
Evalino she fell in, right up to her eyes . . .

Sung by Mr. L. K., Cyclone, Missouri, August 18, 1931. He learned this song near Cyclone, about 1890, but could recall only this one stanza. A "tease" song, on the style of "Peter Murphy" or "At Brighton," Nos. 52 and 238 here, in which the erotic or scatological rhyming word expected is evaded, with some innocuous term following on after the opening syllable. The present song is based upon, though it does not precisely parody, a well-known sentimental favorite, "Sweet Evelina," in Brown, vol. V: p. 424, with further references; and Pound, *American Ballads and Songs* (1922), which Dr. Schinhan calls "an interestingly different version, of which the text is well known." Randolph adds note of other polite texts in Chapple, *Heart Songs* (1909) pp. 417–18; Ford, *Traditional Music of America* (1940) p. 403; and his own *Ozark Folksongs* (1950) vol. IV: p. 344. The tune to which the present song was sung is "The Auld Irish Washerwoman" or "The Wild Irishman," No. 140 here, but in 3/4 time; and so also "Afore Daylight," No. 185, but with a different ending. However, this is not identical with the tune used for this song in Brown, vol. V: p. 424. Note that a highly erotic, in fact purposely dysphemistic parody version, as "Down in the Valley" or "Sweet Abelina," is begun above at No. 166.

187. PECKERWOOD

Way down south in Arkansaw,
Peckerwood fucked his mother-in-law;
The judge he says, It ain't no sin,
Because them peckerwoods ain't no kin . . .

Fragment sung by Mr. J. H., Joplin, Missouri, July 12, 1924. It was part of a long "ditty," he said, that used to be popular at Pea Ridge, Arkansas. In 1:2, *peckerwood,* a "hillbilly," also a woodpecker; 1:4, *ain't no kin,* the meaning being that the mountain "hillbillies" don't bother to get married anyhow, which works out as a brilliant evasion of the laws against incest, or marriages within forbidden limits of consanguinity. The tune is "Ta-ra-ra-*Boom*-de-ay!"

Ray Wood, in *What Happened to Mother Goose?* (1946) p. 74, prints what appears to be a cleaned-up version of this song, and particularly weak in its last two lines. This turns on the phrase "kissing-kin," ostensibly meaning within the family relationships permitting marriage:

Down in the swamps of Arkansaw,
A bullfrog kissed his mother-in-law;
The jaybird said it was a sin
To kiss one another when they were kin.

188. JAYBIRD SETTIN' ON A LIMB

> Jaybird settin' on a hick'ry limb,
> He winked at me an' I winked at him;
> Picked up a rock an' hit 'im in the ass,
> Knocked old jaybird down on the grass.

A. Sung by Mr. E. H., Hot Springs, Arkansas, April 8, 1938. He heard it near Fort Smith, Arkansas, in 1891. The tune is the same as the preceding song ("Peckerwood," No. 187), namely "Ta-ra-ra-*Boom*-de-ay!" Ray Wood, in his *Mother Goose in the Ozarks* (1938) p. 41, has one of his usual mild versions of this, on the same style as that of "Peckerwood" preceding, not really Mother Goose's fault at all.

B. Mr. F. S., Eureka Springs, Arkansas, June 24, 1951, contributed this version of the last two lines as an isolated couplet. He heard it in Yell County, Arkansas, about 1935. G. Legman, at the same period, in Ann Arbor, Michigan, collected from a southern student a similar couplet, but with the second line beginning: "R'ar back, scare back . . ." and the frank statement that the meaning was a polite threat to bugger the person spoken to:

> Jaybird, jaybird, setting in the grass,
> Draw back, draw back, shoot him in the ass.

C. A text, possibly fragmentary, from Mrs. M. M., Springfield, Missouri, April 30, 1946:

> Jaybird a-settin' on a hickory pole,
> Draw back, draw back, shoot him in the hole.

This would seem to be related to an eighteenth-century nursery rhyme in *Tommy Thumb's Pretty Song Book* (about 1744) vol. II, in which the bird involved is "Little Robin Red Breast," which is discussed further at "Cock Upon a Pear Tree," No. 217*B* below. The stanzaic pattern there is briefer and more staccato, and will not fit the "Ta-ra-ra-*Boom*-de-ay!" tune here. These two evidently overlapping strains are therefore treated separately.

189. MY LITTLE ORGAN GRINDER

> *Rio, Rio, son-of-a-bitch!*
> *World's biggest bastard,*
> *Bully I feel!*
> *Straight from the whorehouse,*
> *Pecker like steel,*
> *With my little organ grinder!*

> When I was young, my damfool luck,
> All the maidens I did fuck;
> Fucked 'em all, an' knocked 'em up,
> With my little organ grinder.

> Laid 'em on their mother's bed,
> Rubbed their titties till they bled,
> Busted through their maidenhead,
> With my little organ grinder. . . .

A. Sung as above by Mr. R. K., of Mena, Arkansas, April 1954, in New York City, to Beverley Legman-Keith, my wife, and his own, for purposes of the present work, during my absence in France. The singer stopped in his ultra-*macho* song after the first two stanzas, and stated that he had made a mistake and wouldn't sing any more of this song for an audience of women because it was "too rough." This sort of gallant masculinity, at least when not alone "with the boys," is not always observed. Some male singers obviously erotically, but hatefully, enjoy singing what they consider the vilest songs possible before women, especially if the women are young and beautiful.

When the objection was made, in this case, to encourage the singer to continue, that the song was "pretty crude already," he replied: "Well, it gets a lot cruddier." Which is a fact. The complete text, which has been recovered only once (Stanford, California, 1961, recollected as learned there in 1950) is seven stanzas long and continues with inflicting all sorts of erotic bodily harm on the woman, always with the singer's "little organ grinder," and this is described in a gloating and humiliating way, finally killing her with it, and putting her in her tomb (rhyming with "womb," of course), and then masturbating on her grave (rhyming with "knave"). A complete macho *primer.*

The present singer would not allow his tune to be transcribed, nor any further stanzas to be written down (even without his singing them), as hesitant singers sometimes will. A tune is given, however—probably not the same one—in Logsdon-Neal, *The Whorehouse Bells Were Ringing* (University of Illinois Press, 1989) pp. 235–37, entitled "Old Horny Kebri-O," with text recollected from about 1920, and a different chorus, beginning: "Shagging away . . ."

B. As Text *A* above shows very little of the development of the song, a more recent text is given here for comparison, in which the wording of the opening and chorus are as usually collected. It too stops without concluding. It is taken from the ROTC Southwest Ordnance *C.A.C. Folio* (1945?) p. 4. As usually sung, the song begins with the chorus, very fast and driving:

> I took my girl to the City Hall,
> Spread her legs from wall to wall,
> Fucked her till I made her bawl,
> With my little organ grinder.
>
> > *Rio! Rio! bully-O Rio!*
> > *Jesus Christ, how bully I feel!*
> > *Straight from the whorehouse,*
> > *A pecker of steel,*
> > *Is my little organ grinder!*
>
> I took my gal to the country-side,
> And on her belly I did slide (ride),
> Fucked her till I (she) damn near died,
> With my little organ grinder.
>
> I put my gal against a stump,
> Took a crack at her big rump;
> Missed her rump, split the stump,
> With my little organ grinder . . .

Variants in parentheses in the text above are as collected in the Stanford, California, 1950–1961 version mentioned earlier. Note in 2:3, *till I (she) damn near died,* which goes on to the woman's actual death in the Stanford version, thus expressing very openly the Freudian/Wagnerian "sadistic concept of coitus" which is basic to this song, and involves killing, or fantasying the killing during intercourse of one or both participants, "preferably" the woman in this Tristan and Isolde confrontation.

The song can perhaps be dated by the approbatory interjection *"Bully!"* which I have heard still seriously used in conversation by old-timers of the 1900s period, as recently as 1948. This was made fashionable, in his outdoorsman pose, by President Theodore Roosevelt (1901–1908), whose favorite word it was, as meaning "Well done! Fine!" It is doubtful that the "Rio! Rio!" chorus dates earlier than that. Compare the identical opening lines of *macho* brag from the 1890s with version *A* here, from "When I Was Young" ("The Battleship *Maine*") at No. 51.

Care should be taken to avoid confusing the present song, "(My Little) Organ Grinder," owing to its "Rio! Rio!" opening chorus, with "Hi Rio Randy-O" ("The Galloping, Ralloping Dandy-O"), No. 148 above. The present song is also entitled by various singers: "Hickabrineo," "Mickabrineo," "Shagging Away," and "Rio! Rio!" Herbert Halpert found a version in southern New Jersey, about 1939, with titling chorus line, "With my old Horny Knickabriney-O"; and the 1920s text and tune given in Logsdon-Neal, pp. 235–37, are entitled "Old Horny Kebri-O." This is evidently a very popular song among men—of a certain kind—despite its brutality, or rather *because* of its brutal sexual swagger: that is its key.

190. KATY MOREY

> Come gentlemen and ladies all, and listen to my story,
> And I'll relate to you how I ruined Kitty Mallory . . .

A. Fragment as above from Mr. J. E., Webster Groves, Missouri, April 8, 1948. Randolph's field-note: "A long ballad popular in the 1880s, he says, but he can remember only the first two lines." This is perhaps the most striking example in the Randolph Collection of the "tragic delay" in frankly collecting the authentic bawdy texts of folksongs, because of waiting until most of the old-time singers have died off, and the others surviving are clearly suffering from large memory-lapses if not actually the Alzheimer's syndrome of old age. Here a singer recollecting a "long ballad," from over fifty years before, can deliver only the *two opening lines.* While just below at *B,* another singer, perfectly in possession of his faculties, can remember only the *two closing lines* of the chorus or text from forty years earlier.

In the center, as very often, between these two fragments, Randolph leaves us with a large blank, perhaps in part due to the striking fact that although he began noticing Ozark folksongs as early as 1916, he did not seriously collect them, owing to his difficult struggle making a non-academic living otherwise, until the mid-1920s and early 30s. He made his most active but least productive sweep-around almost too late, as many of his dates of collection silently witness, only in the 1940s in preparation for his forthcoming *Ozark Folksongs* collection in four volumes, which might have been five if they had not been expurgated by the press editor.

B. Mr. Jack Conroy, on whom see further Logsdon, pp. 160–61, remembered a fragment of a similar song he heard at Moberly, Missouri, about 1912, when he was fourteen years old. The chorus ends:

> . . . I thought I had the best of Maggie Reilly,
> But the son-of-a-bitch she got the best of me!

C. By the greatest of good fortune, Dr. Kenneth Goldstein collected the complete text, in both bawdy and "polite" versions, from one and the same singer, a fifty-two-year-old former farmer and handyman, at Asheville, North Carolina, in August 1957. See further in the notes following:

> Come all you friends of fun and sport, and listen to my story,
> I'll tell you how I made a plan to cheat young Katy Morey.
> I went into her father's house just like a bright young fellow,
> I told her that the plums were ripe and getting full and mellow.

I told her that my sister Peg was down among the flowers,
And wished that she would come that day and spend a happy hour.
I waited then till she was gone, and then I followed after,
And when I saw no one in sight I swore I'd have my way, sir.

I went to her and squeezed her hand; she seemed quite pleased but whispered,
I fear my dad might come this way, and sneak up unbeknownst, sir.
Then Kate she says, You climb that tree till he has passed away, sir,
Then we can go to yonder field, and sport the day away, sir.

I climbed the tree she pointed to, not being the least offended,
And Kate she stood down there and smiled, to see how I ascended.
I swung and switched to climb that tree, and at the top I stopped, sir,
I tore my shirt and scratched my shins to stop sweet Katy's fears, sir.

Then Kate she laughed to see my plight, You're nothing but a goat, sir,
You can pick the plums and eat the grapes; my father's nowhere near, sir.
If you were but one half the man that you pretend to be, sir,
You'd have laid me down and plied my cunt to see what fruit grew there, sir.

Then Kate she turned and ran away; I swore myself a fool, sir,
I promised that I'd have that maid before the year was done, sir.
I swore I'd stretch that maiden's cunt and taste the fruits within, sir,
And prove to her that men and goats have cocks to plumb those depths, sir.

(I swore I'd screw that maiden down, and fuck till I grew tired,
And if she had a child by me, she'd find no goat I'd sired.)
And if that maiden liked the sport, and ask to drink of love, sir,
She'd find my cock was like a straw from which she'd have to suck, sir.

Now Katy's mine and lives with me and never tires of fucking,
But if she should she bends right down and turns her mind to sucking.
And if sweet Kate should like the taste and ask to drink of more, sir,
I'd have her then play with my balls till I could come again, sir.

(And now I'll stop, I've sung enough, I married her that year, sir,
And every time she smiles at me, I think of climbing trees, sir.)
And now I'll stop, I've sung enough, this song grows kind of rough, sir,
But when I'm in sweet Katy's arms I fuck and fuck and fuck, sir.

Note in 1:1, *sport,* once referred almost exclusively to sexual play, as in the King James translation (1611) of *Genesis,* 26:8, "And behold, Isaac was sporting with Rebekah his wife." See also 3:4 and 7:3 here; and also in such now out-dated phrases as "sporting house" (of prostitution), "sporting life" (once the name of a brand of condoms), and "a sport" ("big sport," or "hot-shot sport," etc.) as meaning a gambler and/or pimp and criminal. This meaning has been progressively driven out since the 1900s by the connotation of athletic games and contests as "sports."

In 1:4, *plums were ripe and getting full,* a covert allusion to the mystical or mythical affliction of "stony gullions" (from the French *couilles, couillons,* testicles) or "swollen balls," by means of which "horny" young swains in the 1920s and 30s, and perhaps since, attempted to elicit pity from their over-cautious sweethearts and convince them to be "kind." 2:1, *Sister Peg was down among the flowers,* was having her menstrual period ("the flowers," also from the French) and was emotionally depressed over the "loss" of that month's possible child. 3:3, *passed away,* accidental Freudian slip, since "passed away" usually refers to dying, here of the repressive father figure, who never actually appears in the song but is conjured up mentally (internalized super-ego) to prevent the sexual "sport." 5:1, *goat,* fool, chump, patsy, usually in verbal phrase, "to make one the goat," originally a Biblical reference to the scapegoat of the wilderness of Azazel, in *Leviticus,* 16:21–22; and compare the young lamb *vs.* old ram at the intended sacrifice of Abraham, of his son Isaac, in *Genesis,* 22:6–13.

In 7:4, *have to suck,* the oragenital act is here considered by the man to be a humiliating subservience by the oral participant (whether male or female), as is still widely felt in Anglo-American *mores,* despite the presumed New Freedom increasingly since the post-War 1920s, the fellational training-film *Deep Throat* in the 1970s, etc. But compare the calmer acceptance by the woman in 8:2–4 here; though again the observation by the singer in 9:3, that his oragenital reference is "kind of rough," i.e., obscene.

This extraordinarily complete and unexpurgated text of 1955 may perhaps stand-in for the many fragmentary relics of lengthy but now forgotten bawdy songs and ballads of the 1880s to the 1920s, tantalizingly incomplete as reported in Randolph's and other modern British and American collections. It was transcribed three times by Dr. K. Goldstein, at Asheville, North Carolina, from the same singer, Mr. S. H., a fifty-two-year-old former farmer and handyman, first in 1955, then in July and August 1957, the first and last times before all-male audiences. The second time, singing before a mixed audience of men, women, and children, the singer stopped after stanza 6:1–2 (having expurgatorily omitted 5:3–4), and ended abruptly with bracketed lines 9:1–2, thus delivering the usual published version. At his final male-audience rendition, August 1957, here given, he sang basically the same version as in 1955, but omitted bracketed lines 7:1–2 (for reasons unknown) and added lines 8:1–2, one of the rare oragenital references in country folksong in English, and one of the most detailed. But compare "The Whorehouse Bells," No. 196 below.

D. Kittredge has noted in *Journal of American Folklore* (1922) vol. 35: p. 385 that this is the male counterpart or riposte to Child Ballad No. 112, "The Baffled Knight," on a fifteenth-century French tale, often retold; but the two songs have only this non-textual plot connection. (It is *not* Kinloch's modern Scottish rewrite, "Jock Sheep," mentioned by Child, vol. II: p. 480, in which the man tricks and decoys the girl to the forest by disguising himself with a pillow as a pregnant woman!) He cites a broadside text, "Katy Mory and Poll and Mistress," dating from 1830, which is apparently now lost. The oldest extant form is in the Jones-Conklin manuscript (American, about 1850) ending with frank yonijic symbolism, in which *split,* tree-crotch, is metaphoric for *cunt:*

> And now I climb as sweet a tree as ever plumb grew on, sir,
> I will try the split and graft it in, and see what fruit 'twill bring, sir.
> My song grows rough, I've sung enough, and now I'le quit my rhyming,
> And ev'ry time she smiles at me, she makes me think of climbing.

E. Gordon manuscript 3359, from Ben A. Ranger in Santa Rosa, California, 1927, entitled "Miss Kitty O'Horey," has similar lines and a chorus. The girl's rejection and ending are as follows, but there are no other bawdy lines. As in all versions, they finally marry:

> I climbed the tree, she pousted (?) me, not being the least offended,
> Kittie she stood and looked at me, to see how high I ascended.
> > *Tiddie oddie, ing-I-O; tiddie oddie, ing-I-O.*
> Your ugly looks I do despise; you look like one big owl, sir,
> You fuck your plums and snap the stones, you may have your own fun, sir . . .
>
> And now I've climbed the prettiest tree that ever bore peach or pear, sir,
> I have split the limbs and I've grafted in, to see what fruit it would bear, sir.
> Now I have sung enough of this poor stuff, so now I will cease my syning,
> But every time Kittie winks at me, good Lord I feel like clim'ing.

Other than the Jones-Conklin manuscript of 1850, and the "lost" broadside of 1830, as above, see polite texts (listed chronologically): Laws, N-24; Harold Thompson and Edith Cutting, *A Pioneer Songster: The Stevens-Douglass MS. of Western New York, 1841–1856* (1958) pp. 9–11, also printed in Thompson's splendid upstate New York chronicle, *Body, Boots and Britches,* p. 411; Sharp, *Appalachians*

(1932) vol. II: pp. 119–21, No. 115, three texts, all with choruses, collected in 1916, noting that: "The tune is a variant of 'The Dowie Dens o' Yarrow,' several versions of which are given in *The Journal of the Folk-Song Society* 5:110–13"; G. L. Kittredge, in Tolman and Eddy, "Traditional Texts and Tunes," in *Journal of American Folklore* (1922) vol. 35: pp. 385–87; Colonel Henry W. Shoemaker, *North Pennsylvania Minstrelsy* (1923) p. 130; Bess Alice Owens, "Songs of the Cumberland Mountains of Kentucky," in *Journal of American Folklore* (1936) vol. 49: p. 232; Mary O. Eddy, *Ballads and Songs from Ohio* (1939) p. 64; Gardner and Chickering, *Ballads and Songs of Southern Michigan* (1939) pp. 393–94; Earl C. Beck manuscript, pp. 400–03, in his *Folklore of Maine*, p. 110, collected in Kingman, Maine, 1948.

Lomax, *Our Singing Country* (1941) p. 122, has a version sung by Aunt Molly Jackson, who explains prefatorily that this song was in her time considered too "rough" for children; and see also Norman Cazden, *Abelard Folksong Book* (1958) Part 2: pp. 32 and 119, ridiculing the idea of a relationship to Child-Bronson No. 112, and discussing the 1830 broadside. A polite text was also reported by Herb Greer from Manchester, England, 1959 (though not necessarily British) beginning: "Come all you joky boys and listen to my story, I'll tell you a plan I fell upon, to steal Miss Katey Dorey." This is much like the Campbell and Sharp Appalachian texts of 1916, but far more complete, and with chorus: "*Lye too-lye, ring dee ring-dum, Lye too-lye, ring dee ring.*" The evidence suggests that the song has always been considered in America as erotic, merely omitting the bawdy stanzas when sung for an unsuitable audience.

F. Aside from the old unexpurgated fragments recovered by Randolph, *A* and *B* above, and Goldstein's recovery of the complete text *C*, in 1957 in North Carolina, the latest bawdy fragment or survival is a two-line opening sung by an old-time bookseller in New York City in 1944, Mr. Ed Lipton; though this may be connected instead with "Molly Monroe" ("Old Moll Roe"), No. 18 above:

> As I was going down the street last night,
> I met Miss Katie Morey,
> I grabbed her by the cheeks of her ass,
> And I rammed it home to glory.

191. BRIDGET O'DONAHUE

> Bridget Donahue, I'll tell you what to do,
> Go upstairs and get in bed, and I'll come up there too.

A fragment from Mr. J. E., Webster Groves, Missouri, April 8, 1948. He said it was sung in rural Missouri in the 1880s. This is part of a parody of a popular song of the 1870s, of the same name, credited to "Johnny Patterson, the Great Irish Clown." See Ford's *Traditional Music of America* (1940) p. 227, giving one stanza; and compare the brief text in Randolph's *Ozark Folksongs* (1950) vol. IV: p. 300.

192. THE LEG OF THE DUCK

The leg of the duck, the leg of the duck,
I gave it to Nelly to stick in her belly,
The leg of the duck, the leg of the duck.

A. Fragment from Mr. J. W., St. Louis, Missouri, October 2, 1948. Mr. W. had it from a lady-friend whose family was Irish—came from Galway, Ireland, *via* New Haven, Connecticut, to St. Louis. See a further account of unembarrassed bawdy singing in this woman's family during her childhood in Ireland, elsewhere in this collection. In the refrain: *the leg of the duck*, the penis, from its shape; by implication used as a dildo.

B. Also apparently from Galway, Ireland (see Brenda Maddox, *Nora: A Biography of Nora Joyce*, 1988, an admiring feminist biography of the vulgar and practically illiterate Galway street prostitute who became the wife and sado-masochistic Egeria of James Joyce), a somewhat fuller text is given in the opening pages of the remarkable "Nighttown" play-within-the-play of *Ulysses* (1922) by James Joyce, as of a spring night in 1905 in the prostitution slum of a great Irish city: *"In a room lit by a candle stuck in the bottleneck, a slut combs out the tatts from the hair of a scrofulous child. Cissy Caffrey's voice, still young, sings shrill from a lane" :"*

I gave it to Molly because she was jolly,
The leg of the duck, the leg of the duck.

I gave it to Nelly to stick in her belly,
The leg of the duck, the leg of the duck.

She has it, she got it, wherever she put it,
The leg of the duck.

Another fragment or allusion to this song appears in the brief street-ballad collection included in the Francis Place manuscripts in the British Museum Library, dating from about 1820 in London.

193. THE DOMINECKER ROOSTER

Shit, says the rooster to the hen,
I ain't had any since God knows when. —
Shit, says the hen unto the rooster,
You don't come around like you use-ter.

A. Sung by Mr. F. G., as above, Pittsburg, Kansas, April 21, 1916, to the tune of "Turkey in the Straw." This is one of the earliest dates of collection in the Vance Randolph "Unprintable" manuscript. The singer heard it in Green County, Missouri, in the 1880s.

B. From Mr. C. B., Joplin, Missouri, November 24, 1940, and fitting the same tune somewhat better than *A* preceding. In line 2, *had a piece*, "of tail" or "of ass," understood, meaning sexual intercourse; so also, even more elliptically above, *had any*, and *have a little*, below. The *old red rooster* here openly typifies or speaks for the human penis:

Says the old red rooster to the little red hen.
I ain't had a piece since God knows when.
Says the little red hen to the old red rooster,
You don't come around as often as you useter.

C. Mr. Carl Withers, folklorist, New York City, November 7, 1948, recalled the following as a children's rhyme heard in southern Missouri. This version is strictly "dominecker" (dominant?) *macho* sexual announcement or brag, and does not include any riposte by the hen, representing the woman. In line 1, *bow-legged*, when referring to a girl or woman almost always means having had extensive sexual experience. This rhyme was also known among men (though not among children, who know only the forms above) on both the east and west coasts of the United States, as late as 1986. *"Dominecker"* refers literally to gray-barred rose-combed Dominique chickens:

Said the dominecker rooster to the bow-legged hen,
I ain't had any since the Lord knows when,
So rustle up your feathers an' h'ist up your tail,
'Cause I'm goin' to have a little if I have to go to jail!

D. A cowboy-poet, Mr. G. R., employed as a publicity man in Phoenix, Arizona, April 1986, who recited a version very close to *C* above, to G. Legman, added the information that there were more stanzas he couldn't remember, one of them being *a mock epitaph for the singer's own penis* "when it wouldn't stand up any more." And that it all formed part of a minstrel song he had heard a Negro cowboy, "down on his luck" sing, when cadging for drinks in a local beer joint about twenty or more years before. Answering pretty closely to this description is "Here Lies the Body uv Po' Little Ben" (without any "Dominecker Rooster" stanza) at Brown, *North Carolina Folklore*, vol. III: p. 523, collected about 1920, concerning which Dr. Newman I. White notes at Brown, vol. III: pp. 529–30, that it "Has the refrain of the 'Watermillion Song.' I can sing this refrain from memory . . . A fairly familiar 'coon' song of the early 1900s." The tune for this refrain is given in Brown, vol. V: pp. 302–03, noting that there is "a different version" in *Minstrel Songs, Old and New* (Boston: Oliver Ditson Co., about 1920) p. 160. The following is presumably the self-epitaph for the singer's impotent penis:

Here lies de body uv po' little Ben,
We ain't gwyne to see 'im in I dunno when.
'Twus hard to part, but it could 'a' been wuss,
'Case Ben mou'ter been a no-'count cuss.

Ham bone am sweet, beats all de meat,
'Possum am very, very fine,
But give me, O, give me de bestes' thing of all,
'Tis de watermillion hanging on de vine.

E. The following appears as a "tease" reduction merely to a joke or catch, in *Apples of Eden* (about 1980?) p. 28, entitled "Admiration," and refers to taboo sexual relations between white women and black men:

Said the little red hen to the big black duck,
You look like hell, but you sure can swim!

194. POLECAT GREASE

Polecat grease and 'possum belly,
All you gals come taste my jelly.

All I want in this whole creation
Is a likely yaller gal and a big plantation.

Called her Fuzz 'cause her hair is wavy,
Pull out my peter and dip it in the gravy.

Sung by Mr. G. P., Reeds Spring, Missouri, February 10, 1947, as above, to the tune of "Black-Eyed Susan," No. 125 here. He had it from Mr. F. K., also of Reeds Spring, at a much earlier date. In 1:1, *polecat*, a skunk, here invoked simply to be crude. In 1:2, *jelly*, semen; the invitation is not so much actually to taste, as stated, but to sample. 2:2. *likely*, Barkis's "willing," available for love-making; 3:2, *gravy*, often semen, but here refers to the woman's *cyprine*—its correct but little-used name, from Kypros, Cyprus, one of the Greek names of Venus—the vaginal pre-coital lubricant liquor. *Fuzz*, in 3:1, often refers to crinkly head-hair, here of the "yaller gal," refers here to the similarly curly pubic hair.

The term "yaller gal" used in 2:2 is not only a euphemism for avoiding the contemptuous term "nigger" (from the Spanish *negra*, black), but also avoids any concern with such mock scientific or racial "color" nuances as "mulatto," "octoroon," and so forth. This recurrent "yaller gal" theme also indicates and implies the preference since slavery times, for "high yaller" Negro women as sexual partners (also in houses of prostitution), and as projected mothers of continuously lighter-colored children, themselves being born as slaves however.

Compare "'Possum Sop an' Polecat Jelly" in Randolph's *Ozark Folksongs* (1949) vol. III; p. 154, and "Black-Eyed Susan," No. 568, ed. Cohen, pp. 410–11. For similar lines in other play-party and dance songs, see Lomax, *American Ballads and Folk Songs* (1934) pp. 286–88, in nine stanzas and chorus; and Wood, *Mother Goose in the Ozarks* (1938) p. 43, these being essentially polite versions of "All I Need to Make Me Happy," No. 32 here; but see also "The Girls around Here," No. 109.

195. THE ELEVENTH STREET WHORES

I rowed my boat out in the ocean,
I rowed my boat up to the shore
. . . .
I rowed right up to the 'Leventh Street whores.

I saw a sign, Won't you please come in?
. . . .
She says, Kind sir, would you like to jazz?

. . . . in eight days,
I got a dose of the bull-headed clap.
I rolled my dick out on the table,
And the gooey goo comes oozin' out.

. . . . if I ever get well,
And the 'Leventh Street whores can go to hell!

These fragments are all that could be transcribed of a long venereal disease ballad sung by Mr. D. M., Walnut Shade, Missouri, April 4, 1942. He learned it two or more years before in a Civilian Conservation

Corps war-preparation camp near Gainesville, Missouri. In 2:4 *to jazz*, to have sexual intercourse; this was the original meaning of the word in America, spreading from Negro to national white use after about 1915, via New Orleans, St. Louis, and Chicago, both with this meaning and in reference to *jazz* music, therefore called by other less contraband names at first, such as *barrelhouse*, *ragtime*, and *race*. Humorous mock-definition: *"A Whore's Life—Three weeks of jazz, and one week of ragtime."* In 3:2, *the bull-headed clap,* not "bull-headed," stubborn, but of the penis, swollen up at the glans or head (like a catfish or blackfish, sometimes so denominated) owing to *the clap*, gonorrhea; 3:3, *dick*, penis; 3:4, *goo*, sometimes semen, but here purulent matter.

196. THE WHOREHOUSE BELLS

A. Recited by Mr. R. C., Eureka Springs, Arkansas, January 4, 1955. He heard it sung near Green Forest, Arkansas, about 1914. Note that aside from the more rustic conclusion here, than that in the Arizona version below, the entire wording of the song is different except for the *rhymes:*

> The whore-house bells were ringing clear,
> A man stood at the door,
> Stood all day long with a big hard on
> A-waiting to screw a whore.
>
> He picked his choice, they went to bed,
> They both pulled off their clothes,
> He says, I want you to suck this juicey prick
> And blow it through your nose. —
>
> I can't do that, the old whore said,
> With her underlip full of snuff;
> I'd like to suck your juicey prick,
> But the blowing would be tough.
>
> I know a game we both can play,
> Before that we get through,
> Just stick your face in this old twat of mine
> And I'll suck your prick for you. —
>
> I can't do that, the old boy said,
> 'Twould make me go stone blind;
> Just turn your old ass round to me
> And I'll give it the boar-hog grind.

B. As this song has been collected only twice, complete, from oral tradition in America, the other quite different variant is given for comparison. It formed part of the remarkably preserved repertory of 155 cowboy songs and others, of Mr. Riley Neal, a retired cowboy of Gisela and Payson, Arizona, in 1969, then seventy-nine years old. He was born in 1891 in Gisela, died in 1983, and learned most of his songs before 1920. He sang, "wrote out," and transmitted his entire repertory to the collector, Guy Logsdon, of Tulsa, Oklahoma, who courageously included fifty of Neal's songs, not omitting or expurgating the bawdy ones, in his unparalleled collection, *The Whorehouse Bells Were Ringing, And Other Songs Cowboys Sing* (University of Illinois Press, 1989) this one at pp. 145–48, with tune, and complete repertory list, pp. 12–14, using the title of the present song as the main title of the book.

This title of course involves the classic pun on "bells" and "belles," beautiful women, but refers literally to the large, loud, old-fashioned "twist 'em" doorbells on the front doors of American 1900s bawdy-houses (under their ostentatiously large street-numbers, imitated from those in New Orleans' "Storyville," as in France), which would begin ringing more and more frequently as the men's workday ended and night drew on. Note that only the story-line and the main rhymes are similar to version *A* preceding; the rest of the wording and the final stanza are entirely varied and different, owing to oral transmission:

> The whorehouse bells were ringing
> And a pimp stood at the door,
> He'd had a hard on all day long
> To screw some dirty whore.

> At last his choice being made,
> They went upstairs and pulled off their clothes,
> He asked her if she'd suck him off
> And blow it through her nose.

> Oh no! Oh no! the old bitch cried,
> Her head was full of snuff;
> I'd like to suck your juicy cock,
> But blowing is too tough.

> But I know a game we both can play,
> You'll like it when we are through;
> I will suck your juicy prick
> While you lick out my flue.

> The whorehouse bells were ringing
> While this pair's upstairs in bed,
> Trying to get their guns off first
> Into each other's heads.

Except for the client's demanded "specialty" (see below), there is little here that requires glossing. In *A* 3:2, *her underlip full of snuff*, a joke by the singer, as snuff would cause an intense burning sensation to the man's glans penis. *A* 5:4, *the boar-hog grind*, "unknown to the literature," as some special coital motion, but evidently an allusion to the boar-pig's strangely *spiral* penis, of which the physiological use or purpose is unknown, and a subject of much speculation among country children. In *B* 5:3, *get their guns off*, to achieve orgasm, a phrase dating from the era of uncertain flintlocks, which continued to be used in the backwoods until the Civil War. Compare the French *tirer un coup*, to fire a shot (said of males only).

C. Sung by Mr. J. C., Eureka Springs, Arkansas, August 24, 1951, who stated it was the beginning of a song he heard in Moberly, Missouri, about 1912:

> The whore-house bells were ringing,
> A man stood in the door,
> He'd fucked all night the night before,
> And was back to fuck some more . . .

As indicated by Guy Logsdon (1989) pp. 145–48, this song "appears to be a bawdy version of the 1893 sentimental song 'The Fatal Wedding,'" of which he gives the melodramatic story line. "The music was composed by Gussie L. Davis, the first successful black Tin Pan Alley composer," with words by H. W. Windom, and "quickly became a favorite in minstrel shows and vaudeville. The melody used phrases from Mendelssohn's 'Wedding March,'" appropriately. Logsdon notes texts and tunes of the original song in Spaeth, *Read 'Em and Weep* (1927) pp. 172–74; Randolph, *Ozark Folksongs* (1948) vol. IV:

pp. 277–79; and W. K. McNeil, *Southern Folk Ballads* (Little Rock, Arkansas, 1987) vol. I: pp. 110–12.

Extraordinary even for oragenital acts (on which see the unusually frank "Katie Morey" song-text at No. 190*C*, above), the somewhat peculiar erotic activity the client here demands of the old prostitute—who offers him the more classic "*soixante-neuf*" or "69" instead—is a standard French whorehouse joke or specialty, no longer much in style. It was brought to French New Orleans and Mexico during the early or mid-nineteenth century, when erotic books were legally published in the United States, especially in New Orleans, until the Comstock Law of the 1870s, and now again a century later.

It is described in the principal French manual of erotic technique, *Les Paradis Charnels* by "Dr. A.-S. Lagail" (anagram of Alphonse Gallais), first published in Paris, 1903, where it is reserved as the 136th and final posture or promised paradisiacal carnal ecstasy, among the well-named section of "Erotic Clowneries." There it is called—all the postures and specialties having allusive mnemonic names, to assist in remembering their details—"The Judgment of Solomon, or The Baby Cut in Half," this owing to its unexpected nasal snorting climax, which is the point of the present song. See further: G. Legman, *Oragenitalism* (1969) pp. 283–84, noting: "It is only a joke, of course . . . This has to be seen in profile."

Jocular erotic songs and ballads of this type would be sung typically in American whorehouses, until well into the 1930s and beyond, by either the prostitutes (for extra tips) or the waiting clients themselves, who would also drink whiskey or beer and play cards, sometimes to upright piano accompaniment by a Negro or white musician always addressed as "The Professor" (of music), who also often sang. See another such typical "whorehouse song" at No. 241, "The Boarding-School Maidens," and the end-notes on "Frankie and Johnny," No. 153, which is the most famous such modern song, having escaped into the general population during the 1920s.

197. TILL COCK GETS HIGHER

A. This is a *cante fable*, or folktale turning into a song-dialogue at some point, usually as part of a repeated element, and almost always as part of a controversy between the characters. See other examples of this kind at "The Fiddler's Bitch," and "The Bowl Is Yet to Fill," at Nos. 101 and 102*B* above. "*Cock*," here used interchangeably with "cunt," in line 1:2, is a southern dialect term only, from the French *coquille*, cockleshell or cowrie, metaphorically virginity, and also the vulva from its external shape. Mr. B. W., Eureka Springs, Arkansas, March 31, 1950, told this tale as heard near Berryville, Arkansas, about 1900:

A smart country boy went to a whore-house and asked a woman about rates, and she said the price was one dollar. The boy was horrified, and said flatly that he'd pay fifty cents, but not a penny more. The woman sang scornfully:

> Before I'd fuck for fifty cents
> I'd screw my cunt with a monkey wrench,
> I'd pull it off an' hang it on a wire,
> An' let it hang till cock gets higher.

The boy listened contemptuously, and replied:

> Before I'd pay a dollar for cock
> I'd let my prick get hard as a rock,
> I'd pull it off an' throw it on the floor,
> An' let it lay till cock gets lower.

B. Certainly not a version of the *cante fable* above, and connected with it only as to the subject of female prostitution as a profitable, and therefore to some degree socially acceptable activity (here projected on the presumably "immoral" backwoods or hillbilly mountain women of the Appalachian and Ozark uplands). The following once nationally popular song is sung to a tune very similar to "She'll Be Comin' Round the Mountain When She Comes," and variously titled "Nancy Brown" or "The West Virginia Hills":

> Out in West Virginia lived a girl named Nancy Brown,
> Such beauty and such talent there never had been found.
> Nancy and the deacon climbed the mountainside one noon,
> They went up in the mountains, but they came back mighty soon . . .

Sung by an unnamed lady in Galena, Missouri, June 17, 1942, and recorded by Vance Randolph for the Library of Congress Folklore Archive. Nine stanzas, with intermittent chorus about "*She came rolling down the mountain*, etc." delivered of this evidently musical-comedy style imitation hillbilly ballad, of which the stanza above is only the first. The plot is crudely prostitutory: Nancy refuses the deacon's advances, and also those of a cowboy (in West Virginia), but succumbs to the "city slicker with his hundred-dollar bills," who takes Nancy back up into the mountains in a Packard limousine, where this time she stays. However, "along came the Depression" (thus dating the song about 1930 to 1932), and "kicked the slicker in the pants; He was forced to cut expenses, so he had to cut out Nance." She comes back to the mountains "mighty pore," where, now, "the cowboy and the deacon, They are getting what they're seekin', And she's just like any West Virginia—lady!" (rhyming with "pore").

The original piece, entitled "She Came Rollin' Down the Mountain," was copyrighted by Buddy DeSylva, Brown and Henderson, who are almost certainly the composers, in 1932. The song was popular at the folk level until well after World War II, an unusually long period of popularity for a Tin Pan Alley production, clearly because of its presumably titillating subject. A six-stanza parody by Elliot Springs, to advertise his Spring Mills "Spring Maid" bedsheets, "with sprightly illustrations in color," was published in the *American Legion Monthly* and other national magazines (January 1952). This parody is without any allusion to the amateur prostitution which is the actual subject of the song, but is considered too common and economically necessary to be thought of as really disgraceful, at the folk level, especially during periods of mass unemployment, except when the prostitutes (principally to homosexuals) are boys.

198. ST. JAMES INFIRMARY

> I went down to St. James Infirmary,
> Saw my ba-*hay!*-bee layin' there,
> She was stretched out on a table
> (*spoken:* Stretched out on a *marble* table),
> So cold!—so sweet—so fair.
>
> Let 'er go, let 'er go, God *bless* 'er!
> (*spoken:* You know what I mean, fellas),
> Let 'er go, let 'er go, God bless 'er,
> Where-ever sh-*eee!* may be,
>
> She can look this whole world over,
> But she'll never find a *pimp* like me!
> No, never find a . . .
> (*spoken:* Sweet-lovin', hard-fuckin')
> Man like me! Yas . . . *man* like me!

A. Sung by Miss G. M., a young Mormon woman, at San Diego, California, October 1964, who had just returned from a semester at the University of Arkansas, Fayetteville, where she stated she had learned this "and all (her) sinful songs" from other girl students, having never been allowed to sing anything at home in Utah except "hymns and classical." She sang with great emotion, which seemed absolutely real and upset her small audience, singing in a low register to the well-known blues tune, and in an exaggerated Southern accent (not her own), intended to suggest a male Negro, and perhaps to "distance" her somewhat from the pimp-and-dead-whore situation described. In 2:2 *You know what I mean*, i.e., for "God *bless* 'er" in line 2:1 understand *"damn!"* The italicized words represent the singer's own heavily stressed emphasis, the voice soaring up climactically at 1:2, "ba-*hay!*-bee" (meaning lover, not infant), and 2:4, "sh-*hee!*" When I asked the singer after she had finished, since this was all there was to her song, what she thought the woman had died of, she surprised me by replying, "Oh, a disease, I suppose. Probably t.b. [tuberculosis]. Maybe she died having her baby." A very similar version was heard sung by a Negro lesbian professional singer, by G. Legman, in a midnight "beer-joint" in Dunmore, Pennsylvania, 1935, purposely as if sung by a man, the pimp. See his *Peregrine Penis: An Autobiography of Innocence* (1990).

B. Descended from an eighteenth-century English or Irish graveside lament, appearing on nineteenth-century British broadsides as "The Unfortunate Rake," and concerning a young soldier who has died of syphilis from consorting with "flash girls," the slow pace of the song is explained by the reference in the early versions to the dying man's directions for his funeral cortège with muffled military drums. In a nineteenth-century broadside version, sung by A. L. Lloyd in an album of *English Street Songs* (Riverside RLP 12–614, about 1958), the plain details are stated in the 3rd and 4th stanzas as to the venereal nature of the young man's fatal disease, which might have been treated with "salts of white mercury":

> As I was a-walking down by St. James' Hospital,
> I was a-walking down by there one day,
> What should I spy but one of my comrades
> All wrapped up in flannel though warm was the day.

> I asked him what ailed him,
> I asked him what failed him,
> I asked him the cause of all his complaint. —
> It's all on account of some handsome young woman,
> 'Tis she that has caused me to weep and lament.

> And had she but told me before she disordered me,
> Had she but told me of it in time,
> I might have got pills and salts of white mercury,
> But now I'm cut down in the height of my prime.

> Get six young soldiers to carry my coffin,
> Six young girls to sing me a song,
> And each of them carry a bunch of green laurel
> So they don't smell me as they bear me along.

> Don't muffle your drums, and play your fifes merrily,
> Play a quick march as you carry me along,
> And fire your bright muskets all over my coffin,
> Saying, There goes an unfortunate lad to his home.

C. A very large number of offshoots and parodies of this song exist, some adaptations to other professions and some frankly farcical, whistling in the dark by mocking the ugly death of the venereal diseases everyone has feared for five centuries since syphilis was brought back from the island of Haiti in the

1490s by the sailors of Columbus, and now, strangely enough, AIDS from the very same island, about 1950, though not recognized for thirty years. The serious cowboy version is called "The Streets of Laredo." Among the would-be mocks are the rowdy sailor ballad, "Wrap Me Up In My Tarpaulin Jacket" (about 1830), in which the dying sailor finally requests "six jolly fellows" whom he wants to carry his coffin, and then "let me fall with a bump" (an allusion to his expectation of going to Hell):

> Let them all start cursing and swearing,
> Like men that are going to go mad,
> Just tip a glass over my coffin
> Saying, There goes a brave jolly lad.

D. Another parody or "mock" is grafted onto a more recent form of this lament, "The Young Girl Cut Down in Her Prime," under the title of "Gambler's Blues." The present text *A* above is of this blues family, which has not been traced earlier than "race" recordings of the 1920s, and is not believed to be older than the 1900s. The farce version is sung by Dave Van Ronk—a 1950s white singer famous for his Negro-style singing, especially of a laceratingly intense rendition of "The House of the Rising Sun," No. 62 here—on a recording, *Ballads, Blues and a Spiritual* (Folkways FS-3818, about 1960), as first printed in Dr. Kenneth Goldstein's monograph on the whole history of this song, *The Unfortunate Rake: A Study in the Evolution of a Ballad* (1960) p. 8. This is supposedly sung to "the usual crowd" in Old Joe's barroom, by Big Joe McKennedy, "And his eyes were bloodshot red," who has just been down to St. James Infirmary, where his sweetheart is laid out dead, as above, but who ends with irreverent details in Negro gambler style as to his own eventual funeral:

> . . . When I die please bury me
> In my high-topped Stetson hat,
> Put a twenty-dollar gold piece on my watch chain,
> (So) my gang will know I died standing pat.
>
> I want six crap-shooters for pallbearers,
> A chorus girl to sing me a song;
> Put a jazz band on my hearse wagon,
> (To) raise hell as I stroll along.
>
> Well, now that I've told my story,
> I'll take another shot of booze,
> And if anyone should happen to ask you,
> Well, I've got those gambler's blues.
>
> *Let her go, let her go, God bless her,*
> *Wherever she may be;*
> *She may search this wide world over,*
> *Never find a sweet man like me.*

As can be seen, the only hint left here, almost invisible, as to the actual identification or fatal disease of the dead prostitute and her gambler-pimp who plans to die "standing pat" (covering his bets), is the term *sweet-man*, a Negro euphemism for pimp, but this is seldom realized by the generally unwitting folksong-revival audience. Compare, in version *A* 3.3 above, the frank and even insistent extension of "sweet-man" to "Sweet-lovin', hard-fuckin' *man*," which makes the matter quite clear.

E. In fact, the Van Ronk reconstitution, to consider it in its most favorable possible light, is really far less unrepentant than the authentic "Old Time Gambler's Song" it is attempting to recreate, almost unnecessarily, since the original exists in Gordon manuscript No. 1720, and has now been printed by the Fifes, in

Thorp's *Songs of the Cowboys* (ed. 1966) pp. 173–74, though not a cowboy version. It ends—to compare with *D* above—dripping with authenticity, as supplied about 1925 by Terrell McKay, who notes, "Widely known here among the old timers":

> When I die, just bury me in a box black suit,
> Blue shirt, roller hat, pair of shoes with toes so tall;
> Put whiskey in my coffin, deck of cards in my hands,
> Don't let them weep and wail, don't let 'em moan at all.
>
> Put marihuana in my coffin,
> Smoke it as you carry me along;
> Take even-rolling dice shooters for pallbearers,
> Coke sniffers to sing my funeral song.
>
> Put a twenty-dollar gold piece on my watch charm
> So the boys'll all know I'm standing pat,
> Put ice on my feet, for in the place where I'm going
> I won't even be cool with that . . .

It is notable that in this "Old Time Gambler's Song" the gambler finally admits, in poetic justice, that he is dying of the same thing as his sweetheart:

> You may search this wide world over,
> You'll never find another pal such as she . . .
> But if you follow me to the end of my story
> You'll find a blonde was the cause of it all.

See: most valuably, Dr. Goldstein's monograph *The Unfortunate Rake: A Study in the Evolution of a Ballad,* a twelve-page leaflet accompanying a recording of the same name (Folkways FA-2305, issued in 1960) giving twenty different historical texts, tunes, and parodies, and an incisive discussion of their development over two hundred years; also, as cited by Goldstein, Laws' *Native American Balladry,* p. 131, and *American Balladry from British Broadsides,* pp. 285–86; Wayland Hand, "Wo sind 'Die Strassen von Laredo'?" in *Festschrift für Will-Erich Peuckert* (Berlin, 1955) pp. 144–61, and Hand's "The Cowboy's Lament," in *Western Folklore* (1958) vol. 17: pp. 200–05; and Kenneth Lodewick, "'The Unfortunate Rake' and his Descendants," clearing the way for later researchers, in *Western Folklore* (1955) vol. 14: pp. 98–109. Also, on a much broader scale of access to modern texts, Belden, pp. 392–97; Brown, vol. II: pp. 614–18; MacKenzie, *Ballads and Sea Songs from Nova Scotia* (1928) pp. 301–02, the primary research done on this song; Randolph, *Ozark Folksongs* (1946) vol. I: p. 179; Reeves, *Idiom of the People,* p. 188; Scarborough, *On the Trail of Negro Folk-Songs* (1925) p. 94; and Sharp, *Appalachians,* vol. II: pp. 164–65.

Alan Lomax in his large popular conspectus, *The Folk Songs of North America* (1960) gives three different versions of the song, pp. 193–94, 362–64, and 384–86, with tunes to each; then stating concerning one of these, p. 496, of the great Negro prisoner singer, James "Iron Head" Baker, that "his version of 'The Sailor Cut Down in His Prime' has the finest of all recorded airs," but not giving it in this volume! (It is given in Lomax's *Cowboy Songs,* ed. 1938, pp. 420–21; and in Thorp, ed. Fife, 1966, p. 167.)

The Fifes do a tremendous round-up job in Child Ballad style, forty pages long, marred only by some unfortunate "reconstructed" conflations, in Thorp's *Songs of the Cowboys* (ed. 1966) pp. 148–90, on the totally expurgated "Cowboy's Lament" ("Streets of Laredo") version of this song. Though they truly observe, in animadverting on John A. Lomax's cheapjack populist bowdlerization and hoking-up of certainly all the purported cowboy songs he ever published, that: "The seven stanzas of 1908 ["Thorp's"] have a stamp of authenticity and realism that Lomax's bowdlerization lacks. Let us recall that our dying cowboy's literary progenitors, 'The Unfortunate Rake' and 'The Bad Girl's Lament,' were grim songs about the ravages of venereal disease and the ills of indulgence in cards, whiskey, and "wild, wild" women. It is true that in most of the cowboy forms of the song, these unpalatable images are attenuated, even replaced in some texts, by a namby-pamby transcendentalism compatible with Victorian *mores*."

Actually, the same could be said for all the profitably faked presentations of presumed cowboy songs, until Guy Logsdon's recent powerful and courageous publication of the old ex-cowboy Riley Neal's unexpurgated repertory as *The Whorehouse Bells Were Ringing* (University of Illinois Press, 1989), a volume that instantaneously made wastepaper of the whole namby-pamby literature of transcendentally falsified and attenuated "unpalatable" cowboy songs, which is basically most of them. A similar house-cleaning is long overdue as to the even more heavily expurgated sea-chanties, which have never yet been published anywhere complete, in the large and inappropriately shy and pussyfooting literature devoted to them for over a hundred years. It is hoped that my proposed but everywhere-rejected publication of the wholly unexpurgated and finally authentic *Sailing Ship Shanties* (manuscript 1958), consigned just that once to paper by Stan Hugill, the "Last of the Shantymen," will be the one last chance there will now ever be to set the sea-chantey record right.

199. SHORTENIN' BREAD

> Two little niggers layin' in bed,
> One turned over to the other'n an' said:
> > *You pee'd in my warm place!* (4 times)
>
> The doctor come an' the doctor said,
> Feed them niggers on shortenin' bread.

A. Sung as above by Mrs. M. M., Springfield, Missouri, October 21, 1941. She heard it in Stone County, Missouri, in the early 1900s. Recorded by this singer for the Archive of American Folksong, Library of Congress. A parody or continuation of the minstrel song, "Shortenin' Bread," on which see Brown, vol. III: pp. 535–36.

B. Sung by Mrs. E. H., Hot Springs, Arkansas, March 26, 1938. She heard it about 1921, but cannot remember the rest. The reference is of course to sexual intercourse, as in version *A* above: *my warm place*, my vagina:

> You pissed in my warm place (3 times)
> Shortenin' bread, shortenin' bread . . .

C. Gates Thomas, in *Publications of the Texas Folklore Society* (1926) vol. V: p. 163, courageously printed the following:

> Two little nigger babies layin' in the bed,
> One turned over, and t'other one said,
> > You've wet in my warm place,
> > Gwain tell my mammy,
> > You've wet in my warm place,
> > Gwain tell your mammy.

D. Various northern white-culture versions exist, some of them replacing the invidious reference to Negroes with an equally invidious reference to "old maids," in this case implied to be Lesbians as well.

These versions, which have been heard as recently as 1985, also often use unexpurgated *dénouement* lines for their humorous effect, in this case medleying-in the key line from a 1930s pop song. Collected from a sexually obsessed thirty-seven-year-old Irish-American engineer, New York, N.Y., 1939, only the opening, or a "tease" or "throwaway" (no more existing):

> (Briskly:)
> Two old maids in a folding bed,
> Two old maids in a folding bed,
> One turned over to the other and said:
> (Slow:)
> *I've got you under my skin!* . . .

E. In a brief collection entitled "Jody Cadence" of army marching songs, made at Shippensburg University, Pennsylvania, about 1985 by Major Joe E. Semon, item No. 17 shows the most recent form used in cadence-call marching, here referring covertly to masturbation, and ultimately to orgasm:

> Two old maids were lying in the bed,
> One rolled over to the other and said:
> I gotta go.—All the way.—
> Drive on.
>
> A little harder.—A little further.—
> I can't stop.
> I won't stop.—I gotta be.—
> Airborne.—*All the way!*

200. DAN, THE LAVATORY MAN

A. Text from Mr. J. W., St. Louis, Missouri, March 2, 1949. He learned it "in speakeasies and at parties back around 1930 and 1931. It is sung slowly and sadly. Each line has the same melody—three rising notes, three descending notes":

> Dan, Dan, Dan, the lavatory man,
> He takes care of the crap in the can,
> He dishes out the soap and he dishes out the towels,
> And all he gets is a *p-pf-f-ft* from the bowels.

B. Mr. Bill Zeleski, Elk Creek, Missouri, October 27, 1949, wrote to Randolph that he "composed this parody" in 1912, when he was in the United States Navy. He says that the Bosun's Mate chooses a member of the crew to serve as "Captain of the Head," which means latrine orderly. "If a man's name is Daniel," he writes, "he is traditionally the first choice for this detail. Don't ask me why, because I don't know." Here is the "Shit House Rag" as reported by Captain Zeleski, which is very close to the first report of the song, in *Full Dress Suits and Plenty of Whores*, as edited by Hilaire Hiler (manuscript Paris, 1928), as "The Crap-House Rag," with line 4 sarcastically *"Love* to hear the sound of the moving bowels":

> Dan, Dan, the lavatory man,
> Chief inspector of the crapping can,
> Picks up the papers, hangs up the towels,
> Listens to the music of the moving bowels.

> Now and then a fart is heard
> Accompanied by the music of a drowning turd.
> *With a rah, rah, rah! siss-boom-bah!*
> *That's the shit house rag, P-p-f-ft!*

C. Allen Walker Read, *Lexical Evidence* (1935) p. 39, found a similar wall-scribbling in a privy in the western U.S. in 1929:

> Tom, Tom, the lavatory man
> He's overseer of the cumpany can,
> Oh he picks up the papers
> And rolls up the towels,
> And listens to the music
> Of the discontented bowels.

See also, chronologically, other texts, of which only the first indicates the tune, as "Turkey in the Straw:" *Aloha Jigpoha* (Denver? 1945) p. 61; Starr, *Fighter Pilots Hymnbook: Smegmafax Addenda* (1959) p. 125; McWilliam manuscript (1961), "Dan Van"; *Snatches and Lays* (1962, ed. 1975) p. 39; *Be Pure!* (Perth, Australia, 1963) p. 2, reprinted in *"Argus Tuft" Folio* (1970) No. 4; Morgan, *More Rugby Songs* (1968) p. 98, a British rewrite, and compare p. 144, "The Sheik of the Lavatory"; De Witt (1970) p. 25, a *different* British rewrite; Hart, *"Complete" Immortalia* (1971) pp. 252–54, with music; Edwards, *Australian Bawdy Ballads* (1973) p. 85, similar to De Witt.

D. In the later versions, in which the toilet-attendant's name is more often "Sam," if he is named at all (as in a text in the Indiana Folklore Archive), it is made specific that this humiliating job is given to a Negro: "A little black porter," as one 1954 version puts it. Here is the opening of the more usual recent form, in this case collected in Scranton, Pennsylvania, in 1943, as in various later printed sources:

> Down in the subway, underneath the ground,
> There's an old colored man a-shufflin' round and round,
> A-sweepin' up the papers, a-pickin' up the towels,
> A-listenin' to the music ob the discontented bowels.

This is considered, in the mining town of Scranton at least, and possibly for the same reason in the Pittsburg, Kansas, mining area where Randolph was born, as a conscious parody of a rather disliked popular Irish song, attempting to sentimentalize the cruel and brutalizing work of coal-mining by referring aesthetically to the chunks of shining coal, ripped or blasted out of the underground seams, as "black diamonds" or even "dusky diamonds," since theoretically with a couple of thousand tons more of prehistoric pressure the coal would have turned to diamonds. Compare the much more honest, briefly popular work-song by Merle Travis (1946), a hit-tune of the 1950s about the life and work of miners, "Sixteen Tons," in Archie Green's *Only a Miner* (University of Illinois Press, 1972) pp. 295–323. The 1880s song here parodied, "Down in a Coal Mine," is from Howerth's *Hibernica*, a traveling American-Irish magic lantern and vaudeville show:

> Down in a coal mine, underneath the ground,
> Where a gleam of sunshine never can be found,
> Digging dusky diamonds all the season 'round,
> Down in a coal mine, underneath the ground.

201. SHE WOULDN'T AND SHE COULDN'T

> Sally on the railroad
> Coming from a ball,
> She wouldn't and she couldn't
> And she wouldn't come at all,
> But she h'isted up her petticoat
> And showed it to us all.

A. Mr. R. S., Galena, Missouri, February 24, 1947, said he heard this one, as above, near Hurley, Missouri, about 1897. Although the climactic line about "showed it to us all" is reminiscent of "Sweet Betsey from Pike," No. 82 above, who "showed her bare ass to the whole wagon-train," this is an entirely different song, to the tune of "Jenny on the Railroad." And, as differing from unrepressed if drunken Sweet Betsey, the erotically impotent girl here is, in desperation or defiance, showing not her backside but her front. Note that each of the three versions here uses a different term or aspect for her impotence or unwilling "frigidity": "wouldn't come," "wouldn't go," and "wouldn't fuck." Compare "Pretty Gal, Pretty Gal," No. 202 following.

B. Mr. J. C., Eureka Springs, Arkansas, August 24, 1951, heard it this way at Moberly, Missouri, in 1912:

> Oh, she wouldn't and she couldn't
> And she wouldn't fuck at all;
> She lifted up her petticoat
> And showed it to us all.

C. Mr. G. B., Reeds Spring, Missouri, October 17, 1950, recalled this following fragment, which was sung to the fiddle-tune "Jenny on the Railroad." In a joke version where: *The girl asks for more money than the man will pay, she pisses against the wall (or in the dust), saying contemptuously, "Here, take soup. Meat is too expensive." Or the man asks her to do so.* The gesture is ancient; see "pissing against the wall" as a sign of contempt in the cursing of Jezebel, in *2 Kings*, 9:8–37.

> Oh, she wouldn't and she couldn't,
> And she wouldn't go at all,
> But she lifted up her petticoat
> And pissed against the wall.

202. PRETTY GAL, PRETTY GAL

> Pretty gal, pretty gal, walkin' by the water,
> Rollin' of her eyes like Tooby-Jooby's daughter,
> Pulled up her dress to show her behind,
> Sights like that makes a man go blind!
>
> Pretty gal, pretty gal, better find your britches,
> Pretty gal, pretty gal, better tie your shoes,
> Pretty gal, pretty gal, better find your britches,
> Try to get to heaven 'fore the Devil hears the news.

> Whistle up a jaybird, whistle up a crow,
> Whistle up her snatch till she jumps just so,
> Keep on a-bobbin' till she begins to holler,
> Stick it up her ass an' give her half a dollar!

Sung as above by a lady in Carroll County, Arkansas, January 7, 1952. She heard it near Green Forest, Arkansas, in the early 1900s and said it was sung "to an old fiddle-tune." Presumably this was "Jump Jim Crow," on the possible unexpected origin of which see elsewhere in this collection. In 3:2, *snatch,* vagina, a seventeenth-century term.

In 1:2, *Tooby-Jooby's daughter* is difficult to identify, but may refer to the daughter of Jephthah (in *Judges,* 11:30–40, folk-identified as Jubal-Cain in *Genesis,* 4:21, the inventor of the harp and organ), whose classic folktale tells how he rashly vows to sacrifice the first to come forth out of the doors of his house when he returns from his victorious battle—expecting it to be the dog, the commentators explain—but it is his only child, a daughter, "come out to meet him with timbrels and dances." Instead of being put to death, she "goes up and goes down the mountains, and bewails [her] virginity," for two months, after which "she knew no man," this being considered, then as now, a virtual death. In the song here, 3:2, *snatch,* the vagina, an old slang term, played upon in Urquhart and Le Motteux's late-seventeenth-century translation of Rabelais as *snatch-blatch.* In 1:4, *Sights like that makes a man go blind!* The punishment of blindness for "sin" is Biblical, as in Sodom (*Genesis,* 19:11, and compare *2 Kings,* 6:16–29—one for the book!) and specifically for sexual peeping in such legends as that of Lady Godiva and Peeping Tom. Compare "She Wouldn't and She Couldn't," No. 201 preceding.

203. THE FOOT-LONG JOCK

Did you ever see a nigger with a foot-long jock?
It'll make you feel all juicy in the wrinkles of your cock.
You got to rub it up and shove it up,
And shake it with your hand,
Or the god-damn thing just *will not stand!*

Clearly sung to the rhythm or tune of "Turkey in the Straw," Song No. 132 here, which is also the inspiration of the final lines. Parody sent to G. Legman by the social critic, John Clellon Holmes, Fayetteville, Arkansas, 1984, as recited or chanted to him privately by one of his female students, "evidently as a challenge." According to Professor Holmes, she said she had learned the song "at a pajama-party with other girl students, and had doubtless confused" him with the erotic motion-picture actor, John "X." Holmes, celebrated precisely for his foot-long phallic over-development. Both men died in the same month of early 1988. Compare Randolph's Ozark folktale, "Twelve-Dollar Jack," in *Pissing in the Snow* (1976) No. 60, legendarily autobiographical.

The real interest of this present parody-admonition is in its unusual reference to the *labia minora* as "cock" is a confusing common southernism for the vagina, from the French *coquille,* cockle-shell, metaphorically the vulva or virginity; (already recorded in English as *cockle* in the late seventeenth century in John Aubrey's *Remaines*), and the perfectly frank allusion to female-dominant seduction and sexual relations between Negro and white. On the folk-belief that the Negro penis never really erects (which is missing from section *H,* "Unprintable" Ozark Folk-Beliefs, below), but "just waggles around like a donkey's prick" during erection, see G. Legman, *No Laughing Matter (Rationale of the Dirty Joke,* 1975, vol. 2: pp. 474–483) in chapter 13: "Castration: Negroes and Jews," where this and other similar superstitions are discussed.

204. MY PETTICOAT'S BROWN

All around my petticoat's brown, God knows,
All around my petticoat's brown,
I want you to fuck me like a hound.

I ain't had none, can't get a bit, God knows,
I ain't had none, can't get a bit,
If I got a little, I 'spect I'd shit.

Sung by Mr. Fred High, Berryville, Arkansas, October 21, 1950. In 1896 Mr. High traveled with a bunch of "cat-wagon" whores—young girls from Carroll and Washington counties, Arkansas, who made all the little towns along the Indian territory (now Oklahoma) border. It was a rough life, says Mr. High. Drunken women dancing naked, cowpokes firing pistols at random. One customer complained "This here shooting throwed me off! I had a stake raised, and now it's fell!" Mr. High recalled only the above fragment of a bawdy song the girls used to sing. In 1:3, *like a hound*, does not mean from behind, "dog fashion," but violently and intensely, like a "cunt-hound," a sex-obsessed man; 2:3 *'spect,* expect; in 2:1–3, *had none*, *get a bit*, and *got a little*, all refer to "getting" sexual intercourse.

As to the 1890s horse-drawn *cat-wagon*, or ambulant brothel, mentioned by the informant, John A. Lomax describes a very luxurious one, traveled in by a Gypsy mock beggar-and-prostitute couple, in *Adventures of a Ballad Hunter* (1947) pp. 42–44, the man referring to the woman as "My wife [who] shakes down the saps who like to hold her hand while she reads their fortunes in the stars." This type of prostitution flourished again briefly around U.S. Army training camps during World War II, the car-drawn trailers or even medium-large closed trucks used being still called *chippie-wagons*. A rare mimeographed erotic novel using that for title was published in America about 1942.

205. ARKANSAS IS A GOOD OLD SAW

Arkansas is a good old saw
But I don't like the set that's in it,
All day they whore, all night they snore,
And that's why I'm ag'in it.

There ain't no law in Arkansas
And the folks all fuck like foxes,
And all the stills in the Cookson Hills
Are made out of cundrum boxes.

Sung by Mrs. M. B., Springfield, Missouri, December 7, 1935. She heard it in Christian County, Missouri, probably in the 1920s. The Cookson Hills of the second stanza—and their bootleg whiskey stills—are not in Arkansas, but in eastern Oklahoma. In 1:2, *set*, word-play on the "-saw" in the pronunciation of Arkansas, and the *set* of sharpened saw-teeth; it is also found in other songs and wisecracks, for example in Marion Hughes, *Three Years in Arkansaw* (1905). In 2:2, *fuck like foxes*, alliteration only; no canines are observably very passionate, to compare with goats, or rodents like minks. This particular folk-alliterative has been extended by the 1970s to the comparison: "as hot as a fresh-fucked female fox in a forest-fire," *fox* also being used to refer to an attractive woman. In 2:4, *cundrum*, the folk pronunciation of *condom*, which is seldom the would-be elegant word used for the object in mind (more usually *rubber*, *stripper*, *safety*, *Merry Widow*—from a 1910s brand-name—and the hateful *scum-bag*). The mispronunciation *conundrum*, is a jocular Malapropism.

613

206. THE GALS IN ARKANSAS

Look at them gals in Arkansas,
Slippin' around, slippin' around,
They think fuckin' is against the law,
That's why they're slippin' around.

A. Sung by Mr. L. J., Farmington, Arkansas, February 5, 1942. He said it was a fragment of an old minstrel piece.

B. Black and Robertson, *Gold Rush Song Book* (1940) pp. 38–39, reprint "Sacramento Gals" from *Put's Golden Songster* published in the 1850s, with the following stanza:

There's many a gal from Arkansaw
Nipping 'round, around, around,
Who well remembers hollowing "haw,"
As she went nipping around.

207. MOON BIRD

Oh Moon Bird won't you be,
To a moon-struck Cherokee,
What you have always been,
And sure, it ain't no sin.

I'll bring that prick of mine,
And ram it into your spine,
It's ready all the time,
Sweet Moon Bird mine.

Sung by Mr. H. W., Joplin, Missouri, September 12, 1921. He learned it in Pittsburg, Kansas, about 1914. Parody of a sentimental song, popular about 1911. "Moon Bird" is the name of an Indian princess, in the "Redwing" tradition: see No. 178 above. Note the Irish music-hall diction "And sure," in 1:4.

208. AUNT JEMIMA

My Aunt Jemima climbed a tree,
As high as any steeple,
An' there she set the livelong day
An' pissed all over the people.

A. Sung as above to the tune of "Yankee Doodle" (see at "School Days," No. 88, preceding) by Mrs. H. B., Joplin, Missouri, September 4, 1929. There is also a "decent" version of this, which Randolph recorded for the Library of Congress, one presumes the expurgated lady up the tree here throws *apples* at the people, like Mother Eve in the Garden of Eden. Hudson's *Folk Tunes from Mississippi* (1937) p. 39, has a related piece called "Angie Mimey," clearly the same title in spite of the difference in perceived pronunciation.

B. Another stanza from Mrs. O. T., Farmington, Arkansas, October 30, 1951, which may however be more correctly part of "Yankee Doodle," No. 209 immediately following:

> Linus Barton was a-startin'
> With a load of hay,
> Elder Martin went to fartin'
> And blowed it all away.

209. YANKEE DOODLE

> Well, Yankee Doodle went to sea,
> Aboard a cutty clipper,
> He filled his ass with broken glass,
> An' circumcised the skipper.

A. Sung as above by a lady in Forsyth, Missouri, May 14, 1943. She first heard it in Taney County, Missouri, about 1900. The tune is of course "Yankee Doodle"; see at "School Days," No. 88. See also, for another use of the same quatrain, "She Sprang Aloft," No. 160, and "The Good Ship *Venus*," both at that number and in G. Legman, *The Limerick* (1953) pp. 107–08, and annotations pp. 403–04. On the special anal-aggressive type of castratory humor, see my *Rationale of the Dirty Joke* (vol. II: *No Laughing Matter*, 1975) pp. 174–83, "The Ganymede Revenge," a subject no longer considered at all humorous since the advent of AIDS in the 1980s.

B. From Mr. J. E., Webster Groves, Missouri, October 9, 1948. He heard country children sing these verses in the late 1880s. In 1:2, *'lasses,* molasses; 2:4, *Macaroni,* both here and in the usual version, does not refer to a type of spaghetti, but to the homosexual Italianized British dandies, who formed an ostentatious coterie in the late eighteenth century and were briefly imitated in America:

> Yankee Doodle went to town
> Upon a load of 'lasses,
> He swore he could not see the town
> For the gals and their big asses.

> Yankee Doodle went to town
> And rode his spotted pony,
> They stuck a feather in his ass
> And called him Macaroni.

C. W. L. McAtee, *Grant County, Indiana, Speech and Song,* Supplement 2 (1946) p. 2, gives the following as heard in the 1890s. Line 4, *To get its pecker pointed,* must be an old blacksmith shop joke, just the sort of "mock" castratory threat made by workmen, still today, to little boys hanging around gawping at them work. The line also floats into the sea-chantey "When I was a Little Boy" or "Haul Away, Joe!" at No. 95*B.*

> Yankee Doodle had a cat,
> And it was double-jointed,
> Took it to the blacksmith's shop
> To get its pecker pointed.

D. It should be observed that bawdy parodies of "Yankee Doodle" already date from the late eighteenth century. One such bawdy broadside has survived and has been reproduced in various works in facsimile and its text reprinted in T. R. Smith's *Immortalia* (1927) pp. 148–50, in fourteen stanzas and chorus. It concerns the troop encampments in the Revolutionary War, in a type of countrified humor exactly like texts *A* and *B* above, as well as 208*A* and *B* immediately preceding. The allusion to George Washington in the last stanza given below is of course a standard humorous libel—really a brag—on the war leader, and not intended to be taken seriously. Washington was in fact more often accused of homosexuality, and of having advanced young Alexander Hamilton meteorically in the government for that reason, beginning as his aide-de-camp:

Father and I went down to camp,
Along with Cap'n Goodwin,
And there we saw the whores and pimps
As thick as hasty puddin'.

Yankee Doodle, keep it up,
Yankee Doodle dandy,
Mind the action and the pep,
And with the girls be handy!

And there we see a thousand men,
As rich as Squire David,
The cocks they wasted every day
I wish they could be savèd . . .

And there I see a private's gun,
Large as a bullock pintle,
So deucèd large it was he'd run
It into father's cattle . . .

And there was Cap'n Washington
With gentle whores about him;
They say his cock's so 'tarnal proud
He cannot ride without 'em.

All this so scared me I run off,
Nor stopped, as I remember,
Nor turned about 'til I got home,
Locked up in mother's chamber.

210. THE ALPHABET SONG

A is for ass-hole all covered with hair,
B is for ballyx which longed to be there,
C is for cunt all be-shit an' be-pissed,
D is for dill-balls as big as your fist.

E is for the end of a snotty-nosed prick,
F is for fool who has fucked himself sick,
G is for a girl all greasy an' fat,
H is for the hairy ass-hole of a cat.

I is for idle prick that always hung down,
J is for the jolliest old whore in the town,
K is for kiss my ass, you son of a bitch,
L is for a lousy old whore with the itch.

M is for monkey with ballyx of brass,
N is for nigger got fucked in the ass,
O is for otter who sucked the hind tit,
P is for pack-horse all loaded with shit.

Q is for a queen who fucked for pure gold,
R is for the rusty side of her ass-hole,
S is for shit-house which no one could approach,
T is for turd that upset the mail-coach.

U is for unick who couldn't fuck a bit,
V is for vack-balls all covered with shit,
W is for waxed cunt as slick as a mole,
X is for ten pricks dead at the hole.

Y is for a yoe who was always in heat,
Z swelled up an' busted an' sp'iled all the meat.

A. Manuscript text and tune as above, from a lady in Springfield, Missouri, August 18, 1938. She said it was sung (to her?) by Mr. John Gold, of Stone County, Missouri, as long ago as 1892. In 1:4 and 6:2, *dill-balls* and *vack-balls,* (or *clutter-balls* manuscript 1949), "dilberries," the German *Klabusterbeeren,* adhesions of various bodily exuviae to hairs around the anus, etc. 1:2, *ballyx,* ballocks, testicles; 6:1, *unick,* eunuch; 7:1, *yoe,* ewe. In 6:3 the meaning of *waxed cunt* is unknown, but may refer to *wax,* semen.

B. A very similar text to *A* above, begun by Mr. B. W., Eureka Springs, Arkansas, March 6, 1948:

A is for ass-hole all covered in hair,
B is for Ballyx who longs to be there,
C is for cunt-hole all shit an' bepissed,
D is for diddle-balls as big as your fist . . .

C. Manuscript text mailed from Reeds Spring, Missouri, April 27, 1948. According to a note on the margin, Miss E. G. wrote it down from the singing of a Springfield, Missouri, housemaid in 1927. At letter I: *hicks,* probably "micks" is meant. At S: *safety,* a condom; *fish-skin,* a sheepgut condom. In 1:2, *eternal,* singer's error for "external." At Q: *blow off your lump,* have an orgasm; at R: *in bloom,* "having the flowers," menstruating; at V: *Johnny,* the penis; at T: *fresh,* in milk.

A is for ass, upon it we sit,
The eternal end and a passage for shit.

B is for balls, each man has a pair
In a wrinkled old sack, all covered with hair.

C is for cunt, so juicy and slick,
It's home sweet home for a seven-inch prick.

D is for diddle, that never grows stale,
For there's nothing so good as a nice piece of tail.

E is for eggs that are laid in the grass,
That object that comes from a speckled hen's ass.

F is for fart that perfumes the cool breeze,
It's fully as bad as limberger cheese.

G is for guts, that tangled-up mass
That separates your belly from the hole in your ass.

H is for hair that surrounds her cunt,
To find the hole men mightily hunt.

I is for Ireland, the home of the hicks,
They fight all their battles with crowbars and pricks.

J is for jism that's sticky like cream,
It specks up the sheets when you have a wet dream.

K is for king, who wears a crown on his bean,
His favorite sport is the hole of the queen.

L is for love that fails to stick,
It begins in your head and ends in your prick.

M is for marriage, when a man gets a wife,
And lives in misery the rest of his life.

N is for nuts that furnish the sap,
And is sometimes the making of a big dose of clap.

O is for old, or rather that time
When your prick don't stand up like it did in your prime.

P is for prick, the petrified prong,
They range from four to twelve inches long.

Q is for quiver that comes with a thump,
It's a funny sensation when you blow off your lump.

R is for rags, that are used I presume
To wrap up a cunt when it's nicely in bloom.

S is for safety that is made of fish skin,
It usually breaks when you shove Johnny in.

T is for tits, supposed to be sucked,
They never get fresh till a woman's been fucked.

U is for urine, a pot full of piss,
Gee, but it's awful to use language like this.

V is for Venus, a shape we all love,
You jump on her frame and give Johnny a shove.

W is for woman, a cradle of sin,
She is split from her ass clear up to her chin.

X is for X-ray, a magnifying glass
That's used by doctors to look up your ass.

Y is for yes, when a girl gets hot
There is nothing but peckers will cool off her pot.

And Z is for zero, supposed to be cold
Like a man's balls get when he's eighty years old.

D. Fragments of a similar piece, recalled by an aged man in Joplin, Missouri, June 26, 1938. He heard the whole thing near Joplin in the late 1880s, but this is all he could remember:

C is for cunt, so fuzzy an' slick,
A fine little home for a seven-inch prick.

H is for hairs that surround her old cunt,
To find that hole is a man's mighty hunt.

J is for jism, slick like cream,
The spot on the sheet when you have a wet dream.

E. Given as "The Tramps' Alphabet," first collected (or composed?) at hot springs, Arkansas, about 1930, and concerned with the treatment of venereal disease by thalassotherapy baths at the Hot Springs, in this case for impecunious gamblers and hoboes. See further details, and glossarial notes, following the text:

A stands for Ass, (as) you all know,
B for Blue balls in your groins grow,
C stands for Cunt that causes disease,
D for the Doctor who treats it with ease.

E stands for Edith the doctor did make.
F stands for Fucking he neatly did take,
G stands for Girls I screwed on the dock,
H for Hot Springs where I went for the pock.

I stands for Iron Mountain, the road I did beat,
J for Joe Diamond, on the road I ruined my feet,
K stands for Kitty by whom I was burned,
L for Lesson that now I have learnt.

M stands for Mercury without which we die,
N for Nuts that was hung up to dry,
O stands for Ozark, the gamblers' resort,
P stands for pecker, the frisky old sport.

Q stands for Quinine to keep off the chill,
R stands for Rall can we often did fill,
S stands for Shankers that made the boys howl,
T stands for Turkish, the best kind of Towel.

U stands for Ulcers that come on our leg,
V for Vagrants, around the town beg,
W for good Whiskey that we all use,
X for Xmas when we get on a booze.

Y stands for Yaps with the rotten town guard,
Z stands for Zigzags in the back yard.

This particularly interesting Ozark text, apparently from Hot Springs, Arkansas, about 1930, was collected by Godfrey Irwin for his work on tramp and hobo songs and slang, but was not used, and was then turned over to (or newly collected by) George Milburn, for his heavily expurgated *Hobo's Hornbook* (1930) and again not used, and finally given to G. Legman, in 1938. From an unknown source it was then privately printed in a rare ephemeral pornographic "reader" pamphlet, as a poetic filler, where the erotic adventure text ran short (Hollywood? 1940), entitled "The Tramps' Alphabet," word-for-word identically with the hand-circulated text. The song describes, on the alphabetical framework, a session of treatment at Hot Springs, for syphilis ("the pock"), which it was believed such springs alleviated if not cured.

Note: at letter R: *Rall can*, the venereal disease was known jestingly as "The Old Ral," as differentiated from the mere "*New* Ral" (neuralgia!) For humanitarian and religious reasons (Jesus treating Simon and the lepers, in *Matthew*, 8:2–4; *Mark*, 1:40–41; and especially *Luke*, 17:12), sick hoboes and other paupers were allowed access to the natural springs without payment, though in a special plain enclosure called "the (Old) Ral Can," from *can*, slang for a jail-pen. This on the basis of the superb admonition of Jesus to his Twelve Disciples, in *Matthew*, 10:8, "Heal the sick, cleanse the lepers, raise the dead, cast out devils: freely ye have received, freely give." This is the motto, still today, of the volunteer "Médicins du Monde" international organization. Perhaps it should be everyone's.

Glossary: At letter B: *Blue balls*, swollen inquinal glands or testicles in gonorrhea. E: *make*, seduce. F: *fucking*, in this aggressive sense means a cheating, "reaming," "shafting." H: *the pock*, "pox," syphilis, so-called from its skin lesions, a very old word. I: *the road I did beat*, cheated the railroad by "riding the rods" underneath, or in empty freight-cars, to arrive free at destination, Hot Springs. J: *Joe Diamond*, meaning unknown, but the "Jack of Diamonds" (or three of Spades) is considered by card gamblers the unluckiest card in the deck (see Brown, vol. III: pp. 80–81). K: *burned*, infected with venereal disease, a seventeenth-century term. N: *nuts*, testicles. P: *Pecker*, penis. S: *Shankers*, chancres, venereal sores. U: *Ulcers*, polite medical euphemism for the syphilitic ulcerations or lesions typically appearing on the shins and forehead. V: *Vagrants*, tramps begging in the streets for handouts of money. X: *on a booze*, on a drunken spree. Y: *Yap*, a fool, a "chump," "hick," *town guard*, narrow-minded local residents. Z: *zigzags*, attempts by a thief or bilking gambler to run and escape from gunfire by tacking and turning.

The basic purpose of erotic alphabets of this kind is evidently educational, presenting the organs and instrumentalities of the erotic life. They circulate mostly therefore among sexually curious children and adolescents—especially girls—with the extra "delight in the forbidden" that has been troubling women and men since Eden, Mother Eve, and Pandora, her Graeco-Roman congener. This is expressed with charming naïveté in version *C* above, via two women, date 1927, at the letter U: "*U is for Urine, a pot full of piss; Gee, but it's awful to use language like this.*" (The word *language*, in colloquial American English, almost always refers only to *maledicta* or "*bad* language," meaning cursing or bawdry.) Another handwritten text, essentially identical but with oral-transmission variants throughout suggesting revision by a boy, was bought by a male folklorist for twenty-five cents from a grade-school girl, age twelve, in Minneapolis, Minnesota, 1949.

Related to this form of sexually educative verse are the counting-and-touching game songs included above under "Kind Betty," No. 173, particularly "Mit Hands on Mine Shoulders" and "Dot's Vot I Learn in Shkool." These move on quickly to didactic bodily erotic itineraries, showing the proper order and development of a physical seduction (*"Tits first!"*), as in all songs like "Kind Betty" and "Gently Johnny My Jingalo," No 173*F*.

The literature on such alphabets, both nursery and erotic, is extensive, beginning with Eric Partridge's rather superficial *Comic Alphabets* (1961) pp. 49–51. Randolph notes:

> There are several of these songs, historical, occupational, and biblical. The Aurora, Mo., *Weekly Advertiser* (Feb. 18, 1937) printed a page of old-time songs including a "Spanish War Alphabet" with mention of the battleship *Maine*, Admiral Dewey, General Shafter, and so on. Compare "The Lumberman's Alphabet" in Linscott, *Folk Songs of Old New England* (1939) pp. 235–37: "There are several variations of this song," says Linscott, "the most popular ones unprintable." See also the Brown collection, *North Carolina Folklore* (1952) III. 259–60, for extensive references and a sailor's alphabet song, in which the line for V "V is the Virgin, we fly to our (whore)," left the presumably Protestant Brown editor with "no interpretation to offer."

In addition, there are two too-polite "Lumberman's Alphabets" in Doerflinger, *Shantymen and Shantyboys* (1951) pp. 207–09, and references p. 344; while the Opies' *Oxford Dictionary of Nursery Rhymes* (1951) pp. 47–52, begins with a tremendous marshaling of historical materials on *ABC* didactic play-rhymes of this type back to 1670. Randolph's own *Ozark Folksongs*, No. 873, ed. Cohen, pp. 388–89, gives three versions, one collected from Mrs. May Kennedy McCord, in Springfield, Missouri, 1939 (compare version *A* above) with the tune; Mrs. McCord observed: "There were many verses, some not at all suitable for children to sing." The tune used, as for version *A* here, is almost identical with that for "Rub It Up, Shove It Up," No. 113 above.

Erotic versions, which are now generally transmitted in America by handwrit copies, typewritten, or photocopy "Xeroxlore" most recently, owing to the difficulty of memorizing the twenty-six-stanza texts, are in *Cleopatra's Scrapbook* (1928) p. 40, which is closely followed by Randolph's versions *A* and *B*, and by Larson's Idaho manuscript (recollected from 1932) p. 39; *Anecdota Americana: Series II* (1934); Legman Archive, "Zambuck Alphabet," from a Canadian Army dentist, Gander, Newfoundland, 1944; *Snatches and Lays* (Australia, 1962; ed. 1975) pp. 55–56; *Be Pure!* (Perth, Australia, 1963) p. 64, reprinted in "Argus Tuft," No. 65; Parker *Folio* manuscript (England, 1965) p. 112; Morgan, *Rugby Songs* (London, 1967) vol. I: p. 31; *Rugger Hugger* (Denver, 1976) p. 68, of British Rugby origin. All the above are of the same type, except that in *Anecdota Americana II* (1934) which is an essentially new recension, never collected in folk transmission. There is also a more erotic story type as "The Lovers' Alphabet," in Schweinickle's *Book of a Thousand Laughs* (1928) p. 2; "ABC of Love" (Zambuck) in Bold, *Making Love*, p. 207; and a similar "Mephipha Alphabet," in *Immortalla* (1927) p. 136.

British versions are still mostly *sung*, and have a chorus following after each two letters of the Alphabet "lined-out," on the style of: "*Singing, Roley-poley, Up 'em and stuff 'em; Heigh-ho, says Anthony Rowley!*" This is better known for its use with the sixteenth-century "Froggie Would a-Wooing Go," but the chorus dates only from about 1800. See Opie, pp. 177–81, to which may be added that in an anti-Napoleonic song chapbook, *Boney's Wedding* (London: John Reed, about 1808: copy in Legman Collection, Ohio State University Library) p. 24. This is given in the form of an anti-woman item—forgetting for the moment about Napoleon, as against this more traditional enemy-of-man—"Heigho! says Thimble. Written by George Colman, Esq., and sung by Mr. Liston in the Farce of *Killing No Murder*—Tune: *Heigho! says Rowley.*"

This was made famous for the next twenty years, as "featured" by the then most popular Italian-English clown, Joey Grimaldi. It is to be observed that the austere British *Dictionary of National Biography* (edited by Sir Leslie Stephen, the father of Virginia Woolf) considered it worth pinpointing, of the author, George Colman the Younger, that this jolly hypocrite "published coarse comic poems, 1797–1820; [but] showed great scrupulosity as examiner of plays, 1824–36." The same was also true—not to mention the great John Milton—of the even-less expected Giacomo-Girolamo Casanova, author of the world's most famous erotic autobiography (manuscript 1797) when he lost his job as a French government spy and became theatre-censor and police spy for the Inquisition at Venice. *Eheu fugaces!* Colman's anti-woman gloat, on the usual excuse that the wife was a "scold," begins:

> Thimble's scolding wife lay dead,
> > *Heigho! says Thimble*,
> My dearest duck's defunct in bed;
> Death has cabbag'd her, Oh! she's fled!
> > *With her roley, poley,*
> > *Gammon and spinnage*;
> > *Heigho! says Thimble.*

211. GRANDPAW'S PRICK

My grandpaw had a great big prick,
'Twas most as big as a flagpole,
And every night, as sure as heck,
He'd stick it in grandmaw's ass-hole.

Oh, his balls were big and round,
They hung down to the ground,

There was no hick with such a prick
For many miles around.

Recited by Mr. G. P., Reeds Spring, Missouri, July 5, 1946. He had it from a gentleman at Garber, Missouri, at unknown date, probably up to thirty years before. Intended to be sung to the tune of "Yankee Doodle." Stanza 2 (or chorus, if more exists to the song?) takes its first two lines from the chorus of "Christopher Columbo," No. 160B. There seems to be no relationship to a more recent piece, "My Grandfather's Cock," in *Snatches and Lays* (1962, ed. 1975) p. 17, a bawdy Oedipal parody of the favorite nineteenth century recitation, "My Grandfather's Clock," which stopped, dead-still, "when the old man died." Note the childish misapprehension of the nature of sexual intercourse, in stanza 1, as described by Freud before 1905, in which the child—here the grandchild—believes that it takes place anally, with the surrogate belief, on the analogy of defecation, that the resultant child is born the same way.

212. SUCKING JENNY AND FUCKING JOHN

Suckin' Jenny and Fuckin' John,
Went to bed with their britches on,
Johnny let a fart and Jenny give a cough,
Both of 'em blowed their britches off.

A. From a lady at Eureka Springs, Arkansas, January 4, 1950. She learned it as a little girl in the late 1890s. Parody of *C*, below.

B. Ray Wood, *Fun in American Folk Rhymes* (1952), p. 18, has an obviously expurgated version, demonstrating that the forthright form *A*, above, was known to Wood's informant or staff-expurgator:

Spinning Jenny and Hoppin' John
Crawled in bed with their gaiters on;
One shoe on and one shoe off,
And both of them caught the whooping cough.

C. The original nursery-rhyme form, of which version *A* is a bawdy parody, is traced by Opie, *Oxford Dictionary of Nursery Rhymes* (1951) pp. 245–46, to *The Newest Christmas Box* (about 1797), with tunes by Reginald Spofforth, unfortunately not reproduced in Opie. They give the first two lines of the text from the *Diary* of Robert Haydon, at date December 28, 1817, as sung by Charles Lamb; the last two lines also as traditionally, dated 1803. The melody used as recently as 1923 in the eastern United States is "Little Brown Jug":

Diddle diddle dumpling, my son John
Went to bed with his breeches on,
(One shoe off and one shoe on,
These were the deeds of my son John.)

As *diddle* still means, in slang, to masturbate, and therefore by extension to "fuck" or cheat, the last word has not yet been said on "diddle" as a presumed nonsense-word in nursery rhymes and the like. In some of its oldest appearances (about 1600) it refers frankly to the sexual substitute or phallic succedaneum, "*dildo*" or "*dildol*," in some refrains, an Italian or Venetian word then newly imported (from *diletto*, delight) along with the objects celebrated, as in "The Choyce of Valentines, or Tom Nash his *Dildo*" (manuscript 1601; printed first in John S. Farmer, *Merry Songs and Ballads*, 1895, vol. I: pp. 13–25; reprinted in T. R. Smith, *Poetica Erotica* (ed. 1930). As a purported nonsense refrain in nursery rhymes, even when reduced to "dilly-dilly" (or dally), the Sense of Nonsense has never been very hard to discern here. Its most classic appearance is in the still-popular "Lavender's Blue," first published as *Diddle Diddle, or The Kind Country Lovers* (Black Letter broadside, London: J. Wright, about 1675; the first four stanzas reprinted in Opie, pp. 265–67), of which the last half is still as alive, word-for-word, and as clear today as three centuries ago. In fact, the modern version ends even more clearly: *"While you and I,* dilly-dilly, *Keep ourselves warm."*

> Some to make hay, Diddle diddle,
> Some to the Corn,
> Whilst you and I, Diddle diddle,
> Keep the bed warm.

213. WILLIE, OH WILLIE

Willie, (oh) Willie,
Take me out in the grass,
Roll me over and stick it in,
Run it out of my ass!

My cunt is as hot for a wennie,
I can take twelve inches, if any;
So stick it in and work it around,
I'll bet six bits there can't be found
A happier pair, if any.

From a student, Mr. J. M., at Fayetteville, Arkansas, April 27, 1957, who heard it from a man in Bentonville, Arkansas. Parody of the favorite 1890s song by Harry Dacre, "Daisy Bell" (1892), known as "A Bicycle Built for Two." Original words in B. Stevenson, *Home Book of Quotations*, 1211:9. In 2:1, *wennie* (forced pronunciation, to rhyme with "any"), a *wienie*, or wiener-sausage, "hot dog," a common metaphor for the penis; 2:4, *six bits*, seventy-five cents, a still-surviving allusion to the old Spanish "pieces of eight" or "bit," worth twelve and one-half cents, used in French Louisiana, being eight to the old Colonial dollar.

Note that, as sung here by a young man, this is entirely a male wish-projection or erotic fantasy *in the character of the woman*, whom he is pretendedly quoting, to express the extremity of her (hoped-for) passion. This is very common in male fantasies in verse and prose—compare "Violate Me in Violet Time," No. 235—especially in classic pornographic fiction, from *The Dialogues of Luisa Sigea* (1665) really by Nicolas Chorier of Grenoble; *The Memoirs of a Woman of Pleasure* ("Fanny Hill," 1749) really by John Cleland; *Les Chansons de Bilitis* (1896), an imitation, which fooled the scholarly world, of the presumed Lesbian poems of Sappho, here really by Pierre Louÿs; and *The Memoirs of Josefine Mutzenbacher, a Viennese Prostitute* (1908) really by Felix Salten, author also of *Bambi*. So far as is known, no graphic erotic fiction actually written by a woman was ever openly published before the books of Anaïs Nin, Nancy Friday, and Erica Jong in the 1970s. See further the introduction by G. Legman, in Patrick Kearney, *The Private Case: British Museum Library* (London, 1981) pp. 52–59; revised as "The Lure of the Forbidden" in Martha Cornog's excellent recent symposium concerning *Libraries, Erotica, and Pornography* (Phoenix, Arizona: Oryx Press, 1991), which offers a good deal more than the title suggests.

214. SWEET ANTOINETTE

Sweet Antoinette,
Your pants are wet,
I think it's sweat,
It's piss, I bet.

In all my dreams
Your bare ass gleams,
You're the wrecker of my pecker,
Sweet Antoinette.

From a college student, Mr. J. M., at Fayetteville, Arkansas, April 27, 1957. In stanza 1:2–4, the pretended question as to whether the girl's damp panties are wetted by "sweat or piss" is intended to imply that it is really her *cyprine*, the vaginal pre-coital lubricant secretion, that is making her "wet." A close parody of the once ubiquitous "Sweet Adeline" by Richard H. Girard (1903), the original words given in Burton Stevenson's *Home Book of Quotations* (1944) 2287:4–5, calling it the "Old Faithful of all (four-part) harmonic geysers," a perennial barbershop quartet favorite, sung in traditional lachrymose caterwauling style: *"Sweet A-do-liiiiine! My A-do-liiiiine!"* G. Legman heard the original song and the above parody sung together in sequence, in November 1963, at a private fraternity folksong and (as it turned out) sex-party at Ohio State University, Columbus, Ohio, during which four naked girls, stated to be coeds at the University, competed as to who could bring her chosen one of four fraternity members first to orgasm by means of fellation, "without (using) any hands."

Note that the singing of love-songs and presumably bawdy songs in all-male barbershops, and later at mixed theatre parties or among gangsters, gamblers, or pimps, with actress-prostitutes (witnessed in 1937 and often since) dates from the time of Shakespeare or earlier. Shakespeare lived and worked over a barbershop, for the music. See: *Twelfth Night*, Act I, Scene i, line 1, "If Music be the food of love, play on." And compare *First Part of King Henry IV*, Act III, Scene iii, line 14, this prophetic colloquy (about 1598) on psychosomatic "stress":

> *Bardolph:* Sir John, you are so fretful, you cannot live long.
> *Falstaff:* Why, there it is: Come, sing me a bawdy song; make me merry.

215. ON THE OUACHI-TAW

I was shacked up in the mountains
With Big-Ass Sal, my squaw,
Doin' no harm, just a-runnin' my worm,
When they come after me with the Law.

We hauled ass outa there mighty fast,
Me an' Sal an' her maw,
As hot-cocked a bitch as you'd ever see,
And we went for the Ouachi-taw.

> *Low bridge! Low bridge!*
> *Just get yourself a squaw,*
> *And fuck the brains right outa your head*
> *Down on the Ouachi-taw . . .*

The squaws are in the whorehouse,
The captain is in jail,
And I'm the only son-of-a-bitch
Alive to tell the tale.

Sung by Mr. R. K., of Mena, Arkansas, in New York, April 1954, for my wife, Beverley Legman-Keith, and his own, to the tune of "The E-R-I-E Canawl," of which this is evidently an Ozark parody. Unfortunately, the missing central stanzas, giving the whole action of the piece (a burlesque boat-voyage on the Ouachi-taw or Wichita River of northwest Arkansas and thereabouts), have been lost in the transmission of the written-out text. In stanza 1:3, *runnin' my worm*, an illegal spiral-coil distilling apparatus for making moonshine whiskey; 1:4, *the Law*, the Revenue agents scouring the hills to repress illegal bootleg whiskey-making; 2:1, *hauled ass*, departed quickly, decamped; 2:3, *hot-cocked*, "cock" here is equivalent to "cunt," from the older British *cockle*, from the French *coquille*, cockleshell. In chorus, line 3, *fuck the brains right outa your head*, from the very common superstition or folk-belief that "excessive" masturbation or sexual intercourse will make a boy or man insane—on the observation that the insane masturbate openly—whereas it will make a woman "purr like a kitten," and she will eventually therefore also "melt the fat right offa your bones!" (This last from the observation of the great loss of weight, called "pissing their tallow," by male deer during the rutting season.)

No authentic text of "The E-R-I-E Canawl" seems ever to have been published, and the only such text recovered is apparently that in Hilaire Hiler's *Full-Dress Suits and Plenty of Whores* (manuscript, Paris, 1928), being bawdy texts from American informants, including two professional Negro musicians. The conflated text given in John A. Lomax's autobiographical *Adventures of a Ballad Hunter* (1947), pp. 244–47, does not at all closely resemble the *Full-Dress Suits* text, except in the lines about "Sal," who is here the canal-boat mule, and was admittedly cobbled together by Lomax from stanzas from various informants. It is printed in the song collections by his son Alan, with the lively tune. This re-worked "fakelore" version is now thought of by many as the actual song and has been recorded as such by Oscar Brand and other folksong revival singers. See further the perhaps related "Skinner on the Dock," No. 150 above.

216. THE RICH SEÑORITA

He married a rich señorita
And set her ass up on a shelf,
Kept forty young Injuns to fuck her,
And slept with Matilda himself . . .

A. Sung by Mr. G. B., Reeds Spring, Missouri, October 19, 1950. He heard it about 1890 and thinks it is part of a cowboy song not otherwise identified. The situation posed in the last two lines is very enigmatic, not only as to the "wittol" husband, but concerning the sexual relations not with the Indian squaws, as usually described, but here with the gigolo bucks. Compare "On the Ouachi-Taw," No. 215 preceding, and line 3 below.

B. A clearly related song, of which the stanza above is an evident parody *or its source*, is given as "He's the Man for Me" in Eleanora Black and S. C. Robertson, *Gold Rush Songbook* (San Francisco, 1940) p. 7, from an 1850s chapbook, with the stanza as follows. In line 3, *greaser*, a Mexican:

I'll marry a rich señorita
And live on a ranch in the West,

> Have forty young greasers to greet her,
> And fifty, if put to the test.

217. COCK UPON A PEAR TREE

> Cock upon a pear tree,
> Prick out on a pole,
> Jump cock, dodge prick,
> Shoot her in the hole.

A. Sung by Mr. B. W., Eureka Springs, Arkansas, June 25, 1948. He learned it about 1910, near Berryville, Arkansas. His tune was unfortunately not transcribed. Note that "cock" here is the Southernism meaning "cunt."

B. This is clearly connected with a text of "Jaybird Settin' on a Limb," at No. 188 above, which is not in the same stanzaic metre or rhythm as version *A* here, since it is sung to the tune of "Ta-ra-ra-*Boom*-de-ay!" It was given by Mrs. M. M., Springfield, Missouri, April 30, 1946:

> Jaybird a-settin' on a hickory pole,
> Draw back, draw back, shoot him in the hole.

C. In turn, this seems to be related to an eighteenth-century British nursery rhyme in *Tommy Thumb's Pretty Song Book* (about 1744) vol. II:

> Little Robin red breast,
> Sitting on a pole,
> Niddle, Noddle, went his head,
> And Poop went his hole.

D. Surviving almost without change in America over a century later, this was given as follows by Mr. J. E., Webster Groves, Missouri, who said it was popular among "little boys and girls" in the 1880s:

> Robin, robin redbreast,
> Settin' on a pole,
> Wiggle-waggle went his tail,
> *Poop!* went his hole.

E. In their handsomely researched but lamentably expurgated *Oxford Dictionary of Nursery Rhymes* (1951) pp. 371–72, Iona and Peter Opie—the expurgator being Peter, not Iona—give one of their innocuous twentieth-century versions for this, as usual of unknown provenance, but do observe that: "Early recordings show that this rhyme was originally a rude [British for obscene] little jest. Latter-day editors have shown ingenuity in making it suitable for their collections." Their own ingenuous solution is to *end*, "Wiggle waggle went his tail." Some of the other endline revisions since 1744 (see version *C*, the original, preceding), have been: "Which made him look quite droll" (1815); "And warbl'd merrily" (1830); "With a pair of speckled legs, And a green girdle" (James O. Halliwell, 1853). However, the end of the Opies' note indicates that no child was ever really fooled, since they received from an unnamed correspondent so' late as 1950, "an interesting survival of the 18th-century version learnt from a nanny [children's nurse]." This is still a bit "ingenious," but fairly translucent too, and quite close to the American Ozark text at *D:*

> Little Robin Redbreast
> Sat upon a pole,
> Wiggle waggle went his tail,
> Pop! through the hole.

F. The last Ozark text recovered, from Mr. J. C., Eureka Springs, Arkansas, August 24, 1951, who heard it in Moberly, Missouri, about 1912, does not have quite the form of the others, and may be related to the one most frankly sexually perverted of all the British nursery rhymes, the female-dominant flagellation rhyme, "Dapple Gray," or "I Had a Little Pony (Husband)," dating from about 1630, which the Opies divide into three different versions and locations, at pp. 143, 209–10, and 216–17 (and compare 313), of which the first and last, "I Had a Little Husband," are straight sado-masochistic fantasy.

> I had a little monkey
> His ass-hole was red,
> *Razz-pole, bazz-pole,*
> Shot him in the ass-hole,
> Now my monkey's dead.

218. SLOW MASTURBATION

> In the latrine with a sex magazine,
>   *It's slow masturbation,*
> It gives me a buzz to feel of her fuzz,
>   *It's slow masturbation,*
> To feel of her thighs makes my peter rise,
>   *It's slow masturbation . . .*

Fragment from Mr. B. D., Oklahoma City, Oklahoma, November 2, 1950. He heard it sung to the (pop tune) "Sleepy Lagoon" melody by a race-track driver named Tommy Davis, who had it from an old sergeant major at the Oklahoma Military Institute. Note in line 1, *latrine*, indicating its military origin; in line 2: *buzz*, thrill; *fuzz*, pubic hair.

Admissions as to masturbation are rare in male folklore, and almost non-existent in materials supplied by women, as being considered a disgraceful failure of sexual aggressiveness or attractiveness. Compare the riotous and defiant "Last Night I Stayed Up Late to Masturbate," to the tune of "Funiculi, Funicula"—itself a Neapolitan scatological joke in its *-culi, -cula* chorus, not understood by singers outside Italy—in Cray, pp. 108–09 and 213; and Reuss, pp. 211–14, noting that it is of recent vintage, probably British, of the 1940s, as is the present American parody.

219. PULL DOWN YOUR VEST

> Pull down your vest, pull down your vest,
> For Pa's a-coming, and you know the rest.
> Although we're engaged, love, I think it is best
> Before Pa comes in, love, to pull down your vest.

Sung by Mrs. B. M., Monett, Missouri, September 15, 1942. Vance Randolph recorded the singing of this stanza for the Library of Congress Folksong Archive. The informant could recall only this fragment of a long piece, popular at St. Louis in the 1880s. She said it was considered a very "dirty" song, which may be an overstatement. So far as the present fragment suggests, the situation is just the standard "courting" of a young man and woman, where the father traditionally tries to prevent them from "going too far" before marriage, although simultaneously it is understood that they have a certain latitude for testing their body-shapes and sexual compatibility beforehand, as in "necking and petting" (kissing and caressing) and dancing. This item is given only in the 1949 recension of the Randolph "Unprintable" manuscript with note: "I record this fragment, hoping that some of the bawdy stanzas will turn up later."

220. AFTER THE BALL IS OVER

A little maiden climbed a young man's knees.—
Come let me feel it, do Charley, please.
Why is it hard, dear? Why, Charley dear,
I will not hurt it, never, never fear.—

I have a feeling that's very queer,
Can't you do something for me, Lucy dear?
Down fell her panties, Charley gave his all,
Lucy got a promise, after the ball.

> After the ball is over,
> After the break of dawn,
> After you get a queer feeling
> And want to take some girl home.
>
> Many a dick is aching
> If you could see them all,
> Many the loads that have vanished
> After the ball.

Three nights have passed and dear Lucy said,
I must see Charley and take him to bed,
Charley came at last and said, Lucy dear,
I've had an awful time a-getting Jasper here.

Lucy grabbed dear Charley and pulled him on the bed.—
I gave it to you, darling, my maidenhead.
In shot old Jasper, Lucy got it all,
Lucy got a baby, after the ball.

From Mr. H. F., Kansas City, Missouri, January 14, 1955. In 4:1, *dick,* and 5:4 *Jasper,* humorous names for the penis; 4:3, *loads,* ejaculations. Parody of the popular song of the same title by Charles K. Harris (1892), "One of the greatest hits in the history of Tin Pan Alley, first sung by a famous baritone, J. Aldrich Libby, at a matinée of Charles Hoyt's *A Trip to Chinatown*, at the Bijou Theatre, Milwaukee, Wisc.," according to Burton Stevenson, *Home Book of Quotations*: Appendix (1944) p. 2288:1, giving the original tear-jerker text; the second part of the chorus ending—compare the parody above:

> Many a heart is aching,
> If you could read them all,
> Many the hopes that have vanished—
> After the ball.

221. THAT BALD-HEADED DRUMMER

Is there a blood spot on my ass?
Was the question that she asked
As she set upon the pot one summer night.

She was feeling rather blue,
For she was three months over-due;—
I believe I'm knocked up higher than a kite.

Oh that bald-headed drummer
Who slept with me last summer,
He sneaked away and never told his name!

In a whorehouse now she sings,
And the kid wears golden wings,
For the checks were cashed the day that it was born.

Recited by Mr. D. C., Eureka Springs, Arkansas, October 21, 1954. It is part of a song he heard in Joplin, Missouri, about 1915, to the lugubrious tune of "In My Prison Cell I Sit" ("Tramp, Tramp, Tramp"). In 1:3, *pot*, chamberpot. 2:2, *over-due*, as to the expected menstruation; 2:3, *knocked up*, pregnant; 3:3, *checks were cashed*, the baby died. In the chorus, *drummer*, a traveling salesman, but the image of the *bald-headed drummer* is perhaps also intended metaphorically for the penis.

"In a whorehouse now she sings": note the direct statement being made at that date (1915 and before), that the seduced, pregnant, and abandoned girl has no recourse but to become a prostitute. Compare the cynically cruel folk-phrase covering the case (in which "buggered" means cheated or befooled): "bitched, buggered, bewildered—and far from home!" In Josiane Balasko's tender but corrosive motion-picture comedy, *Sac de Noeuds* (*Bunch of Pricks*, 1984), the young blonde wife, beaten by her husband, runs out of their apartment without money, friends, relatives or a job to fall back on, finds herself immediately forced into the position of an oral street prostitute or "mouth-whore" and holdup-woman in order to survive.

222. WHEN MY FLIVVER IS A WRECK

Will you love me in that good old-fashioned way
When my nuts are dropping all along the way?
. . . . will you kiss me that sad day
When my cotter-pin has all been worn away?

A. A fragment recalled by Mr. H. F., Kansas City, Missouri, February 9, 1955, and stated to be a parody of "When My Golden Hair Has Turned to Silver Gray," a popular song of the early 1900s, of which a text has not been found for comparison. It is in the vein of the still-remembered "Darling I am growing old, Silver threads among the gold," by Eben E. Rexford (1873), but is closer to the rather repellent "Will You Love Me When I'm Old?" of which a text is given in Randolph's *Ozark Folksongs*, vol. IV: pp. 344–45, and another, with further references, in Brown, vol. III: pp. 321–22, the last stanza beginning: "When my hair shall shame the snowdrift, And mine eyes shall dimmer grow . . . It is this that I would ask you: Will you love me when I'm old?"

The Brown editor notes that there is a polite parody as well, "Will You Love Me When I'm Bald?" and adds: "Parody is an unfailing evidence of popularity." This is not quite what is involved here, where the parodists are evidently nauseated by the groveling and unvirile demandingness of the song, and wish to show it up ludicrously for what it really is: a not-very-symbolized demand for love even when the male singer will be sexually impotent, whether frankly or symbolized as "baldness," since *nuts* here frankly means the testicles, and *cotter-pin* the penis.

B. A full text of this fragment is fortunately preserved in the very rare private club songbook *The "Wrecks,"* edited anonymously by T. R. Smith, editor also of *Immortalia* and *Poetica Erotica*, and issued in de luxe style for The Reno "Wrecks" (Reno, 1933) p. 28, as "The Ballad of Lizzie," referring to the "Tin Lizzie," as the early Model-T (or T-upside-down) Ford car was called until the mid-1930s when the current model was streamlined:

> Will you love me when my headlights are all shattered,
> Will you love me when my top is rent and torn?
> Will you love me when my fenders are all battered,
> Will you love me when my cotter-pin is worn?
>
> Will you love me when my spark-plugs are all missing,
> Will you love me when the brakes have ceased to grip?
> Will you love me when my intake starts to hissing,
> Will you love me when my clutch begins to slip?
>
> Will you love me when my bumper has quit bumping,
> Will you love me when my tires are soft and flat?
> Will you love me when my bearings are all thumping,
> Will you love me when I can't do this or that?
>
> Will you love me when my nuts and bolts are falling,
> From a frame that's bent entirely out of line?
> Will you love me when I hear the junk-pile calling,
> Will you love me when I'm old, oh, Lizzie mine?

Another somewhat funnier version of this circulated in the later 1930s as "Will You Love Me When My Flivver Is a Wreck," from its refrain-line. This was recorded with a brief introductory stanza, and main text beginning: "Will you love me when my carburetor's busted . . . When I haven't got a cent, And my *connecting-rod* is bent!" Issued (1940) on 78-rpm label Radio 471, and sold under-the-counter then in record stores as a "party record," sung by Bennie Bell, an old-time burlesque performer, in a lachrymose vaudeville "belt-it-out" style, heavily accentuating all possible mechano-human erotic metaphors, until finally the singer's "rear-end's worn and torn . . . And my nuts and bolts are loose."

There is a similar erotic recitation in verse, "Driving Rules," in *Immortalia* (1927) p. 145, along with its revision into an unrhymed art-poem by E. E. Cummings, "She Being (Practically) Brand-new," in *Poetica Erotica* (1927) p. 761; Cole, p. 280; and Bold, *Making Love*, p. 200. These are both strictly descriptions of a girl's first sexual intercourse, in the machine metaphors of an automobile trip. Paul Oliver's *Really the Blues*, has an excellent discussion of off-color Negro blues songs of the 1920s and 30s in "automobile" metaphors. *Immortalia* (1927) includes two more of these, both concentrating on images of the man's sexual impotence, in mechano-morphic terms: "A Sport Model to a Truck," p. 71, and "Your Radiator's Busted," p. 79.

C. All these are certainly to be compared with a heavily castratory cowboy song, more usually collected in an Air Force version during World War II, as "The Dying Airman," in which, in Sorcerer's Apprentice fashion, Man and Machine have become one—by destroying the man and completely cannibalizing his sexuality, of which nothing now remains but the metaphors of death, destruction, and non-operating impotence. As versions of this appear in all the Air Force songbooks, both public and private, such as

Getz, Starr, Wallrich, and others, and especially from Australia as of a dying "stockman," only the two opening stanzas will be given here, in a text from Gander Bay, Newfoundland, the Canadian Air Command, 1944, a version quite close to its cowboy original:

> A handsome young airman lay dying,
> And while on his deathbed he lay,
> To the friends who around him were sighing
> These last dying words he did say:
>
> Take the piston-rings out of my backbone,
> The connecting-rod out of my brain;
> From the small of my back take the crank-shaft,
> And assemble the engine again . . .

Under their gallows-laughter mockery, the songs of this group represent an important grassroots statement of modern terror of the Machine, as a social and sexual substitute for the now-devalued human male. See further, G. Legman, *The Limerick* (1953) Note 1325, pp. 447–48; and especially *Rationale of the Dirty Joke* (Vol. II: *No Laughing Matter*, 1975) pp. 646–62, chapter 13, "Castration;" section 3, "The Mechanical Man."

223. THE TATTOOED LADY

> I'd give a dime to see
> That tattooed lady,
> She was a sight you know,
> Tattooed from head to toe.
>
> On her left cheek was a bust of the Prince of Wales,
> And on her right was the Eddystone Light
> And a pair of spouting whales.
>
> Right where it shouldn't be
> Was the Royal Family,
> And on a certain spot
> Was a blue forget-me-not.
>
> When I asked her who had done it
> She answered frank and free,
> Don Gorman and Hank Barrison
> Were the boys who tattooed me.
>
> I'd give a dime to see
> That tattooed lady,
> She was a sight, you know,
> Tattooed from head to toe.
>
> On her right side was a British man-o'-war,
> And on her back was a Union Jack—
> That's worth while fighting for.
>
> Up and down her spine
> Were the King's own guards in line,
> And right across her hips
> Was a fleet of battleships.

> And over one kidney
> Was a bird's-eye view of Sidney,
> Across her chest was what I like best,
> My home in Tennessee.

A. Sung as above by a nameless lady in Galena, Missouri, June 17, 1942. This song was popular in Galena about 1936. The names "Don Gorman and Hank Barrison" replace those actually sung, which were the names of local men, well known in the village. Randolph recorded this singer in this piece for the Library of Congress Archive of American Folksong. It is considered quite mild and appears in numerous sing-along songbooks.

B. Contributed by Mrs. E. C., Anderson, Missouri, November 1, 1947. She said that some subsequent lines were "nasty," but could not recall them:

> Oh come and see my tattooed lady,
> She's tattooed from her head to her heels,
> And over her liver is the Catachocee River,
> And on her spine is the King's own firing line.
>
> And on her kidney is the Bay of Sidney,
> And on her hips is a fleet of battleships,
> But the part I like best is my tattooed lady's chest,
> Carry me back to the hills of Tennessee . . .

224. LITTLE MABEL TUCKER

> Goosey goosey gander,
> Who's comin' yander?
> Little Mabel Tucker,
> Who's a-goin' to fuck her?
>
> Little Jimmy Green
> Nowhere to be seen,
> Big Tommy Stout
> Pull his pecker out!

A. Sung by Mrs. C. H., Fayetteville, Arkansas, November 4, 1951. She says it was chanted by little children in Jasper County, Missouri, about 1910. Certainly a lesson in the practical logistics of sex, the way both women and men look at the matter in fact: "Men are replaceable—women too." It is worth observing that this is the only bawdy item collected from Mrs. C. H., and apparently the only such she had remembered. In 2:3, *Stout*, not fat but strong, "doughty."

B. Ray Wood, in *Mother Goose in the Ozarks* (1938) p. 16, prints the following "related" text: read, expurgated:

> Goosey—Goosey—Gander
> Who stands yonder?
> Little Betsy Baker,
> Pick her up and shake her.

225. MY GAL'S A HIGHBORN LADY

My gal's a highborn lady,
She's dark but not too shady,
Struts like a peacock, just as gay;
She's not colored—she was born that way.

She's got a form like Venus,
Every night she takes my penis,
Whatever they do they can't outscrew
This highborn gal of mine.

A. Fragment of a parody recalled by Mr. H. F., Kansas City, Missouri, January 14, 1955. Note the "inevitable" rhyme, in bawdy poetry and song, of *Venus/penis*, as in "A Letter from the Postman" ("Footprints on the Dashboard Upside Down"), in section B, No. 45. Randolph notes: "This was one of the 'coon songs' popular about 1900."

B. The original "coon" song of the 1900s, parodied above, runs as follows for the two stanzas given:

My gal's a highborn lady,
She's dark but not too shady.
Feathers like a peacock, just as gay;
She ain't colored—she was born that way!

She's got a form like Venus,
No coon can come between us,
Along the line they can't outshine
This highborn gal of mine.

This is a striking example, in both the original song and the parody preceding, of Negro "self-hatred" on the basis of low social status—the bittersweet pretence or delusion of being "highborn," i.e., of unacknowledged white paternity, thus making the child's skin-color lighter—and the whole overmastering concern with *not being black*: here "dark but not too shady," and the punning "not colored—she was born that way." This concern was challenged by Negro grassroots movements ("Black Is Beautiful") during the brief hippie fake-revolt period of the 1960s and 70s in America; but hair-straightener preparations still sell massively in the Negro ghettoes of New York (Harlem and increasingly The Bronx), Detroit, and many Southern cities; while Negro newspapers, as in New York and Pittsburgh, have a whole vocabulary of "color" adjectives to describe society belles, farther and farther away from black: "dusky pink," "coffee-colored," "light-cream beauty," "Morocco tan," and many others; though "high-yaller" is almost never used, as still contaminated with its post- and ante-bellum sexual exploitation of Negro women. The implied admixture of white "blood" as the enhancing element is also never mentioned, though always immanent and understood.

226. MAMA, LOOK AT SIS

Oh mamma, mamma, look at Sis,
Out in the back yard fuckin' her fist!—
Come in here, you dirty little sow,
Tryin' to make a whore and don't know how!
. . . .
You ought to be arrested, and it ain't no lie!

A. Recited as above by Mr. B. W., Eureka Springs, Arkansas, March 6, 1948. He learned it in the early 1900s, near Berryville, Arkansas.

B. Compare the text below, alternatively the original of the preceding or a cleanup, recorded by Mary Wheeler, *Steamboatin' Days* (Baton Rouge, Louisiana, 1944) p. 98, as part of a Negro song called "Take Your Time," which is almost always a disguised erotic admonition, referring to the man's slowing down during sexual intercourse to avoid premature ejaculation before the woman will also have had her orgasm. The Twist is an erotic "showoff" solo/couple dance of Negro origin, popularized among whites by the 1960s:

Mamma, mamma, look at Sis,
Down in the back yard doin' that twist.
Mama says, Come in the house,
You dirty little wench,
You ought to be down on the Mourner's Bench.

227. MATCHES, MATCHES!

Matches, matches, strike 'em on the grass,
Once knew a man who would strike 'em on his ———
Ash-tray! Ash-tray!

Once knew a gal from Kansas City,
She could strike 'em on her ———
Compact! Compact!

Once knew a man from Niagara Falls,
He could strike 'em on his ———
Bald head! Bald head!

Cherries are ripe and ready for plucking,
Girls in high school are ready for ———
College! College!

From the Parler-Randolph manuscript, Fayetteville, Arkansas. Contributed by a college girl from Fort Smith, Arkansas, who heard it sung by students at the Little Rock Junior College, March 25, 1957. "Tease-song" type, with evaded rhyming words: *ass*, *titty* (breast), *balls*, and *fucking*, considered obscene.

228. CUT IT ONCE

Cut it once, cut it twice,
Third time I cut it was gooey and nice.

> *Keep your hands off it,*
> *It don't belong to you,*
> *Wouldn't give you any*
> *No matter what you do.*

Grandpa said just before he died,
Give me one more piece and I'll be satisfied.

Now if you've got the wrong idea, take my advice,
It's my birthday cake and it's awfully nice.

Text from the Parler-Randolph manuscript, Fayetteville, Arkansas, contributed by a college girl from Fort Smith, Arkansas, March 25, 1957. "Tease" song, of Negro fake-blues Andy Razaf type; the second stanza floats here from numerous other songs, such as "Casey Jones," usually in bawdy versions. In 1:1–2, *cut* is here used in double-entendre for having sexual intercourse.

229. ON TOP OF OLD SUSIE

On top of old Susie
All covered with sweat,
I used fifteen rubbers
But she hasn't come yet.

I've fucked and I've fucked
Till my root it is raw;
Can't hold out much longer,
But I'll try it once more.

A. Sung by a male college student, Mr. J. M., Fayetteville, Arkansas, April 27, 1957, learned in Bentonville, Arkansas. Parody of the popular "On Top of Old Smoky" ("Courting Too Slow"), on which see Brown, vol. III: pp. 287–90, and tune in vol. V: pp. 170–73, which shares its melodic line with the much older sailing-ship song "My Little Mohea" ("Lass of Maui"), in Colcord, p. 199. Note in 1:3, *rubbers*, condoms; 2:3, *hold out*, for the man to continue sexual intercourse gallantly without allowing himself to arrive at orgasm. The final word *more* is to be pronounced here "mo'," to rhyme with *raw* (and not the contrary: "*rawr*" with excrescent *r*, to rhyme with "more"). Of particular interest, and indicating the song-parody's relatively modern date, post-World War I, is the reference to the man's presumably self-imposed duty to help the woman achieve her orgasm by "holding out." (But see version *C* below.) Despite the crude vocabulary and illiterate rhyme, this is a modern and perfectly gallant *complainte d'amours*.

B. For a "parallel inspiration," not a recasting of the song above into limerick metre, compare Legman, *The Limerick*, No. 99, and p. 378-note, dated 1939. Voted the "favorite" or "best" limerick by a gratifying number of modern connoisseurs (male: most women dislike limericks), meaning that they identify and sympathize with the limerick-poet's problem or plight. Note: time indicated is A.M.:

635

My back aches. My penis is sore.
I simply can't fuck any more.
   I'm dripping with sweat,
   And you haven't come yet,
And, my God! it's a quarter to four!

C. Several brief versions of the song-parody have been published, some reduced to two-line jibes, as in Hart's *"Complete" Immortalia* (1971) p. 446. There are also texts (all quite different) in the Dorson Indiana Folklore Archive, from Michigan, 1955, and the Wilgus Western Kentucky Folklore Archive, 1956, as well as a Scottish version in Goldstein, *Buchan Bawdry* manuscript (March 28, 1960) from a fifteen-year-old girl. The earliest complete text is in *Lost Limericks* (1949) p. 15, from which a scatologized Australian version is derived in *Snatches and Lays* (1962, ed. 1976) p. 62. Here is the American *Lost Limericks* original. In 1:4, *come,* and 2:2, *comin',* having an orgasm; 4:1, *root,* penis.

On top of old Sophie,
All covered with sweat,
I've used fifteen rubbers
And she's never come yet.

For screwin's a pleasure
And comin's a relief,
But a long-winded lover
Is worse than a thief.

So, come all you fellows
And listen to me:
Never place your erection
In a long-winded she.

For your root it will wither,
And your passion will die,
And she will forsake you,
And you'll never know why.

230. THE SHADE OF THE OLD APPLE TREE

In the shade of the old apple tree,
Between that girl's legs I could see
A little brown spot, 'twas the hair on her twat,
And it certainly looked good to me.

So I asked as I tickled her tit
If she thought that my pecker would fit,
She said it would do, and we started to screw,
In the shade of the old apple tree.

A. Sung as above by Mr. R. H., Springfield, Missouri, April 16, 1945. He heard it at Springfield, about 1915. Parody of the very popular American song of the same name by Harry Williams and Egbert Van Alstyne (1905). In 1:3, *twat,* the female pubis, an old word.

B. In its earliest printed appearance, in *Poems, Ballads and Parodies* (Detroit "1923": 1928) p. 54, this erotic parody began almost as Randolph's text above, but adds two further stanzas, ending with quasi-

"divine" punishment: (Reprinted in Legman, *The Limerick*, No. 110, p. 23; then in "De Witt," p. 55; also faked-up in "Vicarrion," No. 9, and this reprinted in Morgan, *Rugby Songs*, vol. I: p. 151).

> . . . In the shade of the old apple tree
> I got all that was coming to me,
> In the the soft dewy grass I had a fine piece of ass,
> From a maiden that was fine to see.
>
> I could hear the dull buzz of the bee
> As he sunk his grub-hooks into me,
> Her ass it was fine, but you should have seen mine,
> In the shade of the old apple tree.

The Larson Idaho manuscript (1952, recollected from 1932) p. 1, raises the ante in the punishment to the usual venereal disease: "She handed a package to me: A dose of the claps, the shankers perhaps . . ." but this is followed in no other version. See also: Indiana Archive; McWilliams manuscript (from Squaw Valley, Idaho, 1960); *Lost Limericks* (1949) p. 55; Reuss, pp. 252–54, ending with an Indiana sorority version to the tune of "Sweet Little Alice-Blue Gown"; Cray (1969) pp. 53 and 207–08, stating it was recollected from Hull, England, 1936; *"Argus Tuft" Folio* (Australia, 1970) No. 95; and Hart, *"Complete" Immortalia* (1971) p. 211, a fragment.

231. BLUEBIRD SHIT

> She painted her belly with bluebird shit,
> And the sun shone down on the nipple of her tit.

A. Fragment recited by Mr. J. C., Eureka Springs, Arkansas, August 24, 1951. He heard it years ago, in Moberly, Missouri.

B. Fragment recalled by Mr. J. E., Webster Groves, Missouri, October 9, 1948. Part of a long poem he heard recited in 1885:

> The natural gas escaped her ass
> And scorched off all my whiskers.

This is perhaps the most striking example of the worst problem of Vance Randolph's "Unprintable" Ozark materials: the almost ununderstandable fragmentary nature of the materials he was able to recover, owing to his having waited far too late—in fact until his main multi-volume collection, *Ozark Folksongs*, was already in process of publication—to fill in some of the large holes in that collection, especially as to bawdy songs, by inquiring of very old informants of already failing memories, whom he could have and should have questioned and recorded up to thirty years before. Many modern collectors have made this same mistake. However, in the case of this song, and a very few others, it is possible to determine what the songs were that could not be remembered except fractionally, from other published or manuscript texts. All these are forms of "The Wayward Boy," sometimes known as, and always sung to the rapid march-tune of, "The Girl I Left Behind Me," which see for the further history of this song at No. 138 above.

C. In the rare "Dave E. Jones" collection, mostly of sea-songs (United States, about 1928: only one copy known to have survived) No. 8, p. 9, a fragment entitled "Pearl":

> I knew a girl, her name was Pearl,
> And she was pretty flighty,
> The moonlight lit on the nipple of her tit,
> Oh, Jesus Christ, almighty.

D. The first recovered text to give any real idea of this form or strain of the song is part of the unfinished and unpublished American manuscript collection made by Hilaire Hiler, *Full Dress Suits, and Plenty of Whores* (manuscript Paris, 1928), abandoned when the editor learned of the publication in New York of *Immortalia* (1927–28), anonymously edited by Thomas R. Smith. The Hiler manuscript contains the following self-styled fragment, titled "The State of Maine," with note, "This song is to be sung with a mouth-organ accompaniment":

> The moonlight shone on her flea-bitten teat,
> And she brushed her teeth with blue-bird shit.
> The moonlight shone on the middle of the floor,
> And she wiped her arse on the knob of the door.
>
> > When she got started
> > She shit and she farted
> > She squirted green maggots
> > All over the carpet . . .

The purposely ugly and anti-gallant scatological "break" here is part of another song, not uncommonly mixed in (to the tune of "Sweet Evalina," in Brown, vol. V: p. 24), of which a similar text is printed by G. Legman, *The New Limerick* (1977) No. 1938, p. 391, entitled "Abelina," noting p. 652 that it was "collected as a song fragment from a college freshman from the U.S. southwest, at Ann Arbor, Michigan, 1935. The 'maggots' are evidently a puzzled reference to tapeworm-section infestation."

E. Collected from a young marijuana-grower and peddler, by G. Legman, in Archbald, Pennsylvania, 1940, who did not know where he learned it, but said there was more to the song that he could not remember:

> The moonlight shone on the nipple of her tit,
> And she painted her ass with bluebird shit.
> Oh, she ripped and roared and shit on the floor,
> And the blast of her ass blew the cat out the door!

Other versions are given in Morse (1948) p. 97; and the West Kentucky Folklore Archive (from Norfolk, Virginia, 1956), ending: "And she washes her teeth with Canary-Bird shit."

232. I SCREWED AN OLD WOMAN

> I screwed an old woman in Guinea,
> God damn her old soul, she was dead,
> The maggots crawled out of her ass-hole,
> And the hair it slipped off of her head.

Oh fol da de lol da de loddy,
Oh fol da de lol da de day,
There was never a jinny so ugly
But could get her a jackass to bray.

A. Recited by a lady in Springfield, Missouri, April 30, 1946, who said she had it from Professor Bob Crow, of Salem, Missouri. A sea-song; the tune is "My Bonnie Lies over the Ocean," with *fol-lol* chorus. On these purposely ugly and anti-gallant images, see "Bluebird Shit," No. 231 immediately preceding, and No. 233, following. As to the psycho-dynamics of this sort of maniacal attack on the mother-figure of the "old woman," see Legman, *Rationale of the Dirty Joke* (vol. II: *No Laughing Matter*, 1975) "Anti-Gallantry and Anti-Woman," pp. 704–44; and especially "The Defiling of the Mother," pp. 392–419. An American motion picture on this repellent subject of erotic corpse-profanation, based on a story by Charles Bukowski, a would-be imitator of Henry Miller, was shown officially at the Cannes (France) Motion-Picture Festival in May 1991, along with two other European films on the latest perversion spectacle, erotic cannibalism; the beautiful heroine in both cases being killed and *eaten* by her "snuffy" lovers; as, long ago, in the mystery story "Two Bottles of Relish," by Lord Dunsany. What next? Compare the recent fad for mock-cannibalistic cakes in sexual-organ shapes.

B. Text from Mr. J. E., Webster Groves, Missouri, April 8, 1948. He heard about it in 1885:

I fucked an old nigger in Guinea,
God damn her old soul, she was dead,
The maggots worked out of her ass-hole,
The wool all slipped off of her head.

C. Mr. B. W., Eureka Springs, Arkansas, June 22, 1948, recalled the following:

I fucked an old nigger named Ginny,
God damn her old soul, she was dead,
While the maggots worked out of her ass-hole,
And the hair slipped off of her head.

D. Fragment from Mr. J. C., Eureka Springs, Arkansas, August 24, 1951. He heard it in Moberly, Missouri, about 1912:

The maggots rolled out of her ass-hole,
And her eye-balls burst in her head.

233. HER HAIR WAS LONG

Her hair was long and woolly,
And her nose was flat and level,
And every time I gave a job
She farted like the devil.
        Bugaroo! Bugaroo!
You bet I had to take it slow.

Fragment from Mr. J. E., Webster Groves, Missouri, April 8, 1948. He heard it in the late 1880s.
This is connected with and may form part of "I Screwed an Old Woman," No. 232 immediately preceding, though the metric pattern is not the same. In line 3: *job*, a jab or shove. As the hair-and-nose

description makes clear, reference is to intercourse with a Negro woman or an Australian (New Guinea) "aborigine." "*Bugaroo!*" is evidently a somehow magical or evil-averting apotropaic word, responding to the mention here of the (black) Devil. It is often corrupted to the otherwise meaningless "Boogy-boo," "Bugaboo," or even "Foggy-foggy Dew," as in song No. 64 above, but is here perhaps connected with "booger" (bugger) or "boogie," also an allusion to the demon, but referring more directly to the Negro.

234. SIT ON MY FACE

Now, my father said to me, When you marry a wife
You're going to have to fuck her for the rest of your life.
You're going to have to keep her dressed in silk and lace,
So you better have her sit right down on your face.

> *You got to sit sit sit, sit on my face,*
> *Honey, sit sit sit, sit on my face,*
> *Moon-time, noon-time, sit on my face,*
> *You got to sit sit sit on my face!*

Well, I took my father's word, and I got me a wife,
And on our wedding-night I had the time of my life.
You just should of seen us—what a disgrace—
She climbed up on the bureau and *jumped* on my face!

Well, my dear wife died just the other day,
She died for the lack of a satisfying lay,
And on her headstone these words I placed:
Here lies a girl who just sat on my face.

Sung by Mr. M. M., a Mormon student about twenty years old, from Fayetteville, Arkansas, then at San Diego, California, October 1964, to a familiar tune I was not able to place. Although on first sight, this presents itself as a song about oral-erotic technique, it is basically a masochistic and self-admittedly supine husband's complaint about a domineering and sexually frigid wife. Note that she dies "for the lack of a satisfying lay." Her death is his fantasy punishment of her, for her metaphorical "sitting on his face," in which it is the erotic statement which hides the social reality, instead of the usual reverse. In the chorus, line 3, *moon,* the buttocks.

At the level of erotic technique, here cunnilinctus, on the man's part, as something needed and demanded by the woman to bring her to orgastic satisfaction, the *date* is very significant, as also the social and cultural milieu. The idea of women's erotic *right* to orgasm, like and as often as their husbands, does not date appreciably in America before the 1930s, and not before the 1950s on any broad scale. Another version of the song (without the 3rd line of the chorus) was heard by Markoe Rivinus, Philadelphia, before 1959.

235. VIOLATE ME IN VIOLET TIME

Oh, violate me in violet time
In the vi-o-lest way you know.

Screw me and use me;
Fuck me, abuse me,
In the violest way you know—
On me no mercy show!

From now on, to weak men
I'm wholly oblivious,
I want a man who is
(Shouted) *Lewd and lascivious!*

So, violate me in violet time
In the vi-o-lest way you know!

A. Sung by Mr. R. K., of Mena, Arkansas, in New York, November 1953, for my wife, Beverley Legman-Keith and his own, for the present work, during my absence in France. This is that tremendous rarity, *a folksong by a living author who is positively identifiable*, but of whom the singers have little or no cognizance, in this case William Soskin. Two other modern more-or-less bawdy examples, both also of World War II prominence, are "King Farouk" by Hamish Henderson; and "The Second Front Song" by Ewan MacColl, printed in Martin Page, *Kiss Me Goodnight, Sergeant Major* (London, 1973) pp. 115–20; the first anti-Egyptian, the second anti-American.

B. The original song "Violet Time" was written, without any forthright erotic terms as in *A* above, by William Soskin, later a publisher in New York, as part of a humorous skit in the private Dutch Treat Club show, in 1933, which also included "Four Prominent Bastards Are We" by Ogden Nash in a skit called "Pedigree"; and compare Nash's line in a poem read at the same show: "Seduction is for sissies—A he-man wants his rape!" "Violet Time" was first published in *The Bedroom Companion* (New York, 1934–35, anonymously edited by Philip Wylie) pp. 209–11, giving its author's name, and the tune: a weak sentimental waltz, of which the best a Michigan State College coed was able to say of it in 1953 is that the "Tune is non-descript." The text given below is its first known reprinted form, already from folk transmission and with minor changes from the original, here as appearing in a West Coast Trotskyite private publication, *Unexpurgated* (Los Angeles? 1943) p. 55, combining both Marxist and sexual revolt in print for perhaps the first time in English:

> Violate me in violet time,
> In the vilest way that you know—
> Ruin me, ravage me,
> Brutally, savagely,
> On me no mercy bestow!
>
> To the man who is gentle and kind
> I'm oblivious;
> Give me a man who is
> Lewd and lascivious! (So,)
> Violate me in violet time,
> In the vilest way that you know.

The author's open intention was to satirize masochistic Tin Pan Alley pop-songs, of which the 1940s were the high (or low) point, in such items as "I'm Nothin' But a Nothin'," ("But Love Me Anyway!")

These are of course not new, since all sexual perversions and inversions, such as sado-masochism and homosexuality (which are very often combined, as in hazing, war, and so forth), are very ancient. See Alvin Scodel, "Changes in Song Lyrics, and Some Speculations on National Character," in *Merrill Palmer Quarterly* (1961) vol. VII: pp. 39–47, and compare the "sexual supplement" to this pioneering study by Lance and Berry (1978). In the "pop" line, perhaps the most forthright has been Alfred Bryan's song, introduced by Lillian Lorraine at the New York Winter Garden in 1914: "Smother Me With Kisses, Hon, and kill me with love, Wrap yourself around me like a serpent 'round a dove." At the unconscious humorous level, this is reminiscent of the worst masochistic excesses of Swinburne's in his alliterative "Lady of Pain" paean to his whip-mistress Adah Isaacs Menken, which have been poniarded forever in the greatest parody in English language poetry, "The Octopus" by A. C. Hilton, about 1880, in J. M. Cohen's *Yet More Comic and Curious Verse* (Penguin, 1959) pp. 289–90, ending:

> Ah! thy red lips, lascivious and luscious,
> With death in their amorous kiss!
> Cling round us, and clasp us, and crush us,
> With bitings of agonized bliss . . .

This is not the area in which William Soskin's light-hearted *macho* love song operates, which might instead be styled the acceptably "normal masochism" posited by Freud as to all female mammals (including humans) who must be deflowered painfully by the male. As such, his song is slyly presented as an offer or demand expressive of *eager female passion from the woman's standpoint* and in her own pretended words. It was tremendously popular during World War II, and appears in folk-transmitted form in all the main private armed-forces mimeographed songbooks then and since. It was sung just as heartily and enthusiastically by nurses, WACs, and other servicewomen, both American and British, as by servicemen, and later by homosexual entertainers. William Bradford Huie in *The Revolt of Mamie Stover* calls it the "theme song of the nurses' corps."

The main garblings of the text occur in the (parenthetical) violent verbs. See: *Unexpurgated* (1943) p. 55; perhaps preceded by the Ben Keller manuscript (Socorro, New Mexico, 1944, collected about 1938); *Aloha Jigpoha*, p. 58 ("Brutally ravish me, Rudely and savagely"); *Airdales in the Pacific*, p. 17 ("Rape me and ravage me, Cruelly, savagely"); *Mess Songs*, Australian Air Force, p. 68 ("Ruthlessly ravish me, Lusciously lavish me"); Dorson-Indiana Folklore Archive: fifteen texts, twelve being from girls, such as one from Greenbriar College, 1945 ("I'm just a gal who is fast and fasticidiars [sic]; Give me a man who is lude and lucidicious" [re-sic!]); Morse, p. 98 ("Ruin me, ravish me, Utterly lavish me"); Nancy Evans manuscript, p. 9 ("Rape me and ravage me, Brutally savage me"); Starr, *Fighter Pilots Hymn Book* p. 76 ("Ravage rne, savage me; Utterly damage me"); *Songs of Raunch* (1958) p. 6, sandwiching the original song between two chuckleheaded opening and closing newly added double-stanzas; McWilliams manuscript, tape VI-15 ("Ruin me, ravish me; Utterly depravish me"); *Be Pure!* (Perth, Australia, 1963) p. 53, reprinted in "Argus Tuft" Folio, No. 59 ("Ravage me, savage me, Bruise me and damage me"); *Wild Weasel Songbook*, No. 104 ("Ravage me, savage me; Utterly damage me"); Morgan, *More Rugby Songs* (1968) p. 24 ("I want a man who is generous and lecherous"); also J. Barre Toelken, "The Folklore of Academe," in Jan Brunvand, *The Study of American Folklore* (1968) p. 324; and G. Legman, "Bawdy Monologues and Recitations," in *Southern Folklore Quarterly* (1976) vol 40: p. 110.

In all this outpouring of presumed wild *machismo*, under the convenient stalking-horse pretense that it is a woman who is expressing her overwhelming eroticism (as in "The Yeomanette's Prayer," 1920s, beginning shyly, "Put your arms around me honey," and ending in the wild castratory blaze of "Break it off and let it stay!") it is observable that the one and only text that dares that he-man word "rape" is in the Nancy Evans manuscript (San Diego, California, 1951–60).

Compare the best-selling and *for the first time frank and unexpurgated* female autobiographical fantasies and fictions, in Nancy Friday's trail-blazing and courageous amateur symposiums *My Secret*

Garden (1973) and *Forbidden Flowers* (1975); and Erica Jong's even more courageous first-person *Fear of Flying* (1974), presumably favoring the high New Freedom "zipless fuck" or unemotional, wholly physical sexual encounter; and her *How To Save Your Own Life* (1977), equally candid about sex but actually about the difficulty of falling in love for fashionably "hip" and massively under-reacting modern women and men. Also Anaïs Nin's artistic erotic storiettes, *Delta of Venus* (1977) and *Little Birds* (1979), these written however between 1940 and 1944 at the suggestion of G. Legman. See further my introduction to Patrick Kearney, *The Private Case of the British Museum Library* (1981) pp. 52–55, and as revised and enlarged in Martha Cornog's symposium on *Libraries, Erotica, and Pornography* (Phoenix, Arizona: Oryx Press, 1991).

236. ROLL YOUR LEG OVER

I wish little girls were like bells in a tower,
And I was a clapper, I'd bang 'em every hour.

Oh roll, roll, roll your leg over,
Oh roll, roll, roll your leg over,
Oh roll, roll, roll your leg over,
I'm the man in the mood.

I wish little girls were like B-29s,
And I was a spitfire, I'd buzz their behinds.

I wish little girls were like statues of Venus,
And I was a Mercury with a petrified penis.

I wish little girls were like bats in a steeple
If I was a bat there'd be more bats than people.

A. From a student at the University of Arkansas, Fayetteville, Arkansas, April 27, 1957, *College Folklore* manuscript, p. 88. He learned it from a boy at Rogers, Arkansas, who sang it to the tune of "Blow the Man Down," given above at "Wings of Gold," No. 105. The last line of the chorus and full title of the song originally, is "Roll Your Leg Over the Man in the *Moon!*" "In the *mood*," politely ". . . for love," means sexually willing or desirous, "horny." In stanza 2, *B-29s,* and *Spitfire* (polite for Spanish *cacafuego*, shitfire), and in version *B* following, *Mustang*, are types of transport and fighter planes in World War II; *buzz*, to fly dangerously close to something. This is a very brief version of what was perhaps the most popular American armed forces song in World War II, later remaining popular in the universities, sometimes with as many as twenty or more stanzas, each expressing a similar wish or theorem of sexual mastery.

B. A fuller and more typical version follows, sung by James McWilliams, Berkeley, California, 1961. It was sung together by both young male and female skiers, mostly college students, while climbing the ski slope at Squaw Valley, Idaho, 1952. In 1:2, *ball,* testicle; 3:4, *to go (twice as) far,* to handle a woman's body sexually. 5:2, *boobies,* bubbies, breasts (see *Hamlet* [1603] Act III, Scene ii line 258: "If I could see the *poopies* dallying."); 8:4, *plucker,* rhyming on "fucker"; 9:2 and 4, *bang,* and *lay,* have sexual intercourse, as transitive verbs; 10:2, *meddle* (or *interfere*) *with,* deal with sexually; 10:4, *clitóris,* common colloquial pronunciation, with accent on the 2nd syllable; 12:4, *goose,* to tickle rectally; 13:2, *eat,* meaning cunnilinctus:

If all the young ladies was up for improvement,
I'd give them some help with a *ball*-bearing movement.
  Oh, roll, roll, roll! your leg over,
  Roll your leg over the Man in the Moon!

If all the young ladies were little white kittens,
I'd be a tomcat, I'd make them new fittin's./
If all the young ladies were B-29s,
And I were a Mustang, I'd buzz their behinds.

If all the young ladies were bats in a steeple,
And I was a bat, there'd be more bats than people./
If all the young ladies were wheels on a car,
And I were a piston, I'd go twice as far.

If all the young ladies were little blind moles,
Then I'd find their burrows and fill up their holes./
If all the young ladies were mares in a stable,
And I were a groom mounting all I was able!

If all the young ladies were diamonds and rubies,
And I were a jeweller, I'd polish their boobies./
If all the young ladies were trout in a pool,
And I were a pike with a waterproof tool!

If all the young ladies were little white rabbits,
And I were a buck, I would teach them bad habits./
If all the young ladies were rushes a-growing,
I'd take out my scythe and start in a-mowing.

If all the young ladies were fish in the ocean,
And I were a shark, I would show them the motion./
If all the young ladies were sheep in the clover,
And I were a ram, I would ram them all over.

If all the young ladies were little white vixen,
And I were a fox, I would chase 'em and fix 'em./
If all the young ladies were grapes on a vine,
And I were a plucker, I'd have me a time.

If all the young ladies were bells in a tower,
And I were a sexton, I'd bang on the hour./
If all the young ladies were bricks in a pile,
And I were a mason, I'd lay them in style.

If all the young ladies were like Hansel and Gretel,
And I were Hansel, I'd meddle with Gretel./
If all the young ladies were trees in a forest,
And I was a woodman, I'd chop their clitóris.

If all the young ladies were far better skiers,
And better beer-drinkers and less constant pee-ers./
If all the young ladies were singin' this song,
It would be twice as dirty and ten times as long.

I wish all the girls were like Mount Shasta ski-tow,
You pay your five dollars; you get on and go./
I wish all the girls were like cars on the highway,
I'd clutch them and goose them, and make them go my way.

I wish all the girls were like pancakes from Texas,
And I was a chef, I would eat them for breakfast.

In the 11th stanza, "beer-drinkers and constant pee-ers" is a *macho* brag on cause and effect: that a "real man" can *hold his liquor*, whereas the problem of a woman in long pants, on skis, squatting to piss through the snow-crust is thought humorous and sexually exciting by male skiers, standing up to do so. It is also considered witty to invite a girl companion to assist a boy *pissing in the snow* (see Vance Randolph's book title, 1976), by "holding his pen"—which is mightier than the sword—or "signing his name," or their heart-entwined initials in the snow. This game is known to children as young as five years old. Young mothers—seldom fathers, except by example—sometimes play this game with their boy-children (not always consciously) as *"Pee for Mama . . ."*

C. The earliest known text "A Hunting Song"—but see the endnote below for the Child Ballad *ur*-form, "The Twa Magicians"—is in Samuel Lover's novel of Irish life, *Rory O'More* (1837). In 2:4, *ate mate*, eat meat:

> If all the young maidens was blackbirds an' thrushes,
> 'Tis then the young men would be batin' the bushes.
> If all the young maidens was ducks in the water,
> 'Tis then the young men would jump in an' swim arter.
>
> If all the young maidens was birds on the mountain,
> 'Tis then the young men would get guns an' go grousin'.
> If the maidens was all trout an' salmon so lively,
> Oh, the divil a man would ate mate on a Friday!

D. Cecil Sharp collected two versions of this in Somerset, England, 1906, one from Bridgwater with the women as ducks, and the men turning into drakes to "soon follow after." Only text *B* above seems to have preserved the obviously rustic lines, in stanza 6, about the young ladies as "rushes a-growing," and the singer taking out his scythe to "start in a-mowing," which may fairly be assumed to be a survival of a much older form, if only from the "a-" prefixes. Sharp's other 1906 text, from Porlock Weir, Somerset, *Collection*, No. 109-H, singer seventy-six years old, is tacked onto another song, "Sally My Dear," probably for its *fal-the-dal-dal* (dildo) chorus. The *strip* and *cock* (gun) metaphors in the last lines speak for themselves. In 1:2, *nest*, vagina:

> If young women could build like blackbirds and thrushes,
> There's many a young man would soon find out the nest-es.
>
> If young women could swim like fishes in water,
> There's many a young man would strip and swim after.
>
> If young women could fly like birds in the air,
> There's many a young man would cock and let fire.

E. Although it is usually not possible to cite non-English congeners of bawdy songs that follow anything but the inspiration very closely, in this case the modern French students' song, "Bel Alcindor" is almost identical, if franker. In a remarkable article on witchcraft and English folksong, in *Come All Ye: The Vancouver Folk Song Society Journal* (1973) vol. 2, No. 11: pp. 6–11, Dr. Murray Shoolbraid cites the probable original, the older French and French Canadian "transformations" song, "Si tu te mets anguille—Je me mettrai pêcheur, *etc.*," given in Gagnon's *Chansons populaires du Canada*, pp. 78–81 and 139–41, noting further the art-poem, "Magali," on this same theme, by the nineteenth-century French Provençal poet, Mistral. The text of "Bel Alcindor" below is from the very rare *Anthologie Hospitalière et Latinesque* (1913) vol. II: p. 331 (reprinted in *Chansons de Salle de Garde*, 1962, p. 318), and in Staub, at "Alcindor," omitting a long medley-style opening chorus beginning, "Bandais-tu, bel

Alcindor?" ("Did you have an erection, handsome Alcindor?") In the final schoolroom stanza, on Rolle's Theorem, *colle* is a pun on its two meanings as both semen (paste) and to flunk on a "poser," a difficult question. Note: *con*, cunt; *vit* and *pine*, penis; *couilles*, testicles (cullions, goolies):

> *Si les cons poussaient comme des pommes de terre,*
> *On verrait les vits labourer la terre./*
> *Si les cons nichaient comme des hirondelles,*
> *On verrait les vits monter à l'échelle.*
>
> *Si les cons volaient comme des bécasses,*
> *On verrait les vits prendre des permis d' chasse./*
> *Si les cons nageaient comme des grenouilles,*
> *On verrait sur l'eau cent mille paires de couilles.*
>
> *Si les cons pissaient de l'encre de Chine,*
> *On verrait s'y tremper toutes les pines./*
> *Si les cons savaient le théorème de Rolle,*
> *On verrait les vits leur pousser des colles.*

James Reeves, in *The Idiom of the People* (1958) p. 119, has observed, possibly on the basis of a note by Cecil Sharp whose manuscripts he was editing, that the present song in English is a form of the older ballad "The Twa Magicians" (Child No. 44; Bronson, vol. I: p. 350), concerning a duel in magical transformations between the hero and an ensorcelled virgin maid attempting to preserve her virginity. At least four other folklorists have, apparently independently, also arrived at this same conclusion at later dates. (See Reuss, pp. 232–39; and especially Cray, p. 233, erroneously adding the name of G. Legman to this group.) See further Margaret Dean-Smith, *Guide to English Folk Song Collections* (1954) at "Hares on the Mountains" and "Sally My Dear," and all the basic research fully and magistrally set out by Shoolbraid (1973) as in headnote *E* above.

The only extant text of "The Twa Magicians" was recovered by Peter Buchan, *Ancient Ballads of Scotland* (1828, and reprint 1875) vol. I: pp. 24–27. Beginning as two doves, the lovers' transformations go from eel/trout and duck/drake, to mare/saddle and griddle/cake; and when the fearful virgin eventually transforms herself into a ship, "To sail out ower the flood; He ca'ed (struck) a nail intill her tail, And syne the ship she stood." As to the straight-shooting erotic symbolism here—Reeves' delicately expressed "folk idiom" or "*lingua franca* of the folk"—as Dr. Shoolbraid remarks, "If that isn't your folk idiom, I don't know what is."

Curiously, though Child traces the theme of both the ballad and underlying tale-form through many European and Asiatic versions, he does not mention the earliest such magical reference, in the duel with rods turned into serpents, between Aaron and the sorcerers of Pharaoh, in *Exodus*, 7:8–12. Also, though Buchan's *ur*text of the ballad ends pointedly with the final "unhexing" of the woman by her deflowering , Child does not observe here, but only at "Tam Lin," No. 39, vol. I: pp. 335–39, the obvious parallels in the Greek legendary loves of Jupiter and the competing god Apollo chasing nymphs (especially Daphne), and even more closely the rape by Poseidon/Neptune of his sister Demeter, he being disguised as a horse and she as a mare (this trait is notably retained in Buchan's "Twa Magicians" text). Also, only at "Tam Lin," vol. I: p. 337, does Child admit, where the ensorcelled maid lastly becomes a loathsome snake, that she is liberated when "The knight makes a sufficient incision (!) for blood to come," and that this "incision" and blood are the essence of her devirginizing and thus of her unhexing. See further G. Legman, *Rationale of the Dirty Joke*, vol. I: pp. 527–30, "Ophelia's 'Nothing,'" and especially vol. II: pp. 429–34, "Tooth-Breaker."

Other sources on polite forms of the song: Bronson, No. 44, vol. I: p. 350; Kennedy, No. 169, pp. 395 and 425; Colm O'Lochlainn, *More Irish Street Ballads* (1965) p. 100; Reeves, *Idiom*, p. 119, and *Everlasting*, p. 150; and Williams, p. 224. The American play-party song, "Sourwood Mountain," may involve another strain of this, as in a 1910 version in Brown, vol. III: p. 282, No. 251-C: "A pretty little girl went a-floating down the river, Ef I could-a swum I'd-a went with her."

Unexpurgated sources: *Airdales in the Pacific* (1944) p. 16; *North Atlantic Squadron* (Gander, Newfoundland 1944) p. 11; Matt Carney manuscript (1945); Dorson-Indiana Folklore Archive (20 texts); Wilgus-Western Kentucky Folklore Archive; Bess Lomax Hawes manuscript (1950); *My Bonny* (Ottawa, 1950) p. 2; Nancy Reeves manuscript (1957); *Songs of Raunch* (1958: 49 stanzas); Lillian Zahrt manuscript (1962); Starr, *Fighter Pilots Hymn Book* (1958) p. 77, reprinted in *Wild Weasel* (1968) No. 42; Burson manuscript (Los Angeles, 1959; 17 stanzas); Mack McCormick manuscript (1959); Don Laycock manuscript *Obiter Dicta* (1960) pp. 163 and 187; also in its printed version as *The Best Bawdry* (London 1982); Oscar Brand, (1960) pp. 72–73, and sung on his "Bawdy Ballads" recordings; Walsh (1962) p. 99, reprinted in Babad, p. 111, with tune; Sandra Stolz manuscript (1961) No. 13; Reuss manuscript (1963; medley of 60 stanzas), and in his published monograph, pp. 232–35; *Dirt: An Exegesis* (UCLA 1965) p. 11; Fagan manuscript "*U.S. Navy Folklore*" (1966) p. 47; Cray (1969) pp. 112–13 and 233–34, with tune; Silverman (1982) p. 141, with tune, which Reuss identifies as a Dutch song "Rosa" or "Louisa."

Latest, and far from least, is Carol Burke's searingly powerful article and collection of gruesome Vietnam War cadence calls, in her "Marching to Vietnam," in *Journal of American Folklore* (1989) vol. 102: pp. 424–41, at pp. 425–26, and observing p. 438, note 4, that this song favorite among both women and men in World War II, though only a "playful sexist objectification of women," is an "exercise in metaphor making, this call typically . . . comparing 'girls' or 'ladies' to holes in the road, telephone poles, bats in a steeple, hammers in a shed, bells in a tower, hoops in the gym, nails in a board, fish in the ocean, and clouds in the sky . . . it is scarcely heard today."

237. CARELESS LOVE

What will Mammy say to me,
What will Mammy say to me,
What will Mammy say to me
When I go home with a big bell-ee?

I'll tell her to hold her tongue,
I'll tell her to hold her tongue,
I'll tell her to hold her tongue,
She loved pecker when she was young.

A. Fragment from an elderly gentleman, Mr. J. E., Webster Groves, Missouri, April 8, 1948. He learned it about 1880. In 1:4, *a big bell-ee*, pregnant; 2:4, *pecker*, penis. In polite versions this becomes: "She loved *the boys* when she was young."

B. Below is given a more complete version of this beautiful old Scottish or English song, in which it should be noted that the lovely tune is even lovelier on the triple repeats of the first line. As sung by Judith Evans, later Legman; San Francisco, California, 1950, age ten; recollected 1989. She learned it from her Irish-American mother. In 1:2, *in the family way*, pregnant; and so also 3:1, *wear my apron high:*

Love, oh love, oh careless love, (3 times)
You've seen what careless love can do.

What, oh what, will Mammy say (3)
When she sees that I'm in the family way?

> Once I wore my apron low, (3)
> You'd follow me where-e'er I'd go.
>
> Now I wear my apron high, (3)
> You see my gate and pass it by . . .

C. In another strain, recovered only once, by Herbert Halpert in New Egypt, New Jersey, August 1939 (informant C. G.), the "Row the boat ashore" chorus of "The Hog-Eye Man," No. 126 above, is used. The opening reference to *fifteen cents* is obscure: either the boy or the girl involved in this colloquy has paid the other that ludicrously small sum, evidently for some sexual "show-and-tell" display or permission, which is now being refused out of fear of pregnancy (the "big bell-y" of stanza 2:2).

In 3:3, *musharoon*, a conscious allusion to erotic symbolism in dreams: the mushroom and fast-growing springtime wild asparagus are among the most common rural folk symbols for the erect penis. This is taken cognizance of in the scientific nomenclature of mycology: one of the deadliest mushrooms is called *Amanita Phalloïdes*; another is commonly known as *Dog's Prick*, both because of their shape; and compare the common *Phallus Impudicus*, or "shameless penis," the large arum or "Cuckoo Pintle," this being another old term for the penis, and therefore expurgatorily abbreviated to "cuckoo pint," "wake-Robin," or "Jack-in-the-pulpit," unless the *Robin* and *Jack* (the modern "john"), also imply the same. W. L. McAtee has published an entire monograph, *Nomina Abitera* (Privately Printed, 1945), on this type of erotic and erotico-scientific nomenclature. In the chorus: *hog's-eye* and *pig's eye*, the vagina, or its split "upright diamond" symbol. (Not to be confused with the nautical slang, *dead-eye*, the anus, or a Turk's-head knot in rope.) *Hog's-eye man*, an inveterate wencher or "cunt-hound," a man obsessed with women and sex, also called "Jody." See texts at No. 126 above. The first and last stanzas here are in the metrical pattern of "Yankee Doodle," No. 209:

> Oh, pay me back my fifteen cents,
> Pay me back my money;
> Pay me back my fifteen cents,
> And I'll go home to mommy.
>
> *Row the boat ashore with a hog's eye,*
> *Row the boat ashore with a pig's eye,*
> *Row the boat ashore, and I don't give a damn,*
> *'Cause all I want is a hog's-eye man.*
>
> Now, what would my mommy say to me
> If I went home with a big bell-y?—
> Oh, tell your mommy to hold her tongue,
> For she liked boys when she was young.
>
> Oh, my sister Sal she dreamt a dream,
> She dreamt she went a-huntin',
> She thought she found a musharoon,
> As big as any punkin.

Revived by Cecil Sharp about 1905 in its original form (*B* above) as "The Water Is Wide," and split into two *complaintes*, "Deep in Love" and "Died for Love," see also Lomax, No. 309, pp. 574–75, and p. 585 for the superb tune, which is also used for the chorus; and with further references, Kennedy, Nos. 149 and 160, in the notes only, pp. 372 and 381; also Sharp, *Appalachians*, vol. II: p. 268, as "Every Night When the Sun Goes In"; and Randolph, *Ozark Folksongs*, vol. III: 306, who also notes the related version as "Careless Love" in Lunsford and Stringfield, *30 and 1 Folk Songs from the Southern Mountains* (1930) pp. 40–41. Reeves, p. 90, "Make me a pallet on the floor (3 times), So your good man will never know," implies a theme of ancillary marriage (as with the Patriarchs' lesser wives in *Genesis*) or adultery, on which this song seldom touches. According to Vaughan Williams, the "apron low-and-high" lines come from a different song, "A Brisk Young Soldier Courted Me," in Sharp, vol. II: p. 76, which may in fact be the *story* missing in this song which, as we have it now, is strictly an emotional outcry.

Compare also the famous "O Waly Waly, or The Apple and the Orange," in Ramsay's *Tea-Table Miscellany* (1724), discussed by J. W. Allen in *Journal of English Folk Song* (1954) p. 161, with tune in Thomson's *Orpheus Caledonius* (1733) vol. I: pp. 71–73; and the certainly related "My Apron, Deary," at vol. I: p. 68. The lines in the present versions *A* and *C*, in which the "errant" girl sasses back her mother, in fantasy, by telling her she too "loved pecker when she was young," are to be compared with the full-scale *controverse* between mother and daughter, in that same tone and with the identical line, in at least one other song, "Long Peggin' Awl," No. 71 here.

The present title and chorus have now been used (Winter Solstice, 1989) for an excruciating, whistling-in-the-dark would-be humorous condom-advertising parody or travesty, only too appropriately, on the current AIDS epidemic and panic, "See What Careless Love Can Do." With this compare the perfectly sincere, if mawkish, "Tumble O'Lynn's Farewell: An Innocent's Dirge—Slow," with its evident acronymic subtitle and powerful mourning-tune, "Packington's Pound," reported by G. Legman, with tune, in *Journal of American Folklore* (Jan. 1990) vol. 102, No. 407.

238. AT BRIGHTON

There was an old gent at Brighton last year
Whose hobby was swimming round the government pier,
He'd swim and he'd dive away out to a rock
And amuse all the ladies by shaking his—

Fist at the copper who walked on the shore,
It was the same copper who pinched him before.
They pursued him in small boats but never could pass
Because the old scoundrel would show them his—

Wonderful maneuvers and swimming so fine,
He would leave his pursuers all far behind.

The old gent had a daughter at Brighton that year,
Whose hobby was swimming around the same pier,
She could swim like a fish and dive like a duck,
And showed by her motions she knew how to—

Dabble in the water 'way up to her chin
Without being drowned as others had been.
When tired of swimming, for shells she would hunt
And go through all the motions of washing her—

Clothes in the ocean so deep and so blue,
A-hoping thereby to make them like new.
When through with her bathing, for shore she would start
And enjoy the strange pleasure of letting a—

Wave roll up to cover her nose,
And wash the sand off of the ends of her toes.

A. The text above and the three following are versions collected without tunes, of No. 53C, "The Handsome Young Farmer." This from Mr. H. F., Kansas City, Missouri, January 28, 1955, stating that it was popular in the late 1890s. A "tease" song, evidently derived from a British music-hall song of that period, as shown by the reference to the popular English bathing-resort, Brighton.

B. From a manuscript book in the possession of Miss M. L., Notch, Missouri, September 12, 1934, who had borrowed the book from a neighboring family named Stevens:

> There was an old farmer who lived by a rock,
> He set in the meadow a-shaking his ———
> Fist at some boys who was down by the creek,
> Their feet in the water, their hands on their ———
>
> Marbles and playthings. And in days of yore
> There come a young lady who looked like a ———
> Nice young lady who set in the grass,
> She pulled up her dresses and showed us her ———
>
> Ruffles and lace and a nice little tuck,
> She said she was learning a new way to ———
> Bring up her children and learn them to knit,
> While the boys in the barnyard were shoveling ———
>
> Refuse from the stable and tilling the soil,
> You think I've composed it, but I haven't at all!

C. Recited by a lady in Anderson, Missouri, August 10, 1947, who preferred to remain nameless. She called it "In the Springtime." Note the dialectal pronunciation in the first line, of *creek* (as "crick"), to rhyme with the unspoken *prick*; and so also in version *B,* 1:3 above.

> In the springtime the old man would sit by the creek
> Teaching the young boys to play with their ———
> Tops and their marbles as he did of yore,
> When along came a lady who looked like a ———
>
> Decent young lady who sat in the grass,
> Then she stooped over so you could see her bare ———
> Ruffles and tuffles that formed like a duck,
> She told him she'd teach him a new way to ———
>
> Bring up the children who thought they were it,
> While the boys in the barnyard were raking up ———
> Contents of gravel and dirt for the sod,
> And if you don't believe me, you're a liar, by God!

D. A fragment as sung by Mr. F. S., Eureka Springs, Arkansas, May 29, 1952. He heard it in Yell County, Arkansas, in the 1930s:

> There was a young maiden who lay in the grass,
> And when she turned over you could see her ———
> Ribbons and buttons and panties of lace,
> . . . .
>
> . . . . in the old days of yore,
> He met a young maiden he thought was a ———
> Nice little girlie . . . .

To bring up her children and teach them to knit
While the boys in the barnyard were shoveling out ———
Contents of the stable all over the sod,
If you think I composed this you're a liar, by God.

E. From a student, Mr. J. M., at the University of Arkansas, Fayetteville, Arkansas, April 27, 1957. He got it at Pine Bluff, Arkansas, and said that "it is sort of chanted or sung to your own tune, as you make it up." This has also been heard performed to a dismally worn-down and unidentifiable cantillation or recitative, exactly as the Pine Bluff informant stated:

There was a young lady in the old days of yore
And they say that she was a ———
Decent young lady who sat in the grass
And when she rolled over she showed us her ———

Fashionable clothing. She looked like a duck,
She said she was learning a new way to ———
. . . .

While men in the barn just shoveling up ———
Contents from the stable to put on the sod,
You may think I composed this,
But I didn't, by ———.

F. This and the following are versions of "There's Fun in the Country," No. 53D above, but collected without tunes, though with the same refrain. Sung by Mr. W. S., Fort Smith, Arkansas, February 25, 1951:

There was a wild Irishman, friend of my dear,
Who went to the sea-shore to bathe twice a year,
He could swim like a fish and dive like a duck,
You could tell from his actions he knew how to f———

Frolic in water plumb up to his chin
Without getting drownded like others had been.
And all the young maidens was right down in front,
Waded out in the water plumb up to their c———

Calicoes, they were fleshy, indeed they were fat,
He taught the young ladies to swim on their back.
He held a young maiden close up to his heart,
Dove under the water and let a big f———

Roll back with the waves while he swum all around,
There's fun in the country as well as in town.

G. Sung by Mr. R. C., Eureka Springs, Arkansas, November 20, 1953. He stated that it was a fragment of a long piece popular near Green Forest, Arkansas, about 1910:

There was a fat Dutchman that she loved so dear,
Went to the sea-shore to swim once a year,
The boys and the girls on the bank they would stick,
Just for to amuse them he'd show 'em his p———

Precious delight, just a-swimming around,
He's at home in the country the same as in town.
He'd dive to the bottom and sea-shells he'd hunt,
Just like a young maiden a-washing her c———

Clothes at the spring branch, a-swimming around,
He's at home in the country the same as in town.
He grabbed a young widow so dear to his heart,
He swum under water and let a big f——

Fall wave roll over him and bury him down,
He's at home in the country the same as in town.

239. STRAWBERRY ROAN

I was hanging round town in the house of ill fame,
Spending my dough and a-laying the dames,
When a hotheaded pimp with his nose full of coke
Beat me out of my gal and left me so broke.

A stranger steps up and he says I suppose
You're a bronc-busting man by the looks of your clothes.—
Oh you're damn right, that's one thing I can do,
I'm a second-rate pimp, but a good buckaroo.
          Oh, that strawberry roan!

He's got gonorrhea and shankers and siff,
He is pictured with clap but his cock is still stiff.—

The lump of it was that I found myself hired
A-snapping out broncs that great stud had sired.
They were hotheaded cayuses just like their dad,
The most of them roan, but all of them bad,
          Oh, that strawberry roan!

With their feet in my pockets, them bastards did fight
Till my ass drug my tracks out long before night,
With my balls in my boots and my mouth full of dung,
My ears were all scratched, where my spurs hung.

The boss come around and he says that's enough,
The strawberry roan's colts are too God damn tough.
I'm plumb sick and tired of taking them falls,
Rope that windmilling stud, and we'll cut out his balls,
          Oh, that strawberry roan!

So I builds a big loop and goes in the corral,
I roped his front feet, and he farted and fell,
The boss held his head while I hogtied his legs,
Then I opened my jack knife and went for his eggs.
When I opened his bag he let out a moan,
He squealed like a pig when I whittled one stone,
But all I could locate was one of his nuts,
The other'n was hid away back in his guts,
          Oh, that strawberry roan!

So I rolls up my sleeves, and a-swimming in blood
I frisked for the nut in the gut of that stud,
I thought I had found it when I felt something pass,
But 'twas only a turd on the way to his ass,
          Oh, that strawberry roan!

Of a sudden I heard a blood-curdling squall,
I seen that the roan had the boss by the balls,
I stomped on his head, but it wasn't no use,
The boss says to turn the son-of-a-bitch loose.

So I untied his legs and he got on his feet,
But the boss's voice changed, and I knew he was beat.
He's a ball-bearing stud with only one ball,
But the boss is a eunuch with no balls at all,
 Oh, that strawberry roan!

A. Usually known in full as "The Castration of the Strawberry Roan," this is a bawdy version of "The Outlaw Bronco" or "The Strawberry Roan," a cowboy song written by Curley Fletcher in 1914, who is also supposed to be the author of this bawdy version. The present text is from a former cowboy, Mr. M. M., Fayetteville, Arkansas, December 7, 1951. In 1:3, *coke*, cocaine; 1:4, *beat me out of my gal*, on the belief that cocaine is an aphrodisiac; 3:1, *siff*, syphilis; 3:2, *pictured*, mis-hearing for *strictured*, unable to urinate; 3:3, *lump*, upshot, conclusion; 4:2, *my ass drug my tracks out*, i.e, "was dragging on the ground" from the relaxation and extrusion of the anus (in horse and man) as a result of fatigue; 6:1, *loop*, rope-loop in lariat; 6:4, *eggs*, testicles, also *stones* (or *seeds*, and *nuts*) in 7:2. These are all ancient metaphors; see, for example, "He that is wounded in the stones," in *Leviticus*, 21:20 (King James translation, 1611).

B. Collected by Bruce Jackson, from the singing of a cowboy, Mr. Glen Ohrlin, Mountain View, Arkansas, June 27, 1964, who said he learned it from "an old cowboy I knew from North Ridge, California," but had heard the song for twenty years before learning it. In stanza 1:2, *twist*, a woman, *hustlin'*, prostitution; 1:3, *hop-headed pig*, drug-addicted policeman; chorus, line 3, *blueballs*, venereal buboes; 3:2, *the meat*, the penis; 7:1, *bone*, the penis, especially if erect; 9:1, *bag*, scrotum:

I was just hanging 'round in a house of ill fame,
Laid up with a twist of a hustlin' dame,
When a hop-headed pig with his nose full of coke
Beat me out of my whore and left me stone broke.

When up steps a stranger; said he, Say, my lad,
Are you any good ridin' horses that's bad?—
I said, You're damned right, that's one thing I can do;
I'm a second-rate pimp but a good buckaroo.

Oh, that Strawberry Roan, how many colts has he thrown?
He's got gonorrhea, the glanders and syph,
The blueballs and claps, but his tool is still stiff;
Look out for that Strawberry Roan.

When a good-looking filly would come into heat,
Was the Strawberry Roan that throwed her the meat.
The upshot of it was, I found myself hired
To snap out some broncs that this Roan stud had sired.

They're knot-headed cayuses just like their dad,
Most of them's roans and all of them's bad;
With their feet in my pockets them bastards would fight
Till my ass drug my tracks in, long before night.

With my balls in my boots and my mouth full of shit
I was plumb tuckered out and ready to quit;
Whenever I thought I had one of them rode,
He busted my ass and I found myself throwed.

Then the boss come around; he said, That's enough,
That Strawberry Roan's colts are too tough,
I'm getting damn sick of you taking them falls;
We'll get that windmillin' stud 'n' we'll cut out his balls.

Oh, that Strawberry Roan; we went out to unbend his bone;
I built a big loop and went to the corral,
I roped his front feet: he jumped, he kicked, he snorted,
He farted and fell; I flattened that Strawberry Roan.

Well, the boss held his head while I hogtied his legs,
I got out my knife and I went for his eggs.
He knowed what I wanted, he knowed it damned well,
'Cause he fought like a tiger and he squealed like hell.

I opened his bag and he let out a moan,
He squealed like a shoat when I cut out that stone,
But all I could lo-cate was one of his nuts,
The other was hidden someplace in his guts.

. . . .
I reached up inside him and felt something pass,
But it's only a turd on the way to his ass.

Well, the boss said, I'm sick of this hard-bucking breed,
If it takes us all night we'll get that other seed.
Just then I heard one o' them blood-curdling squalls
And the Strawberry Roan had the boss by the balls.

I stomped on his head, but it was no use,
He's just like a bulldog, he wouldn't turn loose.
I untied his legs and he got to his feet,
The boss's voice changed and I know he was beat.

Oh, that Strawberry Roan; I advise you to leave him alone,
He's a knot-headed cayuse with only one ball,
But the boss is a eunuch with *no* balls at all—
Look out for that Strawberry Roan.

The missing lines opening the 10th stanza are given in version A preceding, and in the very similar version sung by a student, Mr. James McWilliams, Berkeley, California, 1961 (Tape VII-8):

And I rolled up my sleeve, and, swimming in blood,
I fished for the seed in the guts of that stud.

Note in this gruesome ballad the open identification by the cowboy singers with the untamed stone-horse in his victorious struggle with the castratory father-figure of The Boss, who ends up castrated by and instead of the rebellious horse. A clear Oedipal reversal of the age-old sacrifice of Isaac by his Patriarch father Abraham (as Oedipus by his father King Laius, for the later presumptive sin of incest with his mother), in *Genesis*, 22:1–18. Though the ballad seems cruel and unnecessarily detailed, it is far short of the violent reality of the cowboy's life, never more incisively described than in Ron Edwards' *Australian Bawdy Ballads* (Ram's Skull Press, 1973), concerning the real life of the Australian stockman, which is identical except for rattlesnakes ever-present in the American west.

See: Lomax (1934) pp. 392–95; Randolph, *Ozark Folksongs*, vol. II: pp. 232–34; and especially Logsdon, *The Whorehouse Bells* (1989) pp. 86–96, with tune, and further references, identifying the author of both the bawdy original and non-bawdy cleanup as Mr. Curley W. Fletcher, first published in the Globe, Arizona, *Record*, December 16, 1915, as "The Outlaw Bronco," and giving also a completely different bawdy version, pp. 94–95, learned by another cowboy, Mr. Dallas Turner, from his mother.

See also: Austin Fife, *"The Strawberry Roan and his Progeny,"* in *JEMF Quarterly* (1972) vol. VIII: pp. 149–65; and Getz, *The Wild Blue Yonder* (vol. II, "Stag Bar Edition," 1986), reprinted in Logsdon, p. 96, from Getz's pp. BB-21 and TT-2–3, "Bumming Around Town," a non-cowboy bawdy parody sung in the Air Force, about a sex contest with an unbeatable ugly old woman representing the horse to be tamed!

The singer of version *B* above, Mr. Glenn Ohrlin, is discussed, with portrait, in Logsdon, pp. 16–18, noting his own book of cowboy songs, *The Hell-Bound Train* (University of Illinois Press, 1973), and his private recording of "Strawberry Roan" on *Just Something My Uncle Told Me* (Rounder Records, 0141, about 1965). An earlier unexpurgated recording by an unknown singer was issued privately as a "party-record" on the High Society label about 1942, as reported by D. K. Wilgus, 1956; copy in G. Legman Archive. Two other private recordings by the "Sons of the Pioneers" are in Country Music Foundation, Nashville, Tennessee.

240. THE BASTARD KING OF ENGLAND (II)

The minstrels sing of an ancient king
Who lived so long ago,
He ruled his land with an iron hand,
And his balls hung free and low.

He loved to hunt the royal stag
And roam the royal wood,
But best of all he loved the sport
Of pulling his royal pud.

His only undergarment
Was a filthy undershirt,
Which always hid his pride and joy
But never hid the dirt.

So wild and woolly and full of fleas,
His whang hung down below his knees,
All hail the Bastard King of England!

Now the Queen of Spain was a sprightly jane,
And a sprightly jane was she,
She heard of the Bastard Englishman
So far across the sea.

So she sent a special message
By a special messenger,
To ask the King of England
To spend the night with her.

When Phillip of France did hear of it
He summoned the royal court,
He said, I have a rival now,
Because my tool's too short.

Then he ordered the Count of Zippety-Zap
To give the Queen a dose of clap,
To revenge the Bastard King of England.

When the King of England heard of this
He roared through all his halls,
He swore by his filthy undershirt
He'd have the Frenchman's balls.

He offered half his kingdom
And a night with fair Hortense,
To any noble subject who
Could mock the King of France.

So the noble Duke of Sussex
Betook himself to France,
Proclaimed himself a fruiter
And the King took down his pants.

He wrapped his thumb around his wong,
Jumped on his horse and galloped along,
Back to the Bastard King of England.

When the King of England saw them
He fainted to the floor,
For in the ride the Frenchman's pride
Had stretched a yard or more.

Now all the girls of England
They flocked to London Town,
And shouted round the palace gates,
Down with the English crown!

When Phillip of France ascended the throne,
His scepter was his Royal Bone,
With which he crowned the Bastard King of England.

A. Sent to Vance Randolph as above by a friend in Columbia, Missouri, November 17, 1948, who said he obtained it from a college student. This and the text following are versions collected without tunes, of "The Bastard King of England," on which see earlier texts and full annotation at No. 161 above. In 3:3, *his pride and joy,* his penis (and testicles), the "family jewels." 4:2, *whang,* penis, from "whang-string," a narrow leather strip; 10:2, *mock,* mis-remembering for *to nut,* castrate, as the scenario shows; 11:3, *fruiter* or *fruit,* a homosexual (the fruit implied is unknown); 12:1, *wong,* penis, identical with *whang* in 4:2 above; 13:3, *pride,* penis, "pride and joy," as in 3:3 above; 15:2, *bone,* penis. Some versions openly pun, in stanza 10, on the king's offer of a reward being "the half of all his kingdom and the *whole* of Queen Hortense." In all versions, at 2:4, the king's favorite amusement is stated to be "pulling his royal pud," (pudding), masturbating.

B. From Mr, J. S., Chicago, Illinois, February 23, 1949. He had it from a graduate student who learned it at the University of Arkansas, Fayetteville, Arkansas. For lexical details see end-note on *A.* In 1:4 here, the king's mind is "weak and low" presumably because of his habitual masturbation in 2:4. In 10:4 *de-nut,* castrate.

Oh the minstrels sing of an English king
Who lived many long years ago,
He ruled his land with an iron hand,
But his mind was weak and low.

He loved to hunt the royal stag
That roamed the royal wood,
He loved to sit in the royal shade
And pull the royal pud.

His only nether garment
Was a dirty leather shirt,
With which he tried to cover his hide
But never could hide the dirt.

He was wild and woolly and full of fleas,
And a terrible tool hung down to his knees,
God save the bastard King of England!

The Queen of Spain was a sprightly dame,
And an amorous dame was she,
She loved to fool with His Majesty's tool
In the kingdom across the sea.

So she sent a special message
By a royal messenger,
Inviting the King of England
To spend the night with her.

When Louis of France got word of this
He said to all his court:
I fear she loves my rival,
For my pud hangs down too short.

So he sent the Duke of Siff-an-Sap
To give the queen a dose of clap,
God save the bastard King of England!

When news of this foul deed was heard
Round old Westminster Hall,
The King of England solemnly swore
He'd get the Frenchman's balls.

So he offered half his kingdom
And a night with Queen Hortense,
To any loyal son of a bitch
Who'd de-nut the King of France.

Up sprang the Duke of Essex
And sped across to France,
He swore he was a fruiter
And the king took down his pants.

He fastened a thong to His Majesty's dong,
And merrily, merrily galloped along,
Back to the shores of merry England.

The Queen of England fell in a faint,
The king pissed on the floor,
For during the ride His Majesty's pride
Had stretched a mile or more.

He held it like a scepter
Over the mighty throng,
The most inspiring emblem
Of poetry, prose, or song.

And women and men and children
Round old Westminster Hall,
Cried, Down with the bastard monarch!
Cut off his slimy balls!—

And all the virgins of London Town
Shouted, To hell with the British crown!—
So Louis of France usurped the throne of England.

241. THE BOARDING-SCHOOL MAIDENS

Two boarding-school maidens, sweet, charming and bright,
Had gone to their room to retire for the night,
When as young ladies do, as they slowly undress,
Each her most secret feeling did freely express.

Said Nellie, the younger, a most luscious young dear,
I wish at the moment my Johnny was here,
For he is a darling, as smooth as a duck,
And I am half dead for the want of a fuck.

She pulled off her chémise, her drawers she left fall,
And stood naked like Venus, the fairest of all,
With her sweet little bubbies, so round, soft and white,
And crowned with red nipples delicious to sight.

'Neath her plump little belly, like drifted white snow,
The soft mound of Venus rose plain, right and left,
With the hair circling 'round in the valley below,
And showed, partly open, its vérmillion cleft.

Said Katy, I'll play like I am a man,
And give you a fucking the best that I can.—
I'm with you, said Nellie, but where is your prick?—
Said Katy, A candle will do for the trick.

Just put it in gently, the nice rounded end,
You can't tell the difference when you come to spend.
So lie down on the bed and close both your eyes,
And open quite widely your beautiful thighs.

But first I must blindfold you, sweet Katy said,
When lo, Nellie's lover sprang from under the bed;
He had been hid by Katy and was in good luck,
And like Nellie was almost half dead for a fuck.

His prick stood erect like a drum-major's stick,
And Johnny he wanted it into her quick.
Extending his hand with his light finger-tips
He tickled her cunt just within its red lips.

Her bosom heaved up like a wave on the ocean,
Her ass moved rapidly in an upward motion;
He could stand it no longer, not a moment did he wait,
But entered at once into love's finest strait.

And shoving it quickly clean up to the hilt,
Love's extract supreme in her belly was spilt.—
Oh Katy, was that just a candle I felt?
It seemed in my cunt to tickle and melt.

But really I think you have played me a trick;—
She tore off the blindfold and grabbed hold of his prick,

She did not get angry or show any pain,
But made it all right and said, Fuck me again.—

Oh no, cried poor Katy, you've had your turn;
I'll take him awhile, for my cunt it does burn.
So she pulled Johnny over on top of her belly
And he gave her a dose like the one he gave Nellie.

Poor Johnny he got himself into a bother,
For they kept him all night, fucking one then the other,
And just at daylight when he took his last bout,
He said, Good-morning ladies, my prick is wore out.

And so he sprung out from between them in the bed,
And left their cunts gasping, all shining and red.

From Mr. H. F., Kansas City, Missouri, February 18, 1955, who got it in 1891. He said: "Lots of the saloons used to have such pieces printed on the backs of their business cards. But if it was real *hot* like this one, they left the other side of the card blank. News-butchers on the trains used to carry these poems too, and sell them for twenty-five cents." It should be observed that the average workingman or clerk was then paid (until World War I) less than a dollar a day.

This is a typical "whorehouse song," recited or sung by either the prostitutes, or the clients waiting for a favorite prostitute to be unoccupied, usually with piano accompaniment by either a Negro or white pianist, always known as "the Professor," i.e., of Music. In 6:2, *spend,* have an orgasm, a British term. The tune here is unknown, but the piece is very much on the style of "The Rolling Stone," a husband-and-wife duet or *controverse* dating, according to Norman Cazden, *The Abelard Folksong Book* (1958) p. 121, to a popular songbook, *The Mock-Bird* in 1805, that is to say, traceable over a century earlier. This is in sestet stanzas, not quatrains, but with various similar doggerel lines, as in Randolph's *Ozark Folksongs* (ed. Cohen, 1982) No. 194, pp. 186–88:

Oh husband, remember, your land of delight
Is surrounded by Injuns who murder by night.

242. JOHN HARLOSON'S SALTPETER

Montgomery, Alabama, 1864

NOTICE—The ladies of Montgomery are respectfully requested to save all the chamber lye that accumulates on their premises, so that the saltpeter can be extracted from it to be used in making gunpowder for the Army. A barrel will be sent around each morning to collect it.

John Harloson,
Agent, Confederate Army.

John Harloson, John Harloson,
You are a wretched creature,
You've added to this bloody war
A new and useful feature.

You'd have us think that every man
Is bound to be a fighter,
While the ladies, bless the pretty dears,
Must save their pee for nitre.

John Harloson, John Harloson,
Where did you get the notion
To send your barrel 'round the town
To gather up the lotion?

We thought the girls had worked enough
In making shirts, and kissing,
But you have put the pretty dears
To patriotic pissing.

John Harloson, John Harloson,
Do pray invent a neater,
And somewhat less immodest way
Of getting your saltpeter.

For it's an awful idea, John,
Gunpowdery and cranky,
That when a lady lifts her skirts
She's killing of a Yankee.

(The Confederate wits had a lot of fun with the "John Harloson" poem. Then the Federals got hold of it, and some Yankee wrote his version:)

John Harloson, John Harloson,
We've heard in song and story
How women's tears through all the years
Have moistened fields of glory.

But never have we heard, John,
That 'mid such scenes and slaughter,
Your Southern beauties dried their tears
And went to making water.

No wonder Rebel boys are brave;
Who wouldn't be a fighter
When every time he fired his gun
He used his sweetheart's nitre?

And *vicè versa*, what could make
A Yankee soldier sadder
Than dodging bullets fired by
A pretty woman's bladder?

They say there is a subtle smell
That lingers in the powder,
And as the smoke grows thicker
And the din of battle louder,

That there is found in this compound
One serious objection:
No soldier boy can sniff it
Without having an erection.

A. From Mr. H. F., Kansas City, Missouri, February 9, 1955, roughly as above, including both the original Confederate piece and the Yankee reply to it. He did not say where he obtained this material, apparently about 1891. In the original "Notice," signed by the otherwise unidentified Confederate officer or agent John Harloson, *chamber lye* is an old euphemism for urine kept in chamberpots under beds until morning. In the Yankee reply, stanza 3:3, *fired his gun,* a sly erotic reference, being a common "ordnance metaphor" referring to male ejaculation; 5:1, *subtle smell,* referring (subtly) to the characteristic vaginal odor, and showing that this is the work of a cultivated poet, who recognizes that he appreciates and is excited by that odor; whereas, at lower social levels, and in most folk-poetry or humor, any reference to the vaginal odor is usually an insult. Compare also note on No. 244*B,* below; and the "Pharmacist's Aria" ("The Secret Balm") sung by Zerlina in the libretto by Da Ponte to Mozart's opera *Don Giovanni* (1787), a subject not publicly handled at any later date, despite the presumably modern "New Freedom."

B. During World War I this song and its reply were revived, with the identical story and most of the same lines, but now all run together as of the hard-pressed Germans being forced to use the ladies' "chamber lye" after the American entry into the war in 1917. The title and opening line were accordingly changed to "Von Hindenburg, Von Hindenburg," and most texts recovered use the inner-rhyme in the long lines, as in stanzas 1:3 and 6:1 of the "Reply," in *A* above, evidently to fit the tune of "Maryland" ("O Tannenbaum"). See: *Immortalia* (1927) pp. 101–02, entitled "Chamber Lye," though giving the Von Hindenburg version; reprinted in Cray (1969) pp. 140–41 and 173, drawing on Legman, *The Horn Book,* p. 378. This version is much updated (and was again updated in World War II, with only the matching title-change: "Oh, Adolf Dear," referring to Hitler). For example, the Civil War "making shirts and kissing, and patriotic pissing," become: "keeping house and diddling, and patriotic piddling;" and now the "fraulein fair of golden hair . . . Must join the line and jerk her brine, To kill the bloomin' Briton." As usual, two additional stanzas are also added at the end by the anonymous re-editor, as follows, to show his manly mettle; taking off on the gunpowder's newly aphrodisiacal odor. In 2:3, *have a piece,* i.e., "of ass" or "of tail":

> . . . And it is clear now why desertion
> Is so common in your ranks;
> An Arctic nature's badly needed
> To stand Dame Nature's pranks.
>
> A German cannot stand the strain;
> When once he's had a smell,
> He's got to have a piece or bust—
> The Fatherland to hell.

It is not by any means certain that all this tempest-in-a-chamberpot is based on any authentic incident during the Civil War, not to mention World Wars I and II. The authority taking it most seriously, as follows, is Fred Allsopp, who seems to be quoting a printed or manuscript text ("the Yankee view of it"). And it will be observed that he places the action in Selma, Alabama, where the purported "Notice" above refers to Montgomery, some fifty miles away, in his version of the chamber-lye story—or chamber-story lie:

"To provide for making gunpowder during the war," writes Allsopp, *Folklore of Romantic Arkansas* (1931) vol. 2: p. 219, "the Confederates had to resort to all sorts of devices, such as digging out and leaching the earth from smoke-houses, barns, and caves, and making beds of nitrogenous refuse. It will be remembered that the agent of the Confederate government at Selma, Alabama, put out a public advertisement in the Selma newspaper, requesting the people to be careful to preserve all *chamber-lye* to be used for the purpose of making nitre. A ballad was written on this subject, which was circulated all over the South, and when it crossed over the line, a Yankee poet wrote 'the Yankee view of it.' Both of which are highly amusing, if not in good taste."

Both the original text and its "Reply" were printed as a leaflet, apparently at Philadelphia, about 1865 (copy in the New York Public Library, 3*** Collection); and at least one reprint was made, about 1930 (in Brown University Library: American Poetry Collection). The offending Confederate government agent is called also either John Harrolson or John Haroldson, and the verses are sung to the old Scottish tune, "John Anderson, My Jo," or sometimes even forced to the tune of "Maryland, My Maryland" ("O Tannenbaum"). See further on the many topical songs of the Civil War period, of just this kind and often bawdy, S. Foster Damon, *Series of Old American Songs* (Brown University Library, 1936); and Willard and Porter Heaps, *The Singing Sixties*: "The Spirit of Civil War Days Drawn from the Music of the Times" (University of Oklahoma Press, 1960). An erotic Civil War songster of the period, *The Rakish Rhymer* was published in New York, about 1864, but no copy has survived. There is fortunately a reprint made in Paris by Charles Carrington in 1917—imagining it would do for the newly arriving Yankees in World War I as well!—of which the only depository copy is in Brown University Library.

243. THE ELECTION IS OVER

The election is over,
The time of strife is past,
I will kiss your Elephant,
And you can kiss my Ass!

Sung by Mr. R. K., of Mena, Arkansas, in New York City, November 1953, for my wife, Beverley Legman-Keith, and his own, during my absence in France. Early November is the usual date of government elections in the United States, where the Elephant is the totem of the Republican Party and the Jackass (or "Donkey") that of the competing Democratic Party, since the time of the Civil War a century earlier. The age of this "catch" or jest is therefore at any time between. Vance Randolph collected two variants, at about the same period, without tune, which he considered as "Rhymes" for that reason. The present version was reported sung to a nursery-rhyme tune "fairly close to 'I had a little poney, His name was Dapple Grey,' with an extra trill on the *El* of *Elephant*."

244. THE FROST IS ON THE PUNKIN

When the dew is on the lily
Then the Ozark hilly-billy
Is scratching ticks and chiggers all the day.

But when the frost is on the punkin
That's the time for peter-dunkin',
With his wife knocked up,
And crops all laid away.

This weather-saw or bit of farmyard homiletic wisdom was recited by Captain B. Z., Elk Creek, Missouri, December 16, 1949. Another cultivated Ozarker, Mr. R. K., of Mena, Arkansas, in New York City, November 1953, sang the second stanza (only) to a "nondescript tune," to Beverley Legman-Keith, my wife, and his own, jestingly asking first if they knew the song about "Peter Duncan," as though a man's name. Actually, *peter-dunkin'*, (from *dunk*, originally food-symbolic, to dip a doughnut into coffee or milk before eating it) refers, of course, to sexual intercourse. (And in 2:3, *knocked up*, pregnant.) *Peter* is probably, with *Dick* and *John*, the most common pet-name in English for the penis. Compare Rabelais, *Gargantua and Pantagruel* (1552) IV. i, for "Jean Jeudi," or "John Thursday," as the penis, an agnomen still current in English though long-since forgotten in French. See further: Martha Cornog, "Tom, Dick, and Hairy: Notes on Genital Pet Names," in *Maledicta*: *The Journal of Verbal Aggression* (1981) vol. V: pp. 31–40; Ms. Cornog's *hairy* contribution being immediately added to by the editor, Reinhold Aman, and friends: "What Is This Thing Called, Love?—More Genital Pet Names," in *same*, vol. V: pp. 41–44.

Although Vance Randolph generally made himself the defender of the Ozark hill-folk against all detractors, and even objected usually to the term "hillbilly" to describe them, his own field notes are sometimes less guarded than his public defensive pose. For example on the matter of "scratching ticks and chiggers all the day," in line 3 here. In his field note on "The Drunkard's Horse," in *Ozark Folksongs*, quoted in the abridged edition by Norm Cohen, No. 318, p. 269, Randolph describes the singer as follows: "Woodruff is a real backwoodsman, a long-haired snuff-dipper who lives far off the highway. Dirty and crawling with bugs. My other singers are mostly villagers, and look down on Woodruff. He can't read or write, but knows a lot of good songs, and sings them in the real old-time fashion. About fifteen years old, perhaps less . . ."

B. Additional stanza from Markoe Rivinus, Philadelphia, Pennsylvania, October 29, 1989, who noted that it "might fit many a tune although I have never heard it sung":

> Shall we sink the sacred sausage?
> Shall we split the bearded clam?
> Shall we dunk the old love-muscle
> In the sweetest soup what am?

All obvious metaphors: *sausage* and *love-muscle*, the penis (but note "sacred"); *bearded clam*, the external female genitals. In last line, *sweetest soup* (in other versions: *sweetest sauce*); compare in No. 242, "John Harloson's Saltpeter," on version note *A,* on the unusualness in English-language folksong or folklore of any appreciative reference, as here, to the female vaginal liquor, or *cyprine*.

SECTION B

Vulgar Rhymes from the Ozarks

PREFACE

The verses which follow have little in common except that they are all circulated in the Ozark region, and nearly all of them contain "unprintable" words. Some are doubtless fragments of old songs, others seem to be parodies, still others are literary efforts of comparatively recent composition.

Most of these items were recited from memory by my informants, and I wrote them down verbatim. Some of the longer pieces were brought to me in manuscript, usually with the understanding that I was to copy them and return the originals. Occasionally one finds bawdy verses in old ledgers, diaries, manuscript collections of songs, recipes and the like. I recall one such "friendship book," borrowed from Miss M. L., of Notch, Mo., in 1934. She had it from Mrs. L. S., who lived near Marvel Cave in Taney County, Mo. I'm quite sure that Miss L. didn't read the manuscript carefully. The L. girls felt that vulgarity is a bad business wherever found, and they wanted no part of it. If Miss L. had known of these bawdy verses, she would never have allowed me to see the book.

This attitude is not uncommon, and the collectors of such material may have prejudiced many worthy people against folklore in general. Years ago, at a tourist-camp near Eureka Springs, Ark., I met with a group of amateur folklorists from Missouri and Illinois. We sat up most of the night, roaring out vulgar songs and recitations. Roscoe Barbee, manager of the tourist-camp, made no comment at the time. But a few days later some gardeners were digging a ditch across the lawn, and one of the men accidentally struck his pick into a tiled sewer. It smelled pretty bad as Mr. Barbee walked over to inspect the damage. "Boys," said he, "I believe we've struck folklore!"

Despite such criticism, it seems to me that some of these bawdy rhymes have considerable folkloristic value. I believe that literary parallels and scholarly annotations could be supplied by the learned folklorists who sit around in libraries. I am not learned, and have no library. Nevertheless, I feel that it is worth while to set down this raw material for the record.

Vance Randolph

Note: All paragraphs of annotations and bracketed materials in the following pages are by the editor, G. Legman, who is *also* not "sit[ting] around in libraries," as above.

1. WHEN A MAN GETS OLD

> When a man gets old his balls grow cold
> And the end of his pecker turns blue,
> When he begins to diddle it bends in the middle
> —Did it ever occur to you?

A. Heard by Vance Randolph in Pineville, Missouri, about 1929, evidently a recitation.

B. From Mr. G. P., Reeds Spring, Missouri, September 21, 1946. He learned it in the early 1900s. In line 3: *get a little*, refers to sexual intercourse:

> When a man gets old his cod turns cold,
> And the end of his pecker turns blue,
> When he starts to get a little it bends in the middle,
> Did that ever occur to you?

C. Recited by a lady in Eureka Springs, Arkansas, October 21, 1948. In line 2: *ellick*, Ozark dialect word for the penis, from the Scottish name Alec, as in "smart Alec":

> When you get old your balls get cold,
> And the head of your ellick gets blue,
> And when you go to diddle it bends in the middle,
> Did it ever occur to you?

In all versions this refers to the relaxation in old age of the scrotal cremasteric muscle, by means of which the testicles have been kept close to the warmth of the lower abdomen, to protect the proliferation of spermatozoa from excesses of heat or cold. In Shakespeare's *Henry V* (1599) II.iii.30, the Hostess puns that all above the dying Falstaff's knee was "cold as any stone." (In Olivier's movie version this was expurgatorily shown to refer to his elbow!) After the old-age relaxation of the cremasters, the testicles hang noticeably lower than before, as noted in Francis Grose's *Classical Dictionary of the Vulgar Tongue* (1785), calling it "the whiffles," also "the whifflesack," terms no longer common. Compare the song in vol. I preceding, which begins: "Do your balls hang low?—Can you swing 'em to and fro, etc.," No. 49.

D. McAtee, *Grant County, Indiana, Speech and Song*, Supplement 2, (1946) p. 4 prints this as of the 1890s:

> When a man grows old,
> His stones grow cold,
> And the head of his pecker turns blue;
> When he goes to diddle
> It bends in the middle—
> Did this ever happen to *you*?

E. Still very commonly collected among U.S. adult males, this is a survival of one of a series of humorous prognostications printed as "Madrigals," followed by five pages of riddles, as "Questions and Answers," at the end of *Cobbes Prophecies, his Signes and Tokens* (London, Robert Wilson, 1614, leaf C3v–C4; facsimile reprint by Charles Praetorius, as *Antient* (sic) *Drolleries*, No. 1, London, Printed for Private Circulation, 1890):

When a man is old,
And the wether blowes cold,
    well fare a fire and a fur'd Gowne:
But when he is young,
And his blood new sprung,
    his sweete hart is worth halfe the Towne.

When a Maid is faire,
In her smocke and haire,
    who would not be glad to woo her:
But when she goes to bed,
To loose her maiden-head,
    how kindly her Good-man goes to her.

Note the reversal, in all the modern forms, of this cock-crow of youthful sexual potency into a sardonic lament over the presumed impotence of the old—*and* including the listener, suddenly entrapped in the punch-line at the end. The oldest version printed of the modern form, close in date and style to that of McAtee, at *D* above, is given in *The Stag Party* (Chicago? 1888?) edited by Eugene Field, unnumb. p. 256. Compare the musical form of this same homily in vol. I preceding, *Roll Me in Your Arms*, "The Battleship *Maine*" ("When I Was in My Prime"), Nos. 36*B* and 51.

2. LADY LIL

Little Lil taught school when she first came West,
But she soon give it up to fuck and rest,
There was a standin' bet around our town
That no living man could hold Lil down.

Across the street come a half-breed brute
From over the top of Mount Janute,
He slowly strode across the street
And says no whore has got *me* beat.

He layed his jong out on the bar,
By God, it stretched from thar to thar!
We knowed that Lil had met her fate,
But to back out then was too damn late.

So we decided to hold the mill
Behind the shit-house on the hill,
Where every man could get a seat
And watch the half-breed sink his meat.

Lil started like a little breeze
That blows the tops of cypress trees,
Then she jumped and flounced which was plenty slick
Till the half-breed lost control of his dick.

She pumped and pumped and double-pumped
With tricks unknown to a common cunt,
But he called her hand on every trick
And just kept pouring on the prick.

At last poor Lil she missed a shot
And the half-breed pinned her to the spot;

> The sod was tore for miles around
> Where Lil's old ass had plowed the ground.
>
> But she died brave, I want to tell,
> She had her boots on when she fell,
> So we cut off Lil's drawers all full of gore,
> And nailed 'em on the shit-house door.

A. Recited as above by Mr. S. N., Pineville, Missouri, July 20, 1934.

B. A lady in Joplin, Missouri, July 5, 1940, recalled some fragments of it from her childhood in the 1890s:

> She started like a gentle breeze
> That bends and sways the cypress trees . . .
> The way Lil bucked was plenty slick,
> But he just kept letting out his prick.
>
> He had a hell of a time with Lil,
> They wore the grass plumb off the hill . . .
> The man that never diddled Lil
> Don't know what diddling is, nor never will.

C. Contributed by Mr. G. P., Reeds Spring, Missouri, August 5, 1946. He learned the poem from a man named Blair, who called it "Piss-Pot Pete":

> Lil was a schoolmarm from the West,
> That's where she found the fuckin' best,
> The word it come from miles around
> That no two men could hold Lil down.
>
> When out from the hills of Bare-Ass Creek,
> Come a son-of-a-bitch called Piss-Pot Pete,
> Lil knew damn well he was her fate,
> But backing out was too damn late . . .
>
> So off to the mountains to get a seat
> And watch the half-breed sink his meat . . .
>
> The ground was tore up for miles around,
> Where Lil's old ass had plowed the ground,
> And Lil passed out with a sigh and a cough,
> While Piss-Pot Pete started jacking off.

D. Text from Mr. A. M., Columbia, Missouri, October 3, 1948. He heard it recited at Kirksville, Missouri in 1918. In 2:1, *Greek,* a Creek Indian is evidently meant, or was originally, as in *C* above:

> Down in Louisville on a hill
> There lived a gal, her name was Lil,
> The fact was known for miles around
> That no two men could hold her down.
>
> When down from the hills came a bare-assed Greek,
> That son-of-a-bitch was Piss-Pot Pete . . .
>
> Now Piss-Pot Pete and little Lil
> They chose a spot upon a hill,
> Behind a shit-house by the mill.

When Piss-Pot Pete pulled out his cock,
. . . .
Lil knew that she had met her fate,
But to back out now it was too late.

People came for miles to gain a seat
To see that half-breed take his meat.

He threw her down into the mud,
And mounted her ass like a Belgian stud.
They fucked and fucked for hours and hours,
A-tearing up trees and shrubs and flowers.

The earth was tore up for miles around
Where Lil's poor ass had hit the ground.
Lil passed out with a sigh and a cough
While Piss-Pot Pete stood jacking off.

E. A final opening fragment, from a male college student, at Hot Springs, Arkansas, April 27, 1957. In 1:4, *goose,* to tickle the anus as an aggressive or teasing act, especially between men, alluding (or presumably inviting) to homosexual intercourse:

What? You ain't heard of Lil?
Why, she's the best this town ever produced.
Why, them that ain't been fucked by Lil,
Well, they ain't been much more than goosed.

. . . .
When he laid his cock upon the bar
I'll swear it reached from thar to *thar!*
And stink—God damn! it stunk . . .

In his incisive article on this piece, Ronald L. Baker observes (in *Journal of American Folklore,* 1987, vol. 100: pp. 191–99), the rustic appropriateness of the reference, in *D* above, to the sexual hero mounting the woman "like a Belgian stud," a type of enormous farm-horse that can weigh a ton or more. But as the final line shows, he is still not satisfied after killing her. That the woman has merely "passed out" (fainted) modifies her actual death, usually, in this sex-*as*-murder ballad. Her "sigh and a cough" are, however, the signs of her incipient death from heart-failure due to lung oedema and cardiac arrest, the newly so-called "motel death" or "Rockefeller syndrome," on the belief that sex with a stranger or new person is "the hottest." Compare the story of the patriarch Judah and Tamar, in *Genesis,* 38:11–26, a brief but superb scenario that would make an excellent motion picture, *Tamar,* Biblical or neo-biblical.

The usual title of the present piece is "Our Lil" or "Lady Lil." See the extended text, from a woman, and study of this dramatic recitation (rarely given as a song) on the prototypical "War between the Sexes," as intercourse, by G. Legman, in *Southern Folklore Quarterly* (1976) vol. 40: pp. 98–102, in a monograph on "Bawdy Monologues and Recitations," essentially the first time any learned folklore journal in English has ever published texts this graphic; also Ronald L. Baker, "Lady Lil and Pisspot Pete," mentioned above, just as courageously ten years later in *Journal of American Folklore* (editor: Bruce Jackson) 1987, vol. 100: pp. 191–99.

The attribution of this piece to the children's poet and erotica fancier, Eugene Field who died in 1895, in *Immortalia* (anonymously edited by Thomas R. Smith; New York: Macy-Masius, 1927) p. 8, with a variant text, presumably the original, has never been confirmed. There does not appear to be any copy of "Lady Lil" in the very complete Willard Morse Collection of Field's manuscripts, including his erotica, in the Denver Public Library, nor does it appear in *The Stag Party* (Chicago? 1888 or 1889) anonymously edited, if not published, by Field himself (Copies: Denver Public Library, Kinsey Institute, Indiana University; and, incomplete, Sterling Library, Yale.) George Milburn's *Hobo's Hornbook* (1930) pp. 140–41, gives a 5-stanza version, but the text is so full of asterisks that it is purposely impossible to make head or tail of it. "This ribald recitation," Milburn adds, "is sometimes merged with 'Down in the Lehigh Valley,'" song No. 67 above.

In a different order of historical or psychological interpretation, there is a full discussion of this favorite American sex-contest piece by G. Legman, *The Horn Book* (1964) pp. 418–20, setting Lady Lil in the genealogical line of an older heroine celebrated in the song "The Northern Lass," in *Folly in Print* (1667) p. 107, where the sexual contest is restricted politely only to *dancing:* "She was the Fair Maid of Doncaster, named Betty Maddox; who, when an hundred horsemen woo'd her, she conditioned, that he who could dance her down (*note well*), she would marry; but she wearied them all, and they left her a maid for her pains." Or, rather, for *their* pains. This is evidently the female-dominant version of the sex legends of Hercules and of Roland, on which see further, *The Horn Book* (1964) pp. 222–27.

F. When reprinting the text of "Lady Lil" from *Immortalia* in *Folk Poems and Ballads* ("Mexico City, 1945"; really Cleveland, 1948) pp. 79–80, the anonymous editor, the famous Dali collector A. Reynolds Morse, names the sexual hero "Shorthorn Pete," and adds the opening two lines, as above, in *A* and *C* accidentally omitted from the *Immortalia* text, which also gives a variant on Lil's sexual *expertise*, in stanza 6:

> She tried her twists and double biffs,
> And all such m'neuvres known to quiffs.
> But Pete was thar with every tack,
> And kept a-lettin' out more jack.

This passage is a principal focus of variants collected in the field: "She tried out shunts and double-bunts, And tricks unknown to common cunts" (New York, 1938); "She laid her victims out in heaps, With body-English tricks—*for keeps!*"—(La Jolla, California 1965). So is the origin of the hero: "a Mexican (half-breed, pint-sized) galoot, Who wandered in from Scruggins' Chute," indicating that the scene of the action is a western mining-camp. In *D,* 2:1 *Greek,* may therefore have been intended for *Creek* (Indian). In his back-of-the-book "Commentary," pp. 120–21, A. R. Morse gives an unusual first-person note on sex contests of this type:

> In Nevada one time I witnessed a fucking bout, but not as spectacular a one as described in "Lady Lil." We left the mine, and walked some seven or eight miles to the nearest saloon, a lonely desert saloon with a gas pump out in front, kept by an old woman and her daughter. There an argument ensued about whether an old miner could still get an erection, and bets were made. The old lady and miner in question repaired to a pile of rags by the pot-belly stove, and for about 45 minutes the old fellow did his best, with the old girl's help. But nothing happened [meaning, the man could not "perform," or ejaculate], and he lost the bet. Thus among our people are found all the roots of their poetry given here.

Yes, but there might have been a different ending if the old miner had tried with the daughter instead, as in the *First Book of Kings,* 1:1–4, telling how when "King David was old and stricken in years, and . . . he gat no heat," there was sought out for him Abishag the Shunamite, "a young virgin . . . a fair damsel" who was to "lie in [his] bosom, that my lord the king may get heat." Admittedly, the ending was exactly as here, for in the upshot, "The damsel was very fair, and cherished the king, and ministered to him: but the king knew her not." *Knew,* in this passage, is the usual Biblical euphemism for sexual intercourse, as in *Genesis,* 4:1, "And Adam knew Eve his wife; and she conceived and bare Cain."

Sexual contests of the kind in the poem and anecdote above are not always judged strictly on "length and strength," as here, but more often on *frequency*: the number of times the man is able to ejaculate during one bout, or the number of women he can "satisfy" (legend of Roland and "Oliver's Brag," as in the short story of that title by Anatole France); or, most often, the number of men one woman can "take on," which is in fact relatively unlimited, as opposed to the little that men can do.

The queens of both India and Tahiti were reliably reported to have performed in this way, as late as the middle nineteenth century; and the story of the disgrace of Queen Vashti, and the patriarchal *pronunciamento* with which the *Book of Esther* begins in the Bible, 1:9–22, are based on her refusal to allow herself to be required to liven up King Ahasuerus' royal party—on its 181st day!—by appearing (naked, according to the tradition, as with Lady Godiva), "to shew the people and the princes her beauty: for she was fair to look on. But the Queen Vashti refused to come at the king's commandment . . . therefore was the king very wroth, and his anger burned in him." It would appear that the real performance expected of Vashti, with the princes, was not just a striptease, but a one-woman orgy on the East Indian or Tahitian style, as is described elsewhere, with full details, in *Ezekiel*, chapters 16 and 23. An oral contest of this kind is reported by Roman historians as of Cleopatra, the last Queen of Egypt, and one hundred and ten centurions of the Roman guard, to celebrate ritually her arrival in Rome.

See further the toasts or epigraphs in honor of whores, as "A Toast to the Biggest Whore," No. 60, below. There is also a British enlargement of the present "Lady Lil," into a much longer sex-contest epic, called "Eskimo Nell" (not in this collection), known in the United States but not as popular there as in Britain and Australia. This is printed in several bawdy-song collections: by Donald Laycock (who wrote a private continuation of it, on passive pedication, as "The Eskimo's Death-Knell," before dying after a brief sickness in 1987); and by Alan Bold, who actually included "Eskimo Nell," in a 57-stanza text, in his collection *Making Love: The Picador Book of Erotic Verse* (London 1978) pp. 208–214. This on the private grounds that although the anti-hero Mexican Pete, in desperation, ultimately fires his "tough-nosed Colt" revolver into Nell's vagina, this merely makes her "squeal in ecstasy" (it says here), and she wins the sex contest "pants down," thus making the poem a glorification, not a humiliation of the woman. Believe it who will.

3. SHE'LL WIN IN A WALK

> The old man sat in the grandstand chair,
> With shit on his boots and lice in his hair,
> And his voice rang out on the balmy air,
> She'll win in a walk, by Jesus!
>
> Why, if I had money, if I was rich,
> I'd bet my wad on the son-of-a-bitch,
> . . . .
> She'll win in a walk, by Jesus!
>
> The first race run, she come in third,
> The second heat, she slipped on a turd
> And fell in a ditch, the son-of-a-bitch,
> And *lost* the race, by Jesus!

A. Recited by Mr. P. W., Joplin, Missouri, December 20, 1930. He learned it about 1910.

B. A 7-stanza text is printed in *Immortalia* (1927) p. 7, as "A Seventy Year Old Follower," which supplies the missing line above (the mare becoming a stallion) as follows: "When he gets a-goin' he'll make 'em all itch"; and apparently many other stanzas are also missing. Here following is the full text as given in *Immortalia*. The pee-culiar spelling of *turd* as "terd" in the climactic line of the final stanza is as given:

An old sport lounged in a grandstand chair,
There was dung in his whiskers and hay in his hair,
And his voice rang hoarse in the sultry air—
  He'll win in a walk, b'Jesus!

Just wait 'til you see them turn him loose,
He'll go through that field like shit through a goose,
He'll do it as easy as *ace* takes a *deuce*—
  He'll win in a walk, b'Jesus!

His breeding is right, he can't go slow,
He's out of Black Bess by Hungry Joe;
Of that bunch of skates he'll sure make a show—
  He'll win in a walk, b'Jesus!

I ain't got no money, but if I was rich,
I'd go dead-broke on that son-of-a-bitch;
When he gets a-goin' he'll make 'em all itch—
  He'll win in a walk, b'Jesus!

They've sent 'em away—gave him worst of the start—
It don't make no difference—he don't care a fart—
The suckers are yellow, but he's game—got a heart—
  He'll win in a walk, b'Jesus!

From the nineteenth position, 'way out in the grass
Where weeds are so tall they tickle his ass,
He's just nosed out of place Scotch Highland Lass—
  He'll win in a walk, b'Jesus!

They are swung in the stretch and the bastard is third—
He has worked up to second—now he's slipped on a terd,
He's slipped in the ditch, the son-of-a-bitch—
  He wasn't in it, b'Jesus!

The debt or inspiration, situationally at least, is very visible here to Ernest Lawrence Thayer's famous humorous baseball *loser* recitation, "Casey at the Bat" (1888), with its ultra-famous final stanza:

Oh, somewhere in this favored land the sun is shining bright,
The band is playing somewhere, and somewhere hearts are light,
And somewhere men are laughing, and little children shout,
But there is no joy in *Mudville*—mighty Casey has struck out!

4. THE HIGHER UP THE TREE

Recited by Mr. G. P., Reeds Spring, Missouri, March 4, 1947. He had it from an old man at Garber, Missouri:

In the fall of the year when the leaves turn brown,
The coon climbs a tree and the possum comes down,
The higher the coon climbs up the tree,
The dimmer his ass-hole gets to me.

In Katrina Johnson's novel, *Evening Street* (1947) p. 153, the author quotes the last two lines in modified form:

> The higher the raccoon climbs the tree,
> The smaller his fanny seems to be.

5. MONKEY ON THE FLAGPOLE

> The monkey climbed the flagpole
> On top of the steeple,
> The monkey climbed the flagpole
> And showed his ass-hole to the people.

A. From Mr. G. P., Reeds Spring, Missouri, July 5, 1946. Nothing more is known about this verse, which of course shares its *steeple/people* rhyme with a favorite nursery handgame and the violently dysphemistic jazz-song, "Shave 'Em Dry," in vol. I, *Roll Me in Your Arms*, No. 149.

B. There is also possibly some relationship with a 1918 army parody of a bugle-call or favorite march, heard by the editor as sung by pre-adolescent children at Lake Winola, Pennsylvania, in 1926, and incompletely learned from them. The missing word in the final line had at least two syllables but is forgotten:

> Oh, the monkey wrapped his tail around the flagpole,
>   An' up his *ass*-hole, an' up his *ass*-hole!
> Oh, the monkey wrapped his tail around the flagpole,
>   And you can all just . . . kiss my ass!

6. RISE UP, BALDY

> Rise up, Baldy, bold and brave,
> Between these two white thighs you shall dig your grave.
> Grab him, Cunt, right by the snout,
> And squeeze his head till his brains squirts out!

Contributed by a school marm in Christian County, Missouri, May 14, 1943. This quite remarkable brief item is a *charm* or invocation, of unknown age, but in all probability several centuries old. The woman here addresses the man's penis, whom she names "Baldy," referring to the *glans penis* with the foreskin retracted, and encouraging the man to erection. She then invokes her own vagina in no uncertain *vagina dentata* terms, in which "till his brains squirts out" refers of course to the seminal ejaculation by the man.

There is a related folk-phrase and superstition that a man can "fuck his brains out" by excessive intercourse, matching the typification of a stupid young man as "all balls and no brains" (or, "and big feet"), sometimes politely paraphrased as having "a strong back and a weak mind." The comic-strip antihero in Al Capp's enormously popular "Dogpatch" strip, "Li'l Abner," from the 1940s to the 70s, was invariably drawn in such a way as to contrast his large and powerful body against his presumed sexual stupidity, the despair of his frustrated nymphomaniacal girl friend Daisy-Mae. See further the introduction to vol. I, *Roll Me in Your Arms*.

7. KEEP YOUR PUSSY GREASY

Buy a dime's worth of butter,
And a nickel's worth of lard,
Keep your pussy greasy
Till his pecker gets hard.

Recited by an elderly lady in Neosho, Missouri, October 23, 1948. She learned it in Newton County, Missouri, about 1910. It was also probably intended as a sexual *charm* (compare No. 6, preceding), for the purpose of insuring the man's potency. A favorite nineteenth-century sea chantey gives somewhat similar advice to a girl in its chorus-and-title, "Jinny, Keep Your Arsehole Warm." A more recent Negro sex-brag or "toast" includes an antisemitic line about the sexual superman, John Hardy, stating that "A li'l bit of pussy and a nickel's worth of rice, Made him crucify his prick" with excessive intercourse. The spicy food is in this case, as in most aphrodisiacal superstitions, supposed to be the at-least partial exciting cause! In the present homiletic advice or "charm" the vaginal lubricant is to replace the woman's natural pre-coital fluid or *cyprine*, apparently insufficient with the slow-starting lover, or which has been rubbed off ("burned away") with his fumbling or delay.

8. THE PIG AND THE BUTTERMILK

If a pig drank a gallon of buttermilk before it started,
And ran a mile before it farted,
And the more it farted the farther it gits,
How far would it run before it shits?

A farmer said he saw the pig pass
With buttermilk shooting right out of its ass,
The farmer was a mile from where the pig started,
And the pig passed the farmer just as it farted.

Now if the pig is lucky and can control its gas,
And runs a mile with a puckered-up ass,
It seems to me if it keeps its wits,
It can run five miles before it shits.

Vance Randolph notes: "*Recited* by a pretty little girl in Eureka Springs, Ark., Nov. 28, 1948. She learned it in southeastern Kansas." A good example of scatology as female non-sexual "naughtiness," a preference or evasion often observed, scatology being considered by the woman or girl as less compromising or invitational than sexual humor might be.

This piece has circulated in America at least since the 1910s. In the G. Legman Archive-Collection there is a small printed business card or miniature broadside, dating from about 1915 (the usual form for circulating such "undercover" materials before the advent of duplicating machines and modern "Xeroxlore," after 1920–50), entitled "A Riddle" and with a stock cut of a pig as decoration. Note that this is only a *mock-riddle*, to which no true or actual answer is expected. That is considered part of the fun.

9. THE PLAINS OF TIMBUCTOO

As Tim and I were hunting
Out on the plains of Timbuctoo,
We found three maidens in a tent,
I bucked one and *Tim bucked two.*

From Mr. J. E., Webster Groves, Missouri, April 8, 1948. He remembered it from the late 1880s. This is a survival as a mere quatrain or punning *catch* (if not simply an incomplete fragment) of a longer bawdy British music-hall chant or recitation, dating from the mid-nineteenth century. The complete text is given in John Camden Hotten's faked *The Merry Muses* collection (1872, usually with the reversed date of "1827" in its many reprints), which for nearly a century was passed off as the real collection of Scottish bawdy folksongs made by Robert Burns under the full title of *The Merry Muses of Caledonia* (Edinburgh? 1799).

10. R'AR BACK, JAYBIRD

R'ar back, jaybird,
Jig her up behind,
You skin your doodle
And I'll skin mine.

Recited by Professor A. B., Manhattan, Kansas, April 12, 1935. He learned it near Galena, Missouri, in the 1890s. This is a children's or adolescents' *challenge*-rhyme, many of which are often in exactly this brief two-footed quatrain format. G. F. Northall in his splendid but expurgated collection of *English Folk-Rhymes* (1892) pp. 298–318, gives a whole group of these as "Quips and Cranks," including one at p. 318 (from *Notes and Queries*, 2nd Series, 12:380) very similar to the above challenge, but showing the usual modification of any sexual reference to "mere" aggression and killing:

Tit for tat,
Butter for fat,
If you kill my dog
I'll kill your cat.

In the present specimen, in which *doodle* (German *dudel*, bagpipe) means the penis; *skin* or *skin-back* means the retracting of the foreskin. The reference is to mutual masturbation by boys, here separately but in each other's presence, without mutual touching, which would be considered too overtly homosexual. A similar scene almost as frankly detailed ends the opening chapter of the humorous Australian autobiography, *Unreliable Memoirs* by Clive James (London 1980), which also notes that the boys begin, as often, by comparing their penis size. See Vance Randolph, *Pissing in the Snow* (University of Illinois Press, 1976) No. 60, "Twelve-Dollar Jack," about a similar show-and-tell contest among adult males in the Ozarks, the winner's penis being as long as twelve silver-dollars lying flat side-by-side.

For the record, I might mention that a Chicago university professor, visiting me the year after Randolph's book appeared, told me absolutely seriously that he "understood from certain people" that Twelve-Dollar Jack referred to Randolph himself, and the story was autobiographical! He added: "Of course, that may be more folklore than truth." Compare, "more truth than poetry," and the reverse.

11. THE FUCKIN' LITTLE SPARROWS

The fuckin' little sparrows
Built in the fuckin' spout
A fuckin' rainstorm came and washed
The little fuckers out . . .

A. Quoted by a waitress at Rockaway Beach, Missouri, May 30, 1929. She had it from some children in the wilds of Carroll County, Arkansas, as above; this being in fact only the first stanza of two.

B. A text from a manuscript collection made at the University of Arkansas was contributed by Mr. D. H., Little Rock, Arkansas, November 10, 1955. This modifies the "interruptive and inevitable" adjective *fuckin'* to the innocuous *rooting-tooting*, but gives the second stanza missing above, clearly drawn from the old legend of King Alfred being inspired by an indomitable spider:

The rooting-tooting spider
Went up the water-spout,
The rains came down
And washed the spider out.

The sun came out
And dried the rain,
And the rooting-tooting spider
Went up the spout again.

In Emrich and Korson's *Child's Book of Folklore* (1947) p. 109, almost the identical first stanza (only) is given, with "eensy, weensy spider," meaning a very small one; and there is a related item in Ray Wood's *Fun in American Folk Rhymes* (1952) p. 58.

Robert Graves in his *Lars Porsena* (1927; revised as *The Future of Swearing*) gives another mild text from World War I, but sets it in an anecdote about a soldier shocking a superior officer by the profanity of this almost-nursery rhyme! It would appear therefore that the bawdy version is certainly the original, and of British Army provenance, in or before World War I. Note the typical *tmesis* here of the in-fixed or interruptive *past-participle* adjective "fucken," which is not really the *present*-participle "fuckin'," as usually written and believed. Compare "damned," also "blasted," etc., and for the relevant old but still surviving form: wood*en*, fitt*en*, writt*en*, brok*en*, rott*en*, stink*en*, bitch*en*, which certainly do not mean "rotting," "stinking," or "bitching," though, again, usually so believed. This last, *bitchen*, is a common westernism (first heard by me in Southern California, 1964) and refers to an admired, not a reprobated, woman, or other person or thing.

The satirical poem, "The Cowboy," by G. Legman, using the expletive "fucken" in every line (also interruptively, as "abso-*fucken*-lutely") circulated during World War II, and is based on the older "The Great Australian Adjective," in which the heavily-overused term is—presumably—"bloody," but in fact really identical. A version of "The Cowboy," artfully expurgated, is printed by Wallrich as circulating in the U.S. Army Airforce during the Korean War of 1950, but he purposely omits the final lines, in which the main moral or linguistic lesson is intended to reside: "And there with all his *fucken* force, Had sexual-*fucken*-intercourse."

12. BEHIND A ROCK

I took my girl behind a rock
And introduced her to my cock.

I gave her a dollar not to holler,
I gave her a dime to be on time,
I gave her a nickel to suck my pickle,
I gave her a cent and in it went.

Recited by Mr. E. W., Eureka Springs, Arkansas, February 17, 1949. Note the diminishing sums of money offered to the girl, presumably as her sexual excitement increases.

13. NO BALLS AT ALL

There was a young lady named Sylvia Cox,
Blonde hair on her pussy, and a nice juicy box.
She was wooed in the springtime and married by fall,
But her husband, the bastard, had *no* balls at all!—
No balls at all? No balls at all,
Her husband, the bastard, had *no* balls at all!

The night they were married they jumped into bed,
His pecker was dripping, her legs they were spread.
He reached for her titties, her titties were small;
She felt for his balls, he had *no* balls at all!—
No balls at all? No! NO *balls at all,*
She'd married a man who had *no* balls at all!

Oh mother, dear mother, oh what shall I do?
I've married a man who don't know how to screw.
His dooflicker's long and his dornick is tall,
But the son-of-a-bitch never fucks me at all!—
Never fucks her at all? Never fucks her at all,
The son-of-a-bitch never fucks her at all!

Oh daughter, oh daughter, now that's very bad,
It's the very same trouble I had with your dad.
But there's many a man who will answer the call
Of the wife of a man who has *no* balls at all!—
Never fear, dry your tears, they will answer the call
Of the wife of the man who has *no* balls at all!

Oh mother, dear mother, I took your advice,
They fucked me, they buggered me; God! it was nice!
And a bouncing young boy will be born in the fall
To the wife of the man who has *no* balls at all!—
They fucked her, they buggered her; God! it was nice,
And now she is glad she took mama's advice!

Yes! In front and in back, she was pinned to the wall,
She's the wife of the man who had *no* balls at all!

A. Chanted rhythmically, in "galloping anapests," rather than sung (though it is evidently a *song*, since it has choruses, "artfully varied" in the British music-hall style of the late nineteenth century), by Mr. R. K., of Mena, Arkansas, in New York, November 1953, to my wife and his own during my absence in France—perhaps not a very diplomatic choice of repertory, under the circumstances. In 1:2, *a nice juicy box*, referring to the woman's vagina; in less gallant versions (probably earlier) "and cheese in her box," referring insultingly to the preputial smegma of the clitoris, as of the male foreskin. In 3:3, *dooflicker*, foreskin; in the Ozark speech more usually "whickerbill"; *dornick*, penis, often used in slang of a thrown rock, derived from the German word for "thorny."

B. This is an imitation or bawdy parody of an extremely popular American recitation of the Civil War period (1857) "Nothing to Wear," by William Allen Butler (of which there were many parodies, such as "Nothing to Say" by "Phil. Doesticks"). A long extract is in Burton Stevenson's *Home Book of Quotations* (ed. 1944) 487:3, beginning:

> Miss Flora McFlimsey, of Madison Square [has] . . .
> Dresses for breakfasts and dinners and balls;
> Dresses to sit in and stand in and walk in;
> Dresses to dance in and flirt in and talk in.
>
> Dresses in which to do nothing at all,
> Dresses for winter, spring, summer, and fall;
> And yet . . . last time we met was in utter despair,
> Because she had nothing whatever to wear!

In its bawdy form, at *A* above, this is given as a typical *complainte* or "*Mal-Mariée*," in a rhymed or sung controversy between the daughter and the mother who has married her off unsuitably, which is the standard background of the girl's sexual frustration and dissatisfaction, here made very plain. *Controverses* and complaints of this mother-daughter kind are common in the older Scottish folksong, and in French folksong where they are a favorite form and have been collected until a relatively recent date.

The version given here is the most florid ever collected in English, with changes rung in the "3rd-person" choruses in music-hall style, and probably dates from the late nineteenth century, when Butler's original, "Nothing to Wear" was still current and famous. Oscar Brand, pp. 30–31, gives a frighteningly expurgated version, with "hips" substituted for "balls" and other broken-field-running censorship throughout; Cray, pp. 52–53, gives the usual modern text, set to the tune of "Strawberry Roan," but with a note on a completely different song, p. 2. Other texts in Logue-"Vicarrion," No. LVI; and *Songs of Raunch* (1958: reprinted in Walsh, *Songs of Roving and Raking*, p. 60); and a recorded version on McCormick's *Unexpurgated Folk Songs of Men*. In the present version *A*, the frank references in the final stanza and the extra chorus, or *envoi*, to the pleasures of anal erotism for the "passive" participant are very uncommon in non-homosexual contexts. See also the end-note on "Little Mary MacAfee," as to anal erotism, at No. 50 below.

14. CRABS AS BIG AS BUZZARDS

Here's to you, God damn you,
May bleeding piles torment you,
And boils grow on your feet,
May crabs as big as horse-turds
Crawl on your balls and eat.

> And when you're old and worthless
> And a syphilitic wreck,
> May you slip through your rusty ass-hole
> And break your God damn neck.

A. Contributed as above by a nameless lady in Neosho, Missouri, October 23, 1948. In 1:4, *crabs* refers to crab lice, *Phthirus pubis*.

B. Recited by Mr. J. B., Eureka Springs, Arkansas, June 22, 1948. "Only a bit," he says, "of a long *dialogue* between a lady and a gentleman"(!)

> Before I'd touch your scurvy cunt
> Where a million maggots bit,
> I'd eat ten thousand syphilitic scabs
> And wade through liquid shit.
>
> When you get old and become a syphilitic wreck,
> [*Line missing?*] . . . .
> I hope you fall through your own ass-hole
> And break your fucking neck.

C. Allen W. Read, *Lexical Evidence* (1935) p. 54, has this fragment, rather condensed and decayed, as can be seen:

> May crabs as big as lobsters
> Attack your balls, a treat,
> When you are a goner,
> A hopeless fucking wreck.

D. A mock-toast or formalized insult or curse, often collected throughout the United States in the 1920s and 1930s, as by myself, heard declaimed over a chess-table by the loser, a young man from a western state, at the Michigan Union, University of Michigan, Ann Arbor, autumn 1935, beginning:

> May itching piles molest you,
> And boils grow on your feet;
> May crabs as big as buzzards
> Light on your balls—and *Eat!!*

And ending as in both of Randolph's Ozark texts above. His field note on the second of these is of great interest, calling it a fragment of a rhymed "flyting" or contest-in-insult, in a "long *dialogue* between a lady and a gentleman," presumably alternating their insulting stanzas, with each trying to "top" the other. See further on this very ancient form, Balaam's Curse, in *Numbers* xxii–xxiv; and the older alliterative Scottish materials cited and quoted in G. Legman, *No Laughing Matter* (*Rationale of the Dirty Joke*, vol. 2, New York, 1975) chapter 14.II.1, "Contests-in-Insult," pp. 779–788 *ff*. Another version of the present curse or "toast" forms stanza 2 of "Here's to Mag," No. 15*B* following.

15. HERE'S TO MAG

Here's to Maggie, the son-of-a-bitch,
Her cunt broke-out with the seven-year itch,
Before I'd mount that bony frame
And suck those scaley tits,
I'd drink a gallon of drunkard's puke
Diluted with liquid shit.

A. Anti-gallant "toast" (see others at Nos. 60–72 below), of a style once proposed when drinking, and still encountered infrequently, especially in Britain and Australia. Recited by Mr. J. C., Eureka Springs, Arkansas, August 24, 1951, who according to a manuscript note by Randolph may have mispronounced the first word of the last line as "*Biluted.*" He learned the verse at Moberly, Missouri, in 1912. Compare No. 14*B,* preceding, a version of the last four lines here.

B. Text from Mr. D. S., Eureka Springs, Arkansas, February 12, 1949. The first stanza used to be sung, he thinks, but there was no tune for the second verse:

I met her in a graveyard,
She was dirty, she was dead,
And through her maggoty ass-hole
My discharge went to her head.
Before I kissed those moldy lips
And sucked those rotting tits,
I drank a quart of dead man's puke
And a pint of liquid shit.

May bloody piles torment you,
And corns adorn your feet,
And crabs as big as crocodiles
Sit on your balls and eat.
And when you are old and feeble
And a syphilitic wreck,
I hope you fall through your fuckin' ass-hole
And break your God damn neck.

C. From a male student at Fayetteville, Arkansas, April 27, 1957, who stated it was part of a longer piece once popular at Helena, Arkansas In line 2, *slimmery* is a nonsense extension of the usual "slimy," here reduplicating "slippery." In 1:3, *matter*, pus, etc.

Here's to Mag, the dirty old hag,
The slippery, slimmery slut.
Between her toes green matter grows,
And maggots crawl through her gut.

Before I'd climb those scaley thighs
Or suck those festered tits,
I'd drink barrels and barrels of buzzard puke
And die with the drizzly shits.

Note that these last three texts concern or are addressed as a "toast" to a woman (and not to a man), in ultimate anti-gallant insults, including gloating over the repellent physical details of her death, in one of these, *B*, of February 12, 1949. Except for these "graveyard" lines, all three texts have clearly developed from the contest-in-insult form. The "graveyard" form is in fact an importation of lines from the even uglier and more anti-woman (also anti-Negro) song No. 232, "I Screwed an Old Woman," presumably in New Guinea, the woman being dead. Note also that the first text there was given to Randolph *by a woman*, who said "she had it from Professor Bob Crow," of Salem, Missouri; "Professor" in such a context usually referring to the piano player in a bar or whorehouse, often a Negro.

Several further closely related texts, also purposely vying with each other in nastiness of image, are given in Bruce Jackson's *Get Your Ass in the Water* (Harvard University Press, 1974) Nos. 97–98, "Here's to You, Mag, You Dirty Hag." Studies in anti-gallantry, on which see further, G. Legman, *Rationale of the Dirty Joke* (vol. 2: *No Laughing Matter,* 1975) especially chapters 12.IV.6, "Narsty-Narsties: The Defiling of the Mother," and 14.I.3, "Dysphemism and Insults: Anti-Gallantry and Anti-Woman," pp. 392–419 and 704–27 *ff.*, giving numerous congeners and forerunners of the present verse "toasts." And compare song No. 149 here, "His Balls Hung Down," a fragment of the violent Negro insult-song or chant, "Shave 'Em Dry," recorded by a woman.

16. POON-TANG

Poon-tang, poon-tang, I don't want it,
Sleep all night with my hand right on it.

A fragment, possibly of a toast to, or rather against, the female genitals. Heard from Mr. G. P., Reeds Spring, Missouri, July 5, 1946. Randolph notes on this: "Boys in Missouri and Arkansas used to speak of *getting some poon-tang* when they meant 'a little fucking' or 'a piece of cock.'" The word is related to the French *putain*, whore, doubtless nasally pronounced as in the Marseille area, *putaing*, from the Latin *puta*. Wentworth, *American Dialect Dictionary* (1944) p. 468, defines *poontang* as "copulation, especially between Negro and white." Compare Thomas Wolfe's novel *Look Homeward, Angel* (1929) pp. 166, 174, 343.

Note that in Randolph's observation cited above, "a piece of cock" is the southern U.S. usage of *cock*, for what a northerner would call *cunt*. This is derived from the French *coquille* or *coquillage*, seashell, as a descriptive noun for the external female genitals and virginity. Usually thought to have come to the South through French New Orleans, this usage is also fairly old in England, as in various nursery rhymes (where "cockles all in a row" replace the presumably less polite "cuckolds"); in the flagellational game of "hot cockles" (here the buttocks), etc. In a long note on the ancient magical charm or custom of "kneading cocklety bread" with the buttocks to ensnare a recalcitrant lover, from John Aubrey's *Remaines of Gentilisme and Judaisme* (1687; ed. J. Britten, 1881), G. F. Northall in *English Folk-Rhymes* (1892) pp. 153–56, ends with the plain statement: "It is significant that the *labia minora* are still termed 'cockles' in vulgar parlance." Compare the rare allusion to the *labia minora* in "The Foot-Long Jock," song No. 203 above.

17. WE'LL FUCK TOMORROW

Work in pleasure,
Work in sorrow,
Sleep tonight,
We'll fuck tomorrow.

A. Recited by Mr. E. W., Pineville, Missouri, December 21, 1920. An old saying, he told Randolph, popular on Cowskin River in the 1890s.

B. Communicated by a lady in Hot Springs, Arkansas, April 12, 1938. She said it was "a kind of toast" learned from old settlers near Hot Springs. Actually a *charm* or invocation:

> Brew in pleasure,
> Bake in sorrow,
> Work today,
> Fuck tomorrow.

C. The Brown *Collection of North Carolina Folklore*, (1952, vol. I: p. 470) prints this:

> Help me to salt, help me to sorrow,
> Brew me my malt, and —— on the morrow.

with references to Apperson, *English Proverbs and Proverbial Phrases* (London 1929) pp. 548–49; also Smith and Heseltine, *Oxford Dictionary of English Proverbs* (2nd ed., 1948) p. 291.

It is unfortunate that this charm or invocation is not studied further in the sources cited and also seems to be missing from John Aubrey's seventeenth-century collection, *Remaines of Gentilisme and Judaisme* (1687), the earliest British folklore collection, other than folksongs. It is possible that it is connected with Jehovah's great *Curse* to Adam and Eve (but compare the preceding note on Song No. 108, "Turn to Your Wives": "The Old Hundredth"), that the man shall earn his bread in the sweat of his brow, and the woman bear her children in pain "and sorrow," in *Genesis*, 3:16–19. Observe that this curse was first openly abrogated by Queen Victoria (who had her queenly status and power to protect her from it . . .) who first publicly accepted anesthesia during childbirth in the early-middle nineteenth century.

Compare Princess Marie Bonaparte's neurotic operation (performed upon herself) in the early twentieth century, to "liberate" her clitoris and make it into a sort of male-protest penis. In an early feminist attack on men, Ruth Herschberger's *Adam's Rib* (New York 1948), the position is seriously taken that the clitoris is superior to the penis even etymologically: that "clitoris" should really be pronounced with a long vowel, *clite-oris*, and "penis" with a short one: *pennis*. This is not intended as a joke.

18. I BOOGIED THIS MORNING

> I boogied this morning,
> And I boogied the night before,
> You come over to my house
> And we'll boogie some more.
>
> Four and four makes eight,
> And one makes nine;
> Give me a little of yours
> And I'll give you a little of mine.

A. Contributed by two matrons in Green County, Missouri, November 12, 1944. This presumably means they chanted it together.

Note: *boogie*, to fuck, probably from "booger," bugger, but here used as a euphemism. So also in connection with Negro jazz music, "boogie-woogie," a type of rolling "barrel-house" piano playing (probably of European *Tingel-Tangel*, low beer-house origin: compare the fast movement of Schubert's "Trout" Quintette, exactly in that style!) Note that "boogie" is also low American slang for any Negro, on same *booger* origin, with "bogey" (goblin, demon) over-ride. The word *jazz* itself was also used originally as meaning to fuck. See Legman, *The Limerick* (1953) note 1389.

B. Observe that stanza 2, in *A* above, is a *numbering charm*, a very ancient type, often found in the Bible, especially the *Book of Proverbs*, in "triadic" form ("Three things are . . . Yea, and four . . .") Modern charms of this kind are generally connected with sexuality, specifically with masturbation, as in one rhythmic "accompanying" verse to the strokes, used by adolescent boys in Scranton, Pennsylvania, about 1930, when having contests in *speed* of achieving orgasm while swimming "bare-ass" (naked) in Roaring Brook. Note that this is intended to "unhex" with a dicing-formula the threat or danger of going insane (or blind), supposedly caused by masturbation:

> Six times six are sixty-six,
> And *seven-come-eleven!*
> I don't care if I go crazy,
> As long as I get to Heaven.

19. CHEWING GUM

> Oh fuck me quick, the youth insisted,
> While his arms around her waist he twisted.
> I will, said she, if you'll agree
> To buy some chewing gum for me.
>
> The youth was wise and bought the gum,
> And then he told her he wanted some;
> She turned to him and then replied,
> The gum for me you never denied.
>
> So he laid her down upon the grass,
> She chewed her gum and wiggled her ass;
> She chewed and chewed till he started to come,
> Then she grabbed him close and swallered her gum.

Recited by Mr. J. B., Eureka Springs, Arkansas, June 22, 1948. He heard it in Carroll County, Arkansas, about 1936. This is an interesting recognition of the oral components in sexual excitement, and of externalized *oral needs* at orgasm, often expressed by shouting or even biting, as in the *Kama Sutra*.

20. I HAD A LITTLE MONKEY

> I had a little monkey,
> His ass-hole was red.
> Razz-pole, bazz-pole,
> Shot him in the ass-hole,
> Now my monkey's dead.

A. Mr. J. C., Eureka Springs, Arkansas, August 24, 1951, recited a stanza he heard at Moberly, Missouri, about 1912, as above.

B. From Mrs. O. T., Farmington, Arkansas, October 30, 1951, with a variant ending following on:

> Had a little monkey,
> Took him to the country,
> Fed him on ginger bread.
> Ass-tard, bass-tard,
> Kicked him in the ass-tard,
> Now my monkey's dead.
>
> Ass-to, bass-to,
> Kicked him in the ass-hole,
> Now my monkey's dead.

C. Ray Wood, *Fun in American Folk Rhymes* (1952) p. 84, prints a cleaned-up version:

> I had a little monkey, I sent him to the country,
> And fed him on ginger bread.
> Along come a choo-choo and knocked him coo-coo,
> And now my little monkey is dead.

21. THE BOY STOOD ON THE BURNING DECK

> The boy stood on the burning deck,
> Eating peanuts by the peck;
> Along came a little gal dressed in blue,
> She says, I'll take a pecker, too!

A. Recited by Mr. G. P., Reeds Spring, Missouri, July 5, 1948.

B. A related verse contributed by one of Mr. P.'s neighbors; but not disguising the word *pecker,* penis, under the slurred pronunciation, as in *A* above, of "a peck or two."

> The boy stood on the burning deck,
> Grabbed his pecker by the neck;
> His father jumped from where he stood,
> But alas, the boy had pulled his pud.

In line 4, *pulled his pud* (pudding), refers to masturbation. An openly mocking parody on Mrs. Felicia Hemans' "Casabianca" (before 1835) beginning: "The boy stood on the burning deck, Whence all but him had fled." Mrs. Hemans later nervously "corrected" this schoolmarmishly to read: "Whence all but *he* had fled"! See, for several "innocent" parody stanzas: Botkin, *Treasury of American Folklore,* (1944) p. 784, and Ray Wood, *What Happened to Mother Goose,* (1946) p. 54, also Wood's *Fun in American Folk Rhymes* (1952) p. 76, possibly a clean-up of the above. An entire collection of these polite parodies is now announced as "in progress."

22. PORE OLD LO

A. From Mrs. B. M., Lees Summit, Missouri, June 3, 1947. She said that *nisty* was a common word for penis in the 1880s. *Trusty* refers to a rifle; *jock* to the penis.

> Pore old Lo, setting on a rock,
> One hand on his trusty,
> The other on his jock,
> A-thinking of the good old days
> When there were no laws,
> When his trusty plugged the white man,
> And his nisty plugged the squaws.

B. Mr. J. C., Eureka Springs, Arkansas, August 24, 1951, heard this at Moberly, Missouri, about 1912, which suggests that the reciter of *A*, above, had misunderstood "Lo" as a name:

> Lo, the poor Indian,
> Sits on a rock,
> One hand on his rifle,
> The other on his cock,
> Dreaming of the days
> When unhampered by the law,
> With one he plugged the white man,
> With the other plugged his squaw.

23. SHE'S A RAILROAD GAL

Recited by Mrs. M. M., Springfield, Missouri, June 16, 1946. She had it from her husband, who learned it in the early 1900s. The initials in line 2 apparently stand for Missouri, Kansas, and Topeka Railroad, justifying the opening line.

> My old gal is a railroad gal,
> She lives by the M., K., and T.
> She stands on the steeple
> And pisses on the people,
> But she can't rub her ass on me.

B. The cliché about *standing on a steeple to piss on the people* occurs in other songs or chanted recitations as well, and derives from the old nursery rhyme or hand-game, using both hands:

> This is the house (*or* church: *fingers linked inside*),
> This is the steeple (*two fingers pointed up*);
> Open the house (*underside of linked fingers*
>   *is shown with a turnover gesture*),
>
> And see all the people! (*wiggling fingers!*)

When we kids played this, about 1926 to 1930, in Eastern Pennsylvania, we would substitute: "And piss on the people!" (As in the song.) We had many other impolite intrusions into, or finish-offs for, "sappy" polite songs. Said under our breaths when singing under supervision in schoolrooms or the school playground, and mockingly loudly when unsupervised. See also similar "inevitable rhymes" in the song above, "Shave 'Em Dry," No. 149.

24. RICH MAN, POOR MAN

If a rich man wants to get pore,
Get him a car, also a whore;
If a pore man wants to get rich,
Sell the car and strangle the bitch.

From Mrs. E. C., Anderson, Missouri, August 10, 1947. She had it from one of her neighbors, at unknown date. Essentially an aggressive rhyming version updated, of an ancient proverb first noted by Plautus, *Pœnulus* (ca. 200 B.C.) I.ii.210: "Whoever wishes to be very busy, let him equip these two things: a ship and a woman." This becomes, in the anonymous English play, *Lingua: or, The Five Senses* (ca. 1650) IV.v, "A ship is sooner rigg'd by far, than a Gentlewoman made ready." Thoreau, in the first chapter of *Walden* (1854) combined this with a pun on the old proverb about a woman's work never being done: "Clothes . . . a kind of work which you may call endless; a woman's dress, at least, is never done." This in turn may have inspired William Allen Butler's famous American satirical poem on women's clothing, "Nothing to Wear" (1857), on which see further the note at 13B, above.

25. BIRDS DO IT AND FLY

Birds do it and fly,
Bees do it and die,
Dogs do it and stick to it,
So why not you and I?

A. Quoted to Vance Randolph, possibly with seductional intent, by a waitress at Rockaway Beach, Missouri, May 30, 1929. She heard it in Carroll County, Arkansas, about 1910. Contains almost as many folk-errors as it has lines: Bees' death after stinging is here confused with their copulation; though the slow relaxation of the male dog's erection does make it seem to "stick" to the female, whom it may drag along in this way afterward.

B. In another version, also from a woman, Mrs. O. T., Farmington, Arkansas, June 6, 1956, the lines have been extended to fit another rhythm or "mental tune," which is not the original:

The little birdies do it on the fly,
The little girlies do it, then they cry,
The little doggies do it, and stick to it,
So why not let's try it, you and I?

C. There is a version similar to *A*, given as a graffito, in Allen Walker Read's *Lexical Evidence* (Paris 1935) p. 20. In all forms it is either the original, or a worn-down relic of a splendid Scottish song or recitation, "They A' Do't," by or in the style of Robert Burns, and first published in a posterior edition of his *Merry Muses of Caledonia* ("Dublin" 1832). A later revision appears in the erotic magazine *The Pearl*

(London: Lazenby, February 1880) No. 8, intruded into Part IV of "Lady Pokingham, or They All Do It," an erotic novelette, with note that it is sung to the tune of Burns' famous "A Man's a Man for A' That." The full text is given in Legman, *The Limerick* (Paris 1953) at Nos. 369–78, where it is well worth examining. The 7th and 9th of the ten stanzas and chorus are given here, to compare with the folk original or compressed relic, as above:

> The wee-bit cocks an' hens do't,
> The robins and the wrens do't,
>   The grizzly bears,
>   The toads an' hares,
> The puddocks in the fens do't . . .
>
> The kings an' queens an' a' do't,
> The Sultan an' Pasháw do't,
>   An' Spanish dons
>   Loup off their thrones,
> Pu' doon their breeks, an' fa' to't.
>
> *For they a' do't—they a' do't,*
> *The beggars an' the braw do't,*
>   *Folk that ance were,*
>   *An' folk that are—*
> *The folk that come will a' do't!*

This openly allusive phrase, "They all do it," became a favorite for a century or more in both Britain and America, as a not very covert reference to sexual intercourse; and was used at least once in a musical-comedy song of the 1930s, "Let's Do It— Let's Fall in *Love!*" the romantic ending being tacked on as polite disguise. See further note on 41 below, on "Some Do It." A charming French television "clip" with the pop-singer Michel Polnareff, *Toi et Moi* ("You and Me," 1980?) humorously jazzes up into foxtrot rhythm authentically photographed mating dances and couplings of "all creatures great and small," from ladybug to rhinoceros, with romantic lyrics to match.

26. THE OLDER THE BUCK

> The older the buck, the stiffer the horn,
> The younger the buck, the oftener he's on.

A. Mr. A. B., at the Veterans Hospital in Fayetteville, Arkansas, March 21, 1944, chanted this rhymed folk-proverb, of which the first line may be "more poetry than truth."

B. Another patient in the same hospital supplied another version, in which *nanny* means a young female goat; referring of course to a young woman, as in *1 Kings*, 1:1–4, concerning the aging King David and Abishag the Shunamite:

> The older the buck the harder the horn,
> The younger the nanny the sooner he's on.

27. THE JILL-FLIRT MARE

My old jill-flirt mare goes a-trotting down the road,
With a *plosh*, *plosh*, *plosh*, *plosh* . . .

A. Fragment from Mr. J. E., Webster Groves, Missouri, October 9, 1948. "Of course you know what a jill-flirt mare is," writes Mr. E.: "It's a mare that in borning her colt splits her hole, so that the two holes are one. Whenever such a mare trots, her one hole makes a noise something like *plosh*, *plosh*, *plosh*, *plosh*. To the small clodhopper, whose ears are always attuned for unconventional sounds, a jill-flirt mare was the source of great hilarity."

B. A related item from Mrs. H. K., Camdenton, Missouri, March 2, 1949, with which compare the reference to this unfortunate accident during childbirth, in Grose's *Classical Dictionary of the Vulgar Tongue* (1785) in the theatrical metaphor of "setting pit and boxes into one." In line 1 here, *tear*, a gallop or run:

The old gray mare she took a tear,
And through the fence she run.
She rammed a rail right under her tail
And tore both holes in one.

Randolph notes the applying of *jill-flirt* in non-Ozark speech to a woman with many lovers, the implication being the superstition that she has been "enlarged" vaginally by much intercourse. He says: "The noun *jill-flirt*, according to Webster, means 'a light, wanton woman,' but in the Ozarks it is merely a woman who farts frequently and noisily; this is caused by a cut or wound connecting the perineal orifices, usually a tear suffered in childbirth. A female in this condition has little control over the expulsion of gas from the lower bowel." See Randolph and Wilson, *Down in the Holler* (1953) p. 116.

28. WHEN NATURE CALLS

When Nature calls at either door
Do not refuse her,
For many an ail is sure to come
If you abuse her.

When Nature calls, do not delay
Or try to bluff her,
But haste away without delay
Or else your health will suffer.

Recited by a man named Perkins, in the courthouse at Pineville, Missouri, July 7, 1929. "When a man wants to piss *or* shit," said Perk, "he'll do well to drop his other business and attend to pissin' or shittin', as the case may be."

"A Call of Nature," is the sensation of needing to "go to the toilet." Public-school teachers, all women, in Scranton, Pennsylvania, mid-1920s, sometimes explained to us at the opening of the school term that "if we felt a Call of Nature," we were to raise one hand as a signal to the teacher, who would nod in assent, or sometimes say: "You may *leave the room*." To "leave the room" thus became a further euphemism, and was used as a joking remark, to rally any fellow student who farted in the playground.

Hygienic proverbs, of the kind clumsily rhymed above (compare "To Shit with Ease," No. 77), were common in the late Middle Ages, in Latin, such as: *"Mingere cum bumbis, Res saluberrima lumbis,"* roughly rhymed as follows, as a presumed preventive of heart-attacks:

> To piss and fart,
> Is good for the heart.

29. THE BULLFROG JUMPED

> Bullfrog jumped from bank to bank,
> Skinned his pecker shank to shank.

A. Fragment from Mr. G. P., Reeds Spring, Missouri, March 4, 1947. He had it from Mr. F. K., also of Reeds Spring. On *skinned his pecker* see note following.

B. Recited by a lady in Joplin, Missouri, July 6, 1948. She heard it chanted by children in Benton County, Arkansas, about 1910. *Skinned his pecker back* means retracted the foreskin, in this case as a preliminary to intercourse, *socked it in . . .*:

> Way down south in Rackensack,
> Bullfrog skinned his pecker back,
> Socked it in clear to her heart,
> You ought to hear them bullfrogs fart.

C. From Mr. J. C., Eureka Springs, Arkansas, August 24, 1951. In line 4, *frig*, to masturbate, in this case by retracting and replacing the foreskin: "to skin back":

> Way down on the Rackensack
> They don't do nothing but skin 'em back.
> It would pain you to the heart
> To see those bullfrogs frig and fart,
> For they've got nothing else to do.

D. Ray Wood, *What Happened to Mother Goose* (1946) p. 88, has this related stanza: replacing expurgated sex with bodily injury:

> Down on the river Yank-te-hank,
> The bullfrog jumped from bank to bank,
> He spread his legs from shank to shank,
> And split his hide from flank to flank.

30. CONDEMNED BY THE LAW

> Here I set condemned by the law
> For catching a preacher a-frigging a squaw;
> He had her dress up and her ass was bare,
> If he wasn't a-frigging her, why was he there?

A. Contributed by Mrs. M. M., Springfield, Missouri, June 15, 1946. She had it from somebody at Jefferson City, Missouri.

B. Mr. B. C., Cane Hill, Arkansas, October 21, 1948, says it like this:

> I stand here condemned in the eyes of the law,
> For catching a preacher a-frigging a squaw.
> She had her dress up, and his ass was right bare,
> If they wasn't a-frigging, why was he there?

"A lady from Tahlequah, Okla., tells me of a similar stanza written on the wall of a prison for Negro girls. If a black woman in the South did see a preacher frigging a squaw, and was foolish enough to go around talking about it, she might well be thrown into jail on some pretext, to shut her mouth." (Vance Randolph's field note.)

C. Randolph is in error to take this so seriously. In fact, it is a floating use of the rhyming end of a well-known *cante fable* collected in Easton, Pennsylvania, in late 1938, in which a witness to a rape is being condemned for contempt-of-court for having used the word "fucking" (here "frigging," as a synonym) in his testimony, and lapses into this rhyme indignantly as he is being led away, ending:

> His pants were down, his ass was bare,
> His balls were dangling in mid-air,
> His you-know-what was you-know-where,
> And if that wasn't fucking,
> > *Then, I wasn't there!*

31. MY OLD FIDDLE

> Riddledy raddledy, my old fiddle,
> Bends in the middle when I go for to diddle.
> Sally says fuckin' ain't no sin—
> Mighty good fucker for the shape she's in.

A. From a lady in Harrison, Arkansas, April 4, 1948. She said it was part of a Negro song popular in the 1890s. On the "bends in the middle" reference to male impotence, see "When a Man Gets Old," No. 1 above.

B. On the whole idea here, and the sardonic final trait, "for the shape she's in," compare a traditional humorous item circulated in America since at least the 1910s in the form of a small printed card (the ancestor of modern "Xeroxlore") given away by saloons, sometimes with their name and advertisement printed on the other side, the front. One from New York, about 1915, was headed "*Raffle For A Dog*," as a mock announcement, with a stock cut of a white dog "with a star on his head." Another is printed by Morse, *Folk Poems and Ballads* (1948) p. 97:

> A nice brown dog, as sound as a ring,
> He will be eight years old if he lives till Spring.
> He will piss on the carpet, shit on your grass;
> He has three white feet, and a hole in his ass.
> His eyes bulge out, and his cock caves in,
> But he's a damn fine dog—*for the shape he's in!*

No longer in rhyme, this is now usually collected in Xeroxlore form (Shippensburg, Pennsylvania, 1991) in a purposely bathetic prose version, illustrated with a stock drawing of a heartrendingly cheerful one-eyed, flop-eared mutt, as a public advertisement for a—"LOST DOG. 3 legs; Blind in left eye, Missing right ear, Tail broken, Recently castrated . . . Answers to name of 'Lucky.'"

C. Unexpectedly, perhaps, this joke is centuries old, and appears as a *catch* in Christ Church, Oxford, manuscript 439, printed in Wardroper, *Love and Drollery* (1969) p. 162, No. 275, noting: "This is from Thomas Morley's *First Book of Airs* (1600), but in the only known surviving copy—in the Folger Library (Washington, D.C.)—the pages with this song and five others are missing [*i.e., torn out, perhaps centuries ago.*] It is one of many pedlars' songs full of double meanings":

> Will you buy a fine dog with a hole in his head?
> > *With a dildo, with a dildo dildo,*
> > *With a dildo dildo dildo dildo.*
> Muffs, cuffs, rebatoes, and fine sister's thread,
> > *With a dildo, &c.*
>
> I stand not on points, pins, periwigs, combs, glasses,
> Gloves, garters, girdles, busks for the brisk lasses,
> But I have other dainty tricks—
> Sleek stones and poking sticks,
> > *With a dildo, dildo, &c. . .*

The pedlar is announcing here his stock-in-trade, with heavy accent on the *dildos* and "other dainty tricks" available (under the secret tray in his pack) "for the brisk lasses." Chapmen and pedlars of this itinerant kind have always stocked erotic "novelties" and bawdy books, usually of small size, "that can be read with one hand." In Ann Arbor, Michigan, October 1935, such a pedlar, or "bagman," selling bobbins of thread and similar to a crippled tailor sitting at his sewing-machine in his tiny shop, also offered to seventeen-year-old me razor blades and with an enormous wink (I being an accidental customer just walked in), erotic comic-books, called "squeezers," and pornographic pamphlets ("readers"), for twenty-five cents apiece, marked on their cardboard covers: "Havana, Cuba. Price: TEN DOLLAR."

As to Elizabethan dildos, the *locus classicus* is Thomas Nashe's *A Dildoe, or his Valentine* (manuscript 1600) first printed by John S. Farmer in *Merry Songs and Ballads* (1895–97) vol. I, and reprinted in Thomas R. Smith's *Poetica Erotica* (ed. 1927), a long satirical poem on the subject. In early-eighteenth-century nursery rhymes and popular songs these "dildo" refrains, as above, were modified to "*diddle*," which itself refers to erotic fingering, so not a very good disguise. Shakespeare says it all, on the subject of "bawdy-basket pedlars" and their wares, in the character of Autolycus in *The Winter's Tale* (about 1610) IV.iv: who had "the prettiest love-songs for maids; so without bawdry which is strange; with such delicate burdens of *dildos* and *fadings*."

32. TWO LITTLE PILLOWS

Two little pillows covered with lace,
Two little sweethearts face to face,
Hand full of titty, mouth full of tongue,
Pussy full of peter—yum, yum, yum!

A. Recited by Mrs. M. M., Springfield, Missouri, October 21, 1948, as a sort of celebrational "album-verse," complete in a single stanza and ending-off as shown.

B. This is a fragment, or relic worn down to a quatrain, of a fairly long *tour-de-force* formulaic poem, in which all or most of the lines begin with the words "Two little," "A little," or similar. Texts from both Chicago and San Francisco, about 1900, as below, appear to be a *Lesbian love-poem*, from the reserved romantic rather than graphic male ("obscene" or *machisto*) tone, and especially from the covert formula or technique chosen, in which *the sex of the loved-one is never revealed*, nor of the reciter-poet. In the same oblique way, homosexual male singers formerly in burlesque shows (and in general since the 1920s as "crooners," "pop-" and "rock-singers," etc.) make use of song-texts addressed continuously to "You" in all vocative lines, to avoid any betrayal by third-person pronouns, "he" or "him," for the presumed female lover; here as "A Little Poem":

A little nod, a little walk,
A little drink, a little talk,
A little hope that I can be
As close to you as you to me.

A little restaurant discreet,
A little dinner—what a treat!
A little private room upstairs,
(Where no one sees and no one cares,)
A little kiss snatched unawares.

A little bodice trimmed in lace,
A little breast, a blushing face,
A little hug, a little kiss,
A little hour of Sacred Bliss.

A little hope that now and then
We can do it all again.

33. IT'S HARD TO BE GOOD

Said the good little girl to the bad little girl,
It's awfully hard to be good;
Said the bad little girl to the good little girl,
It's *got* to be hard, to be good.

From a lady in Stillwell, Oklahoma, May 14, 1943. She first heard it about 1900. Essentially "celebrational," or didactic advice. "Good" is here to be understood as meaning sexually repressed. Also often collected by the 1940s as a mere prose witticism, on the "hardness" of the penis, and which may well be the original of the poem. Note also *parody song-title* sometimes ascribed to Mae West or other mother-image sex-goddesses since the 1930s: "A *Hard* Man Is Good to Find" (for "A Good Man Is Hard to Find," thus spoonerized).

34. A BREATH OF AIR

> A sigh is but a breath of air
> Breathed upward from the heart;
> But when it takes a downward course
> It's nothing but a fart.

A. Recited by Dr. L. M., Anderson, Missouri, January 12, 1931.

B. Another version, from Mr. C. S., Galena, Missouri, August 14, 1938:

> A belch is but an echo
> A-coming from the heart,
> But if it takes a downward course
> It then becomes a fart.

The "inevitable" rhyme of *heart/fart* refers to the old belief (not entirely false) that the retaining of farts can cause a heart attack in arterio-sclerotic persons: given as a cause of death in the famous passage on *musical farting* in Montaigne's *Essays* (1588). See also note on No. 28, above.

Various eighteenth-century humorous poems send this dangerous *afflatus* even higher, to the brain, pretending that held-in farts "rise to the brain" and cause temporary insanity! Or worse, as in note to No. 28, above. Compare also the 1950s prose recitation, a girl's "wild" rhetorical flights about sherry (or champagne) ending: "But beer?— Beer just makes me fart!" First heard in Rome, 1954, from an American girl tourist, as a "mild" scatological announcement of her sexual availability. (The girl in the recitation is refusing —with this indirect "fart"—a man's seductional offer of a mere glass of beer.)

35. HAM AND EGGS

> Ham and eggs between your legs,
> Beefsteak and gravy.
> With your thing and my thing
> We could make a baby!

Recited by Mrs. O. T., Farmington, Arkansas, October 30, 1951. Openly a female approach of sexual invitation, essentially a magical "charm," it is significant that the woman is thinking of sex as *baby*. "Ham and eggs": here equaling penis and testicles; also "beefsteak and gravy" (not a traditional *and*-connective?) as penis and ejaculated semen owing to its viscosity, also thought of as a *food*-item feeding the woman's "lower (or: other) mouth." Any connected element formed of *three* objects is unconsciously considered, in dreams etc., and at the folk-level, as equivalent to penis and testicles, "prick and balls," but only if formed of *one-plus-two* elements (or one plus a larger or more "plural" object, e.g., *gravy*, as above), not if of three separate units, such as pawn-shop "balls."

With the "ham and eggs" here, compare the similar food metaphor (originally homosexual *camp*, U.S. about 1940), "All that meat and no potatoes!" for a large penis coupled with normal-sized balls. This type of mock-complaint also occurs in "No Balls At All," No. 13 above, stanza 3:3–4, "His dooflicker's long and his dornick is tall, But the son-of-a-bitch never fucks me at all!" Here both the foreskin and penis (dooflicker and dornick) are satisfactory as equipment . . . but the performance is lacking, as are the testicles.

This involves an ancient and elemental principle, the folk-superstition of predestination: that "you can't have everything (or, it all)"; and that at a baby's or hero's christening, the gifts of the good fairies (angels, or mere godparents) are likely to be countered by the one bad witch (demon, Lilith, or old aunt) who angrily spoils everything by adding or refusing one essential gift. The most famous modern example is the O. Henry castratory-disappointment story, "The Gift of the Magi," concerning the man pawning his heirloom watch to buy a fancy comb for his wife's hair—which she has cut off to buy him a watchchain.

Many of O. Henry's stories have similar trick twists or surprise endings, based on this notion of the inevitability of one's destiny, in particular his *Roads of Destiny* (1909). Others are on even deeper, almost conscious symbolic elements, such as his most popular story, "*Alias* Jimmy Valentine," several times made into a motion picture, almost openly on womb-return and birth-danger fantasies, concerning the child locked into the enormous unopenable safe, and in danger of suffocation and death unless the safe-cracker-obstetrician "gone straight," will drop his disguise as a good citizen, and get the child out by means of his sensitive (obstetrical) fingertips. In one of the motion-picture versions this is hoked-up into practically a Caesarean section, with an oxy-acetylene blowtorch cutting into the recalcitrant womb or "safe." The great Hungarian-American magician, "Houdini" (Erich Weiss) took this a step further into water- and womb-symbolism, by making his famous escape, manacled and leg-ironed, from inside a locked safe, *thrown into the river!* See also Note 47 below, on "Screwy Dick." The fictionalized biography of Houdini, by E. L. Doctorow, *Ragtime* (1975), has a good deal on Houdini's "womb-return" escapes, clearly recognized as such.

36. OLD MISTER FLANNIGAN

Old Mister Flannigan
Will never be a man again,
There's a hole in his ass
You could roll a bale of cotton in.

A. Mr. J. E., Webster Groves, Missouri, April 8, 1948, recalled this fragment as part of a long recitation he heard in the 1880s.

B. The Irish original song is given in Padraic Colum, *Treasury of Irish Folklore* (New York 1954) p. 594:

Ma'am dear, did ye never hear
Of pretty Molly Brannigan?
In troth, then, she's left me,
And I'll never be a man again.

An American version of this "polite" original appearing in Mary O. Eddy, *Ballads and Songs from Ohio* (1939) p. 319, also gives this as of Irish origin, and even more sentimentally: "Did you never hear tell of pretty Polly Brannigan? For she stole me heart and I'll never be a man again." Irish names on this pattern lend themselves easily to favorite anapestic songs of this kind, such as the comedy recitation on the Irish drunkard in-and-out of jail: "Off ag'in, on ag'in, in ag'in, Finnegan!" And the never-ending nonsense song of "Michael Finnegan, who grew the whiskers on his chinigin," in *The Oxford Song Book*, ed. Thomas Wood (1928) vol. II: p. 99, No. 64. Unfortunately, none of these give us any lead to the rest of the bawdy version, above, from the Ozarks in the 1880s.

37. A SPINDLE-ASS GIRL

A spindle-ass girl is hard to beat,
The closer the bone, the sweeter the meat,
The harder the prick, the tighter the skin,
The quicker she wiggles, the sooner it's in.

A. From a lady in Bentonville, Arkansas, July 3, 1924. She learned it from her mother in the late 1890s.

B. Recited by Mr. F. S., Eureka Springs, Arkansas, May 29, 1952. He heard it in Yell County, Arkansas, about 1935.

High on the mountain, deep in the grass,
The fairer the maiden, the better the ass,
The plumper the maiden, the tighter the skin,
The shorter the pecker, the quicker it's in.

Note that apart from the formulaic opening of *B*, in the "Fire on the Mountain" style of songs Nos. 115 and 174, these two otherwise quite different versions are both entirely composed of erotic two-part homiletic folk-phrases or proverbs. As *modern proverbs* have not often been collected, nor published— let alone the erotic ones, such as these—it is hard to trace or study those above, and they must be accepted as the welcome rarities they are. See also rhymes Nos. 1, 4, 17, 24, 25, 26, 34, and 35 above; and song No. 203, "The Foot-Long Jock."

C. A similar "nationalistic" or *blason* couplet was heard in New York, New York, Summer 1949, from a young white woman, comparing Negroes and Germans sexually:

A long-pricked Nigger is hard to beat,
But a big-assed Dutchman *drives that meat!*

With this compare the defiantly "miscegenational" song No. 203 above, "The Foot-Long Jock." A similar anecdote or encounter is given in French eighteenth-century jestbooks concerning a small, short French politician with a very long penis, whose opponent snorts, "But where is the ass to drive it?" symbolizing idle political projects.

38. HE FUCKED MY WIFE

He fucked my wife,
He fucked my daughter,
And he shook his prick
At my old dog Towser!

Recited by Mr. Jack Conroy, Eureka Springs, Arkansas, August 24, 1951. A *fragment* of a long poem entitled "A Rambunctious Guy," heard near Moberly, Missouri, about 1912. This "A Rambunctious Guy" poem has not been recovered, and apparently never collected in any form. The implied scenario is classic in various European peasant bawdy tales, from both France and Russia.

Observe the *anti-woman* farcical equating of the "insult" to the man's dog with the affront to the two women, presumably the man's most dearly beloved. Compare *Deuteronomy*, 23:17–18, "There shall be no whore of the daughters of Israel, nor a sodomite of the sons of Israel. Thou shalt not bring the hire of a whore, or the price of a dog, into the house of the Lord thy God for any vow: for even both these are abomination." From other Biblical passages using these terms it would appear that "dog" here is to be understood metaphorically, as of the same sodomite prostitutes reprehended above, but the presumed contempt for the animal itself is clear.

39. A COMICAL CRITTER

> Cunt, oh cunt, thou comical (curious) creature,
> Whiskered around like a Baptist preacher,
> Like a polecat's ass, thou smellest bad,
> But oh thou cunt! thou must be had!

A. Collected by Vance Randolph in the Ozark area, about 1930, but without exact provenance in his field notes, presumably as a *toast* from a man; but observe that version *C* below—admittedly not much less forthright—was heard from a woman. Although apparently insulting, this toast or tribute shows a definitely ambivalent love/hatred (or fear) of the female genitals, for the power exercised over man's emotions and impulsions. See further the notes on the other versions below. The present version may perhaps be dated by the reference to the preacher's "Dundreary" side-whiskers, uncommon before or after the second half of the nineteenth century.

B. See Allen Walker Read, *Lexical Evidence* (Paris 1935)) p. 46, for a similar stanza found as a *graffito:*

> Oh cunt, oh cunt, thou slimy slit,
> All covered with hair, besmithered with shit,
> Like a polecat's ass thou smelleth bad,
> But oh cunt, thou must be had.

C. Recited by a lady in Springfield, Missouri, August 18, 1938. She had it from Mr. John Gold, of Stone County, Missouri, in the early 1900s. There were many stanzas, she said, but she remembered only one. (The "many stanzas" may be an erroneous recollection.)

> A cunt is a comical critter,
> Its face all covered with hair,
> It smells like a rotten potater,
> And resembles the ass of a bear.

D. Mr. J. B., Eureka Springs, Arkansas, June 22, 1948, heard this in Carroll County, Arkansas, about 1927:

> Here's to the cunt, the comical creature,
> All covered with bristles and hair,
> Looks like hell and damnation,
> And smells like the ass of a bear.

E. From Mr. Jack Conroy, folklorist, Eureka Springs, Arkansas, August 24, 1951. He heard it in Moberly, Mo., about 1912:

> It smells like a rotten potater,
> But I wish, by God, I was there.

A personal testimony. The present writer heard version *B* above, cited by Read, which is just about the nastiest and most hateful or resentful, recited by a young California ex-Marine to a mixed group of equally young American tourists in Paris in 1954. To my astonishment, not only the young men, but also the young tourist girls (average age about twenty) applauded his rendition with apparent enthusiasm. When later I asked one young married woman present why she had applauded so elaborate an insult to herself and the other women present, she answered with what seemed to me pretty clear masochistic self-hatred or brainwashing, "Well, it's the truth, isn't it?" Compare the man-to-woman provenance of *C,* above.

Anti-womanism, expressed as fear and hatred of the female genitals, is very ancient, as for example when the open love-song of the *Song of Songs* was pretended by early Biblical annotators to refer only to divine love; or when a purported slur against the "mouth of the vagina" is found in the profound statement in *Proverbs,* 30:15–16, as to the biological female need for maternity: "The horseleach hath two daughters, crying, Give, give. There are three things that are never satisfied, yea, four things say not, It is enough: The grave, and *the barren womb*; the earth that is not filled with water; and the fire that saith not, It is enough." On the basis of this obvious misinterpretation the medieval St. Odon of Cluny made his notorious "close optical assessment": *Inter faeces et urinam nascimur*: "We are born between shit and piss." (Compare note 40, following.) It is this that is artistically varied in W. B. Yeats' strabismic revamp, in his poem "Crazy Jane and the Bishop": "Love has pitched his mansion In the place of excrement." A statement that for some reason tens of thousands of college women are expected to study and admire, including those who might feel that Yeats' belovèd Ireland is now perhaps a bit closer to "the place of excrement."

The Ozarker, as a presumed "primitive," is allowed an extreme license in this kind of anti-gallant assessment, and especially to express all the insulting hostility, against his no-longer sexually attractive or aging wife, that the presumed non-primitive urban male does not allow himself. As in the Ozark folk-tale retold by Vance Randolph: *The old hill-dweller tells his wife that when they were first married her cunt looked like "a fresh peach with a dimple in it," but that now it looks like "a pile of cow-shit that a wagon-wheel ran through."* See further G. Legman, *Rationale of the Dirty Joke* (vol. 2, *No Laughing Matter*, 1975), the chapters "Anti-Gallantry and Anti-Woman," pp. 704–27, and especially "The Defiling of the Mother," pp. 392–419, and 449–67, "The Overlarge Vagina (Dentata)," which go about as far as a male writer can allow himself to go. The further history, sociology, and social pathology of this matter are a subject with which women folklorists and scholars, such as Shulamith Firestone, should certainly concern themselves.

F. The would-be humorous tone striven for in calling the present anti-toast "A Comical (*or* Curious) Critter," is a shade less hateful than the outright insults, to be sure. Or anciently inventing legends of the fearsome "Toothed Vagina" or *vagina dentata*; or starting modern contests of the kind engaged in by the heavily over-reacting "oral masochistic" cartoonist, Al Capp, of "Li'l Abner" fame in the 1940s and since, offering prizes for the ugliest and most nauseating drawings submitted of the mythical modern Medusa, "Lena the Hyena," whom all men fear.

Compare, two centuries earlier, the humorist Ned Ward's *A Dutch Riddle, or Paradoxical Character of An Hairy Monster, often found under Holland* (London, about 1725; reprinted several times by 1737: two editions in the British Museum Library, *Private Case,* Nos. 1033 and 1867). The final pun here, on "under Holland," meaning under a woman's underwear, is for the benefit of the dumb-bells who do not understand this "hairy" joke at first sight. See David Foxon's magistral bibliography of British humorous and satirical verse of the early-eighteenth century. Further details appear in the even more famous prose satire on the vagina, Thomas Stretser's ("Roger Phequewell's") *Merryland: A New Description of Merry-Land,*

"Containing a Topographical, Geographical, and Natural History of that Country" ("Bath," 1741; and many reprints including one by the Panurge Press, "Robin Hood House," New York, about 1932). One edition, now lost, is also reported to have included a set of mock geo-anatomical "maps" of the exact location of Merry-land. For matching male phallic satires and *obscœna*, see notes on No. 42 below, on "P-R-I-C-K Paddle."

G. The present rhyme and the two following, Nos. 40–41, are of particular interest not for their open aggressiveness against the woman and her body, but for their clear ambivalence of fear and hatred, combined with love and overwhelming attraction to the woman's body: precisely the psychological situation alluded to in the Homeric legend of the goddess Circe turning men into swine, and the more lethal Germanic form of this same legend, in the Rhine maidens whose song and beauty "drag men down" to their watery (vaginal/uterine) death. This is also sometimes expressed as an ambivalence in the woman herself: the legend of the serpent-bride Mélusine (the Gorgon Medusa), who turns into a monster only at midnight—i.e., in bed—when her female-phallic serpentine charms stiffen men like stone, again in death. See Oliver Wendell Holmes' novelized version of this legend, *Elsie Venner* (1861), noted as one of his sources by Freud, and the more modern and historical materials in G. Legman, *Love & Death* (1949), chapter 3, "Avatars of the Bitch-Heroine."

Probably the most interesting example of this ambivalent love/hatred, since the author-poet clearly is struggling to love and not to hate the woman, nor to fear her sexual strength, is the superb modern erotic sonnet-sequence, "Romeo and Juliet," by H. Phelps Putnam, about 1928 printed in *Neurotica* (New York, 1949) No. 5: p. 22, of which an inferior early draft is given in Putnam's *Complete Poems*. This masterpiece-cum-mistresspiece has to be read in full to be appreciated. The hateful "Juliet" half begins:

> Mother of men, and bearded like a male,
> Loose lips that smile, and smile without a face,
> Our nursery and whorehouse, you whose stale
> Unconquered stench no purging can erase . . .

But the poem ends transfigured in half-grudging love and adoration. For all its intensely modern air, this sonnet-set is actually a translation, or rather a free adaptation of Pierre de Ronsard's two most famous "Sonnets Masculin and Féminin" (1565), beginning, *"O vermeillette fente*: "Oh, vermillion slit . . ."

40. I WOULDN'T FUCK

> I wouldn't fuck a nigger,
> I'll be damned if I would,
> Their hair's all kinky
> And their pussy's no good.
>
> A white woman smells
> Like Castile soap,
> But a nigger gal smells
> Like a damned billy-goat.

Recited by Mr. J. C., Eureka Springs, Arkansas, August 24, 1951. He heard it in Moberly, Missouri, about 1912. (Compare the opposite sentiment in rhyme No. 41 following.)

This is an anti-Negro parody, or otherwise uncollected stanza of the older song, beginning, "I wouldn't marry an old man (*or*, a soldier, *or* farmer, etc.), And I'll tell you the reason why."

Formulaically, at least, this is connected with an early-seventeenth-century woman-rejecting song, preserved in post-Jacobean plays, disdaining numerous women—all presumably prostitutes being proposed to the drinkers—by their rhyming names: Molly who is jolly, etc.

Note the unconscious contradiction in the anti-Negro rejection of the present rhyme, as with St. Odon of Cluny, that it strongly implies an exact knowledge of the pubic-hair character, odor, anatomy, etc., of the presumably rejected "nigger gal." In actual fact, through all the centuries of Negro slavery in America (and still), Negro women and girls were considered and used as erotic sub-social fare by white men and boys, in both the southern and northern states: in the North as prostitutes.

41. SOME DO IT

Some do it by the babbling brook,
Some do it in the glade,
Some do it in the meadows,
Some do it in the shade . . .

Some do it by the sea,
But a nigger's ass
In the tall blue grass
Is good enough for me.

A fragment recalled by a lady at Anderson, Missouri, September 27, 1942. She had it from some boys at Lanagan, Missouri, about 1930. Lines are evidently missing between the 4th and 5th here. (Compare the opposite sentiment in rhyme No. 40 preceding.)

In line 7, *ass*, is to be understood metonymically, as "the whole for the part," referring to the woman's entire genital area. There is also a widespread folk "reminiscence" here, or instinctual survival, based on our quadruped mammalian-anthropoid past, when the male actually approached the female ideally or originally from behind, aiming at the buttock *target-area*, as do all other anthropoids and most other living creatures. This explains the modern slang division of male sexual choices, as to women, into "ass-men" and "tit-men": back or front. There are presumably no "face-men," for all the fetichistic talk of female beauty.

The catch-phrase, *They all do it*, has been an open allusion to sexual intercourse for over a century now (see end-note on No. 25, "Birds Do It and Fly"); and a recent American verbal fad has been for adverbially punning phrases on "How They Do It": Lawyers do it *briefly* (or: on a trial basis)—Porcupines do it *carefully*—Beavers do it *busily*—Cardiologists do it *heartily*—The French do it *frankly*; and so forth; that on porcupines apparently having started the fad. Collections of these are published (and perhaps invented in part) by Reinhold Aman in his yearbook *Maledicta*, and his *How Do They Do It? A Collection of Wordplays Revealing the Sexual Proclivities of Man and Beast* (1983), with a second volume promised.

42. P-R-I-C-K PADDLE

P-R-I-C-K paddle,
C-U-N-T canoe,
Will you paddle me over
In your canoe?

A. Mr. J. R., Harrison, Arkansas, April 5, 1950, recalled this as a "spelling riddle" he heard in the 1890s.

B. Another such erotic spelling-out item, from a woman, white, about thirty-five years old, from a southern seaboard state, Mrs. G. E., in New York City, 1952, who had come to New York to act as liaison-woman for a southern sado-masochistic "Society of Pain and Pleasure," she being an avowed masochist. Note submissive phrasing; referring to whipping, not buggery?

If I ask you for it nicely
Will you lay me on my back,
And give me your P-R-I-C-K
And make my ass-hole crack?

When I broke down in laughter over this (not at first recognizing the reference to flagellation), she repeated the last two lines—in perhaps the original phrasing?—as "And make my C-U-N-T crack!"

Direct phallic humor of this kind is not common, as the display of the penis is considered the final "obscenity" under patriarchy, where the display of the nude female and any of her organs is considered "charming," meaning sexually exciting. See on this important status difference the remarkable work by Mathilde and Mathias Vaerting, *The Dominant Sex* (English translation, 1923), a work half a century ahead of its time, worth reprinting now.

Eighteenth century humorous *phallica* included: *Arbor Vitæ, or The Natural History of the Tree of Life* (London, 1741) by Thomas Stretser, author of the matchingly yonijic *Merryland* (also 1741), on which see at end-note No. 39F above; likewise *The Potent Ally, or Succours from Merryland,* with *Erotopolis*: *The Present State of Bettyland; The Electrical Eel, or Gymnotus Electricus* by "Adam Strong" (about 1774); and *Teague-Root Displayed* by "Paddy Strongcock" (1746). All these in British Museum Library, *Private Case*, Nos. 1749, 1750–59, 1483, 1760, and 1767.

Only two centuries later, in the 1970s did the first open glorifications and mock-histories of the penis appear again in English, under such allusive titles as *Man's Best Friend*, and similar. An enormous file on literary and folkloristic references to the penis was compiled by the late Harry P. Johnson, of Arlington, Virginia, in the 1940s and 50s, extending to over one million index cards and cross-references, both heterosexual and homosexual; but this has never been published nor is the file's present whereabouts known. (Dr. Clifford Scheiner collection, Brooklyn, New York?) As one corner of the subject, see Martha Cornog's study of pet-names for the penis, with additions by Dr. Reinhold Aman, in *Maledicta* (1981) vol. V, "What Is This Thing Called, Love?"

43. IF YOU WANT TO GO TO HEAVEN

If you want to go to Heaven
I'll tell you what to do,
Just grease your ass
With an Irish stew.

When Old Scratch gets you
In the hot frying pan,
You'll slide right over
To the Promised Land.

A. From Mr. J. E., Webster Groves, Missouri, April 9, 1948. He heard it recited by schoolboys in the 1880s. In 2:1, *Old Scratch*, the Devil. Compare "A Trip to Heaven," No. 54 below.

B. An expurgated song version (note failure of rhyme and meter at the polite *chicken soup*) is given as "Negro humor," with further references, in Brown, *Collection of North Carolina Folklore* (1952) vol. III: p. 525:

> If you want to go to heaven I'll tell you how to do:
> Grease yourself with chicken soup.
> And if the devil get after you with the red-hot pan,
> Just slide over into the Promised Land.

44. NEVER TOUCHED A HAIR

A. Mr. B. H., Joplin, Missouri, October 13, 1932, recalled this jingle which he had learned in the early 1900s:

> Bigfoot Riley killed a bear,
> Shot him in the ass and never touched a hair.

B. Below is another fragment, possibly of the same piece, from Mr. J. B., also of Joplin, Missouri, December 29, 1930, heard near Lanagan, Missouri, in the 1890s:

> Brush tore up and bushes bit,
> Bear sign and painter shit!

See also Ray Wood, *What Happened to Mother Goose* (1946) p. 26, and Emrich and Korson, *The Child's Book of Folklore* (1947) p. 60 for related "polite" items. Various American tall tales (as in the nineteenth-century southern "Sut Lovingood" stories) have versions of the Baron Munchausen story in which the bear is killed by having him swallow the gun flint, then turning and being "shot in the ass" with the steel, with resultant explosion. The "never touched a hair" idea appears in other folk-jokes as well, such as the riddle: *How do you kiss a chicken's ass without getting feathers in your mouth?*—Answer (not spoken, but acted out): "*Blow! then kiss! Blow! then kiss!!* (Now adding, in words:) "BUT FAST!!"—Bronx, New York, 1948, from a middle-aged male pharmacist who was a treasury of bawdy lore, proverbs, catches, etc.

45. FOOTPRINTS ON THE DASHBOARD

> There's a whipstock that is broken,
> That is left us as a token,
> And a lap-robe that's been dragging on the ground;
> There must have been some pushin',
> For there's blood upon the cushion,
> And there's footprints on the dashboard upside down . . .

A. Manuscript copy (incomplete) from Mrs. L. W., Reeds Spring, Missouri, August 26, 1947. There is a tradition in the neighborhood that the verse was "made up" by Dr. Lafayette Henson, a physician who came to Stone County in 1884 and practiced medicine there for many years. Note that the "dashboard" is that of a horse and buggy, complete with whipstock. In line 4, *pushin'*, sexual intercourse; line 5, *blood, i.e.,* of defloration.

B. Recited by Mrs. M. M., Springfield, Missouri, April 4, 1948. There were several stanzas, but she recalls only the following:

> There's a whipstock that is broken,
> Which is left me as a token,
> And a saddle-blanket laying on the ground;
> And the grease spots on the cushion
> Which tell of some good pushin',
> And footprints on the dashboard upside down . . .

C. There is a text from the 1890s, as below, also incomplete, or possibly considered to be complete in this one stanza, in W. L. McAtee, *Grant County, Indiana, Speech and Song*, Supplement 2 (1946) p. 4. The *upside-down footprints* of which all versions make a special point are, of course, those of the man, in "missionary" intercourse with the woman. Compare note at *E,* below, at end.

> The whipstock had been broken,
> And I took that for a token,
> The lap robe had been trailed along the ground;
> A wet spot on the cushion
> Showed there had been pushin',
> There were footprints on the dashboard upside down.

D. The complete version, in two stanzas, includes an Answer from the swain, as in *Immortalia* (1927) p. 100, entitled "A Letter from the (Village) Postmaster," where the Answer begins boldly: "I'm the guy that done the pushin', Put the grease-spots on the cushion, Made the footprints, *etc.*" Also in the first, best, and largest modern British collection, *Camp Fire Songs.* (Madras ca. 1939) f.8, "About a Buggy." This is reprinted in Legman, *Bawdy Monologues* (1976) p. 104. Mr. J. C., Eureka Springs, Arkansas, August 24, 1951, heard the complete version at Moberly, Missouri, about 1912, with the "enclosing" prose story in *cante fable* style:

> A traveling salesman took a country girl out buggy-riding. Her name was Venus, and
> they had a pretty good time. Two months later came a letter from the girl's father:
>
> > This letter is a token of a whipstock that is broken,
> > And a lap robe that was spread upon the ground;
> > There's a grease spot on the cushion
> > That is evidence of pushin',

> And some footprints on the dashboard upside down—
> And my daughter Venus has not yet come round.

The salesman wrote the following answer:

> This letter is a token of the whipstock that is broken,
> And the lap robe that was spread upon the ground;
> Since I met your daughter Venus
> I've had trouble with my penis
> And I wish I'd never seen your God-damn town.

E. A physician in Scranton, Pennsylvania, summer of 1935, gave a sixteenth-birthday party for his pretty and vivacious daughter, unfortunately afflicted with a slight neck malformation (which she successfully hid under her flowing back hair, on the style of the then similarly afflicted young movie-singer, Deanna Durbin), and invited all the late-adolescent boys in the neighborhood. During the course of the party this broad-minded and solicitous father, who sang numerous jolly songs at the piano, recited the above complete version in two stanzas (without any prose explanation). He included without expurgation the climactic line about the daughter who "hasn't come around," i.e., has missed her menstruation and is pregnant. All of us young bucks (who believed that the "dashboard" was that of an automobile) danced with the girl, who was in Seventh Heaven; and we agreed that her father, the physician, was the "greatest guy in town." Edward Tatum Wallace, in his *Barington* (1945) p. 8, refers to "jokes about finding footprints on the dashboard upside down" at a village in western Arkansas. In other joke versions, the girl's high heels have also torn holes (for her part of the dashboard action) in the cloth roof of the buggy or sports-car, when lifted in her ecstasy.

46. THE JOY-PRONGS

> Mabel was a little girl,
> Itched where she couldn't scratch;
> Little boys they used to put
> Their joy-prongs up her snatch.

From Mr. J. D., Clinton, Iowa, March 5, 1951. He heard it in MacDonald County, Missouri, about 1910. Outlandish, perhaps, but perfectly authentic U.S. folk-term for the penis, "joy-prong" (also "joypronger") is matched by "joy-box," cunt. In 1986, in a large Arizona town, the woman proprietor of a sex-shop called "The *Toy* Box," to allude to her stock of vibrators, illegal dildoes (under one disguise or other), and sexy underclothing, told me that her local newspaper advertisement, with rather swash italic capitals in the name of her store, was usually read by the public—and perhaps so intended?—as "The Joy Box."

As to the *vagina dentata* term "snatch," in Sir Thomas Urquhart's mid-seventeenth-century translation of Rabelais, one of the listed terms for the woman's sexual parts (a list much enlarged by Urquhart from Rabelais' original, as usual in that translation) is: "snatch-blatch." It is a reference to the vagina-dentata fantasy, presumably; as in an American "Negro" story where *A man's wife becomes pregnant even though he has been castrated to prevent this: "That woman's cunt'd suck up a tack!"* This "aspirational fantasy of the Sexual Superwoman" is trick-photographed (with magnetic balls disappearing up under her skirt) in Federico Fellini's bitter anti-feminist "comedy" film, *City of Women* (1976).

47. SCREWY DICK

I sing the ballad of Screwy Dick,
The boy that was born with a cork-screw prick,
He spent his life in a valiant hunt
To find a girl with a cork-screw cunt.
But when he found her, poor Dick dropped dead,
For the goddam thing had a left-hand thread.

A. Recited by Mr. L. J., Farmington, Arkansas, December 4, 1941.

B. Found written on the wall of an outdoor toilet at Gateway, Arkansas, June 18, 1954:

Did you ever hear the tale of Moby Dick,
The poor bastard had a corkscrew prick,
And all of his life was a great long hunt
To find a gal with a corkscrew cunt,
And when he did he fell over dead,
The god damn bitch had a left hand thread.

C. This is driven out artificially, by means of extended lines in another meter, into a limerick-sequence of two stanzas, dated 1941, in *The Limerick* (1953) Nos. 1155–56, and note p. 439, calling the original poem "Screwy Dick with the Spiral Prick." Morse, *Folk Poems and Ballads* (1948) p. 96, prints this as:

This is a story of woeful Dick,
Whose life was cursed with a spiral prick.
He spent his days in endless hunt
To find a girl with a spiral cunt.
But when he found her, he near dropped dead
For the God damn thing had a left-hand thread!

The nineteenth-century "clap-doctor" manual, William Acton's *Functions and Disorders of the Reproductive Organs* (1858) is cited as saying: "The boar pig takes his time very leisurely, his penis being of a corkscrew shape . . ." Note that most breeds of male pig do actually have a somewhat spiral twist to the penis, as photographed gloatingly in *Suck*, a Danish hippie-film (made about 1975 by a Japanese photographer and far-out sculptor, whose white girlfriend sold his sculptures on the Paris bar-*terrasses* in the 1950s out of a purse made from a bull's scrotum), in which a heavily-cosmeticked young woman has intercourse with various animals and performs fellation on a pig. She "explains" that she "got into" this through her job, helping in the artificial impregnation of farm animals, though one wonders which came first.

At the broader folk-level, the essential thrust or meaning of the "Screwy Dick" poem is the ancient idea that our fate is predestined, including our sexual anatomy; and that it is foolish and even dangerous to attempt to change or meddle with this; and that if we *do*, in the words of that modern proverb which is Murphy's First Law: *"If anything can go wrong—it will!"* Usually disastrously. This is the point of many Oriental folktales, such as the one about *The foolish Arab who wishes for his whole body to be covered with penises (or to have one a yard long), and ends up with none at all, or at best, with his own back again* ("The Three Wishes" form which is given in *The Arabian Nights*, and in Nafzawi's later *Perfumed Garden*, largely a sex-technique manual). See further on "sexual predestination," note on 35 above, and Mark Twain's *The Mammoth Cod, and Address to The Stomach Club* (ed. G. Legman, 1976).

48. TOMCAT SET ON A RAIL

Tomcat set on a high rail fence,
Pussy cat set on the ground,
Tom made a pass at the pussy cat's ass
And they both went round and round.

From Mr. O. P., Fort Madison, Iowa, April 8, 1953. He heard it in Stone County, Missouri, about 1920. Some other versions end, "And the world went round and round," suggesting origin or relationship with the British suggestive song, early eighteenth century, "See the Yorlin" (or "Goslin"), in which the world "going round and round" actually refers to the woman's orgasm. As in Ernest Hemingway's novel of the Spanish Revolution, *For Whom the Bell Tolls*, in the 1930s, in which the only line anyone remembered of the book was the young virgin Spanish girl's telling the virile American narrator-hero (guess who?) that she did truly have an orgasm, expressed in the terms: "The earth moved." The presumed Spanish original of this phrase, if one exists colloquially, has not been determined.

49. THE T'RANTLER AND THE SANTA FE

The t'rantler jumped on the santy-fay's back
And rode him across the ditch;
Says, If you bite me, I'll bite you,
You pizen son-of-a-bitch!

Recited by Mr. R. C., Eureka Springs, Arkansas, February 9, 1951. He heard it years before near Green Forest, Arkansas. "Tarantula" is pronounced *t'rantler* in the Ozarks: see Randolph and Wilson, *Down in the Holler* (1953) p. 32. Many hillmen call a centipede, by assimilated pronunciation, a *santy-fay*, exactly as they pronounce the name of the Santa Fe railroad: see Archer Taylor, in *Dialect Notes* (1923) vol. V: p. 219. In line 4, *pizen*, poisonous.

This ancient folk-idea, of two dangerous creatures mutually endangering or destroying each other, is treated in Chaucer's *Canterbury Tales* (1393), "The Pardoner's Tale," and in one of Shakespeare's grimmest adaptations, as the ending of *Hamlet* (1603). It is used as the basic plot in the first, best, and last motion pictures by one of the best American film-directors, John Huston: *The Maltese Falcon* and *The Treasure of the Sierra Madre*, in which one miner kills the other for their mutual treasure of gold-dust, not knowing that the other has already poisoned his drink. (Tale Type 763, here from a text by the German novelist, "B. Traven"). The wind then blows away all the gold-dust they have killed each other for. Compare the Oriental belief in predestination, as in notes on 35 and 47 above. The last is Huston's ugly "black-humor" farewell, *Prizzi's Honor* (1985), a parody of the Mafia-glorifying "Godfather" films now being pushed on the public by certain interests, and a satire on Women's Liberation. The effect is of an anti-gallant valentine: the male and female Mafia killers' marriage (which includes a motherhood-defiling paid murder the woman performs on another woman, with a mock-baby in her arms), ending when they both kill each other simultaneously "on contract." Total message: "uninvolved" sex, and mutual treachery—the motto of the "ME Generation" and the cop-and-spy glorifying coming century.

50. LITTLE MARY MACAFEE

Little Mary MacAfee
Wouldn't let me watch her pee;
Stuck my finger up her ass,
Then she pissed all over me.

Recited by Mr. J. B., Joplin, Missouri, December 1930, in the standard quatrain form of many nursery rhymes such as "Peter, Peter, Punkin-Eater." The reference to the woman being sexually excited (to the point of orgasm: "Then she pissed all over me") by anal erotism is very uncommon in folksong or verse. Compare note on 13*B*, above, on "No Balls At All," in which a similar and much more frank reference occurs. The erotic excitability of the perineum and anus and their para-genital nerves (the "*First Chakra*" of Tantric Yoga, since several thousand years ago) is only admitted to with difficulty in the Anglo-American or non-Latin cultures, as being unhygienic, i.e., "dirty," and too close to homosexual. Even touching the area, through the clothing, by another person, called "goosing," is likely to be responded to violently in panic response as if to a homosexual approach, by men, sometimes whinnying like a horse, or even leaping into the air.

51. LISTEN, LISTEN

Listen, listen, the cat's a-pissin',
Where, where, under the chair.
Run, run, get the gun.—
Ain't no use, the bastard's done.

A. Recited by Mr. G. P., Reeds Spring, Missouri, March 4, 1947. He learned it from Mr. R. W., Garber, Missouri.

B. Text from Mr. R. P., Granby, Missouri, January 8, 1948. He learned it about 1900. The *powder,* in line 1 is that of old-fashioned shotguns, kept in a powder horn at the hunter's belt.

Listen, listen, the cat's a-pissin' powder!
Where? Where? Under granny's chair.
Get the gun, get the gun!—
Aw, pussy's done.

C. Here's one from Mr. C. W., New York, November 7, 1948. He got it in Wheatland, Missouri, about 1940:

Listen, listen, the cat's a-pissin',
. . . .
Run, run, get the gun.—
Shit, fart, now it's done.

D. Randolph notes that Ray Wood, in *What Happened to Mother Goose* (1946) p. 34, "prints a defecated version." Like Hamlet's "the mobled Queen," *defecated* is good:

Listen, listen, the cat's a-hissin',
Where, where, under the chair.
Run, run, get the gun.—
Aw, 'tain't no use, he's gone.

Note that "The cat's pissin'," is commonly used by children as a smart retort or interruption to anyone saying prefatorily, "Listen . . ."

52. BALLING THE JACK

Papa takes in washing,
Making lots of jack,
Mama's in the bedroom
Laying on her back.

A. Recited by Mr. G. P., Reeds Spring, Missouri, July 5, 1946. In line 2, *jack*, money. The lightly disguised statement made by the rhyme is that under the pretense of being a washerwoman the mother is a prostitute and the father is her pimp. See G. Legman, *Rationale of the Dirty Joke* (vol. II, *No Laughing Matter*, 1975) sections, "Anti-Gallantry, Anti-Woman, and Anti-Family," pp. 704–44, and 985–87.

B. Carl Sandburg, *American Songbag* (1927) p. 188, has the discreet lines:

My sister takes in washing
And the baby balls the jack.

"Balling the jack," a phrase which occurs in several erotic versions of this song or chant, refers to rotatory or other inspired female motions during intercourse—see note on 46 above—sometimes also to male hip-weavings of erotic significance, as those affected by various male rock-singers since Elvis Presley and Jim Morrison (now dead but still the subject of survival-legends like Emiliano Zapata: "He was seen . . . riding in the mountains . . .") The phrase, which is now usually abbreviated to *balling*, referring to sexual intercourse in general, is said to refer literally to the rocking motion of fast-moving freight trains.

C. From a white girl, Miss A. D., age eighteen, New York, 1946, who said she learned it from a Negro jazz musician, and that it was part of a rock-and-roll or "bop" song, entitled and with chorus, "Hey Baba Leeba (Rebop)":

Mama's layin' on her back,
Papa's up on top,
Baby's in the cradle
Hollerin', *Jam* it to her, pop!

53. ROSIE MCQUEEN

Just picture a girl with plenty of zip,
Who looks swell in a sweater, really a pip,
With fine slender legs and dangerous curves,
A gal who does things to upset a man's nerves.

Now just such a girl was Rosie McQueen
Who came to the city when she was eighteen,
To work in an office for fifteen a week
And see what adventures a live girl might meet.

Her first day of work was one of delight,
She dated the boss the very first night.
He met her at seven, they wined and they dined,
And hit all the high spots the boss had in mind.

At one in the morning with Rosie quite gay,
Up to his apartment they tiptoed their way,
They sat down together on the long wide settee,
Nor did Rosie mind his hand on her knee.

He kissed her, and then shy Rosie cared less,
And gently his hand stole under her dress

(*The bottom of the sheet is torn off here,
and on the other side of the page is written:*)
LOOKS LIKE SOMEBODY TORE OFF A PIECE!

Manuscript copy sent by Mr. H. B., Springfield, Missouri, October 25, 1948: "I know nothing of its history." It is a "sell," or swindle-version of the long and highly erotic "Adventures (or Troubles) of a Young (or French) Stenographer," in verse, circulated since ca. 1920 in typewritten or manuscript form, as boy-and-girl adolescents' spontaneous sex-education, and detailing all usual sexual acts in the first person, as by the stenographer protagonist with her various employers. In the *dénouement* of the present version, "to tear off a piece (of ass, *or* tail)" means to have sexual intercourse, here punned upon.

54. A TRIP TO HEAVEN

It was but a simple maiden with dimpled rosy cheeks,
Who went to church and Sunday School and prayed in accents meek.
There was a reverend minister who loved to see her face,
So full of true devotion, and pity, love and grace.

Who walked each Sabbath home with her when services were o'er,
That he might speak of Heaven and the shining golden shore,
Until the maid took courage and to the preacher said she,
Oh, I would give the world if we that golden shore could see.

Then come up to my cottage, the minister did say,
At nine o'clock this evening, an hour or two to stay.—
I will, kind sir, she answered, and happy I will be
To catch a glimpse of Heaven and to commune with thee.

When she reached the parson's cottage the clock was striking nine,
Ha, said the reverend gentleman, I see you are on time;
Pray step into my chamber where the lights are burning low,
And soon I will be with you, and heavenward we'll go.

708

He shortly joined the maiden and unto her he said,
We will soon be with the spirits and those who long are dead,
But before we make the journey we must ourselves prepare,
Take off your earthly garments, for they wear no clothing there.

The maiden seemed reluctant until to her he said,
Take off your coat and dress, my dear, and lay them on the bed . . .

The maiden blushed a moment and then threw her fears aside,
She thought nothing could harm her with the preacher by her side;
The preacher then took off his pants and other clothing too,
And stood as God had made him, a noble man and true.

She silently obeyed him, doing just as she was told,
While he with nimble fingers did her petticoat unfold;
He took her garments one by one and placed them on a chair,
And then she stood before him, all naked, pure and bare.

Now we are as God made us, the minister did say,
And surely will reach heaven if nothing bars the way.
He took the maiden in his arms and placed her on the bed,
And then laid down beside her, and this to him she said:

Oh reverend sir, please tell me what is that funny trick
That stands so straight and shiny, so stiff and slim and slick?—
That is the key to Heaven, child, and you have got the lock,
It has the works and movements just like an eight-day clock.

He gently laid her on the bed and spread her legs full wide,
To fit the key into the lock, for half an hour he tried;
At last the key was fitted within her little nest,
He gently pushed the button, and Nature done the rest.

Incomplete text, received as above from Miss. E. G., Springfield, Missouri, October 21, 1949, who got it from a girl at the Young Women's Christian Association in Springfield. Also apparently source of No. 53, preceding. Complete texts proceed to further stanzas detailing the seduction of the maiden by the hypocritical minister, whose subterfuge of the "Trip to Heaven"—representing her orgasm—harks back to the famous "Putting the Devil in Hell" of Giovanni Boccaccio's *Decameron* (1353) Day III, No. 10, used in the same way. In the final stanza the girl "victim" turns the tables on the minister, telling him vindictively that she has given him a venereal disease, and ending: "You thought you'd get to Heaven, *but you tumbled (wound up) straight in Hell!*" Compare: "If You Want to Go to Heaven," No. 43 above. The allusion in the final line of the version, as above, to the woman's orgasm being caused by hand-stimulation of her clitoris ("He gently pushed *the button*, and Nature done the rest") is unusual and important as of that date, about 1900. Compare the Negro jazz-song of the 1930s, often sung by a famous black lesbian singer, "Press My Button, Give My Bell a Ring!"

The usual title of the present piece is "The Preacher and the Maiden." It is one of a number of sarcastic anti-clerical recitations and poems popular from at least the 1880s through the 1930s in America, mostly on the above simple pattern. One a bit more elegant, "The Rehearsal," also called "Deacon Foster's Pew" (in T. R. Smith's *Poetica Erotica*, ed. 1927; and in his anonymous *Immortalia*, 1927, pp. 47–48), ends each stanza in the old "medley" style with various lines from well-known *hymns*, here sardonically misapplied to the erotic pleasures of the girl choir-singer and her male friend, who have hidden in a church-pew on "a rainy night" after the rest of the choir and congregation "had hurried home."

The present item is certainly intended to mock or recount the enormous anti-clerical divorce scandal in America in the 1870s, of the seduction of Mrs. Elizabeth Tilton, one of his parishioners and the wife of his friend, by the Reverend Henry Ward Beecher, of Brooklyn Heights, New York, the most prominent

709

male Protestant minister and Women's Suffrage advocate of the nineteenth century in America, and brother of Mrs. Harriet Beecher Stowe, author of *Uncle Tom's Cabin.*

The best study of this case, important in the history of American public morals and religion, is "Abominable in His Lusts," by Ormonde de Kay, appearing in four parts in a luxury-oriented private real-estate magazine, *Quest* (New York, 1988–89). Another much milder work in progress, on Beecher's "life and trials" by Alice Scoville Barry, of New Hope, Pennsylvania, was announced in *Quest* (February 1989) p. 5, in an indignant letter by her concerning "Abominable in His Lusts," certainly a rather hypo-critically out-of-date but titillating title for the jet-setter audience of so "in" a magazine. Note that the cuckold husband, Theodore Tilton, an obscure religious journalist, was not acting out of moral outrage, but was suing Beecher for "criminal conversation" with, and alienation of the affectations of his wife, to the tune of $100,000, considered a truly enormous sum in 1875. But he had so intentionally and obvi-ously been conniving at his wife's adultery, that his chief lawyer stated during the trial that Tilton "would be lucky if he got six cents!"

55. IF YOU'RE TIRED AND WEARY

If you're tired and weary, my darling,
There's a game that I know we can play,
It was taught us by Adam and Eve, dear,
Come quick, and I'll show you the way . . .

Nine days have passed since I met you,
God damn it, I wish you were dead!
I have suffered the sorest of itches,
And the dewdrops have dripped from its head.

Recited by Dr. V. A., Pineville, Missouri, August 3, 1929: evidently missing stanzas in the center: The man's symptoms in stanza 2 are those of gonorrhea.

56. THE NARRY-ASSTED MEN

They say all men are equal,
I'm not sayin' it ain't so;
I've been observin' through the years,
And watched 'em come and go.
If I were pickin' men to live
Their four-score years and ten,
I'd try and pick from out the lot
The narry-assted men.

Another thing I've noticed,
Big strong women, when they mate
Will pick a long, tall, ganglin' man,
They'll do it sure as fate.
And maybe Fate does take a hand
And slips from out her den
To mate these husky Amazons
With narry-assted men.

Take Widder Jones for instance,
That's her cabin down the lane,
Been married six or seven times
And will be soon again.
All the men she's laid to rest
Were short and stout. Now then
She's a-pickin' Ezra Kunkle,
A narry-assted man.

Ezra's nothin' much to look at,
Wears number fourteen shoes,
His hat is five and seven-eighths,
And he never touches booze.
His adam's apple's juttin'
Out in front just like a wen,
And I've heerd other things about
This narry-assted man.

So far the widder's childless,
Not her fault, so it would seem,
For she's a mighty husky wench,
Three feet across the beam.
I'll bet old Ezra gits results
In nine months, or maybe ten,
They always prove a fruitful bough,
Them narry-assted men.

Manuscript copy from Mr. H. B., Springfield, Missouri, October 25, 1948. He credited it to Dr. Harry L. Riggle, of Seymour, Missouri. Compare No. 57, following, also supposed to be the work of Dr. Riggle, a dentist, and author under his own name of a book of Ozark verse, *Rhymes of the Ozark Hills* (1944), which see at its p. 48. As to the subject and title of the present piece, compare the remark of Mr. Charley Short, of Galena, Missouri, reported by Randolph, as quoted from "an old woman: 'For a good, s'archin' kivverin', give me a narry-assted man!'" Here *s'archin'* searching, means profound or complete; and *kivverin'*, covering, an act of sexual intercourse, usually only in reference to farm animals. But compare John Donne's famous sardonic line to his coy lady going to bed (about 1600): "What needst thou have more covering than a man?"

The idea that small buttocks or "buns" ("narrow-assed") in a man must be paired with a large penis is based on folk-notions of Natural justice and *equilibrium*, or predestination; and is in contradiction to the more famous sex superstition or "sign," alluded to in stanza 4:5–7, that a jutting-out Adam's apple in a man's neck, or large nose on his face, implies ("other things") a matchingly large penis. The end reference to a "fruitful bough" is proto-Biblical and is also a discreet reference to the penis, as are old-fashioned gnarled or heavily veined trunks and boughs on genealogical family-tree drawings, such as were often placed in family Bibles. In some of the oldest such "Tree of Life" drawings known, in Europe, early fifteenth century, the main trunk of the family tree rises grandiosely from the chest or belly of the founder of the family, shown laid out in his tomb, and sometimes frankly as his penis—a naively punning reference to the "Resurrection of the Flesh."

57. KILL-PECKER CREEK

Kill-Pecker Creek, so the legend goes,
Rises up in the land of the Arapahoes,
Where furtive-eyed cowboys from high mesas peek
Down that sinister stream called Kill-Pecker Creek.

This legend *en toto* is a very long tale
Of cowboys, prospectors that passed down this trail,
Scanning current and eddy, a ford they did seek,
And like babes in the woods forded Kill-Pecker Creek.

Superstition, maybe, but the fact must be borne
That all men must stand and be sheared and shorn
Of all vestige of manhood, and the waters still speak
A challenge to men who cross Kill-Pecker Creek.

Pistol Bill he was tough, he scoffed at the tale
Of lost manhood, lost hormones, bow-ties and travail,
With his basso profundo and a stout aspen stick
He hazed both his jacks towards Kill-Pecker Creek.—

White Horse Rapids I've shot, and I've done Thirty-Mile,
And if you say I'm lyin', smooth it out with a smile;
Says he, if the Yukon failed to make my knees weak,
Why the hell should I fear this here Kill-Pecker Creek?

I've gambled and romanced a sight in my day,
I fit with Zack Taylor at old Monterey;
Thar's gold in them hills that I'm aimin' to seek,
So I'm campin' tonight beyond Kill-Pecker Creek.

The jacks they sensed trouble, but the joke was on Bill,
They stopped in midstream and were drinking their fill,
And when Bill waved them on and started to speak,
His voice it had changed; he'd crossed Kill-Pecker Creek!

At the sound of a shot Bill's friends rallied around,
And found Pistol Bill stretched out on the ground,
In a feminine voice that was pitifully weak
He said, Boys, she got me; damn Kill-Pecker Creek!

This is only one instance of many that's told
In this quaint old legend of men that made bold
To heed not advice and their fortunes to seek
On the opposite side of Kill-Pecker Creek.

When Fate, the old Vixen, has pointed you out,
One can blaze a new trail by turning about,
But the trail that you blaze or the trail that you seek
Like a lost man, will circle to Kill-Pecker Creek.

All of life's trails lead at last to this stream,
Let us jest of lost heritage, we still have our dream,
As we amble along with a rheumatic squeak,
May we gracefully bow and cross Kill-Pecker Creek.

Manuscript copy from Mr. H. B., Springfield, Missouri, October 25, 1948, transmitted with the similar "The Narry-Assted Men," No. 56 preceding, and also probably the work of Dr. Harry L. Riggle, a dentist of Seymour, Missouri. It should be understood that in including these author-linked pieces in the present collection of folk-rhymes, even though not, or not *yet* folk-transmitted (except by Mr. H. B., so far), Vance Randolph was not insisting on any folk-status for them, except as the work of a backwoods folk-poet, obviously very much of the kind who writes the anonymous pieces already in oral transmission.

"Kill-Pecker Creek," representing the moment when all old men, presumably inevitably, become sexually impotent, is to be compared with those other legendary rivers, separating this world from the next, or from death: the Styx, the Rubicon, and the unplaceable Talmudic river Sambatyon, which keeps all Postlapsarian humanity away from the Garden of Eden by erupting boiling geysers of stones six days a week. (On the Sabbath it rests, but no orthodox religious person would venture to cross the river then, and risk losing Paradise!!) There is an actual Killpecker Creek in Wyoming, according to an official highway sign cited by W. L. McAtee, *Nomina Abitera* (1945) p. 4. Compare also "When a Man Gets Old," rhyme No. 1 above. In the end, "Kill-Pecker Creek" represents, perhaps jealously and unconsciously, the vagina, for which there is no set age of impotence arriving.

The allusions here to male impotence are all very clear. "Stand to be sheared and shorn, Of all vestige of manhood," actually implies a sort of Samson-like castration, if only of the hair, i.e., the advancing baldness of old age. The idea of the male voice "changing" to a "feminine voice that was pitifully weak"—the opposite of the change in adolescence to a deeper voice—is naturally connected with the folk-belief that a *basso profundo* male voice immediately becomes *falsetto soprano* upon castration: this is played upon in numerous jokes, tales, and limericks. As to the "bow-ties" alluded to in stanza 4:2, the matter is not clear, but such ties (like cigarettes and wristwatches before World War I) were once definitely considered effeminate. Professor Alfred Kinsey, of *Sex Behavior* fame in the 1940s, was sometimes rallied about this behind his back, since he almost invariably sported a bow tie; and he became indignant when this folk-belief was hesitantly brought to his attention.

58. JUST A WATER SPOUT

> Happy days have come and gone,
> The fire of youth has all burned out,
> That which was once my pride and joy
> Is nothing but a water spout.

A. Recited by a waitress at Rockaway Beach, Missouri, May 30, 1929. She learned it in Carroll County, Arkansas.

B. From Mrs. B. M., Lees Summit, Missouri, January 20, 1948. She had it from her husband, who heard it elsewhere in Missouri about 1932. This complete (or extended?) version is seldom collected:

> Now that I'm old and feeble,
> My pilot light is out,
> What used to be my sex appeal
> Is just a water spout.
>
> I used to be embarrassed
> To make the thing behave,
> For every single morning
> It would stand and watch me shave.
>
> But now I'm growing old,
> And it sure gives me the blues,
> To have the thing hang down my leg
> And watch me shine my shoes.

C. Recited by Mr. J. C., Eureka Springs, Arkansas, August 24, 1951:

> Here's to the flame
> That all too soon burned out.
> What used to be my sex appeal
> Is now my water spout.

Obviously a mock "toast," with which compare rhyme No. 1 above, this is the commonest old man's complaint in English at present, along with a rather similar joke about: *The old man's penis which once looked up at his chin every morning while he was shaving, and now looks down at his shoes.* Note Vance Randolph's own intentionally wry observation, elsewhere in the present collection, about the purportedly aphrodisiacal waters of an Arkansas spa that "worked" very well for him with one lady (noted elsewhere in a reference to a lady of the theatre checking into a hotel with him as "Georgina Spelvin," a standard theatrical pseudonym later actually used by a sex-movie actress of the 1970s), but that didn't seem to work as well when he tried the same waters again a decade later!

D. Collected as a photocopied item of Xeroxlore in Shippensburg, Pennsylvania, 1990, the complete text, with title "Retirement," and a hand-drawn illustration of a Sad Sack type of middle-aged male, with crumpled hat, unpressed pants, shoes visibly out at the toes, and his necktie, ears, and penis large but *hanging down*:

> My nookie Days are over,
> My pilot light is out.
> What used to be my sex appeal
> Is now my water spout.
>
> Time was when of it's own accord,
> From my trousers it would spring.
> But now I have a full time Job,
> To find the blasted thing.
>
> It used to be embarrassing,
> The way it would behave,
> For every single morning,
> It would stand and watch me shave.
>
> (But) As old age approaches,
> It sure gives me the blues,
> To see it hang its withered head
> And watch me tie my shoes.

59. THE PERSIAN KITTY

> A Persian kitty, perfumed and fair,
> Strolled to the back yard to get some air,
> An old tomcat, both lean and strong,
> And dirty and yellow came along.
>
> He sniffed at the perfumed pussy cat,
> She strutted and preened with great eclat.
> Kitty, said Tom, I know this town,
> Come along with me, I'll show you around.

. . . .
There's a catnip bed just over this fence,
You need a little experience.

The morning after the night before,
Kitty came in at the hour of four,
The innocent look in her eye had went,
Giving place to a wondrous sweet content.

In after days when the children came
To look at the kittens of Persian fame,
They were no Persians, but yellow and tan,
Kitty said their Pa was a traveling man.

A. Recited by a waitress at Rockaway Beach, Missouri, the same informant as of No. 58*A*, just preceding, May 30, 1929. She learned it in Carroll County, Arkansas. A similar text is printed by W. T. Pace, *The Lawyer* (1938) pp. 2–3, alleged to have been quoted in court by H. W. Morgan, Esq., an attorney of Anadarko, Oklahoma. It is commonly collected and often printed in off-color publications, owing to its mildness. In 5:3, *yellow* (or *black*) *and tan*, implying that high-society Kitty's progeny had a "touch of the tar-brush," or presumably Negro "blood." In the incomplete stanza 3:1 (compare version *B*, here complete), *catnip*—also *valerian*—is supposed to be aphrodisiac, or "tonic," to cats. In 2:2, the pronunciation of *éclat* to rhyme with "cat" may be intended as humor, if not dialectal.

B. Typescript from Mrs. M. M., Springfield, Missouri, October 21, 1948:

A Persian kitty with perfumed hair
Strolled out on the backyard fence for air,
A tomcat lithe and lean and strong
And dirty and yellow did come along.

And thinking the time of day to pass,
He whispered, Kiddo, you've sure got class!—
That's fitting and proper, was her reply,
As she arched the whiskers over her eye.

Each day I'm bathed in certified milk,
At night I sleep on a pillow of silk,
But we're never contented with what we've got,
I try to be happy, but happy I'm not.—

Cheer up, said the tomcat with a smile,
And trust your new-found friend awhile.
You need to escape from your fine back fence,
My dear, all you need is experience.

The morning after this night before,
The cat came back at the hour of four,
The look in her innocent eyes had went,
But the smile on her face was a smile of content.

And in after days when the kittens came,
To the Persian kitty of pedigreed fame,
They didn't look Persian, but black and tan,
And she told them their Pa was a traveling man.

60. A TOAST TO THE BIGGEST WHORE

> The biggest whore was Lucy Hicks,
> She drank the juice of a thousand pricks,
> And if you want to do her honor
> Pull down your pants and jack-off on her.

A. Heard by John Clellon Holmes, Fayetteville, Arkansas, October 1976, from a student who said he learned it "from some fellows hanging around a garage." Although not beginning in traditional fashion, "Here's to . . ." or "Here lies . . ." this is a drinking toast, or mock-epitaph (compare "Here's to Mag," No. 15 above), and has probably the oldest genealogy of any item in the present collection of rhymes, as follows. The name "Lucy" is intended as a humorous slur (*loose-y*) referring to the woman's vagina, presumably enlarged by her sex-life, though really usually only by childbirth. In line 4, *jack-off*, to masturbate, said of boys and men only, also *jerk-off*, which may be the original form. Variant in line 2, *drained* the juice, thus not necessarily a reference to fellation, though such references are not rare in U.S. southern folklore.

Note that the "thousand pricks," in line 2, offered as a very large number here, are only formally so, as in the Arabian *Thousand-and-One Nights*. In fact, low-level prostitutes in working-class "cribs," in Neapolitan or Dutch street-brothels, or in wartime, may service sexually as many as fifty men in one working day or night, and sometimes more, meaning *ten thousand men or more per year*, and this over a career lasting twenty years or more. See further the end-note on "Lady Lil," at No. 2 above.

B. In A. Reynolds Morse's anonymous anthology, *Folk Poems and Ballads* ("Mexico City: Cruciform Press, 1945," in reality, Cleveland, Ohio, 1948) p. 96, is given the modern educated urban form, from an unknown source, in which observe the almost obsolete word "scabbard":

> Here lies the amorous Fanny Hicks,
> The scabbard of ten thousand pricks,
> And if you wish to do her honor
> Pull out your cock and piss upon her.

C. Scottish folk-form, collected by Hamish Henderson among a group of secret rhymed "toasts" used in private ceremonies of the farm workers' club, the "Horseman's Word," in Turriff, Aberdeenshire, in 1952; first printed by G. Legman, "Bawdy Monologues and Rhymed Recitations," in *Southern Folklore Quarterly* (1976) vol. 40: pp. 115–17. Note that all other forms omit the Scottish lines here on witchcraft, hell and damnation:

> Here's to aul' Belle Dick,
> She's skinned mony a standin' prick.
> She lived a whure an' died a witch,
> And intae hell she's hurled, a bitch.
> An if ye want to do her honour,
> Tak oot yir cock and pish upon 'er.

Dr. Kenneth Goldstein learned a version of this, combined with another favorite toast, on "fucked her flying," from a woman in Strichen, Aberdeenshire, 1960; given in his unpublished manuscript collection *Buchan Bawdry*. And see note on *E*, below.

D. The Sloane manuscript (seventeenth century?) No. 1965, gives the oldest known form in English:

> Underneath this stone and brick
> Lies one that once loved well a prick.
> All you that pass by, do her this honour:
> Pull out your pintles and piss upon her.

This is printed in John Wardroper, *Love and Drollery* (London, 1969) p. 171, no. 298; with another form, of similar date at p. 286, from Corpus Christi manuscript 327. And likewise an announced epitaph "On Isabella, a Courtesan," p. 202, no. 358 ("He who would write an epitaph . . . Must get upon her, and write well: Here underneath lies Isabell"); and a formal "Epitaph on a Whore," pp. 212–13, no. 376, as an admiring twenty-eight-line epic signed by the seventeenth-century burlesque poet and translator (of Montaigne), Charles Cotton, calling her in the same open oral metaphor as text *A* above, "The Sucking School-Mistress of Love." (Published in *Wit and Drollery*, 1656; ed. 1661, pp. 31–32; preceded by a similar but cruder "On Luce Morgan, a Common-Whore," also reprinted by Wardroper, p. 213, no. 378.)

Cotton's "Epitaph on a Whore" was reprinted in his *Poems on Several Occasions* (1689), two years after his death, then first ungallantly identifying the woman by her initials as "M. H." Fashionable "court favorites" of both sexes, as well as highflying plain whores and the kept mistresses of the rich and noble, usually assimilated to opera-singers, dancers, and actresses, remained very much in the public eye throughout the seventeenth to nineteenth centuries, and also in our own, under the same polite disguises, and those of "jet-setters," "media-personalities," "pop singers," and the like, both female and male.

E. There is an intermediate version of the present "piss upon her" erotic tribute—which is *not* really intended as an insult, but more like a grateful celebration by satisfied clients—in a colored British engraving in the style of Thomas Rowlandson, probably late-eighteenth century, in the form of an unobtrusive inscription on a gravestone in a country churchyard; thus already at folk-level. It is also said to be given in early-eighteenth century Scotland, in the erotic *Records of the Beggar's Benison Society* (1892, and reprint), but I have not been able to find it there.

F. Nevertheless, the piece is not English in origin. It was supposedly written by the Italian satirist, Pietro Aretino, in the early sixteenth century, as of a fashionable courtesan, Maddalena, who had died rich. It was already translated into French in almost the final chapter, novel 125, of the important folktale collection, *Les Nouvelles Recréations et Joyeux Devis* of Bonaventure des Periers (1st edition, 1558), here cited from the modern-spelling edition by "P.-L. Jacob," of 1841, p. 356. As can be seen, the requested "pissing" is in fact intended as an appropriate but honorific burial rite:

> *De Madelaine ici gisent les os:*
> *Qui fut des vits si friande en sa vie,*
> *Qu'après sa mort tout bon faiseur supplie,*
> *Pour l'asperger, lui pisser sur le dos.*

G. The fashion of these irreverent epitaphs, on prostitutes and others, apparently came first from Spain, and another such very famous in English is erroneously attributed to the Earl of Rochester in the middle seventeenth century, no doubt as similarly far-fetched in its eroticism to his "Insatiate Desire" (Wardroper, p. 226, No. 392, beginning: "O, that I cou'd, by some strange *Chymick* Art . . .")

> She was so exquisite a whore
> That in the belly of her mother
> She turned her cunt so right before,
> Her father fuckt them both together.

Wardroper, p. 197, No. 344, "On an Arrant Whore," quotes this from B. M. Additional manuscript 22582, which adds a further incestuous two-line "topper" in the way of anatomical impossibilities, much in the style of the modern French poet, Pierre Louÿs' erotic novel *Trois Filles de Leur Mère* (1926). Wardroper notes, p. 296:

> This is a translation of an epigram which James Howell, the traveller and letter-writer, found circulating in Madrid in 1622. He wrote to one Captain Thomas P.: " . . . Hereunto I will adde a strong and deepe fetcht *Character*, as I think you will confesse when you have read it, that one made in the Court of a Courtesane." (*A New Volume of Letters*, 1647.) In Spanish it is:

> > *Eres puta tan artera*
> > *Qu'en el vientre de tu madre*
> > *Tu tunistas de manera*
> > *Que te cavalgue el padre.*

The insulting intention here is visible in the familiar use of the second person singular, in the Spanish original. This is changed to the third person in the English translation above, obviously by way of softening the blow, since it was then purported to have been written (by Rochester) on Nell Gwynn, the favorite mistress of King Charles II. Professor Ernest Moncada adds, in *Notes and Queries*, March 1964, that this piece was also applied to other Restoration courtesans: "to the Duchess of Cleveland (Barbara Villiers/Castlemaine)," as in B. M. Harleian manuscript 6914. He also indicates the Spanish original, but this had long since been identified in the polymathic Captain Francis Grose's *The Olio* in 1792.

61. THE MERRY FARMER

> Here's to the merry farmer
> In this land of milk and honey,
> The bedbug sleeps in the crack of his ass,
> And Sears-Roebuck gets his money.

A. Recited by Mr. L. B., Pineville, Missouri, August 17, 1927. On Sears-Roebuck see the end-note below.

B. Mr. J. E., Webster Groves, Missouri, April 8, 1948, contributes the following which he learned from a hired man in the 1880s. An "Alliance man" is a member of the Farmers' Alliance:

> The Alliance man set on the fence,
> Screwing his nuts with a monkey-wrench;
> Weeds grew up and tickled his balls,
> And his gun went off in his overalls.

A further but incomplete version, consisting of only the first two lines of *B* (but with "Old Man Spence" instead of "The Alliance man") was recollected by Mrs. O. T., Farmington, Arkansas, October 30, 1951. The joke in line 2 about "Screwing his nuts with a monkey-wrench" also appears in folk-humor as a catchphrase concerning any presumably hard or violent person. For example, army humor in World War II concerning the verbally crude and courageous General George Patton, well-liked by his troops who called him "Old Iron-Balls," ludicrously expurgated in the home-folks newspapers to the pantywaist "Old Tuffy-Pants," and who was rumored to be "so tough that his orderly had a special set of wrenches to unscrew his balls at night, so he could get some sleep." This is a marvelous typification of Reichian "character-armor," and of the rapidly advancing and dehumanizing mechanization and robotization of the human being since the early nineteenth century, when the British Luddite "machine-breakers," and Heinrich Heine (in *Venetian Nights*) expressed the first warnings on this subject. In *Pissing in the Snow*, Vance Randolph gives another joke form, of a big hunting dog whose "asshole has to be sized down" with a set of wrenches so he can hunt squirrels.

C. From Mr. J. C., Eureka Springs, Arkansas, August 24, 1951. He heard it in Moberly, Missouri, about 1912:

> Sears-Roebuck farmer didn't have much sense,
> Spent his time a-setting on the fence;
> The grass grew up and tickled his balls,
> And his gun went off in his overalls.

Sears-Roebuck, and Montgomery ("Monkey") Ward were the two main mail-order firms from whose catalogs American farmers bought their many necessities in the late-nineteenth and first half of the twentieth centuries. In the early years these catalogs even included classified advertisements by young immigrant women, ex-prostitutes, "grass widows" (abandoned wives), and similar, often with young children, who were willing to become western farmers' wives, sight-unseen.

After a long period of quiescence, sex advertisements—mostly for perverted pleasures—were started up again in so unlikely a publication as the *Saturday Review of Literature* (New York, 1947 *ff.*), despite a completely unexpurgated *exposé* of the sex materials actually being circulated, printed in *Neurotica*, edited by G. Legman (1949) No. 5, as "Answers to an Ad," which caused the banning of that magazine. Such advertisements became the staple of the "underground" hippie newspaper press throughout the 1960s and to the present time, in both America and Europe. They now (1990) form almost the entire contents—along with illustrated advertisements for the same sort of "oral" prostitutes' communications (paid) over the telephone, or by "midnight" computer keyboards in private homes—of the main surviving sex newspaper, *Screw*, published in New York, of which the editors state that these erotic prostitutory advertisements, phone calls, and computerized masturbational "contacts" are an "essential social service for the prevention of AIDS!" *Sè non è vero, è ben trovato.*

62. THE TWO SENATORS

A toast, given by the Senator from Illinois:

> Here's to the American eagle,
> That grand old bird of prey,
> She eats her food in Illinois
> And shits on Ioway.

The Senator from Iowa responded with this:

> Here's to the state of Iowa,
> Her soil is firm and rich,
> She needs no turd from your damned old bird,
> Go to hell, you son-of-a-bitch!

A. From Mr. J. R., Harrison, Arkansas, April 5, 1950, who learned this in Boone County, Arkansas, about 1889, as above.

B. Recited by Mr. F. P., Kansas City, Missouri, December 23, 1935, with "enclosing" introductory text referring to the presumably recent Civil War (Southern) "rebels" thus: The story goes that the senator from Illinois and the senator from Arkansas were drinking in a tavern.

The gentleman from Illinois offered a toast:

> Here's to the golden eagle
> That eats wild rebels raw,
> Flies over the plains of Illinois
> And shits on Arkansas.

The Senator from Arkansas replied:

> Here's to the State of Arkansas,
> With soil so goddam rich,
> We want no turd from a federal bird,
> You Yankee son-of-a-bitch!

C. Anecdota Americana, Series II (1934) p. 87 gives the following, and so also does "O. U. Schweinickle," *The Book of a Thousand Laughs* (1928) p. 16:

The congressman from Maine gave a toast:

> Here's to the American eagle,
> That beautiful bird of prey;
> He flies from Maine to Mexico
> And he shits on Ioway.

The congressman from Iowa responded:

> Here's to the State of Iowa,
> Whose soil is soft and rich,
> We need no turd from your beautiful bird.
> You red-headed son-of-a-bitch!

D. "Crossing" of toasts (or proverbs) in this way, as a sort of contest-in-insults, has an ancient lineage in the "flytings" of the early Scottish poets, and one very aggressive will be found recorded (on British *vs.* American naval rivalry) in *The Pearl*, 1879, No. 1. All the British bawdy men's-club songsters and reciters of the nineteenth century give lists of *one-line* erotic toasts (the last and fullest list being in the published *Records of the Beggar's Benison Society*, in the 1890s, this club then being disbanded after existing in Scotland for two centuries), but the "crossed" or *duello* types in two contrasting and answering toasts are uncommon. See further, Legman, *Rationale of the Dirty Joke* (vol. II, *No Laughing Matter*, 1975) pp. 779–809, "Contests-in-Insults" and "The *Dozens*," which reprints complete at pp. 795–96, "The Rival Toasts" from *The Pearl*, 1879, No. 1; here politely omitting the Britisher's reply!

> A Yankee officer suddenly stood up, and said he wished to
> propose a toast . . . Then shouted the American exultingly:

720

Here's to the glorious American flag,
Stars to enlighten all nations,
And Stripes to flog them.

63. LUCK TO THE DUCK

Here's luck to the duck
That flew over grandpappy's barn
And shit a blue turd!

A. Mr. L. K., of Irish descent, Cyclone, Missouri, August 17, 1931, recalled this fragment of "an old Irish piece" that he heard about 1900. In spite of the definite statement here, turds are never, apparently, really *blue*, and the reference seems to be to animal or bird feces on which blue mould has formed when it is found, much later, also called "a beard." There is a reported Irish bawdy song (which it has not been possible to recover) entitled "The Blue-Moulded Turd"—reported from a Scottish singer in Paris, 1955. Observation of the wild and farm-animals' bodies and sexual and excretory habits, including anus, feces, etc., is an important folk activity, whether by hunters or farmers.

B. An American husband-and-wife team of "revival folksingers" (New York, 1953) delivered a parody to the pop tune of "Smoke Gets in Your Eyes," beginning:

They asked me how I knew,
Raccoon shit was *blue*?
But I just smiled and said,
You must be out of your head—
Raccoon shit is *red*!

64. THE ISLE OF MAN

Here's to the little tree
The ladies love to span,
It stands between two little stones
Upon the Isle of Man.

Recited by Mr. B. C., Cane Hill, Arkansas, October 23, 1948; also called "The Little Tree." In line 2, *to span*, presumably with the legs, not with the fingers. See the end-note on the "Tree of Life" at No. 56 above, "The Narry-Assted Men." The New Testament also puns (in Syriac-Aramaic: *Matthew*, 16:18, and compare 7:25) on the founding of the eternal monument upon "Petra," a *stone*, as an everlasting testimonial.

65. HERE'S TO THE BULL

Here's to the bull
With the dangling cod.
Without that dangling cod
We wouldn't have no beef,
By God!

Manuscript from Mr. O. P., Verona, Missouri, July 20, 1951. He heard it on Horse Creek, in Stone County, Missouri, about 1930. See the discussion of this folk-poem in my first publication of Mark Twain's impotence poem, "A Weaver's Beam" (on a Biblical reference), in his *The Mammoth Cod* (Waukesha, Wisconsin: Maledicta Press, 1975).

66. THE CRACK THAT NEVER HEALS

Here's to the crack that never heals,
The longer you rub it the better it feels,
But all the soap this side of hell
Can't wash away that fishy smell.

Recited by Mrs. M. M., Springfield, Missouri, June 15, 1946. It came from her husband, who learned it in Stone County, Missouri, about 1900, and who recited it to her as a tribute or compliment. Compare the similarly ambivalent toast or tribute to the female genitals, the woman simultaneously being called a whore, at No. 72 "Pussy Pays for It All," below.

This "fishy smell" is the standard *macho* insulting allusion to the vulvar odor; but elsewhere in this collection Randolph records a boarding-house mistress who attracted male boarders precisely by boiling up a *granny-rag* (menstrual cloth) in the soup.

67. THE PERFECT VINE

Here's to the woman, most perfect vine,
That blooms every month and bears every nine,
The only monkey this side of hell
Can get meat out of nuts without cracking the shell.

A. Recited at Jane, Missouri, August 17, 1927, by a lady who learned it in Joplin, Missouri.

B. Allen Walker Read, *Lexical Evidence* (Paris 1935), p. 64, prints this, collected as an outhouse epitaph:

Here's to the . . . . human vine
Who blooms every month and bears every nine,
The only thing this side of hell
Can get juice from a nut without cracking the shell.

The missing words in Read's text are *woman: the.* The reference to menstruation as a "bloom" or blossom, "the flowers," is one of the few non-insulting or unfrightened references in male folklore. As is

722

well known, the Jewish Bible (also its enormous commentary, the Talmud) shows an absolute terror of female menstruation, which it surrounds with every sort of folktale or taboo. For example, when one of the Patriarchs' wives, Rachel, hides an object by *sitting* on it, in *Genesis*, 31:34–35, stating she is menstruating, thus preventing the male searcher from even daring to look there. Also heavily codified rituals of "purification," which are still observed by Primitive Orthodox Jews (the Chassidic sects) in Israel and in America, principally in Brooklyn, New York. Of these rituals, certainly the most significant is the specification in *Leviticus* 12:2–5, that a woman is ritually "unclean" (i.e., her husband is not permitted to have intercourse with her) for thirty-three days after the birth of a male child, but is twice as unclean— sixty-six days: verse 12:5—for a girl child. Compare the satirical poem cited at note 60*G* above; and the Christian form of this "purification" in the precise observance of Lady-Day, or at Candlemas, after the Virgin Mary's giving birth. See further G. Legman, "Body Taboo and Verbal Expurgation in Western Folklore,"submitted to *Journal of American Folklife* (1991).

68. HERE'S TO THE SPANIARD

> Here's to the Spaniard, the son-of-a-bitch,
> May his balls rot off with the Cuban itch,
> May his prick shrivel up like a bamboo cane,
> And his ass-hole whistle "Remember the Maine."

A. Recited by a lady at Camdenton, Missouri, September 7, 1949. She heard it near Camdenton about 1901, as an echo of the Spanish-American War.

B. In a revision of this heard in my Pennsylvania school days just after World War I, about 1928, the "Spaniard" is up-dated to "The Kaiser" or "Dirty Bill" (later to "Adolf Hitler," in the late 1930s):

> Here's to the Kaiser, that son-of-a-bitch,
> His balls et off with the seven-years' itch,
> We'll beat on his prick with a two-ton hammer
> Till his ass-hole whistles "The Star-Spangled Banner."

This is an interesting example of an imprecational brag, or fantasy folk-humiliation of a feared enemy. Another such up-dating was of the libelous folk-poem "John Haroldson," a Civil War poem about the (purported) use of ladies' "chamber-lye," to manufacture gunpowder, at song No. 242, and compare "Saddam Hussein," song No. 180*D*, in vol. I here, *Roll Me in Your Arms*.

69. THE HORSE'S ASS

> Here's to the glass and the little Scotch lass,
> They go mighty well together,
> So we'll have a glass, and feel of her ass,
> And make the little lass feel better.

A. The above invitational toast was given by a woman, Mrs. O. T., Farmington, Arkansas, June 6, 1956. This delightfully reverses the direction of the proposed seduction, as intended to "make the little *lass* feel better." However, this also is intended to hide a classic "slurred" pun; for what is really being pronounced is "make the little *ass* feel better." Though collected later in date, the present form may be the romantic original, of which the "horse's ass" version following is the anti-gallant "mock" or parody topper.

B. Recited by Mr. T. K., Pineville, Missouri, August 19, 1927. A "horse's ass" is any disprized person:

> Here's to the lass, and here's to the glass,
> And both are fair to see;
> But a lass's ass and a whiskey glass
> Made a horse's ass of me.

C. The Hollywood movie-writer, Mr. Ben Barzman, in Cannes, France, 1958, told about having worked twenty years before on a presumably "socially conscious" musical revue, where he protested against a proposed song on the 1930s social ferment, just after the end of the Depression, in which *all* political parties were anathematized with the following chorus, rather similar to this toast:

> Masses, classes!—classes, masses!
> What a bunch of horses'—(*pause*)
> Donkeys, and jack-asses!

70. HERE'S TO THE GIRL

> Here's to the girl with the big white tits,
> Who plays with her twat all day;
> She can't shoot jelly in the other girl's belly,
> 'Cause girls ain't built that way.

From Mr. T. S., Joplin, Missouri, recited at Randolph's cabin near Pineville, Missouri, August 17, 1927. The unexpected Lesbian conclusion here is most unusual in its open reference to Ozark female homosexual practice, in this case tribady. Such practices however, must of course always have been common, in harems, prisons, and other nunnery-or-school situations where women are segregated, often under sadistic and flagellational disguises, but were never publicly mentioned in America until the middle 1920s, and then always as an awful scandal.

Meanwhile, two eleven-year-old Oregon girls told me, when I was the same age, in 1929, and we were "playing doctor" in our cellar, that they had done "lots worse than that" with other little girls up to twice that old, using bananas as dildoes, as elsewhere in the present collection, and in "The Romping Party," in Randolph's *Pissing in the Snow, and Other Ozark Folktales* (1976) No. 30, collected in 1950, and originally heard "from some boys near Berryville, Ark., in the early 1890s." In this tale form a young man is hidden among the girls in the dark, his being "that *good* banana." In another castrational Ozark version, but of Levantine origin by methods of transmission unknown, *The man puts his penis up through a hole in the flooring to satisfy two old maids who think they are using a candle stuck upright in the hole.*

71. THE CANDLE AND THE FIST

Here's to the girl that's not afraid
A gentleman's prick to handle,
But damn the girl who sets on her ass
And fucks herself with a candle.

Here's to the boy who's not afraid
A nice soft cunt to twist,
But to hell with the boy who sets at home
And does the job with his fist.

Recited by a nameless schoolgirl at Pineville, Missouri, August 17, 1927 (same date as No. 70 preceding). A message for the coming "Safe Sex" masturbatory era, owing to the AIDS panic and the end of the New Freedom.

72. PUSSY PAYS FOR IT ALL

Here's to the girl with the white cravat,
Silk shirtwaist and big white hat,
Patent leather shoes and blue parasol,
Poor little pussy pays for it all.

A. Recited as above by Mr. R. J., Pineville, Missouri, August 19, 1927. Compare the two following versions from women.

B. A lady at Noel, Missouri, August 20, 1927, heard it like this. Note the total difference, except for subject and "scenario," from *A*, preceding, of same area and date:

Here's to the girl with lace on her hat,
Lace on her pants and things like that,
Lace on her shirt and her parasol—
Little brown spot that pays for it all.

C. From Mrs. O. T., Farmington, Arkansas, June 6, 1956. The clothing described in all versions suggests a date of origin no later than the 1910s. Note the frank acceptance of the statement of the woman's prostitution, in the final line, in *B* and *C*, both from women:

Here's to the girl in the leghorn hat,
White shirtwaist and black cravat,
Polka-dot hose and Spanish shawl,
And her little you-know-what paid for it all.

73. A YOUNG GIRL'S ASS

How well do I remember yet
How very proud I used to be
When like a little queen I'd set
    Upon my ass.

When seated on his springy back,
My little tiny whip I'd crack,
And with my dainty hand I'd smack
    My sleek fat ass.

And when through muddy roads he'd scud
And get himself all over mud,
I'd put some water in a tub,
    And wash my ass.

When horse flies 'round would buzz and bite,
And make him itch from morn till night,
'Twas then with tender touch and light,
    I'd scratch my ass.

Boys too, would play so mean a trick,
At first they'd stroke him with a stick,
And then with heavy boots and thick,
    They'd kick my ass.

At this my grief was most sincere,
Because I loved my donkey dear,
So come, kind friends, and shed a tear,
    And kiss my ass!

A. Manuscript copy from Mrs. M. M., Springfield, Missouri, August 9, 1954. See a related item in J. M. Elgart, *Over Sexteen* (1951) p. 8.

B. "Catches" or "sells" of this kind, in which the basic humorous surprise aimed at is the final invitation, "Kiss my ass!" Being centuries old, they are noted as the main type of court and society humor among young ladies, in Alexander Pope's *Peri Bathos, or The Art of Sinking in Poetry* (1727) p. 111.

They are often mentioned by Swift, as quoted by Grose (1785) *s.v.* "bargain, selling"; and in Legman, *The Limerick* (1953) note 1384. At song No. 243, above, "The Election is Over," another rhymed form of this entertainment is given, similar to the following. This was found anonymously in her mailbox, in Springfield, Missouri, November 1952, shortly after the election, by a lady prominent in Republican politics. (The *elephant* is the totem animal of the Republican party, and the *jackass* that of the Democrats):

    The election is over, the result is known,
    The will of the people has now been shown.
    Let's all get together, let bitterness pass,
    I'll pet your elephant—
        And you kiss my ass!

74. SWEET ROSE MARIE

In a pawpaw patch when the pawpaws were ripe,
I was loving sweet Rose Marie,
When she said, If you have a hot pawpaw
I'll let you tickle me. (2 times)

I laid her down in the cool, cool shade
Beneath a pawpaw tree,
I tickled her once and I tickled her twice,
And she said, Let's make it three. (2)

She grunted and giggled, she twisted and wiggled,
She said, Oh my, oh me!
I thought she was going to toss me up
To the top of the pawpaw tree. (2)

Of all the sweet girls that I have loved
There was none so dear to me,
There was none could tickle me half so well
As darling Rose Marie. (2)

The years have come and the years have gone,
Father Time has played hell with me,
'Twould do no good to meet Rose again
Beneath the pawpaw tree. (2)

Manuscript copy from Mr. J. C. Edwards, Webster Groves, Missouri, April 9, 1948. Randolph's field note adds: "I suspect that he wrote it himself." Almost certainly a private poetic effusion, not traditional, it has not been collected elsewhere. It was also indexed by Randolph under the variant title, "The Pawpaw Tree," a well-known southern fruit-bearing plant. Compare rhyme No. 75, following.

75. PRINCESS PAPOOLIE'S PAPAYA

The Princess Papooli's got plenty paypia,
She loves to give it away,
And all the neighbors they say,
Oh me-a, oh my-a, you really should try a
Little piece of the Princess Papooli's paypia.

The Princess Papooli's a little unruly
To give-a so much-a paypia each day,
And all the neighbors they say,
Oh me-a, oh my-a, you really should try a
Little piece of the Princess Papooli's paypia.

Manuscript copy from a lady in McDonald, Missouri, August 10, 1947. The curious spelling of "papaya" is as in the manuscript. Compare "The Pawpaw Tree," No. 74 preceding ("Sweet Rose Marie"), possibly also the work of the same local poet. "Princess Papoolie" is, however, in folk circulation, sometimes as a song, unlikely as this may seem, considering its stupid "pop" words. It is printed, with tune, in Hart, *The Complete Immortalia* (1971) vol. III: pp. 128–31.

76. ODE TO THE FOUR-LETTER WORDS

Banish the use of the four-letter words
Whose meanings are never obscure,
The Angles, the Saxons, those bawdy old birds
Were vulgar, obscene and impure.
But cherish the use of the weaseling phrase
That never quite says what it means;
You'd better be known for your hypocrite ways
Than as vulgar, impure, and obscene.

When nature is calling, plain speaking is out,
When ladies, God bless 'em, are milling about.
You may wet, or make water, or empty the glass,
You can powder your nose, or "the johnny" will pass,
It's a drain for the lily, or man about a dog,
When everyone's drunk it's condensing the fog.
But as true as the devil, that word with a hiss,
It's only in Shakespeare that characters ———.

A woman has bosoms, a bust, or a breast,
Those lily white globules you spy neath her vest;
They are towers of ivory, or sheaves of new wheat,
In a moment of passion, ripe apples to eat.
You can speak of her nipples as fingers of fire
With scarcely a chance of arousing her ire,
But by Rabelais' beard she'll give you ten fits
If you speak of them roundly as good honest ———.

There's a cavern of joy you are thinking of now,
A warm tender field awaiting the plow,
It's a quivering bird caressing your hand,
Or the Star Spangled Banner—you're ready to stand.
Believe it's a flower, a grotto, a mink,
The hope of the world, or a bottomless sink.
But friend, heed this warning, beware the affront
Of playing the Saxon and calling it ———!

Though a lady rejects you, she'll always be kind,
As long as you're hinting at what's on your mind.
You can tell her you're horny and need to be swung,
Or invite her to see how your etchings are hung.
You can speak of your ashes which need to be hauled,
It's a lid for her sauce-pan, and "lay" is not too bold.
But the moment you're forthright, get ready to duck,
The woman's not born yet who welcomes "Let's ———."

So banish the words that Elizabeth used
When she was a queen on her throne,
The modern maid's virtue is easily bruised
By four-letter words alone.
Let your morals be loose as an alderman's vest,
If your language is always obscure.
Today not the act, but the word is the test
Of the vulgar, obscene and impure.

Typescript copy from Mr. E. I., Forsyth, Missouri, June 13, 1949. He got it at Columbia, Missouri, in 1944. It is obviously a modern literary piece, and of American origin from the slang terms used. It has been very popular since the 1940s, seldom recited but circulated in typescript and (despite its length) manuscript copies, also in mimeographed duplicated form, and most recently as "Xeroxlore." But it is no longer often encountered, due to the broad relaxation of verbal taboos among adolescents since the 1960s, during the main decades of the New Freedom.

In the 1880s Eugene Field wrote a much more elegant "dictionary" piece of the present kind, on the rhymed framework of an epic sexual adventure, "A French Crisis, or The Fair Limousin," printed in *Immortalia* (1927) pp. 15–18. And a mere alphabetical listing of erotic synonymies (taken from Farmer and Henley's *Slang and Its Analogues*, 1890–1909), strung together and broken up into short lines to pass it off as "modern poetry," has been produced by Joel Oppenheimer, as "The Poetry of Porking" (!) printed in *Maledicta* (1988) 9:94–104, a sad descent from the effervescent charm, in the same line, of Field's "Fair Limousin" and her light-horse gallop.

77. TO SHIT WITH EASE

If you want to shit with ease
Put your elbows on your knees,
Count to six and twiddle your thumbs,
Give a squeeze (*grunt!*) and out it comes.

Supplied by Professor John Clellon Holmes, Fayetteville, Arkansas, November 1976, having been found as a *graffito* in "a local lavatory." Hygienic advice of this kind, in versified and humorous form, is centuries old, and a very large literature of such *scatologica* exists, in many languages, to which the key—now badly out of date—is Jannet's *Bibliotheca Scatologica* (Paris 1850, and modern reprint), and its supplement by Gustave Brunet, *Anthologie Scatologique* (Paris: J. Gay, 1862?) The advisory piece above is unusual in being extremely good advice and containing the correct medical and physiological handling of problems of constipation. It should be observed that "Count to six and . . . Give a squeeze" is to be understood as meaning that these two actions should be *repeated* ten or a dozen times, rhythmically, or as often as necessary for the result desired.

78. THE BREEZES

The breezes, the breezes,
They blow through the treeses,
They blow the chemises
And through the girls' kneeses,
(They know that it teases
Both he-ses and she-ses.)
The college boy seeses,
And dooze what he pleases,
The he-ses with she-ses,
The she-ses with he-ses,
Which causes diseases—
By Jesus, by Jesus!

Found by a student of Professor John Clellon Holmes, Fayetteville, Arkansas, November 1976, as a *graffito* in a local bar. Very out-of-date, having been considered eligible for the mildly naughty *College*

Humor type of campus magazines in the 1920s and until World War II. The word "chemise" and concern with "girls' knees" are also very typical of the 1920s short-skirt era and "Revolt of Modern Youth," now fairly dead. The lines about the permutations of "*he-ses with she-ses, etc.*" are apparently more recent, and have not been seen in any other version printed earlier. With the climactic *Jesus/diseases* rhyme (always recited very fast), compare limerick No. 80*B,* below.

79. THE KINSEY REPORT

> Said Hone on the Kinsey Report,
> I have not read it, in short,
>   For I prefer screwing
>   To reading and viewing;
> I'm not just a spectator sport.

Randolph's field note: "From a lady at the University of Arkansas, Fayetteville, Ark., Apr. 23, 1952. Said to have been made up by a local woman, whose husband was called Hone." Formulaic wit: technically a limerick (see No. 80 following), this is essentially closer to the more refined limerick spin-off called a Clerihew, which usually ends suddenly in its third line. The Kinsey Reports on male and female "sexual conduct" created enormous publicity in America in the late 1940s and early 1950s, and much news-media discussion of sex—in a *statistical* sense only, that being the discreet approach taken by Professor Alfred Kinsey and his backers. Although believed to have precipitated the New Freedom (a phrase originally publicized politically by President Woodrow Wilson in 1915, with almost as little result), this relaxation of sexual taboos did not arrive in any broad sense until over a decade later, in the "hippie" period of the middle 1960s and since.

80. LIMERICKS

> Here's to the girl from Swiss,
> She had so much joy and bliss,
>   She screwed herself silly
>   On the stalk of a lily,
> And set on a sunflower to piss.

A. Randolph's field note: "Recited at my cabin in Pineville, Mo., Aug. 17, 1927, by a near-illiterate girl from Jane, Mo." On the general subject of limericks, and printed sources, see the end-note below. As limericks are seldom liked, repeated, or almost never written by women, those collected from girls or women in this research are given first, as *A* through *F* (except *C,* a variant of *B*), followed by those from men. Compare also the elegant Clerihew, "The Kinsey Report," at No. 79 preceding.

B. Randolph's field note: "Contributed by a lady from Jane, Mo., Aug. 17, 1927. She heard it in Joplin, Mo., about 1924." Note the similarity of both provenance and the "toast" format of the opening line, to *A* preceding. And compare the *Jesus/diseases* rhyme with No. 78, "The Breezes," also of 1920s origin:

> Here's a girl who would like to be wild,
> But keeps herself modest and mild,
>   By thinking of Jesus,

And loathsome diseases,
And the danger of having a child.

C. From Mr. B. D., Oklahoma City, Oklahoma, September 16, 1950:

There was a young girl from Carlisle
Who was kept from being wild,
    By thoughts of sweet Jesus,
    Contagious diseases,
And the fear of having a child.

D. Randolph's field note: "From a young matron in Springfield, Mo., Nov. 12, 1944. She had it from a peddler":

There was a young girl in Alaska
Who wouldn't fuck if you'd ask her,
    But she took down her britches
    For rich sons-of-bitches
Like Jay Gould, and Morgan, and Astor.

E. From Mrs. M. M., Springfield, Missouri, October 27, 1948. She heard it in Stone County, Missouri, about 1906:

There was a young lady from Clyde,
Who had no money to ride.
    She told the conductor,
    Who immediately fucked her,
And gave her two dollars beside.

F. From Miss A. M., Eureka Springs, Arkansas, November 7, 1951:

There was an old man in Racine,
Invented a fucking machine.
    Both concave and convex,
    It would fit either sex,
The damndest thing ever seen.

G. Recited by Dr. V. A., Pineville, Missouri, July 12, 1929. Not strictly in the limerick format, but obviously intended as an extended form, this example has circulated orally in Britain and America since the 1880s:

There was a young man from Calcutta
Who greased his ass with soft butter
And inserted therein his own prick.
    He didn't do this for money,
    He didn't do it for pelf,
But to satisfy some son-of-a-bitch
Who told him to go fuck himself.

H. Recited by Mr. G. P., Reeds Spring, Missouri, March 4, 1947. He had it from Mr. F. K., also of Reeds Spring. As Norman Douglas observes, this is one of the first limericks usually learned:

There was an old woman from Wheeling,
She had a remarkable feeling.
    She laid on her back
    And tickled her crack,
And pissed all over the ceiling.

I. From Mr. G. P., Reeds Spring, Missouri, March 4, 1947. He learned it from a man in Springfield, Missouri:

There was an old woman in France,
She hopped on a freight-train by chance,
    The fireman he fucked her,
    So did the conductor,
And the brakeman went off in his pants.

J. Recited by Mr. W. H., Eureka Springs, Arkansas, July 12, 1948. The casual reference to *wine* suggests an origin before U.S. Prohibition in 1919:

There was a young sinner named Skinner,
Who took a young lady to dinner.
    At a quarter to nine
    They opened the wine,
At a quarter to ten it was in her. (*Pause*.)
The dinner was in her, not Skinner.

K. Recited by Mr. W. H., Eureka Springs, Arkansas, July 12, 1948:

There was a fair maid from Cape Cod,
Thought babies were made by God.
    But it wasn't the Almighty
    That lifted her nightie,
'Twas a roomer named Gordon, by God!

L. Recited by Mr. L. J., Farmington, Arkansas, October 23, 1948. He learned it years before in a saloon at Fort Smith, Arkansas, in this "toast" form:

Here's to the man from White Hall,
His pecker was quite small.
    He diddled a goose,
    And behaved very loose,
But the goose didn't feel it at all.

M. From Mr. B. D., Oklahoma City, Oklahoma, September 5, 1950:

There was a shrewd nude from Bermuda,
She was shrewd, but I proved to be shrewder.
    She said it was crude
    To be screwed in the nude;
I got cruder and ruder and screwder.

N. Recited by Mr. F. S., Eureka Springs, Arkansas, May 21, 1952. He heard it in Yell County, Arkansas:

> There was a young man named Adair
> Who was screwing a girl on the stair.
> The railing it broke,
> So he doubled the stroke,
> And finished it off in mid-air.

O. Also from Mr. F. S., Eureka Springs, Arkansas, May 21, 1952:

> There was a young man named Trent
> Whose prick was so long that it bent.
> To save him the trouble
> He put it in double—
> Instead of coming, he went.

Randolph here groups all his fifteen or sixteen Arkansas-collected limericks at the end (with the exception of a Clerihew, immediately preceding, in a slightly other stanzaic pattern). This seems to be the only "subject" or "formulaic" group he makes of song or rhyme materials, unless collected from children, or as dance-calls, both of which have their own separate collections, following. It is apparently not that he doubts the limericks' folkloristic authenticity, but that he is uneasy about considering them strictly Ozark or "Arkansas" materials; though little of the other material in any of his collections is really or exclusively of Arkansas *origin*, and very much is provably general American or of even older British origin.

For a discussion of the historical background of erotic limericks, see the introduction to G. Legman, *The Limerick* (Paris, 1953, and reprints), giving about 1700 American and British orally circulated examples; and for the psychological substructure, nowhere else ever seriously discussed, and the introduction to the Second Series of the same work, published as *The New Limerick* (New York: Crown, 1979: reprint title, *More Limericks*). All the fifteen classic limericks collected by Randolph, as above, are given in *The Limerick*, First Series, with full annotations, and can rather easily be turned up there, for further study, by the index of names and rhymes.

One note certainly worth making here concerns No. 80*F*, "The Fucking Machine," above, of which this is the only text known to have been collected from a woman. On this see further *The Limerick* (1953) No. 1325, with mock-translations in Latin and French, p. 272 and notes pp. 447–48, and especially *No Laughing Matter* (1975) vol. II: pp. 646–71, "The Mechanical Man." Very much more could be said, and probably will be said, and far more textual and pictorial material collected, in the future on this erotic fantasy or fear, first recorded in France in 1793. Since about the mid-nineteenth century in particular, the open fear of the All-Powerful "Machine" (now politely "computer") and the expected robotization—or even replacement!—of human beings by these machines has become endemic in the "high-tech" Western, or rather Northern Hemisphere culture. This is concomitant with the compulsive creation and playing with complex gadgetry and machinery, in a widespread attempt to banalize and control such machines. The sexualization of these aspirations and fears, in the broadly increasing demand for mechanized sexual substitutes and assists since 1938 (date of the invention of the vibrating dildo by Dr. Vladimir Fortunato and G. Legman) is one of the most significant symptoms.

The bawdy limerick as a folk-poetry form reached its highest point of popularity between the 1880s and the 1950s, in both Britain and America, in particular in the university world. It is no longer as popular, even there, and lives on fitfully as a private entertainment among over-educated professional people principally, who enjoy its complex erotic wittiness as a form of disguised sex-fantasy or autobiography.

The largest showing of recent examples will be found in the 2nd volume of *The Limerick*, as *The New Limerick* (1979: reprint title, *More Limericks*). The best of these, forming the major part of that volume, are all by a single folk-poet and artist, the late John Coulthard of San Francisco, whose contributions are given there from his posthumous manuscript, *The Cathouse of Time* (1967). Coulthard's mantle in the writing of thousands of limericks, bawdy and otherwise, by one single person, seems to have fallen upon Mr. Albin Chaplin, who has published several thousand of his own witty originals in various volumes dedicated to these. It is important to observe, however, that practically none of the new limericks composed since the 1950s have ever entered into folk-transmission anywhere, in any classic "oral" sense. The bulk of recent limerick creation in the bawdy (or any) line is currently edited and published by Dr. Arthur Deex, of Los Altos, California, as *Limerick Sig* (for *Signal*), now called *The Pentatette*, a Mensa club private magazine issued as an elegant computer printout.

Bawdy Lore from Ozark Children

The material in this paper all came from children under fifteen years of age. I did not collect it directly from children, however. My informants were adults, mostly teachers who overheard their pupils recite many such pieces. Sometimes they were written on the blackboard, or on slips of paper which were passed from one child to another until finally captured by the schoolmaster. Children often write bawdy jingles especially for the teacher's benefit, and a pretty schoolmarm gets many obscene notes. The older boys are usually responsible for these, but educators tell me that "some of the vilest" are written by girls under twelve.

Many teachers destroy such scribblings at once, but others save them. A school administrator had a trunk full, accumulated over a long term of years. And a retired principal at Springfield, Mo., showed me a large collection of such items neatly pasted into a scrapbook, representing twenty-five years of teaching experience. "Country children write the nastiest ones," she told me. "But it is surprising what these gently reared town kids can do, when they set their minds to it."

Most of the bawdy stuff that comes the teacher's way consists of short pieces, recited, or written on scraps of paper; but there are occasional drawings, carved figures (*scrimshaw*), and obscene toys. As recently as 1925 some small boys set up a wooden phallus in an Ozark schoolmarm's front yard; the thing was four feet high, painted red and yellow, with names and initials added in pencil.

In late years it has become a fad, in some of the larger towns, to send naughty phonograph records to the school authorities. In 1949, at Hot Springs, Ark., three teen-age boys made a disc recording and left it on their instructor's doorstep. "The teacher became hysterical when she played the record, but recognized the voice of one of the boys," according to a newspaper account. Sheriff I. G. Brown, who conducted an investigation, said that the record "contained the foulest and most obscene language I have ever heard." The Garland County Board of Education listened to the recording "in a closed session of Municipal Court." The three boys were arrested, but I don't think they were ever prosecuted. (*Arkansas Gazette,* Little Rock, Ark., Jan. 28, 1949.)

It is difficult for an adult to collect obscene folklore from children, and I am afraid that this paper does not adequately represent the existent material. I am sure that many a rural school-teacher could do better. But even a small collection may have some value, and I set it down for the record. Perhaps other folklore collectors, especially those connected with elementary schools, will some day be encouraged to work in this neglected field.

Vance Randolph

Note: All paragraphs of annotation, and bracketed materials in the following pages are by the editor. Various recent works have attempted to collect and present the authentic and sometimes erotic or scatological folk-rhymes and scribblings, games, etc., of children, as suggested above by Vance Randolph, an attempt at least as old as Rabelais' list (included in the final book of *Gargantua & Pantagruel,* 1535, *ff.*) of French children's games; and Norman Douglas's collection of children's games in England, during the 1910s, published then only in expurgated form. See in the bibliography below, at Borneman, Gaignebet (on French children), Wendy Lowenstein, Sutton-Smith, Turner, and especially Sandra McCosh. None of these, however, with the exception of Borneman on German children's folklore, even approaches the lighthearted and unflinching unexpurgaiety of Randolph's materials collected in the Ozarks.

1

Some of the forthright bawdiness of the adolescent mind is addressed directly to the teacher. A strapping young school marm near Fort Smith, Ark., in 1937, showed me a note somebody had slipped into the pocket of her raincoat.

> Dear Miss Brown:
>
> You sure have got pretty legs
> and I sure would like to get my
> pecker between them and you would
> like it too.
> Respectfully,
> James Bowen

The girl's first impulse was to wallop little Jimmy Bowen, but the handwriting was not his. Some other boy had written the note, and thought best to sign Jimmy's name. The teacher was indignant, but amused. "It's the word *respectfully* that slays me," she giggled.

2

Another teacher near Fort Smith, Ark., in the 1930s collected seven notes within a few hours, and every one of them read:

> What makes teacher wiggle her
> ass when she walks?

3

At Van Buren, Ark., in 1932, a teacher opened her lunch box. Here's what she found, written in pencil on the shell of a boiled egg:

> Miss Blank walks like she had somebody's
> corncob between her legs.

4

When I lived near Pineville, Mo., in the 1920s, somebody wrote on the blackboard of a rural school:

> MISS SPELVIN IS FUCKING OLD
> MAN CARTER AGAIN

5

In Newton County, Mo., a woman passing a country school heard the children on the playground singing:

> Rich man, poor man, beggar man, preacher,
> Mister Henderson screwed our teacher!

6

Here's one from Christian County, Mo., collected in 1924. It is not clear from my notes whether the teacher heard this recited by the children, or found it written somewhere:

> Teacher's name is Jenny Brewer,
> Wouldn't let nobody screw her,
> Till Johnny Burns pulled her panties down,
> Now she fucks all the boys in town.

The teacher's family name was not Brewer, but it was so much like Brewer that there was no doubt about the identification.

7

Here's a cynical observation scribbled on the door of a rural school near Southwest City, Mo., in the 1920s:

> Miss Lilley keeps one of the big
> boys after school.

Beneath this inscription, in another hand:

> The biggest prick is the
> teacher's pet.

8

Near Granby, Mo., they used to tell of a big boy who stayed after school, and propositioned the pretty schoolteacher. She seemed willing enough, but a little doubtful. "Can you do it without taking my corset off?" she asked. "I reckon so," said the boy. "I fucked the old mare, and she had the *harness* on." [In text, *propositioned,* attempted verbally to seduce.]

737

9

Little boys from Joplin, Mo., in the 1920s, chanted this in derision of an unpopular school marm:

> Popcorn, peanuts, jelly cake,
> Teacher's got a belly-ache,
> Milk in the pantry, butter in the bowl,
> Couldn't get fucked to save her soul.

10

In McDonald County, Mo., one of my neighbors told me of his son's exploit. "The schoolmarm kept my boy in, to whip him," the old man chuckled. "But Floyd just pulled up that gal's dress and paddled her ass till she squealed like a pig. And then he give her a good fucking, just to show there wasn't no hard feelings!" The hero's father laughed loudly, adding that Floyd and the teacher were always good friends after that. "Floyd just topped her whenever he wanted to, and she give him the best grades of anybody on the creek!"

11

This is from a rural school-teacher, who collected it near Joplin, Mo., in 1931:

> I see London, I see France,
> I see teacher's under-pants.

12

Another item from the same informant:

> Teacher, teacher is a daisy,
> Teacher, teacher she is crazy.
> Tommy's mother give her a clout,
> Turned her ass-hole inside out.

Compare: Dorothy Mills and Morris R. Bishop, "Songs of Innocence," in *The New Yorker* (Nov. 13, 1937) p. 32.

13

There is some obscenity in the taunts or "sassy rhymes" that children shout at each other on the playground. A retired schoolmaster tells me that this was common in rural Missouri about 1885:

> You lie, you link, you fart, you stink,
> You suck your daddy's poodle-dink.

14

Here is a variant collected in Washington County, Ark., as recently as 1942:

> You poop, you fart, you shit, you stink,
> You suck your brother's bobolink.

15

Children at a rural school in Washington County, Ark., in 1940, used to shout this at a "sissy" little boy:

> Cry-baby crispy,
> Suck your mommy's titsy!

16

A plump little girl who came to school at Ozark, in Christian County, Mo., was greeted with this cry:

> Fatty, fatty, two by four,
> Can't get her ass through the kitchen door.

17

Some small girls near Farmington, Ark., whenever a certain little boy appeared, chanted this in chorus:

> Oh you dirty little devil,
> Does your mother know you're out,
> With your pants wide open
> And your pecker hanging out.

18

Shouted by two little girls, fifth-graders, at Forsyth, Mo., in 1940:

> Silly Dick cut off his prick
> And hung it up to dry,
> All the girls began to laugh,
> And Dick began to cry.

Compare: Scarborough, *On the Trail of Negro Folksongs* (1925) p. 154; and Brown, *North Carolina Folklore* (1952) p. 184.

19

This one is from a retired teacher at Joplin, Mo. She heard it recited by little children in Jasper County, Mo., about 1910.

> Goosey goosey gander,
> Who's a-coming yonder?
> Little Mabel Tucker,
> Who's a-going to fuck her?
>
> Little Jimmy Green
> Nowhere to be seen,
> Big Tommy Stout
> Pull his pecker out.

See: Ray Wood, *Mother Goose in the Ozarks* (1938) p. 16, for a polite version. There is another elsewhere in the present work.

20

A little boy in Yell County, Ark., about 1930, went to school for the first time at the age of six. One of the older boys greeted him with "You don't know your ass from a hole in the ground." The other children laughed, but the little boy was outraged. "Why, I do so!" he cried. Then the big boy took a sharp stick, and made two round holes in the ground. "Well, which one is your ass?" he asked. The little boy stared at the two holes, completely nonplussed. This was considered a great joke.

21

Two schoolgirls in Carroll County, Ark., showed a boy a card bearing the words "POLISH IT IN THE CORNER," and persuaded him to read the sentence aloud. Then the girls pretended to be much embarrassed. "She did?" cried one. "Who'd have thought Polly would do such a thing!"

See: McAtee, *Rural Dialect of Grant County, Indiana in the 1890s,* Supplement 1, (1942), p. 7. Compare similar slurring puns on "her ear" as *her rear,* also "pecker" and others, as at Nos. 27–29 below.

22

A boy said to a ten year old girl: "I bet you can't spell *up*." When the little girl answered "U-P," the boy said, "Sure I do. Don't you?"

23

At Fayetteville, Ark., as recently as 1949, children thought it a great joke to tell some greenhorn that the school principal's name was I. P. Freely, or sometimes P. A. Little. Other proper names used in children's jests were R. U. Cumming, Mike Hunt, I. C. Hare, C. R. Peters, and Eileen Back. A highschool boy in Springfield, Mo., kept talking about a new novel entitled *The African Princess,* claiming the author's name was Erasmus B. Black!

Lists of up to fifty different mock book-titles of this type, out of which the punning authors' names added create an erotic joke or allusion, have been popular in American humor at least since the 1920s, when brief lists of them appeared in such folk-erotic collections as *Cleopatra's Scrapbook* and *The Book of a Thousand Laughs,* by "O. U. Schweinickle," apparently on an earlier German humor format.

A few of these were noted in Alan Dundes and Robert Georges' "Some Minor Genres of Obscene Folklore," in *Journal of American Folklore,* (1962) vol. 75: pp. 221–26; and a full traditional group is printed by "Henry Clerval," *pseud.,* as "Clap Books," in *Maledicta,* (1988) vol. 9: pp. 139–41, including a few of his originals, and followed by an entire group of originals by the editor of *Maledicta,* Reinhold Aman, vol. 9: pp. 141–42, as "Bawdy Books," ending with the frank plea: "Someone please hose me down before I get carried away again!" These coinages of the *"Maiden's Nightmare,* by Mister Period," type do seem to be habit-forming or infectious, and I have more than once received lists of fifty or more newly invented by correspondents.

24

A child complained to the teacher at Noel, Mo., that an older boy had stolen his lunch, but he didn't know the big boy's name. Asked to describe the culprit, the little boy said: "Teacher, he was a freckledy son-of-a-bitch. You know, like a cow had farted and throwed shit in his face."

25

When a young man at Granby, Mo., boasted of his skill as a figure skater, the children all laughed. "Yeah," said one, "we seen you make an *i* and dot it with your ass!" That is, he made one straight mark on the ice, and then fell backward.

26

A little boy at Sallisaw, Okla., was very proud of a silver watch. The other children got to kidding him about it. One of the big girls rushed up to him and asked "What time is it, Johnny?" The little boy scowled, then consulted his watch gravely. "Half past friggin' time, and time to frig again," he answered. [Usually reported politely as "Half-past kissing time."]

27

Near Camdenton, Mo., a boy said to a girl "What's the three best vegetables there is?" The girl named several, but the boy shook his head. "All right, Mister Smarty," she said, "what do *you* like best?" The boy grinned. "Lettuce, turnip, and polk!" said he. This was considered very daring, because it sounds exactly like "Let us turn up, and poke." [*Turn up* refers to the girl's skirt.]

28

Naughty boys at Eureka Springs, Ark., used to bet that a little girl couldn't name the parts of a kitchen stove as they were pointed out. If they could get her to say "Lifter, leg, and poker" they all burst out laughing, and then shouted that nice girls shouldn't talk like that.

29

In Gainesville, Mo., a ten-year-old girl was asked to define the word A-W-L. When she said it was "a shoemaker's tool" the other children all laughed. "I'm surprised you'd go around talking about Mr. Burton's pecker," cried one boy. Mr. Burton was the village cobbler. [Little girls in grade schools in Eastern Pennsylvania in the late 1920s would be similarly trapped into innocently "defining" the word *friction* as "two bodies rubbing against each other," *as in the schoolbook.* One big girl refused when asked by the teacher, and said indignantly, "I don't see why I should be asked a question like that!"]

30

Near Joplin, Mo., when one little boy told another to "Shut up!" the second boy replied in verse:

> I don't run on shutters,
> I run on gas,
> And when I get tired
> I set on my ass.

31

Here's a variant collected at Farmington, Ark., in 1951:

> Don't run on shutters,
> Always run on gas,
> If you don't like it
> You can kiss my ass.

32

Children in the Ozarks use a universal finger-sign as an insult. When a child puts his thumb to his nose and wiggles his fingers, it means "Kiss my ass." Sometimes he makes this sign with both hands for additional emphasis, joining the thumb of one hand to the little finger of the other. Many school-ground fights are precipitated by these signs. [This is ancient, of Levantine or Italian origin, and is mentioned in Rabelais' *Gargantua* (1535) and as "biting the thumb" in the opening scene of Shakespeare's *Romeo and Juliet* in about 1597.]

33

A teacher at Columbia, Mo., in 1949, described a *finger game* thus: "With hands about four inches apart, put thumbs together, also the first, second, third, and fourth fingers. Then put right thumb to nose, and wave right four fingers to the following words: *MY—TEACHER—TOLD—ME—TO—DO—THIS*."

34

At Pineville, Mo., in 1919, several boys were punished for making "vulgar signs with their fingers" at some little girls, who complained to the school principal about it. A boy just held up his right hand with the fist clenched, and the thumb sticking out between the first and second fingers. A teacher told me that this sign is used by bad boys everywhere, and its significance is known to all school children. "Well, what does it mean?" I asked. The schoolmarm hesitated. "If you really don't know, I'll tell you," she said. "It means *Let's fuck!*"

The hand-sign here described, which is of Roman origin, is the original of modern nose thumbing, as above. It is known still in Italy by the name of *la fica,* the cunt, to be distinguished from *lo fico,* the fig, and does not usually mean what the "schoolmarm" above says, but is rather the insulting invitation, of Devil-worship origin, to "Kiss my ass." Rabelais, in *Gargantua and Pantagruel* (1535) gives a folk etymology of this sign, concerning defeated Neapolitans required to pluck a fig out of a donkey's anus with their teeth; but it is far older than the story he tells to "explain" it, as is usually the case with folk-etymologies. Compare international items Nos. 35 and 36 following, of which No. 36, scratching or tickling the palm, is of Knights Templar origin, and possibly Gnostic before them. The modern middle-finger-up gesture since World War II known as "The Finger," insultingly for "Fuck you!"—compare No. 79 below—is also of ancient Roman origin, then called the *digitus impudicus,* or shameless finger.

35

Another sign, with the same meaning, is made by holding the left thumb and forefinger so as to form a circle, and thrusting the right forefinger into it. I don't know if this is known "everywhere" as the schoolmarm said. But it is certainly familiar to children in many parts of Missouri, Arkansas, and Oklahoma. Nice little girls always resent such signs, or at least pretend to resent them.

See Otis W. Coan, *Rocktown, Arkansas* (1953) p. 96, for an account of a naughty little girl who propositioned a boy: "She held up one clenched fist, then jiggled the forefinger of her other hand back and forth in the hole made by the fingers and thumb of the clenched hand."

36

Near Neosho, Mo., in the 1920s, a common way of "feeling out" a girl was to tickle the palm of her hand with the forefinger. This could be done in such a way as to attract no attention from others. Little girls in school sometimes raised a great outcry about this, and the boy who did it was severely punished. A farm boy told me that he tried this sign on a village girl about fourteen years old. "She was kind of tough," he said, "and made me look like a fool." I learned later that the girl cried out in a loud voice, before a whole room full of people: "Ask for it like a man, don't scratch for it like a dog!" [Compare: McAtee, *Rural Dialect of Grant County, Indiana,* Supplement 1, 1942, p. 8. In the text "feeling out" means "propositioning" or attempting to seduce.]

37

A woman in McDonald County, Mo., told me that when she was a girl in the 1890s her mother insisted that she carry a handkerchief wadded up in her right hand at play-parties. During the dancing games it was necessary for boys to take her hand, but the handkerchief discouraged any nasty finger-signals. I have seen country girls at dances and play-parties with handkerchiefs held as this woman describes. Even very small girls, who play kissing-games freely, sometimes seem reluctant to touch hands with the boys. They feel, or their parents feel, that holding hands "in a certain way" is much more intimate than kissing.

38

In Yell County, Ark., about 1930, if somebody farted, children used to hold their noses and cry:

> Peaches, peaches,
> My nose itches,
> Here comes Pete
> With a hole in his britches.

See related rhymes in Randolph's *Ozark Superstitions* (1947) p. 54, and Ray Wood's *Fun in American Folk Rhymes* (1952) p. 82.

39

A lady at Springdale, Ark., in the 1940s, said that the following chant "refers to a bad breath or body odor." [The boy's surname was chanted too, as often in such rhymes, but has been omitted here.]

> My nose itches,
> I smell peaches,
> Little Johnny ———
> Shit in his britches.

40

A teacher near Warsaw, Mo., in 1934, told me that: "If somebody let a fart, and somebody else made a face, the other children all cried out:

> The fox is the finder,
> The fault lays behind her.

Meaning that the girl who made the face is also responsible for the stink." [The Germanic word "fox" often refers to any bad odor.]

41

Ralph W. Church, Pittsburg, Kan., Aug. 10, 1935, says that the children at Stuttgart, Ark., used a different version:

> The fault's in the finder,
> The stink's in his hinder.

42

Ray Wood, of Houston, Texas, told me in 1946 that the folks around Fort Smith, Ark., had a saying:

> Foxy finder,
> Stinks behind her.

It meant that the guilty person always seemed overcome or disgusted by the odor, so as to make it appear that somebody else let the fart.

43

Two little country boys stood at the crossroads, when along came a young man from town, with a fine horse and buggy, and a pretty girl beside him. Just to make fun of the little yokels, and show the girl how smart he was, the fellow asked "Which way is it up the hill?" The country boys looked at him blankly, and finally one of them answered "Just follow your pecker, Mister." This happened in Barry County, Mo., in the summer of 1932. I heard some grown men laughing about it later. "That's the way to put them town smart-alecks in their place," said a villager.

Compare an anecdote in J. L. Hedgecock's *Gone Are the Days* (1949) pp. 112–13.

44

Small boys near Sallisaw, Okla., in the 1920s played a game they called "Tickle-Tackle." If they could get a little girl seated in a chair, they tickled her hands, arms, elbows, face, and neck, reciting a little rhyme with each tickle. The girl's part was to refrain from laughing. My informant, a schoolteacher, recalled several of the rhymes used toward the end of the game:

> When I tickle you on the knee,
> If you laugh you don't love me.

> When I tickle you on the thigh,
> Do not laugh and do not cry.

At this point the girl usually giggled and stopped the game. If she did not, the next verses were:

> When I tickle you on the cunt,
> Do not laugh and do not grunt.

> When I stick my finger in,
> Do not laugh and do not grin.

Compare: McAtee, *Grant County, Indiana, Speech and Song,* Supplement 2 (1946) p. 4. Also Brown, *North Carolina Folklore* (1952) vol. I: pp. 188–189. This is clearly a game version of the song "Thigh-Thickle," or "Tickle My Toe Some More," No. 173 above, in vol. I, but going on unusually to its genital conclusion.

45

Jack Short of Galena, Mo., told me of a "sell" practiced by little boys near Hurley, Mo., about 1895. Three boys offer to show a greenhorn how to catch birds, especially the kind of bird called the peewee. They take a broadbrimmed hat and stand close together, so that each holds one side of the hat between his teeth. This brings the four heads close together, with the crown of the hat open to the sky. Without dropping the hat they all cry "Peewee! Peewee!" Unknown to the chump, who cannot see what is going on under the hat, three of the boys prepare to urinate on him. When one gives the signal by crying "Peewee! Peemore!" they all let fly together. The greenhorn is pretty wet before he realizes what is happening, and the whole thing is considered a great joke.

46

In McDonald County, Mo., about 1920, country boys who could get a deck of cards used to play "Peter Poker" on rainy days. It was not really poker, as there was no betting. Each player was dealt five cards face up. The boy with the lowest hand stood up, and exposed his penis. The other players, each holding five cards together, rapped the loser's organ, and they rapped pretty hard sometimes. If the loser fled rather than submit, as often happened, he was pursued and held by force until each of the other players took a whack at his pecker.

See: McAtee, *Rural Dialect of Grant County, Indiana, in the 1890s,* Supplement 1 (1942) p. 7.

47

Some little children near Poplar Bluff, Mo., in 1930, were fond of "initiating" people. In one ceremony two boys in outlandish costumes sat on chairs, with a larger chair between them. The middle chair was called the throne, and contained a pan of water covered with a cloth. After some mumbo-jumbo ceremony, the girl being initiated was saluted as "Queen," and led to the seat of honor. She sat down, but sprung up immediately, with everybody shouting "Sally got her ass wet! Sally got her ass wet!"

The children who took part in Sally's coronation were in the sixth grade, which would make them about eleven years old. Sometimes these ceremonies really are friendly initiations into the group; more often such business is just a trick to play on some "stuck-up" child, usually a newcomer to the community.

Compare: Brown, *North Carolina Folklore* (1952) vol. I: p. 42; and Brewster, *Non-singing Games* (1953) p. 121. The identical "coronation" ceremony was played as a prank originally on any sailor or passenger on old sailing-ships who was crossing the Equator for the first time. This *rite de passage* has been revived in recent years on cruise steamers, the victim being in a bathing suit; and even on airplane flights, squirting the victim with ejaculatory champagne as his-or-her ritual bath.

48

At Rocky Comfort, Mo., about 1925, the schoolboys used to seek out a student who was good in arithmetic. "Let's play store," they proposed, and the chump undertook to record an imaginary customer's purchases. "Black felt hat, six dollars," said one boy, and the "bookkeeper" wrote it on his slate. "Gray flannel shirt, a dollar fifty," cried another, and the chump wrote it down. So on with undershirt, drawers, socks, shoes, and necktie. After each entry the speaker asks "Got that down?" and the bookkeeper answers "Yes." Finally somebody calls out "Blue jeans pants, two dollars," and after a pause "Got my pants down?" When the bookkeeper answers "Yes," the players all shout "Kiss my ass, then!" Everybody laughs at the bookkeeper, and the game is over. [A typical "sell." Compare: Brown, *North Carolina Folklore,* 1952, vol. I: p. 174.)

49

At Sallisaw, Okla., in the 1920s they used to inveigle a "green" child into playing a game; the victim was to shout "Just like me!" no matter what was said to him. Here is part of the dialogue:

> Went upstairs,
> *Just like me.*
> Looked in the looking-glass,
> *Just like me.*
> Saw a little bastard,
> *Just like me.*
> Playing with his pecker,
> *Just like me.*

Then all the other children would laugh very loud, and begin to shout "Johnny plays with his pecker! Johnny plays with his pecker!" until poor Johnny fled.

Compare: Newell, *Games and Songs of American Children* (1883) p. 141; Johnson, *What They Say in New England* (1896) p. 167; Brown, *North Carolina Folklore* (1952) vol. I: p. 172. In another such "trap" on the word *key,* the victim is entrapped into saying, "I am a monk-key." So also on *hole* and "ass-hole," for the very unwary.

50

Near Pineville, Mo., in 1921, children would line up on the playground, being careful to place the "sucker" or "chump" eighth in line. Then the leader sang out: "There's a pile of cow-shit! I one it!" The next child cried, "I two it!" Others followed with "I three it!" and "I four it!" So the count goes on until the chump shouts "I eight it!" This is the end of the game, and all the children begin to chant "Tommy ate the cow-shit! Tommy ate the cow-shit!" which is considered a great joke.

See the Brown *Collection of North Carolina Folklore* (1952) I. 173; and Brewster, *American Nonsinging Games* (1953) p. 123.

51

This is "a kind of riddle" used by children at Forsyth, Mo., in 1940:

> Adam and Eve and Kick-my-Ass
> Went to the river to catch a bass,
> Adam and Eve they both got drownded,
> Who do you think was saved?

If any chump is so incautious as to reply "Kick-my-Ass" the other children are ready to oblige him. [In older forms, the third person is named "Pinch Me," and Adam and Eve go "down to the river to bathe," rhyming assonantly with "saved." However named, the third person here distinctly represents the Devil or the principle of Evil, in the original Biblical sub-erotic trio of Adam and Eve and "the Serpent" in the Garden of Eden.]

52

Rural children are often amused by parodies of party-game rhymes. A lady in Little Rock, Ark., told me that back in 1900 they thought it very smart to recite:

> Chicken in the bread-tray
> Kicking out dough,
> Granny, will your rooster peck?—
> No. child, no.
> His pecker was cut off
> A long time ago.

53

G. H. Pipes, Reeds Spring, Mo., heard it like this in the 1930s:

> Mammy, will your rooster peck?—
> Hell fire, no,
> His pecker's cut off
> A long time ago.

The rhythm or tune here is that used above for "Fire on the Mountain," Songs No. 115 or 174. See Scarborough, *On the Trail of Negro Folksongs* (1937) p. 194; Ray Wood, *Mother Goose in the Ozarks* (1938) p. 39; and Brown, *North Carolina Folklore* (1952) vol. I: pp. 199–200.

54

An old man near Green Forest, Ark., says that when he was a child (in the 1880s?) the country boys chanted this "game song" on the school ground:

> Cock upon a pear tree,
> Prick out on a pole,

> Jump cock, dodge prick,
> Shoot her in the hole.

55

Here is a related item from a teacher at Webster Groves, Mo., who says it was popular with little boys and girls in the 1880s:

> Robin robin redbreast
> Setting on a pole,
> Wiggle-waggle went his tail,
> POOP went his hole.

See: Brown, *North Carolina Folklore* (1952) p. 203. This is eighteenth-century British, at latest, as seen in Section A, Songs, above, No. 217. In the erotic rather than scatological form, No. 54 here, "cock" is a southernism for "cunt," from the French *coquille,* cockleshell, from its external shape and metaphorically representing virginity.

56

This one was heard at Pineville, Mo., in 1929.

> Here I stand all ragged and dirty,
> Show me your pecker, I'll run like a turkey.

There are two related stanzas in the Brown *Collection of North Carolina Folklore* (1952) vol. I: p. 193.

57

A Barry County, Mo., teacher heard seventh-grade children chanting this in 1921:

> Johnny's prick is getting bigger,
> Went upstairs to fuck a nigger,
> Stuck his pecker in her crack,
> Pull it out and put it back.

58

Chanted by small children in Washington County, Ark., during the winter of 1941:

> Old Jack Daley, old Jack Daley,
> Had a wife and three little babies,
> One in the corner, one in the cradle,
> One in the shit-pot eating with a ladle.

59

[Compare, at the same date as No. 58 preceding, about 1941, the following chanted by Negro and white children in New Rochelle, New York, to the tune or rhythm of the "Soldiers' March" from Gounod's opera, *Faust,* 1859:]

> Hey, Aunt Jemima,
> Lookit your Uncle Jim,
> There in the piss-pot
> Learning how to swim.
>
> First he does the breast-stroke,
> And then he does the side,
> And now he's under the water
> Swimming against the tide!

60

Mr. A. M., Columbia, Mo., in 1949, recalled a counting-out rhyme used by Missouri children:

> The old cow shit in the barn door,
> And the old man had to clean it out.

The child doing the counting pointed to a prospective player with each syllable, and the one indicated as he uttered the last word was *OUT.*

61

Here is a counting-out jingle heard in Carroll County, Ark., in 1950:

> Diddle diddle dominecker,
> Every boy has got a pecker;
> How many peckers do I see?—
> One two three and out goes he.

Compare, in another part of this collection, *Pissing in the Snow* (1976) No. 89, the same rhetorical question "How many peckers do I see?" inflated into an anti-clerical pretended "real occurrence," in which a "buckbrush circuit-rider a-preaching" gets carried away by his rhetoric in the story of St. Peter's third betrayal "when the rooster (sic!) crowed," and "so all of a sudden he hollered out: 'How many Peters is in this room?'"

62

A lady at Eureka Springs, Ark., remembered the following rope-skipping rhyme used by school children about 1895. Compare: Randolph, "Jump Rope Rhymes from Arkansas," in: *Midwest Folklore* (1953) vol. III: pp. 77–84:

> Paw fucked Maw, it was a sin,
> Turned around and fucked her ag'in,
> How many inches did it go in?
> One—two—three—four, etc.
>
> Johnny give me apples,
> Johnny give me pears,
> Johnny give me fifteen cents
> And fucked me under the stairs,
> One—two—three—four, etc.
>
> Cinderella dressed in yellow,
> Went down town to meet her fellow,
> Jumped so high her britches busted,
> How many people were disgusted?
> One—two—three—four, etc.
>
> Nigger in the grass,
> Kick her in the ass,
> How many kicks?
> One—two—three—four, etc.

63

Here's a variant used by little girls jumping rope at Reeds Spring, Mo., in 1932:

> Oh my goodness, oh by golly,
> Freddie is a-diddling Molly.
> How many inches did it go in?
> One—two—three—four, etc.

Often in "polite" form as a jump-rope rhyme: "Mary, Mary, sat on a pin, How many inches did it go in?—One—two—three, etc." (Ian Turner and Wendy Lowenstein, *Cinderella Dressed in Yella,* 1978, No. 12–045, "Jarlie, Jarlie," i.e., "Charlie Chaplin.")

64

A teacher near Pineville, Mo., in 1926, contributed some fragments of jump-rope rhymes:

> Little Sally Big-a-Rump
> Shows her twitchet every jump,
> Jump so high, kick the sky,
> Come back on the Fourth of July.
>
> Fancy dancer, do a high kick,
> Get a-hold of Tommy's prick,
> Fancy dancer, throw her down,
> Kick her ass right out of town.

65

A related item collected at Rocky Comfort, Mo., in 1931:

> Look at little Thunder-Pump,
> Shows her ass at every jump.

66

Naughty little girls jumping rope at Joplin, Mo., in the 1920s, used to wait till the boys were watching them, then call the signal *"High-water pants."* Whereupon they flipped the rope so as to pull the jumper's dress clear up about her ears, so as to show her panties. And some little girls didn't wear any panties.

Another jump-rope cry was *"Hot pepper, there's a pecker!"* At this, the rope was turned very rapidly, and the jumper pulled her skirts very high, to give the little boys a treat.

Compare Brewster, *American Non-singing Games* (1953) pp. 118–19. Morganatic or exhibitionistic little girls who did this, also in the 1920s and 1930s, in Scranton and Honesdale, Pennsylvania, would call out "Free show!" or "Red pepper!" (though never with any open mention of peckers) or, if turning with two ropes, would call out "Double Dutch!" as a signal that they were about to start turning as fast as possible, so that the skirt of the girl jumping would fly very high and show her panties. Us pre-teen or adolescent boys considered this to be a further or hidden signal that the "turners" or "jumpers" who didn't run out of the game at that point could later be invited to private sex-games such as "Doctor" or the oral-masochistic "Pocahontas," in a nearby cellar, club-shack, or under a convenient porch in a lying-down position.

67

When the children were "speaking pieces" at school in Montevallo, Mo., about 1916, a seven-year-old girl recited:

> Langshang rooster grows so tall,
> Takes two days for a turd to fall.

The teacher explained that *turd* was not a nice thing to talk about. But the child answered "My daddy says it, and I reckon he knows!" (*Langshang,* i.e. "long-shank," long-legged.)

68

A gentleman at Granby, Mo., told (about 1930) of some country folk insisting that their little boy speak a piece for the visiting preacher. Finally the child stood up and recited:

> A great big bird with a great big turd
> Flew over Mammy's threshold,
> He stretched his neck and shit a peck,
> And then closed up his ass-hole.

69

A parody repeated by fourth-graders at Hot Springs, Ark., in 1938:

> Listen, my children, and you shall hear
> Of the midnight ride of Paul Revere,
> He jumped in the seat and stepped on the gas,
> Slipped on a turd and fell on his ass.

This is only the opening of a long bawdy parody, in numerous stanzas, recited by adolescents and adults elsewhere in the United States from the 1920s through the 1950s, mocking the standard nineteenth-century recitation on the same theme. The present abbreviated version in which Revere's ride is by automobile, is both uncommon and obviously transitional, combining as it does both gasoline locomotion and horse-turds.

70

Small children near Jefferson City, Mo., used to mutter a mock blessing over their food:

> Lord, bless this bread,
> And bless this meat.
> You sons-of-bitches
> Pitch in and eat.

71

Here's one [of erotic connotation] from Van Buren, Ark., collected in 1932:

> God bless the meat,
> God damn the skin,
> Open your mouth
> And suck it in.

72

A little boy in McDonald County, Mo., in 1929, was punished for mumbling this at the table:

> Amen, Brother Ben,
> Killed a rooster,
> Fucked a hen.

See: Francis Very, "Parody and Nicknames among American Youth,": in *Journal of American Folklore* (1962) 75: 260–62, on other similar sacrilegious parodies of prayers and graces. See also Nos. 73*a* and *b,* following.

73

Another mock prayer from Pineville, Mo., collected in 1930:

> Father, Son and Holy Ghost,
> Who eats fastest gets the most.
> Blessings on them every one,
> Fuck 'em all before I'm done.

[In a similar parody of the slumber-prayer of children, reported in World War I:]

> Now I lay me down to sleep,
> I pray the Lord my soul to keep.
> If I should die before I wake,
> Fuck 'em all, for Jesus' sake!

74

At Joplin, Mo., in 1939, a five-year-old girl was given a new dress. "Hot dog!" she cried, "I guess *this* will make the boys' peckers stick out!" The child's mother was horrified. She was never able to find out where a five-year-old got such an expression.

75

This one sounds pretty grown-up, but a twelve year old boy wrote it on a blackboard in Joplin, Mo., in 1931:

> Life is short and death will come,
> Do your fucking while you're young.

[Sign supposedly displayed on a Florida real-estate "boomer's" store-front, 1950:]

> GET LOTS WHILE YOU'RE YOUNG—
> LATER IT WON'T STAND TO REASON!

76

A wisecrack which seemed very funny to children near Neosho, Mo., in 1933. ("Wall-flower," an ugly girl. *Dandelion,* to be pronounced slowly: "a *dandy, lyin'* in the grass.")

> Don't never slight a wall-flower. She
> might be a dandelion in the grass.

77

A schoolmarm near Galena, Mo., in 1943, found this in a child's copy-book:

> The night was dark and dreary,
> Sally rolled in the grass,
> She rolled into a bramble bush
> And scratched her little—never mind.

78

I have never seen any openly ribald verse in the autograph albums or "friendship books" formerly so common among young people in the Ozarks. But sometimes one finds a suggestive crack concealed in an apparently innocent memory verse. Here's one from Pineville, Mo.:

> *When* Winter's days are past and gone
> *May* pleasant calms appear,
> *I* know sometimes in ashes deep
> *Sleep* hidden coals of fire.
> *With* these few lines
> *You* will a question find.
> *Sweet* is the answer, mark it well,
> *Friend,* farewell, farewell.

The question is found in the first word of each line; just read 'em from top to bottom.—*V.R.* In line 5, *With* should probably read: *Within.* According to tradition, an acrostic almost this primitive, telling the location of a secret passage in the chapel where he was allowed to say his final prayers before his execution in 1649, might have saved the life of King Charles I, but he was unable to decipher it. See Randolph and McCord, "Autograph Albums in the Ozarks," in *Journal of American Folklore* (1948) vol. 61: pp. 188–89. And compare: Joseph C. Hickerson, Alan Dundes, and Robert A. Georges, "*Mother Goose* Vice Versa, and Some Minor Genres of Obscene Folklore," in *Journal of American Folklore* (1962) vol. 75: pp. 221–26 and 249–59.

79

Backwoods smart-alecks delight in slipping some vulgarity into an unsuspecting maiden's album. This verse is from one belonging to a nice old lady near Forsyth, Mo.

> *F*rom all the signs of evil flee
> *U*nder a sky of gold,
> *C*ome to me when the rising sun
> *K*eeps love from growing cold.
> *Y*our heart is warm, your mind is set
> *O*n every thing that we begun,
> *U*ntil I'll win you yet.

Read the first letter of each line downward for the tender sentiment. The lady has kept that album for more than sixty years. I am not sure whether she has ever found the hidden meaning in this verse.—*V.R.*

The use of hidden messages in the acrostic first letters or words of poems is very old. See note 78 preceding. By far the most complicated and difficult—upside-down, or using the first, then second, then third, letter of each line, etc.—will be found in the poetry of Edgar Allan Poe. James Branch Cabell ends his mock-"modern" poetry spoof, *Sonnets from Antan,* about 1920, with an acrostic in the final sonnet reading: "THIS IS NONSENSE." On this inspiration the last ranking male American poet using rhyme, John Peale Bishop, includes in his *Collected Poems* another such nonsense sonnet, apparently on cunnilinctus with a two-tailed mermaid, in which the acrostic reads, similarly to the present "album" message: "FUCK YOU, HALF ASS." This was pointed out by a young American college woman on her "Junior year abroad, in Paris," in 1954, who stated that her professor of poetry had shown it to her class.

80

From a girl's album near Notch, Mo., is this entry dated 1927:

> May is the month of pure delight,
> I love to see the pale moonlight,
> Screw up your face and kiss me sweet,
> You know the secret can't be beat.

Read the first word of each line for the "secret."

81

In the same album, someone has written in fine shaded script:

> Virtue is like a bubble. Once pricked,
> and it is gone forever.

82

A thirteen-year-old girl near Pineville, Mo., in 1930, sent this couplet to a bashful lover of seventeen:

> I'll be the watermelon, you be the knife,
> You be the husband, I'll be the wife.

In this locality, women often marry at thirteen, or even younger. I knew this child and her family very well. She was a very "nice" girl, carefully brought up, well educated according to the local standards. She would have been grossly insulted if any strange man had used such a word as *bull* in her presence. But she regarded this verse as very clever and delicate; a little suggestive perhaps, but not vulgar.

SECTION D

Ribaldry at Ozark Dances

What the Ozarker calls a "frolic" is an old-fashioned square dance, but it is very different from a square dance, which the casual visitor sees at the summer resorts along the highway. This latter affair is just a tourist attraction, although some hotel keepers hire wild-looking natives to lend an authentic Ozark atmosphere. The real backwoods frolic is quite another thing, and few outsiders know much about it. For a general discussion of these dances see my *Ozark Mountain Folks* (1932) pp. 63–82.

Religious people in the hill country have always opposed the frolics. When I lived at Pineville, Mo., in the 1920s, the citizens refused to have a children's dancing-class in the village; I heard a prominent merchant declare that he'd rather see his daughter dead than dancing. At Galena, Mo., the authorities permitted round dances, such as waltzes and foxtrots, but would not allow a square dance inside the city limits. The church people believe that the fiddle is "the Devil's own instrument," and that all square-dance music is aphrodisiac. They say that certain fiddle-tunes will "make an old man's prick stand up," and cause young women to "squirm around like minks on a griddle." Compare a vivid description in Constance Wagner's fine novel, *Sycamore* (1950) pp. 62–74; the author lived in Carroll County, Ark., for many years.

For many years I was accustomed to disport myself at backwoods frolics. They are not so bad as the preachers would have us believe. But there is a good deal of drinking, some sexual irregularity, and a lot of coarse talk. Many of the young men carry weapons, and bloody fights are not uncommon. Quarrels between rival clans and neighborhoods often come to a head at dances. If the boys from one settlement attend a frolic in another, and feel that they are not treated with proper consideration, the dance often ends in a general uproar. Sometimes the roof is riddled with bullets, the lamps thrown down and broken, and other serious damage done before the entertainment is over.

The worst features of the frolic derive from the Ozark tradition of indiscriminate hospitality. The only way a quiet family can give a private dance is to keep it secret. One is often invited to a frolic with the caution "Don't say nothing, or them Collins boys will get wind of it." Nobody can be turned away unless he commits some gross breach of the peace or the proprieties. Even then the attempt to eject an intruder is not to be undertaken lightly. I have seen very few backwoods dances at which there were no unwelcome guests, people who came uninvited and whose presence was resented by the host. [Known in slang as *crashers* or *gate-crashers*; in French as the similar *casseurs,* presumably from their damage and breakage.]

In those days I wanted to write a book about the Ozark frolic, with transcribed tape-recordings and uncensored photographs. But the foundations and learned societies refused to finance such a study, and I never had money enough to do it at my own expense. Once in the 1940s I borrowed a recorder from the Library of Congress through Alan Lomax and made more than a hundred fiddle-tune recordings for their Archive of Folksong. I gathered some material in manuscript also, but most of it was then considered too coarse for ordinary publication. The items which follow were all collected in the Ozark region since 1920, and are here presented for the first time.

Vance Randolph

757

Editor's Note: Although one of the shortest, this is also one of the most interesting and unusual sections of Vance Randolph's "Unprintable" collection, and the one responsible for its publication now. Randolph listed some of the less indecorous items in his preliminary article, "The Names of Ozark Fiddle Tunes," in *Midwest Folklore* (Summer 1954) vol. IV: pp. 81–86, and though some of these were allowed to pass, such as "The Biggest Prick in Town" (No. 4 below), certain others such as "Dog Shit a Rye Straw" (No. 1) were cut out of the galleys by the editor, apparently Professor W. Edson Richmond, as he observes drily above.

This "last straw" disillusioned Randolph completely as to the possibility of publication of his collection in America, in the repressive cultural climate of that period. And he was inspired to re-edit and retype the entire "Unprintable" manuscript, and to offer it for unexpurgated publication then in France by the present editor. See further the introduction to vol., *Roll Me in Your Arms*. All annotations and bracketed materials here are by the editor.

1

The titles of fiddle-tunes are many and varied, but some of them are pretty crude. Perhaps the most popular of these latter is "Dog Shit a Rye Straw." I included this title in a list of Ozark dance tunes for a folklore journal (*Midwest Folklore,* in 1954), but the editor cut it out of the galleys. Years ago Marion Hughes wrote: "There is one tune I think every fiddler in Arkansas can play. It has a great many names, but is commonly called *A Dog in a Difficulty,* or *The Unfortunate Pup.*" (See his *Three Years in Arkansaw,* Chicago, 1905, p. 75.) My old friend George Baize always referred to this piece as *Lady's Fancy,* but I heard him play it near Reeds Spring, Mo., in 1939, and the caller shouted *"Rye Straw!"* at intervals during the dance. The male dancers barked aloud, and the ladies wagged their tails in a singularly canine fashion.

2

Bob Duncan, of Oklahoma City, told me in 1950 that he had recorded a dance-tune called *Fucking Bull* in eastern Oklahoma. I haven't heard this one, but Duncan says it is "a graphic musical description of the title." Cowpokes used *fucking-bull* as a nickname for a rider who spends too much time running after women. "It wouldn't do to play that tune at a dance fifty years ago," an old cattleman told Duncan, "because it made the womenfolks blush and was apt to start a fight. But nowadays, the young people think it's just another fiddle-tune." [The cowboy slang term *fucking-bull,* noted above, is politely expurgated to *raging-bull,* as in a popular motion-picture title about prize-fighting, ca. 1980.]

3

Near Day, Mo., in 1940, an old fiddler played a fine hoedown called *Fucking in the Goober Patch,* but wouldn't allow me to make a recording of it. "We used to play lots of tunes like that," he said, "but the folks that knowed 'em has mostly died off now. Them that's left don't dance no more, because they're all crippled with rheumatism, or else got religion."

4

Lon Jordan of Farmington, Ark., in 1941, played an old favorite which he called *Biggest Prick in the Neighborhood.* Seven years later, at Eureka Springs, Ark., I heard the same tune played by A. L. Pierce, of Newton County, Ark. "What's the name of that tune?" I asked him. Pierce said it was just an old hoedown, and that he never heard any name for it. But finally he grinned a little. "If you must know," said he, "the boys used to call it *The Biggest Prick in Town*." [This is listed by title in Randolph's article, "The Names of Ozark Fiddle Tunes," in *Midwest Folklore,* Summer 1954, vol. IV: pp. 81–86; but that editor cuts certain other titles, such as No. 1.]

5

An old fiddler near Pine Bluff, Ark., in 1938, played *The Hickory Hornpipe,* a wild tune with a lot of thumps and shrill squealing in it. "Back in slavery times," he told me, "if a nigger wench didn't behave, they just fanned her ass with a hickory. A young yaller gal will holler and dance mighty lively, and that's what this here tune is about."

See Homer Croy, *Wonderful Neighbors* (1945) pp. 75–76, and Walker F. Lackey, *History of Newton County, Arkansas* (1950) p. 296, for references to similar sadistic material on phonograph records.

6

The dance tune known as *Forked Deer* is regarded as vulgar in the Ozarks, because the title has a double meaning. *Forked* might refer to the deer's antlers, but it is also the common Ozark term for *horny,* which means sexually excited. The word is always pronounced *fork-ed,* in two syllables. I have seen nice young girls leave a dance when the fiddler began to play *Forked Deer.* Lon Jordan, veteran fiddler of Farmington, Ark., always called it *Forked-Horn Deer* when ladies were present. Buster Fellows once played it on a radio program, but the announcer was careful to call it *Frisky Deer*! (Station KWTO, Springfield, Mo., May 3, 1947.)

7

Nancy Rollin is a well known dance tune, but the same title applies to a bawdy song, the words of which I have been unable to obtain. Lon Jordan, of Farmington, Ark., told me a long story about it in 1948. "About forty years ago," said Jordan, "a prominent citizen at Harrison got drunk, and sung that song. He took off his clothes and acted it all out, right there in the street. He had a tool like a jackass, and when he come to *the verse about how Nancy was a-coming,* he shuck his old prick at the womenfolks. There was a big scandal about it. He was a well-to-do man, but he died a pauper. A fine feller too, that never done anything out of the way except when he got drunk."

[Note this early reference, publicly in America about 1908, to a woman's orgasm, and the reported proud or defiant gesture accompanying it on the man's part.]

8

Rufe Scott, an elderly attorney at Galena, Mo., was a left-handed fiddler. In the 1930s I heard him play one very fine tune, always greeted with grins by the villagers, because the title of it was *Big Limber.* Allen McCord, who lived near Galena, could play the same piece. But I have not found many fiddlers who ever heard of it.

[The humorous reference in the title is in the word *limber,* meaning heavy and soft, not stiff, alluding to the penis. It is an item of folk belief, and may even be true, that very large penises never can become very stiff.]

9

Since fiddle tunes are not announced by title, the significance of the music is known only to initiates. City folk may attend country dances and hear the tunes without the least suspicion that the yokels are laughing at them. At a dance in Taney County, Mo., in 1934, a fat lady from Chicago joined one of the sets. Instantly the fiddler began to play *The Big Ass Rag.* The villagers suppressed their amusement as best they could; the tourists saw nothing to laugh at, because they didn't know the name of the tune.

10

The common *Irish Washerwoman* tune was regarded as very naughty in the early days, because the vulgar words set to it were so widely known. Mrs. M. M., of Kirbyville, Mo., said that when she was a girl in the 1890s, "decent girls would get up and leave a dance if a single bar of that tune was played." [For the "vulgar words" to this tune see "The Wild Irishman," song No. 140, in vol. I, *Roll Me in Your Arms.* See also note 6 above, on "Forkèd Deer."]

A dance tune called *The Nightingale* is another item which the hillfolk think is very wicked. Mrs. M. M., of Springfield, Mo. (not the same informant as in No. 10 preceding), told me that her mother, in the early 1900s would not allow it to be played in her house.

For the innocent words to this tune see Randolph's *Ozark Folksongs,* (1946) vol. I: pp. 266–69. However, the "Nightingale" song objected to is in all probability another old love song of the same name, surviving in the Ozarks: either that given in *Pills to Purge Melancholy,* 1719, vol. V: pp. 86–87, on which see further Claude M. Simpson, *The British Broadside Ballad and Its Music,* 1966, pp. 511–13; or a simpler Scottish song of which the old words are in the Pepys and Roxburghe collections of black-letter ballads: Simpson, pp. 572–73, at "Peggy and the Soldier." Another even stronger possibility is the erotic stage-song in Thomas Durfey's *Trick for Trick,* (1678) known as "See the Gowlan," in *Pills to Purge Melancholy,* (1719) vol. II: p. 150, discussed by Simpson, pp. 464–65, of which the bawdy scenario would probably seem objectionable to the public prudery affected in the Ozarks.

11

The following titles are regarded as obscene in the Ozarks. I am listing them separately because it may be that they depend for effect upon the Ozark dialect and manner of speech, not always understood by outsiders: *Clabber Cod Stomp, Come Get Your Nubbin, Goober-Grabbin' Mamma, Granny Rag, Hog Eye Sally, Hold Your Jemson Steady, It's Good For Your Knockers, New Ring on My Horn, Put Sugar On It, Red Onion Stomp, Red River Rising, Tie Your Scabbard Down.*

The erotic references in these titles—all 1954—are roughly as follows: *Clabber,* or *clobber,* the semen; and *Cod,* the penis. *Nubbin',* the penis, and by extension sexual intercourse. *Goober,* testicle. *Granny-rag,* a menstrual cloth or clout. *Hog eye,* the opening of the vagina. *Jemson,* or *jimpson,* also *Johnson* or *Johnson-bar,* the penis, with reference to the dangerous jimpson weed, ("deadly nightshade," *Datura stramonium*), of which the toxic effect is considered aphrodisiacal by country boys; it is also used in Eastern Pennsylvania, and sometimes with fatal effects. *Knockers,* testicles. *Horn,* the erect penis; the *new ring* meaning a new girl's vagina. *Put Sugar On It,* a humorous incentive to oral erotism by either sex. *Red River Rising,* an allusion to the beginning of menstruation, when it is believed, apparently correctly, that a woman is very likely to be erotically inclined. *Tie Your Scabbard Down,* alludes to the inconvenience of sword belts in the days, as late as the Civil War in the South, when they were still worn and found in the way while men were dancing; here suggesting that the inconveniently erect penis should be tied to the man's leg in the same way. Compare No. 23 below. *Red Onion Stomp,* the "red onion" being the glans penis when swollen with blood during erection; this is also used as the title of a famous New Orleans jazz piece, with a wild fiddle or clarinet obbligato.

12

Here are the titles of some other fiddle-tunes of the same type: *Belly to Belly, Big Ass Rag, Big Prick Coming to Town, Big Balls in Nashville, Big Bottom Wabble, Everybody Knows How Maggie Farts, Frigging on the Floor, Fucking in the Kitchen, Fuck Her Under the Stairs, Grease My Pecker Sally Ann, Grease On My Prick, Hard Pecker Reel, Josie Shuck Her Panties Down, Keep Your Pecker in Your Pants, Kick Her Ass Out in the Rain, Kiss My Ass Says Rosie, Lucy Needs Fucking So Bad, Mamma Don't 'Low No Diddling Here, No More Cock in Texas, Pecker On a Pole, Piss-Ellum Blues, Pissy-Ass Breakdown, Poontang On the Levee, Quit Shaking My Prick, Ragged-Ass Bill, Sally Fucks on the Floor, Shake It Up Julie, Slippery Ass Wiggle, Something Under My Apron, Stick Your Pecker Where It Belongs, Take Your Fingers Out of My Pants, Tickle His Balls Maria, Trade My Name For a Piece of Tail, Where Is My Pants At?* and *Wiggle-Ass Jig.*

As with No. 11 preceding, all these titles were reported by Vance Randolph, Eureka Springs, Arkansas, November 1954. A few lexical notes: *Big Ass Rag,* for "ragtime," punning on menstruation cloth. *To Wabble,* or wobble is to wriggle when dancing. *Grease,* joking on the need for coital lubricant, when the woman is "dry" or has become so from protracted intercourse. *Shuck (Shook) Her Panties Down,* a joke on a presumably common accident while dancing wildly, or when entering trance by a woman during "holiness shoutin'." *Kick Her Ass Out in the Rain,* here "ass" represents the whole body or person. *No More Cock,* a southernism for what would be called "cunt" elsewhere, from the French *coquille,* cockleshell. *Piss-Ellum,* the elm tree, because its supple twigs with the bark slipped off are used for backwoods abortions. *Pissy-Ass,* bepissed because of excitement, laughter, etc., presumably more often of women than of men. *Breakdown,* a wild kind of dance. *Poontang,* sexual intercourse, from the French *putain,* whore, in the nasalized Marseille and New Orleans pronunciation, *putaing. Ragged-Ass,* slovenly, wearing old or torn clothing; a proud army song, referring to the honorably torn clothing of battle, is entitled "The Raggedy-Ass Cadets." *My Apron,* always refers to pregnancy, from the old Scottish phrase and famous song about "Now I wear my apron up (or: high)." *Trade My Name,* means: I'll get married to anyone for her "piece of tail."

13

Here is a verbatim account of a disreputable dance in Carroll County, Ark., about 1893. I had it from an old gentleman at Harrison, Ark., April 10, 1950. [Compare the notes on "backwoods" frolics in Randolph's preface, and at No. 15 below.]

> Back in the nineties, some of the people in this town was kind of tough, not to say wild. There was one of the Burdock girls, a right pretty girl too. But she was awful dark complected, and tanned like saddle leather. She went to a square dance out on White River, not too far from Beaver. Out in front of the dance place some other girls got to kidding her.

They said she was black as a nigger. "I'm just as white as any of you-uns," she says. And with that she pulled off her waist. The other girls kept egging her on, so she pulled off her dress too. A minute later off come her petticoat, and there she was without a stitch on but her shoes and stockings, with red carpet-rag garters a-holding 'em up. She was white enough, but it like to busted up the dance, because them wild young folks was a-whooping and hollering after her. Pretty soon two other girls, maybe they was a little drunk, pulled off their clothes too. Things got so wild and rough that the respectable folks all went home, but the rough element raised hell, and kept it up till plumb daylight. Before they got done, pretty near half the girls on the floor was naked as jaybirds. And there was some laid down and fucked like a bunch of wild animals, with the lamps still burning and the fiddlers still a-playing! [Compare the Scottish song, "The Ball of Kirriemuir," in note 25 below.]

14

The rhymes shouted out by the caller at ordinary square dances, attended by respectable women, are innocent enough. Otho Pratt, who was raised on Horse Creek near Galena, Mo., said that "right at the end of a dance, when most of the decent people had went home, the caller used to get kind of dirty sometimes." Every old-time caller knows some really ribald calls, which are used at unconventional frolics in the backwoods. [Compare Randolph's *Ozark Mountain Folks* (1932) pp. 79–80.]

15

Wythe Bishop of Fayetteville, Ark., remembered such dances from the early 1900s in Washington County, Ark. When I interviewed him Dec. 19, 1941, he made it plain that most of the square dances were "pretty decent," but things were different in certain tough backwoods settlements. "Some of them white-trash was plumb vulgar," said he. "I've saw dances where big fat country gals would hang every stitch of their clothes on a nail!" When I asked about the calls used on such occasions, he rattled off more than a dozen fragments. During the next three weeks he recalled many more. What follows is Mr. Bishop's entire collection, the largest I have recorded from one individual. [Compare the calls of Nos. 24 and 27, below:]

Lead the ace and trump the king,
Let me feel that pretty little thing.

Up and at 'em, everybody dance,
Goose that gal and watch her prance.

Swing round the mountain, swing Cora Lee,
Gals won't let my tallywhacker be.

Up with her twitchet, down with her heel,
The more you fuck her, the louder she'll squeal,
The louder she hollers, the better you'll feel.

Do-se-do and a rattlesnake pass,
Grease your pecker and stick it up her ass.

Gals all setting a-straddle of a rail,
Boys all running to get a piece of tail.

Swing your opposite all over town,
Look at that pretty gal shake her pants down.

Ladies do the shimmy, down goes her britches,
In goes a little thing about six inches.

Promenade all, she's a-dancing for her dinner,
Went off twice before I got it in her.

Shake that gal with the red dress on,
Hot as a pistol, sure as you're born.

Right hand across and one, two, three,
If you don't like peaches quit shaking my tree.

Swing that gal that's about half grown,
She'll grab your pecker like a dog grabs a bone.

Fuck your opposite, fuck your taw,
Everybody fucking in old Arkansas.

Some folks say that gals can't climb,
I caught two on this tree of mine.

Don't throw her down, boys, don't throw her down,
Folks all say her daddy's in town.

Shirt tail west and dress tail east,
Walk along, John, and get a little piece.

Waltz the hall, remember my call,
Ruby can take it, balls and all.

Corn in the crib, wheat in the bin,
Honor your pardner before you stick it in.

Gent round the lady, quick, quick, quick,
Lady round the gent and grab him by the prick.

Log-chain your sweetie, hog-tie your honey,
Stick it up her ass, get the worth of your money.

Cheat your partner, swing Miss Lucy,
Up with her petticoat, out with your ducey.

Shoo fly back in single file,
Ladies all holler and the gents hog wild,
Look at them floozies a-fucking in the aisle.

Swing your corner, then to your taw,
Pull off your clothes and go at it raw.

Gals promenade, single file,
Wiggle your tail Arkansas style.

Gent's prick forward and it's howdy-do,
Lady winks her twitchet with a how-are-you.

Stick it in her, one, two, three,
Fiddle a-singing like a bird in a tree.

Drink your own whiskey, dip your own snuff,
Fuck your own woman and that's enough.

First lady fell down a rattlesnake hole,
Gent tops the lady, they're a-putting up coal.

Hurry up boys and don't be slow,
Never get nothing that way, you know,
Never get to fuck her if you don't do so,
One more change and home you go.

Plant your 'taters in sandy land,
Promenade back to the same old stand.

Taw in various dance-calls means partner, or the dancer opposite. In the 3rd verse from end, *putting up coal* is a euphemism for copulating; in last verse, *plant your taters* also means to copulate. In 10th from end, *ducey,* a large penis, or other champion, from Eleanora Duse, a famous turn-of-the-century actress.

16

Jean Winkler, St. Louis, Mo., Sept. 21, 1948, contributed a fragment of a square-dance call, heard in rural Arkansas. He says that "when the fiddler had reached a frenzy and the likker was flowing free" the caller would yell:

> Down the roads and over the ditches,
> Swing them whores, you sons of bitches!

17

A lady in Carroll County, Ark., Jan. 7, 1948, adds this one, which she heard near Harrison, Ark., in the early days:

> Little feet high and big feet low,
> Fuck that gal in the red calico.

18

A gentleman in Harrison, Ark., Dec. 4, 1952, recalls this one:

> Cream and peaches once a week,
> Pull up her dress and pat her cheeks,
> Cream and peaches every night,
> Lay her down and fuck her right.

19

From Mr. A. M., Columbia, Mo., Oct. 3, 1948. He learned it about 1918, as part of a vulgar "Turkey in the Straw" dance-call:

> Grab her by the right leg, swing her half around,
> Grab her by the left leg, throw her on the ground,
> Stick it in the middle and a bobble up and down,
> When you come to her ass-hole, go on around.

20

A lady in Green Forest, Ark., Nov. 14, 1947, recalls "a dirty dance-call" that she heard about 1909:

Tickle her bubbies
And keep on a-rubbin',
Down goes her hand
A-feeling of your nubbin.

Up goes petticoats,
Down goes britches,
In goes a little thing
About six inches.

The second verse here—also in No. 15, above, verse 8—is related to "Fire on the Mountain," Songs Nos. 115 and 174, of which the first is also well-known in Britain as a harvest "charm." In this, the sun-ripened "apples" are the girl's breasts, and "nuts" the boy's testicles, in their outdoor love-making.

Apples be ripe
And nuts bc brown,
Petticoats up
And trousers down!

21

Mr. J. P., Picher, Okla., Aug. 24, 1940, recalled these items he heard at "a drunken riot they called a square dance" between Picher and Joplin, Mo., in 1922:

One wheel off and t'other'n a-dragging,
Lets all stop and do a little shagging.

Pigs all a-squealing, ponies all a-bucking,
Choose up sides and do a little fucking.

Alamand left and tromping jimpsons down,
Stick it in the hole, don't run it in the ground.

Balance eight till you get straight,
You diddle Sue and I'll screw Kate.

Swing your taw and slap it up against her,
On to your neighbor while I stick it in her.

Back to the center with a yo-gee-haw,
Fuck that gal from Arkansaw.

Down the center and split the ring,
Keep on a screwing till you hear the birdies sing.

Swing her to the left and then to the right,
Take her home and fuck her all night.

In verse 3, *Alamand,* or *allemande,* a dance movement; *jimpson,* or *jempson,* the penis, from the purportedly aphrodisiacal jimpson weed, the very deadly nightshade (*Datura stramonium*). Verse 7, *split the ring,* to break a girl's hymen.

22

From Mr. J. D., Little Rock, Ark., April 4, 1931. He heard them in the late 1880s.

> Swing right and left and stick it in the middle,
> Stick it in the middle, stick it in the middle,
> Swing right and left and stick it in the middle,
> And go home with the gals in the morning.
>
> Hop light ladies, tiptoe fine,
> Somebody's pecker is bigger than mine,
> Honor your pardner, rise and shine
> And go home with the gals in the morning.
>
> Swing right and left and stick it in the middle,
> Stick it in the middle, stick it in the middle,
> Swing right and left and stick it in the middle,
> And go home with the gals in the morning.

23

An old lady in Russellville, Ark. (about 1940), said that some callers used to "mutter under their breath" such calls as:

> Grab your pardner, swing her around,
> Pocket full of rocks to hold your pecker down.

Compare note on No. 11 above, the identical idea in the last dance-call or tune-title, *Tie Your Scabbard Down*.

24

From an old man in Fayetteville, Ark., Dec. 20, 1941. He was a friend of Wythe Bishop. When Mr. Bishop finished recording a tale, there was still a good deal of room on the disc. So this fellow stepped forward and gave his dance-calls. Bishop told me the man's name, but I failed to record it. [Compare Bishop's own calls in No. 15 above; and No. 27.]

> Left hand across and lady in the corner,
> Shoot out the lights and fuck a little longer.
>
> Bitches to the brush and the gents all foller,
> Stick it up her ass and give her a dollar.
>
> Ladies all wiggle and the gents all waller,
> Piss on the fiddler and shit on the caller.
>
> Drop your hands and circle four,
> Makes no difference who is a whore.
>
> Swing that gal and waltz the hall,
> Fuck her quick or you'll never fuck at all.
>
> Toodle-dee, toodle-dum, seven peckers high,
> Big prick, little prick, root hog or die.

Up to my ass and higher too,
Cotton-Eye Joe says howdy-do.

The final item here shares its first line with a planting "charm" or ritual, elsewhere in the present collection, section H, "Folk Beliefs," No. 39.

25

J. W. "Skeeter," a well-known fiddler at Busch, Ark., Feb. 6, 1952, remembered the following as part of a "whore-house call" he heard on the Oklahoma border:

First lady pass, second lady pass,
Third lady's finger up the fourth lady's ass.

Out with your peckers and balance all,
Fuck them gals and piss on the wall.

Jump and buck, hug that doe,
Finger in your ass and home you go.

Ladies to the center, squat and piss,
Gents to the center and fuck your fist.

The last verse here also occurs in No. 31 below, which see. In verse 3, *home you go,* refers to intromission or anal digitation to bring on the "Chakra" (perineal nerve) orgasm. Observe that the first couplet or call here occurs in various American recoveries of the famous modern (?) Scottish orgiastic bawdy song, "The Ball o' Kirriemuir," of which there is no complete example in Randolph's collection. The relationship is worth exploring between the implied balls as Scottish dance-orgies, the naked whorehouse dances in Britain since the Restoration, noted in Rochester's *Sodom,* in Pepy's *Diary* (about 1660), and by Francis Grose, *Classical Dictionary of the Vulgar Tongue* (1785) at *ballum-rankum* and *buff-ballers*—the latter term surviving in America for three centuries entirely underground as a favorite term for sexual intercourse—and the Ozark "kitchen sweats" and "blackguardy dances" and these "whorehouse calls" at naked dances in New Orleans and west, sometimes openly assimilated to surviving "Devil-worship" or quasi-religious sex orgies in the American south. See items No. 26–32 below, and especially the final section H here, "Ozark Folk Beliefs." The intense American backwoods objection to couple-dancing, especially to fiddle music ("the Devil's own instrument"), and the prudish subterfuges of the invented "play-party" and its anodyne dance rhymes and songs, indicate very clearly a recognition of not-very-well-hidden vestiges of some sinful earlier or surviving sex-orgiastic Diabolism. See also Randolph's rather reserved *Ozark Mountain Folks* (1932) pp. 63–82, on Ozark dance "frolics."

26

An old gentleman in Eureka Springs, Ark., Feb. 17, 1952, recalled these calls from the "blackguardy dances" they used to have about 1900. [In verse 1, *mouth* is a euphemism or endline "tease" referring to the vagina. In 3:4, *shoot the owl,* to ejaculate in the air for birth-control purposes (Onan's sin in *Genesis,* 38:9), when making love out-of-doors at night. Also *shoot the moon* or *the monkey* or *the stork.*]

Lay on your back a-looking south,
Let the moon shine in your mouth,
Balance all!

> In and out, ladies' chain,
> Stick it in, pull it out,
> All down the lane.
>
> Stick it in her ass-hole,
> Listen to her howl,
> Waltz the hall and
> Shoot the owl.
>
> Cheat or swing,
> She's a-sucking honey,
> Double up, boys,
> Get the worth of your money.
>
> Circle the ladies all about,
> Everybody hollers
> Pull your pecker out.
>
> Lady hollers gee,
> Gent hollers haw,
> Fucking right and left
> In old Arkansas.

The dance caller is heavily peppering his texts here with erotic details, hardly hidden in any local slang or "*lingua franca* of the folk," to impel and incite the dancers to the naked sex-orgy in which the dance will presumably end, as described by an eye-witness in No. 13 above. In verse 1, *Let the moon shine in your mouth,* is sometimes also said to refer to the oragenital act called "face-sitting" (*moon,* the buttocks), on which see song No. 234, "Sit on My Face," in section A above. Verse 3, *shoot the owl,* or *moon,* or *stork,* withdrawal or coitus interruptus, as in verse 5: *hollers, Pull your pecker out.* (See Onan in *Genesis,* 38:9–10, there considered a profound sin preventing conception.) Verse 4, *Cheat or swing,* also to *double up,* to trade (sex) partners; also a dance movement, here applied to the erotic practice called *half-and-half,* where one gets "the worth of your money," by the man beginning orally, to excite himself, and ending vaginally; or the exact reverse as the "ideal" method of *coitus interruptus.* In verse 4, *a-sucking honey,* the semen, but sometimes also the woman's pre-coital lubricant liquor or *cyprine,* as in rhyme No. 7, "Keep Your Pussy Greasy." Verse 6, "Gee!" and "Haw!" are calls to a plow-horse meaning "right!" and "left!" as in this case, and sometimes "Start (*Git-up*)" and "Stop (*Whoa!*)"

27

From L. J., veteran fiddler of Farmington, Ark., Feb. 5, 1942. Mr. J. played some fifty fiddle-tunes into my recorder, but wouldn't allow me to make a phonographic recording of his "dirty" dance calls. "I don't mind you writing 'em down," said he, "but I don't want 'em kept in my own voice on them phonograph records." [Compare No. 24, above:]

> Grab your pardner and hit the floor,
> Stick it up her ass about six inches more.
>
> Fuck 'em early and diddle 'em late,
> Swing that gal like you're swinging on a gate.
>
> Ladies a-leading Indian style,
> Kick her in the ass every little while.
>
> Swing your pardner Arkansas style,
> Tickle her twitchet, she'll run hog wild.

Bobcats holler and wildcats squall,
Button up your pants, you can't please 'em all.

Promenade to the shade,
Kiss the widow, fuck the old maid.

First couple out, balance and swing,
Tickle her tits and show her that thing.

Loosen up your belly-bands,
Tighten up the traces,
Grab 'em by the ass
And put 'em in their places.

Swing your opposite, swing her again,
Get her in the corner and fuck her if you can.

All gents left and balance all,
Diddle that widow at the head of the hall.

Pull off your shoes and pull off your socks,
Pull down your pants and show 'em what you got.

Four coming up and four coming down,
Peters going in and out all over town.

Chase that rabbit, chase that squirrel,
Pay that fiddler and diddle that girl.

Lady go gee and the gent go haw,
Swing your neighbor and screw your taw.

Devil on the floor and a whack, whack, whack,
Pull up her dress and stick it in the crack.

Swing her by the waist and rub it on her leg,
Grab that gal and set her on the peg.

Swing your opposite round and round,
Grab your pardner and throw her on the ground,
Such a getting upstairs I never did see,
This kind of fucking it don't suit me.

Where you going, Sally Ann?
Going to get married as quick as I can,
Sift your meal and save the bran,
Wiggle your twat as fast as you can.

Gents fall back, piss on the wall,
Take a chaw terbacker and waltz the hall.

Ducks in the mill-pond, goose on the ocean,
Fuck that gal while she's in the notion.

Bump your belly up against the wall,
Button up your pants and promenade all.

In verse 11, *show 'em what you got,* i.e., the man's penis size. Verse 14, *gee* and *haw,* see end-note No. 26 preceding; *taw,* one's dance partner or "opposite" (as in verse 9). Verse 16, *peg,* penis. Male houses of homosexual prostitution are called *peg-houses.* Verse 17, *getting upstairs,* euphemism for sexual intercourse, because bedrooms in private houses are on the upper floors. The two-dollar bill is called *upstairs* money, because formerly (till World War II) it was the price of an ordinary prostitute; and this bill is therefore often still refused as "carrying bad luck." (See: *Deuteronomy,* 23:18, prohibiting any sacred use of "the hire of a whore, or the price of a dog," the latter meaning a male prostitute.) Verse 19, *Gents . . . piss on the wall, Take a chaw* (of) *terbacker,* dance-party version of what is known politely on busses and in offices as a *pee-stop* (or "rest-stop") or *coffee-break,* also as a *sex-break,* defined in current folk-humor as "when the boss and his secretary do not come back after lunch."

28

Here are some calls collected at a wild backwoods "frolic" in McDonald County, Mo., Sept. 10, 1928:

> Cornstalk fiddle and a shit-skin bow,
> Never get to heaven till you do just so.
>
> Up to her ass and higher too,
> Pull back your rooster and cocky-doodle-doo.
>
> Pull off your boot and smell your sock,
> Pick you a heifer and get a little cock.
>
> Kingbolt gone and axle a-dragging,
> Keep right on with your god damn shagging.
>
> All hands up and circle round,
> Don't let that pretty gal get out of town.
>
> Ducks in the millpond, geese on the ocean,
> Screw 'em both while you got 'em in the notion.
>
> Swing her again and go somewhere,
> You know the place and I don't care.
>
> Grab that gal and hold her close,
> Pull out your pecker and double the dose.

In verse 1, *shit-skin,* refers to the "blue mould" forming on manure. In verse 3, *smell your sock,* i.e., as an aphrodisiac, also to reduce fatigue; the violent odor excites the adrenalin flow, thus "snapping the synapses." Verse 2, *Up to her ass and higher too,* line borrowed from a planting or fertility charm used while sowing wheat; *rooster* usually means penis, but here is applied to the foreskin "and cocky-doodle-doo." Verse 3, *heifer,* young girl; *cock,* southernism for cunt. Verse 4, *Kingbolt* and *axle,* metaphorically of penis and testicles; *shagging,* fucking, or the motions thereof, said of goats. Verse 7, *go somewhere,* etc., indicating that at the milder dance-parties the sex-minded couples go off traditionally to search for privacy in the dark outside, the woods, upstairs, and similar.

29

Mr. C. S., Noel, Mo., Sept. 14, 1928, gave this as a dance-call he heard near Pack, Mo., about 1914.

> Bump your belly against the wall,
> Shoulder your prick and promenade all.
>
> Paint on her face, terbacker in her mouth,
> Fuck that gal like they do down South.
>
> First lady out, cheat or swing,
> On to the next and shake that thing.

> Make your boots go whickety-whack,
> Circle to the left and stick it up her crack.
>
> Swing her high, swing her low,
> Keep on fucking till she hollers Whoa!
>
> Set on your butt, get a hold of your nubbin,
> If you don't get butter, just keep on a-rubbing.

In verse 1, *shoulder your prick,* mock-military ordnance metaphor. Verse 2, *terbacker in her mouth,* note chewing of tobacco by women, and compare end-note No. 27, verse 19 above. Verse 3, *cheat or swing,* see end-note No. 26, verse 4, a dance movement, here to be understood erotically; *shake that thing,* applied to the coital movements of the genitals and buttocks by either sex. Verse 6, *nubbin,* penis; *butter,* or more usually in the Ozarks, *duck-butter,* the semen, from the necessary pounding and churning motions, as in male masturbation, to "make the butter come." See the long, purposely erotico-symbolic description of a woman desperately churning "at the turn of the butter," in Oliver St. John Gogarty's Irish autobiography, *As I Was Going Down Sackville Street* (1937) chapter vi, p. 113, reprinted in *The Limerick,* Note 1350, presumably as observed by a folklore-collecting priest in Tipperary, with the woman finally taking refuge in a *charm* of "the old forgotten gods of the homestead! Twenty strokes for ten! Gasping she sang the following charm":

> Come butter, come butter, come butter, come!
> Every lump as big as my bum!

30

Contributed by Mr. F. P., Galena, Mo., Nov. 12, 1932. He heard many such calls at kitchen-sweats in Stone County, Mo., about 1910:

> Up with your petticoats,
> Ladies to the middle,
> Gents' pants down
> All begin to diddle.
>
> Alaman left,
> To the lady in the middle,
> Everybody fucking
> Keep time with the fiddle.
>
> Bird hop out, crow hop in,
> Hang your clothes on a hickory limb,
> Ladies bow, gents duck under,
> Holler loud and fuck like thunder.
>
> Up the river,
> Around the bend,
> All join hands
> We're a-fucking again.

In verse 2, *Alaman,* from the French *Allemande,* a German dance-step, all these old square-dance directions coming from the period of John Playford's *The Dancing Master* (1651) over twenty times reprinted by 1727, under the French influence of the Restoration in England.

31

Fragments of a "whore-house call" remembered by Mr. R. C., Eureka Springs, Ark., Sept. 24, 1949. Such calls were never heard at ordinary dances, he said; but they were used at certain "tough frolics" in the eastern part of Carroll County, Ark., about 1916.

> Ladies to the center,
> Squat and piss.
> Gents to the corner
> And fuck your fist.
> Balance all. Whoo-ee!
> Rag, women, rag!
>
> Keep your feet on the floor,
> Shit on the wall,
> Take a chaw terbacker
> And balance all!

In verse 1, *Gents . . . fuck your fist,* does not refer to actual masturbation, but to the male dancers handling their penises to keep them (attractively) erect despite the effort of dancing. *Ladies . . . squat and piss,* not merely for bladder relief but presumably as exciting to the men, as seen in the courting of dogs, deer, mooses, etc. This verse also occurs in briefer form in No. 25 above. *Rag* is presumably also intended as a dance indication, if not a reference to the "granny-rag" or menstrual cloth, the modern "kotex."

32

Despite the fact that such items are common in the Ozark region, I do not know of any folklorist who has collected them. I have never seen any of these vulgar dance-calls in print, except a rather mild one in Weldon Stone's Ozark novel, *Devil Take a Whittler* (1948) p. 191, where a precocious child cried out:

> Shake 'em up early, diddle 'em late,
> Pull in your line, spit on your bait!
> Anything goes!

SECTION E

Bawdy Elements in Ozark Speech

The average Ozarker, in polite conversation, is more prudish than the people I knew in New York and Chicago. The hillman's songs and riddles are more suggestive than his common speech. But there is no denying that some characteristic backwoods expressions are a bit salty, and even Mildred Woods learned "a fine lot of four-letter words" from an Arkansas hill woman. (*Arkansas Gazette*, Little Rock, Ark., Jan. 29, 1953.) Long ago I mentioned some of these matters in a paper entitled "Verbal Modesty in the Ozarks," and Louise Pound, then editor of *American Speech*, accepted it for publication. But an official of the printing company was "terribly upset" and didn't want to publish such "questionable material" without consulting the Attorney General of the United States! Miss Pound returned the manuscript to me. Percy W. Long finally published it in *Dialect Notes*, in 1928.

Printers are not quite so squeamish nowadays, but only a few years ago, when Professor George P. Wilson and I wrote a book on the Ozark dialect, *Down in the Holler*, we decided to *omit* everything that could possibly offend the pure in heart. Despite our efforts there were many readers, even some hard-boiled newspaper reviewers, who regarded the material as a bit on the bawdy side. "To anyone not familiar with the language of the Ozarks," wrote Ken Parker, "the chapter on taboos and euphemisms might seem to border on being vulgar . . . enough so to make that chapter alone worth the price of the book." (*Arkansas Gazette*, May 17, 1953.) Another Southern newspaperman thought that "the book will appeal to the stag crowd, but there's a good deal of obscenity in the language that would offend some of the modest among us." (Greensboro, North Carolina, *Daily News*, May 10, 1953.) A nice old gentleman who teaches English literature in a college said that *Down in the Holler* is "the nastiest, filthiest book ever issued by an American university press."

With these criticisms in mind, it is my purpose to record here some words and expressions omitted from earlier works. I'm afraid that some of them might not be acceptable to the journals, even today. These items were all collected since 1920 [to 1957] in the Ozark region of Missouri, Arkansas, and Oklahoma.

Vance Randolph

Editor's Note: The materials that follow, as Randolph's preceding lines make clear, are precisely those expurgatorily omitted from *Down in the Holler* in 1953. (All paragraphs of annotations and materials in brackets in the present Section E, "Ozark Speech," and following, are by the present editor.) It should be observed that the somewhat self-righteous prudery of Ozark speakers, and journal editors, at least in their public attitudes, seemed common in the native response to Randolph's published materials, and those of other serious writers. At the first All-Ozark Folk Festival, at Springfield, Missouri, April 1934, Chamber of Commerce President John T. Woodruff stated, of the one best Ozark novel so far written, Thames Williamson's *The Woods Colt*, that it was: "the rottenest, nastiest stuff I've ever seen in print, and I haven't understood why it was not suppressed long ago."

Randolph himself, who was born just across the state border in Kansas, Mr. Woodruff felt was one of "a lot of carpetbaggers who have come in here," and also "doesn't know much about the Ozarks—he has been consorting with some of the undercrust, and he took them as typical." Robert Cochran, whose biography *Vance Randolph: An Ozark Life* seldom misses an opportunity to badmouth its subject, records in full, pages 199–200, among other even more pawky assessments, this one by Mrs. Ruth Tyler, a lady appearing locally "in granny gown and bonnet to play her hammered dulcimer at festivals."

She is here writing to Otto Rayburn in August 1957, on one of Randolph's last tale collections, *The Talking Turtle*, of which she observes succinctly that "it fair stinks," and concludes somewhat paradoxically, as to Randolph and his friend, the artist Thomas Hart Benton: "I've known many characters who were dirty, low-down talkers, but they *were* comical and amusing—not revolting. He and Tom Benton should swap notes . . . they have twisted minds."

A certain amount of native caution is necessary in judging the objective truth of some of the stories and witticisms retailed here, bearing in mind that the title of another of Randolph's Ozark tale collections is, perfectly candidly, *We Always Lie to Strangers*. Don't we all?

The paragraphs of notes added here should make clear (a sampling appeared in *Maledicta*, vol. I, as "A Word for It") that most of the incidents and anecdotes following are only jestingly presented by the tellers as having authentically happened to them personally. For many of the identical anecdotes are straight-faced jokes, and something very close to the same "spontaneous" remarks or witticisms have also often been collected—also as authentically true, and just as loyally reported—at other locations in New York, eastern Pennsylvania, and elsewhere half a continent away, from the 1920s to the 1980s. *Se non è vero, è ben trovato*: If it isn't true, it's well told.

1

The hillman's talk is full of strange figures, metaphors, similes, cryptic allusions, and backwoods wisecracks. He is not satisfied to observe that an object is cold; he likes to say that it is *cold as a preacher's balls*, or *a well-digger's ass*, or *a witch's tit*, or *a dead man's pecker*. Of a widow who lived near Noel, Mo., a villager remarked: "That woman's butt is *cold as a pumpkin*; the only way to warm her up is to *put pepper on her twitchet*."

One of my neighbors, after several months of exasperation, persuaded a pretty schoolmarm to spend the night with him. But the whole enterprise was a failure. "That gal ain't got no spring in her tail," he said. "She just laid there, *still as a cold turd in a dead eddy*." [Compare, *as dead as a whore's turd in a chamberpot*, heard, as all parenthetical notes following, in eastern United States, 1920s to 1950s.]

2

One often hears a man say that something is *hot as a fresh-fucked goat*, *hot as a goat with a hard-on*, *hot as a whore's cunt*, *hot as a June bride in a featherbed*, *hot as a country girl playing postoffice*, or *hot as a hired man's prick on Saturday night*. Another common figure is *hot as a boar chinch*, which means a male bedbug.

Brown, *North Carolina Folklore*, 1952, vol. I: p. 373, has "hot as a bore chinch." The game of Postoffice—with "Special Delivery hugs and kisses" swapped in a closet—is, along with the older Spin the Bottle, of country-dance origin, the most common kissing game among American adolescents since the late nineteenth century.

The opening image here, of the "fresh-fucked goat," immemorially the typically rutting animal, is enlarged in the extensive Orr collection of Colorado similes, playing on the humor of alliteration, to: "as hot as a fresh-fucked fox in a forest fire," with a side-allusion to "fox" as a passionate girl—a back-formation from "feisty," as in No. 94 below. Compare: "as hot as an asbestos cat fucking a celluloid dog in Hell," or "in a volcano." A significant parallel on the origins of Hell. In the polite form of this, the animals are merely "chasing" each other. The reference to pre-plastics *celluloid* dates the phrase as originating before World War II.)

3

Men who fiddle for the country dances are supposed to be an amorous lot, so that *busy as a fiddler's prick* [i.e., *stick*] is a favorite figure. At Galena, Mo., I heard the remark "Tommy may not have the *biggest* prick in town, but it sure is the *busiest*." In more or less decorous conversation one hears *busy as a fiddler's elbow*, but everybody knows it isn't really his elbow that is meant. Other common sayings are *busy as a cat covering shit*, *busy as a boar coon in rutting time*, *busy as a tumblebug on a cow turd*, and *busy as a goose with seven ass-holes*.

4

If some particular objects are very abundant, the hillman says they are *thicker than pecker-pokes round a schoolhouse*. Since the schoolyard is a good place for young people to park at night, undisturbed by the light of cars on the highway, the place is often littered with condoms in the morning. [*Poke*, a bag or bonnet.] *Thick as mouse-turds in the meal barrel* carries a similar meaning, and needs no explanation.

5

One year the watermelon crop failed in our neighborhood, and a farmer remarked that melons were *thick as turds in a briar-patch*. By this he meant that melons were very rare indeed. There are no turds in briar-patches, for good and sufficient reasons.

6

I have heard an empty cupboard characterized as *bare as a bird's butt*. A similar phrase is *naked as a jaybird's ass*. There are people who apparently cannot use the word *naked* without mentioning jaybirds. When members of the other sex are present, one shortens the phrase to *naked as a jaybird*. It may mean completely nude, or partly clothed. I once heard a hillman in Joplin, Mo., describe some city girls in evening dresses as being *naked as jaybirds*. [*Down in the Holler*, p. 178.] A doctor in Reeds Spring, Mo., has some photographs of Holy Roller nudists. A woman said that these people were *naked as a jaybird's ass in whistling time*. [E. T. Wallace, in *Barington*, 1945, p. 198, has "naked-assed as new jaybirds." Any blushworthy action or thing is said to be *a shame to the red-assed jaybirds*, owing to the bird's tail-flirting gesture.]

7

A very common expression, in the Ozarks, is *ragged as a buzzard's ass*. In some sections one seldom hears a person described as ragged, without some reference to buzzards. In polite conversation, instead of saying simply ragged, one says *ragged as a buzzard*, and several times I have heard *ragged as a buzzard's tail*. ["*Raggedy-assed,*" is ill-clothed or slovenly.]

8

Thin as piss on a plate, weak as skimmed piss, weak as strained piss, weak as cat piss, and *poor as piss in a pumpkin* are all common figures. But any concentrated solution, like strong lye or black coffee, may be described as *strong as Kentucky horse piss.* [Brown, *North Carolina Folklore*, 1952. vol. I: p. 463, reports "as weak as puppy-water." In a Negro comedy-recitation from Texas, 1949, a *macho* cowboy in a barroom orders: "Bartender, gimme a drink—*strong as mule-piss, with the foam farted off!*"]

9

Stiff as a young man's pecker is natural enough, and so is *stiff as a bride's present.* And *limber as an old man's plaything* is understandable, too. *Slick as a soap-maker's prick,* and *smooth as an otter's pecker* are not uncommon. *Clean as a coon's prick* is heard everywhere; one of the Ozark novelists has turned it into "clean as a coon's pretty thing." [Referring to a raccoon.—Stone, *Devil Take a Whittler*, 1948, p. 167. Brown *North Carolina Folklore*, 1952, vol. I: p. 478, has "as slick as a soap-maker's ass." In a letter to the editor in 1957, Randolph referred to problems of publishing his "unprintable" materials as being *stiff as Rasputin's pecker,* evidently a late 1910s locution.]

10

Black as Coaley's ass is often heard, Coaley being an old name for the Devil. *Yellow as baby shit, pink as a spanked baby's ass, brown as a gander's ass-hole, red as a bear's ass in mulberry time,* and *green as goose shit* are well known. *Blue as a possum's cod* sounds a bit strange to city folk, but a possum's scrotum *is* blue, believe it or not. A variety of little bluish apples, buried in the ground to last the winter, are regularly called *possum-cods.*

Brown, *North Carolina Folklore*, 1952, vol. I: pp. 366 and 416, has "red as a bear's ass in pokeberry time," and "red as a goose's ass in mulberry time." A white woman, about forty-five, from South Carolina, 1949, used the phrase "as cute as the pecker on a baby boog," the last word being an abbreviation of *booger*, a devil or imp, and by extension a Negro.)

11

A young man in Pineville, Mo., wore better clothes than the rest of us, and was inclined to put on airs. "That boy *ain't got a pot to piss in, nor a window to throw it out* [or: *through*]," said one of my neighbors, "but he acts *proud as a half-wit with two peckers.*" [Or *as a hunchback whore with three tits.*]

It is a tenet of folk-belief that nature always strikes an equilibrium, or "tempers the wind to the shorn lamb." Accordingly, idiots are believed to have longer penises or "baubles" than anyone else—"caused" by presumed excessive masturbation—whereas large-muscled athletes are supposed to have small penises and no brains at all: "all balls and no brains," modified to "a strong back and a weak mind," stated to be the secret of success in the army, etc. Also given as an army proverb dating from World War I: "Keep your mouth shut, and your bowels open, *and don't volunteer!*"

12

A metaphoric figure like *bright as a sunflower on a pile of shit* is plain enough, and so is *rich as water up* [or *six feet up*] *a bull's ass*. But how about the common expression *cheerful as a basket of cat-shit* [by antiphrasis or irony]? Or, *pretty as a speckled pecker in the barn.* [Compare, in note 10, above: *as cute as the pecker on a baby boog*. In the most famous traditional insult in American political invective, Daniel Webster is supposed to have said of Aaron Burr: "Like a rotten mackerel by moonlight, my opponent shines—*AND STINKS!*"]

13

A poker-player at Pineville, Mo., raised twice under the impression that he had a diamond flush, and then discovered that one of his cards was a heart. "Gentlemen," he said later, "the sweat broke out on me *big as horse-turds!*" One sometimes hears people speak of tears *as big as horse-turds*. And I remember a woman from Oklahoma who was said to wear *diamonds as big as horse-turds* in her earrings. [A Negro musician in Paris in 1927 said he learned the words of "Frankie and Johnny" from "the original Frankie" on a western train about 1908, "wearing diamonds as big as hoss-turds."]

14

Serious as a dog shitting in the road means very serious indeed. One must watch a solemn-looking hound attending to this business, in order to appreciate this figure.

15

Watching a circus acrobat, a backwoodsman was all admiration. "That feller is *nimble as a whore at a fucking-match*," he said.

16

Of a city man who seemed interested in nothing but women, a villager remarked, "His mind is just *as high as a country girl's twat*, and not a inch higher!"

17

Here are some more common [comparative] expressions: *Sour as owl-shit, dry as a cornbread fart, puckered as a hen's ass, puckered as a robin's ass, round as a schoolmarm's butt, tight as Polly's drawers, close as a miner's whickerbill, flat as a cow-turd, hollow as a mare's ass, long* [or *sweet*] *as a whore's dream, cute as a striped-assed groundhog,* and *easy as pissing in a well.*

Whickerbill means prepuce, foreskin; see Randolph and Wilson *Down in the Holler,* (1953) p. 298. The inclusion of this term was one of the main complaints against the book by old-fashioned Ozarkers. In a private bawdy "party record" by Robert Benchley, about 1945, the bathetic conclusion to a long and lachrymose shaggy-dog story being told by an alcoholic old prostitute comes when Little Eva, in *Uncle Tom's Cabin,* being hoisted to Heaven onstage, breaks the rope and "falls *flatter than a turd from a tall cow's ass,*" Compare No. 19.

18

One also hears *scared as a whore in church, loud as* [*two*] *skeletons fucking on a tin roof, noisy as cats a-fucking, mad as a bear with a sore cock, useless as a cut dog at a fucking-match* [or *as tits on a bull*], *helpless as a one-legged man at an ass-kicking* [*contest*], *straight as an Indian going to shit, full of lies as a mule is of piss* [or *farts*], and *quick as a cat can lick its ass.*

The southern dramatist, Tennessee Williams, entitled one of his best plays, made into a successful motion-picture, 1959, *Cat on a Hot Tin Roof,* an allusion to, and combination of the phrases about skeletons and cats, as above. When I asked about this title in 1964, Williams said, "I like to tweak the censor's ear." Other titles punning on erotic phrases—sometimes unconsciously?—usually involve the words "cat" or "pussy," as being the easiest to pass off as innocent. Compare also, elsewhere in this collection, the folk game of inventing mock book-titles on the bawdy style of *The Virgin's Ecstasy,* by "R. U. Cumming," or "Poppet Upper."

19

At the end of a long drought, a gentleman in Carroll County, Ark., cried out "Ain't that rain wonderful? It sounds *like an old cow pissing on a flat rock!*" (Compare Note 17, above.)

20

An old resident of Eureka Springs, Ark., was always bragging up the past glories of his home town. "You boys ain't seen nothing," said he. "Why, I can remember when we had fine big whore-houses all over town, just like Kansas City!"

21

In Forsyth, Mo., there was a thin, fragile-looking [girl] who moved around *like she had caught a fly in her ass, by the wing!* The same girl, according to one commentator, looked *like a lily on a pile of shit.* Another lady, it was said, "puts me in mind of *a Friday fart going to market on Saturday.*" A nervous little merchant always behaved *like he had a boil on his ass.* And a buxom country girl acted *like she'd been fucked with a fence rail.*

22

A man in Carroll County, Ark., complained that his son was a spendthrift. "Money runs through that boy's fingers *like shit through a tin horn*," he said. [Or *through a goose.*]

23

Referring to some detail of village politics, Uncle Jack Short, Galena, Mo., observed morosely that "them Campbellites stick together *like summer hog-turds in a grass pasture.*" Such turds do stick together, when swine are feeding on grass. I've seen rows of little ones strung like beads, on a blade of grass nearly a foot long.

24

Any stout woman is built *like a brick shit-house*, and really does loom up *like a shit-house in a fog.* At Granby, Mo., the boys said of a very fat girl "Whenever Gertrude runs, her ass *looks like two big babies a-rassling* [*under a blanket*]*.

25

A big plane made an emergency landing near our village, and we all walked out to see it. The thing was made of some white metal, like aluminum. Describing this later, one of my neighbors said "It was *a-shining like a country girl's ass in the moonlight.*" [Or *like a shit-house in a fog.* Compare note on 12.]

26

Uncle Jack Short, of Galena, Mo., was in poor health. Asked how he felt, Uncle Jack answered "Like a wildcat." Later on he added "I didn't say all of it." This is a reference to a local character who delivered himself of the immortal statement "I feel *like a wildcat without no ass-hole.*" Elsewhere I have heard it as a riddle: "What makes the wildcat wild?—Why, it's because he ain't got no ass-hole."

This forms part—often the climax—of a favorite, usually bawdy folk-recitation, "The Hamburg Show," or "Van Amberg's Show," also known as "Larry, Turn the Crank!" from its refrain, and dating from the 1870s, in which: *"An 'ere, Ladies 'n' Genumun, we 'ave the Tasmanian Wildcat or Gyrascutus, who eats like a pig all day long and has only this teentsy-weentsy li'l ass-hole, or none at all.—That's what makes 'im so wild!—Larry, turn the crank!"* The last line meaning that this is only a stereopticon show, and not a real menagerie. Sometimes this animal is *"the Shaggy-Assed Hyena, who scorfs it up 364 days in a row, and can only shit once a year.—Do stand back there, little boy; today is the day!—Larry, get the shovel and dig 'im out!"*

27

A man in Protem, Mo., had a prodigious hangover. "My eyes feel *like two galded ass-holes*," he told me. [*Galded*, galled.] Of another fellow it was said "His eyes look *like two piss-holes in the snow.*"

Describing a nervous little man's aimless activity, a woman said "Jim's always in and out, *like a dog piss-ing in the snow*." A ragged, sheepish boy seemed always ill at ease; a neighbor said of him "Tommy looks *like they'd kicked him out of hell for pissing on the fire*." Woodard, in *Publications of the American Dialect Society*, *PADS*, 1946, vol. VI: p. 39, gives "kicked out of hell for sleeping in the ashes."

28

One of my neighbors owned a nice lot on the highway near Aurora, Mo., and somebody asked if he planned to build a filling-station. "No," said he. "Filling-stations *is like ass-holes*, everybody's got one nowadays."

29

If anything seems incongruous, or ill-timed, the hillman says "It's out of place, *like a woodscolt in the family*," or "out of place, *like a pig-turd in the hash*." (A *wood's-colt* means a bastard child, from the presumably "unhallowed" love-making of the parents out-of-doors or at night. This is an extension of the same term originally referring to the colt of a brood-mare who has run off into the woods and been "covered" by an unknown stallion. See the end-note to the preface here, on Thames Williamson's fine Ozark novel of that title. Compare also the ancient idea of the *nightmare*, or ephialtes, as the cause of bad dreams. As to the *out-of-place pig turd in the hash*, compare the modified "food-dirtying" of the mock-Irish song, "Who Threw the Overhauls in Mrs. Murphy's Chowder?")

30

A foolish boy was said to be "*grinning like a possum eating shit*." I have also heard "he had a grin on his face *like a wave in a piss-pot*." [In a famous anecdote, an American Indian inscription about Theodore Roosevelt refers to him "*grinning like a fox*, or *hyena eating shit out of a wire brush*." This really describes more aptly Roosevelt's man's-man *macho* imitator, the novelist Ernest Hemingway.]

31

A country girl in our neighborhood was pretty willing, but inept. "That girl goes at fucking *like she was a-grabbling 'taters*," was one boy's comment. To *grabble 'taters* is to remove small potatoes from the hill without uprooting the plant. One must see a grabbler at work in order to appreciate this figure

32

A young widow seemed a bit coquettish, and it was said that she "keeps a-wiggling *like a mouse had crawled up her twitchet*." [This is the plot of the old song, "Jackie and Mossy," in section A, above, No. 78.]

33

An enthusiastic hunter was delighted with a new rifle; he spent hours cleaning and polishing it. "Jim acts *like a girl playing with her first pecker*," remarked a neighbor. [*Compare: "As happy as an old maid with a twenty-inch candle, or: with a skyrocket!"*]

34

One often hears "sizzling *like piss on a hot stove*," or "steaming *like a fresh turd on a frosty morning*," or "bouncing around *like a fart on a hot skillet* [or *in a wet blanket*]."

35

Of a man who flew into a rage it was said "Jim got so mad, he was shaking *like a dog shitting persimmon-seeds*." The expression "*like a dog shitting peach-seeds*" is also common. Another fellow was so overcome by ire that he "pissed backwards *like a sow pig*."

36

In Pineville, Mo., I was buying some asparagus at the store. "Don't never eat that stuff," an old man said earnestly. "I et a bait of sparrowgrass once, and I shit *like a goose* for seven days!" ["Bait," also "bate," an amount, a serving. Asparagus is also believed to make the subsequent urine markedly "odoriferous."]

37

A woman accused a man of raping her right in the middle of an Arkansas town, with crowds all about. "Why didn't you yell?" asked the sheriff. The woman swore that she did yell, but nobody heard her. "She yelled about *like a rabbit*," muttered an officer who took no stock in the rape story. [Accusations of rape are in general disbelieved unless the woman bears evident marks of violence. Compare No. 184 below.]

38

A girl in Crane, Mo., seemed a bit promiscuous. "If every prick that's been stuck in Lizzie was a-sticking out, she'd *look like a porcupine*," said an old woman. "What men see in that slut I don't know. Why, her *cunt is so big, you could* stand clear across the road and *throw a boot in it!*"

39

An old man kept staring at a country girl on the high seat of a wagon, peering up under her skirt. Finally she pulled up her dress and spread her legs apart. "Didn't you ever see one before?" she shouted derisively. [Line missing here: "You came out of one of those," the girl added.] "Yes," answered the old man, "but that's the first one I ever seen that looked *like I could get back into it!*"

40

At a dance in Stone county, Mo., two village girls were talking about a drunken woman's immodest behavior. "She set there with her knees wide apart," said one, "and her old snatch was a-blaring open *like a cipher's eye*."

41

"When I first knowed you," an old man said to his wife, "your pussy was just *like a peach with a little fuzz on it*. But now it looks *like a pile of shit the wagon-wheel has run through*." [This is a standard ugly anti-gallant line appearing in Ozark jokes.]

42

Old John Ball, Eureka Springs, Ark., was telling about a woman caught in a sudden wind; her dress blowed up, and she didn't have no drawers on, so he seen everything she had. "Did it look nice, John?" somebody asked. "No," he answered, "it looked *like a dead pig's eye*." [Per contra, an eleven-year-old boy who admitted to the older boys that he had to bathe his little sister, and being asked what her cunt looked like, said that "it looked *like a little bread-roll with a dent poked in it*." Scranton, Pennsylvania 1928.]

43

Of a youth with a very large penis, the boys at Granby, Mo., used to say "He's got a cock on him *like a Kansas City sausage*." These long-peckered boys are called *bank-walkers*, because they strut around the swimming-hole while the rest of us conceal our inferior equipment in the water. [Personal remark probably intended sardonically: Randolph was a very tall, powerfully built man of large frame.]

44

I have heard a few bawdy maxims or proverbs, such as *A long prick is easy burnt*; *Every piddle makes a puddle*, *Every dog licks his own ass*; *Short and thick does the trick* [or *like a Welshman's prick*]; and *Faint heart gets little cock*.

45

One of my neighbors listened to a long tirade from his wife, and then remarked "Every dog has his day, and *a bitch for Saturday night*." The same man ended another argument with "*Talk's cheap, but manure costs money*." An old fellow at Noel, Mo., twitted about his age and decrepitude, said "*Alive and limber is better than dead and stiff*." [Brown, *North Carolina Folklore*, 1952, vol. I: p. 397, prints the absurdly edulcorated "Every dog has his day, *and the bitch her evenings*." A common French "*Lapalissade*," or absurdly trite remark, observes that "it's better to be rich and healthy than sick and poor."]

46

A girl near Pineville, Mo., aroused the whole neighborhood, demanding loudly that her lover marry her at once. "Betty wants to get married," said a farmhand, "but she ain't even knocked up yet. That's what I call *putting the cart before the horse!*" [Compare the European peasant demand for premarital pregnancy to prove that the girl is not sterile.]

47

Accused of violating the game law, a man at Hollister, Mo., said "*Kettle can't say black-ass to pot,*" meaning that his accuser also had killed deer out of season. [This is also an old Spanish proverb, on "*cula di negra.*" As used in English nowadays, it is expurgated by omitting *ass:* "The pot *calls the kettle black.*" See another example of this method of disguise in note 48 following.]

48

Asked his opinion about a woman's hat, an old man answered "*Neat but not gaudy, as the Indian girl said when she painted her ass blue.*" Another common saying is "*Every little bit helps, as the old woman said when she pissed in the ocean.*" A man at Neosho, Mo., remarked "*Fire follers frost, as the Devil said when he shit on the ice.*" One hears also "*Each to his own taste, as the fellow said when he kissed the cow's ass.*"

These are a formulaic type of folk-wit usually called "Wellerisms," after Sam Weller in Dickens' *Pickwick Papers,* (1836) who uses them often. The best list is in Vincent Lean's *Collectanea,* (1904). In the older European forms, "Neat but not gaudy" is said by *the Devil, when he painted his "tail" pea-green.* And "Every little bit helps," by "*the old lady when she pisht in the sea.*" On "Fire follows frost," see Brown, *North Carolina Folklore,* 1952, vol. I: p. 408. "Each to his own taste" is often expurgated by the same method, of dropping the crucial word, as seen in note 47 preceding. Thus, also: "*. . . as the old lady said when she kissed her cow.*"

49

"*Sure as shit stinks,*" and "*sure as there's shit in a cat*" are mild oaths. So is "*sure as the Devil fucked Eve in the cool of the evening.*" [Alluding to the old Midrashic legend that the Devil taught Eve the art of intercourse, while his wife Lilith taught Adam: the first "mate-swap."]

50

A miser in Carroll County, Ark., was nicknamed *Snug* because he was so tight. "If a flax-seed ever gets in Snug's ass, it'll be Katy-bar-the door!" said a village loafer. Another man spoke to the same effect. "You can't get a nickel out of Snug, no matter what happens. Might as well try to get a fart out of a dead nigger." [This ends more commonly: "*. . . out of a dead donkey's ass.*" The meaning of the catch-phrase, "Katy-bar-the-door" has not been traced. In Rabelais' *Pantagruel,* Bk. V, 1562, chap. 22, in an extended list of old proverbs being defied by Queen Whim's arsy-varsy officers: "I saw a *spodizator,* who very artifically *got farts out of a dead ass,* and sold them for five pence an ell."—Le Motteux translation, 1694.]

51

A storekeeper in Stone County, Mo., was inclined to be penurious—*tight-assed,* in the local phrase. "He was *so stingy you couldn't drive a flaxseed up his ass with a maul,*" or "*so close that it would take a team of mules to pull a fiddle-string through his ass,*" according to the villagers. Of this same man, a woman told me "Charley sure is tight. Every time he shits, he shakes his fist at the turd." When I asked why Charley did that, the lady said: "Oh, he's mad because it looks like he's [been] done out of something."

52

A fellow at Pineville, Mo., stood more than six feet tall, *so high he could piss over a five-rail fence.* A very short man is *knee-high to a duck's ass,* or *pecker-deep on a gosling.* He could *kiss a tumble-turd's ass without bending his knees.* He was *so low he seen a snake's ass-hole, and thought it was the North Star.* Another comment was that "Tommy's *ass is so close to his mouth, you can smell shit on his breath, and his guts don't know which way to move.*" [Of a very short person it's also been said: *They built the sidewalks too close to his ass.*]

53

A girl in Greene County, Mo., had an impediment in her speech, but was very popular with the boys. "She stuttered so bad, is what done it," I was told. "By the time she could say 'Stop!' the fellow is done fucking and buttoned up his pants!" [Compare the elegant joke heard in Dunfermline, Scotland, 1959, about: *The English girl tourist visiting Paris, whose horse bolts and runs away with her in the Bois de Boulogne because she doesn't know the French word for "Whoa!"* This was specifically told as alluding to tourist girls warding off would-be male seducers, and the horse-symbolism as the uncontrollable sexual *id* is very striking here.]

54

"I'm so goddam hungry," said a boy near Pineville, Mo., "that *I could eat the ass off'n a skunk.*" Another common saying is "I'm so *hungry, my ass-hole* ["*stomach*"] *thinks my throat's cut.*" [Also: "so hungry I could *eat a bear raw,*" or "*eat the ass off a bear—without salt!*"]

55

One of my neighbors was a very poor poker player, but had a phenomenal run of luck that discomfited the local gamblers. "If a man is so lucky as that," a villager said, "*shit will do for brains.*"

Also: "*He's so lucky you could throw him in a shit-house and he'll come up with a goldmine.*" This is used as the plot of many modified folktales, such as the six-thousand-times-told lecture "*Acres of Diamonds*" by the Reverend Russell Conwell, alluding to the discovery of oil in Titusville, Pennsylvania, on the proceeds of which lecture Temple University was said to have been founded. As to shit-and-brains, or "*more crust than brains,*" the medical publisher, Henry Schuman, a gifted raconteur, observed concerning commercial writers turning crime headlines into best-sellers: *"Those fellows just have a fistful of clever snot where they ought to have their brains."* New York, 1951.

56

"So tired my ass is dragging out my tracks," is often heard. A woman at Galena, Mo., told a neighbor: "I'm so tired, *I wouldn't walk ten feet to see a piss-ant fuck a elephant!"*

57

Speaking of the severe winters of his youth, an old-timer said "The snow was so goddam deep, *we had to stand up to shit."* A man from Yell County, Ark., remembered a snow so deep that "it was *ass-high on a nine-foot Indian."*

58

At Granby, Mo., they were talking about a young man who was *cunt-struck*, interested in nothing but running after women. "Freddy is so crazy about the girls," said a loafer, "that whenever he finds where one has took a piss, he sets down to making mud pies." [On the widespread belief that the insane dabble in mud, shit, etc., as in Nos. 71 and 72, below. But compare the urination of mammalian females to excite the males, as discussed in note on dance-call No. 31, in section D preceding.]

59

A villager in Forsyth, Mo., was making wild threats against one of the county officers. "I'll kick that son-of-a-bitch so high," he shouted, "that the *bluebirds will nest in his ass before he comes down!"*

60

Asked whether a local merchant was honest, my neighbor answered "He's *so crooked you could run a corkscrew up his ass and never bust a gut."*

61

Of a man who had concluded a profitable business deal it was said "That fellow is *so lucky he could fall in a barrel of shit, and come out smelling like roses!"* [Compare Note 55, above.]

62

The new schoolmarm at Pineville, Mo., had a pretty face, but she was *wasp-assed,* with no buttocks worth mentioning. Most of the loafers leered at her anyhow, but one fellow thought she was too skinny. "I don't like a *narry-hipped woman,*" said he. "That gal's ass is so sharp she could shit in a beer-bottle!" [Compare: "The Narry-Assted Men," Rhyme No. 56.]

63

The only daughter of our local rich man was pretty skinny, but she had better clothes than any other girl in the village. A poor man's wife, fingering one of the girl's expensive dresses, shook her head. "Fine lace, but *no ass to hang it on,*" she said. [Compare eighteenth-century French witticism, of a small man with a long penis: "Yes, but *where's the ass to drive it?*" Said of impractical plans.]

64

A moonshiner near Jane, Mo., turned out a batch of very inferior whiskey, and the boys kidded him about it for a long time. "My brother took two drinks," said a loafer. "The stuff was so sour it give him the flux, and *so hot he had to shit in the river to keep from setting the woods afire.*"

65

"Them boys on Bull Creek is so tough, they have to *take a wrench and loosen their nuts at night, before they can go to sleep,*" said a peace officer in Taney County, Mo. [Said of General George Patton, in World II. Compare note 123, below.]

66

When the oil boom struck Oklahoma, many Osages suddenly came into large sums of money. "Them Indians is so rich," a solemn fellow told me, "that *they're a-making piss-pots out of solid gold!*" [A personal testimony: at a rich home in La Jolla, California, in 1964, the editor was shown to a bathroom in which the toilet-seat was of 24-carat gold plate.]

67

A man near Day, Mo., was telling about the primitive conditions in the backwoods, before the coming of highways and automobiles. "My folks lived so far back in the timber [or: *boondocks*]," said he, "that *we had to wipe the owl-shit off'n the clock, to see what time it was.*"

68

In Eureka Springs, Ark., an old-timer said: "We was so piss-ant poor in them days, that some winters *we had to fuck our own wives!*" This was a slighting reference to the sex habits of newcomers and tourists. [Burlesque show joke, New York, 1939: "You sending your wife to Florida this year?—No, I think I'll screw her myself."]

69

A young man fell in love with a grass-widow, and his friends said "Bob is so crazy about that woman, *he thinks her shit don't stink.*" [Compare of a proud, "stuck-up" girl: "*She thinks her ass is ice-cream, and everybody wants a bite.*" Also the male's masochistic acceptance: "*I'd eat a yard of her shit for a lick at her hole.*" Sometimes modified politely to "*a look . . .*" To "eat someone's shit" means to toady to them, or put up with their nonsense.]

70

One of our friends had been cheated out of his farm, and a neighbor said: "Poor Tom sure got *the shitty end of the stick.*"

71

A woman had a long series of troubles, and finally cried out, "If things go on this-a-way, I'll be *shitting on the floor and playing in it!*" A fellow at Reeds Spring, Mo., complained of his constipation. "If I don't shit pretty soon," he told a physician, "I'll *take a stick and play in it,*" meaning that he would lose his mind. There is a wide-spread notion that insane persons spend hours playing with their own dung. [See note on 58. There is also a wide-spread notion that constipation or the retaining of farts will "go to the brain" and cause insanity. This idea is very ancient.]

72

An old lady in Yell County, Ark., was denouncing some worthless farm-hands. "If I didn't have nothing better than *that* to do," she cried, "I'd *piss in the sand and get me a stick to stir it!*"

73

Of a man who is "well hung" it is said "he sure has got a fine *soup-bone* hanging on him." The term *peavy bone* or *peevish bone* is heard occasionally. Other common names for the male organ are *cob, cock, dick, dinger, dink, dood, doodle, ducey, family organ* [or *family jewels*], *goober, gun, hammer, hammer-handle, hoe-handle, horn, jemsen* or *jemmison, jock, john, jong, okra, pecker, peter, pintle, pood, poodle, poodle-dink, prick, rhubarb, robin, stalk, tackey, tail, tally-whacker, thing, tickler, tilly-whacker, tool,* and *ying-yang.*

Ying-yang is used in Weldon Stone's Ozark novel, *Devil Take a Whittler*, 1948, p. 9. Isabel France, in the *Arkansas Gazette*, May 24, 1953, says that *priest's pintle* is "an old folk name" for Jack-in-the-pulpit. The reference to the sexuality of priests alludes to sex orgies as part of "Devil worship." There are extensive lists of slang and colloquial synonyms for the penis in Farmer and Henley's *Slang and Its Analogues*, (1890–1909) at "cream-stick" and "prick"—with matching synonymies at "cunt" and "monosyllable," also verbs at "greens" and "ride"—and for prostitute at "barrack-hack" and "whore." See more modern synonyms in John Trimble-Blake's *5,000 Adult Sex Words and Phrases* (Hollywood, 1964–1966) giving about 150 synonyms, at "penis," and other similar synonymies throughout.

74

The common names for the testes are *balls, ballocks, berries, jingle-berries, knockers, nuts, seeds, stones,* and *weights.* Sharpening his knife to castrate a hog, my neighbor said "I'm fixing to take the *weights* off'n him." Soon as the job was done, the animal walked away grunting "*Ruint! Ruint! Ruint!*" A boy at Pineville, Mo., was threatening one of his schoolmates. "If you monkey with me," he shouted, "it'll be your old *tomatoes!*" [There are twenty-two modern synonyms in Trimble-Blake, at "testicles."]

75

The scrotum is called the *bag, cod,* or *craw.* Sometimes *cod* means the scrotum and testicles together, but I have never heard an Ozarker use *cod* to mean penis. When the hillman refers to the male genitals in general, he says *the prides,* or *the privates.*

76

The female sex organ is generally called the *bird's nest, box, cock, concern, cuckoo's nest, cunt, flue, fork, grabber, hog-eye, koosy, koozy, monkey, moosey, muff, nest, pussy, quiff, red onion, road, satchel, snatch, tail, thing, twat,* or *twitchet.* In Weldon Stone's novel about the Ozarks, *Devil Take a Whittler*, p. 167, a woman is invited to come close to the fire and *warm her twitchet,* to which she replies that it's warm enough already. ["*Moosey*" from the German *Möse,* adapted in English as "*mouse,*" as in the "bodice-ripper," or women's "soft-porn" adventure novel, *Duchess Hotspur,* about 1946.]

77

The term *hair poultice* also has reference to the female genitals. There is an old tale about a boy with a perpetual erection who went to a drugstore for treatment. The druggist wasn't in, but his pretty wife examined the patient's organ. "That thing needs a hair poultice," she said. So she took the boy into a back room and locked the door.

78

Fur collar is another term for the female pudendum. A girl near Pineville, Mo., had an affair with a tourist from Illinois. When the tourist left, the girl was both pregnant and diseased. "Molly hung her fur collar on the wrong peg," remarked one of my neighbors. [Used in the 1917 Carrington joke collection, *Some Yarns*. The girl's misfortune is called *the double event,* originally a British sporting term; or *a full house,* from the game of poker.]

79

Of a woman with ovarian trouble it was said "Her *ovals* just riz and busted," meaning that her ovaries swelled up and burst.

80

Another country woman told her physician "My *woon* has fell, Doc. It comes right out into the world, every time I go to the privy." [Third degree *prolapsus uterus*. The word *womb,* usual pronunciation "woom," is also sometimes pronounced "wom" by British and Scottish rustic populations, construed by them as the older *wame,* belly.]

81

The dialect name for the clitoris is *fud-tit*. An aggressive woman with a passion for her own sex is called a *bull-dagger;* the term is sometimes pronounced *bull-diger* to rhyme with tiger. A man in the Veterans Hospital at Fayetteville, Ark., told me a long story about how his wife had deserted him. "It was a red-headed woman tolled her off," said he. "A *bull-dagger* with a big *fud-tit* can take a woman away from any man." Two women indulging in any sort of homosexual practice are said to be *bull-dagging*. The verb *ham* is used in this connection, too. In Stone County, Mo., there was a great scandal when a highschool principal caught his pet schoolmarm *a-hamming it* with a big stout country girl.

The clitoris has the fewest slang, or even any old colloquial synonyms of any part of the sexual anatomy: *bell, button, buzzer, bump, bean, bud, lovebud,* and *rosebud*—as in Welles and Mankiewicz's *Citizen Kane* motion picture, 1940—also *it, clit, clitty, dot, spot,* and the originally Negro *boy in the boat*. Observe, in Randolph's Stone County anecdote here, the two women's use of X-legged vulvar apposition, anciently called *tribady,* and not the mutual masturbation or cunnilinctus thought of as the usual lesbian practice. The folk belief that an aggressive "butch" lesbian necessarily has an enlarged clitoris is quite false.

The word *bull-dagger* is linguistically one of the most interesting in the English vocabulary, since almost all its intermediate forms exist concurrently: *hermaphrodite, morphodite, morphodike; dike, diker, dagger;* plus "bull" as strong, large, or male indicative, giving *bull-dike, bull-diker,* or *-diger, bull-dagger,* and even *boon-dagger,* reported in Robert Goldenson's recent *Sex: A to Z,* (1986).

82

Sexual acts between men and animals are not uncommon; country boys are often found a-fucking calves, mares, sheep, goats and other creatures. But homosexual doings between males are rare, and pederasty is almost unknown in some sections of the backwoods. I remember a great hullaballoo in one settlement, where a young man fled the country to avoid prosecution. "The son-of-a-bitch tried to corn-hole Bert," I was told. "*Corn-hole?* What do you mean?" I asked. "Why, he wanted to fuck Bert in the ass!"

said my informant. [Etymology unknown, possibly from some rustic anecdote or farming detail. Often *corn-haul,* an expurgation?]

83

Menstruation is designated by such terms as *bundled up, courses, the curse, grannies, grandma, grandma's visit, ill, in the flowers, monthlies, moon, moon flowers, moon in the ass, old woman, off the roof, pussy's in the hammock, tied up, unwell, wearing a rag, wearing a granny-rag.* ["To have the flowers," originally French.]

84

Here are some of the common words [verbs] for copulate: *bed, bother, come, coot, correspond, cover, cram, crawl, diddle, doodle, frig* [or *frick*], *fuck, get a piece* [of cock, ass, or tail], *get some nooky, go off, hone, kife, knock off a chunk, knock off a piece, lay, line, mount, plow, pull gravel, plant your 'taters, put the blocks, put up coal, rake, ram, roger, shag, screw, sprunch* [or *spruncing*], *top, top off, tread, wing,* and *yense.*

Yentz is also used in "Pennsylvania Dutch" and Yiddish; also by extension meaning "to cheat," as with many other verbs for genital or anal intercourse. Like *coozy* or *cuzzy* for the vagina, of unknown etymology, *nooky* has perturbed amateur linguists considerably. Mr. Eric Partridge saves for it one of his most amateurish *klang*-etymologies, presumably "from getting into nooks and corners" to engage in it! In fact, it is the standard colloquial Dutch word, *neuken,* for sexual intercourse. Randolph's friend, Thomas Hart Benton, *An Artist in America,* (1937) p. 108, spells it "nucky."

85

A woman near Crane, Mo., found her husband in bed with another woman. "They was a-doing *the thing itself!*" she said, in telling of it later.

86

A very old lady was talking of outrages committed by bushwhackers during the *War Between the States.* They killed her brother, burned the house, stole all the provisions and livestock. "And then," she cried, "they had the nerve to ask me for *the real old thing!*"

87

A countryman with too many drinks under his belt "follered the music" and thus blundered uninvited into a private dance. He stood around for awhile, without disturbing anybody. But at the first intermission he raised his voice. "Well, folks," he shouted, "let's choose up sides and do a little diddling!" Most of the young folks laughed, but their respectable elders hustled the intruder out of the building. This happened more than twenty years ago, and the farmer is a deacon now, but he never lived down that scandalous proposal. Some of the villagers chuckle about it today, whenever the man's name is mentioned. [Note the implication of drunken orgies at dances by "choosing up sides." The same phrase and idea are expressed directly in a dance-call at a country "frolic."]

88

The word *poon-tang* is used in many parts of the South. Wentworth defines it as "copulation, especially between Negro and white." Boys in the Ozark towns used to speak of "getting a little *poon-tang*," when they meant "a little fucking" or "a piece of cock." These boys were not thinking of Negro girls. The term is related to the French *putain,* doubtless from the Latin *puta,* which means whore. See Thomas Wolfe's southern novel, *Look Homeward Angel,* in 1929, pages 166, 174, and 343.

89

In Yell County, Ark., about 1935, the boys used to talk about *poos-turd*—with the accent on the first syllable, which rhymes with *moose.* This word has the same meaning as *poon-tang.* It is definitely not restricted to intercourse between whites and Negroes. [Compare the similarly pronounced Dutch *poes,* cat, pussy. The "turd" element here does not refer to feces.]

90

A pregnant woman is *about to find pups, big, coming fresh, falling apart, falling to pieces, in a family way, ketched, knocked up, looking piggy, otherwise, poisoned, sewed up, springing, sprung, swelling, teeming, too big for her clothes, up and coming,* or *with squirrel.* It may be said that she has *let her foot slip, cut her foot, broke her leg, missed the bus, missed the train,* or *swallowed a melon seed.* [*Coming fresh* literally means "in milk," as any mammal.]

91

A woman at Noel, Mo., was furious at being mistaken for a girl who had *went wrong* and was *with squirrel* by a traveling salesman. "Well, I *ain't* her, not by an apron-full!" she cried. [Any reference to a woman wearing her apron "up" or "down," or "full," as here, or *not being able to tie her apron strings,* is a traditional Scottish allusion to pregnancy, as in the famous song "Love, Oh Careless Love," by the pregnant and abandoned girl.]

92

If a man seems interested in nothing but woman-chasing he is described as *cagey, cock crazy, cunt-struck, fleshy, hard-peckered, horny, peach-orchard crazy, pruney, pussy simple, red-eyed, rollicky, satchel-crazy, twat-foolish,* or *twitchet-struck.* ["Rollicky" refers to the testicles or *bollocks,* as in the bawdy song "Bollocky Bill the Sailor."]

93

I asked an old gentleman at Galena, Mo., what sort of a fellow Buck Thurmond was. "Oh, just a big country boy, *all pecker and feet,*" was the reply. [Theatre slang, New York, 1937, for clumsiness onstage: *all pecker and hair;* or *stepping on your prick,* the implication being that one has a very long penis and is "therefore" probably an idiot, because "the weight of the thing *draws all the blood from your brain,* and you're liable to faint," or "if you get the hiccups sitting on the toilet, *it'll siphon up all the water in the bowl.*"]

94

A lascivious or sexually excited woman is *feisty, forkèd, hot, pecker-foolish, red in the comb, rimmy, rimming,* or *white-livered.* One may say "she's got *fire in her pants.*" The adjective *horny* usually applies to men (and deer), but sometimes one hears it used with reference to a wanton woman.

"Feisty," bold, *full of farts,* is now often pronounced "*foxy,*" *by analogy;* a handsome or passionate girl being back-formed into a "*fox,*" as in note 2 above: "*as hot as a fresh-fucked fox in a forest fire.*" William G. Hall, in an Ozark novel called *Turkey Knob Line,* (1954) p. 229, reports: "them girls got *fire in their drawers.*" A bitch-heroine novel in progress in 1947, on the Duchess of Essex scandal at the court of King James I, was to be entitled *Firetail.*

95

At Forsyth, Mo., I remarked that a certain girl "seemed mighty nice." The woman I was dancing with cried "Nice! She'd *drop her pants* in the cut of an eye!" Meaning promptly, I take it.

96

Lively young girls, inexperienced but passionate, are called *squirmies,* because they "keep a-squirming around so." A man once remarked to me "Them little squirmies can feel their twat without putting their hand on it!" [Compare German *Backfische,* comparable to U.S. *flappers* in the 1920s, and the more openly sexually available rock-musicians' *groupies* of the 1950s and since.]

97

A girl at a dance near Picher, Okla., got drunk and tore off most of her clothes, shouting "*I can kiss, kick, holler, fight, fart, squeal, and fuck!*" Referring to a local beauty, a young fellow at Pineville, Mo., said "She likes running, jumping, dancing, kissing, kicking, wrassling, *and* fucking!" Of another lively young girl it was said "She's awful good when it comes to fighting or dancing a jig, with fucking somewhere in between!"

Homosexual "camp" line—from the French *camper,* to strike theatrical attitudes—heard in New York, 1939: "I didn't know whether to *fish, fuck, faint, or fall over,*" of which "fish" refers to oral sexuality, and "fall over" to passive anality. The opening brag here, as to "Kiss, kick, etc.," also appears as the main final refrain, delivered *accelerando prestissimo,* of a bawdy song describing the ideal wife, "Mary-Ann, Queen of the Acrobats: She can run, jump, fight and fuck, shoot a pistol, drive a truck, and that's the kind of a son-of-a-bitch that's goin' to marry *ME!*" The classical contrasting or combining of "*fight and fuck*" is the frank understructure or inspiration of the world-famous hippie motto of the 1960s and since: *Make Love, Not War!* Compare the *Song of Songs,* in 450 B.C.: "Set me as a seal upon thine heart, as a seal upon thine arm; for *love is strong as death.*"

98

"That gal's been *a-laying betwixt the plow-handles,*" means that she has been fucking farm boys in the fields. It is literally true sometimes, though an awkward position for satisfactory intercourse. I have heard people say of a child, "That baby was got between the plow-handles." [In France, "between the rows of grapevines."]

99

A merchant at Protem, Mo., had a pretty wife who seemed to dominate him, even in the conduct of his business. "She's a-leading poor Lonnie *around by the prick,*" one of our neighbors said scornfully. [He is *pussy-whipped,* or in the old style "be-shrewed"; common in sado-masochistic marriages.]

100

A miner near Joplin, Mo., was very jealous. One evening his wife went out into the darkness, and was gone for ten minutes. "Where the hell have you been?" he demanded when she returned to the house. The woman answered indignantly that she had just stepped out to piss. The husband pulled her to him, and thrust his hand up under her skirt. "Can't fool me! It's too *slick* for piss!" he shouted. And the fight was on. [Same as a joke, on the viscosity of semen, with punchline: "You can't fool me, you bitch! *Piss don't make windows!*"]

101

A young man near Pineville, Mo., got married, and his friends were discussing it next day. "Well," said one, "poor Bill never did have nothing only two tree-dogs and a hard-on." Another fellow shook his head soberly." That's right," he said. "And now Bill ain't got nothing but two tree-dogs."

Also as an urban joke, during the 1930s Depression: *The ruined stock-market speculator had a yacht and a chorus-girl before the crash. After the crash he had a canoe, and a whore with a paper bag over her head—*so he won't see how ugly she is—*Now all he has is a rowboat and a hard-on.* The Ozark joke takes this on to the next step: the impotence of old age.

102

To say that a man has got the *mokus* [rhymes with focus] means that he is "*over-fucked and under-fed.*" It usually applies to men, rarely to women. At Eureka Springs, in 1947, a feeble old man said that he had the *mokus-ee* [accent on the last syllable], meaning that he was impotent. "I still have ideas sometimes, he said, "but I can't do no good." A fellow at Tahlequah, Okla., observed that "after a man has the *mokus* for a few years it develops into the *mokus-ee,* and that's the end of him."

Mogue or *moke,* Gypsy word for a fake or swindle. The American comedian W. C. Fields, a "barrel-fed alcoholic," would refer to "mokus of the ge-kokus" as an imaginary wasting disease, similar to a male deer thinning down in rutting time, when he has "pissed his tallow." This mock-sexual disease is also known as the "snee-witchums," apparently a Pennsylvania-Dutch reference to a Lilith-like "snow-witch." The American artist Mahlon Blaine, who was an old-time friend of Fields, said that he also or really called the disease "*mopery of the ge-kokery,*" and admitted that it referred to his own impotence caused by alcoholism. *Mopery* is usually an imaginary crime, punished at mock-trials or "Kangaroo Courts" by prisoners, as a jail-entertainment at the expense of newcomers, and is defined as "*Indecent exposure to a blind woman on a public highway—between the hours of sunset and sunrise, or during an eclipse of the sun.*" When?

103

Speaking of his waning virility, an elderly farmer at Walnut Shade, Mo., shook his head ruefully. "Every morning," said he, "I have to *poke a black stick up my ass and holler 'Snake!'*" Asked the purpose of this procedure, he answered "It's the only way I can get my pecker out far enough to keep from pissing down my leg."

104

An old man near Joplin, Mo., was accused of raping a young woman. He denied it indignantly, and his wife agreed with him for once. "How could *he* rape anybody?" she said scornfully. "Can you *push a string?*"

Catch-phrase sometimes elaborated into a joke about: *An old man who marries a young bride, and worriedly prepares an aphrodisiac for himself, hidden in his drink. The glasses get mixed, however. When asked later how the wedding-night went, the old man answers, "Have you ever tried pushing a pound of melted butter up a wildcat's ass with a wilted noodle?"* The "melted butter" refers of course to the semen.

105

Referring to old men's troubles, a fellow in Eureka Springs, Ark., sighed. "Well," said he, "there comes a time when it won't stay roostered." He meant that the penis might become erect, but it wouldn't remain so long enough to be of use. This is gun-fighter's talk. When the action of a firearm becomes worn, the hammer or *rooster* fails to catch, and the weapon won't stay cocked. Many old-timers removed the triggers from their six-shooters, or filed the lock so that the trigger ceased to function; they preferred to fire the pistol by snapping the hammer with the thumb.

"*Rooster,*" polite for *cock.* H. L. Mencken told the Chicago newspaper editor, Henry N. Cary, compiler of *The Slang of Venery,* in 1916, that he had lost his faith in religion at an early age when he heard a prudish minister substitute the word *rooster* in reading aloud the dramatic passage in the *Gospel According to St. Matthew,* 26:34 and 74, where the Apostle Peter denies Jesus for the third time: "Then began he to curse and swear, saying, I know not the man. *And immediately the cock crew.*"

106

An ugly old woman ran a boarding-house, and all the bachelors in town ate there. The food was bad, and the place was dirty, and there were many better places to eat in the vicinity. I asked a loafer why the boarding-house was so popular. "Betsy puts a *granny-rag* in the soup," said he, "and them old stags can smell it a mile off."

"Granny-rag," a menstrual cloth: a folk-testimony to the attraction of all male mammals to the genital odors of the female, as opposed to the notion that normal men fear or hate the vaginal or menstrual odor. See also Legman, *Rationale of the Dirty Joke* (1968) chapter "Cunnilinctus," pp. 581–82, a passage for which the editor found himself referred to by one indignant New York reviewer as a "well-known vampire."

107

There are many stories about the aphrodisiac qualities of Arkansas water. An old man in Carroll County said: "I drunk Magnetic Spring water *to draw my pecker out long.* Then I used radium Spring water to thicken it, and done pretty good. Now I'm a-drinking Basin Spring water for hardening and stiffening, but it don't work worth a damn."

108

The water at Hot Springs, Ark., is widely advertised as an aphrodisiac. When I visited the place in 1938, I was almost persuaded that there might be some merit in these claims. But when I returned ten years later, with a different lady, it became evident that the value of the Hot Springs water has been grossly exaggerated.

109

At Bentonville, Ark., according to a local legend, the townspeople had a fruit festival. In the street parade, a wagon full of pretty girls represented Peaches; other floats showed Cherries, Pippins, Winesaps, Jonathans, Ben Davis, and so on. There was one wagon containing Negroes with a sign Arkansas Blacks—the Arkansas Black is a very fine apple. At the end of the parade came a rattletrap buckboard full of drunken old men, who had joined the parade without consulting the program committee. They carried a large sign with the letters *LT.* Many of the tourists didn't know what it meant, but the apple-growers knew well enough, and the whole town rocked with laughter. The old men advertised a variety of apples called *Limber Twigs!*—For another version of this tale see Royal Rosamond, *Bound in This Clay* (1945) p. 23.

110

"Christmas don't mean nothing at our house," said a woman at Eureka Springs, Ark. "All I ever get is a *banana,* and I have to peel it myself."—Near Forsyth, Mo., a young matron complained: "Before we was married, Tom promised me a fine roasting-ear. But it ain't nothing but a *nubbin.* And I have to shuck it myself, at that!"

"Nubbin," an undersized ear of corn. In a matching sex-hate or disappointment story: *A man getting drunk in a barroom on Christmas Day refuses to go home when the bartender suggests that his wife will be waiting to give him his Christmas presents. "Naw," says the man, "all I ever get from her for Christmas is a pair of bedroom slippers and a piece of ass—both of 'em too big!"* Another bitter expression of marital disappointment or disharmony is given as a triad, or riddle: "What are *The Three Most Over-Rated Things in the World?—Home cooking, home fucking, and Los Angeles!*" Heard in a Lesbian barroom in San Diego, Calif., 1965.

111

Of a vivacious girl whose morals the neighborhood was beginning to question, an old woman said: "That gal's *a-fooling with the buttons on the Devil's britches.*" A related crack is "She's *got her hand on the Devil's pecker.*" Note the undisguised Diabolic reference.

112

Near Windy City, Mo., lived a very religious woman, who was somehow persuaded to attend a musical show in Kansas City. Later on she told some of her kinfolk about the perils of such an experience. "When them fiddlers begun to play," she said, "it seemed like I could just *feel* the Devil's fingers in my pants!"

This appears to draw from the very widespread idea that the violin is "the Devil's instrument," and that *string music* in general—even the guitar—will make women uncontrollably erotic, as at dance orgies connected with Diabolism. The great Russian novelist Tolstoy seriously states in his story, "The Kreutzer Sonata" that no virtuous woman can listen to Beethoven's violin-and-piano sonata of that name "without losing her virtue." This idea has been exploited to the hilt in a nineteenth-century Gypsy-violinist-and-lady-pianist painting used as a recent advertisement for *Tabu* perfume. Even Mozart's church Masses were objected to, as "too worldly," while formerly the ordinary key of *C* was frowned upon by church authorities as the *modus lascivus*. The *braying of a jackass* is also believed in some parts of the U.S. south to make a woman who hears it erotic. The jackass is the Devil's (Bacchus') favorite mount, and sometimes stands in for him erotically at the Black Mass.

113

City folk often regard the hillbilly as a guileless, credulous yokel, but nothing could be farther from the truth. Barring his blind acceptance of religious and supernatural notions, the Ozarker doesn't take anybody's word for anything. On the Missouri side, at least, his incredulity has become proverbial. The simple statement "I'm from Missouri" is recognized everywhere as a refusal to credit one's veracity, a demand for objective proof. "You'll have to show me!" cries a Missourian in one of the old stories. "Showing ain't enough," growls the hillman from Arkansas. "I got to *feel* of it!" [Sexual reference here is only implied. Compare the disturbing story of Doubting Thomas, in *Luke,* 24:39, and especially *John,* 20:24–29.]

114

A woman had just died in Neosho, Mo., and one of the neighbors remarked "I believe she was a *baked ass* all her life." The others nodded their agreement, but I had no idea what it meant. Later on I learned that a *baked ass* is a virgin. The expression was common in Newton and Barry counties, Mo., in the 1920s. [Compare the more recent sly high-cuisine reference in calling the French "*omelette Esquimau,*" or hot ice cream pie, a *baked Alaska,* which adds only the disguise of the extra syllables.]

115

Accused of a relationship with a notoriously promiscuous woman, a young man at West Plains, Mo., denied the charge. "Why," said he, "*I wouldn't touch that hussy with a borrowed* [or *with your*] *pecker.*" Another fellow, in a similar situation, was equally indignant. "Before I'd lay up with *her,*" he cried, "I'd bore me a *auger-hole in a tree, and line it with a meat rind!*"

Henry Miller in his autobiographical novel, *Tropic of Cancer,* published in Paris, 1934, has this as "*boring out the core of an apple and lining it with coldcream,*" obviously a citified variant. In eastern Pennsylvania, at the same period, it was considered the height of aggressive wit among adolescents, when a girl would allow "necking and petting" on a date, but would not "go all the way—or the limit"— for the rejected swain to observe bitterly, "Well, back to my *can of hot, buttered worms!*"

116

The act of masturbation, in the male, is called [jerking off] *jacking off, playing with himself, pulling his pud, pounding his meat,* or *lathering a bar of soap.* Trimble/Blake, at "Masturbation," reports a full fifty such American slang locutions. The nineteenth-century "take a whet," used only of boys or men, as in some of the private writings of Mark Twain and Eugene Field, seems to have disappeared with the once omnipresent pocket-knives literally referred to. Terms for masturbation by women have always been, and still are, rare.

117

Near Joplin, Mo., masturbation is often known as *loose-chucking;* this is a miners' term, meaning that the drill has caught, and is just working back and forth in its socket.

118

There is an old tale of the boy who *pounded his meat* without effect, till finally he cried out: "Smoke, run, or bleed! Damn' if I'm going to spit on you again!"

119

A boy who masturbates is said to be "*sparking old Mother Five-Fingers,*" or "laying up with *Mis' Thumb and her four daughters.*" [Apparently translates the French: "*la Veuve Poignet*—Old Widow Fist—*et ses quatre filles.*"]

120

A boy at Green Forest, Ark., remarked that old Dock Thompson had got his arm broke. "How did it happen?" a woman asked innocently. The boy laughed. "Dock was *trying to climb his prick, and the skin slipped,*" said he.

121

Pimples on the face of an adolescent boy are called *pud hickies* or *pood bumps,* as they are believed to be the result of excessive masturbation. [Or *not enough!* The *pud* or *pood* is the penis, seldom used except in the phrase, to *pull one's pud*, or *pudding,* meaning to masturbate. The pronunciation is indicated in the song "The Bastard King of England," who either "hunts the stag in the Royal wood, Or spent his time pulling the Royal pud."]

122

A man in Jasper County, Mo., was always known as *Woback* Spelvin, and many people thought Woback was his given name. But it was only a nickname. The old settlers said that when Judge Spelvin was a boy, they caught him out in the pasture trying to fuck a mare. He was standing on a stump, hollering "*Whoah-back!—Giddyup!—Whoa-back!*" So that's what they called him from then on. [Sometimes given as a joke on "The Laziest Man."]

123

There are numerous common nicknames applied to men, such as *Pewter-Prick, Jingle-Ballyx, Fartin-Britches, Fuddle-Britches, Red-Pecker,* and *Gilt-Balls.* I am not sure that these names have any particular meaning, but I set them down here for the record. [Also: *Telegraph Pole, Stinky-Pink, Fud-Pecker, Horsecock, Ironballs,* this last of a tough person, e.g. General George Patton, usually modified in news papers to "Tuffy-Pants." Compare note on 65, above.]

Obvious phallic allusions are very common, as here. Others refer to digestive accidents, such as farting habitually or, as *Funky-Butt,* to "shitting in one's pants." *Stinky-Pink* refers jealously to a boy who has evident success with girls—the "pinkie" is the little finger—and there were until World War II numerous nouns and nicknames of purported contempt for such boys: *sheik, porch-climber, lounge-lizard, crumpet-muncher*—now *quiche-eater:* no "he-man" does that—*greaser, grease-ball,* or *greasy-head,* from the hair pomade and slicked-down coiffure made popular by the movie actor Rudolph Valentino—*The Sheik*—in the 1920s; and most accusing of all: *tit-kisser!* These could be accepted jocularly, but the ultimate term of *macho* reproach, *cunt-lapper,* referring to a penchant for, or willingness to engage in cunnilinctus, was invariably "fightin' words" until the New Freedom following World War II, after which the term was applied, as an insult, and so also a (*hair-*) *pie eater,* only to a Lesbian.

124

A country girl who lived near us caught the eye of a rich man from Joplin, and he wanted to marry her. But the girl was not impressed by money or big automobiles. She would have nothing to do with the man, because of his dissolute past. "Why, that old feller ain't no good," she said. "Every whore in Jasper County has measured *his* pecker."

125

Backwoods girls use balls of woollen yarn, pieces of tallow, the leaves of various plants, small crab-apples, or even green butternuts as pessaries. "They're always a-sticking things up their cunt," as one man told me. A boy in Yell County, Ark., was complaining of the discomfiture an Indian girl had caused him. "She took and *put sand in her koozy,*" he said indignantly.

Vagina dentata revenge of the self-destructive "Tunic of Nessus" type; often told as a true anecdote of a girl being raped on a sandy beach, as here. Indian girl element probably owing to known cruelties and tortures of Indians. By "pessary" above, Randolph is referring to any intra-vaginal birth control device. An American early nineteenth-century physician referred contemptuously to women making "Chinese toy-shops" of their vaginas, after the Francis Place "Diabolical Handbills" had given working-class women their first birth-control advice by the 1830s, in the form of a small sponge dipped in vinegar or lemon-juice and worn pressed up against the mouth of the womb during intercourse. Actually such devices are ancient, for example, throughout the Middle East small round stones are inserted in a camel's uterus to cause continual abortion, exactly the unavowed purpose of the dangerous human intra-uterine devices today.

126

Warning his daughter against an amorous evangelist, my neighbor said, "Look out that preacher don't jump on your running-board." The girl laughed, and laughed again as she lifted her skirt to show a dagger stuck in the right garter. "If he does, God save his soul," she said, "because the Devil will have his ass already." [Various urban "anti-rape" devices and practices are used today. One confused young married woman in Wilkes-Barre, Pennsylvania, 1975, was found to be simultaneously studying judo and belly-dancing!]

127

In central Arkansas a farmer had built a very fine road. An engineer asked how he had made such a perfect curve without any surveying instruments. "Well, sir," said the farmer, "I done it *by the squat of my ass and the squint of my eye.*"

128

An old farmer near Van Buren, Ark., was threatening his wife with physical punishment. "I'll kick her *rear of the kappa focus,*" he shouted. I am not sure just what this means. But I wrote it down just as it sounded, for the record. [Compare note 102, above.]

129

Sam Leath, of Eureka Springs, Ark., used to make extravagant claims about the curative properties of water from one of the springs. "To hear Sam tell it," said a skeptical villager, "that water will *heal up a dog's ass and hair it over,* in twenty-four hours." [See the legend of Doubting Thomas, in *John,* 20:24–29.]

130

A man at Columbia, Mo., told me that his father used to say "Well, *your butt's the blackest"* when somebody had worsted him in a debate. He meant "Maybe you're right," or perhaps "your arguments are better than mine."

131

At a mining-camp near Joplin, Mo., a very dark Negro woman was a public charge, and several business men were trying to find her a job. "Let's set her to teaching school," said one. The others pointed out that the woman was a cook's helper, not a schoolmarm. "She'd be handy around a schoolhouse," the first speaker persisted, "because they could *use her ass for a blackboard*." [Anti-Negro "joke."]

132

A farmer just across the Oklahoma border had a sure remedy for constipation. "Just poke a piece of yellow cheese up your ass," said he, "and then swallow a live rat." [Also presented as a "Chinese torture."]

133

One Saturday at Eureka Springs, Ark., a troop of tall, long-legged country boys appeared. "They come from Grindstone Mountain," said a villager. "The boys up that way are all *split from their ass-hole to their back teeth*."

134

A tall man near Bentonville, Ark., was known as "High Pockets" because of his long legs. "They had to split that fellow a long ways," said a neighbor, "before they could find *a sound place to drill his ass-hole*."

135

Speaking of his dire poverty, a hillman said: "If turkeys was selling for ten cents apiece, *I couldn't afford to kiss a jaybird's ass!*" This man borrowed from all his friends and neighbors, but refused the federal relief to which he was clearly entitled. "I don't want no charity," said he. "I'd sooner *get me a tin bill and pick shit with the chickens.*" [The line about being so poor one *can't afford to kiss a jaybird's ass,* or similar, is used as the conclusion of a long mock "Debtor Letter" given by both Dundes and Pagter, vol. I: pp. 26–31; and Legman, *Bawdy Monologues,* pp. 83–86.]

136

An old woman in Yell County, Ark., denounced some lazy farm-hands. "If I couldn't beat what you're a-doing, I'd *stick my head in a holler log and let the bears eat my ass off!*" she cried.

137

To say that a man *has got a wild hair in his ass* means only that he's excited or distraught. But when one says "Bill's got a wild ass" the inference is that Bill is lazy, or at least disinclined to continuous labor. A teamster at Day, Mo., insisted on having a soft cushion for the seat of his wagon. *"My ass was raised a pet,"* he said seriously. [In John Steinbeck's migrant-worker novel, *Of Mice and Men,* (1937) one farm-worker is guyed by the others because he wears a single glove containing vaseline: he is *keeping that hand soft for his wife,* meaning for caressing her intimately.]

138

A woman in Springfield, Mo., was caught in a sudden gust of wind; her skirts were blown very high, with a great display of bare thighs and lingerie. An old loafer grinned appreciatively. "The wind sure lifted the feathers off'n *her* ass," said he. [Brown, *North Carolina Folklore* (1952) vol. I: p. 406, reports a proverb: "Fine feathers are lifted when the wind blows."]

139

Of a pompous little man it was said: "if you'd just *stick one feather in his ass,* that fool would strut himself to death." [Compare "Yankee Doodle," and the Macaronic fop with the feather stuck in his "hat," either the original idea (or an expurgation) on the example of chicken-yard strutting. Also often said in satire concerning women's dress styles.]

140

A village boy had a fine new car, and an envious neighbor said: "I wish I had Johnny's new Ford, and he had *a feather up his ass!* Then we'd both be tickled." [In "novelty arcades," and shooting-galleries in the 1930s, one of the novelties peddled was a mock-newspaper printed with the buyer's own name in the headline, as a humorous gift for his wife: "*Mrs. Name Has 9-Pound Baby Born With Whiskers—Mother Tickled.*" Under the punning humor this disguises a daring fantasy allusion to Oedipal cunnilinctus.]

141

A loud-mouthed stranger suddenly appeared in our town, and started telling people what to do. "His *ass seems to be sucking wind,*" said one of our neighbors contemptuously. [Or *be out a yard and sucking wind;* or *blue mud.*]

142

Of a talkative, boastful fellow it was said: "A cyclone hit him in the ass about 1904, and he's still a-blowing." [Or: *and still can't get the fence-post out.*]

143

A woman at Crane, Mo., made a great outcry about something that was none of her business. Finally the town marshal lost patience. "Who's been blowing up *your* ass?" he demanded. [Sometimes "*with a barley-straw*" is added. British catch-phrase in this situation: "Who pulled *your* chyne?" referring to old-style toilets with overhead reservoir and chain for flushing.]

144

A man in Eureka Springs, Ark., was scornful of household gadgets. Looking at a complicated electric mixer, he said: "That thing ain't no good. *I wouldn't have it up my ass, if I had room for a sawmill!*" This is a common expression. May Kennedy McCord, who talked over the radio at Springfield, Mo., used it on the air sometimes; she'd say "in my house" instead of "up my ass," but the old-timers all knew what she meant. [Alluding to an ancient Three Wishes tale, in which, in the modern version, *the wishful wife ends with a newfangled egg-beater up her ass.*]

145

An old woman at Farmington, Ark., remarked that "the boys had real horses in them days, not these here little *pestle-tailed* ponies." This is a euphemism; the term *pestle-assed* is often applied to thin, bony horses. I have heard it used with reference to "scarce-hipped" women. [Also *narry-assted,* in Ozark speech.]

146

In company with a boy from the Arkansas backwoods, I visited the little city of Joplin, Mo. We sat in a car on the main street, and watched the girls go by. After a long silence the country boy spoke. "There sure is a lot of big *churn-assed* women in this town," he said thoughtfully.

147

Of an indolent man, or a very slow worker, one says "He's just *flat-assing* around." This is a saying from the lead-mines. In the early days miners worked sitting down, in a low drift, because there wasn't room enough for a shoveler to stand up. [A slow worker is also said to be "*fucking the dog*," thus explaining his sitting or lounging posture.]

148

In a club at Joplin, Mo., a stranger stood for a long time with his back to the open fire. Finally an old man said "Do you come from West Virginia?" The stranger answered "No, and why do you ask?" The old fellow grinned. "Well," said he, "my first wife come from West Virginia, and she had the coldest ass I ever seen."

149

A young woman had a habit of standing with her back to the fireplace, raising her skirts the while. "They say it takes the wrinkles out of your cheeks," she said demurely. [That is, the heat of the fire is ironing them out. Reversing the phrase, that each new bit of knowledge is *one more wrinkle in your ass*."]

150

To *assle around* is to loaf, or to wander idly about. "Them boys don't do no work, they just assle around town all day." Perhaps it is somehow related to *ass-hole?* In Stone County, Mo., the verb *piddle-ass* is common, with the same meaning, as in the sentence "I seen him *piddle-assing* around, down by the depot." An intoxicated man is often described as *pissy-ass drunk*. [To "assle" is actually a form of *arsle*. See: *Dialect Notes,* 1927, V. 476.]

151

Along the Arkansas-Oklahoma border a certain wading bird is known as the *dollar-ass*. I think it is the bittern, or pump-thunder. [McAtee, *Nomina Abitera* (1945) p. 33, says that the purple gallinule is called the *target-arse* in South Carolina.]

152

A man expresses indifference about another's behavior by saying "Well, it's no skin off *my* ass." To someone giving unwelcome advice, he says "What do you care? It's no skin off *your* ass." At Granby, Mo., when someone tries to interfere in one's personal affairs, he is squelched by the simple statement "*No hair.*" This means "It's none of your business," or literally "It's no hair off your ass."

153

A boy at Neosho, Mo., is the *spittin' image* of his father, and strangers often remarked on this "favorance." A newcomer gazed at father and son, open-mouthed. "That boy looks as much like the old man, as if he'd been *chiselled out of his ass with a peggin'-awl!*" said the stranger.

"Spitting image," also in French, *craché,* sometimes even farther derived as the parataxic "*spit-and-image,*" is itself a disguised or forgotten allusion to the male procreating semen: an excellent example of the Freudian "displacement upward," as in the myth of Jupiter and Ganymede, where the pederastic god attacks the boy in the "back of the neck." The *peggin' awl*—again sometimes "*peg-and-all*"—openly represents the penis in the folksong of that title.

154

A woman at Cassville, Mo., regarded her son as a great man, although he was just a village loafer. "Ellen thinks *the sun rises and sets in that boy's ass,*" said one of the county officers wonderingly.

155

The expression *to show one's ass* is not taken literally, but just means to appear ridiculous, to make a fool of oneself. When a girl in our village played the piano very badly at a public entertainment, an old woman remarked "Ruby sure did *show her ass at the crossroads.*" [Argentine Spanish, "*on the boulevards.*" Urban New York variant: "*in Macy's window—at high noon!*" And of course the more literal and never-to-be-forgotten "Betsey from Pike," who on the way west in a Conestoga wagon, "got drunk and danced o'er the plain, *And showed her bare ass to the whole wagon-train.*"]

156

Ass over appetite means no more than head-over-heels, as in the sentence "Bill slipped on the top step, and fell *ass over appetite.*" A man at Pineville, Mo., standing for some political office, announced that he was "going to stump the county from *ass-hole to appetite,* apparently meaning from end to end.

This has many general slang equivalents: *ass over teakettle, ass over tit*—"politely" *ass over tip*—and a specifically male version, *ass over pecker-head;* all meaning "head-over-heels." The Ohio humorist, James Thurber, refers in a medieval jousting contest to one contestant cutting open the other *from guggle to zatch,* from the German, *gurgel,* throat, gullet; *zatch* being anybody's guess. Compare notes on 133 and 191.

157

If a stranger at Granby, Mo., asked "How are you?" the town smart-alecks would reply "Just so as to be around." They pronounced *so as* to sound like *sore ass,* and it was supposed to be very witty.

158

Some jokers at Webb City, Mo., asked the schoolmaster for light on a grammatical question. "Do you say *is souls* or *are souls?*" the boys wanted to know. Then they pretended to be deaf, so that the man of learning stood in the street shouting "*Arse-holes! Arse-holes!*" at the top of his voice. [This is a "practical joke," meaning acted-out, of which several other forms exist, all usually with the same or similar *dénouement*, such as *"Polish-it-in-the-corner,"* given earlier.]

159

I once asked a man in McDonald County, Mo., for news of local happenings. "Well," he said, "my brother has done got married. And Bay Smith hurt *his* ass on the fence." This is just a way of saying that his brother had made an unfortunate marriage, but it seemed very funny to me at the time.

160

When a hillman says "let's *haul ass* out of here," he just means "let's go elsewhere." To say that a person "ain't worth an ass full of hay" or "an ass full of ashes" signifies that the party is of little importance. One of my neighbors was warning me that the new hired man couldn't keep a secret. "That fellow would *belch his ass up,* if it wasn't fastened right good," said he.

In an earlier tale form or a cautionary proverb: *"Never bet the Devil—or lend anyone—your ass, or you'll end up shitting through your ribs."* As to lack of worth in scatological images: *not worth a fart—in a high wind; not worth shit,* or *a bucket of shit—with a rope of piss for a handle; not worth a pisspot full of crabapples;* or *not worth a quart of soapy farts,* probably referring to an enema.

161

At Gainesville, Mo., I overheard an argument in a barbershop, and one man was pretty sure of himself. "Why," said he, "*I'll bet five dollars ag'in a frosted horse-turd, and hold the stakes in my mouth!*" Some people who use this expression say *road-apple, horse-apple, horse-biscuit,* or *road-walnut,* all common euphemisms for horse-turd.

162

A native of Baxter County, Ark., was telling how he had been throwed higher'n a kite by an outlaw pony. "At the second big jump," said he, "I reached for the saddle-horn, and grabbed a horse-turd thirty steps down the road!"

163

People at Granby, Mo., used to tell a long story about a man who flourished his pistol and forced a singing-teacher named Sneed to *eat a horse-turd.* They say that the case got to the Missouri Supreme

Court, where the pistol-toter's conviction was set aside because the jury had been illegally separated. It seems that one juryman *went into a shit-house and shut the door,* while the other eleven remained outside!

Mock legal transgression, on the style of *"Mopery,"* described in note on 102 above. In one of Eugene Field's legendarily devastating Denver theatrical criticisms: "I can't honestly discuss this play, because I saw it under very adverse circumstances—*the curtain was up."* The Granby, Mo., long story, not told here by Randolph, is an old classic, with a century-long history in Europe, in which: *An army officer catches a sentinel shitting while on duty, takes his rifle and forces the sentinel to eat most of the turd. While he is laughing at him, the sentinel snatches the rifle back and forces the officer to eat the rest. When the officer then has the sentinel brought before court martial, the sentinel explains innocently: "All that happened is we had lunch together. Ask him if it isn't true!"*—See: Legman, *No Laughing Matter,* (1975) "The *Escoumerda,"* vol. II: pp. 937–52.

164

There used to be a man at Galena, Mo., whose face was deeply pitted with smallpox scars. "That feller's face," said Uncle Jack Short, "reminds me of an old soldier's turd, which the birds have picked the beans out of it." [Seed-foods covered by natural integuments, such as beans and corn, cannot be digested unless these integuments have been broken by chewing. *Succotash,* combining both corn and beans, is therefore unusually mashed in cooking.]

165

When our sheriff asked "Where's Jim Bradley gone?" a ruffian answered *"Out to shit, if the hogs ain't got him."* This means "It's none of your business." But the old settlers say that wild hogs did sometimes attack a man who was "hunkered down" when they would not molest him if he was standing. There are old tales of men who climbed trees in order to defecate, with ravenous razorbacks grunting and squealing underneath. [See note on 195.]

166

A salesman was bragging about his experiences, telling how he had visited every state in the Union, even crossing into Canada and Mexico. Most of the villagers were impressed, but a country boy who had followed the guns in Africa was not. "I've traveled further than that, *around a piss-pot looking for the handle,"* said the veteran.

In a similar put-down of a braggart, in this case concerning his bravery and fighting abilities, he is told *"You couldn't fight your way out of a paper bag full of shit, and tied in the middle with a pussy-hair."* The reference to *pussy* is an implied statement of cowardice or effeminacy, which to the *macho* speaker is *"to be,* or *turn, pussy."* Compare note on 188.

167

A boy at Carterville, Mo., was always pursuing the "hired girls" in his parents' home; several of them became pregnant, and made considerable trouble. "Cliff is a good boy," his father said. "The only thing is, *he shits too close to the house."* [See *Hoosier Folklore Bulletin,* June 1944, vol. III: p. 37.]

168

One of my neighbors was complaining because his wife demanded new furniture, expensive clothes, and better food. "That woman thinks *I can shit money!*" he cried. Another time, she suggested that he sell the farm and get a job in Joplin. "I won't do nothing of the kind!" he shouted. "Why, I'd sooner *have my bag slit and both legs stuck through it!*" [As in trussing sheep carcasses, or slaughtered pigs for hanging on a hook. *Bag* here means scrotum.]

169

Laborers hired by the hour often spend a good deal of time in the privy, in order to shorten their day's work. Ask for one of these fellows by name, and the boss will answer, "He ain't here right now. I reckon he's gone *to shit a rest.*" [Anti-labor privy joke, 1934: "*Union Rules:* There got to be two goin', two comin', two shittin', an' two workin'—*at all times!*"]

170

A farmer near Camdenton, Mo., was bragging about his son, who had distinguished himself in the military service and elsewhere. "My Tommy is the *best boy that ever shit down two boots!*" said the proud father. One sometimes hears a variant, "the best boy *that ever shit between two shoes.*"

Of dysphemistic pro-female, grudging "compliments" of this type, compare, from a New York City bookseller, 1940: *the best woman that ever pissed squatting;* and this tribute to the American poet Edna St. Vincent Millay, by one of her former lovers: "She was the best damn' woman *that ever wore her ass split down the middle.*" Congener of the Shakespearean *split-arse,* for a medlar fig.

171

An enraged woman spoke unfavorably to her true-loving husband. "There's a *streak of shit up your back,*" she said, "and there *ain't no starch in your pecker.* You ain't *fit for a decent woman to wipe her ass on.* I hope you *die of the piles, and they bury you under a piss-ellum tree!*" ["Streak of shit," this is the *yellow streak* more politely ascribed to cowards. A young married woman in The Bronx, New York, 1957, who wanted to leave her husband admitted: "I'm afraid to do it. I guess *I've got shit in my blood.*" On extravagant curses and rejections of the type reported here, see the text beginning "May itching piles molest you, etc." at rhyme No. 14 above.]

172

In the midst of a political discussion, one of the disputants cried out "Oh, shit!" His opponent smiled. "Jim," said he, "you said a mouthful, *as usual.*" [In France the similar retort to the expletive "*Merde—Mange!*" meaning, "Eat it!"]

173

A related crack came to me from the University of Missouri, where a pompous fellow had been goaded into an argument, and was getting the worst of it. Finally he lost his temper. "Shit!" he cried loudly. "Yes," said one of his tormentors, "*in the highest and best sense of the word!*"

174

One of my neighbor's little boys had some minor accident at the table—he spilled the gravy, or something of the sort. The boy cried out "God damn it!" whereupon the father scowled. "*Shit-fire, son, mind your manners!*" said he. "That ain't no way to talk before company."

Typical of a whole style or series of jocular anti-hillbilly and anti-family anecdotes, current in America. Nevertheless, something very similar happened to the present editor in Southern France in 1965, when he used the mild slang word for gobbling food, *bouffer,* to an elderly native, an egg-farmer, only to be reprimanded patiently: "I know you just learn words like that from those Paris tourists. Otherwise, I'd say, Get out of the shit by yourself!—*Démerdez-vous!*"

175

A man at Fayetteville, Ark., said "Boys, I'm hockey-proof," meaning that he couldn't be moved by lies, cajolery, or bullshit. Yankees never seem to realize it, but *hockey* means nothing but *shit* in the Ozarks, and in many other parts of the South. [Compare: *don't know hockey from tar,* or *chaw-terbaccer,* in No. 177 following.]

176

Referring to a state of indecision or mental confusion, the hillman says "I was *between a shit and a sweat.*" A related expression is "Them gamblers got me so bumfuzzled, I didn't know whether *to shit or go blind.*"

The term "bumfuzzled," used here for confused or intimidated may be a combination of the British *bum,* arse, and *foozzle* or *fizzle,* the "soft" or wet fart of fear or nervousness; or may simply involve a back-formation on "bamboozle." The "going blind" is almost always of drunken or erotic trance. Joke on: *The country girl who wants to become a big-city prostitute, and is told that she should ask for the money when the John's eyes "go glassy." Later she admits she has made no money at all, because "When his eyes go glassy, I go stone blind!*"

177

Of an ignorant or stupid man, it is said that he *don't know hockey from tar*, or *shit from apple-butter,* or *sheep-shit from brown coffee,* or *baby-shit from wild honey.* One of my neighbors was known as a man who *couldn't tell his ass from a hole in the ground.* This last expression has some amusing variants. We once heard a woman say to some tourists: "I been so dizzy here lately, *I can't tell my husband from a hole in the ground!*" The man of the house just stood there, looking outraged and baffled, but he didn't say anything.

A visitor to New York from Mena, Arkansas, April 1954, varied this as: *don't know his ass from a gourd*; also collected as *from punkin pie,* or *from third base,* an allusion to the game of baseball. A folk-circulated poem pretends that "ass" in these phrases refers to the farmyard animal, or that *horses' asses* are those of a Norse warrior named Horsa.

Of generalized ignorance: *don't know chaw-terbaccer from hockey;* see in No. 175, "hockey" here meaning feces. In the following urban alliterative witticism, "shinola" is shoe-polish: "*He don't know shit from shinola,*" with topper: "—and do *his* shoes stink!" Rabelais' old proverb, in *Pantagruel,* V. xxii, Motteux trans., (1694): *not to know honey from a dog's turd,* is slurred or disguised in a well-known *mal-mariée* folksong, "The West Virginia Boys."

> Come all ye pore deluded gals,
> An' listen to my noise . . .
> When they come a-courtin'
> They'll tell you about love;
> First three months it's honey,
> Then it's tur*dle-dove* . . .
>
> Marry you in summer,
> Beat you come next spring—
> Git up an' git my breakfast,
> You good-fer-nothin' thing!

178

Clutter-balls are round hard bits of fecal matter attached to hairs about the anus. Sometimes they are called *vack-balls.* A physician named Doggett, who practiced at Crane, Mo., in the 1920s, told of a pregnant woman who had so many clutter-balls that he called for scissors to cut them off. "They were just like you see on sheep sometimes," said Dr. Doggett.

179

Dill-balls or *dill-berries,* also attached to hairs, are composed mostly of dried [menstrual] blood. It is explained to me, delicately, that women have dill-balls or dill-berries in front, while either sex may have *clutter-balls* or *vack-balls* behind.

Intended as a straight-faced joke, which Randolph is perhaps innocently retailing. All these words are used interchangeably. "Vack-balls" are also called *wax-balls,* as a euphemism, or plainly *shit-balls.* The German *Klapusterbeeren,* or *Klabauter-beeren,* "witch-berries," are usually ascribed only to Bavarian peasants, who serve the same purpose in the German *blason* of insult, as hillbillies in America. On the household demons or pixies tangling knots in the unspecified hair of "slovenly wenches" while they sleep, see Malvolio's great "Queen Mab" soliloquy as enlarged by Shakespeare in the 2nd quarto of *Romeo and Juliet* in 1599, I. iv. 60.

180

The common phrase *up Shit Creek without no paddle* means in a serious predicament. A badly frightened man is said to be *scared shitless.* [Compare note on 218.]

181

An old lady in Yell County, Ark., said of the hired man "He ain't got no more sense than *to shit and fall back in it.*" This is not to be taken literally; it just means that the fellow made a sorry mess of whatever he tried to accomplish. [Grose's *Classical Dictionary of the Vulgar Tongue* in 1785 describes a prank involving doing this to victims on purpose. So also tipped-over privies in backwoods America as a Hallowe'en prank, with the same result. See 185 following.]

182

The same woman, referring to another dubious character, remarked: "Elmer might be honest. But *I wouldn't trust him in a shit-house without a muzzle.*" [Referring to the omnivorous habits of dogs and hogs.]

183

When anybody keeps calling first for one thing and then another, without prospect of success, he is told "You might as well *wish in one hand and shit in the other.*" It means, I suppose, that idle desires are no better than shit. A variant of this is applied to a man engaged in some futile enterprise. "He's just pissing in one hand and shitting in the other, *to see which will get full first*" [or *faster*]. A related expression is "you just *shit in one hand and rub it off on the other,*" referring to an unsuccessful attempt to clear up a bad situation. [Spider Rowland, in *Arkansas Gazette,* June 3, 1948, printed this as "*wishing* in one hand and *spitting* in the other." Sometimes as "shitting," with the addition "—and see which gets full faster."]

184

On the witness stand in a rape case, a young girl refused to repeat a rapist's conversation that she had overheard. "I would blush to say such filthy words," she told the judge. An old woman in the audience cackled, and then spoke in a loud whisper: "Anything that makes *her* blush, would start a *blind horse a-hunting a dark place to shit!*"

Compare No. 37. This is an example of the standard folk-denial that rape ever exists; contending that the woman is always essentially willing and has only been "leading the man on." The reaction to this, on a feminist basis, has led to the legal position where nearly half of the United States will now (1990) prosecute a husband for the rape of his own wife, on no evidence but her own statement. This even includes "wedding-night rape," though that assumes the legal absurdity of an unconsummated marriage not being automatically annulled. Husbands can also sue wives for rape, genital or anal, but this is still uncommon.—The *blind horse* reference is to a folk-phrase delightfully expurgated by Partridge as "*lead the blind monkeys to evacuate,*" of a clumsy or incompetent person.

185

Some village boys had moved the hotel privy on Hallowe'en (as a prank). A drunken farmer came into town, stopped at the hotel, and fell into the pit. This was at Pineville, Mo., and the Cowskin River is only a few yards away. Covered with shit from head to foot, the poor chap said "It must be soap, fellers! I better run to the river, and see what kind of suds it'll make." [See note on 181, above.]

186

A girl near Bentonville, Ark., was reared in poverty, but became the wife of a wealthy man in Little Rock. Someone was talking to the girl's mother about her sudden prosperity. "Yeah," said the old woman, "Mabel's *a-fartin' through silk* nowadays." [In *Anecdota Americana,* 1927, the columnist "Bugs" Baer is quoted as saying that a poor chorus-girl *has never farted through silk,* meaning has never worn silk underwear or other clothing. In New York, 1939, the novelist Jack Hanley punned, as a topper on a "career-gal" who married rich: "That chorus-kicker never farted through silk in her life—*And that's straining it!*"]

187

At Cassville, Mo., a woman "set in to raising hell" and her husband fled the house. Later that night I met him in the tavern. "Polly has been *a-farting fire* all evening," he said. "I ain't going home till her ass cools off." [Spanish *cacafuego,* literally "fire-shitter," of any violent and choleric person.]

188

A candidate for office had just made a rousing speech from the courthouse steps. Asked what she thought about his chances of election, an old country woman sniffed. "That feller thinks he's going to *cut a big hog in the ass,*" she said. "But the truth is, he don't amount to *a fart in a whirlwind.*"

Or, "*in a high wind.*" Compare: Brown, *North Carolina Folklore,* 1952, vol. I: p. 405. "Cut a big hog in the ass," means to create a large effect or success. Baumann, *Londonismen,* (1887) quotes Dickens in 1836 using an elliptical form, perhaps the original: "Gentlemen 'cutting it uncommon fat,'" for *cutting a dash,* showing off. Inadequacy or lack of courage is also sometimes stated as: "*He couldn't fart*—or *fight—his way out of a paper sack full of shit.*" See further note on 166, above.)

189

One of my friends near Sulphur Springs, Ark., had sold most of his property, invested the money in government bonds, and looked forward to his retirement. "Everything's in fine shape," said he. "No more farming for me. All I got to do is lay in bed, and *draw farts* from now on out."

190

The president of our village school board sat on the platform during an "entertainment," but he seemed ill at ease. My neighbor noticed this, and remarked: "Lee looks like he's just *turned loose a bird,*" let a fart, that is.

Also, in the eastern United States, 1948, *to turn one loose, drop a shoe, fire a torpedo, lay one,* or *lay a depth-charge,* or *cut a stinker.* To *cut one,* used in the western United States by the 1880s, referred originally to a cowboy separating a steer from the herd while on horseback. Refraining from farting is called *holding a fart, baking it,* or *sitting on it;* lifting one buttock to fart while sitting is *tilting.* Disguising the act silently and inobtrusively, instead of being appreciated by others is considered sneaky and dishonest: *sliding out one of those silent stinkers.* A printed humorous drawing still circulates anonymously, showing various such individual "styles," or as "Types of Men (*or* Gals) in the Restroom," including urinary styles as well.

191

One of my neighbors in McDonald County, Mo., was shouting threats against the sheriff. "I'll knock that feller *loose from his ass!*" he cried. Similar expressions are "I'll whip him *till he pisses like a pup,*" or "I'll beat him *till his ass chaws terbacker,*" or "I'll make him *piss a ring round himself,*" or "I'll whip him till his *britches won't hold corncobs,*" (i.e., till he "shits himself") or "I'll *pull off his head and stick it up his ass.*"

I once heard a little storekeeper speak his warning to an up-the-creek bravo. "Get out of my store," said he, "or I'll take this knife and *rip you up from cock to collar!*" I believe the little man would have done just that, but the bully kept well out of his reach thereafter. Compare *"from guggle to zatch,"* quoted earlier from James Thurber, in note on 156. Other threats of this self-evident anal sadistic type are: *"I'll knock you back through your asshole,"* in rhyme No. 14 above, also, *"I'll kick your ass up around your neck, like a horse-collar,"* heard as part of a "toast" contest or game of insults called "The Dozens"—from the Scottish, *dose,* to stun, as in "bull-dozer"—among Negro adolescents in Harlem, New York, 1938.

192

Near Hollister, Mo., a man spoke contemptuously of another. "That fellow? Why, I *wouldn't piss on him if his ass was afire!*" A related crack is *"If he was a-dying of thirst, I wouldn't give him the sweat off of my balls!* No sir, I wouldn't lend him the *froth off of my piss!*" [Also, *"I wouldn't piss up your ass if you were dying of thirst*—and your tongue was tangled around your prick!"]

193

A friend of mine was worried because his son couldn't pass a civil service examination. "Johnny can read and write pretty good," said the father, "but when it comes to arithmetic, he *can't piss a drop.*"

194

An aged man, watching his grandchildren move truck-loads of furniture into their new home, spoke wistfully of his youth. "Moving was a lot easier in them days," he said. *"All we had to do was piss on the fire and whistle up the dogs."*

195

An energetic young fellow is said to be *full of piss and ginger,* or *full of piss and vinegar.* A man near Hot Springs, Ark., [or his penis?] was described as *full of piss and blue veins,* but I'm not sure what this means. To say that somebody is *full of shit* is to cast doubt upon that person's veracity or reliability.

A person believed to be lying or grievously in error is sometimes said to be *"so full of shit that I'm surprised the pigs don't eat you."*—Compare earlier note on 165, on pigs.—Also: *" . . . that your eyes are turning brown."* Enthusiastic fan letter to a male writer, from a Chicago sex-magazine editor, Ms. Marianna Beck, 1988: "Your writing is always *full of pith—and vinegar.*"

196

A lady in Fayetteville, Ark., told me of the dying man who said to a physician: "When I shit, I shit like a horse. And when I piss, I damn nigh wash up the steps." This in the presence of his wife, daughters, and other weeping relatives. By *wash up,* he meant wash the dirt from under the steps, so as to loosen or dislodge them, like a flood or a sudden cloudburst. [Compare: Rabelais, *Gargantua,* (1535) Bk. I, ch. 17, on his horse's heroic pissing.]

197

Of a harum-scarum, unpredictable young man at Picher, Okla., a friend remarked: "Jim is the kind of a fellow that will piss his pants any minute, and he *don't care which leg it runs down.*" [Another remark of angry dismissal, especially if to a woman: *"Go piss up a rope—and play with the steam."* Or: "You can *go shit in your hat, and pull it down over your ears—and call it curls!*" Both of these are U.S. theatre and motion-picture "camp," 1930s.]

198

A man in McDonald County, Mo., spoke unfavorably of a widow, saying that *"her and the Devil piss through the same quill,"* but I'm not certain just what he meant. At Hot Springs, Ark., an irate citizen was denouncing the candidates of both major political parties. "Them fellows all piss through the same quill," said he, "with the Devil holding the pot!" [To *piss in a quill together* means to agree, especially if secretly, or to be plotting together. The full form of this old proverbial phrase, *"with the Devil holding the pot,"* does not seem to have been recorded before Randolph, here. In Bulgarian Yiddish, men who are old friends are said *to have pissed together in the same hole.* The young man who used this phrase, in New York, 1939, and also glossed its meaning, said to the editor, "I don't have to tell you *what* hole they shared."]

199

In the mines near Granby, Mo., a man who shovels out the ore is called a scoop-ox. It is said that a good scoop-ox can stick his head through a coil of fuse, but *can't get his ass into a bushel basket.* One must go into a lead-mine and see the shovelers at work, in order to appreciate this crack.

200

An old fellow near Cyclone, Mo., used to say "Well, *keep your pecker up.*" All he meant was "Don't be discouraged." Some of the womenfolk thought this was a very improper expression; they tried to get the old man to say "Keep your *chin* up" instead, but he was still saying *pecker* as late as 1921.

Compare Brown, *North Carolina Folklore,* 1952, vol. I: p. 456. When a young professor at the University of California told another in 1965 that he was "dickering" with a different school, he was told mockingly: "Well, just *keep your dicker up,* and use all the strength of your *dickerer,*" playing on the present phrase. In a similar Missouri anecdote, usually told about President Truman, *A politician has used the phrase "horse-manure" in a public speech. When his children complain about this to his wife she says, "Oh, I'm satisfied. It's taken me twenty years to get him to say 'manure.'"* (Told by Mrs. L.K., St. Louis, Mo., 1948.) Note in both anecdotes the figure of the wife or "women-folk" as the traditional frontier tamer or "civilizer" of men, as in the most popular 1930s newspaper comic-strip, George T. McManus' "Maggie and Jiggs, or Bringing Up Father."

201

A woman in Hickory County, Mo., complained that the coffee was too weak. "I could *stick one coffee-bean in my ass and swim the ocean,*" she cried. "It'd make better coffee than that!" [Compare: the "toast" recitation, "Shine and the *Titanic,*" on the heroic Negro stoker who swims ashore after the shipwreck, using his thumb and palm, like the coffee bean here, as rudder.]

202

In a roadhouse near Pineville, Mo., somebody gave a young woman a glass of beer. She tasted the stuff, and handed it back. "*Run it through the horse again,*" she said shortly. [Folk-wit everywhere in the United States. A similar Belgian witticism calls bad beer "Drink-It-Twice" brew.]

203

A drunken man appeared in our village one Saturday, when the street was full of people. The constable told him not to holler so loud, whereupon the fellow decided he was being persecuted by the townsfolk. He climbed up on a fence and clapped his hands for attention. "You can all *kiss my ass, and bark at the hole!*" he shouted.

204

A man near Galena, Mo., married a feeble-minded girl, and she kept having babies every year, depending on the charity of her neighbors for a livelihood. "You can't blame that poor half-wit woman," said the lady who lived next door. "It's *his* fault, and he orter be worked on like a hog!": She meant that the woman's husband should be castrated.

205

Speaking of an idle, worthless fellow, whose wife bore many children and supported them by taking in washing, my neighbors at Pineville, Mo., said: "With them people, it's *butt for best, and belly half the family.*" I don't know exactly what this means, but it isn't complimentary. ["Belly half the family" probably refers to the wife; and possibly "butt" too. *"Butt and ben"* is an old Scottish phrase for the back and front ends of a one-room cabin.]

206

If a person is unfortunate, subject to many trials or hardships, the general situation is described as *tough titty.* One often hears of somebody being forced to *suck the hind tit,* which means getting the worst of a deal. A man in Barry County, Mo., thought himself mistreated by those in authority, so he announced publicly: "I'm getting tired of being browbeat and bulldozed, and having to *suck the hind tit!*" [Brown, *North Carolina Folklore* (1952) vol. I: p. 487, says that *tough titty* means hard trials, and gives the example: "It is a tough titty to suck, but she sucked it." But on page 602 *tough titty* is defined as "a dangerous person." In Dr. Paul de Kruif's *Why Keep The Alive?* (1937), milk-deprived slum children are described as looking like the *tit-man* of a large brood of *tit-kitties,* meaning the one that is shoved back by its siblings to nurse at the *hind-tit.*]

207

If a woman is infatuated with a worthless man, the neighbors wonder "What can she see in that fellow?" The stock answer is, "He must *have sugar on his prick.*" A mountain man in Stone County, Mo., said seriously: "I'd like to be postmaster, all right. But I ain't going *to poke sugar up no congressman's ass* to get the job." ["Sugar" is meant metaphorically here, as money, for purposes of bribery. Grose's *Classical Dictionary of the Vulgar Tongue,* 1785, the first true dictionary of slang, gives "to *grease a fat sow in the arse,*" now usually politely shortened to *grease a fat sow,* or *pig,* as meaning to bribe a man already rich. The phrase is also sometimes used of flattery. The "sugar on his prick" phrase, above, implies fellation.]

208

When someone tries to flatter a woman, he is said to be *crawling up in her.* This does not necessarily mean a sexual approach; it may be financial, or even political. [Note that it is also expurgated by omission of the final anatomical noun, as with No. 207 preceding, and other examples earlier, as *"The pot calls the kettle black-ass."* This in Spanish is frankly *"cula di negra."* The Ozark phrase here exactly parallels the German locution *"kriechen im Arsch,"* literally, to *crawl up someone's arse,* as meaning to cringe, fawn, or toady. Also used in exact translation in English, meaning to ingratiate oneself by subservience, sometimes with the addition "—*and suck the hole from the inside!*"]

209

The expression *till the cows come home,* meaning a long time, is common everywhere. But May Kennedy McCord tells me that when she was a child at Galena, Mo., they always said "till the cows come home *with bulls on their backs.*" May's father ran a little store, and loafers used to argue religion and politics. Some infidel from Springfield was belittling the Bible, and old man Belton finally said, "The Word of God will stand thar—*right thar*—*till the cows come home with bulls on their backs!*" May's father laughed about this, and told her mother. He got the biggest laugh of all when his wife didn't see the joke, but with a far-away look in her eyes, she said "Amen!"

210

On hearing any loud noise, the boys used to say "It sounds like *Maw's got her tit caught in the wringer again.*" Another one was "I ain't heard such a racket since Uncle Joe *got his balls caught in a crack.*" [Compare line rallying a man who says he has caught cold: *"You must've been sleeping by a crack,"* meaning the vagina. A current (1990) Xeroxlore item illustrates the first of these anti-woman slurs in cruelly graphic detail, showing a screaming woman whose breast is being ground through a laundry mangle by a fiendishly laughing child. In another version, this is modified to "merely" a cow and its udder.]

211

Two backwoods ruffians, with pistols drawn, held a group of villagers at bay. "What'll we do with these son-of-a-bitches, Joe?" said one. Joe looked contemptuously at the crowd. "Oh, fuck 'em all but six, and save *them* for pall-bearers," he answered.

A similarly "true" anecdote is given in *The Pearl*, September 1879, No. 3, complete with provenance, as having happened "*In the wars in India, in the year 1800,*" to *Major Torrens at a drinking party among the officers, when the Sergeant brought in two prisoners, one old and one young. When he asked what to do with the prisoners, "the Major merrily answered: 'Oh, take them away and frig them.' The Sergeant retired. In an hour he returned, and respectfully made this report: 'Please, your honour, we have frigged the young one, but we can't make the old man's cock stand.'"* In the sense meant, *frig them* equals " . . . and damn them!"

212

Uncle J. S., Galena, Mo., told me of a woman who had never been ten miles from home. When she married, her husband insisted upon moving to a farm twenty miles distant. The woman claimed that the climate was very different from that of her old home. "The weather is so changeable here," she complained. "I went out to get a bucket of water, and the wind blowed three hailstones into my twitchet. I wasn't at the spring-house but a few minutes, and on the way back to the cabin it blowed sand up my ass!" [Typical tall tale, but referring to midwest cyclones.]

213

Denouncing a politician at Joplin, Mo., a citizen cried: "Foolishness runs in the family. That feller's grandpa *stuck a lighted candle in his ass,* and jumped off a three-story hotel. Thought he was Halley's comet!"

Reference to the comet presumably dates this story back to 1835; probably really only to 1910. Mark Twain, who was born and died with Halley's comet, had prepared an account of a somewhat similar lighted-candle frolic as "The Royal Nonesuch," for use in *Huckleberry Finn* (1885) but was persuaded by the usual well-meaning friends to omit it. Such stories usually end, as here, with impersonating a sky-rocket, the "fartoblast," an imaginary "arse-musica," or more mundanely by farting the candle out. During World War II, a frisky young army nurse used to do the latter, to win bets at drinking parties with officers in the Pacific theatre-of-operations. She would "top" her performance by stating that she was also learning, from a bar-girl in Hawaii, "how to smoke cigarettes and squirt ping-pong balls" with her vagina, both also authentic exhibition feats, since then often seen in Manila pick-up bars and Bangkok.

214

With reference to another deluded mortal, one of my neighbors said: "He might as well set on a cake of ice, hire a nigger to *throw horse-shit in his face,* and pretend like he's taking a sleigh-ride!"

215

Near Granby, Mo., a man boasted that he was a pretty good fiddler. "Shucks," said one of his fellows, "you might play the *swinnet,* or the *fuzzy-wuzzy,* or *three hairs stretched over a hog's ass.* But it takes brains to play a fiddle." [Leg-pull experts in New York, 1948, defined the "*swinette,*" as "Three cunt-hairs strung over a pig's ass—and you pluck it with your teeth!" Other imaginary musical devices of this kind are also referred to, such as the "Hoo-hah trumpet," "arse-musica," or "fartoblast," on which see further note on 213. The "fuzzy-wuzzy," mentioned by Randolph, has not been identified, but may refer to pubic hair. The similar "Chinese violin" is supposedly a horn funnel strung with cats' whiskers, inserted anally, and then "Chopsticks" is plucked on it for a transcendental thrill.]

216

In Stone County, Mo., is a place known as *Raw-Bag Holler.* Uncle J. S. told me that an old man was so tortured by ticks and chiggers that he scratched his scrotum plumb raw; a woman herb-doctor who treated him "with soft soap out of a gourd" gave the name to the valley in which the patient lived.

There are tall tales of *Hockey Center, Duckbutter Knob, Shit City, Jingleberry Junction,* and *Chippy's Delight,* more or less mythical mining camps in Jasper County, Mo. See Randolph's *We Always Lie to Strangers* (1951) p. 242.

217

In Southern Arkansas there is a village called Fouke. The natives pronounce it *fowk,* but visitors usually say *fook* or *fuck.* The tourists' puns are considered very funny in some quarters, and there are many references to the town in humorous writings. W. H. Elzey tells how he and his wife lay in bed at Texarkana, some sixteen miles away, trying to decide "whether they were going to Fouke or not." Elzey is a real Ozarker, but most of the wisecracks about Fouke are credited to "furriners," therefore I do not list them here. [Elzey, *Things about Things,* Eureka Springs, Arkansas, 1946, p. 17.]

I have heard a few vulgar Ozark place-names, but nothing to compare with the variety reported by McAtee from other parts of the United States. There is a *Chicken-Shit Ridge* in Newton County, Mo., and a *Horse-Turd Bluff* near Pineville, Mo. A place in Taney County, Mo., used to be called the *Bump-Ass*

Barrens. Piss Mountain is a jocular name for Pea Ridge, Ark., and a peak not far off is sometimes known as *Pissing Squaw Knob.* [See: McAtee, *Nomina Abitera,* pp. 1–4. There are also imaginary Ozark towns with scatological names, such as *Hockeyville* and *Durgenville,* from "hockey" meaning feces, and "durgen," an obscure Ozark adjective for anything filthy, "ornery," or disprized; also *Shitville,* politely *Mudville,* as in "Casey at the Bat," and *Shit Junction near Ass Corner.*]

218

The town of Eureka Springs, Ark., is built on steep hillsides, and the civic boosters advertise "The Switzerland of America," but a county official told me that *"The Ass Hole of Creation"* would be more appropriate. The little stream that runs through the town carried all the sewage in the early days, and the old-timers still call it *Shit Creek.* [Standard slang phrase for the situation of any benighted traveler, or discouraged or defeated person: *to be up Shit Crick without a paddle—and no map.* Compare note on 180 above.]

219. THE WORN OUT PUSSY

Old Man Benfry's wife left him and she put in for a divorce. And then she took up with a young fellow that run the filling station in Pineville. But her and Old Benfry was educated and terrible broadminded, so they was still acting friendly and even kidded each other when they would meet up, just like they done before she got the divorce. They used to joke about it sometimes, specially if somebody was a-listening.

One day in the drugstore he says to her, "How does your new boy-friend like it, when he sticks his pecker into your old wore-out twitchet?"

She looked kind of flustered for a minute, and then she spoke right up. "Oh, he likes it just fine, soon as he gets it past the worn-out part!" she says. And then she grinned kind of innocent-like, and them young folks all laughed, pretty loud.

Old man Benfry didn't have no more to say, so he walked right out of that drugstore.

Note that *pussy* is not used (but *twitchet*) in this story, as told by an anonymous lady in Fayetteville, Arkansas, November 1976. She heard it in Hot Springs, Arkansas, "maybe about a year ago." A very similar tale was collected from Mr. E. L., Joplin, Missouri, in the summer of 1930.

According to Robert Cochran's biography, *Vance Randolph: An Ozark Life* (1985) p. 84, Randolph sent a transcript of this tale to his friend and former tale-annotator, Professor Herbert Halpert, November 30, 1977, asking him for parallels in the folktale literature; but Halpert answered, December 29, 1977, "that he never heard the story, and finds no parallel in the folktale literature." The tale, which has circulated in America since the 1950s with the *two men* speaking, was then sent to G. Legman, in France, January 1978, for inclusion in the present work. (See also No. 200), although Randolph had identified it, in his earlier accompanying letter to Halpert, as "the title story of my second book of bawdy tales." This refers to his successful first such book, *Pissing in the Snow,* just published then courageously by the University of Illinois Press, in 1976, an excerpt or "out-take" from the present collection.

In fact, Randolph never intended or expected to be able to compile any such second book, and was only joking with Halpert, who was of course aghast at the idea of trying to get a volume with the word *"pussy"* in the title—let alone *twitchet!*—commercially published. Curiously enough, a book doing exactly that was successfully published at that time, *The Doom Pussy,* concerning the ill-fated American recent military campaigns in Asia, to which the title referred in the sense of a jinx or hex. But it was correctly assumed that the general public would disguise or mis-identify the "Pussy" in the title as meaning a feline cat or kitten, and not in the intended *vagina dentata* sense of the phrase.

According to Professor Speer Morgan, writing under the pen-name of "Doctor Jekyll" in *Boone County Fare,* a Missouri anthology edited by Karlana Gentile and Eric Staley (Singing Wind Press, 1975) p. 35, the bawdy-talking novelist Norman Mailer, known as "the poor man's Hemingway," told the "Worn Out Pussy" tale in a public lecture at the University of Missouri, to demonstrate some point now obscure. Or to shock his audience with the anti-woman hatred and penile-insufficiency fear, predominant in much or most of his best-seller output, as in that, earlier, of Hemingway and Henry Miller.

220. THE MAGIC WALKING STICK

One time a fellow had a magic walking stick that would ask questions and get answers. He pointed the stick at a tree and says, "You ever had any acorns?" and the tree answered, "Sure, lots of 'em." So the stick says, "What went with 'em all?" and the tree answered. "The hogs et 'em up."

So there was three sisters a-living there. The fellow pointed the stick at the oldest one's cunt, and the stick says, "Have you done any fucking?" The cunt answered, "Lots of it," and the man says, "You ain't the one I want."

Then he pointed the stick at the middle sister's cunt, and the cunt answered, "Just once in a while," so the man says, "You ain't the one I want, neither."

Finally he pointed the stick at the youngest sister's cunt, and the stick says, "Have you done any fucking?" The youngest sister's cunt answered, "No," and the fellow knowed it was the truth. So he says, "You're the one I want," and that's the one he married.

There was an old girl a-living there that heard about the magic walking stick, and she wanted to try it. So she stuffed her cunt full of rags. The walking stick says, "Have you done any fucking?" but the old girl's cunt didn't make no answer; it just kind of whistled like wind was a-coming out. The stick asked the same question again, but the old girl's cunt just blowed soft and whistled low. So then the stick turned to the old girl's asshole and says, "What's the reason cunt don't answer me?" Asshole spoke right up and says, "Cause it is stuffed full of rags." The old girl scowled back over her left shoulder. "If I had known *YOU* was so loose-mouthed, I'd have filled you up with rags, too," she says.

The preceding, only known American text of this most interesting old folktale was collected by Vance Randolph in 1958, in Eureka Springs, Arkansas, from a gentleman who had it from a man in Carroll County, Arkansas, about 1900. It was first published by G. Legman, *Rationale of the Dirty Joke (No Laughing Matter,* 1975) vol. 2: pp. 875–76, in the chapter on "Scatology," as the collection for which it was intended, Randolph's *Pissing in the Snow, and Other Ozark Folktales* (University of Illinois Press, 1976) accidentally omitted this tale as published, owing to its having been collected in 1958, after the date of that manuscript (1954). It is based on an ancient folktale motif, the *vagina loquens,* or "talking cunt," of which the connection with farting will be seen at once, the two apertures involved being separated only by the famously small and sensitive isthmus or perineum.

Under the effect of a stronger external magic than its own, the ensorcelled vagina is required to *speak,* by the action of some magical object or charm, and is usually made to admit to its own unchastity. (Aarne-Thompson, *Types of the Folktale,* Helsinki, 1961; Tale-Type 1391, Motif H451.) The most famous literary treatment is Denis Diderot's *Les Bijoux Indiscrets* (1748), especially in chapter 47, where the "bijou" bragging or confessing—in English, among other languages!—is that of the king's mistress, lightly disguised. This was consciously inspired by Garin's thirteenth-century fabliau, "Le Chevalier qui faisoit parler les cons et les culs" (text reprinted in *Nocrion, conte Allobroge,* Bruxelles, 1881, in which title "Nocrion," or nock, is *con,* cunt, reversed.) Note that in this original, both the vagina and the anus speak, as in Randolph's folktale collected in the Ozarks; although this is not the case in *Les Bijoux Indiscrets,* of which an amusing "X-rated" erotic motion-picture was issued in France about 1976 by Frédéric Lansac, completely modernized under the title *Le Sexe Qui Parle,* reissued on videotape in America as *Pussy Talk.*

It is evident, of course, that it is the "speaking" anus with its ghost voice, that is the original inspiration, while the *pudenda loquens* is conceived of simply as an analogue. The humorous trait, of the woman scowling back over her (always unlucky or disfavored) left shoulder and reprimanding her own anus for speaking out of turn, derives obviously from the various catch-phrases in many languages by which one rallies another person's or one's own fart, by pretending to reprimand the buttocks (which are sometimes also slapped) or the anus, as though it were an autonomous person or *vox humana.* There is also perhaps some remote influence here of the East Indian Tantric Yoga idea of the main perineal *chakra* as the seat of the personality and the erotic *kundalini* "Serpent Power."

One of the most interesting self-rallyings was told the editor as a reminiscence of a Polish overseer for the Dutch in Sumatra (at the beginning of World War II), speaking in either Malay or French, if not Dutch, who would say to his buttocks chidingly, "If you're going to talk, I'll be quiet." Compare Franco Sacchetti's *Trecento Novelle* (before 1400) No. 29; also *Kryptádia,* 1884, vol. II, p. 149, "Les Gens bien élevés," collected in Picardy by E. Henry Carnoy. In another Picardy tale in the same important series, vol. XI: p. 148, "Un Vieux polisson," *An old woman who is cleaning the statue of her favorite male saint in church is led to believe that the saint is pulling up her skirts, and addresses him angrily.*

This is unquestionably some "coded" reference to a (formerly) phallic saint, of the kind still made the object of a famous public quasi-religious cult or ceremonial by women, including embroidered surplices changing in color with the seasons, for the *Manneken-Pis* statue of a naked urinating boy in Brussels, Belgium. See further on phallic religious vestiges of this kind, Roger Goodland's remarkable *Bibliography of Sex Rites and Customs* (1930), and most recently Ed Schilders' *De Voorhuid van Jezus* (*Jesus' Foreskin,* 1985). A fascinating monograph could be written on these themes of all the speaking privates, or anus, of both sexes; not forgetting the fabulous *locus classicus* for much early-modern erotic folklore, Antonio Vignale's *La Cazzaria* (*The Book of the Prick,* about 1530), concerning the Great and Bloody War Between the Sexual Organs. An excellent English translation, done anonymously by Samuel Putnam, was ignobly printed in California, 1968, as *Dialogue on Diddling,* "by Sir Hotspur Dunderpate," a true folklore classic well worth rediscovering and salvaging now.

SECTION F

Obscenity in Ozark Riddles

The true old-time Ozarker was very fond of conundrums, enigmas, puzzles, catch questions and wise-cracks, which he lumped together under the name of riddles. Young folks used to sit around the fire and "riddle theirselves" through long winter evenings. Riddles served the purpose of modern intelligence tests, and the ability to solve puzzles was often taken as an index of general mental development. "Workin' out riddles" was supposed to be an excellent intellectual discipline. Many people put riddles to their children in order to train their minds, just as more sophisticated parents insisted upon the study of Latin and mathematics.

In the late 1880s, it is said, strangers even stopped each other in the street to try out the latest riddles:

> There was a teamster with a four-horse wagon just west of Rolla, Mo., and he was stuck in the mud plumb to the hubs. He was whipping the horses, and cussin' loud as he could. A preacher happened along, and was shocked by all this blasphemous caterwauling.
> "My friend," said the minister, "do you know the name of Him who died for sinners?"
> "I got no time for conundrums now!" shouted the teamster. "Can't you see I'm stuck in this son-of-a-bitching mud?" [Compare: Randolph, *Funny Stories about Hillbillies,* 1944, p. 9.]

It is surprising to hear Ozark women, who are absurdly prudish in some ways, and would be insulted if a strange man pronounced such a word as *bull* in their presence, use very broad expressions in connection with riddles. I know a schoolmarm who sat with a bunch of hillfolk near Fort Smith, Ark., in 1928. There were both men and women in the group, and they told a lot of very suggestive riddles.

In leaving, the schoolmarm said that she'd like to come up later in the Fall and gather some nuts on the place. The whole group looked embarrassed, and some of the men walked away. "Riddles is riddles," an old woman explained later, "and you can say anything *then*. But when you're a-talking sense, you don't never say nasty words like *nuts* in a mixed crowd. Leastways *decent* people don't, specially women-folks." [Note formalized abrogation of taboo by riddling.]

Only four collections of riddles from the Ozark region have ever been published, so far as I know, over the twenty years from 1934 to 1954 [ending with Vance Randolph and Mary-Celestia Parler, "Riddles from Arkansas," in *Journal of American Folklore,* vol. 67: pp. 253–59]. In each of the three papers with which I was concerned, the number of items was reduced when either my collaborator [Archer Taylor] or the editor insisted that the "obscene" pieces be eliminated. It is my purpose to set down the rejected riddles here. They were all collected in the Ozark region subsequent to 1920 and before 1954.

V. R.

Editor's Note: "Obscene" Riddling. The peculiarity which Randolph comments upon, that the Ozark verbal taboos are lifted during the telling of riddles, has its parallels in many other countries. As he observes, it seems extraordinarily out-of-keeping with the exaggerated verbal prudery affected by the

Ozark dwellers—though in public only. See his "Verbal Modesty in the Ozarks," in *Dialect Notes* (1928) vol. 6: pp. 57–64, for some almost ludicrous examples, such as "cow-critter" for a *bull*; and further in his volume of folksay with George P. Wilson, *Down in the Holler* (1953).

Obscene riddling is, in many countries, closely connected with ritual obscenity in jokes, songs, and even gestures during *rites de passage* concerning birth and death, such as at weddings and in particular funerals. This sort of permitted, or rather required jocular obscenity, in stories and riddles at such times, is an intentional invocation of the immanent power and magic of sexuality, to drive off occult dangers perceived as omnipresent and particularly threatening at moments of either great happiness or sorrow, and the passage into or out of the "other world" of death. See in this connection the fine monograph by the Abbé Augustin Nadal, added to his *Histoire des Vestales* (1725), on the right enjoyed by Roman soldiers to recite bawdy satires against their own victorious generals: the origin, in part, of the famously bawdy soldiers' songs still today. (For further commentary on Nadal's study see G. Legman, *The Horn Book,* 1964, pp. 384–85 and 408–09).

Modern permitted or required obscenity at funerals is an *anti-taboo,* or form of contradictory relief from verbal taboo, and is particularly marked in Ireland and in the Hispanic cultures. In the latter there is even a formalized song, well-known today, "*El Bobo en el Velorio*" ("The Fool at the Funeral, or Wake"), entirely turning on the fool's riddles which appear to be bawdy as told, but to which there is invariably an "innocent" solution offered by the erotically jesting fool. One of many examples: "I put it in hard and dry, and took it out soft and wet. What is it?—Answer: *Chewing-gum.*" This is the type of riddle, or riddling format, most common in the Ozark examples collected by Randolph, as seen in the following pages.

Certain of the Italian tale-tellers or *novellieri* of the sixteenth century, in particular Gian-Francesco Straparola, whose *Piacevoli Notti* or "Facetious Nights" were published in 1550–53, presenting materials already surely old and traditional at that date, divides up his stories with little courtly scenes among the ladies and gentlemen presumably telling the stories, in imitation of Boccaccio's *Decameron* (manuscript 1350). But here the interludes or story-framework of this mixed company's entertainment are precisely the telling of riddles, most of them bawdy, of the two classic sorts: A) those that seem bawdy when told, but have innocent solutions; and B) those that seem innocent when told, but have bawdy solutions. These two sorts, already classic then in Italy, have stayed current in the West at least since then.

In the parent British and Scottish cultures from which the Ozark highlanders originally came, word-games of all kinds, including riddles, acrostics, spoonerisms (*chiasmi*), and so forth were extremely popular, especially in the sixteenth to the eighteenth centuries. Many will be found recorded in some of the very oldest jestbooks in English, and in old country-house commonplace or "autograph" books such as that of Richard Hill, as edited by Dyboski (see the bibliography following). They are frequent also in the most popular of the seventeenth-century drollery and "compliment" books, which were anthologies of gallant and satirical poetry, bawdy songs, models for love-letter writers, etc. One drollery was even neatly illustrated—*Wits Recreations* (1640), the long section entitled "Fancies and Fantasticks," reprinted in *Musarum Deliciae,* 1870, vol. 2—with woodcut rebuses, and grotesque drawings reprinted from the so-called *Songes Drolatiques* falsely ascribed to Rabelais a century before.

The key to much of this older literature is the unpublished Harvard thesis by Courtney Craig Smith, *Restoration Drolleries and Jest Books* (1944: Harvard Archival Film Laboratory, No. 3277) running to 620 pages. This type of jocular word-game and its literature are by no means extinct, though admittedly less common than in the early 1900s. For example, Jackie Martling's *Raunchy Riddles* and *More Raunchy Riddles* (New York, 1984–85), two modern pocketbook volumes for stand-up comedians, in which "raunchy" means bawdy, demonstrating clearly the continuing popularity of bawdy riddles at the folk level.

One form of what are only by courtesy riddles will be found at Nos. 46–54 following. These are generally proposed as "Differences" ("What's the difference between . . . ?"). They turn strictly verbally and usually nonsensically on the ancient Greek rhetorical device of *chiasmus,* or "crossing," so called from the

Greek letter *X, chi*. Such crossings of words often occur accidentally, when emotionally upset or tired—as also similar inversions of intended hand-motions, as in typewriting or playing a musical instrument—and in non-riddle form they are thus known as "tongue twisters." Since the nineteenth century they have been called in English "Spoonerisms" (in German, *Schüttelreime,* shuttle-rhymes), and are assimilated to an unfortunate Oxford don to whom all such invented slips were ascribed, such as having begun a formal allocution before Queen Victoria: "Your Majesty, I have in my bosom a *half-warmed fish . . .*"

However, they are recorded first in Rabelais' *Pantagruel* (1533) chapters 16 and 21, as "*contrepéteries,*" or "cross-fartings," where both examples that Rabelais retails are bawdy, and presumably a form already old and traditional: "There was but an *antistrophe,* or little more than a literal inversion between a woman, *folle à la messe,* and *molle à la fesse*: that is, foolish at the mass, and of a pliant buttock." (Urquhart translation.) The modern development of such erotic spoonerisms in France since Rabelais is astonishingly complex: best seen in Louis Perceau's *La Redoute de Contrepéteries,* or *"Cross-fartings"* (1934), and in the continuations of this work by "Luc Etienne" (Professor Perrin). On the inevitable psychological anality of all such upside-down humor, see my *No Laughing Matter,* vol. II: pp. 982–85, "All to Shit." And consider also reversible palindromes, as Adam (to Eve): "Madam, I'm Adam."

The antecedents and superstitious importance of riddles are extremely ancient (see further note on 44 below), for example in the story of Samson and his attempts to evade the treachery of his wife and mistress Delilah through his lion riddle, in *Judges,* 14:12–18, and the secret of his heroic strength in his hair. The anxiety anciently—and still!—expressed about deciphering and interpreting the riddle or mystery of dreams, and of the stars in their courses, is also very prominent in the Bible, particularly in the stories of Joseph in Egypt (*Genesis,* chapters 40–41), and of Daniel in the lions' den (*Daniel,* chapters 2–6), where the first known reference to graffiti also occurs, presumably about 540 B.C., in the fateful handwriting on the wall at Belshazzar's Feast.

Note: All annotations in paragraph form and materials in brackets in the following pages are by the editor. Solutions to the riddles are given in italics.

1

In many cases the vulgarity lies in the riddle before it is answered. When the solution is given, the whole thing seems innocent enough. Take this example from Van Buren, Ark.:

> Belly to belly, hand on back,
> Piece of fresh meat to stop up the crack.

2

Here's another version of the same riddle. An old man in Joplin, Mo., told me that he heard it when he was a little boy:

> Belly on belly, hand over back,
> Take a piece of meat and stick it in the crack.

This sounds a bit suggestive of coitus, but the answer is merely: *A woman nursing her baby.*

3

Mrs. E. B., Hot Springs, Ark., collected this from some children in 1938:

> Laying on a hillside, belly to the sun,
> Wiggledy, wiggledy, the juice begun to come.
>
> *Old sow with pigs sucking.*

4

This one was contributed by a schoolteacher in Crawford County, Ark.; she learned it about 1930:

> Dead in the middle,
> Alive at both ends.
>
> The answer is not an old man's penis, but: *A young man plowing corn.* The horse and the man are alive, but the plow is not alive.

5

I got the two riddles which follow from the same informant near Pineville, Mo., in 1931:

> Hairy all around the hole,
> In slipped Birdie.
>
> *A bird's nest.*
> [Very rare in English, the reference to the penis as a *bird* is the commonest Annunciatory metaphor in Italian: *uccello*.]

6

> It's not round,
> And it's not square,
> It's ringed all round
> With a little bunch of hair.
>
> *An eye.*

7

Here's a variant from West Plains, Mo., where the man said he heard it in the 1880s:

> A little hole,
> Hair all round it,
> Red at the rim,
> Water comes out of it.
>
> *An eye.*

8

A lady in Christian County, Mo., in 1941, remembered this one:

> Hairy all around the hole,
> Wet at the end,
> In slipped a little thing
> Too stiff to bend.

A bearded man, eating with a spoon.

9

Related item contributed by Lon Jordan, Farmington, Ark., in 1942:

> Under your apron,
> Black as a crow,
> Hair all around
> Like grass it doth grow.
> If you don't touch it
> It will do you no harm,
> Stick something in it,
> To keep something warm.

A woman's muff.

10

Here's one from Mr. C. B., Little Rock, Ark., 1938. He learned it near Sweet Home, Ark., about 1912:

> Black without, red within,
> Raise up your leg and stick it in.

"The answer is not a nigger wench," says Mr. B., "but *a rubber boot*. Nearly all boots were lined with red cloth when I was a boy."

11

A variant contributed, without comment, by a schoolmarm near Fort Smith, Ark., in 1932:

> Black on the outside, red within,
> Hoist up your leg and stick it in.

A boot.

12

From Mr. J. E., Webster Groves, Mo., April, 1948. He learned it in the Missouri Ozarks, about 1885:

> What stands up in the bed
> And has a round head?
> It goes in easy,
> Slobbers all around,
> When it comes out,
> Makes the belly all greasy.

A head of cabbage, cooked in the pot with pork. [Compare the Hispanic riddle on *chewing-gum* quoted in the editor's note, above.]

13

Remembered by a lady in Pineville, Mo., 1933:

> Goes in hard, comes out easy,
> Comes out limber, slick and greasy.

Cabbage cooked with pork.

14

Heard in Fayetteville, Ark., 1942:

> It goes in stiff and stout,
> Limber and greasy when it comes out.

Cabbage boiled with meat.

15

Some children at Galena, Mo., in 1933, repeated this riddle as learned from their parents:

> The old man went out
> And shuck it and shuck it,
> The old woman bent over
> And tuck it and tuck it.

The old man shook *an apple* off a tree, and the old woman took it—picked it up, that is. [Note position of coitus indicated, from behind during field work, as in many rural cultures.]

16

A variant found in Reeds Spring, Mo., about 1936:

> The old man he shuck it and shuck it,
> The old woman up with her dress and tuck it.

> The old man shook *fruit* off a tree, and the old woman pulled up her dress to catch it, as in an apron.

17

Collected by a schoolmarm near Fort Smith, Ark., in 1932: [Compare: *Journal of American Folklore, 1934, vol. 47: p. 84.*]

> The old woman she pet it and pat it,
> The old man took off his britches and went at it.

> *A bed.*

18

From Webster Groves, Mo., in 1948. It was well known in the 1880s, according to my informant:

> Riddle me, riddle me, riddle me ree,
> What does a little boy hold in his hand
> Whenever he goes out to pee?

> *The latch-string, or doorknob.*

The old gentleman who gave me this riddle said: "How well do I remember the wintry nights when, just before going to bed, I'd step out into the dark and hang onto the door-handle while I emptied my bladder. I always expected a ghost to come around the corner of the house and grab me." [For the underlying superstition see section H, "Unprintable Ozark Folk-Beliefs," No. 17.]

19

Contributed by a nameless lady in Springfield, Mo., about 1935:

> Riddle-me, riddle-me, riddle me riss,
> What does an old man hold
> When he goes out to ————?

> [Answer missing: *Doorknob.*]

20

Here's a variant from Huntsville, Ark., 1948:

> Riddledy, riddledy, riddledy rout,
> What does a little boy hold in his hand
> When he goes out?

The doorknob.

21

Contributed by the artist Rose O'Neill, Day, Mo., in 1940. She had it from a neighbor:

> The old man went to bed and forgot it,
> The old woman went to bed and forgot it,
> Then the old man got up and stuck it in.

The door pin, a little peg used to bolt the door on the inside.

22

A text from Walnut Shade, Mo., 1941:

> Uncle John and Aunt Sue to bed had gone,
> Uncle John had left a job undone,
> So Uncle John climbed over Aunt Sue
> And put it in the hole. What was it?

The door pin.

23

Sent to me in 1939 by an old gentleman from Cedar County, Mo.

> Stiff a-standing in the bed,
> First it's white and then it's red . . .

My informant had forgotten the last two lines [See No. 24, following, with fellatory conclusion], but said that the answer is "*A radish.*"

24

This one was collected in Washington County, Ark., in 1941. [Compare No. 23 preceding, and 32 below.]

> It's stiff and red and stands in the bed,
> There's not a lady in the land
> That wouldn't take it in her hand
> And shove it into her mouth.

A radish.

25

A girl at Tahlequah, Okla., in 1944, thought this riddle had been "made up" by one of her boy-friends:

> Pretty fellow dressed in yellow,
> Dressed without no stitches,
> Mabel grabbed it by the head
> And off come his britches.
>
> *A banana.*

26

From Mr. C. C., Eureka Springs, Ark., in 1953. He heard it about 1915. [Castrated males are believed to speak and sing in high voices, as in the conclusion of the cowboy song, "Strawberry Roan," in section A, No. 239.]

> What is it that has six nuts, and sings?
>
> *A barber-shop quartette; we ain't sure about the tenor.*

27

Contributed by a lady in Joplin, Mo., in the middle 1920s:

> What is it that's six inches long, with a head on it and all the women like it?
>
> *A dollar bill.*

28

A related item from Hot Springs, Ark., in 1938:

> What's six inches long, just the right size,
> And ladies take it between their thighs?
>
> *The horn on a side-saddle.*

29

This one was common in Barry County, Mo., about 1930, perhaps much earlier:

> What is it that a girl does setting down, a boy does standing up, and a dog does on three legs?
>
> *Shakes hands.*

[Compare *Anecdota Americana,* 1934, p. 150, which adds "—of course!"]

30

Reported by a lady in Van Buren, Ark., July, 1932. She had it from rural school-children. [Pretended scatological reference:]

> Down she squat, out it come,
> Up she jumped, home she run.
>
> *Girl milking a cow.*

31

Variant from a schoolmarm near Mena, Ark., in 1936:

> Up she jumped, out she run,
> Down she squat, and out it come.
>
> *Girl went out and milked a cow.*

[*Journal of American Folklore*, 1934, vol. 47: p. 87.]

32

Related riddle from the same lady, who learned it in southwest Missouri when a school girl, about 1926. [Note the fellatory conclusion, as in Nos. 23 and 24 above.]

> White thing hangs down,
> Bag swings loose,
> Pull the white thing,
> Drink the juice.
>
> *Girl milking a cow.*

33

This one was given me in Van Buren, Ark., in 1932:

> Wooden belly, iron back,
> Fire in the hole, goes off with a crack.
>
> *A rifle.*

34

A. From a woman named Freese, Joplin, Mo., 1936. She heard it in Benton County, Ark., about 1890:

> Big long slim fellow,
> Pinch his cock and make him bellow.
>
> *A rifle.*

B. A variant form heard in Pineville, Mo., about 1928:

> Long slim slick feller,
> Pull his cock, hear him beller.
>
> *A rifle.*

35

Collected near Fort Smith, Ark., in 1932. [References like this to defloration and to its bleeding are very uncommon, owing to the folk-taboos as to both virginity and blood:]

> Sally had a hairy thing,
> John had a long thing;
> John stuck his long thing
> Into Sally's hairy thing,
> And it bled.
>
> *John took his butcher-knife and killed Sally's pig.*

36

This was a favorite with young people near Branson, Mo., in the middle 1940s:

> Great long thing,
> Fumbles in the hole.
>
> *A stove lifter,* a long handle to remove the lids from a cookstove.

37

Vaguely remembered by a very old lady at Galena, Mo., in 1933:

> One going in,
> And two a-shaking . . .
>
> (*Answer missing.*) The ostensible reference is to the penis and testicles during sexual intercourse. In the older Scottish form: "The master goes into the dark cave, and his two valets are shaking with fear (or dancing) outside the door."

38

Beside the harmless-when-answered riddles noted above, there are many items with "unprintable" words in the question or the answer, or both. Here are three examples gathered at Reeds Spring, Mo., in 1934:

> What's quicker than thought?—
>
> *Shit*: I shit before I thought.

Do you know what thought did?—
No, what?—

*Went to bed like I did, and shit the bed,
like you did.*

39

What is the sharpest thing in the world?—

A fart: It goes through your pants without
making a hole.

40

Collected near Joplin, Mo., in the late 1920s:

Riddledy, riddledy, riddledy rye,
Two fat cheeks and one black eye.

A man with a sore ass.

41

An old gentleman at Carterville, Mo., in 1927, assured me that the following riddle was more than a
hundred years old:

Black and green
And yellow between.

A nigger shitting in the grass.

42

I heard this one at West Plains, Mo., in 1934:

Redhot feet, cold ass,
Pick it up or let it pass.

Fire tongs.

43

This one came to me from Jasper County, Mo., in 1932. My informant heard it near Pine Bluff, Ark,
in the 1880s. [This is a "neck-verse," which saves the endangered person. In the text: *snatch,* vagina, a
seventeenth-century term. In 1:2, *Bugle,* the foxhound's name:]

A man had a prize foxhound to die on him, and he thought a nigger woman had poisoned it. He was going to whip her, but if she knowed a riddle he couldn't figure out, he would turn her loose. She cut off the dead dog's tail and stuck it up her snatch, and then she says:

> Riddle riddle runt,
> Bugle in my cunt,
> Riddle riddle rout,
> Tail a-sticking out.
>
> Riddle riddle riss,
> If you riddle this,
> Riddle riddle rass,
> You can whip my ass!

The man tried a long time, but he couldn't figure out the answer. So then the nigger wench told him, and showed him old Bugle's tail, and he had to turn her loose.

44

Contributed by a schoolteacher in Crawford County, Ark., in 1931:

> In it went, out it come,
> Saved the lives of seven sons.

An old woman had seven boys, and they were to be hanged unless she could spin a riddle that the King couldn't solve. She walked through the timber and saw a woodpecker enter a hole in a tree, and then come out again. So she gave the riddle as above. The King failed to answer it, and the seven sons were saved.

Compare *Journal of American Folklore* (1934) vol. 47: p. 87. This and the preceding "neck-verse" No. 43, are "*stumping* riddles," in which the person propounding the riddle escapes some danger or evades a persecutor who cannot solve the riddle, as with Samson trying to foil Delilah and the Philistines in *Judges* 14:12–18; or the Child Ballad No. 3, "The False Knight Upon the Road." More often it is the dangerous person who propounds the riddle: to discover his name (Rumplestiltskin) or hidden desire Sir Gawain and the Hag: made into Puccini's last opera, *Turandot* (1924); or to discover the meaning of an obscure but disturbing riddling dream or omen, as in the Biblical stories of Joseph and of Daniel; or the solution to some difficult mathematical problem or impossible numbering task set, such as counting the sands of the sea, or doubling the volume of a cube; almost always in order to avoid some evil fate. This largely explains the ancient popularity of riddles.

45

Written out for me by a citizen of Mena, Ark., in 1938:

> I had a hard time to get it,
> I liked it fine when I got it,
> The longer I had it, the less I liked it,
> I gave away more of it than I got,
> And still had more of it than I wanted,
> I paid a lot of money to get rid of it.

A dose of the clap.

833

A *paradoxical* or "negative" type of riddle, of ancient or Oriental origin, based on the idea of the immutability of one's destiny, a main tenet of ancient Greek philosophy. In the famous Greek form of the riddle, which has no sexual reference—and therefore no version of line 2, here, about "liking it fine when I got it"—the answer is: *fleas*.

46

See further the editorial note, at the end of the Preface here, on the following change-ringing or "Spoonerism"—[*chiasmi*]. All the four "difference" items were collected in Eureka Springs, Ark., in 1949:

> What's the difference between a baby and a shitepoke?—
>
> *A shitepoke flits around the shore.*

47

> What's the difference between a goldfish and a mountain lion?—
>
> *A goldfish is always mucking around the fountain.*

48

> What's the difference between a rooster and a lawyer?—
>
> *A rooster clucks defiance.*

49

> What's the difference between a hot whore and the Panama Canal?—
>
> *The Panama Canal is a busy ditch.*

These four examples are of the evasive or "sophisticated" type in which the final answers are left to the listener to work out, on the hints given: *shits around the floor; fucking around the mountain; fucks the clients;* and *a dizzy bitch.* The last is earlier in Samuel Roth's expurgated *Anecdota Americana,* (1934) p. 186.

50

An old man at Cane Hill, Ark., in 1941, asked me this one:

> "What's the difference between me washing my overalls here, and Mary and Lucy baking a pie in Little Rock?" I did not know the answer. "Well," said he, "*one is a pair of old pants in the country, and the other one is a pair of old cunts in the pantry.*"

51

While I was writing this down, my informant recalled another of the same type.

"What's the difference between a sewing machine and a piece of tail?" he asked. *"One sews seams good, the other seems so good."* [Not actually of the same type, as here only the vowels are change-rung, in "inner" assonance; and not the opening consonants, in alliterative reversals.]

52

Collected near Van Buren, Ark., in 1932: [Compare *Journal of American Folklore,* 1934, vol. 47: p. 86.]

What's the difference between a watermelon and a sweet pea?—

The watermelon always comes first.

53

Another item from the same informant:

What's the difference between a potato-bug and a bedbug?—

A potato-bug sets on potatoes and peas:
a bedbug sets on pillows and sheets.

54

And another, also from the same informant:

What's the difference between circus acrobats and the gals in a whorehouse?—

The acrobats have cunning stunts; and the whores
have stunning cunts.

55

In Eureka Springs, Ark., in 1946, a smart-aleck asked one of the local virgins:

"What's the difference between a man and a woollen blanket?" The girl pondered awhile, then said that she didn't know. "Well," said the village wit, "you better find out, before you get under one!"

56

Here's another such catch-question heard in Joplin, Mo., in 1940.

"What's the difference between a sin and a pity?" The answer is "Well, *putting it in is a sin. But it's a pity to pull it out.*"

(*The Limerick,* Paris, 1953, p. 425, no. 896, gives this from the editor's own early memories as: "Children's riddle, Pennsylvania, ca. 1925: 'What's the difference between a sin and a shame?—*It's a sin to put it in, but it's a shame to take it out.*'")

57

From a lady at Eureka Springs, Ark., in 1947:

What has a nigger got in his pants that
will kill a cow, but won't hurt a woman?—*Blackleg.*

Blackleg is a dreaded bovine disease, of the hoof-and-mouth type.

58

Here's another from the same informant:

What is the silliest bug in the world?
The lightning-bug: He not only shows his ass, but holds a light so everybody can see it.

59

Contributed by a schoolmarm in Carroll County, Ark., in 1948. [Current slang, *to make,* seduce.]

What did the rooster do when it started to rain?
He made a duck under the porch.

60

Sent me by Carl Withers, folklorist, New York, 1948. He heard it at Wheatland, Mo., about 1940:

What is the best tea in the world?—C-U-N-T.

Also heard among children about 1928, and in *Anecdota Americana,* also 1928, as a coded message: "See You When Tea Is Ready." This is given in Joyce's *Ulysses* as by an adult, in Dublin, 1905.

61

From a lady in Barry County, Mo., 1936:

What did the fruit-jar say to the cover?—

You can't screw me without a rubber.

Also seen as a little anthropomorphic drawing on a vest-pocket "novelty card," 1964, with the lady fruit-jar speaking; not as a riddle.

62

Here's one that was heard around Sallisaw, Okla., in the middle 1920s. [Sometimes "politely," as: When are *all* holes open?"]

When are women's holes open?—

In planting time, of course.

A woman making a garden stands astride the row, with her feet wide apart.

63

Collected near Van Buren, Ark., in 1932. [*Crabs,* crab-lice.]

Why does the ocean roar?—

If you had as many crabs on your bottom
as the ocean, you'd roar too.

64

Contributed by a schoolmarm near Fort Smith, Ark., in 1932; as also the following item:

Why is a boy's pecker like light-bread?—

Neither one is any good if it don't rise.

65

How is a woman like a skillet?—

You have to get both of 'em hot, or they
ain't worth a damn.

In the editor's *Peregrine Penis: An Autobiography of Innocence,* manuscript 1988, chapter 8, "Girl Crazy," *temp.* 1933, he describes a scene of private sex education of an adolescent boy by an older man, a retired vaudeville comedian, explaining to him the importance of female passion and of satisfying it: "*First get the pan hot!—Then put in the meat!*"

66

Collected in Van Buren, Ark., in 1932:

> How does a fat woman act on a hot night?—
>
> *She takes off her hat, and pants.*

67

From a lady in Fort Smith, Ark., in 1932. *Goober* means peanut, but it is also a dialect word for penis. [Compare riddle 52, above.]

> If it takes a watermelon two months to water,
> And a cantaloup three months to lope,
> How long will it take a peanut to pea?
>
> *Just long enough to get the goober out.*

68

I heard this near Van Buren, Ark., in 1932: [*Sorghum* is molasses.]

> Did you hear about the boy who ate too much sorghum?—
> No, what happened to him?—
> Nothing happened to *him*. But the tumble-turds had
>   a candy-breaking that lasted four months!

69

Some of these catch-questions have the appearance of [pretended] spontaneous creations. In Carroll County, Ark., in 1948, we were talking about somebody's twins, a girl and a boy. Our village humorist said:

> "One baby was born just before midnight, the other a few minutes after midnight. Which one was the boy?" Another man scratched his head. "Why, I don't know," he answered. "Lots of people don't know about that," said the first speaker. *"The boy is the one with the pecker between his legs."*

70

The school children at Rocky Comfort, Mo., in 1930, thought this one was very funny:

> I see they cut down all the walnut trees.—
> What did they do that for?—
> They had to, in order to keep down scandal;
> Them trees was showing their nuts to the womenfolks!

SECTION G

Folk Graffiti from the Ozarks

About 1915 the late G. Stanley Hall of Clark University told me that somebody should do a Ph.D. dissertation on the wall-scribblings in public toilets. I was not impressed at the time, and thought no more about it until 1938, when Professor Robert A. Caldwell, at the University of Arkansas, showed me Allen Walker Read's scholarly monograph, *Lexical Evidence from Folk Epigraphy,* privately published in Paris in 1935. Read was a professor at the University of Missouri, and his book is a collection of back-house inscriptions gathered in the summer of 1928. This opus begins with a defense of the vernacular, since Read apparently thinks that Americans who do not say *shit, piss,* and *fuck* must be crazy: "That anyone should pass up the well-established colloquial words of the language and have recourse to the Latin *defecate, urinate,* and *have sexual intercourse,* is indicative of grave mental unhealth."

The colloquial words are not passed up in Read's work: *shit* appears 73 times, *fuck* 53 times, and *piss* 22 times, the author observing that the latter word is used eight times in the Authorized Version of the Bible. [As shown in *Dialect Notes,* July 1934, vol. VI: p. 389.] See also "An Obscenity Symbol," in *American Speech,* for December 1934, vol. XI: pp. 264–78, in which Read discusses the term *fuck* at great length, yet somehow avoids using the "unprintable" word.

Read's book aroused my interest in this type of material, and I searched the *inscriptoria* of many an Ozark town and village, in the years since. Similar scribblings are found in wagon yards, livery stables, berry sheds, and even in doorways where village boys gather to watch the girls go by. I have seen a few in the lobbies of small-town hotels. But public toilets are the best places to look for such items. Obscene writings are more numerous in open privies than in coin-operated toilets. One finds better stuff in crappers connected with railroad stations, cheap pool-halls, and workingmen's saloons than in expensive establishments. This may mean only that tile or marble walls are less easy to write upon than the painted wood or plaster of the poor man's privy. Also the porters in better-class places are more assiduous in erasing inscriptions.

It appears that women are somewhat less prone to this sort of writing than men. My first thought was that this must be due to feminine delicacy and refinement. However, the inscriptions which do appear in women's toilets are quite as nasty as those found in back-houses frequented solely by men. Most men use lead pencils, while many inscriptions in women's toilets are done in lipstick. It may be that the ladies write less merely because they do not carry pencils, and are disinclined to waste lipstick which is comparatively expensive.

Detectives and other knowledgeable folk say that some of these wall-scribblings are code messages. R. Havelock-Bailie, in "Fools' Names and Fools' Faces" (*Official Detective Stories,* Oct. 1947), tells how a murderer was identified and captured at Blytheville, Ark., by reason of such an inscription in a bus-station toilet. Konrad Bercovici thinks that Gypsies leave *patterans* in toilets "at every railroad station in the United States. No white person knows anything about them, yet the smallest Gypsy child can discover and read them." (*American Magazine,* Mar. 1929.)

Elderly persons tell me that obscene back-house epigraphy was unknown in the good old days; they regard its prevalence as marking the degeneracy and depravity of modern youth. But the fact is that the pioneers had no privies—see my *The Ozarks*, pages 39–40—and most of them couldn't write, anyhow. The foremost historian of Carroll County, Ark., where I now live, says that "Ninety per cent of the people here during the 1870s would be classed as wholly illiterate." (J. L. Russell, *Behind These Ozark Hills*, 1947, p. 61.)

Having no access to the literature of the subject, beyond the work of Read and McAtee, I do not know whether the Ozark *latriniana* differs from that found in other parts of the United States. Such material as I have, I set down here for the consideration of the learned. The items which follow were collected from 1938 to 1954, in southern Missouri, northern Arkansas, and eastern Oklahoma.

V. R.

Editor's Note: Graffiti: The inadequacy of the term "oral transmission" to limit folklore has always been evident, if only because so narrow a definition would omit all such non-verbal manifestations and folk-traditions as artifacts and methods of doing things: building houses, dancing, working, planting seeds, making love, having babies, taking medicine, living and dying. Most of these essential acts are not done or learned "orally." The term will also certainly not apply to those actually written forms of authentic folklore that are wall *graffiti*—wherever found—and the century-old printed or handwrit satirical broadsides they became, sometimes scaled down to vest-pocket "novelty cards," for ease of concealment when their subject would be sexual, scatological, political, irreligious, or otherwise taboo.

These written items of ephemeral nature, or *Flugschriften,* fly-sheets, are nowadays grouped as "Xeroxlore" or similar, from the name of their most recent mechanical photoprint method of amateur reproduction. Up to a very recent date we were often still handwriting, or mimeographing, or typewriting them—sometimes even with the carbon-paper slipped in backwards, to make a secret copy illegible except in a mirror. The private, and often the surreptitious nature of such materials is not essentially changed by their being finger-tapped or keystroked out now, at a midnight "computer break," for an *electronic billboard* suddenly appearing out of nowhere on a thousand screens the next morning, nationwide, trickling along in little green letters line-by-line and then falling anonymously into the laser print-out tray. This too is folklore, of our new century, and many of these only-externally electronic scripts clearly show their origin in the ancient anonymous wall scrawls that are *graffiti*.

Ancient; very ancient. The imperial tombs of Pharaonic Egypt, cut into the rock in the third and fourth millennia B.C., are quite covered on their inner walls with sacerdotal writings and hieroglyphic symbols. The walls of the prehistoric rock-caves, that the tombs imitate, have held their superb animal pictographs since tens of thousands of years earlier. But these are all a formalized, and probably a subsidized priestly art. They lack the true human spontaneity of real handwriting or lettering. Of this, the first firm record we have is at Belshazzar's Feast and the downfall of the Chaldean Empire: of historic date in 538 B.C., whether or not one believes literally the legend attached, of the Handwriting On the Wall—mysteriously appearing, then as now—in the *Book of Daniel,* V. 5–31:

> In the same hour came forth fingers of a man's
> hand, and wrote over against the candlestick upon
> the plaster of the wall of the king's palace: and
> the king saw the part of the hand that wrote . . .
> And this is the writing that was written:

> MENE, MENE, TEKAL, UPHARSIN

This arch-famous Aramaic line is believed to have been one of the main inspirations of Joseph Smith's translation of *The Book of Mormon* (1830), from the long-buried Golden Plates delivered to him by the Angel Moroni on September 21, 1823, near Palmyra, in upstate New York. For here we learn, in the *Book of Alma,* X. 2: "Now these are the words which Amulek preached: I am Amulek . . . descendant of Aminadi; and it was that same Aminadi who interpreted the writing which was upon the wall of the temple, which was written by the finger of God."

Since at least those days, *graffiti* have always been a favorite form of folk communication, almost always anonymous, yet put up prominently in public places. There are whole volumes published of the corpus of authentic inscriptions of antique Greece and Rome, of which these and the rather similar inscriptions on coins are among the oldest existing records. The poet and novelist, Pierre Louÿs, in his masterpiece *Aphrodite* (1896), a sensually pagan reconstitution of the life of a prostitute in the ancient Greek world about 400 B.C., does not overlook to record in the second chapter, how the young girl prostitute, Seso, finds a chalk inscription on the jetty of Alexandria, on the special Ceramic Wall devoted to such rendezvous appointments, the cash offer in silver addressed to her: "*Seso of Knidos—Timon son of Lysias—One mina.*" "She paled slightly: 'I remain,' she said."

This same significant scene could have taken place today—wall-*graffito* and all—at the "Meat Market" corner of 42nd Street and Eighth Avenue in New York City, or the similar "Buckets of Blood" rendezvous in London, Los Angeles, Chicago, Paris, Amsterdam, or a score of other great world capitals, except that the wall-scrawled offer would more likely be made to a male prostitute than to a female. This is a point that will be returned to below.

It was the custom in early Roman times to mark off the limits of large country estates and gardens with roughly hewn statues of wood or stone pillars, called Hermæ, outfitted only with a bearded head and a large erect wooden penis—sometimes merely stuck upright into a fig-tree trunk—and usually a monumental foot or foot-and-a-half long. This, of course, in the style of the ithyphallic Greek satyr statues, of which a very few have been miraculously preserved unmutilated. These Roman field-marker statues or Hermæ represented the so-called tutelary or protective god of gardens, Priapus (he of the Large Penis), also called Mutunus or Tutunus; and at a later period the large erect penis would be pudibundly veiled with sculptured drapes. At their classic period the Hermæ would necessarily be decorated with small signs, roughly lettered or cut into a small slab of wood, or on papyrus, and hung over the statue's penis, warning that the god Priapus would bugger, with his outsize figwood penis, any robber who trespassed on the fields or stole the fruit.

Later, during the high years of the Roman Empire, convivial drinkers at private parties out in the fields would entertain themselves in competition writing bawdy poems to hang over Priapus's wooden penis. These poems were often just brief rhythmic distichs or inscriptions, imitating or topping the statue's traditional buggery threat. These pieces, obviously formalized *graffiti,* under the name of *Priapeia,* were gathered into a famous manuscript collection and edited, according to tradition reported by Servius and Donatus, by the greatest Roman poet, Virgil, "in his youth," or by Ovid, and presumably including some of his own originals in the vein. The *Priapeia* have always been printed in the "Appendix Vergiliana" or "Juvenilia" of the poet Virgil since the earliest incunabular editions, and several good translations have been made over the last century, especially in German and English. Some of the later books of erotic and satirical *Epigrams* by the classic Spanish-Roman poet Martial are also often in the "obscene" Priapean style, and are therefore usually missing from most translations.

By the time of the Renaissance in Italy, this type of rhymed and witty graffiti, sometimes merely in the sardonic question-and-answer style of statements followed by comments and toppers by other (anonymous) hands, were formalized as the "Pasquinades." These were critical and satirical complaints and statements on public affairs and personalities, and were hung in the night in the form of anonymous placards—rather similar to the output of modern scandal-and-exposé columnists—on an ancient old ruined and shapeless Roman statue called "Il Pasquino," discovered in the year 1503 "near one of the entrances of the ancient amphitheatre of Alexander Severus." (See further William S. Walsh's first-rate article on the Pasquinades, in his *Handy-Book of Literary Curiosities,* 1892, still the best and only reliable of the amateur "Treasuries of Serendipity.") There was also a competing statue, Marforio, and eventually an interloper, Facchino the porter, when the *graffiti* traffic got heavy, each statue representing the anonymous point of view of the competing social classes, thus politicizing the originally merely sexual and scatological wall-scrawls.

The outstanding satirical poet and playwright, Pietro of Arezzo, called Aretino (whose real family name is unknown since he refused to carry it, being illegitimate), was essentially the Pasquino of Italian literature of the early sixteenth century, and his purposeful insolence and obscenity can only be understood in this connection. A small collection of Pasquinades was published as *Pasquillorum: Tome duo,* in 1544; but they have never really received the attention they deserve, along with the fabulous Spanish satirical and rogue literature of the same period.

A century later, similar farces and privately printed brief lampoons against the French prime ministers were quite a fad, especially concerning the Italian politician in France, Cardinal Mazarin. Many were published then as single-sheets or broadside pamphlets, under the title of "Mazarinades," often resulting in jail-sentences for their authors when they could be found. A particular target of such poetry in England, during the Revolution of the 1640s, was the "Rump" Parliament, and a whole volume of drollery poetry lampooning it scatologically was published under the appropriately logical title of *The Rump.*

As can be seen, the *graffiti* of the old Greek and Roman walls—not to mention those of the *Book of Daniel*—had been tamed and politicized into a minor literary genre, by way of the Priapeia and the Pasquinades. The French and English drollery collections of songs and poems for drinking parties, from the 1560s to the 1660s and beyond, were filled eventually with nothing but love poems and bawdy songs, competing for space with political sardonics in the Pasquinade and Priapean style. See in particular, from this optic, the last and largest of the drolleries, *Pills to Purge Melancholy* (1699–1714), edited by Henry Playford in its final edition (1719–20, in six volumes!) under the straw-man signature of a fashionable theatre comedian, singer, and playwright of the period, in the later music-hall style, one Thomas Durfey. In fact, the political poetry overran the cup so lavishly by then, that there was even a competing, and solely political, drollery entitled *Pills to Purge* State *Melancholy.*

True British *graffiti* were also fortunately first collected and published at that same period, under the pseudonym of "Hurlo-Thrumbo"—never identified—as *The Merry-Thought,* or *Glass-Window and Boghouse Miscellany* (1731) in four parts: a *Merry-thought* being "that part of a chicken that goes over the fence last," and a *Boghouse* simply an out-house or privy. As to the "Glass-Window," the meaning here is that some of these gems were inscribed by their patrician poets with their diamond rings on the windows of then fashionable inns and boozing-kens. Some such, dated from the early-eighteenth century, are still to be seen so etched on the glass windows of old barrooms of the period at Oxford and Edinburgh, and probably elsewhere.

Almost no further literature on the subject of *graffiti* was published from that date onward for nearly two centuries, until a few examples were offered in 1899 in the final pages of the erotic folklore yearbook, *Kryptádia,* vol. VI: pp. 390–97, under the elegant title of "La Muse Latrinale," collected in various locations in southwest France since 1872. Vance Randolph also thought at first to ornament his small collection, following, with the title "Latriniana," but thought better of it later. As he notes, the first serious modern work other than that in *Kryptádia* and in its sequal series, *Anthropophytéia,* was the private monograph published at his own expense in Paris, 1935, by Professor Allen Walker Read, a Rhodes scholar at Oxford, from Missouri, and a very serious philologist and lexicographer.

In recent years, as one of the first (and least expensive) exploitations of the New Freedom of the 1970s, there has been a good deal of what can only be called junk-journalism connected with *graffiti:* a slew of humorous books, mostly by a librarian, Robert Reisner; and a few articles, most of which have sadly limited themselves to transcribing—and sometimes frankly faking—only the "clever" type, turning on word-plays or mock-satirical social and sexual complaints. Many of these clever-type items are cast in the colloquy or statement-and-comment style of the old Pasquinades, presumably by various hands replying to each other, and are to be found principally only in public toilet-rooms in or near the universities, as their over-intellectualized approach generally shows.—The same problem as with limericks, also basically only a male educated-class bawdy entertainment.

The only really insightful book on *graffiti* has been that by Drs. Ernest Abel and Barbara Bickley, *The Handwriting on the Wall* (1977); but there is real documentary value in the photo-illustrated collections by Dr. Luquet in *Anthropophytéia,* edited by F. Krauss (1905), and more recently William McLean—again published only in Paris, 1970—and by Ronnie Ellis, *Australian Graffiti* (1975).

A final point: Although one would not even suspect this from the contents of most of the recent published works on the subject, except a few psychological articles and the book *Tearoom Trade,* the largest percentage of all modern toilet-room epigraphy of this kind, except perhaps in toilets of and adjacent to the universities, concerns itself with homosexual assignations, both amateur and prostitutory, exactly as Pierre Louÿs describes in *Aphrodite,* as of Greek Alexandria in the fourth century B.C. As one attempted collector complained: "All they ever say is, '*Show it stiff, and get it sucked,*' and then no one ever turns up!"

Only a few authentic collections of modern graffiti have therefore ever been made, and none of these have been published until Randolph's now. The two largest such collections are those made by Professor Pelham-Box in London, just before World War II (now in the Legman Archive Collection), and another by Professor John Del Torto and G. Legman, just after. The latter is preserved in the Kinsey Institute for Sex Research Library, and is catalogued by error under the name of a patron, Thomas Painter. It includes the drawings traced from the walls at the same time. This is true of no other collection except that of Dr. Luquet, published in Krauss' large sexual folklore yearbook, *Anthropophytéia* in 1905. Another recent collection, by the British folklorist Venetia Newall, "The Moving Spray-Can" (in *Maledicta,* 1988, vol. 9), is restricted only to amusing examples, as the title suggests. Vance Randolph's present collection, though clearly selective, does not overlook to give at least a sample of the homosexual and prostitutory epigraphs, in a way typical of his unremitting and intransigent honesty as a folklore collector.

Note: All paragraphs of annotation and materials in brackets in the following pages are by the editor.

1

A. Perhaps the commonest of all latrine verses is a couplet found in many parts of the Ozark region:

> Some come here to sit and think,
> I come here to shit and stink.

B. There are many variants based on the same fascinating rhyme. A gentleman near Pine Bluff, Ark., writes it thus:

> I come here to shit and stink,
> But all I done was sit and think.

C. At Hot Springs, Ark., it was elaborated by some right-thinking visitor:

> Some go to church to doze and nod,
> But I go there to worship God.
> Some folks come here to set and think,
> But I come here to shit and stink.

D. Here's one from Argenta, Ark.:

> Some come here to sit and think,
> Some come here to write on walls,
> But I come here to shit and stink
> And scratch my poor old rusty balls.

E. From Forsyth, Mo.:

> Some come here to sit and think,
> Others come to shit and stink.
> But I come here to scratch my balls
> And read the poems on the walls.

F. A related item from Tahlequah, Okla.:

> Some come here to sit and think,
> Others come to shit and stink,
> But I come here to take a drink.

G. Variant from a Joplin, Mo., railway station:

> Some come here to sit and sit,
> I come here to shit and shit.

2

A. This one was found in Bentonville, Ark.:

> Some come here to shit and stink,
> I come here to fiddle my dink.

B. A man in Joplin, Mo., recited this as part of an anecdote, which he heard at Anderson, Mo., in 1929. [*Cock* and *pussy* both here refer to the vagina; *to pull my pud*[*ding*] is to masturbate:]

> Some come here to sit and think,
> Others come to shit and stink,
> But I come here to pull my pud,
> The cock in this town ain't no good.

C. Here is a text from Carthage, Mo.:

> Some come here to sit and think,
> Others come to shit and stink,
> But I come here to pull my pud,
> Cause Carthage pussy ain't no good.

3

A. Wise counsel from Sallisaw, Okla. Slightly different versions are common elsewhere; [including the final suggestion to "squeeze in rhythm," rhyming with "Push your head right down with 'em."]

> If you want to shit with ease,
> Rest your elbows on your knees,
> Put your hands beneath your chin,
> Work your ass-hole out and in.

B. Here's one from Pineville, Mo.:

> If you want to shit with ease,
> Rest your elbows on your knees,
> Work your ass-hole out and in,
> Let a fart and then begin.

4

A. This is a common inscription around Springfield, Mo., and Rolla, Mo.:

> Here I set in silent bliss
> Listening to the flowing piss,
> Now and then a fart is heard,
> Mingled with a falling turd.

B. Sometimes the last line reads:

> Barking at a passing turd.

5

A. From a hotel restroom in Aurora, Mo. [*Drop a tear,* to urinate.]

> Enter in silence, friend, and drop a tear,
> Full many a weary ass has rested here.

B. Similar sentiment from a Bentonville, Ark., comfort station. [*Pratt,* the buttocks, of unknown origin.]

> Tread softly, friend, and drop a furtive tear,
> For many a weary pratt has rested here.

6

In Golden City, Mo., it reads like this:

> Oh hungry stranger, gently close the door,
> Many good dinners lay beneath this floor.

[Compare the related French classic (Chalons, France, 1955; in translation:) *"Here tumble in ruins the masterpieces of French cooking."*]

7

This one is contributed by Mr. B. C., Salem, Mo. He says his grandfather found it in a local privy during the War Between the States, and that the tax was a war measure of the 1860s:

> When you come here to leave your wax,
> Don't forget the old War Tax,
> Article second, chapter third
> Says put a stamp on every turd.

8

Beneath a lot of exhortatory verses at Tahlequah, Okla., some critic has scribbled:

> I don't need this bull,
> My cow is already bred.

9

This one is from a pay station in Joplin, Mo., but I've seen the same verse in many other places. [See G. Legman, *The Limerick,* Paris, 1953, p. 142 for a British variant on this theme.]

> Here I set all broken hearted,
> Paid a nickel to shit and only farted.

10

A related lament from Webb City, Mo.:

> Here I played a hell of a caper,
> Paid a nickel, but there ain't no paper.

Note: The *paid-a-nickel-to-shit* verses are found in free toilets and rude outdoor privies, nearly as often as in coin-operated places.

11

A. In a hardware store at West Plains, Mo., the proprietor has written on the wall of his toilet:

> Shit where you trade. We don't want the
> ass end of your business.

B. Here's one from a barbershop in Anderson, Mo., apparently the work of a professional sign painter:

> Do your shitting
> Where you do your shaving.

We do not want the ASS END
Of your business.

12

From a self-styled "university" at Siloam Springs, Ark., comes this admonition:

A man that will stand with his cock in his hand
And piss on a shit-house seat,
He ought to be thrashed and his old cock mashed,
And his ass kicked out in the street.

13

The proprietor of a barbershop in Little Rock, Ark., has a regular painted sign:

Don't piss on the floor,
Hold your cock over the trough.

14

Above a urinal in Hot Springs, Ark., is the legend:

IN IT, NOT AT IT.

15

Another one from Hot Springs, Ark.:

Don't lope your mule in [here]. This
is a private race track.

[To *lope one's mule,* or *donkey,* or *antelope:* to masturbate, of a boy or man, from the wrist motion involved.]

16

From a business college in Springfield, Mo.:

Never sacrifice accuracy for speed.
In other words, don't piss on the seat.

17

A. In the jail toilet at Pineville, Mo., there is a large painted sign on the wall, above the depression in the concrete floor which serves as a urinal:

PLEASE PISS HERE

B. Someone has written below the sign:

Sorry, sheriff, I can't piss that high.

18

Almost every village in the region has such inscriptions as:

Bulls with short horns
Stand up close.

19

A. Beneath such a sign at Neosho, Mo., a customer has written:

Don't try to kid yourself,
Just stand close.

B. In Tahlequah, Okla., it reads (unusually):

Don't stop to measure your
pro-bob. Just stand up close.

20

In the Army and Navy Hospital, Hot Springs, Ark., I found this old one:

Old soldiers with short muskets
Please stand close to the target.

21

A. In the court-house toilet at Berryville, Ark., is the admonition:

Stand up close, the next fellow may be barefooted.

B. Just below this, in another hand:

Hell, I am barefooted!

C. This is from Vinita, Okla.:

> Better stand close to the stool, the
> next man may come in barefooted. Help us
> keep this place clean.

22

A friend reports this from a hotel toilet at Aurora, Mo.:

> Ducks with short bills, please
> stand up close. The next duck may
> be barefooted.

23

Here is one from Webster Groves, a suburb of St. Louis, Mo.:

> Steady hand and steady eye,
> Keeps the toilet clean and dry.

24

A very subtle pronouncement from a tourist court urinal near Eureka Springs, Ark.:

> We aim to please.
> You aim too, please.

[Sometimes found as: "We aim to keep this place clean.—Your aim will help."]

25

Here is one from Harrison, Ark.:

> If your pecker is short,
> If your pecker is weak,
> You better lean over
> Or you'll piss on your feet.

26

A. Printed sign put up by the management over the urinal in a barroom in St. Louis, Mo.:

> PEACOCKS INN

B. Outside the toilets for men and women in this bar are signs marked *POINTERS* and *SETTERS* with a drawing of a dog on each sign appropriately posed. [Compare signs, *TENOR* and *SOPRANO,* at No. 48, below.] In a bar in Plainfield, N.J., 1948, were similar signs marked: *BUCKS* and *DOES.* Someone had changed the first by scraping it, to read: *FUCKS,* and under the *DOES* was added:

> *US BUCKS DOES TOO*

27

In almost every roadside urinal one finds such instruction as:

> Shake well before using, or Shake well
> *after* using.

28

At Yellville, Ark., someone has written:

> Shake it all you want to. The last drop
> always goes down your pants leg anyhow.

29

Near Conway, Ark., I found this admonition in a cheap boarding-house. [This is a folk-saying or proverb, known nationally in the United States among adolescent boys. To *play with it* means to masturbate:]

> If you shake it more than three times,
> you are playing with it.

30

A. The owner of a filling station near Blue Eye, Mo., writes in his privy:

> This is the place we all must meet,
> Let's try to keep the damn thing neat,
> So sit on the hole and not on your feet,
> And shit in the hole and not on the seat.

B. Here is one signed "Janitor" in a bawdy-house at Kansas City, Mo. [*throne,* self-mocking slang term for a toilet-seat or privy.]

> This little throne I call my own,
> Please help me keep it clean and neat.
> So wipe your ass with a piece of glass
> And don't shit on the seat.

C. Another text from Carthage, Mo.:

> This little house we call our own,
> We try to keep it clean and sweet,
> So pull the chain when you get done,
> And don't shit on the seat.

31

From a newspaper office in Springfield, Mo.:

> We want you to feel at home.
> If you shit on the seat at home,
> do so here.

32

A. A typewritten card in a drugstore toilet, Fayetteville, Ark., reads as below. ["Cob," meaning a corn-cob, as in many rustic privies; used for toilet paper:]

> Don't stand on the seat. If you are afraid to sit down,
> go where you can get a cob too, as you will feel
> more at home.

B. Some (female) visitor has added a comment, written in vivid lipstick:

> They tell me not to stand on the seat,
> But I think more of my ass than I do of my feet.

33

A. Here is a related bit of customer-reaction from Monett, Mo.:

> A man don't think much of his ass, that will
> stick it down the hole in a public water closet.

B. Underneath, in another handwriting:

> What would you suggest?

34

A. Near Joplin, Mo., I found the following rhyme in the privy behind a barbecue pit, or "pig-stand":

> No use to stand upon the seat,
> These pig-stand crabs can jump six feet.

B. Here's one from a tourist camp at Eureka Springs, Ark. [*Crab,* crab louse, *Phthirus pubis*:]

> Why put paper on the seat?
> An Arkansas crab can jump six feet.

35

A fellow who runs a restaurant at Mansfield, Mo., put up a sign in his outdoor privy:

> Don't be so nasty in a public toilet,
> Treat it as you would your own.

36

A customer added the following comment in pencil:

> If it was mine, I'd lock the door and
> keep these crabby bastards out.

37

In a brand-new two-holer at Billings, Mo., someone wrote:

> Two good holes for your legs, Hot Dog!
> And a nice clean board to shit on!

38

Here's one from Sallisaw, Okla.:

> When a *GENTLEMAN* has to shit
> He hits the hole and wipes a bit.

39

Also from the vicinity of Sallisaw, Okla.:

> God damn a man, and damn his soul,
> That can't shit in a ten-inch hole.

40

From the men's toilet in an Aurora, Mo., hotel [during World War II:]

> In case of an air raid, hide under the toilet
> seat. It's never been hit yet.

41

A. Advice from a honky-tonk privy near Mountain Home, Ark.:

> Don't leave the stool when the bowels are in motion.

B. [Compare the mournful college song, to thc tune of Dvorák's "Humoresque," sometimes called "The Pullman Porter's Song," stanza 2:]

> While the train is in the station
> Please refrain from moving bowels;
> Ask the porter—just politely,
> He will (surely) bring you towels.

42

A. This one is common around Picher, Okla.

> Don't leave change on the counter
> when you do business here.

B. From Waco, Mo., comes this text:

> When you make a deposit in this bank,
> don't leave your change on the counter.

C. In a hotel at Little Rock, Ark., we found a carefully painted sign:

> This is no bank. Don't leave change
> on the counter.

43

A related item from Russellville, Ark. [Again pretending the toilet is a bank, as in 42 above, on the classic unconscious idea of *gold* as feces.]

> Make your deposit, don't forget your change,
> No corrections made after leaving window.

44

A. In the Blue Goose Hotel at Noel, Mo., there used to be a painted sign:

> Please put nothing but toilet paper in the stool.

B. Underneath this sign somebody scribbled:

> My God, have we got to shit on the floor?

C. On the wall nearby is the following, carefully written in a fine business-college hand:

> It seems to me that this defeats the
> primary purpose of the toilet. I doubt if
> many of the citizens will come here, just
> for the pleasure of tearing off toilet-paper
> and putting it in the stool.

45

From the outdoor water closet behind a tourist camp at Lamar, Mo.:

> Don't Throw Matches in the Can.

46

In a public building at Mount Vernon, Mo.:

> Do not empty any dirty water in this toilet.
> *MATRON*

47

Formal statement in a Mindenmines, Mo., store:

> If you boys don't stop throwing rubbish in the
> hole we will have to close this place up. Please
> try to cooperate with us.

48

A. A beer parlor at Eureka Springs, Ark., has one toilet marked *TENOR,* the other *SOPRANO.* Over the urinal in the *TENOR* compartment is a printed sign. (Compare No. 26*B*):

> Don't throw cigarets in here,
> It makes them hard to light.

B. [Another form of this sign, hand-printed, is pasted over the urinal-bank in the "Luna Park" entertainment grounds, Brooklyn, New York:]

> Please don't throw your cigarets here,
> It makes them soggy and hard to light.

C. A rational request, reported by Prof. John Clellon Holmes, unofficially placed over the urinal in the men's room in the university library, Fayetteville, Ark. [about 1975:]

> Don't throw your butts in the bowl;
> Do we piss in your ashtrays?

D. Related request causing the arrest of the owner of a "Tin Lizzie" touring-car on which it was lettered, in Natchitoches, La., about 1928:

> All You Ladies That Smoke Cigarets,
> Throw Your *BUTTS* In Here.

"*Butts*," buttocks, here punning on the metonymic sense, also of *arse,* as referring to the entire body or person. Note cigaret-smoking by women as implying sexual immorality too.

49

In the outdoor privy behind a little hotel at Noel, Mo., is a wooden box with this sign [referring to menstrual pads, called "sanitary napkins"]:

> WOMEN, discard articles of wearing apparel
> here. Do not throw them into the toilet.

50

This one is from a women's toilet near Camdenton, Mo.:

> Please don't put pads in the stool. I wood
> lots rather carry them out than to dig this
> sewer line up and clean it. Just throw them
> in a corner.

51

A privy near Mammoth Springs, Ark., is provided with a wooden box of toilet paper; the paper is not in rolls, but in separate pieces. Above the box is a printed sign:

> Don't use two
> Where one will do.

52

This is a scribbled inscription in a railroad toilet in Joplin, Mo.:

> Owing to our inability to get people to
> use both sides of the paper, the privilege
> has been discontinued. Use your finger,
> and the hell with you.

53

A. In the courthouse at Carthage, Mo., is a large sign painted above the urinal:

> $25 fine for Marking or Defacing
> in Any Manner the Walls, Woodwork,
> or Any Part of this Building.
> By Order of the County Court.

B. Just below the sign, someone has written in equally large letters:

> Fuck the County Court in the Ass.

54

In a public building at Clarksville, Ark., a stencil sign *DON'T SPIT ON THE FLOOR* has been carefully altered with a knife and pencil. It now reads:

> *DON'T SHIT ON THE FLOOR.*

55

Here is a painted sign in a very dirty crapper near Rogers, Ark.:

> This is a white man's toilet,
> Please use it as such.

[Until as recently as World War II, and in certain localities even later in the south and southwest of the United States, and as far north as—and including—Washington, D.C., the national capitol, white and Negro users of both sexes had separate public toilets, and often drinking fountains as well.]

56

From a cheap hotel in Joplin, Mo.:

> If you are a hobo,
> Write on the wall.

If you are a tramp,
Piss on the floor.

57

Under some filthy drawings in a toilet at Harrison, Ark., someone has written:

Fool, stay thy hand!

58

A. Here's one from a filling station, run by a woman near Crane, Mo.:

Please do not draw such pictures or write
such dirty writings in my toilet. You are
just showing your ignorance.

B. Someone has added below, in a large masculine hand. [Compare the "Twelve (Silver) Dollar Jack" references elsewhere in this collection.]

Lady, I don't want to show my ignorance. But
I sure would like to show you my prick, which
it is twelve inches long limber, and never been
measured hard.

59

From a privy near Marionville, Mo. [*Drummer*, a traveling salesman:]

Drummer's wit and tobacco spit,
Always mixed with hateful shit.

60

In a hotel toilet at Springfield, Mo. is a crude drawing of a naked couple, with the following inscription:

Eve: Would you like a piece?
Adam: Don't care if I do, soon as I
   finish this here apple.

61

From a filthy outdoor privy at Neosho, Mo., comes this bit of cryptic wisdom:

Have thy tools ready,
God will find thee work.

62

A. In another toilet at Neosho, Mo., some local moralist writes in red paint:

> Men, sleep with your own wife.

B. Below, somebody has written in even larger letters:

> Suck your own cock, for all I care.

63

A. In the privy behind a boarding-house at Kiowa, Okla., someone wrote:

> Read about ADULTERY in Leviticus 20 chapter,
> start it at verse 10 and read to 21.

[Citation is to the main Biblical anti-sexual passage, but is *not* restricted only to adultery.]

B. Among a lot of obscene drawings and inscriptions in a toilet at Berryville, Ark., is the following:

> *ISAIAH, 55, 6*

[Cited passage is apostolic only and has no anti-sexual reference: "*Seek ye the Lord while he may be found; call ye upon him while he is near.*" Note the implication that every person reading these will have access to a Bible.]

C. In the courthouse toilet at Eureka Springs, Ark., painted above the trough-type urinal in letters four inches high:

> *HONOR GOD, MY SON.*

64

In the same toilet, at Eureka Springs, Ark., I found this verse:

> Fuck a duck and screw a pigeon,
> Kiss my ass and get religion.

65

This one is from a hotel toilet in Rolla, Mo.:

> I set here now for quite a while,
> I can't shit cause I've got the piles.

66

Just below, in another hand:

> If your ass is sore, you cannot shit,
> Just wipe the hole and call it quits.

67

The following inscription was found on the wall of a public toilet at Fayetteville, Ark. [To *do a job,* or *one's job,* to shit. Parody of "Tom, Tom, the Piper's Son."]

> I come in here to do a job,
> Took down my pants and shit a gob,
> Pulled the chain and flushed the can,
> Wrapped up my cock and away I ran.

68

Also from Fayetteville, Ark., [*Old frost:* hoar frost, punning on "whore."]

> Behind these prison bars I sit
> With my fingers dipped in shit,
> And the old frost is growing thick
> Between my ass-hole and my prick.

[A fragment of "The Prisoner's Song: In Barlinnie."]

69

Bob Duncan, Oklahoma City, Okla., sends me this one. Somewhere in eastern Oklahoma, it was painted on a clean wall above a tile urinal:

> Be Careful, the Future of the World is in Your Hands.

70

From a toilet on the campus of the University of Missouri, at Columbia, Mo. I like to think of it (a pun?) as the reflection of a student who has just received his diploma:

> On the Whole, I Have Done Well Here.

71

Above the urinal in a poolhall, Springfield, Mo., is the inscription:

> Who stands here is empty of piss,
> A yard of hose held in his fist.

72

In a cigar-store toilet at Fort Smith, Ark. [*Dick* means both penis and detective.]

> Crooks beware! This is where all the
> dicks hang out.

73

In a ladies' restroom at Springfield, Mo., was the scribbled reflection:

> A big prick is better than a small finger.

74

On the same wall is a crude drawing of an erect penis, with the words:

> Nine inch long and one inch around!

75

Just below, in a different handwriting. [Note homosexual "camp" use of feminine pronoun *she* where "he" is meant:]

> Seems pretty thin, and maybe she is confusing
> circumference with diameter. But still pretty thin.

76

Beneath a large picture of a phallus in the railroad station at Joplin, Mo. somebody has written [also satirical homosexual "camp."]:

> Oh dearie, I'm all of a twitter!

77

It is unusual to find prose anecdotes in these inscriptoria, but here's one from a comfort station at Monett, Mo.:

> A little boy in school, playing with his
> peter. Teacher says, Johnny, I don't want to
> see any more of that. Johnny says, hell,
> that's all there is *OF* it!

This item is not only unusual for its locale, as observed, but also in its merely "grammatical" punch-line. This has been enlarged to a whole pretendedly true anti-gallant anecdote concerning various American presidents since World War II, with wives not famous for their beauty: *The president is staying up late worrying about the state of the country, and sees the visiting British prime minister sneaking into the bedroom of the president's wife. When he comes out, the president shakes his finger at him, saying: "Now, I'll have no more of* that, *my friend!" "No," replies the prime minister; "and neyther shall I!"*

78

In the Elks Club toilet at Joplin, Mo., I found this inscription [a "Wellerism," as in Dickens' *Pickwick Papers*]:

> A small thing, but mine own, as Shakespeare
> said when he looked at his pecker.

79

Literary advice from the old Capitol Hotel, in Little Rock, Ark. [Ernest R. Ball, author of "Mother Machree," is only there for the rhyme]:

> If you would aspire to fame
> Write a poem and sign your name,
> Shakespeare, Burns, Longfellow, Ball,
> All began on a shit house wall.

80

A. A related item from Beebe, Ark.:

> Don't be down on the shit house poet,
> You may be one before you know it,
> Longfellow, Byron, Whitman, Moore,
> All begun on a shit house door.

B. From Huntsville, Ark.:

> Oh shit house poets, be of good cheer,
> While you write your verses here,

> Who knows but Shakespeare, Milton, Moore,
> Began their writing on a shit house door?

81

From Green Forest, Ark. [In the added couplet here, "*eggs*" means testicles, as the source of the poets' inspiration.]:

> One might think from this display of wit,
> Shakespeare himself come here to shit.
> All these poets are sure to fall
> And scramble their eggs on a shit house wall.

82

A. From a privy near the old town of Argenta, Ark., which is called North Little Rock nowadays [Compare No. 91.]:

> Of all the writers, the worst of all
> Are them that write on a shit house wall.

B. A variant from Jefferson City, Mo.:

> Of all the poets great and small,
> The shit house poet is worst of all.

83

From the village of Waco, Mo.: [Apparently incomplete?]

> Of all the poets beneath the skies,
> The shit house poet I do despise.

84

Here's one copied out for me by a lady at Neosho, Mo. She got it from a *private indoor toilet,* in a wealthy citizen's residence [combines both Nos. 83 and 85 below]:

> Of all the poets beneath the skies
> The shit-house poet I most despise.
> A man who writes on privy walls
> Should have his crap done up in balls.
> And when he feels so full of wit
> Should eat a ball or two of shit.

85

Variant from a schoolhouse privy at Buffalo, Mo.:

> He who writes on shit house walls,
> Should roll his shit in little balls,
> And he who reads the words of it
> Should eat the little balls of shit.

86

From a men's toilet in Carterville, Mo.:

> Some poets are poor,
> Some poets are rich,
> But the shit house poet
> Is a son of a bitch.

87

A. In the toilet of a pool hall at Little Rock, Ark., someone has set down a personal complaint:

> Damn all these poets,
> The sons of bitches,
> I got to reading
> And shit in my britches.

B. A variant from Rogers, Ark.:

> Fuck all you poets,
> You sons of bitches,
> I stopped to read your poems,
> And shit in my britches.

88

Somebody in a hotel toilet at Aurora, Mo., doesn't care for backhouse rhymes:

> It takes a hick from a town like this,
> to think up such nasty verses.

89

On the same wall, in another handwriting:

> For God's sake, do not erase these
> WONDERFUL poems.

90

Some earnest scribblers seem particularly opposed to the writing of proper names in toilets, and in nearly every good inscriptorium one finds this:

> Fools' names like fools' faces,
> Often seen in public places.

91

Here is a similar opinion from Verona, Mo. [Also very commonly seen. Compare No. 82.]

> A man's ambition must be small
> To write his name on a shit house wall.

92

A. In Anderson, Mo., I found an elaboration of this sentiment:

> A man's ambition is mighty small
> To write his name on a shit house wall;
> But a woman's ambition is smaller still
> To sell her ass for a two dollar bill.

B. A similar elaboration, from the same. [Dialectal pronunciation of "yet" as *yit*.]

> . . . But your ambition's smaller yet,
> To set your hand where others shit.

93

From a bus-station toilet in Joplin, Mo.:

> Any damn fool can write his name in a crapper.

94

A. At Fort Smith, Ark., somebody wrote in the toilet of a railway station:

> When Fort Smith grows up and gets a little
> bigger, maybe they won't charge five cents for
> a shit. Just come to Little Rock and see if
> we have a God damn pay toilet in the depot.

B. One of the local patriots answered this in *green ink:*

> Fuck Little Rock and everybody that lives there.

95

A. In a hotel toilet at Monett, Mo., I came across this inscription:

> Kansas City is the ass hole of all creation.

B. Just below, in another hand:

> So is this lousy dump, you chicken shit rube.

96

In the Frisco Station at Joplin, Mo., was a serious attempt, apparently, to counteract the boastings of the Chamber of Commerce:

> I lived in this ass hole town for 14 years,
> and it is the shits for a good man. What do you
> think, boys, better come to a good town like
> Tulsa as Joplin is the shits. Joplin can kiss
> my ass and everybody in it. Come and see me when
> you get there.
>
> > Jack Popper
> > Tulsa, Okla.
> > Age 19 years

97

A. A reflection from the restroom of a factory in Little Rock, Ark.:

> When bigger turds are shit, they will
> be shit in Little Rock.

B. Below, in another handwriting:

> All shits weighing more than six pound
> must be lowered with a rope.
>
> > *The Management*

98

A. To understand this one, from Ozark, Mo., one must know that both Ozark and Galena are towns on the banks of the James River, and that Galena is down-stream:

> For God's sake pull the chain,
> Galena needs the water.

B. [On the incredible reality of American drinking-water pollution from town to town, with feces—*and worse!*—see *No Laughing Matter,* 1975, vol. II: pp. 929–33 and 983–85, noting for example, from *The Doctors Mayo,* 1941, that: "Every time you drink from a faucet in St. Louis, Missouri, you're drinking from every flush-toilet all the way up the Mississippi." And citing a patriotic sign on the river which flows through Anderson, Indiana, with Muncie the next town down-stream:]

ANDERSON SHITS IN IT AND MUNCIE DRINKS IT.

99

In a hotel at Rockaway Beach, Mo., on Lake Taneycomo, some tourist registered a mild complaint upon the privy wall. [*Cock*, equivalent to cunt in southern American speech, from the French *coquille*, cockleshell. Note that this real sport spent nearly twice as much on gin as on women:]

> Rooms 2.50
> Meals 2.00
> Gin 5.00
> Cock 3.00
> Show 1.00
> —————
> $13.50
> PRETTY STEEP

100

Near Southwest City, Mo., there was a toilet set on the bank of a creek, so that the water often came nearly up to the floor. On the wall was this inscription:

> I have shit in the Red River Valley,
> I have shit in Niagara Falls,
> This is the first place I ever shit
> Where the river splashed up on my balls.

101

In a toilet at Eureka Springs, Ark., somebody wrote [classic Oedipal "regicide" epigraph, 1940s through 50s]:

KILROY WAS HERE

102

Some disgruntled tourist added a comment below:

> He must have died here, the way
> this town stinks.

See the interesting psychoanalytic article on the then ever-present epigraph, "Kilroy Was Here," by Dr. Richard Sterba, in *American Imago,* November 1948, vol. VI: p. 173 *ff.*

103

A. Somebody in a cannery at Crane, Mo., did not think too highly of the superintendent. This is what he wrote in the privy:

> I don't like the bastard's face
> That runs this lousy cock sucking place.

B. Underneath this, in another hand:

> Go to hell, Jim Kane, I mene you!

104

In a similar place at Galena, Mo., I found the following inscription [*sucking ass,* toadying]:

> The old cow lives by eating grass,
> Bob lives by sucking the boss's ass.

105

From a school toilet in Carroll County, Ark.:

> Nathan E. jacks off, and Ted B.
> has got the *CLAP*.

106

A related observation from Huntsville, Ark.:

> Jim ——— fucked his Ma, and he
> is a son of a bitch anyhow.

107

At a local town a man named Jay Frith was the county sheriff. Somebody wrote in the jail toilet:

> Fuck Jay Frith, the old bastard.

108

A. From a roadside toilet near Rolla, Mo., a town that was full of soldiers during World War II:

> Fuck Captain J ———, the old son of a bitch,
> I hope he gets the mumps and goes down on him.

B. Below, in another handwriting:

> Yes, and the spinal magnitis, too!

109

Genial expression from a toilet in the City Hall at Joplin, Mo.:

> Mayor Z—— is a chicken shit, and so is the Chief of Police.

110

Some dreamer in a privy near Noel, Mo., wonders:

> How would Doctor B. look, fucking
> Elizabeth ———?

111

From Sulphur Springs, Ark., comes the following:

> Where else in this town can a man get fucked besides Q's?

A villager explained to me that Q's was a store, where everything was priced too high. [*Fucked,* here meaning also cheated.]

112

During the rise of the Ku Klux Klan (the K.K.K.), many privies in Missouri and Arkansas were decorated with stencil and rubber-stamp inscriptions, such as *TO HELL WITH THE KNIGHTS OF COLUMBUS; DOWN WITH THE GOD DAMN JEWS,* and the like. In a toilet at Van Buren, Ark., I found the following written with heavy black crayon:

Fuck the Pope, also to Hell with the Priests
and all there Children.

113

In a barroom toilet at Joplin, Mo.:

> Anybody play poker upstairs will get horse whip.
>   K. K. K.

114

From a tourist-camp privy in Jasper county, Mo., comes this bit of racist propaganda:

> These yellow nigger wench got no right
> to fuck white men and get their money.
>   K. K. K.

Wench, in U.S. southern usage, is an old British term for a Negro girl, or serving-woman of any age. Also heard as far north as Somerville, New Jersey, 1944, this state having kept elements of "chattel" slavery until a relatively late date.

115

In a railway toilet at Carl Junction, Mo., somebody wrote:

> If you want to cure the clap
> Fuck Miss Josephine Carnap.

See folk-belief No. 3, in section H below. Refers to the gruesome folk-belief that gonorrhea can be cured by giving it to an innocent partner, or to as many as possible! And in particular to a virgin girl! Compare the recent (1990) hostile "tasteless" style riddle-joke: *"Did you hear about the new cure for AIDS?"—"No, what is it?"—"Suicide!"*

116

From the Keystone Hotel, Joplin, Mo.:

> I screwed the maid on the second floor,
> boy she sure is hot.

117

Wise counsel from the Connor Hotel, Joplin, Mo.:

> Date the redhead in the coffee shop,
> boys, but lay off the blonde.

118

Enthusiastic comment in a privy at Lanagan, Mo.:

> Miss Pearl D——— is the best piece of
> tail in this town.

119

Praise for a lady, written on the wall of a public toilet in Webb City, Mo. [Probably a pimp's advertisement, like 118 above.]

> Thelma H. sure knows how to fuck,
> nice and juicy, no fool talk.

120

This is written in the washroom of a saloon in Joplin, Mo., with furnished rooms upstairs. [A pimp's advertisement. *Pussy,* vagina, as metonymy for the sexual enjoyment of the woman.]

> Good fresh country pussy,
> one flight up.

121

Enigmatic advice in the privy of a tourist court near Cape Fair, Mo. ["two bits," twenty-five cents, implying a one-dollar basic price]:

> Ask Mabel what she will do for
> two bits extra.

122

From a hotel in Carthage, Mo. [a pimp's advertisement.]:

> A good fuck in Room 308 for two dollars.

123

Business card in the toilet of a "club" in Hot Springs, Ark.:

> If gentlemen who can piss properly but know
> also of other uses for their tools wish to exercise
> this knowledge, try Goldie Timms at 802 Cocker Ave.
> Others can go to Schwartz's place on Toddy Street,
> and good enough for them.

124

Here is a group of four inscriptions from the restroom of a bus station in Springfield, Mo.:

> Vivian ———, 502 1/2, Campbell Street, City. A pretty fat girl, young and lively.
>
> Violet ———, 810 Main, Tulsa, Okla. Jolly blonde, rich widow. Loves nobody. Goes places. Sees things.
>
> Zelda ———, 414 Sherman, City. Redhead, thirty years old. Has been to the East. She knows her business.
>
> Juanita ———, 702 Baylor Ave., City. Widow, nineteen years old. Beauty shop and bath house experience. She likes both ways.

Exactly identical to the "Blue Book" whorehouse and pimps' advertisements, circulated in special privately issued booklets, or in semipublic handbills—like these—in England and France since the eighteenth century, and in New Orleans since ca. 1830. Nowadays very prominent in cheap and "underground" newspaper advertisements presumably for *"massage"* and photographic *"models,"* and in publicly advertised telephone sex-call services by women, 1970s through the 90s; including perverted sado-masochistic offerings both as telephone fantasies and as paid services. These telephone and computer "bulletin board" activities are at present just as common and public, in England, France, Germany, and in Southeast Asia, "servicing" western and Japanese visitors willing to pay. Such toilet inscriptions by pimps are therefore now disappearing, except in cheap urban and rural neighborhoods, or isolated work sites.

125

A. From a hotel toilet in Joplin, Mo., comes this announcement:

> If you want to get your prick sucked off,
> go to the Dreamland Rooms and call for Thelma.

B. Just below is an endorsement in another hand:

> Thelma sure knows her onions, just one grand
> big suck after another. Rates reasonable.

C. Still lower on the same wall is the card of a competitor, perhaps a male:

> Reasonable hell, I'll do it for nothing,
> make dates in the bar after 7 P.M.

126

Here's one from a rather plush hotel on the highway near Rolla, Mo. [pimp's advertising *graffito,* if in male toilet]:

> Lots of girls they like to fuck,
> But I know one would rather suck.
>
> Laura B.

127

A similar proposition [perhaps homosexual] in a hotel toilet at Columbia, Mo., near the University of Missouri campus:

> Get your Cock suck Saturday Nite between 8 and 9.
> Where? Room 214. How much? FREE!

128

From a toilet in Jefferson City, Mo.:

> Make a date. Get it sucked. Here in the can.
> Five P.M. I take nine inches two ways for $1.
> Fuck me in the ass once, boy, it sure feels good.

129

In a tourist camp privy near Noel, Mo., a gentleman announces in red ink:

> If you want to suck a big one, meet me here
> six o'clock, Friday, April 14.

130

From the men's room at a hotel in Conway, Ark.:

> In front of hotel at 7 P.M. Be there
> with hard on. Ask for M. J.

131

I found this written on the wall of a public toilet at Rocky Comfort, Mo. [*got to go,* meaning to the toilet]:

> Yoo hoo gitago, gotago, right or wrong,
> When you get a good thing just push it along.

132

A bit of hygienic wisdom from Conway, Ark.:

> Clap is bad, syph is worse,
> Use your hand for safety first.

133

In the village of Blue Eye, Mo., an outdoor privy offers this:

> All you boys that got the clap
> From what you thought was a private snap,
> *MARK HERE.*

Just below this inscription are more than forty X-marks, made with different pencils and several sorts of ink. ["What" refers impersonally to the woman, who is the *private snap* or "sure thing" as to sexual availability.]

134

On the door of a toilet in Mountain Home, Mo., is the inscription *DATE JACKED,* with a column of dates and blurred figures below it. In some cases there are two entries in a single day, then several days without any notation. A physician tells me that this may be the diary of a masturbator; he says that boys sometimes keep such records.

Compare adult sex-diaries, which are not uncommon, and are sometimes kept with exact dates, records, names, numbers of participants and "times," measurements, etc., and occasionally on index cards, since the 1850s at least; as cited—from a cultivated northeastern American woman—by Professor Peter Gay in his recent study of nineteenth-century moral attitudes. Also as cited in the extraordinarily detailed British male erotic autobiography *My Secret Life,* privately issued in 1888–94; and compare with Casanova in France and Italy a century before, who left his *Memoirs* (1797) in manuscript only. Many lengthy and bragging toilet *graffiti,* particularly as collected in large, lonely cities, are essentially public diary entries.

135

Here's one from the jail toilet at Carthage, Mo.:

> In sixty days,
> Shit forty-two times,
> Jacked off twice.

[Note prisoner's less than normal, or diminished sexual appetite. Many prisoners and soldiers masturbate unusually often and feel "sex-crazed," owing to deprivation and sexual frustration.]

136

In the municipal privy, behind the courthouse in Pineville, Mo., a visitor wrote [cowboy, "personals advertisement" style]:

> I am a rider and a roper and a
> fucker and a fighter, and out of a job.
>
> > Herb Carter
> > Sallisaw, Okla.

137

Urgent personal communication from a poolroom toilet in Joplin, Mo.:

> Listen, Jim, don't be a fool. It was
> > Slim Cravens done it.

138

In the Antlers Hotel, at Mena, Ark., I found this on the washroom door:

> Pretty Boy Floyd is still here. Match
> this handwrite with the papers.

That was in June, 1933, and Charles "Pretty Boy" Floyd was a publicity-hungry outlaw from Oklahoma [then at large]. Men who knew Floyd said that it looked like his writing.

139

Except for a few Greek letters, apparently designating college fraternities, I have found only one clear inscription in a language other than English. At Columbia, Mo., in the toilet attached to a restaurant, someone scribbled:

> *AD HADES CUM SAPIENTIA*

A young man assured me that this bit of "dog Latin" means "To Hell with Knowledge," and is the motto of a clandestine student society at the University of Missouri [known as "The Syntaxers"].

140

At a public park near Joplin, Mo., a woman asked me if I could read Dutch. Assuming that she meant German, I said yes. She showed me some marks in black crayon, on the *outside* of the door to the ladies' toilet:

E O A R   Y O 9

I copied this very carefully, and have since shown it to several learned clerks, but none of them could tell me what it means. I set it down here for the record.

This may be an attempt to write backwards in lower-case "mirror script" the words *BOY ARSE* as a homosexual wish or fantasy, disguised. Mirror-writing in this way, as a code, dates at least from the period of Leonardo da Vinci, about 1500, who kept his secret anatomical and mechanical notebook texts in this way, by writing with both hands simultaneously in opposite directions, and then discarding the readable copy.

SECTION H

"Unprintable" Ozark Folk Beliefs

Many many years ago, I published some papers about Ozark witchcraft and folk-belief, and discussed these matters at length in several of my books. Later on, I devoted an entire volume to Ozark superstitions. In these writings I tried to tell the reader what the Ozark hillfolk believe, and how they act upon these beliefs. Since the editorial taboos are mostly verbal, they did not bother me too much in writing about superstition. I described folk-beliefs and physical activities in my own language, with little need to quote the hillman's exact words.

Thus when my informant used the verbs *fuck, shit, piss,* and the like, I wrote "copulate," "defecate," "urinate," et cetera. Such nouns as *prick, cunt, ass-hole* and so forth are easily turned into their Greek or Latin equivalents. The meaning is preserved, and the editors are not offended.

In a few cases, however, I was forced into some evasion, when it would have been better to quote an informant directly. For example, in telling about an aged hillman whose wife died, I wrote:

> Before he drank Bill poured a little whiskey on the ground, and drew a circle about it with his forefinger. He muttered something to himself, but I heard it. "Just an old sayin'," he said gently, "for them that's gone." It is not a saying to be written down in a book.

(See my *Ozark Mountain Folks*, 1932, pages 189 and 278.) This is good enough for a "popular" book, perhaps. But the old man really said:

> All you've et
> Turns to shit
> And never comes no more.

I do not know just what this means. But I've heard it three times, from old men in widely separated parts of the Ozark country. And I have several second-hand reports, from persons who do not know each other. A learned friend suggests that it is one of those "family sayings," confined to certain clans or small related groups. This may be true, but my opinion is that the ritual was used by many elderly folk. There may be persons still living, in the Ozarks or elsewhere, who know more about this. If any reader has information on any of these subjects, I hope he will write to me or to the editor about it.

In the following pages I have set down certain other items of this sort, together with related material which has, for one reason or another, been omitted from my formerly published works. These have included: the *Journal of American Folklore* (1927 and 1933) vols. 40: pp. 78–93, and 46: 1–21; *Folk-Say* (1931) vol. 2: 86–93; and *Kansas City University Review* (June 1936) pp. 203–06; and my own books *The Ozarks* (1931) pp. 87–137; *Ozark Mountain Folks* (1932) pp. 30–41, 189, and 278–79; and *Ozark Superstitions* (1947) page 367.

V. R.

Editor's Note: Ozark Witchcraft: All of the materials on Ozark folk beliefs given by Vance Randolph, in the ensuing and final section of his work, are visibly simple and unselfconscious about their superstitious folkways. It seems strange today that these naïve evidences should *all* have been expurgated and rejected in his earlier books and articles, as listed just above, at the demand of the right-thinking busybodies and coldly career-minded academics who held the reins of publication on the folklore books and journals until a very recent date: certainly at least until the advent of the New Freedom in America in the 1960s. Nor are their depradations over yet.

Randolph expressed himself in many letters as being particularly hurt and "disgusted" by the expurgatory antics and prejudices of otherwise first-class academics like Professors Archer Taylor of California and Stith Thompson and Richard Dorson of Indiana, whose basic notion, as another victim, the late Francis Utley—one of America's finest folklore scholars—put it, was that "no one should rock the sex-boat."

Utley himself observed that in his magistral work on "Old Man Noah, Mrs. Noah and the Devil," he was not even allowed, without an enormous struggle, to discuss the jocular legend or "just-so" story of *The leak sprung by Noah's Ark, and Madame Noah saving the ship by sitting on the hole until they landed on Mount Ararat, with the result that "women have always had cold asses ever since."* Sometimes expurgated to her "elbow," or even a dog's nose! This is probably only a jesting echo of the Biblical story in *Genesis,* 31:33–35, of the Patriarch Jacob's wife Rachel *sitting on* the stolen graven images, hidden in the camel's saddle during her menstruation, so that her father Laban could not retrieve them, owing to the menstrual taboo. It is perhaps as good an example as any, of the not-very-frightening "obscenity" that the similar expurgatory taboos of the past have so well succeeded in keeping unprintable and unprinted even now.

The matter of Ozark witchcraft, however, and the related notion of Diabolism and of sexual orgies as the "worship of the Devil" which Randolph reserved discreetly for his last folk belief items here, Nos. 44 through 51—and which should be carefully studied—are subjects on which emotions often run high, even among many who are certain of themselves as *rational humanists,* and on which therefore the effort of repression has always been the most massive. It is clear that Randolph has not told all he knew, or that helpful informants such as the unsinkable Mrs. McCord (on whom see Godsey, in the bibliography following) were willing to tell him of what they themselves had heard or seen, and knew. Such a song, for example, as "Head o' the Holler," No. 43*B* in Volume I, *Roll Me in Your Arms,* openly describes midnight sexual orgies, presumably as part of Diabolistic or witch-coven ceremonies, taking place at some unspecified date in the 1890s, but also no doubt occasionally since, on a hilltop in southwestern Missouri, familiarly known to the singers—and orgiasts—as "Sowcoon Mountain," possibly a polite disguise for Sourwood Mountain, which may therefore still be worth investigating.

It is unquestionable that witch covens, proudly so-called and proudly if secretly observing sexual orgy ceremonies, still exist today in Great Britain and France at least. On a revival basis since about the 1900s, if not as actual survivals from the "old times," meaning the seventeenth century of witch-burnings and hangings. In the Appalachian and Ozark highlands, it also seems certain that such witch covens hung on, but as real survivals, along with other surviving British folksongs and folklore, since the emigration of the original settlers to Canada and the Appalachian south, in precisely that century.

The more recent and more open orgying of "hippie" cults, and other quasi-religious private groups, openly "sex people" and advertising themselves as "wife-swappers" and "swingers" since the early 1960s in America and abroad, do not often bother with any pretended occult backdrops or framework. But sometimes they do, particularly when the real ritual activity is of sado-masochism, flagellation, homosexual "fisting," scatology, and so forth, especially sexual abuse of children, and not the comparatively mild and harmless sexual orgying or adults' "horsing" around. The present writer has been invited to exactly such ceremonials, and with all the occult and sado-erotic trappings and surrealist trimmings, in both England and France, as well as on southern California beaches, as recently as 1975. The use of excitant and inebriant drugs in such occult and "merely" erotic orgying, has been discussed in trenchant fashion over a century ago in the magnificently written *La Sorcière* (*The Sorceress,* 1862) by Jules Michelet, the masterpiece of the witchcraft literature.

When the French minister Colbert ruled, in his revised civil code of 1672, that the sinister witchcraft accusations of that period were entirely "frivolous," and would no longer be taken cognizance of by the courts, he was moved in part by philosophical and humanitarian considerations, to end the gruesome legal persecution and murdering of helplessly neurotic old women being accused and burnt wholesale then as witches. His ruling, however, made the erotic and orgiastic type of "Diabolism" far easier and less dangerous to engage in thereafter; and from a secret Gnostic religious survival it moved on to become an erotic society fad. The secret sex-societies then, of the Earl of Rochester and other courtiers, and especially those of the eighteenth century and since—the Hellfire Club and Medmenham Abbey of Lord Francis Dashwood and later imitators—were never without both erotic and occult elements. The refined "Cosmopolite" orgy club of the Duke d'Aiguillon, on his private estate in eighteenth-century France, is of particular interest, especially for its very private press erotic publications, on which see *Les Muses en Belle Humeur* in the bibliography following, and further in G. Legman, *The Horn Book* (1964) pages 87–90. Zora Hurston in 1938 and Anaïs Nin in 1940 both told me they had been involved in "occult" orgying, the former in actual "voodoo" Black Masses.

The evidence Randolph cites at No. 49 below, that the Confederate General Albert Pike was the peripatetic secret head and tail, and officiating sex-priest of the main American southern witch covens of the late nineteenth century, mainly cite the writings of the eccentric Reverend Montague Summers as to Pike. In fact, Summers is taking his information from the writings on Freemasonry of one of the main European occult exploiters of that century, Léo Taxil (pseudonym of the French journalist Jogand-Pagès), whose "Diana Vaughan" hoax "bluffed even the Pope in Rome." This was put a stop to, and the occult movement essentially took its death-blow then, despite recent sado-masochist cults disguised as Diabolism, or Surrealism, because of the Catholic Church's then increasing caution as to occult pseudo-miracles and swindlers, following the acrid controversy over the "Turin Shroud," and especially Bernadette Soubirous and the "cures" at Lourdes. This is a subject still controversial enough to have been made into a recent and superb satirical motion picture in France, *Le Miraculé* (1987) by the sardonic Jean-Pierre Mocky, which, by an artful tongue-in-your-cheek pirouette, ends its hilarious exposé—with a miraculous cure after all.

Note: All the paragraph-long annotations and materials in brackets in the following pages are by the editor.

1

In describing the magic rituals by which girls identify their future husbands, I discussed *dumb suppers* at some length, but had to omit a fine story that Bob Wyrick, Eureka Springs, Ark., told me in 1946. See my *Ozark Superstitions* (1947) pp. 178–181.

Two young girls near Green Forest, Ark., about 1898, prepared a dumb supper with all the trimmings—absolute silence, dim light, walking backward, and so on. But a local ruffian had overheard their plans. Exactly at midnight the two girls sat down and bowed their heads. The door opened very slowly, and in came a big man walking backward, clad only in a short undershirt. Approaching the table he bent forward, took his enormous tool in hand, and thrust it backward between his legs, so that it stuck right out over the food on the table. One of the girls screamed and fled into the "other house" crying, "Maw, Maw, he's thar! He's come a long way, an' he's only got one eye!" The other girl sat silent as if paralyzed, and the man walked out the door and disappeared in the darkness. Later on the family realized that the whole thing was a joke, and hushed it up "to keep down scandal" in the neighborhood. Nobody was ever quite sure who the man was, though the girls had their suspicions.

The girl who sat frozen at the table was my informant's grandmother. Mr. Wyrick never heard of the incident until one day, when his grandmother was getting pretty old, some teen-age girls asked if she had ever "set a dumb supper." The old lady laughed and replied that she had, adding that one experience was quite enough. And then she told the story.

In Randolph's *Pissing In the Snow,* (1976) No. 30, "The Romping Party," he gives a more detailed anecdote of girls having a midnight "pajama party" in which they use a banana on each other in the dark, as a dildo: "She squealed and farted like a mare, and . . . the boy sneaked out the door again . . . The biggest girl was still a-breathing hard, but pretty soon she begun to holler. 'Mamie,' she says, 'come back here with that *good* banana.'" Compare also the similar scene in song No. 241, "The Boarding-School Maidens," above.

2

It is well known [in the area] that many Ozark women have a superstitious horror of circumcision. They feel that there is something unnatural and revolting about a penis without a prepuce. This has nothing to do with racial prejudice, since there are no Jews in the backwoods. A young man from St. Louis was enamored of a country girl in Benton County, Ark., She liked him, too, but the moment she put her hand on his pecker all bets were off. "No whickerbill!" she cried out. "My God, you ain't *human!*"

The girl told my wife about this, and Sally explained to her that circumcision is common in cities nowadays, and most parents have their male infants circumcised, because the physicians advise it. "Well," said the girl, "if city people want to butcher up their babies, that's their own business. Maybe them women in St. Louis *like* big pricks without no whickerbill! But I wasn't raised that way. No man is going to stick anything in *me,* without it's a regular human pecker!" All the young fellow's pleadings were useless. The girl would have nothing more to do with him, and he went back to the city alone.

3

When backwoods boys acquire a dose of gonorrhea, they believe it can be cured by infecting as many females as possible. Several physicians in the Ozark towns have told me about this belief, and a young farmer at Galena, Mo., expressed his conviction in very plain language. "That drugstore stuff ain't no good," said he. "The only way to cure the clap is to *fuck it out.*" This fellow was not an illiterate hillbilly. He had graduated with honors from the village high school, and spent two semesters at the University of Missouri. [See Randolph, *Ozark Superstitions,* 1947, p. 150; and compare folk graffiti, No. 115, in section G, preceding.]

4

Many hillmen carry luck charms, and the finest of all is the dried baculum from the penis of a male raccoon, euphemistically known as a bone toothpick. A coon-prick not only wards off evil, but is believed to fortify the sexual powers in elderly men. Mr. J. C. Edwards, a school administrator in St. Louis, carried a large *coonbone* in his pocket for more than twenty years. One day a music supervisor, who was born in Germany and knew little of the American hinterland, happened to see the pocket-piece and asked what it was. Mr. Edwards explained that every male coon had a bone in his penis. A few weeks later the German came to the office. He had been watching every Negro who urinated in his presence, and saw no sign of bone. "Their pricks are just as limber as mine," he said. The poor chap was familiar with the word *coon* as meaning Negro, but it never occurred to him that a raccoon had anything to do with the matter. [See Randolph, *Who Blowed Up the Church House,* 1952, pp. 135–137, 216.]

5

The old-timers believe that if a man is hanged for rape, and shows an erection after death, it is a sign that he was surely guilty. And if the dead man's prick *ain't* hard, some say the poor fellow must have been innocent after all. They tell me that when a man dies by hanging, the penis is sometimes erect and turgid. [Reminiscence of the trial-by-ordeal of witches: *If the witch drowns during the ordeal, she was innocent. If she survives, she was guilty and is burnt.*]

6

There is an old proverb "a hurricane always strips a whore." I supposed that it referred to the destruction of an immoral woman's house and property, but some hillfolk take the saying quite literally. When several persons were killed by a tornado in rural Arkansas, the body of one woman was found completely nude. "I don't never speak ill of the dead," an old lady told me, "but you know the old saying."

7

Another yarn concerns a little twister that swept through a mining camp near Joplin, Mo. Several persons were injured, windows were broken, a few ramshackle buildings knocked over. But a prostitute dressed in the elaborate finery of the 1890s happened to be coming out of the postoffice. The storm lasted only a few moments. When it was over, there was the whore in the street, unhurt. But she didn't have a stitch on except her shoes and stockings.

8

The hillman has some peculiar notions about the anatomy of the female sex-organs. Mr. L. S., of Stone County, Mo., told me that "every virgin has got three maidenheads." He believed that the hymen consists of three separate membranes, to be ruptured *seriatim* in defloration. This was a new idea to me, but I have since found that it is widely known, in many parts of rural Missouri and Arkansas.

9

There is a widespread belief that a girl who has lost her maidenhead can restore it by some magic herbs or drugs. Some girls use *love-apple tea,* which means concentrated tomato-juice. I have known women to thrust green tomatoes into the vagina, and have heard of others who "stuck crab-apples and butternuts up their cunt." These things are believed to produce a membrane indistinguishable from the hymen. A physician told me of a girl who used a douche of alum-water on her wedding night, to persuade the bridegroom that she was a virgin. [Brown, *North Carolina Folklore,* 1952, vol. I: p. 523, refers to "*bridal wreath,* a herb bath supposed to restore virginity."]

10

Human urine is highly regarded as medicine. I have discussed elsewhere the use of urine as a remedy for piles and chilblains. [*Ozark Superstitions,* 1947, pp. 99–100, and 109.] In 1944, at the Veterans Hospital in Fayetteville, Ark., I met a man whose hands were disabled by something like eczema. The doctors were giving him all sorts of treatment, but he attributed a slight improvement to the application of urine. "I just piss on my hands every night," he told me, "and it done more good than all them drugstore shots."

On the surprisingly large subject of scatological medicine, see Captain John G. Bourke, *Scatologic Rites* (1891) which dedicates a ninety-page chapter to the matter of "Ordure and Urine in Medicine," pp. 277–369; and from the viewpoint of humor, Legman, *No Laughing Matter,* 1975, vol. II: pp. 928–53, "Dr. Dreck, and The *Escoumerda.*" This belief has been particularly common in Germany.

11

A college professor at Columbia, Mo., in 1948, told me that some of his neighbors regarded urine as a specific for pulmonary tuberculosis. "They just make the patient drink his first water in the morning," said he. A country boy in central Missouri tried this, after the doctors had "plumb give him up," and six months later he was fit as a fiddle.

12

A degree of magic is involved in the medicinal use of urine. For swollen testicles or other difficulties associated with venereal disease, all one needs to do is piss in the fireplace every night. A newspaperman in Fayetteville, Ark., puts it more delicately: "Wetting on a heated fire shovel will dispose of a kernel in the groins in short order." [Fred Starr, *Pebbles from the Ozarks,* 1942, p. 53.]

13

Morris Hull, Eureka Springs, Ark., told me in 1949 of a magic cure for jaundice or "yeller janders." He got it from John Ball, an old-timer who lives in Mill Hollow, near Eureka Springs. "You just face the east when the moon's in the first quarter," said Mr. Ball, "and piss on a row of turnips that ain't come up yet."

14

Urine is believed to prevent certain diseases, and ward off some types of calamity. Boys about to go swimming piss on their legs to keep from getting cramps. I have seen them do this near Pineville, Mo., in the 1920s. A man who has just diddled a strange woman pisses on his legs as a prophylactic against venereal disease. "Don't wash it off, neither," said a man at Joplin, Mo., in 1931. "Just let it dry on your legs, and take a bath the next morning."

15

Many a girl, in southwest Missouri, treats a spotty complexion by rubbing her face with a baby boy's diaper, wet with fresh urine. I have known a dozen backwoods damsels who say they have removed freckles and blackheads by this procedure. They all agreed that a girl-baby's urine won't do.

16

Urine is good for skin cancers too. If the patient is a woman, the urine must be provided by a man, and vice versa. "Get a good healthy young fellow," said one old granny-woman, "and make him piss in a bottle, through a gold wedding ring."

17

Many hillfolk believe that ghosts and spirits stand about near lighted cabins at night. That's why they don't sweep dirt out of a door or off a porch after dark, for fear of throwing dust in a supernatural being's face. For the same reason, few hillmen will stand on a porch and urinate into the darkness. "It's terrible bad luck to piss on a ghost," as one old gentleman told me. The correct thing is to stand on the ground, and direct the stream of urine against the trunk of a tree. [See the old man's recollection on this occult belief, in section F, "Obscenity in Ozark Riddles," No. 18.]

18

A girl who wants to see her future mate has only to urinate on her nightdress, hang it before the fireplace, and go to bed naked. According to the old story, the image of the man she is to marry appears as soon as the dress is dry enough to be turned. Some ribald tales have it that he leaps into bed, in order to give the lady a foretaste of married life. When this happens, he always leaves some token, usually a pocket knife, which the girl shows him after they are safely married. [Compare: Randolph, *Ozark Superstitions,* 1947, p. 177. See also *Journal of American Folklore,* 1953, vol. 66: p. 336. A well-known joke in the 1940s concerned: *A woman who will not accept payment for her sexual favors, but demands a jackknife instead, to seduce young boys with when she is old.*]

19

The use of fresh cow-dung as a poultice for sores and sprains is common everywhere. It is an astringent, and may have real merit for all I know. A few years ago, country girls still believed that an application of this stuff would remove freckles and improve the complexion. A woman at Crane, Mo., told me that she had tried it. "That cow-shit drawed up my face," she said, "till I couldn't hardly move a eyewinker!"

20

One often hears of a "chicken-shit poultice" applied to the chest in cases of pneumonia. There is an element of magic here, for it must be the dung of a *black* chicken. I have seen black hens confined in a coop, to make certain that the material is not contaminated by fowls of another color. Most *healers* moisten the stuff with water, and then mix it with lard. They say that the poultice turns black, after being smeared on the patient's breast.

21

Measles is treated with a tea made of sheep manure: "You just take a handful of sheep-shit, not too fresh, and bile it in a quart of water." Taken internally, this brings out "a good healthy rash" and hastens the recovery. Sometimes a little molasses is added for taste, but the sheep dung provides the active ingredient. Refined people call this remedy "nanny tea" or "sheep noodle tea." A concentrated solution, made by boiling or evaporation, is often put into children's ears as a cure for ear-ache.

22

In one of my books I wrote: "Every backwoods child has heard a little rhyme to the effect that one who defecates in a path will get a sty on his posterior." [*Ozark Superstitions,* 1947, pp. 6–7] The editors wouldn't let me print the jingle, but here it is:

> Shit in the path,
> Get a sty on your ass.

23

A woman at Van Buren, Ark., in 1932, told me that as a girl she was noticeably flat-chested, "didn't have no bubbies to speak of." To remedy this condition, the granny-woman advised her to drink human milk, preferably that of a woman with large breasts. She did not try this herself, but says that it was a common practice along the Arkansas-Oklahoma border in the early 1900s. I have never found a woman who would admit to having resorted to this remedy, but have known several who had heard about it as recently as 1940.

In a well-known Roman legend, intended to inculcate the virtue of respecting one's elders, a young girl nurses her aged father with her own milk. This is refurbished as the climactic chapter, presumably of symbolic intent, in John Steinbeck's novel of the Oklahoma dustbowl emigration of the 1930s to the west coast, *The Grapes of Wrath* (1939), the dutiful and nutritious granddaughter here being named "Rose of Sharon," which would assimilate her to the poet-heroine of the *Song of Songs.* The theme is also reprised, satirically, of an aging billionaire, in Aldous Huxley's *After Many a Summer,* (1939).

24

Women in the Ozarks often nurse their babies for a long time, from twelve to eighteen months. To see a three-year-old child at the breast is not uncommon. A. H. Krappe says that he knew a woman "in the southern part of the state of Missouri who fed a boy nearly four years old with milk from her breast." Women believe that this prolonged lactation prevents another pregnancy, and there are many stories about it. [It is also good for the child's character. See: *Journal of American Folklore*, 1933, vol. 46: p. 10. Also *Ozark Superstitions*, 1947, p. 209–10; and A. H. Krappe, *The Science of Folklore*, 1930, p. 35.]

25

At Pineville, Mo., I heard the tale of a sixteen-year-old boy who had never used tobacco. Suddenly one day he asked his father for a chaw. The man expressed some surprise. "Well," said the boy, "Maw's been eating (wild) onions again, and I got to have something to take the taste out of my mouth." [A well-known mock "hillbilly" joke. See: Legman, *No Laughing Matter*, 1975, vol. II: pp. 704–44, "Anti-Gallantry and Anti-Woman," for much material on such anti-mother or breast rejections.]

26

Another story was related by a deer-hunter near Shaburg, Ark., in 1932. He saw a woman screaming through the woods, hotly pursued by a bearded young man. The hunter pointed his rifle, and forced the young man to stop. "Let me go, Mister," cried the young fellow. "That woman is my maw, and she's a-trying to wean me! It's an outrage, and I ain't going to stand for it!"

This is evidently a farce-reduction of the famous Oedipal incest scene in Henry Fielding's *Tom Jones* (1749) in which, strangely attracted by the breasts of an unknown naked woman he has saved from robbers in the woods, the hero unwittingly engages in incest with his own mother—later stated to be only his foster-mother, in a polite plot-pirouette. In the joke form, *The unwillingly weaned young boy*—no beard!—*is beating his mother with a stick and calling her obscene names for refusing to keep nursing him at her breasts.* Told by a young Irish mother, *jestingly,* of her eighteen-year-old "hippie" son who had just announced, before company, that if she didn't give him twenty dollars at once he would "peddle his ass to the homos on the beach."—San Diego, California, 1965.

27

The editors allowed me to discuss love-charms, amulets, and aphrodisiacs in some of my published works, although the informants could not be quoted verbatim. A tea made from snakeroot (*Cimicifuga*) is highly regarded in some quarters. So is ginseng, particularly if the root is dug by a naked woman. Other vegetable love-potions are made from yarrow (*Achillea millefolium*), love-vine or dodder, mistletoe, and the lady's-slipper or moccasin-flower (*Cypripedium*). [This last is thought to resemble a woman's genitals.]

Some store-keepers used to sell a patent liquid called "*Wonderful Sportine,*" but many country druggists compounded their own love-powders, usually a perfumed mixture of milk sugar and flake whiting, which they sold at enormous profits. [*Sport,* a word formerly restricted to erotic contexts, as "Sporting Life," the name of a brand of condoms. Randolph on love-charms is published in *Journal of American*

Folklore, 1927, vol. 40: pp. 78–80, and 1933, vol. 46: p. 8. Also *Ozark Superstitions,* 1947, pp. 55–56, 112, 166–170, and 262–63.]

28

A young man in McDonald County, Mo., was a great believer in the powerful love-drops sold by a village druggist. "All you got to do," he told me, "is feed a girl that stuff in candy, or put a few drops into her liquor. Then you play with her bubbies, and feel her legs, and maybe tickle her twitchet until the medicine gets to working good. About that time you unbutton your pants, pull out your pecker, and put her hand on it. Then she mostly just falls over backwards, and all you got to do is mount her!" The boy told me this in 1921, and he was still doing well with the "love-medicine" when I last saw him, about 1938.

29

There is an old belief that if a girl drinks from a man's blowing-horn, she is powerless to resist his advances thereafter. The blowing-horn is just a polished cowhorn used in calling foxhounds. Some young people stopped at a spring near my home at Pineville, Mo., in 1928. They were drinking whiskey out of a bottle. There was cold water in plenty, but no cup. A young man held his thumb over the mouthpiece of his horn, filled it with water, and offered the ladies a chaser. The country girls all shook their heads, but a young woman from Joplin drank greedily. "Tom will have his prick in her before midnight," one of the local girls whispered. I believe he did, at that. But I don't think the blowing-horn had anything to do with it. [Possibly the whiskey?]

30

Mountain girls often carry love-charms—turkey bones, the beard of a wild gobbler, small wasp-nests and the like—between the breasts or attached to a garter. Some women wear carved peach-stones or cherry-pits containing a pinkish, soap-like material. A girl at Fort Smith, Ark., in 1930, showed me a tiny "lucky charm" in the form of an erect penis, made of clay and fastened to her garter. Many country girls believe that a drop of menstrual fluid, placed in a man's whiskey, will cause him to fall madly in love. I am personally acquainted with women who have tried this. [See *Journal of American Folklore,* 1927, vol. 40: p. 79. Also *Click Magazine,* December, 1939, p. 20, for photos of love-charms by D. F. Fox, of Galena, Mo. Randolph also tells elsewhere a jocular tale of an Ozark old maid who ran a boarding-house for workmen, and who claimed she attracted new boarders *by smell* simply by boiling up a "granny-rag" (menstrual rag or cloth) in the boarding-house soup!]

31

Sexual acts between human beings and domestic animals are not uncommon in the Ozarks, and many people believe that such unions are sometimes fruitful. In many settlements one hears of girls giving birth to litters of puppies, mares bringing forth colts with human heads, and so forth. When a baby looks like a dog, some hillfolk believe that the mother must have had intercourse with a dog, while others speak of such an infant as "marked," meaning that the woman was frightened by a dog during her pregnancy. [On the belief in animal-human monstrous births, see *Journal of American Folklore,* 1927, vol. 40: p. 83.)

32

Here is part of a letter from a woman at Marionville, Mo., dated March 7, 1941: "Well, here is something more I want to tell you. I come to Missouri from Illinois when I was twelve years old, that was back in 1888. Well, I started to school and I set with a girl that I loved her dearly. Well, here is what she told me. She had a sister who was *marked* like a cat. She walked on hands and feet, was quite hairy all over, did not talk, she ate like a cat, and slept like a cat curled up on a large feather pillow on the floor. The pillow was behind the stove on the floor, because she wouldn't lay anywhere else. Well, when she became *old enough* she would go *wild* by spells. They built an iron cage in the corner of the room and had to put her in there while the spell lasted, *as in animal life*. Well, my cousin lived maybe a mile from there now, and he says the cat-girl is still living, with some kinfolks in the house to take care of her. She still eats like a cat, and walks on her hands and feet like a cat. But she is over sixty now, just sleeps nearly all the time, and pays no attention to any one who comes in."

33

A young matron in southwest Missouri gave birth to a child with a peculiar squint, which her husband thought was positive evidence of "marking" or prenatal influence. "Oh, you can mark 'em, all right," he said. "That baby looks exactly like Jim Bridges, that used to work for me." He believed the resemblance was due to his wife's seeing the squint-eyed man across the table at mealtime! The more obvious explanation apparently did not occur to him at all. [Perhaps an excuse rather than an actual belief?]

34

Another babe, born near the Missouri-Oklahoma line looked very much like an Indian, although neither parent boasted any Indian blood. This was another case of "marking." The woman remembered that, during her pregnancy she had been frightened by a drunken Osage, who had chased her a few yards on her way to the crossroads store. "I reckon he chased her, all right," said a cynical neighbor. "From the looks of that baby, *I believe he must have caught up with her!*" [Standard witticism, here in reference to Osage Indians; more often concerning a Negro.]

35

The practice of water-witching, locating underground streams with a forked stick, has some connection with virility in the hillman's mind. "If a man can't raise a good hard-on," one fellow said, "it ain't no use for him to try water-witching." Some water-finders even claim that a successful dowser actually "feels his tool a-getting hard" when the forked stick moves in his hands. [See Randolph's *Ozark Superstitions*, 1947, p. 85. Also believed in Europe.)

36

Sexual intercourse is involved in many of the old-time planting rituals. A newly cleared field "has got to be fucked over" in order to insure a good crop of corn, turnips, or flax. I published a paper entitled

"Nakedness in Ozark Folk Belief," which dealt with these ceremonies, but the essential sex act was touched upon very lightly. The folklore journals will accept articles about nakedness, but copulation is something else again. [*Journal of American Folklore,* 1953, vol. 66: pp. 333–34. See the six following items, and especially belief 43, below.]

37

Some old-time farmers went to the corn-patch immediately after the crop was planted, accompanied by a nude woman, and paraded up and down the rows. Then the man threw the woman down in the dirt and gave her a good fucking; this was supposed to make the corn grow tall.

38

Near the Missouri-Oklahoma border, in the early 1890s, a man took his wife out to the freshly planted cornfield at midnight. The woman stripped and ran three times around the patch. "Then he would throw her right down on the ground and have at it till she squealed like a pig." The neighbors laughed about this, saying that it was an Indian custom supposed to protect the crop against bad weather and insect pests. The old Indians whom I interviewed, however, said they had never heard of any such foolishness.

39

Near Aurora, Mo., I got the story of a ritual for sowing flax. Just before sunup the farmer and his wife appeared in the field, both naked. The woman walked ahead, and the man did the sowing. They chanted a rhyme with the lines "Up to my ass, and higher too!" [This line occurs in several bawdy dance-calls still remembered in southwest Missouri in 1954. See section D, No. 24, "Ribaldry at Ozark Dances," above.] Every few steps the man threw some of the seed against the woman's buttocks. "Then," as my informant put it, "they just laid down on the ground and had a good time."

Ruth Ann Musick (in the Fairmount, West Virginia, *Times,* May 18, 1952) reports a related flax-sowing ritual, but with no mention of copulation. According to Dr. Musick, the woman chants, "Up to my hips." The man responds, "And higher too." [Centuries older in Britain, for this identical planting "charm" and others similar. Plowing rituals involving copulation in ancient Russo-Scythia are involved crucially in the fine novelized reconstitution of that culture, *The Corn King and the Spring Queen* (1931) by Naomi Mitchison, Part III, chap. 2.]

40

A backwoods clan in southwest Missouri, according to one of my neighbors, produced phenomenal turnips by reason of secret magic. Just before sunrise on July 25, a grown boy and four girls did the planting. They all stripped, and the boy sowed the seed, with the four girls prancing about him. The girls kept a-hollering "Pecker deep! Pecker deep!" When the planting was complete, they all rolled together in the dust "like wild animals." The way I heard it, the turnip-planters were cousins. But some say that a boy and his sisters did the job, if no girl cousins were available. Incest is not uncommon in the back hills, even without any turnip-sowing as an excuse.

[In fact, brother-sister incest is quite common everywhere; and father-daughter incest almost as common. Mother-son incest is, however, the principal Western taboo, and is almost unknown here. In rural and mountain areas the excuse offered for these irregularities is that the roads—to go and find other sex partners—are poor or almost non-existent.]

41

Once in McDonald County, Mo., a giggling farm girl led me to the top of a high ridge. "I'll show you something funny," she promised. Down in the holler was a clearing with a tiny cabin. Pretty soon we saw a naked man and two nude women. They were romping and rolling on the ground, in a freshly plowed garden patch. "Them people belong to thc Ncw Ground church, and that's their religion," the girl told me. "They've got beds in the house, but they think it's better to waller in the dirt." She said nothing about crops or planting. But the earth in that particular spot was prcparcd for sccding, and later in the season I saw turnips growing there. [See *Journal of American Folklore,* 1953, vol. 66: p. 334. And compare beliefs Nos. 52–54, below.]

42

Many hillfolk believe that the size of a cucumber is determined by the size of the planter's genitals, and everybody knows that cucumbers planted by women and children never amount to much. I have heard a man refer to his penis as "my old cucumber." To say that a girl "ought to be raising cucumbers" means that "she needs a good fucking." [The cucumber, carrot, and banana are the classic vegetable succedanea used by women as dildos for masturbation, as in Randolph's story of "The Romping Party," quoted in note on 1, above.]

43

The Ozark country produces some very large watermelons, most of them force-fed through woollen wicks inserted into the stem. According to *Time,* (June 22, 1936), a melon grown near Hope, Ark., weighed 195 pounds. I have seen these melons in the fields, and they look nearly as big as barrels. The old-timers say that all the best melon-patches were "fucked over." Frank P., Galena, Mo., told me of a fabulous melon raised in his neighborhood. When I published the story I wrote: "Payne described the exact method by which this monstrous fruit was fertilized and cultivated, but his description would not pass the censors." (See my *We Always Lie to Strangers,* 1951, p. 88.) Frank said that the melon depended upon human copulation for its very life.

"All during the growing season," said he, "men and women come at night and laid down beside that big melon. The more they fucked, the faster it growed." The grower went down to Lovers' Lane every morning to gather up condoms, and used their contents to fertilize the earth about the melon, but stale semen didn't have much effect. "It takes fucking and loud grunts to raise big melons," said Frank. "The farmer and his wife pretty near fucked themselves to death. So did all their married sons and daughters, and even them that wasn't married took turns in the melon-patch. It got to be kind of a neighborhood joke, with people laughing about it for miles around. But them people raised the biggest melon ever seen in Stone County." Frank's story is just a tall tale, *of course.* But it shows that the narrator was familiar with the ancient planting rituals. [See also further beliefs 36–42 above.]

44

Very few vulgar references are found in ghost stories. But I recall one tale of a man pursued by a headless monster near a Taney County, Mo., graveyard in the early 1940s. He ran down the road and escaped. Later on, asked how he managed to outrun a supernatural monster, the fellow said simply: "I got a head start, because the ghost was running in shit for the first quarter of a mile."

A well-known joke, often stated to be told by a Negro; this is visibly a bawdy version—or else the scatological original—of the legend of Ichabod Crane and the Headless Horseman, in Washington Irving's *Legend of Sleepy Hollow,* about 1820. Note that the Devil often requires his minions to "bet, *or* pay him their head," or soul, or *shadow,* or some other part of their body, generally the buttocks, as the sacrifice or counterpart for his supernatural services. Consider Andersen's folktale of "The Little Mermaid." Such "Faust" bargains often involve sexual power as the Serpent-Devil's gift, as in the myth of Adam and Eve; and compare the Devil's temptations of Job, also in *Matthew,* 4:1–11.

45

There are several old tales about wandering spirits who came into houses, and had sexual intercourse with living women. Most hillfolk are a bit skeptical of such accounts. When it was suggested that the intruders were really villagers in disguise, who only pretended to be ghosts, one indignant woman answered: "You think I don't know the difference between a live man and a dead one? Why, his pecker was just like a icicle! And when the duckbutter come, it was cold as ice too!" [*Duckbutter* is seminal fluid. See *American Speech,* 1933, vol. 8: p. 48. Also Randolph and Wilson, *Down in the Holler,* 1953, p. 114. The Devil's snakelike penis and semen are also usually stated to be ice-cold in witchcraft depositions, as in belief No. 48 below. It is possible that such a pretendedly occult visit is the real situation in the well-known "Foggy, Foggy Dew" song, in volume I, No. 64, where in the original form a disguised "booger" frightens the girl.]

46

In Oregon County, Mo., a man used to come in from the fields and say to his wife "I got something for you, honey." And then he always put three dried rabbit-turds into her hand. The woman would throw them away with a great show of indignation. "It was kind of a family joke, just between them two," I was told. Well, the husband died, and a year later the woman married again. On the first night of the second honeymoon she saw the ghost of her dead husband in the bedroom, and started up with a scream. The second husband got up and lit the lamp. The door was barred and the windows fastened shut. There was nobody in the room, except the honeymooners. But the woman screamed louder than ever, and pointed to a "stand-table" beside the bed. There, on a clean towel, lay three dry rabbit-turds!

47

Many accounts of a witch's initiation contain references to obscene "rhymes and sayings," but I have never been able to obtain the exact words. "Mostly they're just nasty or wicked, about fucking Christ's mother, and shitting on the pulpit, and things like that," I was told. [See *Ozark Superstitions,* 1947,

p. 265–67; also the further remarks on "anti-godlin" obscenity as sacrilege, in the editor's note following the preface, above, and in G. Legman, *No Laughing Matter,* 1975, vol. II. pp. 760–79, "Dysphemism and Insults: Cursing God."]

48

The participants in witch ceremonies are all naked, and the woman who is becoming a witch must give her body, on three successive nights, to the Stranger who is inducting her into the mystery. "She don't get no pleasure out of it," an old woman said, "because the Thing that's a-fucking her ain't no natural man." The fireside legends all agree that the male is either the Devil himself, or one of Satan's deputies. "They tell me," said one famous witch-master, "that Old Ned's tool is two foot long, cold as a snake, with big rough scales on it!" Later on the old man added: "Why, when that Thing was a-screwing Sally Taylor in the graveyard, she hollered so loud you could hear it plumb to the schoolhouse!" [Many further authentic details in the writings, and particularly in R. Hemenway's biography, of the great Negro folklorist, Zora Neale Hurston (1977), who involved herself in voodoo erotism cults.]

Compare belief No. 44, above. Open question whether the woman's crying-out is in pain, or in the perhaps unaccustomed ecstasy of orgasm—not necessarily her usual share in everyday intercourse with a mundane husband.[See also John Updike's *Witches of Eastwick,* 1985.]

49

Long ago it was said that [Civil War] General Albert Pike, one of the outstanding figures in Arkansas history, was in league with the Devil. Within my own memory there were people in the Ozarks who believed such tales. "Pike's tool was fourteen inches long, with bones in it, and scaly like a fish," an old man told me. There are stories of wild orgies in the woods, where Pike sat on a throne, with naked women dancing about and placing wreaths of water-cress on his penis. "Them women was all witches, and some of 'em was his best friends' wives," a Confederate veteran said solemnly.

All this was printed in a book published at Little Rock, according to the old-timers, but I have been unable to find any trace of such a volume. The only printed reference I have seen is in Montague Summers' books, especially the *History of Witchcraft and Demonology* (1926) page 8, where it says that "Albert Pike has been identified upon abundant authority as being the Grand Master of a society practicing Satanism, and performing the hierarchical functions of the Devil at the modern Sabbat." In another work by the same author, Pike is called "the Vice gerent of Lucifer" and "Grand Master of the Witches, comparable to Francis Bothwell, Cagliostro, Jacob Falk, and Adam Weishaupt." (*Witchcraft and Black Magic,* 1945, p. 199.) Summers was an English clergyman, and I do not know where he got his information about Albert Pike. But as recently as 1930, I have met unlettered men in the Ozarks who firmly believed that Pike sold his soul to the Devil. These men did not read books, and never heard of the Reverend Summers. Their stories came from oral tradition. [See further the editor's note, in the preface, above.]

50

There are many old tales of people killed by witchcraft. An evil woman is supposed to toss a little ball of black hair mixed with beeswax, and the victim dies a few hours later. It is said that the hair-ball is always found in the body of a person killed in this manner. A young girl in southwest Missouri died suddenly, and her mother became hysterical. "Witches! Witches! They've killed Milly!" she cried. The relatives tried to quiet the woman, but she kept shouting "Look in Milly's cunt!" The friends who prepared the body for burial did look, and they found the witch-ball. I asked a local physician about this. He said that Milly died of heart disease, and if the granny-women found a hair-ball in her vagina, it was something she had used as a pessary. [See *Ozark Superstitions,* 1947, p. 271–72.]

51

A woman at Springdale, Ark., used to tell about the witch that laid a spell on Peggy D. Poor Peggy was in great pain, and "couldn't pass her water." Her father knew how to fix witches. He pissed in a bottle, dropped in some needles, and hung the bottle up in the chimney corner. Peggy began to feel better almost immediately. But now the *witch* couldn't urinate, so she came to Peggy's house, begging to be released from the spell, and promising not to work any more evil. So Peggy's father took the bottle down and broke it. After that both Peggy and the witch could piss as good as anybody.

"Pissing pins and needles," an old phrase for the typical pains of gonorrhea. Many "hexing"—and unhexing—ceremonials involve the use or manipulation of pointed or cutting objects, such as knives, needles and pins, or scissors. Such objects may never be given as presents, because they "cut love," without some unhexing randle being recited, or side-gift offered. That the fears involved here allude to death is made clear in "The Sleeping Beauty," who is hexed with the prick of a needle, with the result that she sleeps for a hundred years, and can only be unhexed with a "kiss." In the *Pentamerone,* of Basile (1666?), this "kiss" not only impregnates the sleeping beauty but also all the female servants in the house, and "the chamberpot under the bed gave birth to six little chamberpots."

52

Many stories are told about the antics of the "New Ground" Christians known as Holy Rollers. Groups of these fanatics sometimes appear stark naked at religious meetings. They make no secret of this, and citizens of Taney County, Mo., have seen as many as fifty nude men and women at one time. Photographs of these backwoods nudists have been made and sold to the tourists. I have seen some of these photographs myself, and county officials at Forsyth, Mo., showed them freely enough in the 1930s.

See *Journal of American Folklore* (1953) vol. 66: pp. 337–39. See also belief No. 41, above, concerning ritual intercourse by "Holy Rollers" on new-plowed earth. In James G. Huneker's once-banned novel of American classical and operatic musical life, *Painted Veils* (1920) the singer-heroine refuses to admit to the hero, after such a nighttime orgy, that they have made love to each other, and she possibly to the officiating preacher. Compare No. 54, below.

53

At Forsyth, Mo., a fellow named Oss Stockstill marched into town in broad daylight, stark naked, carrying a Bible under his arm. "I'm looking for twelve apostles!" he yelled. A local officer hesitated. "If the damn fool was drunk, I'd know what to do," said he. "But Oss ain't drunk, he's just got religion. There ain't no law against religion." W. E. Freeland, editor of our weekly newspaper, later expressed a similar opinion. "A man started to parade around the square here in Forsyth, clad only in his religious beliefs and with a Bible in his hand. He was arrested as an indecent man. Well, he might have pleaded he was only a religious devotee." (*Taney County Republican,* Forsyth, Missouri, February 26, 1942.) They let him out of jail after a week or so, and the New Grounders held their nude parades in the woods thereafter. But there are many people still living around Forsyth who remember Oss Stockstill's exploit.

54

The truth about the New Ground orgies is lurid enough, but some stories about them are wilder still. [See Nos. 41, 49 (Diabolism), and 52, above.] Lew Beardon, Branson, Mo., told me that he had seen a naked preacher standing on a stump, while the whole congregation lay naked on the ground before him, with "all them men and women a-fucking like minks." Another witness, closely associated with the New Ground faith, said that the people were in such a frenzy that many "didn't even know who they was a-fucking." He thinks some of the women were quite honest in saying that they couldn't tell which man had fathered their children. "It don't make no difference," one female preacher told a reporter, "because we're all children of God, and this world is coming to an end pretty soon, anyhow."

Abbott, George. *Songs for Sinners, Saints and Scoundrels*. (New York, ca. 1925.) Manuscript repositoried at The Lambs' Club, New York, but not now discoverable there.

Abel, Ernest L., and Barbara E. Buckley. *The Handwriting on the Wall: Toward a Sociology and Psychology of Graffiti*. Westport, Conn.: Greenwood Press, 1977. Best study of the subject, but with few examples. Compare: Read.

Abrahams, Roger. *Deep Down in the Jungle*. Hatboro, Pa.: Folklore Associates, 1964. Excellent study of Negro "toasts." Abridged and revised edition, Chicago, 1970.

———. *Abrahams MS*. Philadelphia, 1959. Transcript of tape-recorded "toast" recitations by Negro children.

———. *Negro Folklore from South Philadelphia: A Collection and Analysis*. University of Pennsylvania, 1962. Ph.D. dissertation with numerous field-collected texts not in printed edition above. Compare: Jackson; and Wepman.

Addison, James. "Bawdry, Cancer or Cure?" in: *Chapbook*. (Aberdeen Folklife Soc., 1967) vol. IV, no. 3.

Allred, Judy. *College Fraternity Songs*. (Austin, Texas, 1963.) 25 pp. hektographed. Compare: Reuss.

Aloha Jigpoha. (Compiled by Robert D. Thornton.) Boulder, Colo. and Honolulu, Hawaii, February 1945. 61 pp. mimeographed. Army and Air Force songs. (Copy: Harvard University Library.)

The Amanda Group of Bagford Poems. (MS. 1668.) Edited by J. W. Ebsworth. Hartford: Ballad Society (no. 20), 1880.

Anders, Greg ("Vito"). *17th Wild Weasel Songbook*. (Thailand, ca. 1968.) Mimeographed, air force songs.

Anecdota Americana: Being explicitly, An Anthology of tales in the vernacular. By Mr. William Passemon (*pseud.*, Joseph Fliesler). "Boston: For the Association for the Asphyxiation of Hypocrites." (New York: Printed by "Guy D'Isère"/Joseph Gavorse, for David Moss, Gotham Book Mart, 1927–28.) Repr. as: *The Classic Book of Dirty Jokes*, New York: Bell, 1981.

———. *Anecdota Americana: Second Series*. Edited without expurgation by J. Mortimer Hall (*pseud.*, Vincent Smith). "Boston: Humphrey Adams." (New York), 1934. Repr. as: *The Unexpurgated Anecdota Americana*, North Hollywood, Cal.: Brandon House, 1968.

———. *Anecdota Americana: Five Hundred Stories*. Expurgated and revised by Samuel Roth. New York: "William Faro" (Samuel Roth), 1933. Repr., New York: Nesor (Rosen and Wartels), 1934; and further revised by Roth as: *The New Anecdota Americana*, New York: Grayson, 1944.

Antarctic Fuckup. (Australia, ca. 1960?) 20 p. mimeographed songbook.

Anthologie Scatologique. (Edited by Gustave Brunet.) Paris: J. Gay, 1862? Suppl. to: *Bibliotheca Scatologica* (by Jannet), 1850.

Anthologie Hospitalière and Latinesque: Recueil de Chansons de Salle de Garde. Réunies par Courtepaille (*pseud. of* "Dr." Edmond Dardenne Bernard). Paris: "Chez Bichat-porte-á-droite," 1911–13. 2 vols. First and largest collection of French medical and art students' bawdy songs.

Anthropophytéia: Jahrbuch für folkloristische Erhebungen. Editor: Friedrich S. Krauss. Leipzig, 1904–13. 10 vols., 4to with 9 supplementary side-volumes of regional *"Beiwerke."* Compare: *Kryptádia;* and *Maledicta*.

An Antidote against Melancholy: Made up into Pills, compounded of witty ballads, jovial songs, and merry catches. (Edited by John Playford.) London: Mercurius Melancholicus, 1661. (Copy: Folger Library.)

Apollo's Banquet. London, 1669.

———. *Same*, 6th edition, 1690. (Edited by Henry Playford.)

Apples of Eden: A Private Collection of American Folklore, by A Liberal. (California? ca. 1980.) MS. Cited by Logsdon. Mostly bawdy songs.

The Arabian Nights (*Thousand and One Nights*). Persian work, *Hazar Afsana*, 9th century; in Arabic recension by Ibn 'Abdus al-Jashyari, about 940 A.D. Various translations.

Archive of Folk Culture, Library of Congress. Washington, D.C., 1928 to present.

The Archives. ("A collection of earthy verses and tales.") Cambridge, Mass. (ca. 1960?)

Argus Tuft's Compendium of Verse. (Colophon:) Collected, collated, arranged and edited by Argus Tuft (*pseud.*). Published and printed by R. Supward. (Perth, Australia: S.C.I.I.A. Engineering Society) 1970. Mimeographed revision and enlargement of *Be Pure!* (1963) by same editor.

Arkansas, University of. University Folklore Collection, Special Collections, University of Arkansas Library, Fayetteville. Assembled 1949–65, by Mary Celestia Parler Randolph and others. Over 3,500 tape-recorded songs and other genres; also typed transcriptions in 65 document cases and 10 bound volumes.

Army Song Book. Washington, D.C., 1941.

Arnold, Byron. *Folksongs of Alabama.* University of Alabama Press, 1950.

Arschwische und Scheissereien, ausgemistet von einem Schismatiker. (Witzbuch der Biedermeier-zeit: Sotadisch-skatologischen Witzbuches von, 1836.) Repr., ed. Dr. Lutz Röhrich. Allmendingen: September Verlag, Rainer G. Feucht, *announced* 1989.

Ash, Robert. See: *Union Jack.*

Ashton, John. *A Century of Ballads.* London: Elliott Stock, 1887.

———. *Modern Street Ballads.* London, 1888.

Aubrey, John. *Brief Lives.* (MS. 1680), ed. John Collier, 1944?

———. *Miscellanies.* 1696. First folklore collection in English.

———. *Remaines of Gentilisme and Judaisme* (MS. 1687), ed. J. Britten, 1881.

(Auden, W. H.) *The Platonic Blow.* Designed and Published, Zapped and Ejaculated by Fuck You Press. (New York: Peace Eye Bookshop; Ed Sanders and Tuli Kupferberg), 1965.

———. *Same.* Mimeographed repr. as: *A Gobble Poem.* Snatched from the notebooks of W. H. Auden. London: Fuckbooks Unlimited, 1967. Compare: Bishop; Dylan Thomas; and Updike.

Babad, Harry, ed. *Roll Me Over.* New York: Oak Publications, 1972. With extra songs supplied by Oscar Brand. Reprint of: Walsh, *Songs of Roving and Raking,* 1961.

The Bacchanalian Magazine, and Cyprian Enchantress. London: H. Lemoine, 1793.

The Bagford Ballads, edited by J. Woodfall Ebsworth. Hertford: Ballad Society, 1876–80, 2 vols. Reprinted, New York: AMS, 1968.

———. Supplement: *The Amanda Group of Bagford Ballads.* (Hertford, 1880?) "Reserved" supplement of the erotic ballads.

Baker, George. *Slightly Soiled . . . A group of tales, compiled and retold.* Limited edition. New York: National Advertising Art Center, 1944–47. 3 pamphlets, with other humorous material.

Baker, Ronald L. "Lady Lil and Pisspot Pete," in *Journal of American Folklore* (1987) 100: 191–99.

Baker House Super-Duper Extra Crude Song Book. (At head: The ONE the ONLY.) (Cambridge, Mass.: Baker House, Massachusetts Institute of Technology, ca. 1963.) Hektographed.

The Ballad of Eskimo Nell. (Australia) Printed and Published by Bold Books, 1973.

Baltzer, R. *Knurrhahn:* Sammlung Deutscher und Englischer Seemannslieder. 3 Aufl. Kiel, 1936. 2 vols.

Baring-Gould, Sabine. *Songs of the West: Folk Songs of Devon and Cornwall.* Revised and edited by Cecil Sharp. London: Methuen, 1905. See: James Reeves, *The Everlasting Circle,* 1960, printing the unexpurgated texts collected.

Barke, James. "Pornography and Bawdry in Literature and Society." Preface to Robert Burns, ed. *The Merry Muses of Caledonia* (Edinburgh: Auk Soc., 1959). Repr. New York.

Barkov, Ivan, *pseud.* See: *Luka Mudishchev.*

Barons, Kr., and H. Wissendorffs. *Latuju Dainas* (Riga?), 1898–1915. 6 vols. Principal collection of Latvian folksongs, extending to about 36,000 basic texts, of which 3822 are erotic, including variants. The Kinsey-ISR Library holds a valuable manuscript analysis of these erotic texts, by Prof. Walter Anderson, signed with the initial "S," 1969–79; plus further sheets entitled "Preliminary Analysis of Female-contributed Latvian Folk-songs."

———. *Latviesu Nerátnás.* Copenhagen: "Imanta," 1957. Revised edition of vol. 6 of preceding work, containing only the erotic songs, Nos. 34,379 to 35,789, or 1411 main texts. Nothing on this scale exists elsewhere, in print.

Barph, Toshka (*pseud.*). *Cookie-Tossers and Stomach-Turners.* "Filthadelphia," 1969. MS. collection of purposely disgusting ("but not obscene"!) college songs and "sick" jokes, supplied by a young woman. Compare: *Songs of Sadism.*

Barrick, Mac E. *German-American Folklore.* Little Rock, Ark.: August House, 1987. Riddles and rhymes, pp. 82–88.

Baskervill, Charles R. *The Elizabethan Jig, and Related Song Drama.* Chicago: University of Chicago Press, 1929. Reprinted, New York: Dover Pubs., 1965.

———. "English Songs of the Night Visit," in: *PMLA (Publications of the Modern Language Association,* 1921), 36: 565–614.

Baucomont, J. *Les Comptines de Langue française.* Paris: Seghers, 1961. Children's verse, erotic and other.

The Bawd's Book: Being a Collection of Crass and Curious Limericks and Linoleum Cuts. San Marino, Calif.: (R. A. Billington?), 1965. Not seen.

Beck, Earl C. "The Farmer's Curst Wife (Child 278) in Michigan," in: *Southern Folklore Quarterly* (Sept. 1940) 4: 157–58. Compare: Stekert.

———. *Lore of the Lumber Camps.* University of Michigan Press, 1948.

Beck, Horace Palmer. *Down-East Ballads and Songs.* Ph.D. dissertation, University of Pennsylvania, 1952. Unexpurgated.

The Bedroom Companion. (Edited by Philip Wylie.) New York: Farrar and Rinehart, 1934. Repr., New York: Arden Book Co., 1941.

Bedroom-Party Literature. Privately Printed. Limited Edition. (U.S., ca. 1950.) 70 pp. Erotic miscellany in prose and verse. Cited by C. J. Scheiner, *Compendium* (1989) no. 94.

Beer, Thomas. *The Mauve Decade* (the 1890s). New York: Knopf, 1926. Reprint, Alblabook, 1937. Unreliable.

(*The Beggar's Benison.*) *Records of the most Ancient and Puissant Order of the Beggar's Benison and Merryland.* "Anstruther" (London: Leonard Smithers), 1892.

———. *Supplement to the Historical Portion of the Records, with excerpts from the Toasts, Recitations, Stories, Bon-Mots, Speeches and Songs delivered thereat.* "Anstruther" (London: Smithers), 1892. Repr., 1980?

Beilenson, Peter. See: *Rowdy Rhymes.*

Beiwerke zum Studium der Anthropophytéia. See: *Anthropophytéia.*

Belando, Vicenzo. *Lettere facete e chiribizzose.* Paris, 1588. Compare: Tabourot; and *Wit's Recreations.*

Belden, Henry M. *Ballads and Songs Collected by the Missouri Folklore Society.* Columbia: University of Missouri Studies, 1940. See also: *Brown Collection.*

Bell, Robert. *Ancient Poems, Ballads and Songs of the Peasantry of England.* London: Parker, 1857. See: Dixon.

Bent, Eric. *Laughs in the Loo.* London: Tandem, 1970. ("Loo," British for toilet, from French *lieux.*)

(Bently, Ms. Logan.) *Stovepipe Serenade.* Armed services' and pilots' songs. Editor is a woman. 1954. Mimeographed.

(———, and other eds.) *Stovepipe Serenade.* 2nd edition. Compiled at the Worldwide Rocketry Meet, Vincent Air Force Base, Arizona, 1956.

Be Pure! (Perth, Western Australia: Engineering Students' Society, University of Perth, 1963.) Mimeographed. Bawdy Australian college songs. Enlarged as: *Argus Tuft's Compendium of Verse,* 1970.

Bergson, Boris. *Privat-pornographie in Deutschland: 1789–1960.* Verfemte erotische Trivial-literatur. Darmstadt: Buchdienst (Melzer, 1975). Folk-erotica.

Bernard, Edmond Dardenne. See: *Anthologie Hospitalière; Les Chants du Quartier Latin;* and *Trois Orfèvres;* also *Les Filles de Loth.*

Berry, Henry. *Make the Kaiser Dance.* Garden City, N.Y.: Doubleday, 1978. World War I interviews, quoting bawdy Army songs.

Beware! See: *Parker Folio Manuscript.*

Bible: Old Testament, redactors: Ezra and Nehemiah, ca. 440 B.C.

———. *New Testament,* redactors: Justin Martyr and Tatian (?) ca. 160 A.D. "King James" translation, 1611; reprs.

Le Bibliophile Fantaisiste, ou Choix de pièces désopilantes et rares. Turin: J. Gay et fils, 1869. 12 numbers. Limited to 175 copies. Continuation of Gay's *Pièces désopilantes,* 1866.

Bibliotheca Scatologica. Paris, 1850–65. See: Jannet.

Bibliotheque Erotique. "London" (Detroit: McClurg), 1929. 1 vol. in 2: 616 pp. Obscœna in prose and verse, *in English,* edited by the publisher, McClurg.

———. Reissued as: *Library L'Amour.* "London: Pickadilly Press" (Detroit: McClurg, 1930). 12 pts. in 4 vols.

Bishop, John Peale. *Collected Poems.* New York, 1946?

Bishop, Morris. See: Mills.

Black, Eleanora, and Sidney Robertson Cowell. *The Gold Rush Song Book.* San Francisco: Colt Press, 1940.

Blair, Walter. *Native American Humor, 1800–1900.* New York: 1937. Repr., San Francisco: Chandler, 1960.

Blake, Roger. See: Trimble.

Blankety Blank Verse. Boston: Carol Press, 1910. 18 pp.

Blasons, Poésies anciennes des XV et XVImes siècles (ed. by D. M. Méon.), Paris, 1809.

Blom, Xenia. See: *Ohio State University Sailing Club.*

Blümml, Emil Karl. "Erotische Lieder aus Oesterreich," in *Anthropophytéia* (1905) 2: 70–112; and (1906) 3: 169–217.

———. *Erotische Volkslieder aus Deutsch-Oesterreich,* mit Singnoten. Privatdruck (Wien: Dr. Rudolf Ludwig, 1906–07). See further: F. Bilger, "Einige Urteile über Blümmls schriftstellerische Arbeiten," in: *Das Deutsche Volkslied* (1911) 13: 35–75.

———. "Reime beim Fensterln (Gasselreime) aus Steiermark," in: *Anthropophytéia* (1906) 3: 41–50. Songs of the night-visit. Compare: Baskervill.

———. "Welche hätte die Beste?" in: *Anthropophytéia* (1905) 2: 110. On "Three Old Whores from Baltimore."

———, and "J. Polsterer" (*pseud.* of Josef Latzenhofer), editors: *Futilitates: Beiträge zur volkskundlichen Erotik.* Wien: Dr. R. Ludwig, 1908. Vol. 1: Blümml, *Schamperlieder;* Vol. 4: "Polsterer," *Militaria.*

———, and Gustav Gugitz, editors: *Der Spittelberg und Seine Lieder.* Wien: Privatdruck, 1924. Editors' pseudonyms given as: "K. Giglleithner and G. Litschauer."

The Boastful Yak. By Henri Nicolai (*pseud.* U.S.) "Privately Printed for the Members of the Zoological Society of Paris." (Fully Protected, 1927.) Limited to 51 copies. (Note: This is *not* identical with the erotic poem of the same title by Eugene Field, which uses the gambling term "renegue.")

Boccaccio, Giovanni. *Decamerone.* MS., 1353. Many translations.

Boehme, Franz. *Deutsches Kinderlied und Kinderspiel.* Leipzig, 1897.

The Bog-House Miscellany. See: *The Merry-Thought.*

Bold, Alan. *The Bawdy Beautiful: The Sphere Book of Improper Verse.* London: Sphere Books Ltd., 1979. Compare: *Immortalia,* T. R. Smith; and Whitworth.

———. *Making Love: The Picador Book of Erotic Verse.* London: Picador/Pan Books, 1978. Compare Cole, Laycock, and *Poetica Erotica.*

Boni, Margaret B. *Fireside Book of Favorite American Songs.* New York, 1952.

———. *The Fireside Book of Folk Songs.* New York: Simon and Schuster, 1947.

"Bonmal, Don," *pseud.* See *The Rhyme of All Flesh,* by "Eric E. StAye Scott" (Davis?).

Bontemps, Arna, and Langston Hughes. *The Book of Negro Folklore.* New York, 1958.

The Book of a Thousand Laughs, by "O. U. Schweinickle" (*pseud.* Wheeling, W. Va., 1928.)

A Book of Vulgar Verse. Toronto, 1981. See: *Immortalia.*

"Borde, Victor," *pseud.* See: R. Lehmann-Nitzsche.

Borneman, Ernest. *Studien zur Befreiung des Kindes.* Unser Kinder im Spiegel ihrer Lieder: Die Umwelt des Kindes. Olten, Switzerland: Walter-Verlag, 1973–76. 3 vols.

Botkin, Benjamin A. *The American Play-Party Song.* Lincoln: University of Nebraska Studies, 1937. Compare: Wolford.

———. *A Treasury of American Folklore: Stories, Ballads, and Traditions of the People.* New York: Crown, 1944.

The Boudoir: A Magazine of Scandal, Facetiæ, etc. London: "H. Smith, 1860" (W. Lazenby, 1883). Repr., New York: Grove Press, 1971. A continuation of *The Pearl,* q.v.

Bourke, John G. *Scatalogic* (sic) *Rites of All Nations.* Washington, 1891. Reprint, New York: "American Anthropological Soc." (Panurge Press), 1934. Foreword by Sigmund Freud.

Box, Pelham. See: Pelham-Box MS.

Bradley, S. A. J., ed. *Sixty Ribald Songs from "Pills to Purge Melancholy."* New York: Praeger, 1968. See: *Pills.*

Bramlett, Jim. *The Original Strawberry Roan.* (U.S.) Published by the Author, 1987.

Brand, Oscar. *The Ballad Mongers: Rise of the Modern Folksong.* New York: Funk and Wagnalls, 1962.

———. *Bawdy Songs and Backroom Ballads.* New York: Dorchester Press, Ltd. (Grove Press), 1960. 96 pp. 4to. With a best-selling series of ten equally expurgated phonograph recordings, similarly titled. Texts all rewritten.

———. "In Defense of Bawdy Ballads," in: *Modern Man,* January 1957 (Skokie, Illinois, 1956) pp. 8–11, and 51–52, with self-portrait. Revised in Brand's *The Ballad Mongers.*

———. *Folk Songs for Fun.* New York: Hollis Music, 1961.

Brednich, Rolf W. *Erotische Lieder aus 500 Jahren.* Frankfurt, 1979. (Fischer Taschenbuch, No. 2953.)

———. "Erotisches Lied," in: *Handbuch des Volkliedes* (München, 1973) vol. I: 575–615. Important article.

Brewer, J. Mason. *Worser Days and Better Times: The Folklore of the North Carolina Negro.* Chicago: Quadrangle, 1965.

Brewster, Paul G. *American Non-Singing Games.* Norman, Okla., 1953.

———. *Ballads and Songs of Indiana.* Bloomington: Indiana University Press, 1940.

The Bride's Confession, contained in a Letter to her friend Bella, otherwise entitled "The Bridal Night." Poem attributed to Lord Byron (!) Paris: Printed in the Third Year of the World War (Charles Carrington, ca. 1917).

Briggs, Bill. *Crud and Corruption.* Boston (ca. 1956). Mimeographed college songbook.

Brivio, Roberto. *Canzoni sporche all'osteria.* Milan: Williams Inteuropa, 1973. 159 pp. Supplement to *La Mezzora,* No. 141. Italian students' drinking and erotic songs; the best collection. See: Castelli, *Il Libretto Rosso.*

Broadway Brevities. New York, 1931–35. Vols. 1–13, folio: 125 numbers. Tabloid newspaper of sex scandal and humor. *Rarissime.*

Broadwood, Lucy, and J. A. F. Maitland. *English Country Songs.* London, 1893.

Bronson, Bertrand H. *The Traditional Tunes of the Child Ballads, with their texts.* Princeton University Press, 1959–72. 4 vols. Companion work to Child, q.v. See: Gilchrist.

Brophy, John, and Eric Partridge. *The Long Trail.* London: André Deutsch, 1965. Reprint of:

———, and Eric Partridge. *Songs and Slang of the British Soldier, 1914–1918.* 3rd ed., enlarged. London: Scholartis Press, 1931. Repr. as: *The Long Trail,* London: A. Deutsch; and Freeport, New York: Books for Libraries, 1965.

Brown, Frank C. *Collection of North Carolina Folklore: Folk Ballads and Songs,* edited by Henry M. Belden and Arthur P. Hudson (vols. I–III). *The Music of the Ballads and Songs,* edited by Jan P. Schinhan (vols IV and V). Durham, North Carolina: Duke University Press, 1952–62. 7 vols. See also: Belden.

Brown, H. "Rap." *Die Nigger Die.* New York: Dial Press, 1969.

Brown, Robert Carlton ("Bob"). *Gems: A Censored Anthology.* Cagnes-sur-Mer (Alpes-Maritimes), France: Privately Printed, Roving Eye Press, 1931. Censorship spoof.

The Brown Book of Locker-Room Humor. Toronto: Peek-A-Boo Press (Rexdale, Ontario: Coles Pub. Co.), 1980. 16 mo. Obscœna and verse. In series with: *The Pink* (and *Turquoise*) *Book of Locker-Room Humor.* Compare: *Locker Room Humor,* 1958.

Brüning, H. Enrique. "Erotische Tanzlieder der Peruaner," in *Anthropophytéia* (1910) 7: 341–49, and 399–400; and (1912) 9: 470–72. Erotic dance-songs from Peru.

Brunner, J. C. "Erotik im Soldatenlied," in his *Illustrierte Sittengeschichte: Krieg und Geschlechtsleben.* Frankfurt: Delius Verlag, 1922, with extra plate between pp. 48 and 49.

Brunvand, Jan H. *The Study of American Folklore.* New York: Norton, 1968. See also: *Metafolkloristica,* 1989.

Buchan, Peter. *(Manuscripts of Peter Buchan).* British Museum, Dept. of Manuscripts, 1828?

(———.) *Secret Songs of Silence.* By "Sir Oliver Orpheus" (*pseud.*) MS. Aberdeen, 1832. (Harvard

University Library, 25241:9*) Announced for forthcoming publication. Erotic supplement to Buchan's *Ancient Ballads and Songs of the North of Scotland,* Edinburgh, 1828. 2 vols. (Reprint, 1875.) For details see his biography by William Walker, which also lists full contents of the MS.

Buchan Bawdry, 1960. See: Kenneth Goldstein.

Buckley, Bruce. *'Frankie and Her Man': A Study of the Interrelationships of Popular and Folk Traditions.* Ph.D. diss., Indiana University, 1962. On "Frankie and Johnny."

The Buck's Bottle Companion: Being a complete collection of humorous, bottle, and drinking songs. London, 1775.

The Buck's Delight, or Love's Repository. Presented to the rising members of society, by Timothy Tickle-Pitcher. (London?) Printed in the Year 1779. (Copy: Gichner Collection, Washington, D.C.)

The Buck's Delight, or Merry Companion. Containing a Collection of Comic Songs . . . by the Sons of Comus. London: W. Lane, 1783.

The Buck's Delight: A Collection of Humorous Songs sung at the several Societies, London: T. Knowles (ca. 1790).

Budzinski, Klaus, and Hans R. Schatter. *Liederliche Lieder:* erotische Volkslieder aus fünf Jahrhunderten. München, Bern, Wien: Scherz Verlag, 1967. 448 pp.

Bullen, Arthur H. *Speculum Amantis.* London, 1889. Older erotic art-poetry in English.

Bulletin of the Folk-Song Society of the Northeast. Cambridge, Mass., 1930–37. (Articles by Phillips Barry.)

Burke, Carol. "Marching to Vietnam," in *Journal of American Folklore* (1989) 102: 424–441. Outstandingly courageous discussion and record of American air-pilots' anti-civilian gloat songs of war-horror.

Burns, Robert. See: *Merry Muses of Caledonia;* and *Scots Musical Museum;* and compare: Buchan; Hecht; Herd; Kinloch; Maidment; and Sharpe.

Cabell, James Branch. *Sonnets from Antan.* New York, 1920?

Campbell, Olive Dame, and Cecil Sharp. *English Folk Songs from the Southern Appalachians.* New York and London: Putnam, 1917. See: Sharp and Karpeles, for enlarged 1932 edition.

Camp Fire Songs and Verse. Collected by a well-known Cavalry Regiment. (Madras, India, 1939–40.) 75 p. folio, mimeographed. Only two surviving copies are known of this most important modern British collection of soldiers' unexpurgated songs. Compare: Henderson; Hopkins; Morgan; and Page.

Canà, Ettore, and Lodovico Mosconi. *I Pianeti della Fortuna: Canzoni e vignette popolari.* Milano: Vanni Scheiwieler, 1973.

Cantagalli, R. *Con rispetto parlando.* (Milano?) Sugar, 1972.

Carlisle, Irene Jones. *Fifty Ballads and Songs from Northwest Arkansas.* Master's Thesis, University of Arkansas, 1952.

Carmer, Carl. *Listen for a Lonesome Drum: A York State Chronicle.* New York: Farrar and Rinehart, 1936.
———. *Songs of the Rivers of America.* New York: 1942.

Carmina prose et rithmi, Edite in laudem podice sacerdotalis, contra prosam excusare eonantem scandalosissium concubinatum. (Colophon: Qui faciebat Nicholaus Lebzelter Gundelfingius, V. et T. . . . V. V.) (No place or date, ca. 1505.) 4 f. 4to. (Bodleian, *Antiq.* e.U.20.)

(Caron de Beaumarchais, Simon.) *Le Plat de Carnaval,* ou Les Beignets apprêtés par Guillaume Bonnepâte (*pseud;* Paris, 1802). Limited to 56 sets. Reprints of old facetiæ and modern bawdy pieces in prose and verse. This is Part 7 of Caron's rare *Recueil de poésies anciennes, farces, et facéties,* 1798–1806 (later supplemented by Montaran, and by Du Roure.)

Carpenter, James M. Unpublished manuscript collection of folksongs, folkplays (British), sea-shanties, etc., made without expurgation in America and Britain from 1920s to 1950s. Deposited in Library of Congress, Archive of Folklife. Important collection; indexed in part by Michael Preston. Compare: Gordon; and Henderson.

(Cary, Henry N.) *The Slang of Venery and Its Analogues.* (Chicago: H. N. Cary) 1916. 3 vols., mimeographed. (Copies: Kinsey-ISR Library; NYPL:3*; British Museum, Private Case.) Note: Largely culled from Farmer and Henley, q.v., but the Kinsey-ISR copy also has further MS. materials.

(———,) compiler. See: *Treasury of Erotic and Facetious Memorabilia.*

Cary, Melbert B., Jr. *Mademoiselle from Armentières.* New York: Press of the Woolly Whale, 1930–35. 2 vols. The *locus classicus* on this principal army song of World War I, with an introduction on the musical origins of the song, by Robert W. Gordon. Compare: Winterich.

Case, Arthur E. *Bibliography of English Poetical Miscellanies: 1521–1750.* Oxford: Bibliographical Society, 1935. Comprises the unexpurgated drolleries of the late 17th century; list importantly enlarged by Norman Ault in *Cambridge Bibliography of English Literature* (1940) 2: 173–256. Compare: Day; Foxon; and Simpson.

Castelli, Alfredo. *I Canti Goliardici,* No. 2. (2nd Series.) Milano: Williams Inteuropa (1974). Supplement to magazine *Collna Cabaret.* Study and texts of modern Italian students' drinking and erotic songs and obscœna. First Series issued as: *Il Libretto Rosso.*

Catch that catch can, 1652. See: Hilton.

Caution! See: Nancy Wright.

Cazden, Norman, ed. *The Abelard Folksong Book.* New York: Abelard-Schuman, 1958. Largely the repertory of one folksinger. Compare: Logsdon.

Cela, Camilo José. *Diccionario Secreto.* Madrid: Ediciones Alfaguara, 1968–71. 2 vols., and further volumes in progress.

Chambers, Robert. *Popular Rhymes of Scotland.* London and Edinburgh, 1870.

Chansonnier du Bordel, ou Veillées d'un Fouteur. "Paphos" (Paris, ca. 1830).

———. Nouvelle édition. Paris: Se trouve chez Vénus, à Bagatelle, 1833. Reprs., 1834, and 1840; all very rare. The principal French collection of 19th-century erotic folk-poetry and songs.

Le Chansonnier des Internes de Lille. Association des Anciens Internes des Hôpitaux de Lille, 1927. The first openly published collection of the French medical and art students' bawdy "Chansons de Salles de Garde." Compare: *Anthologie Hospitalière;* also the following:

Les Chansons de Salles de Garde, avec la musique. "Amsterdam: Éditions du Scorpion" (Paris?) 1930. Note: Contents of this edition, and of many others with the same or similar titles, are much abridged from *Anthologie Hospitalière* (1911–13) by Edmond D. Bernard; and where the musical notation is given it is generally taken from his *Chants du Quartier Latin,* (ca. 1931). Compare: Staub.

Les Chansons de Salle de Garde. Paris: Cercle du Livre Précieux (Claude Tchou), 1962. Repr., Paris: Régine Desforges, L'Or du Temps (J. –J. Pauvert), 1972. Introduction, and Bibliography of 25 similar editions, by G. Legman. Text is selected (but not the same selection as in preceding editions) from *Anthologie Hospitalière.*

Chansons Joyeuses du XIXe siécle. "Yverdon: Imprimerie particulière" (Bruxelles: Jules Gay), 1866. 2 vols. Variant edition of Gay's *Les Gaudrioles du XIXe siècle.*

Les Chants du Quartier Latin et de l'Internat. (Paris: Guibal? for E. D. Bernard, ca. 1931.) Edited by Edmond Dardenne Bernard, as a supplement to his *Anthologie Hospitalière et Latinesque* (1911–13) and its partial reprinting in 1930 as *Trois Orfèvres à la Saint-Éloi.* Gives the musical notation, apparently for the first time, for these "Chansons de Salles de Garde."

Chapman, Robert L. *American Slang.* New York: Harper, 1987. Compare: Gillette; Wentworth and Flexner; and Wilson, R. First and unabridged edition of this outstanding work, *New Dictionary of American Slang,* 1985.

Chappell, Louis W. *Folk-Songs of Roanoke and the Albemarle.* Morgantown, W. Va.: Ballad Press (Published by the Author), 1939. Note: This is the *first expurgated* folksong collection publicly published in English since Herd's in 1776. Compare: Fauset (1931).

Chappell, William. *Popular Music of the Olden Time.* London, 1855–59. 1 vol. in 2. Repr., New York: Dover Pubs., 1965. The best edition, but see: Simpson.

———. *Same,* as: *Old English Popular Music,* revised by H. E. Wooldridge. London, 1893. Repr., New York: J. R. Brussel, 1961. This revision (of the music mainly) omits most of the "traditional" songs!

———, and J. Woodfall Ebsworth, eds. The *Roxburghe Ballads.* Hertford: Printed for the Ballad Society, 1879–99. 9 vols. Repr., New York, 1968?

Chapple, Joseph. *Heart Songs, Dear to the American People.* Boston: Chapple, 1909. Compare: Wier.

Charrière, G. *La Signification des Représentations Erotiques* dans les arts sauvages et préhistoriques. Paris: Maisonneuve, 1972? Important contribution on *graffiti*.

Chatterton, Thomas. *The Letter Paraphras'd: An Unpublished Poem* (1769?) Privately Printed for A.B.C. (Metuchen, N.J.: Charles Heartman, 1933.) 6 pp. Introduction signed "M. O. Hunter" (by Prof. Thomas O. Mabbott).

Chenailler, Capt. *Chansons des marins, et autres*. Rassemblées par le Capitaine de Frégate . . . Lorient: Editions et Imprimerie de Bretagne (ca. 1975). 36 pp.

Cheney, Thomas E. *Mormon Songs from the Rocky Mountains*. Austin: University of Texas Press, 1968.

Cheshire, D. F. *Music Hall in Britain*. Newton Abbot: David and Charles, 1974. With section on the "Prudes on the Prowl" affair of 1894. See also: Speaight.

Child, Francis J. *The English and Scottish Popular Ballads*. Boston, Mass., 1882–98. 5 vols. Repr., New York: Pageant Book Co., Folklore Press, 1957; and Dover Pubs., 1965. See further: Bronson.

Choyce Ayres and Songs. London, 1679. Drollery collection.

Choyce Drollery: Songs and Sonnets. London, 1656. Reprinted, edited by J. Woodfall Ebsworth, Boston, Lincolnshire, 1876. A "*Supplement of Reserved Songs from Merry Drollery, 1661*" was also issued privately in 1876 to be inserted between pages 256 and 57, comprising expurgated and omitted songs referred to, p. 243, as "The Chamber of Horrors."

Christie, William. *Traditional Ballad Airs*. Edinburgh, 1876–81. 2 vols.

Cleopatra's Scrapbook. "51 B.C., Blue Grass, Kentucky" (Wheeling, West Virginia?) 1928 Edition. Folk-publication of obscœna and verse.

Clerval, Henry. "Clap Books," in: *Maledicta* (1988) 9: 139–41.

Cobbes Prophecies, his Signes and Tokens. London: Robert Wilson, 1614. facsimile repr. as *Antient* (sic) *Drolleries,* No. 1. London: Printed for Private Circulation (Charles Praetorius), 1890.

Cochran, Robert. *Vance Randolph: An Ozark Life*. Univ. of Illinois Press, 1985. Supplemented by bibliography of Randolph:

———, and Michael Luster. *For Love and for Money*. Batesville, Ark., 1979.

Coffin, Tristram P. *The British Traditional Ballad in North America*. Philadelphia: American Folklore Society, 1950.

———. *Same,* revised and enlarged by Roger deV. Renwick. Austin: University of Texas Press, 1977. Additional listings to Child.

Cohen, J. M. *The Penguin Book of Comic and Curious Verse*. London: Penguin, 1952. With sequels: *More Comic and Curious Verse,* 1956; and *Yet More Comic and Curious Verse,* 1959. The best such anthology.

Cohen, Norman. *Long Steel Rail: The Railroad in American Folksong*. Urbana: University of Illinois Press, 1981.

———. "Tin Pan Alley's Contribution to Folk Music," in *Western Folklore* (1970) 29: 9–20.

———, editor: Vance Randolph, *Ozark Folksongs*. Abridged edition. Urbana: University of Illinois Press, 1982. Dr. Cohen's additions to the notes and discographies are of importance, making this the most useful edition.

Colcord, Joanna. *Roll and Go!* Indianapolis, 1924. Revised and in part de-expurgated as: *Songs of American Sailormen,* New York: Norton, 1938. Reprinted, New York: Oak Pubs., 1964.

Cole, William. *Erotic Poetry: classical to contemporary*. New York: Random House, 1963. Up-dating of T. R. Smith's *Poetica Erotica*. Compare: Bold; and Whitworth; also Laycock.

Coleman, Satio N., and Adolph Bregman. *Songs of American Folks*. New York, 1942.

Collé Charles. *Chansons qui n'ont pû être imprimées et* que mon censeur n'a point dû me passer. (Paris) 1784. Also issued as Collé's *Poésies libertines*.

A Collection of Old Ballads. (Edited by Ambrose Phillips.) London, 1723. 3 vols.

College Folklore: A Collection made on the campus of the University of Arkansas (by Eddie J. McRell, or O'Rell.) MS., Booneville, Ark., 1957. Erotic poems, songs, humorous obscœna, and storiettes. Typewritten sticker on title-page states: "Gift of Vance Randolph, who did not collect it, did not put it together, did not stimulate it." Compare Reuss.

Collier, John Payne. *A Book of Roxburghe Ballads*. London, 1847. See also: Roxburghe.

Colum, Padraic. *Treasury of Irish Folklore*. New York, 1954.

Combined Universities' Songbook. (Sydney, Australia), 1965. Extensive collection; includes a few unexpurgated texts.

Combs, Josiah H. *Folk-Songs du Midi des États-Unis.* Paris: Presses Universitaires de France, 1925.

———. *Same,* original English text as: *Folk-Songs of the Southern United States,* edited by D. K. Wilgus, Austin: University of Texas Press, 1967.

———. *Folk-Songs from the Kentucky Highlands.* New York, 1939.

———. *Pneumatology,* by "Count de la Fartte." MS., Charlottesville, Virginia, ca. 1952. Collection of prose and poetry, 17th century to 20th, on farting.

Conklin-Jones MS. See: Lewis Jones; and Thompson, H.

Contributions au Folklore Érotique, Kleinbronn: Gustav Ficker, 1905–08. 4 vols. Companion set to *Kryptádia.* (Extra volume by Antonin Perbosc, ed. Dr. Josiane Bru, Toulouse, 1986?)

The Convivial Songster. London: Fielding, 1782. Mostly very mild.

Cornog, Martha, ed., *The Libraries, Erotica, and Pornography: A Symposium.* Phoenix, Ariz.: Oryx Press, 1990. Compare: *Private Case.*

Corso, Rafaelle. *Das Geschlechtsleben* in Sitte, Brauch, Glauben und gewohnheitrecht *des Italienischen Volkes.* Nicotera: Im Selbstverlag des Verfassers, 1914. (*Anthropophytéia,* Beiwerke, vol. 7.) With German translation of the songs and "Blasioni licenziosi."

———. "Vom Geschlectsleben in Calabrien," in *Anthropophytéia* (1911) 8: 137–59.

Coulon, Marcel. *La Poésie priapique au XVIe siècle.* Paris: Editions du Trianon; Dr. Kahan, 1933. Compare: Schwob.

Covent Garden Drolery. Written by the refined'st Witts of the Age, and collected by A. B. (Aphra Behn). London, 1672. Reprinted, ed. George Thorn-Drury, London, 1928, the best edition. The earlier Montague Summers reprint (1927) is a mere catch-guinea rushed into print. Note: Original editor of the drollery was not A. or R. Brome, as sometimes stated, but the early woman dramatist Aphra Behn.

The Covent Garden Jester, or The Rambler's Companion . . . by Roger Ranger, Gent. (*pseud.*) London: Walker, 1785. Note: British Museum Library copy is bound with another less interesting jest-book of similar title, *The Covent-Garden Jester,* or Man of Fashion's Companion, London: Sudbury, (1795?).

Cox, John H. *Folk-Songs Mainly from West Virginia.* National Service Bureau of the Federal Theatre Project, W.P.A. New York, 1939. Repr. as: *Traditional Ballads and Folk-Songs Mainly from West Virginia.* Philadelphia: American Folklore Society, 1964.

———. *Folk-Songs of the South.* Cambridge: Harvard University Press, 1925. Reprs., Hatboro, Pa.: Folklore Associates, 1963; and New York: Dover Pubs., 1967.

Crawhall, Joseph. *Olde Tayles Newlye Relayted.* (London), 1883.

(Cray, Edward B.) *The Dirty Song Book: American Bawdy Songs.* Compiled by E. R. Linton (*pseud.*) Los Angeles: Medco Books (Sherbourne Press), 1965. Preliminary edition, without music, of the following item:

———. *The Erotic Muse.* New York: Oak Publications, 1969. Reprinted, New York: Pyramid Pubs., 1972; and as:

———. *Bawdy Ballads: A History of Bawdy Songs.* London: Odyssey Press, 1970. Texts conflated, but useful notes.

———. *Songs from the Ash Grove.* Los Angeles, Calif.: Ash Grove, 1959. 47 pp. 8vo. See also: *Super Stag Treasury.*

The Cream of the Crap. (Unpublished MS. collection, 1968, made by John Newbern, q.v., of the "too-hot-to-handle" jokes, poems, and obscœna sent in by readers of his *Sex to Sexty* and *Super Sex to Sexty* humor magazines.) See: "Victor Dodson."

Creighton, Helen. *Songs and Ballads from Nova Scotia.* Toronto: Dent, 1932. Expurgated.

The Cremorne: A Magazine of Wit, Facetiœ, Parody, Graphic Tales of Love, etc. London: "Cheyne Walk, Privately Printed, 1851" (W. Lazenby? 1882). Sequel to *The Pearl, The Boudoir* and *Story of a Dildoe.*

(Crowley, Aleister.) *The Scented Garden,* 1911. Reprint, 1981. See: Motta.

(———.) *Snowdrops from a Curate's Garden.* "1881 A.D. Cosmopoli: Imprimé sous le manteau, et ne se vend nulle part" (Paris: Philippe Renouard, for the Author, ca. 1904–05).

(———.) *White Stains. The Literary Remains of George Archibald Bishop* (*pseud.*), *a Neuropath of the Second Empire.* (London: Leonard Smithers), 1898. Reprinted, London: Duckworth, 1973.

Croy, Homer. *Wonderful Neighbors.* New York, 1945.

The Cuckold's Nest of Choice, Flash, Smutty and Delicious Songs, with Rummy Toasts. Adapted for Gentlemen Only. (London: W. West, ca. 1865). 48 pp. Compare: Speaight.

Cupid's Horn-book. Songs and ballads of marriage and of cuckoldry. (Edited by Peter Beilenson). Mount Vernon, N.Y.: Published at the Sign of the Blue-Behinded Ape, 1936. Reprints of 17th and 18th century materials.

The Curiosities of Street Literature. See: Charles Hindley.

"Curnonsky." See: Sailland.

"Curran, William" (*pseud.*) *Clean Dirt.* 500 anecdotes, stories, poems, toasts, and wisecracks. Buffalo, New York, 1938. (At head: "Volume I," but no more published.) With supplement of 5 mimeographed leaves of bawdier material.

Cutrell Collection. Santa Monica, Calif., 1961. Private tape recording of 44 songs, sung by the collector, Sandy Cutrell, with transcription of words in photoprint.

Cutting, Edith E. *Whistling Girls and Jumping Sheep.* Cooperstown, N.Y.: Farmers' Museum, 1951. See also at: Thompson, H.

Cutts, John P. *Seventeenth Century Songs and Lyrics.* Columbia: University of Missouri Press, 1959. Anonymous texts only, in supplement to Norman Ault's *Elizabethan Lyrics* and *Seventeenth Century Lyrics* (both 1928). See also: Wardroper.

Cythera's Hymnal, or Flakes from the Foreskin: A Collection of Songs, Poems, Nursery Rhymes, Quiddities, etc., never before published. "Oxford: Printed at the University Press, for the Society for Promoting Useful Knowledge" (London: John Camden Hotten?) 1870. Aggressive and unpleasant; written and edited by Frederick Popham Pike, Edward Sellon, and George Augustus Sala. Compare: *Dirt, An Exegesis;* and *Songs of Sadism.*

Dallas, Karl. *One Hundred Songs of Toil: 450 Years of Workers' Songs.* London: Wolfe, 1974. Contains some unexpurgated materials, with peculiarly truculent notes.

Damon, S. Foster. *Series of Old American Songs.* Providence, R.I.: Brown University Library, 1936.

Dance, Ms. Daryl Cumber. *Shuckin' and Jivin': Folklore from Contemporary Black Americans.* Bloomington: Indiana University Press, 1978. Rhymed "toasts," Chap. 13: pp. 197–239.

"Dardenne, Edmond," *pseud.* See: Bernard; and *Anthologie Hospitalière.*

Das sind unsere Lieder. Gütersloh: Bertelsmann Verlag, ca. 1978. Erotico-humorous songs with purposely repulsive illustrations reproduced in part in Silverman, *The Dirty Song Book.*

"Dave E. Jones" *pseud.* See: "Jones, Dave E."

Davids, R. M. See under: Robert W. Gordon.

Davis, Arthur Kyle, Jr. *Folk-Songs of Virginia. A Descriptive Index and Classification.* Durham, N.C.: Duke University Press, 1949.

———. *More Traditional Ballads of Virginia.* Chapel Hill, North Carolina: Duke University Press, 1960.

———. "Some Problems of Ballad Publication," in *Musical Quarterly* (1928) 14: 283–96. Unusual in its discussion of the bawdy element in ballads.

Day, Cyrus L., and Eleanore B. Murrie. *English Song-Books, 1651–1702.* London: Bibliographical Society, 1940. Invaluably indexes all the songs. An unpublished manuscript notebook supplement prepared by W. N. H. Harding, ca. 1960, is preserved with the bequest of his collection of old song-books at the Bodleian Library, Oxford. This should certainly be published. See also: Case; and Simpson.

Dean-Smith, Margaret. *A Guide to English Folk Song Collections, 1822–1952.* Liverpool, 1954. Valuable index of 19th- through 20th-century collections, with pioneering notes on the "erotic *lingua franca* of the folk."

Death Rattlers. (*Old American Ballads.*) Korea: Marine Air Squadron VMP–323 "Death Rattlers," 1951.) 41 pp. mimeographed. Reprinted secretly (Bloomington, Indiana, ca. 1960), mimeographed entirely in capital letters.

De Boccard, Enrico. *Il Processo di Sculacciabuchi e Ifigonia.* Roma: Edizioni Homerus, 1971. On modern Goliard students' bawdy recitations.

Decamerino: Rime baciate, suonata e agravate, di Ignoti del XIX e XX secolo. La Spezia (Rome? ca. 1965.)

Deleurme, Gaston, and "Charles Brémond" (*pseud.* of Édouard Ramond). *Encore des Histoires de*

Commis-Voyageurs et de Table d'Hôte. Paris: Bibliothèque du Bon vivant. Quignon (ca. 1930). With erotic folksongs, etc., as "Chansons et rimes gauloises" pp. 129–88.

Del Torto, John. See: Painter Collection.

De Sola Pinto, Vivian. See: Pinto and Rodway.

Des Périers, Bonaventure. *Les Nouvelles récréations et joyeux devis.* Paris, 1558; and modern scholarly editions.

Devilcats Songs. (Yellow Sea, off Sasebo, Japan: Marine Air Squadron VMF–212 "Devilcats," aboard aircraft carrier *Rendoa Bay,* 1953?) 56 pp. mimeographed. Re-issued by Xerox, with typewritten annotations by Ms. Nancy Evans, University of California, Los Angeles, 1960.

"De Witt, Hugh" (*pseud.*). *Bawdy Barrack-room Ballads.* London: Tandem, 1970. Unreliable texts, largely faked.

The Diary of a French Stenographer. Limited Edition. (Detroit, Michigan: McClurg, 1929.)

Dick, James C. *The Songs of Robert Burns.* London, 1903. Reprinted, Hatboro, Pa.: Folklore Associates, ca. 1966. See: *Merry Muses of Caledonia.*

Dirt: An Exegesis. (At head: An Introductory Collection of Real Folk and Traditional Songs.) (Los Angeles: U.C.L.A Co-Op House, ca. 1965.) 22 pp. mimeographed. Curiously violent and aggressive bawdy songs. See: *Gloriæ Feminæ.*

The Dirty Song Book. See: Cray, 1965; and Silverman, 1982.

Dixon, James J. *Ancient Poems, Ballads, and Songs of the Peasantry of England.* London: Percy Society, 1846. See: Bell.

"Dodson, Victor" (*pseud.*). *The World's Dirtiest Jokes.* Edited and compiled by Victor Dodson (*pseud.* of John Newbern/"Richard Rodman," and Peggy "Goose Reardon" Rodebaugh.) Los Angeles: Medco Books (Sherbourne Press), 1969. Includes bawdy poetry and obscœna.

Doerflinger, William M. *Shantymen and Shantyboys.* New York: Macmillan, 1951. Reprinted as: *Songs of the Sailors and Lumbermen,* New York, 1972. Thoroughly expurgated. Compare: Hugill.

Dolph, Edward A. *Sound Off!* New York: Cosmopolitan, 1929. Revised edition, New York: Farrar and Rinehart, 1942. Expurgated soldiers' songs of World War I.

Dominique, Jacques. *Chansons gaillardes et bachiques du Quartier Latin.* Paris, 1933. French students' bawdy songs openly published. Compare: Staub.

Doncieux, Georges. *Romancero populaire de la France.* Paris, 1904.

Dorson, Richard. (Archive of college folksong texts from students at Michigan State College and Indiana University, ca. 1947–50ff.) Discussed in *Midwest Folklore* (1955) V. 51–59; repositoried in Indiana University Folklore Archives. See also: Gordon; Kinsey; and Wilgus.

———. *Handbook of American Folklore.* Bloomington: Indiana University Press, 1983.

———. "A Visit with Vance Randolph," in: *Journal of American Folklore* (1954) 67: 260.

Douglas, Norman. *London Street Games.* London, 1916. Revised edition, 1931. Originally published, in expurgated form, in: *The English Review* (Nov. 1913).

———. *Some Limericks.* (Florence, Italy) 1928. Many reprints. Continued as: *The Rhyme of All Flesh* (Paris? ca. 1935), rare. Compare: "Nosti," and *The Rhyme.*

"Dow, W. I." (*pseud.,* i.e., "Widow"). *Anthology of Modern Classics.* "London: Nautilus Society" (U.S.) 1913. Not seen: Cited by Morse.

"Drecken, Gotfried von" (*pseud.*). *Das schmutzige Lied: Was Ist Das?* Non-existent parody monograph presumably delivered before "Die Gesellschaft für Muzikwissenschaft" (by G. Legman?) at Baden-Baden, 1908; according to Jerry Silverman, *The Dirty Songbook* (1982) p. vii.

Dregs of Drollery, or Old Poetry in Its Ragges. "London: Printed," 1660. (Copy: Huntington Library.)

Droke, Maxwell. See: "John H. Johnson."

Drozdanowski, W. von. "Polnische Liebeslieder," in: *Anthropophytéia* (1910) VII: 352–59. Polish erotic folksongs.

The Drunk's Album. (New Guinea, or Goodenough Island, Papua: Royal Australian Air Force, #75 Squadron, 1942.) 11 pp., mimeographed. (Only known copy: Australian War Memorial, Canberra.) Bawdy Australian air force songs.

Dubout, editor (?). *Chansons de Salles de Garde.* Paris: Michèle Trinckvel, 1971.

The Duchess of Portsmouth's Garland. From a MS. in the Library of the Faculty of Advocates. (Edinburgh, 1837.) xvi pages. Ltd. to 25 copies. (Edited by James Maidment), and compare

Ane Pleasant Garland. The manuscript from which these songs were printed, formerly in the Scottish National Library, is now lost.

Dugaw, Diane. *Ozark Folksongs.* M.A. thesis, University of Colorado, 1973.

Duncan, Edm. *Lyrics from the Old Song Books.* New York, 1927.

Dundes, Alan. "Here I Sit: A Study of American Latrinalia," in: Kroeber Anthropological Soc. *Papers* (1966) 34: 91–105.

————. *Mother-Wit from the Laughing-Barrel.* Prentice-Hall, 1973.

————, and Carl Pagter. *Work Hard and You Shall Be Rewarded: Urban Folklore from the Paperwork Empire.* Austin, Texas, 1975. Repr., Bloomington: Indiana Univ. Press, 1978. Xeroxlore, an expurgated collection: also sequel:

————. *When You're Up to Your Ass in Alligators.* Detroit, 1986.

————, and Robert Georges. "Some Minor Genres of Obscene Folklore," in *Journal of American Folklore* (1962) 75: 221–26.

The Dung Heap/Barrel and Cesspool Cleaners Gazette: Life and Laughter in Your Good Ole U.S. of A., 1980. (A Decadent Decade's Greetings—from One Dirty Old Ro-mantic to Another.) MS., San Francisco, Calif., 1980. 24 pp. photocopy issue. Purposely nauseating jokes and verse "in guaranteed bad taste." Compare: "Toshka Barph"; *Dirt, An Exegesis*; and *Songs of Sadism.*

D'Urfey, Thomas, ed. *Wit and Mirth, or Pills to Purge Melancholy.* 1698–1720. See: *Pills.*

Ebsworth, J. Woodfall. See: *Bagford Ballads; Choyce Drollery*; and *Roxburghe Ballads.*

Eckstrom, Fannie Hardy, and Mary Winslow Smyth. *Minstrelsy of Maine: Folk-Songs and Ballads.* Boston: Houghton Mifflin, 1927.

Eddington, Neil A. "Genital Superiority in Oakland (California) Negro Folklore: a Theme," in *Papers of the Kroeber Anthropological Society* (Fall 1965) No. 33. Reprinted in: Alan Dundes, ed. *Mother Wit from the Laughing Barrel,* 1973.

————. *The Urban Plantation: The Ethnography of an Oral Tradition in a Negro Community.* Ann Arbor, Michigan: University of California at Berkeley Ph.D. thesis, 1967.

Eddy, Mary O. *Ballads and Songs from Ohio.* New York: J. J. Augustin, 1939.

Edwards, Ron. *Australian Bawdy Ballads.* Holloway Beach, Australia: Rams Skull Press, 1973. Mimeographed. Bawdy materials supplementing his *Australian Folksongs* (Rams Skull Press, 1972.)

————. *The Overlander Songbook.* Adelaide, 1971.

Eglis, Arsène. "Sex in Folksongs," in: *Sexology* (New York, Nov. 1958) pp. 246–49.

"Elgart, J. M." (*pseud.*). *Over Sexteen.* New York, 1951. With sequels, *More Over Sexteen* (1953), and others similar. Semi-bawdy humor, cartoons, and verse. Compare: *Sex to Sexty.*

Eliot, T. S. *King Bolo* (or *Bungo*) *and his Great Black Queen.* MS. bawdy poems circulated by Eliot in the 1910s and 20s among his friends, especially Conrad Aiken, among whose papers the entire *King Bolo* set is preserved. Printed in part in Eliot's *Letters,* ca. 1985. See also: Whitworth.

Ellington, Richard, and Dave Van Ronk. *The Bosses' Songbook: Songs to stifle the flame of discontent.* A collection of modern political songs of satire. 2nd ed. New York, 1959. 36 pp. Compare: *Unexpurgated.*

Ellis, Ronnie. *Australian Graffiti.* Sydney, 1975.

Elzey, W. H. *Things about Things.* Eureka Springs, Arkansas, 1946.

Emmons, Earl. See in: *Rowdy Rhymes.*

Emrich, Duncan, and Rae Korson. *Child's Book of Folklore.* 1947.

Enevig, Anders. *Lokumsdigte og Retiradenvers: Graffiti — når det er værst.* Odense, Denmark: (Privately Printed,) 1980. 60 pp. Danish graffiti and verse.

Erotopægnion, sive Priapeia veterum et recentiorum: Veneri jocosæ sacrum. Paris: Patris, 1798. Edited by Fr. -J. Noël. Compare: *Priapeia.*

The Eternal Eve: from a Mid-Victorian Manuscript, "The Duchess." Unexpurgated edition, modernized and revised. (Cleveland?) Printed for Private Distribution, 1941.

Evans, David. "The 'Toast' in Context" in: *Journal of American Folklore* (1977) 90: 129–48.

Evans, Nancy. See *Devilcats Songs.*

Evans, Patricia Healy. *Rimbles.* New York: Doubleday, 1957. Children's rhymes.

Facetia Americana. (U.S., ca. 1925.) 8vo. (Copy: Denver Public Library, Morse-Field Collection.) Verse by Eugene Field and others.

Facetiæ: Musarum Deliciæ, or The Muses' Recreation. Edited by Sir John Mennis and Dr. James Smith, 1656. (Reprint edited by Edward Du Bois.) London, 1817. Reprinted, 1872? See further under: *Musarum Deliciæ.*

Fagan, J. S. *Folklore and the Modern Sailor.* (Bloomington, Indiana, 1966.) MS., 50 pp. lithoprint. Bawdy sailors' songs, etc., from experience aboard the USS. *Douglas H. Fox.*

Farmer, John Stephen. *Merry Songs and Ballads,* prior to the year A.D. 1800. National Ballad and Song. (London: Gibbings?) Privately Printed for Subscribers Only, 1897. 5 vols. (Volume I issued separately, dated 1895.) Reprinted, New York: Cooper Square Publishers, 1964, with introduction by G. Legman, and *Musa Pedestris, 1896.*

————, and William Ernest Henley. *Slang and Its Analogues.* London: Privately Printed (Gibbings?) 1890–1909. 7 vols.; with revised vol. I, reprinted New Hyde Park, N.Y.: University Books, 1966, with 75-page introduction by G. Legman, "On Sexual Speech and Slang." Note extended erotic synonymies, grouped at "*cream-stick*" and "*prick,*" "*cunt*" and "*monosyllable;*" and verbs and nouns for coitus at "*greens*" and "*ride;*" and prostitute at "*barrack-hack,*" "*tart,*" and "*whore.*" Compare: Chapman; Trimble/Blake; and plagiarism by Cary, H.

Father Rugby Reveals. See: *Rugger Hugger Presents* . . .

Fauset, Arthur H. *Folklore from Nova Scotia.* New York: Stechert, 1931. (American Folklore Society, Memoir Series, vol. 24.) Includes erotic songs and tales without expurgation, for first time in America.

(Feinhals, Josef.) *Non olet, oder Die heiteren Tischgespräche des Collofino (pseud.), Über den Orbis Cacatus.* Köln: Privatdruck, 1939. 1104 pp. Rare eccentric compilation on scatology and smoking, with songs and verse.

Ferris, William. *Black Folklore from the Mississippi Delta.* Ph.D. dissertation, University of Pennsylvania. Philadelphia, 1969. With a remarkably full classified bibliography. Abridged ed. as: *Blues from the Delta.* London, 1970; and complete ed., New York: Doubleday, 1978.

The Festival of Anacreon. See: Charles Morris.

The Festival of Love, or A Collection of Cytherean Poems, procured and selected by G—e P—e (i.e., Prince George). London: M. Smith, ca. 1770.

(Ficke, Arthur Davison.) *The Hell of the Good: A Theological Epic in Six Books,* by Édouard de Verb (*pseud.*) 22 copies, "Privately Printed: Not to be Sold." (U.S., ca. 1925.) 59 pp.

Fiddle, Seymour. *Toasts: Images of a Victim Society.* New York: Exodus House, February, 1972. 72 pp. lithoprint. Compare: Abrahams; Jackson, B.; and Wepman.

Field, Eugene. See: *The Stag Party,* (1888–89). Also: Mooney.

Fife, Austin E. "Anthology of Folk Literature of Soldiers of the Pacific Theater," in *Bawdy Songs Folder,* Archive of Folk Culture, Library of Congress, Washington, D.C.; and in Fife Collection Archive, Utah.

————, and Alta S. *Cowboy and Western Songs: A Comprehensive Anthology.* New York: Clarkson Potter, 1969. See also: Thorp; and compare: Logsdon.

————. "The Strawberry Roan and His Progeny," in: *JEMF Quarterly* (1972) VIII: 149–65. Note: for Fife collection index, see Walker, Barbara.

The Fighter Pilots Hymn Book. See: William J. Starr.

Les Filles de Loth, et autres poèmes érotiques, recueillies par "le Vidame de Bozegy" (pseud. of Edmond Dardenne Bernard). "A Sodome: Imprimerie de la Genèse" (Paris: Guibal? for E. D. Bernard), 1933. Erotic art- and folk-poems, in supplement to the same editor's *Les Chants du Quartier Latin,* and *Trois Orfèvres à la Saint-Éloi.* Not to be confused with:

Les Filles de Loth: Légende Biblique. "Priapeville: Imprimerie galante, An III du XXe siècle foutatif" (Paris: Jean Fort? 1903). 12 pp. Pamphlet cited by Pascal Pia, *Les Livres de l'Enfer,* col. 470; containing erotic poems.

Finger, Charles. *Frontier Ballads.* Garden City, New York: Doubleday, 1927.

————. *Sailor Shanties and Cowboy Songs.* Girard, Kansas: E. Haldeman-Julius, 1923. Pamphlet. Compare: Shay.

The First Boke of Fowle Ayres. Sydney, Australia, 1944. Not seen. Cited in *Snatches and Lays,* 1962.

Flanders, Helen, and Marguerite Olney. *Ballads Migrant in New England.* New York: Farrar, Strauss, 1953.

―――, and Phillips Barry. *The New Green Mountain Songster.* New Haven, 1939. Repr., Hatboro, Pa.: Folklore Associates, 1966.

Fletcher, Curley W. *Rhymes of the Round-Up.* San Francisco: Privately Printed, 1917. Cited by Logsdon.

Les Fleurs du Mâle. Bruxelles, 1935–38. 2 vols. Rare Belgian collection of students' *Chansons de Salle de Garde.* (Copy: G. Legman.) Compare:

―――. Illustrations de Jean Dratz. (Geneva: Sack, ca. 1955.) Not identical with the preceding. Title puns on Baudelaire's *Fleurs du Mal.*

"*Folklore de la France,*" in: *Kryptádia* (1898) V. 275–400. Erotic folksongs, tales, and riddles, arranged by dialect of origin, with French translations. Important field collection attributed to Gaston Pâris, and Eugène Rolland.

Folk Poems and Ballads. See: A. Reynolds Morse.

Folly in Print. London, 1667. Drollery songbook.

Forbidden Fruit: A Collection of Popular Tales by Popular Authors. (at head: Not for Maids, Ministers, or Striplings.) (Glasgow? ca. 1890.) 2 pts. in 1 vol. (Unique copy: Murison-Burns Collection, Dunfermline; microfilm, School of Scottish Studies, Edinburgh.) Burns' *Merry Muses,* plus a miscellany of erotic prose and Scottish folk verse. Note: Not to be confused with an erotic novel of incest also entitled *Forbidden Fruit,* ca. 1905.

Ford, Ira W. *Traditional Music of America.* 1940. Reprint, Hatboro, Pa.: Folklore Associates, 1965; and New York: Da Capo Press, 1978.

Ford, Robert. *Vagabond Songs and Ballads of Scotland.* Paisley, Scotland, 1899–1901. New ed. 1904.

Foster, Herbert L. *Ribbin', Jivin', and Playin' the Dozens.* Cambridge, Mass.: Ballinger Press, 1974. Negro erotic "toasts," etc. Compare: Abrahams; and Jackson.

The Foundling Hospital for Wit. (Edited by Sir Charles Hanbury-Williams.) London, 1743–49. 7 pts.

Les Fouteries chantantes, ou Les Recréations priapiques des Aristocrates en vie (vit). "À Couillardinos . . . au Vit couronné," 1791. 48 pp. Violent and aggressively obscene anti-Royalist songs.

Fowke, Edith Fulton. "Bawdy Ballads in print, record, and Tradition," in: *Sing and String* (Summer, 1963) vol. II: No. 2: 3–9. The first article on the subject by a woman; in reply to "The Bawdy Ballad—In Print and In Fact," by G. Legman, 1959. Compare: Muir; and Green.

―――. *Bawdy Folksongs from Ontario.* (MS.) Toronto, 1989. Announced for publication, 1990, with Kenneth Goldstein.

―――. *Lumbering Songs from the Northern Woods.* Austin, Texas, 1970.

―――. *The Penguin Book of Canadian Folk Songs.* Harmondsworth: Penguin Books, 1973.

―――. "A Sampling of Bawdy Ballads from Ontario," in: Bruce Jackson, ed., *Folklore and Society* (Hatboro, Pa.: Folklore Associates, 1966) pp. 45–61. Supplement to her *Traditional Singers and Songs from Ontario.*

―――. *Sea Songs and Ballads* from 19th-century Nova Scotia. New York: Folklorica, 1981.

―――. *Traditional Singers and Songs from Ontario.* Hatboro, Pa.: Folklore Associates, 1965. See: "A Sampling," above.

―――, and Richard Johnston. *Folk Songs of Canada.* Waterloo, Ontario, 1954.

Fox Club. (Harvard MS. album of bawdy verse.) See: *Sweet Violets;* and Oxford University.

Foxon, David. *English Verse: 1701–1750.* (*Bibliography of Burlesque and Satirical 18th Century Verse.*) Cambridge University Press, 1975? Admirably continues work on early-18th century by Prof. Richmond Bond.

"The Frankie and Johnny Episode of 1899 (Missouriana)," in: *Missouri Historical Review* (Oct. 1941) No. 36, pp. 75–77.

Freeman, Richard. *Graffiti.* London: Hutchinson, 1966.

Friedman, Albert B. *The Viking Book of Folk Ballads of the English-Speaking World.* New York: Viking Press, 1956.

Friedman, Josh Alan. *Tales of Times Square.* New York: Delacorte Press, 1986. Extraordinary no-holds-barred exposé.

Friedman, Victor A. "Vocabulary Elements in Early Macedonian Lexicons." in: *Maledicta* (1984) VII: 164–66. On Macedonian bawdy song. Compare: Koukoulès.

The Frisky Muse, by "Rigdum Funidos" (*pseud.*), Ballad Master in Ordinary and Composer Extraordinary. London: For the Author, 1749. 56 pp.

The Frisky Songster. (London, or Dublin, ca. 1770.) Reprint copies: (1776?) Bodleian, Harding Collection; (1802), Kinsey-ISR Library. Essential erotic folksong collection in English of the late 18th century. Compare: *The New Frisky Songster,* 1794.

From Bed to Verse: An unabashed anthology . . . collected with diligence and industry by divers idle hands (ed. Kenneth S. Giniger and Talbot Patrick) *for the amusement and delectation of some members of the Army of Occupation in Germany, and their friends.* (Wiesbaden,) Germany: Very Privately Printed, 1945. 20 pp. (Yale University Library, *Zeta.*) Mostly reprinted from Norman Douglas' *Some Limericks* (1928).

Frothingham, Robert, ed., "Old Songs That Men Have Sung," in: *Adventure Magazine,* "for a short time," prior to July, 1923. See: Gordon.

(Fry, John.) *Pieces of Ancient Poetry, from unpublished manuscripts and scarce books.* Bristol, 1814. Private publication of rare pieces, 16th–18th century. Compare: Ritson, and Utterson.

Fryer, Peter. *Mrs. Grundy: Studies in Prudery.* London, 1963.

Fuckup. See: *Antarctic Fuckup.* (Songbook.)

Fuld, James J. *American Popular Music,* 1875–1950. Philadelphia, 1955.

————. *The Book of World-Famous Music.* Rev. ed. New York: Crown, 1971.

Full Dress Suits and Plenty of Whores. (Edited by Hilaire Hiler, with introductory "Apology" by Robert Carlton "Bob" Brown.) MS., Paris, 1928. (Transcript copy: G. Legman.) Brief collection of American and British bawdy folksongs. Compare: *The Slime Sheet.*

Furnivall, Frederick J. See: *Jyl of Breyntford's Testament;* and *Percy Folio Manuscript.*

Futilitates: Beiträge etc. See: Blümml and Polsterer.

Gai (Le) Chansonnier français. (Edited by Gaston Pâris and Eugène Rolland.) In: *Kryptádia* (Heilbronn, 1886) 3: 1–146. First scientific collection of erotic folksongs in any language. See also: *"Folklore de la France."*

Gadpaille, W. J. "Graffiti: Its Psychodynamic Significance," in: *Sexual Behavior* (Nov. 1971) 2: 45–51.

Gaignebet, Claude. *Le Folklore obscène des Enfants.* Paris: Maisonneuve and Larose, 1974.

————. *La Magie sexuelle populaire.* (Forthcoming, 1992.)

Gamo-Tragouda (Fuck-Songs). Athens, 1981. See: Koukoulès; and Lelegos.

The Garden of Priapus, edited by "Mentula" (*pseud.*). "The Dorian Club, 1919." (New York: Samuel Roth? or Millers, ca. 1935). See: "W. I. Dow."

Gardiner, George. See: Purslow; and Reeves.

Gardner, Emelyn E., and Geraldine Chickering. *Ballads and Songs of Southern Michigan.* Ann Arbor, 1939. Reprint, Hatboro, Pa.: Folklore Associates, 1967.

Garrison, Theodore. *Forty-Five Folk Songs, Collected from Searcy County, Arkansas.* M. A. Thesis, University of Arkansas, 1944.

Gatty, Ivor. "The Old Tup and His Ritual," in: *Journal of English Folk Dance and Song Society* (1940) V: 23–30.

Gaudeamus Igitur. (Epigrafi de Laurea, o Papiri dal MDCCXXXI al 1975.) Padova, 1976. Italian students' centenary mock-academic folk-art folio, of University of Padua "Feriæ Matricularum" graduates in political science; edited by Manlio Morgagni and M. Luigi Poli.

Les Gaudrioles du XIXe siècle: Chansons Joyeuses. "Bâle: Bertal" (Bruxelles: Jules Gay), 1866. 2 vols. Not entirely songs; includes erotic art poetry. See: Poulet-Malassis.

Gautier, Théophile. *Poésies de Th. Gautier qui ne figureront pas dans ses œuvres.* "France: Imprimerie particulière" (Paris? Poulet-Malassis), 1863. 84 pp. Various piratical and other reprints, the best edited by René Jasinski, as:

————. *Poésies Libertines.* (Paris: René Bonnel) 1935. (Copies: *Enfer* 1153; G. Legman.) Also published with Gautier's erotic *"Lettre à la Présidente"* (Mme. Sabatier), as:

————. *Obscenia,* "Bruxelles" (Paris: J. Chevrel), 1907; also as: *Lettres etc.,* edited by Louis Perceau, 1927; and by "Pascal Pia," 1960.

Gentile, Karlana, and Eric Staley. *Boone County Fare: A Missouri Anthology.* Columbia, Mo.: Singing Wind Press, 1975.

Getz, Col. Charles Wm. *The Wild Blue Yondr: Songs of the Air Force.* Vol. I. (Vol. II: Stag Bar Edition.) Redwood Press, Box 412, Burlingame, California, a division of Syntax Associates, Phoenix, Ariz., 1981–86. 2 vols. 4to. The bawdy songs are given only in Vol. II. By far the most complete of the Air Force song compilations, based on over 40 privately mimeographed service collections, all rare, mostly of World War II and since. Compare: Burke; Hopkins: and Starr.

The Giblet Pye. "Shamborough: John Knox" (Scotland or England, ca. 1806). (Unique copy: Bodleian, Harding Collection.) In part a reprint of Burns' *Merry Muses of Caledonia.*

Gilbert, Douglas. *Lost Chords: The Diverting Story of American Popular Songs.* Garden City, N.Y.: Doubleday, 1942.

Gilbert, Paul F., and Paul Cameron. *Jody Calls, Cadence Calls, and Marching Songs* (at Georgia Air Force Base, California, 1962.) Austin, Texas, 1963. 9 pp. hektographed.

———. Supplemented by a further fascicule of 7 pp., headed *Jody Calls,* MS. 1963, collected by Paul Cameron, for the same folklore course given by Dr. Roger Abrahams. (Copies: R. Abrahams; G. Legman.)

Gilchrist, Anne G. "Captain Kidd/Samuel Hall," in: *Journal of English Folk Dance and Song Society* (1938) 3: 167–70. Tracing the song's origins and transmutations; as later by Bertrand Bronson as "Samuel Hall's Family Tree," (1942), and George Pullen Jackson (1953).

Gillette, Paul J. *Complete Sex Dictionary.* New York: Award Books, 1969. Compare: Chapman; Goldenson; Farmer; Morton; Trimble; Wilson, R.

Gillis, Frank J. "The Metamorphosis of a Derbyshire Ballad (The Derby Ram) into a New World Jass Tune," in: *Discourse in Ethnomusicology: Essays in Honor of George List,* ed. by Caroline Card; Bloomington, Indiana: Ethnomusicology Group, Archives of Traditional Music, (1978), pp. 117–59.

Ginsberg, Allen. *Journals 50–60.* New York: Grove Press, 1977. With 3-page blitz "Anthology of English Folk Songs," pp. 277–79, collected from an English girl.

Gloriæ Feminæ: Latin Poems, by Mucus Surfus (*pseud.*). Los Angeles, 1965. MS. 42 pp. Crude anti-woman poems and songs (none in Latin). Compare: *Dirt: An Exegesis.*

Godelück, William. "Erotische und skatologische Kinder- und Jugendreime," in: *Anthropophytéia* (1906) 3: 218–43. Alsatian-German children's rhymes.

Godsey, Helen, and Townsend. "May Kennedy McCord: Queen of the Hillbillies," in: *Ozarks Mountaineer* (1977) 25: 14–27.

Gogarty, Oliver St. J. *As I Was Going Down Sackville Street.* New York, 1937.

The Golden Convolvulus. Edited by Arthur Moyse. Blackburn, Lancashire: Screeches Publications (1965). 40 pp., mimeographed. Poetry of revolt, children's rhymes and graffiti; banned from the mails.

Das Goldene Buch, gereimter Erotik. München: Privatdruck, 1919. Not to be confused with *Das Goldene Buch der Liebe* (Wien, 1908) by "L. van der Weck-Erlen" (*pseud.* of Dr. Josef Weckerle), a 531-posture sex technique manual! A recent English translation of Weckerle exists.

Goldenson, Robert. *Sex: A to Z.* New York, 1986.

Goldin, Hyman E., et al. *Dictionary of American Underworld Lingo.* New York: Twayne Publishers, 1950. With section of synonymies, pp. 245–327. Compare: James Morton, *Lowspeak* (London 1989).

Goldstein, Kenneth S. "Bowdlerization and Expurgation: Academic and Folk," in: *Journal of American Folklore* (1967) 80: 374–86. Reply to discussion of academic bowdlerization of collected folk-songs in G. Legman, *The Horn Book* (1964) pp. 336–424, "The Bawdy Song, In Fact and in Print."

———. *Buchan Bawdry: Scottish Highland Folklore.* Strichen, Aberdeenshire, 1960. Unpaginated MS. (references by date of collecting.) Valuable and courageous field-collection; remains unpublished apparently because tunes were not collected with the texts. Compare: Fowke.

———. *"The Unfortunate Rake."* New York: Folkways Records (FS-3805), 1960. Monograph on "St. James Infirmary/The Streets of Laredo" origins.

Goldstone, Sherle. *Unprinted College Songs.* MS., Albany, New York State College for Teachers, 1934. Term paper sumitted to Prof. Harold W. Thompson. (Copy: New York Historical Ass.,

Cooperstown, N.Y., File: H.W.T. 01.363.) The first attempted scholarly collection of bawdy students' songs in English; except those of Gordon; and Legman; and compare: Reuss.

Gomme, Alice. *The Traditional Games of England, Scotland, and Ireland.* London: D. Nutt, 1894–1898.

(Goodwin, Harold L.) *Memorandum.* Noumea, New Caledonia: 1st Marine Raider Battalion, 1943. 7 p. photoprint. Transcript of U.S. Marine songs.

Gordon, Robert W. (*Manuscript collections as follows:*)

———. *Gordon MS.:* 1858 numbered letters and their transcripts containing song texts, sent to Gordon (and before him to Robert Frothingham, 1922–23) as editor of the "Old Songs That Men Have Sung" column in *Adventure Magazine* (New York, 1923–29), 12 vols.; also in response to Gordon's series of articles, "The Folk Songs of America," published in *New York Times Magazine* (Jan. 2, 1927–Jan. 22, 1928). This group includes other songs collected by Gordon, mostly in the west, dated 1921 to 1932; and a MS. of 210 texts from New Hope, Kentucky, sent by Mary Newcomb, 1929–30 with 101 tunes.

———. *Gordon, California MS.:* About 400 songs collected by Gordon in Berkeley, Calif., 1922–23; and similar groups of 555 collected by him in Darien, Georgia, 1926–28; and 374 (plus 125 from T. B. Boyd) in North Carolina, 1925–27. Also a MS. group of 33 songs from R. M. Davids, Cross-X Ranch, Woodmere, Florida, 1924–29.

———. *"Inferno" Collection:* (Vulgar Collection, Reel 8.) MS. of the 236 erotic song texts included in all the above, as grouped by Gordon, with the same realism as Bishop Percy—but two centuries later. Note: The originals and typescript copies of all the above, including *about 700 sound recordings,* are repositoried principally in the Robert Winslow Gordon Collection of American Folksong, R. V. Mills Archive of Northwest Folklore, University of Oregon Library, Eugene, Oregon; and in overlapping part or whole (?) in the Library of Congress Archive of Folksong, Washington, D.C., which was apparently instituted by Gordon, but which he left with two volumes of his materials and recordings, on being suddenly replaced by John A. Lomax.

    See: Melbert B. Cary, *Mademoiselle from Armentières,* with a masterly musical introduction by Gordon; also Karen Grimm, "Prolegomenon to a Catalog for the Robert W. Gordon Collection," in *Northwest Folklore* (1967) 2: 8–10; and especially the full-dress biography of Gordon by Debora Kodish, *Good Friends and Bad Enemies* (1986), which see further. The Gordon folksong collection is outstandingly the most important made in America (along with James M. Carpenter's, q.v.) that remains unpublished, except for a brief sample in his *Folksongs of America* (1938), but has been used by Randolph-Cohen; Fife; Legman; and Logsdon. Note: A valuable detailed description of the various Gordon MSS. is given by Norm Cohen, in Randolph, *Ozark Folksongs,* abridged edition (1982) p. 557, keying the whole collection, except the "Inferno."

Grainger, Percy, and Rose. *Collection of English Folksongs, Sea Chanties, etc.* MS., 1907. Hektographed. (Copies in New York Public Library, and Library of Congress Folksong Archive.)

Graves, Robert. *Lars Porsena, or The Future of Swearing and Improper Language.* London, 1927. Revised as:

———. *Mrs. Fisher, or the Future of Humour.* London, 1928. Unreliable and amateurish, but contains folklore.

(———.) *Silent as the Graves.* MS., Mallorca, 1956. Brief collection of World War I bawdy British army songs, "anonymously" sent to G. Legman.

Gray, Roland Palmer. *Songs and Ballads of the Maine Lumberjacks.* Cambridge: Harvard University Press, 1924.

Green, Archie. "Midnight, and Other Cowboys," in: *JEMF Quarterly* (1975) 11: 137–52.

———. *Only a Miner.* Champaign: University of Illinois Press, 1972.

Green, Jonathan. *The Dictionary of Contemporary Slang.* London: Pan Books, 1984.

———. *The Slang Thesaurus.* London: Penguin, 1988.

Green, Rayna. "Folk is a Four-Letter Word: Dealing with Traditional **** in Fieldwork, Analysis, and Presentation," in: *Handbook of American Folklore,* edited by Richard M. Dorson. Bloomington: Indiana University Press, 1983.

———. Introduction to: Vance Randolph, *Pissing in the Snow, and other Ozark Folktales*. Urbana: University of Illinois Press, 1976. (First in: *Mid-South Folklore*, 1975, III: 89–94.)

———. "Magnolias Grow in Dirt: The Bawdy Lore of Southern Women," in: *The Radical Teacher* (1977) vol. 6; reprinted in: *Southern Exposure* (1977) 4: 29–33.

Greenleaf, Elizabeth B., and Grace Y. Mansfield. *Ballads and Sea Songs of Newfoundland*. Cambridge, Mass.: Harvard University Press, 1933. Excellently researched; but wholly expurgated.

Greenway, John. *American Folksongs of Protest*. Philadelphia, 1953.

Gregory-Boomer-Fouff Collection (No title). At head: "Reproduction in all its forms is to (be) encouraged. No copyright, no classification." George Gregory, Lt. Cdr., UNBR, Special Devices Division; Paul Boomer, Air Marshall, Royal Australian Airforce; François Fouff, Ministère de l'Aire, Etat-Majeur (*pseuds.* of Cornelius Van S. Roosevelt, Frank Wood, Ralph Martinez, and Ralph Mork.) Washington, D.C.: Navy Bureau of Aeronautics, Special Devices Division, 1945.) Limited to 150 copies, mimeographed.

———. 3rd enlarged edition, 1945. 25 pp. mimeographed. Also MS. addenda to 1959; Washington, D.C., 1966. (Copy: G. Legman.) Contents mostly limericks. Compare: *Luka Mudishchev.*

Greig, Gavin. *Folk Song of the North-East*. Peterhead (Scotland): "Buchan Observer" Works, 1914. Reprinted, Hatboro, Pa.: Folklore Associates, 1963.

———. Also: see the enormous *Greig Manuscript Collection,* as described in Legman, *The Horn Book* (1964) pp. 268–69.

Grose, Capt. Francis. *A Classical Dictionary of the Vulgar Tongue*. London, 1785. Revised, 1792 and 1811; and as *Lexicon Balatronicum,* 1823. Reprints, London, 1931; and Northfield, Ill., 1971.

———. *The Olio*. London, 1792.

Grotjahn, Martin. *Beyond Laughter*. New York, 1967?

Guam Air Force Songs. (No title:) At head: "*Warning!!!*" (Guam: U.S. Air Force, 1959?) 35 pp., mimeographed. MS. note gives compiler as Capt. De Marrs, or De Moso.

———. (Austin, Texas; or Bloomington, Indiana, 1963.) 35 pp., hektographed in violet ink on paper watermarked "Manuscript Bond." Very exact counterfeit or reprint, except that in the original, alternate lines are indented until p. 8; whereas all lines are flush-left in the reprint. See also: Kellogg.

Gundelfinger, Nicholas Lebzelter. See: *Carmina.*

Guthrie, Woodrow ("Woody"). *The Wild Oaken Tree*. MS., ca. 1940? (Copy: Prof. Kenneth Goldstein, Philadelphia.) Private group of original songs on eroticism, incest, etc. Title-song, in praise of the "sixty-nine," printed in Laycock, pp. 41–43. Compare: Auden, Putnam, Thomas, and Updike.

Haddington. Thomas Hamilton, Earl of. *Select Poems on Several Occasions*. London? ca. 1730. Reprints. Includes numerous erotic tales-in-verse. Compare: Hall-Stevenson.

Hagen, John Milton. *"Lecherous, Licentious, Lascivious Lyrics* (is NOT the Title of This Book)." True intended title given as: *The Violent Violet*. South Brunswick, New Jersey: A. S. Barnes, 1969. 104 pp. Weakly humorous doggerel, vaguely about sex.

Hall, William G. *Turkey Knob Line*. New York, 1954.

Halliwell, James Orchard. *The Nursery Rhymes of England*. London, 1842; enlarged 1845, and 1853. Reprint, London: Bodley Head, 1970. Compare: Opie.

Hall-Stevenson, John. *Crazy Tales*. 1762. Reprint, London, 1894. Also other volumes of bawdy tales-in-verse by this author. Compare: Haddington; and Head.

Halpert, Herbert. "The Cante-Fable in New Jersey," in: *Journal of American Folklore* (1942) 55: 133–43.

———. "The Cante-Fable in Decay," in: Horace P. Beck, ed., *Folklore in Action* (1962) pp. 139–50.

———. "Some Ballads and Folk Songs from New Jersey," in: *Journal of American Folklore* (1939) 52: 52–69.

Haltaus, Carl. *Liederbuch der Clara Hätzlerin: Aus der Handschrift des Böhmischen Museums zu Prag*. Quedlinburg and Leipzig, 1840. Compare: *Crailsheim MS.,* at Kopp.

Hamer, Fred. *Garners Gay*. London: English Folk Dance and Song Society, 1967.

———. *Green Groves*. London: English Folk Dance and Song Society, 1973.

Hammond, Henry and Robert. See: Purslow; and Reeves.

Hanbury-Williams, Charles. See: *Foundling Hospital for Wit.*

Hand, Wayland. *Popular Beliefs and Superstitions from North Carolina.* (Brown Collection of North Carolina Folklore, vols. 6–7.) Durham, N.C.: Duke University Press, 1961–64. Outstandingly annotated. Dr. Hand left behind at his recent death a million-item card file on folk-beliefs:

———. *A Dictionary of American Popular Beliefs and Superstitions.* This unparalleled MS., deposited at U.C.L.A., Department of Folklore, urgently demands publication. See also: Parler-Randolph: *Folk-Beliefs.*

———. *Schnaderhüpfel.* Chicago, ca. 1950. Ph.D. thesis.

"Harde, Dick." See: *Lusty Limericks and Bawdy Ballads.*

Harding, Walter N. H. (*English Song-Book Index; 17th century.* MS.) See at: Day and Murrie.

Harington, Donald. "Bawdy Ozark Tales: Vance Randolph's Collection of Local Off-Color," in: *Grapevine* (1977) 8: 10.

Harlequin Prince Cherrytop and the Good Fairy Fairfuck, or The Frig, the Fuck and the Fairy. (At head: New and Gorgeous Pantomime, entitled . . .) London, 1879. "Private Reprint: Theatre Royal Olymprick" (London: Erotika Biblion Society, Leonard Smithers), 1905. 52 pp. Bawdy verse playlet (by George Augustus Sala), including many folk catches and sells. In partial folk transmission as "The Sods Opera." attributed to Gilbert and Sullivan (!) and in very decayed form as a recitation, "The King of the Goddam Isles."

Harmonia Musarum. 1843. 8vo. Not seen. Cited in *Bibliotheca Arcana,* 1885 (by William Laird Clowes), no. 516; stating that a copy was sold at auction in 1882.

Haroldson, John. See: *The Lay of John Haroldson.*

Hart, Harold Horowitz. *The Bawdy and the Naughty.* New York: Hart Pub. Co. 1971. See following items:

———. *The Bawdy Bedside Reader.* (Variant title of:)

———. *(The New) Immortalia.* New York: Hart Publishing Co., 1971 (also Bell, 1974); and as: *The Bawdy Bedside Reader,* New York: Bell Pub. Co. 1975. Song texts not expurgated, but heavily edited and gruellingly rewritten. The illustrations by Lindi are charming. Note: This atrocity is NOT an edition or revision of *Immortalia* (1927), q.v., edited by T. R. Smith. See also: Silverman; and *Poems Lewd and Lusty.*

Hartogs, Renatus. *Four-Letter Word Games.* New York: Dell, 1967.

Harvey, James Clarence. See: *The Point of View.*

Hawkes, Daniel. *Erotic Letters and Graffiti.* London: Riverhaven Ltd., Luxor Books, 1971. British narrative-style graffiti. Compare: Painter Collection; and Pelham-Box.

(Hayet, Armand.) *Chansons de la voile, "sans voiles,"* par Jean-Marie Le Bihor (*pseud.*) "Dunkerque: Pour les Amis du Gaillard d'Avant" (Paris: Denoël), 1935. Erotic supplement of French sea-chanteys not printed in Capt. Hayet's *Chansons de bord.* (Paris: Editions Eos, 1927). With a mock-imprecational "Coup de Gueule" by way of preface. Compare: Hugill; and Roy.

———. *Dictons et tirades des anciens de la voile.* Paris: Denoël, 1934. Companion volume to the preceding, especially as to its preface.

Hayward. *"Mr. Hayward's Account,"* 1821. See Place, Fr.

(Head, Arthur, *pseud.*): "Uther Capet." *The Broadway Broadsides and Pamphlets.* (Two privately printed series of chapbooks written and published by Head at his bookstore in New Haven, Conn., ca. 1930.) In all, 21 booklets. (Copies: Yale University Library.) Bawdy jokes retold as tales-in-verse; No. 21 is an *Apologia pro arte poetica sua.* Compare: Haddington; and Hall-Stevenson.

Healy, James N. *The Second Book of Irish Ballads.* 3rd ed. Cork, Ireland: Tyhe Mercier Press, 1968. Compare: Colum; and O'Lochlainn.

Hecht, Hans. *Songs from David Herd's Manuscripts.* London, 1904. See: Herd.

Hedgecock, J. L. *Gone Are the Days.* Girard, Kansas, 1949.

Hemenway, Robert E. *Zora Neale Hurston: A Literary Biography.* Urbana: University of Illinois Press, 1977.

Henderson, Eleanor Evelyn. *An Ozark Song Book: A Collection of Songs and Ballads from the Fayetteville Area.* Master's thesis, University of Arkansas, 1950.

Henderson, Hamish. *Ballads of World War II.* Collected by Seámus Mór Maceanruig (Hamish Henderson). Issued by The Lili Marleen Club of Glasgow, to Members Only (1947). (Copies:

School of Scottish Studies, Edinburgh; Hamish Henderson; G. Legman.) The first unexpurgated collection of soldiers' songs published, including Henderson's "King Farouk," which became traditional among British troops in North Africa.

————. *Notebooks.* MS., Scotland, 1945 ff., arranged chronologically. Textual transcripts of Henderson's important field-collections of Scottish folksongs. Accompanied by very numerous tape-recordings, including one or more "roch (rough) reels," of wholly bawdy sessions at farm-workers' secret societies, etc. (Repositoried at School of Scottish Studies, Edinburgh.) Compare: Burns; Gordon; Greig; and Carpenter.

Henderson, W. *Victorian Street Ballads.* London: Country Life Press, 1937. Compare: Hindley; and Shepard.

Henry, Mellinger. *Folksongs from the Southern Highlands.* New York: J. J. Augustin, 1938. Printed in Germany, and therefore somewhat more free than most such American regional collections. Compare: Chappell, L.; and Fauset.

"Henry, O." (*pseud.* of William S. Porter). *Roads of Destiny.* New York, 1909.

Herber, J. "Essai sur les Graffiti," in *Crocodile—Les Albums du.* (Algiers? 1943.) Also on erotic tattooing.

Herd, David. *The Ancient and Modern Scots Songs.* Edinburgh, 1769, 2 vols. Revised, 1776. Reprints, Glasgow: Kerr, 1869; Edinburgh: Paterson, 1870, 1875. New revision, Scottish Academic Press, 1973. 2 vols. Note: The reprint dated 1791 is entirely expurgated.

————. *Songs from David Herd's Manuscripts,* edited by Hans Hecht. London, 1904. Supplement to the preceding work. Herd's manuscripts are preserved in the British Museum Library, Additional MSS., and contain other songs *not* printed by Hecht, as the "from" in his title indicates.

Herschberger, Ruth. *Adam's Rib.* New York: Pellegrini and Cudahy, 1948. First modern feminist attack on men.

Heywood, Thomas. *The Rape of Lucrece.* London, 1608. Reprint, ed. Alan Holaday, University of Illinois Press, 1950.

Hickerson, Joseph C. "A Bibliography of American Folksong in the English Language," in: Duncan Emrich, ed., *American Folk-Poetry: An Anthology* (Boston: Little, Brown, 1974) pp. 775–816. Very valuable compilation.

————, Alan Dundes, and Robert Georges. "Mother Goose Vice Verse," in *Journal of American Folklore* (1962) 75: 221–26 and 249–59.

————. *Recording* (October 19–20, 1963) of an informal song session; primarily by Jim Hitchcock; in Archive of Folk Culture, Library of Congress, Washington, D.C. (LC–AFS 17022).

Higginbotham, Don. *Folklore of the United States Marine Corps.* (Austin, Texas, 1963.) 26 pp. (Copy: Prof. Roger Abrahams, University of Pennsylvania.) Extraordinary collection of erotic and sadistic usages, traditions, hazings, etc.; with songs and jokes.

Hiler, Hilaire. See: *Full Dress Suits and Plenty of Whores.*

Hille, Waldemar. *The Peoples' Song Book.* New York, 1948.

Hilton, John. *Catch that Catch Can.* London, 1652; also 1658. Collection of drollery verse and "catches," often bawdy.

(Hindley, Charles.) *Curiosities of Street Literature: Comprising "Cocks," or "Catchpennies," a large and curious assortment of street-drolleries, etc.* London, 1871. Reprinted (luxuriously, on various-colored paper) by "The Broadsheet King," John Foreman, London, 1966. 2 vols.

Hirschfeld, Magnus, and Andreas Gaspar. *Sittengeschichte des Weltkrieges.* Mit Beiträgen von Paul Englisch, *et al.* Leipzig/Wien, 1930–31. 2 vols. and Ergänzungsheft. Abridged edition, as: *Sittengeschichte des 20. Jahrhunderts,* Hanau, 1966–68, vol. 1. "Moral History" of World War I: the erotic folk-materials are relegated to the *Ergänzungsheft* supplement.

Hoerner, S. "ABC des Pfurzes," in *Anthropophytéia* (1912) 9: 510–11. Fart-alphabet. Compare: Combs.

Hoffmann, Frank A. *Analytical Survey of Anglo-American Traditional Erotica.* Bowling Green, Ohio: Bowling Green University Popular Press, 1973. Bibliographical notes throughout; useful but highly incomplete in view of its ambitious title. Prof. Hoffmann, of Buffalo, former cataloguer-bibliographer at the Kinsey Institute Library, also holds a fine private collection of older erotic "novelty" printed materials, "Xeroxlore," etc.

"Hogbotel, Sebastian, and Simon ffuckes," (*pseuds.*) *Snatches and Lays: Songs Miss Lilly White Should Never Have Taught Us.* Melbourne, 1962. Repr., Melbourne: Sun Books, 1973; and enlarged ed., Hong Kong, 1975. See: *Snatches and Lays.*

Holbrook, Stewart H. *Holy Old Mackinaw: A Natural History of the American Lumberjack*. New York: Macmillan, 1938.

Holloway, John, and Joan Black. *Later English Broadside Ballads*. Lincoln: University of Nebraska Press; and London, 1975. Fine selection, in part erotic, of 18th-century materials from the Madden Collection of *25,000 printed broadside ballads* at Cambridge University.

Hollywood Bedtime Stories. Hollywood, California: Private Printed, 1930. Includes verse. (Copy: Dr. Arthur Deex, Los Altos, California.)

Holmes, Oliver Wendell. *Elsie Venner*. Boston, 1861. (The legend of "The Serpent Bride.")

The Honest Fellow, or Reveler's Memorandum-Book . . . A Collection of such jocular Songs now in vogue. By Bumper Allnight, Esq. (*pseud.*) London: Printed in the Year 1790.

Hopkins, Anthony. *Songs from the Front and Rear: Canadian Servicemen's Songs of the Second World War*. Edmonton, Alberta: Hurtig Publishers, 1979. Outstanding collection of World War II armed-service songs, three-dimensionally edited with interpretive headnotes and unexpurgated texts. Foreword on wartime obscenity by Bob Godfrey, former Squadron Leader. Compare: Getz; Henderson, H.; and Starr.

Howard, Dorothy G. Mills. *Folk Jingles of American Children*. Ph.D. thesis, New York University, 1938. 4to, typewritten. Not entirely expurgated, but compare: McCosh; and Turner. See also: Mills and Bishop.

Hubbard, Lester A. *Ballads and Songs from Utah*. Salt Lake City: University of Utah Press, 1961.

Hudson, Arthur Palmer. "Ballads and Songs from Mississippi," in: *Journal of American Folklore*, (1926) 39: 93–194. Enlarged as:

———. *Folksongs of Mississippi and Their Background*. Chapel Hill, N.C.: University of North Carolina Press, 1936.

———, and George Herzog. *Folk Tunes from Mississippi*. National Play Bureau Publication No. 25, July 1937.

Hughes, Marion. *Three Years in Arkansaw*. Chicago, 1905.

Hugill, Stanley J. *Shanties from the Seven Seas*. London: Routledge, 1961; New York: Dutton, 1966. Supplemented by Hugill's *Sailortown*, 1967; and mainly by the following:

———. *Sailing Ship Shanties*, by Long John Silver (*pseud.*). MS., Aberdovey, Merioneth, Wales, 1956–57. (Copy: G. Legman.) The unexpurgated texts, supplied for the present work, of all the shanties "camouflaged" in Hugill's *Shanties from the Seven Seas*. Compare: "Dave E. Jones."

———. *Songs of the Seas*. New York: McGraw-Hill, 1977.

Humor Russkago Naroda v Skazkach. See: *Mejdu Druziami:* Second Series.

Humphreys, Laud. *Tearoom Trade*. Chicago: Aldine, 1970. On homosexual graffiti. See also: Sechrest and Flores.

Huneker, James G. *Painted Veils*. New York, 1920?

Hunter, Max F. *Collection of Ozark Folk-Songs,* collected ca. 1957–76. Tape-recordings and transcripts deposited in the Springfield, Mo., Public Library.

Huntington, Gale. *Songs the Whalemen Sang*. Barre, Mass., 1964.

Huston, John. *Frankie and Johnny*. New York: Boni, 1930. See: Hoyt Taylor.

Immortalia: An Anthology of American Ballads, Sailors' Songs, Cowboy Songs, College Songs, Parodies, Limericks, and other Humorous Verses and Doggerel Now for the First Time Brought Together in Book Form, by a Gentleman about Town, (Thomas R. Smith. New York: Macy-Masius and Jacob Baker, Vanguard Press,) 1927. Numerous reprints, to 1969. The essential American source-work. Compare: *The "Wrecks."* (Note: This is NOT identical with the inferior collection with music, edited by Harold H. Hart, 1970, using the same title or similar.) Reprinted by "Arthur MacKay," q.v., 1959; and as :

———. *A Book of Vulgar Verse*. Toronto: Checkerbooks, 1981.

Indiana University Folksong Archive. See: Dorson.

The Indiscreet Muse: Poems of diverse amatory moods. New York: Citadel Press, 1946. (Edited by Hiram Haydn.) The "last" of the drolleries.

Infant Institutes. London, 1797? Contains unexpurgated children's rhymes, some reprinted by Ker, q.v.

Institute for Sex Research. See: Kinsey-ISR.

An Introductory Collection of Real Folk and Traditional Songs. See: *Dirt: An Exegesis*.

Irwin, Godfrey. *American Tramp and Underworld Slang . . . With a selection of tramp songs.* London: Scholartis Press, Eric Partridge; New York: Sears, 1931. Songs, pp. 199–252. Manuscript was expurgated to relative worthlessness by Partridge. Compare: Milburn, another masterpiece of expurgation. Almost the only showing of the real tramp and hobo songs is in the Gordon *"Inferno MS."* See also: *The Slime Sheet,* presumably edited by Irwin.

Ives, Burl. *The Burl Ives Song Book.* New York: Ballantine Books, 1953.

Ives, Edward D. *Joe Scott, The Woodsman-Songmaker.* Champaign, Ill.: University of Illinois Press, 1978.

Jack, Stella. See: *Percy Folio Manuscript.*

Jackson, Bruce, ed. *Folklore and Society: Essays in Honor of Benjamin A. Botkin.* Hatboro, Pa.: Folklore Associates, 1966. See: Fowke.

———. *Get Your Ass in the Water and Swim Like Me: Narrative Poetry from the Black Oral Tradition.* Cambridge, Mass.: Harvard University Press, 1974. Best collection and discussion of bawdy American Negro rhyming "toasts" and similar, impeccably edited.

———. *Wake Up Dead Man: Afro-American Worksongs from Texas Prisons.* Cambridge, Mass.: Harvard University Press, 1972.

Jackson, Richard. *Popular Songs of Nineteenth-Century America.* New York: Dover Pubs., 1976.

James, Clive. *Unreliable Memoirs.* London: Cape, 1980.

Jamet (le Jeune), François-Louis. *Stromates sur les Femmes.* MS., Paris, ca. 1752–77. 2 vols. (Bibliothèque Nationale, *Enfer* 1247.) Very valuable manuscript scrapbook partly in verse, described *in extenso* by Pascal Pia, *Les Livres de l'Enfer,* cols. 1271–6.

(Jannet, Pierre, et al.) *Bibliotheca Scatologica.* Paris, 1850. Supplemented by: Gustave Brunet, *Anthologie Scatologique.* Paris: J. Gay, 1865? Proverbs, *blasons,* etc.

Jest on Sex: Sexplosively sexsational sinerama of life . . . for He and She: Ages from Sexteen to Sexty. New York: Encore Press, 1953. 192 pp. 8vo. Imitation of Elgart's *Over Sexteen,* but with real folk-humor tone, and includes mildly bawdy verse and songs.

Jiménez, A. (Armando Jiménez Farias.) *Picardía Mexicana.* México: Costa-Amic, Libro Mex, 1960. (Often reprinted.) Supplemented by: *Nueva Picardía Mexicana,* 1971. Mexican erotic folklore, in riotous typography, with texts of the main obscene poem, *"El Ànima de Sayula,"* I: 153–60, and 242, on which see further Dr. Américo Paredes, "The Anglo-American in Mexican Folklore," in: *New Voices in American Studies* (Purdue University Studies, 1966) pp. 121–24. See: Lehmann-Nitzsche.

Johnson, Clifton. *What They Say in New England: A Book of Signs, Sayings and Superstitions.* Boston, 1896–97. Reprint, New York: Columbia University Press, 1963, with introduction by Carl Withers.

Johnson, Guy B. "Double Meaning in the Popular Negro Blues," in: *Journal of Abnormal and Social Psychology* (1927) 22: 12–20. Compare: Oliver.

———, and Howard W. Odum. *The Negro and his Songs.* 1926. Reprint: Hatboro, Pa.: Folklore Associates, 1964. Note: Much material expurgated from this work (also from their *Negro Workaday Songs,* Chapel Hill, 1926), is now "lost" among Dr. Odum's papers.

Johnson, James (and Robert Burns). *The Scots Musical Museum.* Edinburgh, 1787–1803, 6 vols. Revised, Edinburgh, 1839 and 1853, 4 vols. with notes by William Stenhouse and David Laing. Reprint ca. 1968.

"Johnson, John Henry" (*pseud.* of Maxwell Droke). *Bawdy Ballads and Lusty Lyrics.* Indianapolis: Droke, 1935. Enlarged ed. 1950; reprinted New York: Pocket Books, 1970. Very mild stuff. Not to be confused (as intended) with "Dick Harde's" *Lusty Limericks and Bawdy Ballads.*

Johnson, Katrina. *Evening Street: a novel.* 1947.

La Joie du Pornographe, ou Nouveau Recueil d'amusemens. "Paris: Mère Godichon" (Bruxelles: Kistemaeckers, 1884). Reprint of *La Lyre gaillarde,* "Aux Porcherons," 1776.

"Jones, Dave E." (i.e., "Davy Jones"). *A Collection of Sea Songs and Ditties, from the stores of Dave E. Jones.* (U.S., ca. 1928). 48 pp. (Unique copy: Kinsey-ISR, formerly in collection of G. Legman.) Compare: Hugill; and Frank Shay, to whom this *Collection* is ascribed.

Jones, Lewis. *Jones-Conklin MS.* East Hampton, New York, ca. 1850. Military and naval song texts, about one-third erotic, mostly copied from printed broadsides, ca. 1825–1850. Repositoried in

Indiana University Library in 1958 by Edmund Conklin; announced for publication by Dr. Kenneth Goldstein. Compare: Thompson and Cutting.

Jordan, Philip D., and Lillian Kessler. *Songs of Yesterday: A Song Anthology of American Life.* New York: Doubleday, 1941.

Journal of American Folklore. Philadelphia, 1962. Vol. 75: (July 1962) pp. 187–265. Entire issue devoted to "*Symposium on Obscenity in Folklore,*" papers read at the combined meeting of the Modern Language Association and American Folklore Society, 28 December 1960, on the initiative of Dr. Tristram P. Coffin and Dr. Roger D. Abrahams, two then-young American folklorists.

Jungbauer, G. *Volkslieder aus dem Bohmerwalde.* Prague, 1930. Vol. 1 includes erotic materials without segregation.

Jyl of Brentford's Testament. Robert Copland, boke-prynter (fl. 1508–1547); "The Wyll of the Devyll, and his Last Testament"; "A Talk of Ten Wives, on their husbands' ware"; and other short pieces. Edited by Frederick J. Furnivall. London: Printed for Private Circulation (Ballad Society, vol. 7A), 1871. 44 pp. The "Talk of Ten Wives, on their husbands' ware" (from the Porkington MS. about 1460), pp. 29–33, is the oldest surviving erotic folksong in English.

Kabronsky, V. (*pseud.*). *Uncensored Russian Limericks.* New York: Russica Publishers, 1978. Not actual limericks, but Russian *chastushki,* or erotic four-liners, given in Cyrillic print without English translation. See: Krauss; Raskin; Spinkler; and Stern-Szana.

Kannon, Jackie. *Poems for the John.* New York: Kanrom, Inc., 1960. Crap.

Karpeles, Maud. See under: Cecil Sharp.

Kate Hand-Cock, or A Young Girl's Introduction to Fast Life. Privately Printed (Paris? ca. 1900.) 36 pp. Text dated "London, 1882." Erotic poems, pp. 23–36.

Kay, Ormonde de. "Abominable in His Lusts," in: *Quest Magazine.* (New York, 1988–89.) Best work on the Beecher-Tilton 1870s scandal.

Kearney, Patrick J. See: *The Private Case.*

Keller, Benjamin. *Chad's Ford Flivver Songs.* MS., Socorro, New Mexico, 1949. Collection of 30 bawdy song texts. (Copy: G. Legman.)

Kellogg, James W. *Fighter Pilot Songs.* (Austin, Texas) 1963. 35 pp. hektographed. Term-paper submitted to Dr. Roger Abrahams' folklore course. Reprints part of the *Guam Air Force Songs (Warning!)* folio, with comments.

Kennedy, Peter. *Folksongs of Britain and Ireland.* London: Cassell; New York: Macmillan, 1975. 4to. Excellently researched and with valuable comparative notes, but silently restricted to the least graphic erotic texts available.

———, and Alan Lomax. *The Folksongs of Britain.* I: *Songs of Courtship.* II: *Songs of Seduction.* New York: Caedmon Records, 1961. 51 and 52 pp. Chapbook pamphlets accompanying phonograph recordings of the same title, and giving the texts and tunes.

Kennedy, X. J. *Tygers of Wrath.* Athens, Georgia: University of Georgia Press, 1981. Magnificently printed anthology of invective in verse. See: Lindsay, H.

Ker, John Bellenden Gawler (called:). *An Essay on the Archaiology of Popular English Phrases and Nursery Rhymes.* Southampton, 1834–40. 4 vols. in two series of 2 vols. each. Rare eccentric work, attempting to demonstrate that English proverbial phrases and children's rhymes are all in a secret "Old Dutch" language, and consist mainly of imprecations against the clergy.

Kick Him Jenny, a tale (in verse). 11th ed. To which is added, *The Female Contest, a Merry tale.* London: W. France, 1737. 24 pp. Compare: Haddington.

Kidson, Frank. *Traditional Tunes: A Collection of Ballad Airs.* Oxford: Taphouse, 1891. Reprinted, Wakefield, Yorks.: S. R. Publishers, 1970.

———, and Alfred Moffat. *A Garland of English Folk Songs.* London: Ascherberg, 1926.

"Kieswetter, Bonifazius." See: *Wirtshaus an der Lahn.*

"Kimbo" (*pseud.* of Bradley Gilman). *Tropical Tales.*

———and: *More Tropical Tales.* Nice, 1925–26. 2 vols. (Copies: Ohio State University.) Jokes and facetiæ, including verse. Under his own name author also issued *Clinic on the Comic* (Nice, 1926).

(Kinloch, George R.) *The Ballad Book*. Edinburgh, 1827. Reprinted, Edinburgh: Goldsmid, 1885. A somewhat less expurgated supplement to Kinloch's *Ancient Scottish Ballads,* (1827), but compare:

———. *Burlesque and Jocular Ballads and Songs*. MS., Scotland, 1829. (Harvard University Library 25242.12.) Comprises the pages totally withdrawn from both Kinloch's main and supplementary volumes (see above), with a satirical titlepage parodying that of Wedderburn's *Book of Gude and Godlie Ballatis*. Note: These materials are indexed in Montgomerie, *Bibliography,* q.v.

Kinsey Institute for Sex Research, Indiana University, Bloomington, Indiana. *Folk Poems and Songs*. Manuscript archive file, ca. 1963, with contents-index prepared by Frank A. Hoffmann.

Kipling, Rudyard. *Putnam*. (New York: The Author, ca. 1905.) Printed in an edition of four copies on toilet paper. Only known George Barr McCutcheon copy held by New York bookseller, Gabriel Engel, in 1950s. An attack in verse on Kipling's American publisher; scatological.

Kirkpatrick Sharpe. See: Charles Kirkpatrick Sharpe.

Kittredge, George Lyman. "Ballads and Songs," in *Journal of American Folklore* (1917) 30: 283–369. Important research notes.

(Klinefelter, Walter.) *Preface to an Unprintable Opus,* by Pedro Pococampo (*pseud.*). Portland, Maine: Southworth-Anthoensen Press. Privately Printed, 1942. 15 pp. Limited to 75 copies. (NYPL: *K) The "Unprintable Opus" is the American bawdy folksong "Christopher Columbo," song No. 160B in vol. I here.

Klingman, Gail. "The Rites of Women: Oral Poetry . . . in Contemporary Romania," in: *Journal of American Folklore* (1984) 97: 167–88. In-depth study; gives a few bawdy *strigâturi* (shouted, rhymed couplets) pp. 178–80, used at Rumanian peasant wedding-feasts.

Klintberg, Bengt af, and Christina Mattsson. *Fula visboken: 50 folklige erotiska visor*. Lund, 1977. (Tiden: Fib's Lyrikklub Bibliotek, no. 196.) 137 pp. Erotic folksong supplement to B. af-Klintberg and Finn Zetterholm, *Svensk Folkpoesi* (Stockholm, 1971). Compare: Rasmussen.

Klose, H. U. *Sexus und Eros* in der deutschen Novellendichtung um 1900. Breslau, 1941. Ph.D. dissertation, issued during World War II.

Knapp, Mary and Herbert. *"One Potato, Two Potato": The Secret Education of American Children*. New York: Norton, 1976. Compare: McCosh.

Kochman, Thomas. *Rappin' and Stylin' Out*. Urbana: University of Illinois Press, 1972. Negro "toast" recitations. Compare: Jackson, B.

Kodish, Debora. *Good Friends and Bad Enemies: Robert Winslow Gordon and the Study of American Folksong*. Urbana: University of Illinois Press, 1986.

———. "'A National Project with Many Workers': Robert Winslow Gordon and the Archive of American Folk Song," in *Quarterly Journal of the Library of Congress* (1978) 35: 218–33. See further: Gordon.

Kohn, Gustav. "Lieder aus Oesterreichisch-Schlesien," in *Anthropophytéia* (1912) 9: 55–56. Erotic songs from Austrian Silesia. Compare: Blümml.

Kopp, Arthur. *Deutsches Volks- und Studentenlied in vorklassischer Zeit*. Berlin, 1899. On the unpublished Crailsheim song manuscript. See: *Futilitates*.

Koukoulès, Mary. *Loose-Tongued Greeks: A Miscellany of Neo-Hellenic Erotic Folklore*. Translated by John Taylor (and G. Legman). With an introduction by G. Legman. Paris: Digamma, Bibliophile Edition (The Author), 1983. Limited to 300 copies. Vol. I only, giving Greek texts of the 302 songs and rhymed recitations, with English translation on facing pages. By far the most important collection of modern Greek erotic folklore in verse. The introduction by G. Legman, and a brief part of Mme. Koukoulès' text in their joint translation, appeared earlier in *Maledicta* (1983), as "In the Time of Masturbation."

———. *Same, complete,* Greek text (only): *Neo-Hellenike Athyrostomia*. (Preface by G. Legman.) Athens: Nefele, 1984–1988. 3 vols. The complete work: 1160 rhymed and other texts, without English translation; the proposed follow-up title, *Loose-Tailed Greeks,* having been rejected.

———. Compare: Ethelyn G. Orso, *Modern Greek Humor* (Bloomington: Indiana University Press, 1979), principally of erotic prose tales and jokes; and Elias Petropoulos, *Rebétika Tragoudia,* and *Kaliardá* (Athens: Digamma, 1968 and 1971), on urban folk-poetry and Greek homosexual slang.

Krauss, Friedrich S. *Das Geschlechtsleben des deutschen Volkes in des Gegenwart: Folkloristische*

Studien und Erhebungen, ed. Dr. Friedrich S. Krauss. Leipzig: Ethnologischer Verlag, 1911. (*Anthropophytéia:* Beiwerke, vol 4.) Part IV includes "Der erotische Vierzeiler: *Die Wirtin an der Lahn,*" 334 bawdy quatrains. Abridged reprint, Hanau: Schustek, 1970.

(———.) "*Grande Russie, Folklore de la,*" in: *Kryptádia* (Paris, 1898) 5: 183–214. Note: It has been questioned whether Krauss was the editor, or actual collector. Perhaps by Th. Volkov, along with 5: 1–182, on erotica of Ukrainia. See also: Raskin.

———. "Die Zeugung in Sitte, Brauch, und Glauben der Südslaven: *Lieder,*" in: *Kryptádia* (1899) 6: 193–382, and (1901) 7: 97–368, and (1902) 8: 149–266. Slavonic, Bosnian, and Croatian erotic songs, with German translation: a remarkable field collection, supplementing Krauss' *Sitte und Brauch der Südslaven* (Wien, 1885).

———, and Karl Reiskel. "Das Wirthaus an der Lahn: Die ungedruckten, erotischen Strophen des Volksliedes," in: *Anthropophytéia* (1905) 2: 113–16.

———, and Alfred Webinger, editors: *Das Minnelied des deutschen Land- und Stadtvolkes.* Leipzig, 1929. (*Anthropophytéia:* Beiwerke, vol. 9.) By far the most important work on German erotic folksongs, with contributions by numerous collectors. Compare: Borneman, on children's songs, later. Abridged reprint, Hanau: Schustek, 1968, which omits the music, etc.

Krauss, Joanne. "*Love and Death* and the American Ballad: A Morphodite of 'Ballads of Family Opposition to Lovers,'" in: *Folklore Annual* (1972–73) nos. 4–5: 91–100.

"Krotus, M." (*pseud.* of H. Göke). *Klappentexte: Materialen zur Psychologie der Dichtung.* Freiburg, 1970.

Kryptádia: Recueil de documents pour servir á l'étude des traditions populaires. Heilbronn and Paris, 1883–1911. 12 vols. 12 mo. Reprinted, Darmstadt, 1970, with introduction by Dr. Will Peuckert. Erotic folklore and folksong collections in many languages (*except* English); yearbook founded by Isidor Kopernicky and Friedrich S. Krauss, and edited by the French and Italian folklorists, Gaston Pâris (who wrote the introduction to vol. I), Eugène Rolland, Henry Gaidoz, E.-Henri Carnoy, and Giuseppe Pitrè. All the editors and contributors were agreed to remain anonymous to protect their professional positions on the companion yearbook, *La Tradition.* Independently continued as: *Contributions au Folklore Érotique,* 1906–09, q.v. See also Krauss' much more important continuation yearbook, *Anthropophytéia,* which remained active until stopped by the Nazis in the 1930s.

Kynett, Harold H. *What Nonsense!* Philadelphia, 1945. "Musical Note," pp. 130–37, on erotic songs.

La Barre, Weston. "The Psychopathology of Drinking Songs," in: *Psychiatry* (1939) 2: 203–12. Mainly on limericks. Reprinted in pamphlet form, ca. 1978 with other of the author's pseudonymous persiflages.

Labov, William. *Language in the Inner City.* Philadelphia: University of Pennsylvania Press, 1972. On Negro recitation style.

Lacht zum Bescheissen! Eine ausgewählte Sammlung erotischer Vorträge, Gedichte, Anekdoten, *usw.,* für Freunde ausgelassener Frölichkeit. "New-York und Philadelphia: bei A. R. Schlecker" (Germany or Austria, ca. 1890). (Copy: G. Legman.) Compare: *Arschwische und Scheissereien.*

Lackey, Walter F. *History of Newton County, Arkansas.* Independence, Mo., 1950.

Lance, Larry M., and Christina Y. Berry. "Has There Been a Sexual Revolution? Human Sexuality in Popular Music, 1968–1977," in: *Journal of Popular Culture* (1978) pp. 65–73. Compare: Scodel's earlier study. Important mass-observation approach to moral standards, giving song titles and discussion. Should be enlarged to cover television "clips," which are probably the real future of cinema.

Langenfelt, Gösta. *Shakespeare's Debt to the Middle Ages.* MS., Stockholm, 1958. Best on erotica in Shakespeare. Compare: Partridge.

Larson, Kenneth. *Barnyard Folklore of Southeastern Idaho: A collection of vulgar verses, jokes, and popular ballads, all of them unprintable, obtained by word-of-mouth from those who* [were] *entertained by them, mostly farmers, laborers, and students . . . during the years from 1920 to 1952.* Salt Lake City, Utah, 1952. 5 pts. (244 pp.) typescript, including music. (Copies: Indiana University Folklore Archives; Idaho State University Archives, Pocatello, Idaho; University of California, Los Angeles, Folklore and Mythology Center; G. Legman.) Note:

As to the title-page statement of "word-of-mouth" transmission, the compiler prepared and circulated *three differently worded* and revised redactions of this same material, the earlier form entitled:

———. *Songs and Ballads: Vulgar Ballads, Jingles, and Jokes,* "collected . . . Idaho, 1932–52." (Copies: Indiana University Folklore Archives; G. Legman.) Larson's authentic text.

———. *Same,* 3rd redaction, as *Countryside Folklore: Songs and Ballads of Bygone Times.* "Collected during 1930–33 in Idaho, and reorganized September 5, 1972." Salt Lake City, Utah, 1972. Mimeographed. (Copy: Archive of Folk Culture, Library of Congress, Washington, D.C.)

———. *The Folklore Trade.* Salt Lake City, Utah: The Compiler, November 11, 1952. Mimeographed. (Copy: Archive of Folk Culture, Library of Congress, Washington, D.C., bound under title above of *Barnyard Folklore.*) See: Legman, *Specimens of Folklore,* ed. Larson, the "trade" referred to.

Der lasterhafte Herr Biedermeyer: Wollüstige Tändeleyen un' ziemlich Reimereyen. (Edited by Leo Schidrowitz. Wien, ca. 1930.) A collection of stanzas of *Das Wirthaus an der Lahn,* q.v.

Lavender, Roy. See: *Lost Limericks and Bar Room Ballads.*

(Lawrence, T. E.) *The Mint.* New York: Doubleday, 1936. (Private copyright edition, not issued publicly. Copy: Library of Congress, *Delta.*) Reprinted, London: Cape, ca. 1958, in both expurgated and complete editions. The latter gives text of the British Army and Navy bawdy ballad, "The Captain's Wife."

Laws, G. Malcolm, Jr. *American Balladry from British Broadsides: A Guide for Students and Collectors of Traditional Song.* Philadelphia: American Folklore Society, 1957. (Bibliographical Series, vol. 8) Important research and indexing tool for folksong studies. Compare: Simpson. Continuation of following:

———. *Native American Balladry: A Descriptive Study and Bibliographical Syllabus.* Philadelphia: American Folklore Society, 1950. (Bibliographical Series, vol. I.) Revised edition, 1964. Continues in the preceding item.

Laycock, Donald C. *The Best Bawdry.* Sydney/Melbourne: Angus and Robertson, 1982. Mostly Australian modern bawdy songs and poems, with interesting introduction; but the folk originals are heavily conflated and editorially revised. Cited therefore to following MS.:

———. *Obiter Dicta.* Canberra, Australia, 1955–61. MS., typewritten folio, with handwrit annotations by the compiler and part-author. (Copies: South Australia National Library; G. Legman.) The original redaction of the preceding item. Compare: *Snatches and Lays.*

The Lay of John Haroldson. Philadelphia? ca. 1862. Pamphlet, 8vo. Topical bawdy poem of the Civil War, on the purported use of southern ladies' *chamber-lye* for nitrates to make gunpowder. See song No. 242, in vol. II. (Copies: NYPL: 3*; Brown Univ. Library, Harris Poetry Collection; and various broadside versions in American antiquarian societies, some with crude woodcut showing the southern ladies squatting patriotically.)

Lazenby, W. (William?) *pseud.* "D. Cameron," Editor-publisher of *The Pearl,* 1879–80, and its sequels, *The Boudoir,* and *The Cremorne.*

Leach, Clifford. *Bottoms Up!* New York: Paull-Pioneer Music Corp., ca. 1933. Folio of semi-bawdy songs with piano music, issued to celebrate repeal of Prohibition (of alcohol) in U.S.

Leach, MacEdward. *Folk Ballads and Songs of the Lower Labrador Coast.* Ottawa: National Museum of Canada, 1965.

Lean, Vincent S. *Collectanea: Proverbs, Folklore, and Superstition.* Bristol, 1902–04. 4 vols. Much on odd linguistics.

Leary, James P. *Midwestern Folk Humor.* Little Rock, Ark.: August House, 1991. Unexpurgated jokes and excellent annotation, with *cante fables* and obscoena.

"Le Bihor, Jean-Marie." See: Armand Hayet.

Lee, Katie. "Songs the Cowboys Taught Me," in: *Arizona Highways* (February, 1960) pp. 34–39.

La Légende Joyeuse, ou Les Cent-et-une leçons de Lampsaque. "Londres: Pynne" (Paris?) 1749–51. 3 vols. 24to., engraved text. Rare vest-pocket collection of erotic tales-in-verse. Reprinted as: *Le Bijou de société,* ca. 1780; *Le Cabinet de Lampsaque,* 1784; and *Les Bons Contes* (Étrennes aux raffinés), Bruxelles, 1882.

Legman, Gershon. *The Ballad: Unexpurgated Folksongs, American and British, of the Twentieth Century, and their Sources.* MS. Archive in progress, begun in 1934.

———. *The Ballast Value of the PHTH-Phoneme* in Anglo-Norse Monophthongisation before 1200 A.D.; by Gonzague Truc (*pseud.*) "Dissertation submitted for the degree of PhthD. Paris: Les Hautes Études" (Auribeau, Alpes-Mmes., France, 1957). 20 pp. Photocopy issue from typewriting, limited to 25 copies. Under the perhaps misleading cover-title, this is a tryout of typographical form for *The Ballad: Unexpurgated,* and includes only variorum texts of one song, "The Ball o' Kirriemuir," 1890–1955.

———. "Bawdy Monologues and Rhymed Recitations," in: *Southern Folklore Quarterly* (University of Florida, 1976) 40: 59–123.

———. "The Bawdy Song . . . in Fact and in Print," in: *Explorations: Studies in Culture and Communication* (University of Toronto, 1957) No. 7: pp. 139–56. First article ever published on this subject; expurgated before publication by the editor, who was nevertheless dismissed for this "goddam breach of taste!" Expanded in *The Horn Book* (1964) pp. 336–426.

———. "Body Taboo and Verbal Expurgation in Western Folklife," submitted to: *Journal of American Folklore* (Autumn 1991) vol. 104.

———. "Erotic Folksong: An International Bibliography," in: *Journal of American Folklore* (Autumn 1990) vol. 103: bibliographically detailed text, but without present lexical and *graffiti* materials.

———. "For Students of Folklore," in: *American Freeman* (Girard, Kansas, June 1949) p. 10/1–2. Newspaper appeal signed by G. Legman-Keith, for erotic ballad materials, listing 46 song-titles specially sought, including "The E-ri-e Canawl" (never found).

———. *The Horn Book: Studies in Erotic Folklore and Bibliography.* New Hyde Park, N.Y.: University Books, 1964. Reprinted, London: Cape, 1970, but withdrawn from circulation in England, and an apology printed in the London *Times* by the publisher, owing to complaint by James Reeves, q.v. as to the final chapter, "Who Owns Folklore?" Spanish translation published in Mexico.

———. *The Limerick: 1700 Examples, with Notes, Variants and Index.* Paris: Les Hautes Études, 1953. Reprinted with historical introduction, New York: Brandywine Press, 1970; and anonymously as: *Bawdy Limericks,* "Canada: Popular Press" (Rexdale, Ontario: Coles Pub. Co.), 1980, an unauthorized reprint; also various piratical abridgements under different title. (This has been the most frequently pirated book in English in modern times, except for *In His Steps,* not copyrighted 1897, by the Rev. Ch. M. Sheldon.)

———. *The New Limerick: 2750 Unpublished Examples, American and British.* New York: Crown Publishers, 1977. With a sociological introduction. Reprinted as: *More Limericks,* New York: Bell Pub. Co., 1980; and unauthorized reprint as: *Lusty Limericks.* "Canada: Popular Press" (Rexdale, Ontario: Coles Pub. Co.), 1981; and the same text issued in 8 pts., 16mo, as *The Pink (Red,* etc.) *Book of Limericks.*

———. *No Laughing Matter.* See: *Rationale,* below.

———. *Peregrine Penis: An Autobiography of Innocence.* Ms. Valbonne (A.M.) France, 1989 ff., in progress. Contains much American erotic folklore, song scraps, etc. Chapter on Anaïs Nin to be published in *Libido.*

———. *Rationale of the Dirty Joke: An Analysis of Sexual Humor. First Series.* New York: (Basic Books and) Grove Press, 1968; London: Cape, 1969.

———. *Same. Second Series.* (*No Laughing Matter.*) New York (Wharton, New Jersey): Breaking Point, Inc., 1975. Reprints, New York: Bell Pub. Co., 1975; London: Hart-Davis, 1980.

———. *Same,* both series reprinted as: *No Laughing Matter.* (*First and Second Series.*) Bloomington: Indiana University Press, 1982. 2 vols.

———, ed., Vance Randolph, *Roll Me in Your Arms,* and *Blow the Candle Out: "Unprintable" Ozark Folksongs and Folklore, Collected by Vance Randolph.* Fayetteville: University of Arkansas Press, 1992. 2 vols. The present work.

———. "Russian Bawdy Songs," forthcoming (?) in: *Maledicta,* 1992? With translation and discussion of the Russian 18th-century erotic folk-recitation, "Now Let Us Preach, and Sing a Song." See also: introduction by G. Legman to A. N. Afanasyev, *Russian Secret Tales* (New York: Brussel, 1969).

————. *Songs of Sadism, Lust, etc.* "by G. Legman." (!) See under title.

————. *(Typical) Specimens of Folklore from the Files of G. Legman.* (Salt Lake City, Utah: Kenneth Larson, 1952), mimeographed. (Copies: Indiana University Folklore Archives; Idaho State University Archives, Pocatello, Idaho; and Library of Congress, Archive of Folk Culture, under title "*The Folklore Trade.*") Unauthorized pre-publication of texts from the Legman "Ballad" archive.

————. "Tumble O'Lynn's Farewell," in: *Journal of American Folklore* (1990) 103: 68–71. The first AIDS folksong, California, ca. 1987; with the music dating from 1560.

————. "Unprintable Folklore?—The Vance Randolph Collection," in *Journal of American Folklore* (Summer 1990) vol. 103.

————. "A Word for It," in: *Maledicta* (1977) 1: 9–18. See also introductions to: Burns; Cornog; Farmer; Kearney; Koukoulès; McCosh; and Randolph.

(Lehmann-Nitzsche, Robert; *pseud.* "Victor Borde.") *La Plata Folklore.* Leipzig, 1923. (*Anthropophytéia: Beiwerke,* vol. 8) Argentine-Spanish erotic folklore and folk-poetry, with German translation; the outstanding work. Compare: Cela; and Jiménez.

————. "Neue Parallelen zum '*Streit der Jungfrauen,*'" in: *Anthropophytéia* (1910) 7: 374. On the vaginal bragging-song known in English as "The Whorey Crew, or Three Old Whores from Baltimore."

————. "Zur Volkskunde Argentiniens," in: *Zeitschrift des Vereins für Volkskunde* (1914) 24: 240–55.

Leisy, James F. *Songs for Pickin' and Singin'.* Greenwich, Conn.: Fawcett Pubs., 1962. With music.

Lelegos, Michael. *Demotikè Anthologia.* Athens, 1868–69. (Copy: Sorbonne Library, Paris.) Modern Greek folk-poetry and songs, including a brief erotic section of "*Priapeia.*" This section reprinted alone: Athens, 1974. Compare: Koukoulès.

Lenoir, Maurice. *Chansons de Salle de Garde, choix fait par le Dr. Maurice Lenoir.* Tirage limité — Strictement réservé au Corps Médical. Paris: Collection du Carabas, Les Presses Modernes, 1926. (Copy: M. Léon Guichard, *acc.* Staub, p. 217.) The first signed "medical" collection of the bawdy "*Chansons de Salle de Garde,*" of French medical and art students.

Leonhardt, Wilhelm. *Liebe und Erotik in den Uranfängen der deutschen Dichtkunst.* Dresden: R. Kraut, 1910. Interestingly reviewed by F. S. Krauss, in *Anthropophytéia* (1911) 8: 500–01; and supplemented by:

————. "Die beiden ältesten Skatologika der deutschen Literatur," in: *Anthropophytéia* (1911) 8: 400–06. Verse items from Hroswitha's "Passion of St. Gongolf" (975 A.D.), and "Salomon and Morolf" (1200 A.D.), with glossarial notes on Old German terms.

Levine, S. "Regression in Primitive Clowning," in: *Psychoanalytic Quarterly* (1961) 30: 72–83. On *graffiti.*

Levy, Lester S. *Flashes of Merriment: A Century of Humorous Songs in America.* Norman: University of Oklahoma Press, 1971.

Library L'Amour. "London: Pickadilly press" (Detroit, Michigan: McClurg, ca. 1930). 12 pts. in 4 vols. 12 mo. A re-issue of McClurg's *Bibliothèque Érotique,* 1929, q.v.

Il Libretto Rosso dell' Universitario: Raccolta di commedie, drammi, ballate, cazzate, sproloqui, e Canti Goliardici. (Edited by Alfredo Castelli? Ferrara, 1968. Reprinted, Bologna, 1972?) (Copies: Guiliano Averna, Lido-Venice; G. Legman.) The modern break-through collection of Italian student bawdy verse and obscœna, similar to the French students' *Chansons de Salles de Garde,* q.v. Compare: Castelli, *Canti Goliardici,* No. 2 (1974), which is the second series of the present *Libretto.*

Lindsay, H. A. "The Bastard from the Bush," in: *Quadrant* (Australia, 1957) 5: 65–7. On the favorite Australian bawdy "mucker-pose" recitation, reprinted in part in X. J. Kennedy, *Tygers of Wrath* (1981), an anthology of invective in verse, at pp. 273–74, as "Bagman O'Reilly's Curse."

Lindsay, Jack. *Life Rarely Tells.* London, 1958. Autobiography of an outstanding Australian literary editor, with notes on bawdy song.

Lingenfelter, Richard E., et al. *Songs of the American West.* Berkeley: University of California Press, 1968. Cowboy songs, not entirely expurgated. Compare: Logsdon.

Linscott, Eloise Hubbard. *Folk Songs of Old New England.* New York: Macmillan, 1939.

"Linton, E. R.," *pseud.* See: Edward B. Cray.

"Literatura popular erótica de Andalucía," in: *Kryptádia* (1884) 2: 223–51. Erotic riddles-in-rhyme and *coplas,* pp. 228–41. Compare: Cela; Jiménez; and Lehmann-Nitzsche.

Lloyd, Albert L. *Folk Song in England.* London: Lawrence and Wishart, 1967. Reprint, Panther Arts, 1969. Excellent conspectus; the outstanding work on English folksong, with chapter on erotic song in reply to G. Legman.

Locker Room Humor: It's a Million Laughs. (Toronto? 1958.) Miscellany of semi-bawdy humor; "Poems and Limericks," pp. 60–71, and 160. See also: *Bar Room Tales,* an inferior sequel; and *New Locker Room Humor.*

Loesser, Arthur. *Humor in American Song.* New York: Howell, Soskin, 1942.

Logan, W. H. *A Pedlar's Pack of Ballads and Songs.* Edinburgh, 1869. Reprint, Detroit: Singing Tree Press, 1968.

Logsdon, Guy. *"The Whorehouse Bells Were Ringing," and Other Songs Cowboys Sing.* Champaign, Ill.: University of Illinois Press, 1989. The best and *only* unexpurgated collection of cowboy songs, largely the repertory of one retired Arizona cowboy singer, Riley Neal, (MS. 1969). Compare: Cazden; and Kinloch; and for cowboy songs, Fife; and Lomax, J.

(Logue, Christopher.) *"Count Palmiro Vicarrion"* (pseud?). *Book of Bawdy Ballads.* Paris: Olympia Press (Maurice Kahane-Girodias), 1956. Reprinted 1961. Texts ruthlessly rewritten, with outrageously poor music: the worst collection ever. *But compare:* Brand; Cray; Hart; and Silverman.

Lomas, Harvey D. "Graffiti: Some Observations and Speculations," in: *Psychoanalytical Review* (1973) 68: 71–89. Compare: Abel; and Reisner.

Lomax, Alan. *The Folk Songs of North America.* New York: Doubleday; London: Cassell, 1960. Excellent socioanalytic and psychological headnotes, but as with all the Lomax popular collections, texts are conflated and revised, and expurgated by means of "judicious selection." See also: Kennedy; and Sandburg.

Lomax, John A. *Adventures of a Ballad Hunter.* New York: Macmillan, 1947. Colorful reminiscences.

———. *John A. Lomax MSS.* Collected at various locations in the U.S., 1900 ff. Repositoried in the Texas Archives, Barker Texas History Center, University of Texas Library, at Austin, these MSS. include a small "Inferno" section of bawdy songs (Box A/9–152 "Bawdy"). This is now even smaller than originally, as it has in part been rifled, then "misplaced," by unknown hands at some date after 1957, when all the materials were fortunately transcribed in MS., and tape-spoken for the present research by Profs. D. K. Wilgus and Austin Fife.

———, and Alan Lomax. *American Ballads and Folk Songs.* New York: Macmillan, 1934.

———. *Cowboy Songs, and Other Frontier Ballads.* Revised and enlarged by Alan Lomax. New York: Macmillan, 1938. Reprinted, with an introduction, by Alan Lomax and Joshua Berrett. New York: Macmillan, 1986. Texts heavily expurgated and conflated originally by John A. Lomax. Compare: Logsdon, for the *real* texts.

———, and Alan Lomax., *Folk Song, U.S.A.* New York: Duell, Sloan, Pearce. 1947.

———, and Alan Lomax. *Negro Folk Songs as Sung by Leadbelly* (Huddie Ledbetter). New York: Macmillan, 1936.

———, Alan Lomax, and Ruth Crawford Seeger. *Our Singing Country.* New York: Macmillan, 1941.

Lost Limericks and Bar Room Ballads. (Edited by Roy Lavender, for World Science Fiction Convention, Cincinnati, Ohio, 1949.) 69 pp., 4to, mimeographed. (Copies: Samuel Moscowitz Science Fiction Fanzine Collection, Roseville, New Jersey; G. Legman.) Valuable collection of folk-verse and obscœna, "mimeographed from stencils cut by many persons," according to the editor, who states that this is the "third and much revised edition." Note: Not to be confused with *Lusty Limericks and Bawdy Ballads,* by "Dick Harde," below.

Love-Poems and Humorous Ones: ca. 1616–1619. Edited by F. J. Furnivall. Hertford: Ballad Society (No. 11), 1874.

Lowenherz, Jack. See: *The Tenth Muse Lately Hung Up.*

Lowenstein, Wendy. *Shocking, Shocking, Shocking! The Improper Play-Rhymes of Australian Children.* Melbourne, and Prahran, Victoria: Fish and Chip Press, 1974. The first unexpurgated handling of children's rhymes in English, replacing the Opies' uncourageous work. Compare: McCosh; Turner; also Borneman, for German materials.

Lüdecke, Hugo. "Grundlagen der Skatologie," in: *Anthropophytéia* (1907) 7: 316–28. On *graffiti*.

Luka Mudishchev. (At head: Ivan Barkov.) 2e Izdanie. "Moskva: Izdatelstve TSK–KLSS 'Gospolitizdat'" (London: Institute of Economics; Coulsdon, Surrey, or "Hexton House," Herts), 1969. 80 pp. Vest-pocket pamphlet. Text in Russian. Aside from the title-page ascription to Ivan Barkov (1732–68), this bawdy Russian ballad in the style of "Eskimo Nell" is also attributed to Aleksandr Pushkin, and more probably to Pushkin's successor in Byronic poetry, Mikhail Y. Lermontov (1814–41), who "wrote a fair quantity of obscene verse," as well as a famously bitter "Farewell to (Czarist) Russia." Printed as a British spy-service legpull or exhibitionistic joke, to demonstrate their technical ability and printing *matériel*. "Luka Mudishchev" was first mentioned in Spinkler's "Gross-Russische erotische Volkdichtung," in *Anthropophytéia* (1913) 10: 353. Compare: *Gregory-Boomer-Fouff Collection.*

Lunsford, Bascom L., and Lamar Stringfield. *30 and 1 Folk Songs from the Southern Mountains.* New York: Carl Fischer, 1930.

Luquet, Georges H. "Sur la survivance des caractères du dessin enfantin dans les *graffiti* à indications sexuelles," in: *Anthropophytéia* (1905) 5: 196–202, and documentary pls. at end of volume. Important early illustrated study. Compare: Ellis; and McLean.

Lusty Limericks and Bawdy Ballads. Compiled and edited by "Dick Harde" (collective *pseud.* of Walter Breen and Robert Bashlow. New York? 1956.) 49 pp. mimeographed. (Copies: Kinsey-ISR; G. Legman.) Ballads, pp. 35–49. Note: Not to be confused with *Lost Limericks and Bar Room Ballads,* above, as seems to have been the editors' intention. The senior editor here also uses the pseudonym "J. Z. Eglinton."

Luther, Frank. *Americans and Their Songs.* New York, 1942.

Lyra Ebriosa: Being certain narrative ballads of a vulgar or popular character, and illustrative of the manners of the times. With An Appendix. (Edited by Littleton M. Wickham. Norfolk, Virginia: Gilpin Withers), 1930. 31 pp. (Unique repository copy: University of Kentucky Library.) Issued privately for members of the University of Virginia secret society "Eli Banana," and including two original songs; one of which, "The Master *Betas,*" immediately entered oral circulation in men's college fraternity beer-bust singing. The "Appendix," pp. 26–31, is Mark Twain's *"1601,"* in the old-style spelling of the edition secretly printed at the West Point Military Academy Press (by Charles Erskine Scott Wood.)

The Lyre of Lord Byron: Operative Music with Ladies of Rank and Fashion . . . Lectures on the Hairy Harp at E*** College; Using his Musical Faculties, with Tit-Bits, Opera Dancers, Actresses and other Ladies of Fashion, Rank and Folly. "Scotland: D. McVitia," (1840). 96 pp. (British Museum, Private Case, 1085.) With apocryphal ascription to Byron; compare the following, which is attributed to Pushkin:

Lyuka Mudishchev. See: *Luka Mudishchev.*

Mabbott, Thomas O. See at: Thomas Chatterton.

McAdams, Nettie F. *The Folksongs of the American Negro.* M.A. thesis, Univ. of California, 1923. (Copy: Library of Congress, Folklife Archive, with index by R. W. Gordon.)

McAtee, Waldo Lee. *Grant County, Indiana, Speech and Song.* (Vienna, Virginia:) Privately Printed, 1946. *Supplement 1: Folk Speech.* 1946. 3 pp. *Supplement 2: Folk Verse.* 1946. 6 pp. *Supplement 4: On Grant County, Indiana, Dialect.* 1954. 3 pp. 8vo. (Copies: Library of Congress, MS. Division; with McAtee MSS.) Very valuable personal memory record. All the supplements listed contain erotic songs or song-scraps, from recollection of materials learned in the 1890s.

———. *Nomina Abitera.* (Vienna, Virginia:) Privately Printed, 1945. On bawdy elements in plant- and place-names.

———. *Rural Dialect of Grant County, Indiana, in the 1890s.* Chicago, 1942.

McCarthy, Tony. *Bawdy British Folk Songs.* London: Wolfe, 1972. 60 tunes and mildly erotic texts, without source indicated, but *extremely similar* to the same songs in the Sharp and Hammond MSS. as published by Purslow, q.v.

McNary, James Leslie. *Sexual Myths and Fallacies.* New York: Van Nostrand, 1971.

McClure, John. *The Stag's Hornbook.* New York: Knopf, 1929? Milk-and-water, for *"milchiges,* modern Hiawathas."

McClurg. (Detroit, Michigan.) See: *Bibliothèque Érotique; Diary of a French Stenographer; Library L'Amour;* and *Poems, Ballads, and Parodies,* all ca. 1928–30. Much of this sub-rosa publisher's poetic output seems to have been written by himself, in the hobo folk-style.

MacColl, Ewan. *Scotland Sings.* London: Workers Music Association, 1953.

———, and Peggy Seeger. *Travellers' Songs from England and Scotland.* London: Routledge; and Knoxville: University of Tennessee Press, 1977. Unexpurgated collection of British Gypsy songs. Compare: Seeger.

McCormick, Mack. *The Unexpurgated Folk Songs of Men.* Berkeley, California: International Blues Record Club, 1964. Booklet of texts and discussion accompanying a phonograph record of same title.

McCosh, Sandra. *Children's Humor: A Joke for Every Occasion.* London: Panther/Granada, 1979. 336 pp. With 40-page introduction by G. Legman, "The Attack on the Child." Parodies, songs, and verse, pp. 143–64, the rest of the text being devoted to tales and jokes. This is the first open publication in English of the unexpurgated folklore of children, other than rhymes. See: Lowenstein.

McCulloh, Judith. "Some Child Ballads on Hillbilly Records," in: *Folklore and Society;* edited by Bruce Jackson, (Hatboro, Pa.: Folklore Associates, 1966) pp. 107–29.

———. "What Is the Tune?" in: Caroline Card, editor, *Discourse in Ethnomusicology* (Bloomington, Indiana, 1978) pp. 89–107.

McDonald, James. *A Dictionary of Obscenity, Taboo, and Euphemism.* London: Sphere, 1988.

McDowell, John H. *Children's Riddling.* Bloomington: Indiana University Press, 1979.

McGlynn, P. D. "Graffiti and Slogans: Flushing the *Id,*" in: *Journal of Popular Culture* (1972) 6: 351–56.

McGregor, Craig (*pseud.*). *Bawdy Ballads and Sexy Songs.* New York: Belmont/Tower Books, 1972. Editing of this pocket collection is attributed to the Canadian folksong specialist, Keith MacMillan, q.v.

"MacKay, Arthur." See: *Immortalia,* "Karman Society (Japan, 1959)."

Mackenzie, Richard C. *Old Favorite Songs and Hymns.* New York, 1946.

Mackenzie, W. Roy. *Ballads and Sea Songs from Nova Scotia.* Cambridge, Mass., 1928. Reprinted, Detroit, 1968. With Cox, (q.v.), the best-researched of the Harvard ballad collections inspired by George Lyman Kittredge.

———. *The Quest of the Ballad.* Princeton University Press, 1919.

McLean, William. (Contributions à l'étude de l') *Iconographie populaire de l'érotisme.* Paris: Maisonneuve and Larose, 1970. With extraordinary photographic *graffiti* illustrations. Compare: Luquet; and Ellis.

MacMillan, Keith, and Hugh Oliver. *The American Limerick Book.* New York: Beaufort Books, 1980. Compare: McGregor.

McNeil, W. K. *Ozark Mountain Humor.* Little Rock, Ark.: August House, 1986.

(McRell, or O'Rell, Eddie J.) *College Folklore: A Collection made on the campus of the University of Arkansas, Booneville, Arkansas, 1957.* MS., 93 pp., 4to. A final collection of bawdy Ozark songs, supplied to Vance Randolph by a male student. (Copies: Kinsey ISR-Library; and G. Legman.)

McWilliam, James. *College and Western Folksongs.* MS., Berkeley, California, 1961. Transcript of tape-recording of bawdy college songs. (Copy: G. Legman.)

Mada. See: *Super Stag Treasury.*

Madden Ballads. (Collection of over 25,000 printed broadside ballads, mostly 18th century, collected by Sir Frederic Madden, d. 1873, Keeper of Manuscripts in the British Museum, which also has enormous further holdings of English broadside ballads.) Now repositoried at Cambridge University Library, and published only in very minor part. See: Holloway and Black.

(Maidment, James.) *The Duchess of Portsmouth's Garland.* (Edinburgh: Maidment) 1837. xvi p. Erotic 17th-century verse, in supplement to Maidment's *Ane Pleasant Garland* (1835) q.v., also erotic.

(———.) *A North Countrie Garland.* Edinburgh, 1824. Reprinted, Edinburgh: Goldsmid, 1884, and 1891. Erotic Scottish folksongs. Compare: Charles K. Sharpe; and *Merry Muses.*

(———.) *A Packet of Pestilential Pasquils.* (Edinburgh: Wm. Paterson, 1868?) 31 pp. A private supplement of the unexpurgated specimens omitted from Maidment's *A Book of Scottish Pasquils,* (1868), itself a supplement to his *Scotish Ballads and Songs, historical and traditionary* (1868).

Makara, Stephen. "Oh! That Strawberry Roan!" (Ca. 1970?) Unpublished MS. article on cowboy composer-singer, Curley Fletcher, cited by Logsdon. (Archive of Folk Culture, Subject File. Library of Congress.)

Maledicta: The International Journal of Verbal Aggression. Editor: Dr. Reinhold Aman. Waukesha, Wisconsin, 1975–1990. 10 vols. Yearbook of verbal-sadistic and erotic linguistics and folklore, in part continuing *Kryptádia* and *Anthropophytéia.*

(Malraux, André, ed.) *La Quintessence satyrique du XXe siècle.* Composée de poèmes de quelques-uns des meilleurs esprits de ce temps qui ne figureront point dans leurs œuvres. (Paris: Malraux, 1926.) 2 vols. (Copies: Bibliothèque Nationale, *Enfer;* G. Legman.) See: Pia, *Les Livres de l'Enfer,* col. 1126–7. Compare: Poulet-Malassis.

The Mantua-Makers: A Poem. From an undated broadside, *circa* 1700. (Lexington, Kentucky?) 1949. 4 pp. (Copy: University of Kentucky Library.) Compare: *The Lay of John Haroldson,* 1862?

Marie: (Tu sortiras de ma maison!). (Paris? ca. 1945?) 6 pp. with music and amateur illustrations, litho-printed. (Copy: G. Legman.) Bawdy *Chanson de Salle de Garde,* not in most collective editions.

Marines in the Marianas. (Mariana Islands: U.S. 9th Marine Battalion, 1948.) 32 pp. mimeographed. (Copy: Kinsey-ISR.) Untitled; the title given here being added on the Kinsey Institute copy. Contents: about half songs, half private erotic storiettes.

Marquis, Don. *Ode to Hollywood.* (Los Angeles? Privately Printed.) 1929. Compare: Ficke; Guthrie; Twain; and Updike.

Martial, Marcus Valerius. (1st Century A.D.) *The Index Expurgatorius Martialis,* literally translated; comprising all the *Epigrams* hitherto omitted by English translators. London: Printed for Private Circulation (J.C. Hotten?) 1868. (Copies: British Museum, Private Case; New York Public Library: 3***). (Translated by Edward Sellon, G. A. Sala, and Frederick P. Pike, authors also of *Cythera's Hymnal,* q.v.) Later complete translations of Martial's *Epigrams* also exist. Compare: *Priapeia.*

A Martial Medley: Fact and Fiction. (Edited by Eric Partridge.) London: Scholartis Press/Eric Partridge, 1931. The editor's own article in this symposium, "From Two Angles," by Corrie Denison (*pseud.*), pp. 59–102, includes World War I soldiers' songs. Compare: Brophy.

Martilla, Luana. "Write On!—Goodbye to Female Compliance," in: *Sexual Behavior* (Nov. 1971) vol. 2: in Gadpaille, q.v. on female graffiti. Compare: Newall.

Martling, Jackie. *Raunchy Riddles.* New York: Pinnacle Books, 1984. One-line gags revamped into bawdy riddles, by a professional nightclub comedian. Compare: McCosh. Further volumes also published.

Marty, Dr. Luc. *La Chanson à l'Internat des Hôpitaux de Montpellier.* Montpellier, 1974. (Doctorat-en-Médicine thesis.) 182 pp. reproduced from typewriting. First serious study of medical students' bawdy *Chansons de Salles de Garde,* q.v. Compare: Staub; and Lenoir.

Mascheri, Nino. *I Piu' volgari canti studenteschi.* Ristampa non autorizzata de "*I Canti Goliardici.*" Milano: Edizioni Studio-sette, 1973. See: Castelli; Brivio; and *Il Libretto Rosso.*

Masterson, James R. *Tall Tales of Arkansas.* Boston: Chapman and Grimes (Printed for the Author), 1942. Courageous openly published work, giving for the first time in America in this way unexpurgated materials in prose and verse, particularly in the notes. Compare: Fauset.

Maurepas, Jean-Fr. Phélypeaux, Comte de. *Recuil dit de Maurepas: Pièces Libres, chansons, épi-grammes, et autres vers satiriques.* "Leyde, 1865" (Bruxelles, Jules Gay, 1868). 6 vols. (Copies: Bibliothèque Nationale, *Enfer;* G. Legman.) Edited anonymously by Anatole de Montaiglon. Includes all the erotic songs and poems of the great *Recueil Clairambault-Maurepas* (MS. 1715–1781: in Bibliothèque Nationale, Paris); the non-erotic pieces later published as: *Chansonnier historique du XVIIIe siècle,* edited by Émile Raunié. (Paris, 1879–84).

Meade, Guthrie T. "The Sea Crab," in: *Midwest Folklore* (1958) 8: 91–100. Historical tracing of this bawdy English folksong.

Medulla Facetiorum: complectens epigrammata jocosa et salsa de qualicunque Venere, feminis et vino. E farragine scriptorum latinorum classici, medii et recentioris vi selecta . . . per Immanuelum Sincerum, juniorem (*pseud.*) Stuttgart: Ed. Fischhaber, 1863. 93 pp. 16mo. (Copies: British Museum, Private Case; G. Legman.) See also: Kühlwein; and *Erotopægnion.*

Mejdu Druziami (Among Friends): *Smiechnyia i pikantnyia shtuki domachnich poetov Rossii*. Piervoye polnoye izdaniye. "Cargrad: Simonius magazinie, Galata" ("Constantinople": really Geneva? ca. 1880.) (Copy: Bibliothèque Nationale *Enfer;* microfilms, New York Public Library, Slavonic Division; University of California at Los Angeles, Folklore and Myth Center.) Presumably the supplement of erotic art- and folk-poetry promised by A. N. Afanasyev in the preface to his anonymous *Russkiya Zavetniya Skazki* (Russian Secret Tales; Geneva, ca. 1872), here edited by his friend and literary executor or legatee, Soldatenkov. See also *Luka.*

————. *Same,* Second Series, as: *Yumor Russkago naroda v skazkach.* "Cargrad" (Constantinople? ca. 1885.) 140 pp. (Copy: Leningrad Library.) Not seen. Cited by V. Hnatjuk (Gnatjuk) in Pavlo Tarasevskyi, *Das Geschlechtsleben des Ukrainischen Bauernvolkes,* I. xi (*Anthropophytéia: Beiwerke,* 1909, vol. 3), and presumably also edited by Soldatenkov.

"*Mélanges de Bulgarie,*" in: *Kryptádia* (1899) 6: 164–77. Sephardic/Jewish (Ladino) erotic songs and parodies, from Bulgaria, with French translation; includes bawdy macaronics, pp. 170–77, based on Biblical and Talmudic phrases. Compare: Samuel Armistead and Jos. Silverman, *Judaeo-Spanish Ballads from Bosnia,* (Philadelphia: University of Pennsylvania Press, 1974).

Memorandum. See: Goodwin.

Mencken, H. L. *The American Language.* 4th ed., New York: Knopf, 1936–61. 2 vols.

Méon, D. M. See: *Blasons.*

Meredith, John. *Australian Folk Songs.* (Tape-recording collection, repositoried in National Library, Canberra, Australia, before 1972.) Includes Meredith's extensive erotic field-collections, which remain unpublished. Compare following:

————. "Bawdy Bush Ballads," in: *Meanjin* (Melbourne, Australia, Dec. 1958) 17: 379–86, no. 75. Note: Meredith's collection of these erotic materials is listed in part by titles in Peter Kennedy, *Folksongs of Britain* (1975) Note 183, but remains unpublished in tape-recording form: see preceding item.

————, and Hugh Anderson. *Folk Songs of Australia, and the Men and Women who sang them.* Sydney: Ure Smith, 1967. Meredith's expurgated published collection. Compare the two preceding items here; also Ron Edwards; and Brad Tate.

Merling, Susanna. "Lieder aus Tirol und Voralberg," in: *Anthropophytéia* (1909) 6: 396–98. From an elderly lady who learned these erotic songs sixty years before.

Merry Drollery, or A Collection of Jovial Poems, Merry Songs Witty Drolleries, Intermix'd with Pleasant Catches. London, 1661. Revised edition, 1670. (Copy: Bodleian Library.) Reprinted, as: *Merry Drollery Compleat,* edited by J. Woodfall Ebsworth; Boston, Lincs., 1875. See further under: *Choyce Drollery,* as to "*Supplement of Reserved Songs from Merry Drollery, 1661,*" issued with that later reprint.

The Merry Muses. "1827" (London: John Camden Hotten, 1872.) Heavily music-hallized revision of Burns' *Merry Muses of Caledonia* (1800), which follows. Essentially *not* the same work.

The Merry Muses of Caledonia . . . Selected for use of the Crochallan Fencibles. "1799." (Edinburgh? Peter Hill? 1800.) *Only two copies known to survive: one *pænes* Lord Roseberry; the other recently discovered, and now owned by Prof. G. Ross Roy, University of South Carolina. Scottish erotic folksongs: compiled from letters and other documents by Robert Burns to members of the Crochallan Fencibles, a men's mock-revolutionary drinking club in Edinburgh. See also: Burns, Robert; and further: Legman, *The Horn Book* (1964) pp. 131–236.

————. Type-facsimile, edited by G. Legman. New Hyde Park, New York: University Books, 1965. With complete bibliography of all editions to date, and analysis of their contents.

————. (Edited by Duncan McNaught. Kilmarnock:) Burns Federation, 1911. — Reprinted (Philadelphia: Nathan Young, *ca.* 1930). Adds Burns' "The Court of Equity."

————. Edited by James Barke and Sydney Goodsir Smith. With . . . some authentic Burns texts (from letters, etc.) contributed by J. DeLancey Ferguson. Edinburgh: M. Macdonald (Auk Society), 1959. Reprinted, New York: Gramercy, 1959; Putnam, 1964; and London, W. H. Allen, 1965; pocket-reprint, London: Panther, 1966. Actually edited by S. G. Smith, after Barke's untimely death, and for the same reason Smith's fine introduction (already published in *Arena,* London, 1950, No. 4; and reprinted with expurgations (!) in *Hudson Review,* New York, 1954, vol. 7) was not used. The most recent "standard" edition of Burns' *Poems and Songs,* edited by James Kinsley (Oxford: Clarendon Press, 1968) takes no significant account of the *Merry Muses* poems and songs authentically written or revised by Burns, and omits most of them.

——. *Faked editions* as: *The Merry Muses* (omitting: "*of Caledonia.*") "1827." (London: John Camden Hotten, 1872, the last two digits of the real date being reversed.) Many reprints, with same false date. Note: All editions omitting the words "of Caledonia" from the title are variously faked and abridged, except that published by Charles Skilton; London: Luxor, 1967.

The Merry Musician, or A Cure for the Spleen. London, 1716. 2 vols. Late drollery collection competing with *Pills to Purge Melancholy.*

The Merry-Thought, or The Glass-Window and Bog-House Miscellany, by "Hurlo-Thrumbo." London, 1731. 4 pts., (Bodleian Library, Oxford, Harding Collection; and incomplete copies, British Museum Library, and Harvard University). Usually known as *The Bog-House Miscellany,* this is the original graffiti collection; but compare: *Priapeia.* Not to be confused with the obscœna (but not graffiti) collection, *The New Boghouse Miscellany, or A Companion for the Close-Stool* (1761), reissued with title expurgated to *The Wits' Miscellany* (1762). Compare: Read.

Mess Songs and Rhymes of the R.A.A.F., 1939–1945. "Ten only complete copies of this book have been issued, printed on paper, duplicating, and bound in paper, Sisalcraft, bearing the musical key signature of the compiler, and number 1 to 10." (Milne Bay?) New Guinea, September 1945. 76 pp., mimeographed. (Unique copy: Australian War Memorial Library, Laycock Bequest.) Royal Australian Air Force bawdy songs, and service gripes.

Metafolkloristica; An Informal Anthology of Folklorists' Humor, ed. "Franz Kinder and Boaz the Clown" (*pseud.:* Jan H. Brunvand). Salt Lake City, Utah, 1989.

"Mexico, Robert De" (Robert Bragg). See: *Songs of Sadism and Lust, etc.*

(Meyer, Gustav.) "Vierzeilen aus den Oesterreichischen Alpen," in: *Kryptádia* (1888) 4: 79–133, Erotic "*Schnadahüpfeln*" (273 four-liners) from the Austrian Alps. Compare: Blümml; Hand; and Krauss.

Mezhdu Druziami. See: *Mejdu Druziami.*

Michel, José Antonio. *Versos picarescos méxicanos.* (Picardía en verso.) México: Costa-Amic, Editor, ca. 1975. Compare: Jiménez. Note: These verses seem to be originals written by Michel, rather than orally collected folksongs.

Michelet, Jules. *La Sorcière.* Paris and Bruxelles, 1862. Translation as *The Sorceress,* Paris: Carrington, 1900? Masterpiece of style and research, to which Margaret Murray's more famous *Witch Cult in Western Europe* is heavily indebted.

Milburn, George. *The Hobo's Hornbook.* New York: Ives Washburn, 1930. Outstandingly expurgated; in "Our Lil," p. 140, one stanza consists entirely of asterisks! Compare: Irwin; and Gordon.

Miller, E. Joan Wilson. "Vance Randolph, Folklorist," in: *Mid-South Folklore* (1975) 3: 63–69. Special number for Vance Randolph.

Miller, Henry V. *Tropic of Cancer.* Preface by Anaïs Nin (Guiler), Paris, 1934. Reprinted, "México: Medvsa" (New York: Jacob Brussel and G. Legman), 1940; also New York: Grove Press, 1961, et al. Section on Miller teaching at a junior college at Dijon in 1932 gives the most convenient sample available of the French students' bawdy "*Chansons de Salle de Garde.,*" q.v.

Mills, Dorothy, and Morris Bishop. "Songs of Innocence," in: *New Yorker* (Nov. 13, 1937) pp. 32–39. On children's rhymes. See also: Howard.

Miscellanea of the Rymour Club. Edinburgh, 1906–28, 3 vols. in 4. Folk-rhymes, etc.

Mockridge, N. (*pseud.*). *The Scrawl on the Wall.* New York: Collier, 1969. *Graffiti,* once-over-lightly.

Mock Songs and Joking Poems. London: W. Birtch, 1675. (Copies: British Museum, Thomason Coll.; New York Public Libr.)

Moeser, D. R. "Erotik und Musik," in: W. Gieseler, *Kritische Stichwörter zum Musik-unterricht* (München, 1978) pp. 78–86.

Monôme. (Editor, "Jérôme Clandestin," *pseud.* No place, publisher, or date: the imprint given is a figleaf. Lyon? ca. 1935.) (Copies: Alain Kahn-Sriber, Paris; G. Legman.) Rare edition of French students' bawdy *Chansons de Salles de Garde.* The "Monôme" is the medical and art students' orgiastic serpentine parade, half-naked, on graduation, when these songs are sung in the public streets. Compare: *Gaudeamus Igitur.*

Monteiro, George. "Parodies of Scripture, Prayers, and Hymns," in: *Journal of American Folklore* (1964) 77: 45–52. Enlarging a milder note on the same subject by Ray D. Browne, also in *JAF* (1959) 72: 94. Compare: McClurg.

Montgomerie, Norah and William. *Sandy Candy, and other Scottish Nursery Rhymes.* London: Hogarth Press, 1948.

Montgomerie, William. "A Bibliography of the Scottish Ballad Manuscripts, 1730–1825," in: *Studies in Scottish Literature* (edited by Prof. G. Ross Roy, 1966 ff.) 4: 3–28, and subsequently. Important index, including the numerous Scottish folksong MSS. collections not published because of the eroticism of their contents.

Mooney, Harry J. "The *Sub Rosa* Writings of Eugene Field," in: *Papers of the Bibliographical Society of America* (1978) 72: 541–52. Based on Field MSS. in the Willard Morse Collection, Denver Public Library.

Moore, Ethel, and Chauncey O. Moore. *Ballads and Folksongs of the Southwest.* Norman: University of Oklahoma Press, 1964.

(Morgan, Harry.) *Rugby Songs.* See: *Why Was He Born,* below:

(———.) *More Rugby Songs.* London: Sphere Books, 1968. Continuation of following item, and letter-expurgated like it. In part reprinted from *Camp Fire Songs and Verse,* q.v.

(———.) *Why Was He Born So Beautiful, and Other Rugby Songs.* London: Sphere Books, 1967. Compiler's name appears only in copyright notice. Texts are letter-expurgated with asterisks ("but not otherwise"!) and in part rewritten and enlarged. Note: This work is not connected with the phonograph recording, *The Compleat Rugby Songs* (London, ca. 1977), giving wholly different texts.

Morris, Alton C. *Folksongs of Florida.* Gainesville: University of Florida Press, 1950.

Morris, Capt. Charles. *A Complete Collection of Songs.* 9th ed. London, 1788. (PC. 1289–91, with other editions.) Compare:

———. *The Festival of Anacreon. Containing a Collection of Modern Songs . . . by Capt. Morris . . . Mr. Hewerdine, etc. London, 1789.* Bawdy drinking-house songs in the taste of the period.

Morrison, Daniel H. *Songs We Love: All the Favorites from Every Land.* Chicago: Monarch Books, (1902?). Compare: Wier, also Chapple.

(Morse, A. Reynolds.) *Folk Poems and Ballads: An Anthology . . . A Collection of rare Verses and amusing Folk Songs compiled from scarce and suppressed Books as well as from verbal Sources, which modern Prudery, false Social Customs and Intolerance have separated from the public and historical Record.* With Commentary, Notes, and Sources. "Mexico City: The Cruciform Press, 1945" (Cleveland, Ohio: A. R. Morse, 1948). (Copies: British Museum, Private Case; Kinsey-ISR; A. R. Morse; G. Legman.) Texts conflated and rewritten in part by the editor. Companion-volume: *The Limerick: A Facet of Our Culture,* "1944" (1948). both volumes suppressed on publication by police action, and are very rare.

———. *Same.* Waukesha, Wisc.: Maledicta Press, 1984. With a new introduction by the compiler, here named.

Morton, James. *Lowspeak: A Dictionary of Criminal and Sexual Slang.* London: Angus and Robertson, 1989. Good vocabulary, but amateur "blitz" folk-etymologies. The strange combination of "criminal and sexual" vocabulary here is an unconscious indictment of the abnormalized sexual ethic of our culture. Compare: Goldin.

Motherwell, William. *Minstrelsy: Ancient and Modern.* Glasgow, 1827. Magnificently produced limited edition.

Motta, Marcelo Ramos, and Aleister Crowley. *The Equinox: The Official Organ of the A.∴ A.∴, The Review of Scientific Illuminism.* Vol. V, No. 4: March 1981 (old style). Nashville, Tennessee, Box 90144: Thelema Pub. Co., 1981. (Jacket title: *Sex and Religion,* by Aleister Crowley: "The Bagh-i-Muattar," etc.) Essentially a reprint of Crowley's homosexual legpull, *The Scented Garden: Bagh-i-Muatter, of Abdullah the Satirist of Shiraz* (pseud.), "Edited by Major Alain Lutiy" (pseud.); privately issued in Paris, 1911, in an edition of 100 (200?) copies, all but two of which were destroyed by British Customs service. This reprint also contains several other of Crowley's *obscœna,* in prose and verse; the entire contents riotously edited by the publisher, Motta, along with extensive italicized notes and mock book-reviews of his own. See also: Crowley.

Moyse, Arthur. See: *The Golden Convolvulus.*

Muir, Willa. *Living with Ballads.* London and New York: Oxford University Press, 1965. The best and wisest book on ballad-*style* and meaning, an education in sensitivity in listening to the hidden voices of folksong. Ends, p. 255, with a courageous plug for the main Scottish bawdy ballad of modern times, "The Ball o' Kirriemuir." Compare: Edith Fowke; Rayna Green; and Sandra McCosh.

Müller, Paul. "Schnadahüpfeln aus Franken," in: *Anthropophytéia* (1912) 9: 454–55. Erotic German four-liners. Compare: Blümml; Hand; and Krauss.

———. "Studentenlieder aus Würzburg," in: *Anthropophytéia* (1912) 9: 457–59.

———. "Zum Liede von den weiblichen Geschlechts-teilen (*Vom Streit der Jungfrauen*)," in: *Anthropophytéia* (1908) 5: 155–56, and (1909) 6: 398–99 gives as "Das schönste Nonnenlied" German versions of the vaginal bragging-song known in English as "The Whorey Crew, or Three Old Whores from Baltimore, Canada, etc." See: Schwaab.

Musarum Deliciæ, or The Muses Recreation. London, 1655. (Edited by Sir John Mennis and Dr. James Smith.) 2nd ed. 1656, reprinted London: (Pearson? 1872–73). 2 vols., including the same editors' *Wit Restor'd,* 1658, and *Wits' Recreations,* 1640, with the curious (rebuses, etc.) "*Fancies and Fantasticks.*" Important drollery anthology. See earlier reprint at: *Facetiæ.*

Les Muses en Belle Humeur, ou Chansons et autres poésies joyeuses. "Ville Franche" (Vérets, Touraine: Private press of the Duc d'Aiguillon), 1742. 260 pp. 8vo. (Copies: Bibliothèque Nationale, *Enfer;* British Museum Library, Private Case; G. Legman). Very rare work, printed in an edition limited to 12 copies, for members of the patrician secret orgy club, "Le Cosmopolite," Probably edited by J.-B. Willart de Grécourt and Paradis de Moncrif. Important not only for its erotic songs but for the *date* of publication, being the first secretly issued anthology of erotic folksong, then finally if not wholly driven underground. Note: The English work following, *The Muse in Good Humour,* 1745, is not a translation of this songbook.

———. "Ville Franche, 1742" (Paris? ca. 1745.) 184 pp. 12mo. (Copies: British Museum Library, Private Case; Bodleian, Harding Collection). A piratical reprint, made for envious non-members of the "Cosmopolite."

Les Muses en belle humeur, ou Élite de poésies libres. "Rome," 1779. 2 vols. (Copy: British Museum Library, Private Case.) Not the same as the preceding collection, though the songs are also erotic.

The Muse in Good Humour: A Collection of the best poems, comic tales, choice fables, enigmas, riddles, etc. London: 1745. Cited in George Daniel sale catalogue, (ca. 1864) no. 1157. *Not* a translation of either of the two preceding French collections.

The Musical Miscellany. London, 1729–31. 6 vols. Excellent collection of current more-or-less bawdy art- and folksongs, competing with the more famous *Pills to Purge Melancholy,* q.v.

My Bonny. (*Tune.*) (Ottawa, Ontario: Eastern Air Command Reunion, 1950.) 11 pp. mimeographed. (Copy: G. Legman.) In part a reprint of the longer similar mimeographed songbook, *North Atlantic Squadron,* q.v. See also: Getz; Starr; and Hopkins.

Nadal, Abbé Augustin. "Sur l'Origine de la Liberté qu'avoient les Soldats Romains de dire des Vers Satyriques contre ceux qui triomphoient," in his: *Histoire des Vestales* (Paris? 1725) pp. 332–86. (Copy: Ohio State University Library, former Legman Collection.) Important and little-known monograph on ancient satirical and obscene soldiers' songs. See further: Legman, *The Horn Book,* pp. 384–409; and compare: Nisard.

Nafzawi, Umar al. *The Perfumed Garden.* (MS., ca. 1500.) Anonymous English translation (from the French of Baron Regnault), (Sheffield: Smithers, 1888?) Later English translation, ca. 1980, adds the omitted final homosexual section. Arabic sex-technique manual which contains many erotic folktales interspersed. Compare: Crowley; and Motta.

Neal, Larry. "And Shine Swam On," in: Leroi Jones and Larry Neal, eds. *Black Fire: An Anthology of Afro-American Writing* (New York: Wm. Morrow, 1968) pp. 638–59. On the prototypical Negro toast, "Shine, or The *Titanic.*"

Neal, Riley. See: Logsdon.

Neale, A. *Twenty Red-Hot Parodies on present song hits.* New York: (The Author), 1921. Reproduced from typewriting. (Copy: G. Legman.) One of several such off-color parody-books advertised in the *Police Gazette, 1921,* (and earlier?) with the deathless line: "BE FUNNY . . . 50¢."

Nettel, R. *Seven Centuries of Popular Song.* London, 1956. Compare, on the music-halls, etc.: Speaight; and Shepard.

Nettleingham, F. T. *Tommy's Tunes: A Comprehensive Collection of Soldiers' Songs, Marching Melodies, Rude Rhymes, and Popular Parodies; Composed, Collected, and Arranged on Active Service with the B.E.F.* London: Macdonald, 1917. Wholly expurgated. Compare: Brophy; and Hopkins.

Neurotica (editors G. Legman and Jay Landesman). New York, 1948–51. 9 nos., of which 1–8 are reprinted as *The Compleat Neurotica.* New York: Hacker Art Books, 1957? and London: Landesman, 1984.

The New Academy of Complements . . . With an Exact Collection of the Newest and Choicest Songs à la Mode, Both Amorous and Jovial, Compiled by the most refined Wits of this Age. London: Samuel Speed, 1669. (Copy: Folger Library, Washington, D.C.) Reprinted 1671 with the same songs; but later works of similar title have entirely different contents. Note: Disguised as a drollery collection of art-songs "*à la Mode,*" this is in fact an important early anthology of folksongs, pp. 85–270. Compare *Pills to Purge Melancholy.*

New Boghouse Miscellany, 1761. See at: *Merry-Thought.*

Newall, Venetia. "The Moving Spray-Can: A Collection of some contemporary English graffiti," in: *Maledicta* (1988) 9: 39–47. Unfortunately restricted to "amusing" examples. Compare: Martilla; and Pelham-Box.

(Newbern, John, and Peggy Rodebaugh.) *The World's Dirtiest Jokes.* Edited and compiled by "Victor Dodson" (*pseud.*) Los Angeles: Medco Books (Sherbourne Press), 1969. Miscellany of prose and verse obscœna, considered "too dirty" for Newbern's Texas *Sex to Sexty* magazine series. Intended title: *The Cream of the Crap.*

Newell, William Wells. *Games and Songs of American Children.* New York, 1883; enlarged eds., 1903, and 1911.

New Frisky Songster, by "Peregrine Penis" (*pseud.*). London? 1794. Cited in George Daniel sale catalogue, 1864, no. 607. Compare: *The Frisky Songster.*

New Locker Room Humor. Revised edition. Chicago: Burd Pub. Co., 1960. Prose and verse obscœna. Compare: *Locker Room Humor.*

Nichols, Cranz. *Bawdy and Obscene Folklore.* (Austin, Texas, 1963.) 20 pp., reproduced from typewriting. (Copies: Prof. Roger Abrahams, University of Pennsylvania; G. Legman.) Paper submitted to Dr. Abrahams' folklore course, entirely composed of erotic songs and riddles.

Nicolai, Henri, See: *The Boastful Yak.*

Niemoeller, Adolph F. *Sex Ideas in Popular Songs: A Study of the strong sex innuendo in most popular song lyrics.* Girard, Kansas: Haldeman-Julius Pubs., 1946. (Big Blue Book, N–523.) 27 pp. Once-over-lightly. Compare: Oliver; and Urdang.

Niles, Abbe. "Blue Notes," in: *New Republic* (1924?) 45: 292–93. Also other very trenchant short columns and reviews by Niles in the same journal on folk songs and their expurgation.

Niles, John J. *Singing Soldiers.* New York: Scribner's, 1927. Compare: Dolph.

———, and Douglas S. Moore. *The Songs My Mother Never Taught Me.* New York: Macaulay, 1929. Reprinted, New York: Gold Label Books, 1930? Expurgated soldier songs, etc. Compare: *Songs My Mother Never Taught Me.*

Nisard, Charles. *Des Chansons populaires chez les Anciens et chez les Français: Essai historique, suivi d'une Étude sur la chanson des rues contemporaines.* Paris: Dentu, 1867. 2 vols. Magistral study. Compare: Nadal.

Normandy, Georges. *Les Chansonniers gaillards.* Paris: Michaud (1910?).

Northall, G. F. *English Folk-Rhymes: A Collection of Traditional Verses.* London: Kegan Paul, 1892. Splendid compilation. Compare: Talley.

North Atlantic Squadron. (Gander, Newfoundland: Eastern Air Command, Canadian Air Force, 1944.) 24 p. folio, mimeographed. (Copy: G. Legman.) The most important of the original American war-song collections of World War II, but compare: Getz; Hopkins; Starr; and abridged reprint as *My Bonny.*

"Nosti" (*pseud.*). *A Collection of Limericks*. With Commentaries, explanatory and critical, as well as geographical notes. Privately Printed in Switzerland (Bern?) 1944. (Copy formerly in the collection of Arpad Plesch; see *Bibliothèque "Le Lèonina,"* 1955, by Jacques Pley.) Illiterate imitation of Norman Douglas' *Some Limericks* (1928), but with interesting would-be humorous notes giving folklore materials.

"*Note allegre: Canti popolari Napolitani,*" in: *Kryptádia* (1899) 6: 97–102. Erotic Neapolitan songs. Compare: Corso; and Pitrè.

Nouveau Parnasse Satyrique. See: Poulet-Malassis.

Odum, Howard W. "Folk-Song and Folk-Poetry as found in the Secular Songs of the Southern Negroes," in: *Journal of American Folklore,* (1911), pp. 255–94 and 351–96.

———, and Guy B. Johnson. *The Negro and His Songs*. Chapel Hill, N.C.: North Carolina University Press, 1925. Reprint, Hatboro, Pa.: Folklore Associates, 1964.

———, and Guy B. Johnson. *Negro Workaday Songs*. Chapel Hill, N.C., 1926. See Also: McAdams; Perrow; Talley; and note on *Lost manuscript* at Johnson.

Ohio State University Sailing Club Song Book. (Columbus, Ohio, ca. 1962.) Mimeographed (?). No copy known except one collected on 96 or more typewritten sheets by Xenia Blom, ca. 1962, and preserved in the Indiana University Folklore Archive, the sheets being scattered in the files by song titles. This should be reconstituted again from the files, as supplied.

Ohrlin, Glenn. *The Hell-Bound Train: A Cowboy Songbook*. Urbana: University of Illinois Press, 1973.

Olajubu, Oludare. "References to Sex in Yoruba Oral Literature," in: *Journal of American Folklore* (1972) 85: 152–66.

Old American Ballads. See: *Death Rattlers*.

Oliver, Paul. *Screening the Blues*. London, 1968. Outstanding work on the American Negro "blues," with wholly unexpurgated texts of these entertainer-songs, and discussion of "The Blue Blues," pp. 164–277. Compare: Oliver's other volumes, *Blues Fell This Morning* (New York: Horizon Press, 1961), and *The Story of the Blues* (1969); also Tobiason below.

O'Lochlainn, Colm. *Irish Street Ballads*. Dublin, 1939.

———. *More Irish Street Ballads*. Dublin, Three Candles Press, 1965.

The One and Only Baker House Super-Duper Extra Crude Song Book. See: *Baker House*.

One Potato, Two Potato. See: Knapp.

Opie, Iona and Peter. *The Lore and Language of Schoolchildren*. Oxford: Clarendon Press, 1959. Thoroughly expurgated by pre-selection of materials. Compare: Lowenstein; and McCosh. See also: Winslow.

———. *The Oxford Dictionary of Nursery Rhymes*. Oxford: Clarendon Press, 1951. Outstanding work on adult rhymes taught to children in English, splendidly researched. A similar but non-alphabetical later work credited to William S. Baring-Gould reproduces "all" the same material.

Oppeln-Bronikowski, Friedrich von. *Deutsche Krieg- und Soldaten-lieder: Volk und Kuntsgesang, 1500–1900*. München, 1911. Non-erotic texts; see further: Blümml.

Ord, John. *The Bothy Songs of Aberdeen, Banff and Moray*. Paisley, Scotland: A. Gardner, 1930.

O'Rell, Eddie. See: McRell.

Orpheus, Sir Oliver, *pseud*. See: Buchan, Peter.

Orr, Cathy M., and Michael J. Preston. *Urban Folklore from Colorado: Typescript Broadsides*. Ann Arbor, Mich.: Xerox University Microfilms, 1976. (Research Abstracts, LD–69.) sm. 4to, reproduced from typewriting. Xeroxlore texts, outstanding. Compare: Dundes; and Smith, P.

———. *Same* (Volume 2:) with Louis M. Bell. *Urban Folklore from Colorado: Photocopy Cartoons*. Ann Arbor, Mich.: Xerox University Microfilms, 1976. (Research Abstracts, LD–79.) sm. 4to, reproduced from typewriting etc. Xeroxlore in pictorial form, cartoons and *graffiti*, matching vol. I.

———. "Similes from Colorado," in: *Western Folklore* (1976?)

Orwell, George (*pseud*. of Eric Blair). *Dickens, Dali, and Others: Studies in Popular Culture*. London, 1946. With a basic chapter, entitled "Rudyard Kipling, etc." on folk-poetry and its audience; also on folk-art.

Ostermann, Valentin. *Villotte Friulane: Appendice*. Udine, 1892. 47 pp. Limited to 50 copies for private circulation. Erotic Italian *vilótis,* or four-line dance songs (equivalent to the German-Austrian *Schnaderhüpfel*) from Friuli near the Austrian border of Italy. Supplement to Ostermann's earlier volumes on Friuli folklore. Note: More than half of the text of this rare "Appendix" is reprinted by Johannes Kostiál, in his review in *Anthropophytéia* (1909) 6: 469–82, giving the Italian song texts with German translation. See further: Kostiál's own Friuli supplement, in *same* (1909) 6: 389–96; also Corso; and Pitrè.

Ostwald, Hans. *Erotische Volkslieder aus Deutschland.* Berlin, 1910. Compare: Blümml; Krauss; and Schidrowitz.

The Oxford Song Book, edited by T. Wood. Oxford, 1928. 2 vols.

Oxford University. Oxford, England. ("House-books" or student albums of bawdy poetry and similar, preserved and added to in manuscript, at most of the colleges at Oxford; also at other great universities and college fraternities in Britain and America, not usually available for public inspection. Also exist in other countries: Italy—see *Gaudeamus Igitur*—and in Germany: called "*Kommers-buchen.*") See: Fox Club; and *Sweet Violets.*

Page, Martin. *Kiss Me Goodnight, Sergeant Major! The Songs and Ballads of World War II.* London: Hart-Davis, 1973. British military songs without expurgation. Compare: Henderson; and Hopkins.

Painful Poems, by "One Who Has Suffered." MS. Bournemouth, England, ca. 1955. 25 pp. Small collection, by a man, of anti-family and anti-gallant songs and verse, including parodies and dysphemizations.

Painter Collection of Graffiti. MS., New York, ca. 1940. New York subway and barroom graffiti, collected without expurgation by Dr. John Del Torto and G. Legman, including illustrations found *in situ.* (Copy: Kinsey-ISR Library.) Compare: Ellis; Luquet; McLean; and Pelham-Box.

"Palmer, Edgar," *pseud.* See: Eric Posselt.

Le Panier aux Ordures, par Armand Gouffé et autres. (London: J. C. Hotten, for Richard Monckton Milnes, ca. 1865.) 36 p. lithographic facsimile of calligraphic manuscript. (Copies: British Museum Library, Private Case, 1392–93; and M. Bottin, Librarie Niçoise, Nice, France: the former Pierre Louÿs copy.) Bawdy songs and art poems, in the French "*caveau*" or music-hall style.

———. Printed edition: *Le Panier aux Ordures, suivi de quelques chansons.* "Libreville" (Bruxelles: Jules Gay), 1866. Enlarged edition. Reprinted, "Canton: W. Field et Tching-Kong," (Bruxelles: J.-J. Gay and Mlle. Doucé, ca. 1978.)

Papers for the W.C.: A Journal for the West Central District, No. 1 (Leipzig, ca. 1876.) Cited in Wm. L. Clowes, *Bibliotheca Arcana* (1885) no. 515. Not seen. Printed on toilet paper, with articles like "Standing Cocks, A Plea for More Hydrants," etc. No copy known. Compare: Kipling.

Pâris, Gaston. See: *Gai Chansonnier Français.*

(Parke, Howard.) *Freudian Folksongs for the Up-and-Coming, or Dildoes, Dollars and Doughnuts: A Trip down Memory Lane with The Aardparke (pseud.).* MS., Los Angeles, California, 1955. 62 pp. typewritten. (Copy: G. Legman Collection.) Bawdy folksong texts and humorous scraps.

Parker, Charles. "Pop Song: The Manipulated Ritual," in: Peter Abbs, editor, *The Black Rainbow* (London: Heinemann, 1975). A *cri-du-cœur* against degenerate "rock" and "pop music vocals" replacing erotic folksong.

Parker, Shane. *Parker Folio Manuscript.* (Caption-title: "*BEWARE!* The owner of this book has V.D.") MS., London, and Colchester, Essex, 1966–71. (Copies: Dr. Shane Parker, South Australian Museum, Adelaide; G. Legman Collection.) Mainly erotic folksongs collected by Dr. Parker in Britain until 1966, with additions from Australia, 1969–71.

Parler Randolph, Mary Celestia. Manuscript collection: 10 vols. of *Folksongs,* ca. 1965, by her students, at University of Arkansas.

———. *Folk Beliefs and Superstitions from the Ozarks.* MS., 1965. 15 vols. (Copies: Univ. of Arkansas Library; UCLA, Hand Collection.)

Le Parnasse èrotique du XVe siècle: Recueil de pièces (ed.) *par J. –M. Angot.* Paris: Sansot, 1908. Compare: Schwob.

Le Parnasse libertin, ou Recueil de poésies libres. Amsterdam, 1769. Many reprints. See detail of contents in Pascal Pia, *Les Livres de l'Enfer* (1978), cols. 999–1002.

Le Parnasse (des Poètes) satyriques, ou Recueil de vers piquants et gaillards de nostre temps, tirez des oeuvres secrètes des autheurs les plus signalez. (Edited by Théophile de Viau.) Paris, 1622. Many reprints, those from 1660 onward under title *Le Parnasse satyrique du sieur Théophile;* and modern scholarly editions since 1861.

Le Parnasse Satyrique de XIXe siècle. See: Poulet-Malassis.

Partridge, Eric. *A Dictionary of Slang and Unconventional English.* London: Routledge, 1937–61. 2 vols. The main volume is mostly an abridgment of Farmer and Henley (1890–1909) omitting all the invaluable quotations.

———. *A Dictionary of Catch-Phrases.* New York: Stein and Day, 1977.

———. *Shakespeare's Bawdy: A Literary and Psychological Essay, and a Comprehensive Glossary.* London: Routledge, 1947, and reprints. Poor work, with many omissions and misapprehensions. (Compare: Langenfelt.) See also: Brophy; Irwin; and *A Martial Medley.*

Paull, Steven. (Caption-title: "*From the Collection of Steven Paull.* Collected by his Mother prior to World War II. From a handwritten MS.") Panorama City, California, 1964. 18 pp.

Peacock, Kenneth. *Songs of the Newfoundland Outports.* Ottawa: National Museum of Canada, 1965. 3 vols.

The Pearl: A Journal of Facetiæ, Voluptuous Reading. "Oxford: Printed at the University Press" (London: Edited and published by "D. Cameron," *pseud.* of W. Lazenby), 1879–80. 3 vols., and Supplements. Pornographic mazagine, including fiction, jokes, bawdy verse, limericks, etc. Various reprints to 1970. See also: *The Cremorne.*

———. Supplement: *The Pearl, Christmas Annual, 1881.* Reprint: Atlanta, Georgia: Pendulum Books, 1967. Contains several bawdy songs interspersed in the prose text.

(Peignot, Gabriel.) *Amusements philologiques, ou Variétés en tous genres.* (3rd ed., enlarged.) Par "G. P. Philomneste," (*pseud.*) Dijon: Lagier, 1842. Opening section: "Petite Poétique curieuse et amusante," pp. 1–202, on formats of bizarre poetry since antiquity. Peignot's *Le Livre des Singularités* is also a serendipitist's delight. Compare: Walsh, W.; and Rhodi.

Peirce, Waldo. *Tit-illations: An Ode.* (New Haven, Conn.: Arthur Head) 1931. 11 pp. Limited to 100 copies.

Pelham-Box, Prof. R. (*London Graffiti, 1935–1940.*) MS., made at University of London, 1940, on sheets and index-cards, now *pænes* G. Legman Archive-Collection. Wholly unexpurgated, outstanding collection. Compare: Ellis; and Painter.

Penoncelli, Abbé. *La Merdeide: Cante tre.* (Con varie altre poesie analoghe.) "In Cacherano: B. Culati" (Torino: Canfari, 1859.)

Pepys, Samuel. *Journal* (*Diary*), MS. 1660–69, edited by Henry Wheatley, London, 1893–97; and later editions with enciphered erotic passages decoded.

The Pepys Ballads, 1553–1702. Edited by Hyder E. Rollins. Cambridge, Mass.: Harvard University Press, 1929–32. 8 vols. Culled by Rollins in *A Pepysian Garland* (1922) and *The Pack of Autolycus* (1927), ballads not reprinted here.

Percy, Bishop Thomas. *Bishop Percy's Folio Manuscript: Loose and Humorous Songs.* Edited by Frederick J. Furnivall. London: Printed by and for the Editor, 1868. Note: The Percy MS. dates from about 1643. Facsimile reprint, Hatboro, Pa.? ca. 1965.

Perdue, Chuck. "I Swear to God It's the Truth If I Ever Told It," in: *Keystone Folklore Quarterly* (Spring 1969) vol. 14.

Los Perfumes de Barcelona: Canción cantable. Palma, ano 1844. 72 pp. Enlarged edition, "*con La Defense del pedo,*" Madrid, 1877. 60 pp., with cover-title: "*La Mierdépolis.*" Scatologica. Compare: Jiménez.

Perrow, E. C. "Songs and Rhymes from the South," in: *Journal of American Folklore* (1912) 25: 137–155; (1913) 26: 123–73; and (1915) 28: 129–90. Important collection of Negro folksongs. Compare: Odum; and Talley.

Peter, Dr. I. *Gasslreim und Gasslspruch in Oesterreich.* Salzburg, 1953.

La Petit Cabinet de Priape: Poésies inédites tirées d'un recueil manuscrit, fait vers le commencement du XVIIe siécle. "Neuchâtel: Imprimé par les presses de la Société des Bibliophiles Cosmopolites" (San Remo? Jules Gay), 1874. Early French manuscript drollery collection, here first published.

Petropoulos, Elias. *Rébétika Tragoudha* (*Songs from the Greek Underworld*). Athens: Digamma, 1968. Reprinted, 1975; enlarged edition, 1980. Modern Greek urban folk poetry. The compiler's imprisonment for this publication of underworld material resulted in his *Kaliardá* (Digamma, 1969), a dictionary of Greek homosexual slang. See further: Mary Koukoulès, *Loose-Tongued Greeks* (Paris, 1983).

Pia, Pascal (*pseud.* of Henri (?) Durand). *Les Livres de L'Enfer*. Paris: Coulet and Faure, 1978. 2 vols. Catalogue of Bibliothèque Nationale, *Enfer*. Compare: Kearney, *The Private Case*.

Pike, Robert E. *Tall Trees, Tough Men*. New York, 1967. See chap. 14 on bawdy lumberjack ballads, such as "The Whore's Lament," which are coyly begun but then stated to be "too scabrous to print."

Pillement, Georges. *La Poésie érotique*. Paris: L'Or du Temps/Régine Desforges, (J.-J. Pauvert), 1970. Anthology of French erotic poetry, 15th to 20th century.

Pills to Purge Melancholy. (Edited and published by Henry Playford.) 3rd ed. London, 1707–14. 4 vols. The last, largest, and most important drollery collection.

———. London, 1719–20. 6 vols. This final edition is stated to be edited by Thomas D'Urfey, who in fact merely added his own theatre songs as vols. 1 and 2. Reprint, London, "1719–20" (Pearson, 1872). 6 vols. Type-facsimile, but reset with "short" *s*'s (for *f*'s). Note: Some volumes have variant title: *Wit and Mirth, or Songs Compleat, Pleasant and Divertive*.

———. New York, 1959. 6 vols. Offset reprint of Pearson's facsimile.

The Pinder of Wakefield: A Pill fit to Purge Melancholy, in this drooping Age. London, 1632. Reprinted, ed. by E. A. Horsman, Liverpool University Press, 1956. Rogue biography, including various outspoken folksongs.

The Pink Book of Locker-Room Humor. Toronto: Peek-A-Boo Press (Rexdale, Ontario: Coles Pub. Co.) 1980. Contains off-color verse. Part of a series including also the *Brown,* and *Turquoise Book*. Compare: *Locker Room Humor*.

The Pink' Un. See: *Purple Plums*.

Pinto, Vivian de Sola, and Allen Rodway. *The Common Muse*. London: Chatto and Windus, 1957. Reprinted, New York: Philosophical Library, 1958? and London: Penguin, 1965. Excellent historical selection, very courageous for its time.

"*Piosenki Polskie* (Chansonnettes polonaises)," in: *Kryptádia* (1886) 3: 304–37; and (1888) 4: 8–75. Polish erotic songs, with French translation. See further: "*Folklore Polski*."

(Pitrè, Giuseppe.) "Spigolature Siciliana: Glanures Siciliennes: Canzoni, satire, parodie, epigrammi, moti spiritosi, e giuochi di parole," in: *Kryptádia* (1886) 3: 164–219. Sicilian folklore, with French translation; erotic supplement to the enormous published collections by Pitrè. Compare: Corso.

I Piu' volgari canti studenteschi: Ristampa non autorizzata de "I Canti Goliardici." Milano: Edizioni Studio-sette, 1973. Compare: Castelli.

Place, Francis. (*Papers.*) *Collections Relating to Manners and Morals*. MS., London, ca. 1825–30, in 6 vols. (British Museum Library, Additional MSS. 27, 825.) Vol. 1, part B: "Grossness: Songs," and especially "Mr. Hayward's Account," dated 1821, principally on bawdy street songs of the 1790s, with texts. Note: Place was the original "oral historian."

Le Plaisir des Dieux. Illustrations de Raymond Lep. Paris, 1946. French students' erotic "*Chansons de Salles de Garde*."

Le Plat du Carnaval. See: Simon Caron.

Playford, Henry. See: *Apollo's Banquet;* and *Pills to Purge Melancholy,* 1699–1720.

Ane Pleasant Garland of Sweet-Scented Flowers. (Edinburgh: Edited and published by James Maidment), 1835. Limited to 25 copies. 31 pp. Erotic Scottish verse and folksongs from old MSS.—now lost. See: Maidment.

"Pococampo, Pedro," *pseud.* See: Walter Klinefelter.

Poemata, auctore Oxon. nuper alumno. Londini: C. Bathurst, 1769. 68 pp. (Copy: Yale, *Zeta* Collection.)

Poems, Ballads and Parodies: A Volume of Collected Verse Hitherto Unpublished. Published for Distribution Among Members only and not for Sale by Benardin Society. "Benares-Paris, 1923" (Detroit, Mich.: McClurg, ca. 1928). 60 pp. (Copy: Brown University Library, Harris Poetry Collection.)

Poems Lewd and Lusty. New York: Hart Pub. Co., 1976. Reprint, New York: A. and W. Visual Library, 1981. Presumably edited by Harold H. Hart, q.v.

Poems of Passion. (Havana, Cuba, ca. 1933) Not seen. Perhaps excerpts from *Immortalia,* then recently reprinted in U.S.

Poésies Sotadiques, G. L. "La Muse du Lutrin et de l'Art poétique, (1960). L'an soixante, a dicté ce recueil hystérique." Paris (1960). 18 pp. Ltd. to 9 copies only. Note: The initials G. L. here do *not* refer to the present editor.

Poetica Erotica. See: Thomas R. Smith.

The Point of View. "London: Hope, Waite and Long; International Press" (Boston?) 1905. Limited edition. (Copies: British Museum Library; Brown University Library, Harris Collection; G. Legman.) Edited anonymously and probably in part written by James Clarence Harvey.

Pope, Alexander. *Peri Bathos, or The Art of Sinking in Poetry.* London: Curll? 1727.

Posselt, Erich. *Give Out! Songs of, by and for the Men in Service.* New York: Arrowhead Publishers, 1943. Reprinted, New York: Femack Co., 1944. Expurgated texts. Revised as:

———. *G.I. Songs,* edited by "Edgar Palmer" (*pseud.*) New York: Sheridan House, 1944.

Poulaille, Henri. *La Fleur des chansons d'amour du XVIème siècle.* Paris: Grasset, 1943. "Chansons libres," pp. 265–350. Compare: Schwob.

(Poulet-Malassis, Auguste.) *Le Parnasse Satyrique du XIXe Siècle: Recueil de vers piquants et gaillards.* "Rome: l'enseigne des Sept Péchés Capitaux." (Bruxelles: Poulet-Malassis and Jules Gay, 1863/4.) 2 vols. Reprinted, "Oxford" (Bruxelles: Vital-Puissant), 1878; also Bruxelles, 1881, in 3 vols. including the following supplement:

———. *Same, Supplement,* as *Le Nouveau Parnasse Satyrique du XIXe siécle.* "Eleutheropolis: Aux devantures des libraries; Ailleurs, dans leurs arrières-boutiques" (Bruxelles: Poulet-Malassis and Jules Gay), 1866. Reprinted, Bruxelles, 1881 with the *Parnasse,* as vol. 3. Important collection of "unpublishable" erotic poetry and songs by all the main 19th-century French poets. For 20th century supplement, see: Malraux.

Pound, Louise. *American Ballads and Songs.* New York: Scribner's, 1922; reprinted 1972.

Preston, Dennis R. "Ritin' Fowklower Daun 'Rong: Folklorists' Failures in Phonology," in *Journal of American Folklore* (1982) 95: 304–26.

Preston, Michael J. See: Cathy M. Orr; and Carpenter.

Priapeia. Satirical and erotic collection of 85 Latin verse *graffiti,* similar to Martial's *Epigrams;* presumably edited by Virgil or Ovid, at Rome or Naples, ca. 40 B.C. First printed in incunabula editions of Virgil, as an "Appendix Vergiliana"; scholarly separate editions, 17th century.

———. English translation, in verse and prose, by "Outidanos" and "Neaniskos" (Sir Richard Burton and L. C. Smithers), "Cosmopoli: Erotica Biblion Society" (Sheffield: Smithers), 1888, and 1890; and other English and German translations since.

The Private Case: British Museum Library. An Annotated Bibliography of the Private Case Erotica Collection. Compiled by Patrick J. Kearney, with introduction by G. Legman. London: Jay Landesman, 1981. Ltd. ed.

A Private Interview between Young William and Sweet Lucy: A Poem . . . designed as a voluptuous Interpretation of Love's Young Dream. (London? ca. 1890.) 19 pp., remounted. (Unique copy: British Museum Library Private Case, 1495.)

Purple Plums Picked from the "Pink ' Un." A carefully Culled Collection of Clippings from the famous London weekly, the *Sporting Times.* Privately Printed. (London: The Sporting Times, 1931?) Mildly off-color limericks, verse, etc., selected from issues of the *"Pink ' Un,"* the British pink *Police Gazette* of the period, from 1914 to 1924.

Purslow, Frank. *Marrow Bones!* English Folk Songs from the Hammond and Gardiner MSS. London: English Folk Dance and Song Society, 1965. From unpublished collections made in England, 1905–09, by Henry and Robert Hammond, and Dr. George Gardiner, with the music. Valuable series of texts and tunes, without expurgation, including those listed below. (See also: McCarthy, Tony.)

———. *The Constant Lovers.* More English Folk Songs from MSS. London: E.F.D.S. Pubs., 1972, as above.

———. *The Foggy Dew.* More English Folk Songs from MSS. London: E.F.D.S. Pubs., 1974.

————. *The Wanton Seed.* More English Folk Songs from MSS. London: E.F.D.S. Pubs., 1968.

Pushkin, Alexander. *Secret Journal, 1835–37.* Milwaukee, Wisconsin, 1987. First translation of this incredible document.

Putnam, H. Phelps. "Romeo and Juliet," in: *Neurotica* (New York, 1949) No. 5: p. 22. Free translation from Ronsard. Printed in Putnam's *Collected Poems,* ed. Charles Walker (New York: Farrar, Straus, 1971) pp. 142–43, as "Sonnets: To Some Sexual Organs," but from an inferior early draft. Compare: Bishop; Dylan Thomas; Updike.

Queri, Georg. *Bauern-erotik und Bauernfehme in Oberbayern.* München: R. Piper, 1911. Reprinted, 1969. Bavarian erotic folk-verse and songs.

————. *Kraftbayrisch: Ein Wörterbuch* der erotischen und skatologischen Redensarten; mit Belegen aus dem Volkslied und dem Volkswitz. München: R. Piper, 1912. Facsimile reprint, 1970. Dictionary of German erotic dialect, with folksongs and jokes.

La Quintessence Satyrique du XXe siécle. See: André Malraux.

Rabelais, François. *Gargantua and Pantagruel.* Lyon, 1533–52. 5 "Books." Many reprints and translations, especially that by Urquhart and Le Motteux, 1650–96, in English. See: Mikhail Bahktin, *Rabelais and His World,* translated from the Russian.

Rainey, Leo. *Songs of the Ozark Folk.* 2nd ed. Branson, Mo.: Ozark Mountaineer, 1976.

Rakish Rhymer, (The), or Fancy Man's Own Songster and Reciter. (New York: "Shang" Andrews? ca. 1864). (Cupid's Own Library, No. 10.) No copy known. Reprint, "Lutetia" (Paris: Charles Carrington): Privately Printed for Members of the Sport's Club, in the Year of the World-War, 1917. (Copies: Brown University Library, Harris Collection; G. Legman.) Erotic songs and parodies mostly of music-hall type, dating from and concerning the Civil War in America.

The Rambler's Flash Songster: Nothing but Out-and-Outers, adapted for Gentlemen only, and now singing at Offleys, Cider Cellars, Coal Hole, etc. (London: Wm. West, ca. 1865.) 47 pp. 24to. (Copy: British Museum Library, Private Case, call-mark 31.g.20/1. Bound with three other erotic music-hall songsters of the same publisher and date: *The Cuckold's Nest,* q.v.; *The Cockchafer;* and *The Flash Chaunter: A Slashing, Dashing, Friskey and Delicious Collection of Gentlemen's Songs.* See on these: *The Cuckold's Nest;* and note unparalleled collection of 50 further such songsters in the British Museum Library, *not* in Private Case, call-mark C.116–a.6–55.

Ramsay, Allan. *The Tea-Table Miscellany: A Collection of Choice Songs, Scots and English.* Edinburgh, and London, 1724–40, 4 vols.; Glasgow, 1768, reprinted in 1 vol. Glasgow: John Crum, 1871; Edinburgh, 1876, 2 vols. Folk texts expurgated and rewritten. See, for the tunes: Thomson.

Randiana, or Excitable Tales: Being the Experiences of an erotic Philosopher. "New York" (London: Edward Avery?) 1884. Reprinted, (New York, ca. 1932). In the text the author is referred to less guardedly as a "cunt Philosopher." Bawdy songs throughout, rewritten in music-hall style.

Randolph, Vance. *Hot Springs and Hell.* Hatboro, Pa.: Folklore Associates, 1965. First American annotated jestbook.

————. "The Names of Ozark Fiddle Tunes," in: *Midwest Folklore* (1954) 4: 81–86. See: section D, here, "Ribaldry at Ozark Dances," preface—editor's note.

————. *Ozark Folklore: A Bibliography.* Bloomington: Indiana University Folklore Institute, 1972–87. 2 vols. Completed posthumously.

————. *Ozark Folksongs,* edited by Floyd C. Shoemaker. Columbia: Historical Society of Missouri, 1946–50. 4 vols. Reprinted, 1980, with introduction by W. K. McNeil. Note: In the original editing, a large proportion of the erotic songs were expurgated of certain stanzas, or else wholly omitted. For these see: *Roll Me in Your Arms,* as below.

————. *Same.* Edited and abridged by Norm Cohen. Urbana: University of Illinois Press, 1982. Remarkably edited, adding much new annotational material, especially as to recordings.

————. *Ozark Mountain Folks.* New York: Vanguard Press, 1932.

————. *Ozark Superstitions.* New York: Columbia University Press, 1947. Reprinted as: *Ozark Magic Folklore.* Dover, 1964. Compare: Hand.

————. *Pissing in the Snow, and Other Ozark Folktales.* Urbana: University of Illinois Press, 1976. Edited by Frank Hoffmann, with introduction by Rayna Green. Unexpurgated tales omitted from all Randolph's earlier published collections.

————. *Roll Me in Your Arms,* and *Blow the Candle Out: "Unprintable" Ozark Folksongs and Folklore, Collected by Vance Randolph,* edited by G. Legman. Fayetteville, Ark.: University of Arkansas Press, 1992. 2 vols. The present work. See: *"Unprintable."*

————. "A Survival of Phallic Superstition in Kansas," in: *Psychoanalytic Review* (1928) 15: 242–45.

————. *"Unprintable" Songs* (and *Folklore*) *from the Ozarks.* MS., Eureka Springs, Ark., 1954–57. See: *Roll Me in Your Arms.*

————. "Verbal Modesty in the Ozarks," in: *Dialect Notes* (1928) 6: 57–64. Reprinted in: Miller Williams, editor: *Ozark, Ozark: A Hillside Reader* (Columbia: University of Missouri Press, 1981) pp. 33–40.

————. *We Always Lie to Strangers.* New York: Columbia University Press, 1951.

————, and May Kennedy McCord. "Autograph Albums in the Ozarks," in: *Journal of American Folklore* (1948) 61: 182–93. See: Godsey.

————, and Ruth Ann Musick. "Children's Rhymes from Missouri," in: *Journal of American Folklore* (1950) 63: 425–37.

————, and George P. Wilson. *Down in the Holler: A Gallery of Ozark Folk Speech.* Norman: University of Oklahoma Press, 1953.

————, and Isabel Spradley. "Ozark Mountain Riddles," in: *Journal of American Folklore* (1934) 47: 81–89.

————, and Mary Celestia Parler. "Riddles from Arkansas," in: *Journal of American Folklore* (1954) 67: 253–59.

————, and Archer Taylor. "Riddles in the Ozarks," in: *Southern Folklore Quarterly* (1944) 8: 1–10. Expurgated at the demand of Prof. Taylor.

Raskin, Victor. *Chastushki.* MS., London? 1976. (Copy: Prof. V. Raskin, Lafayette, Ind.) Collection of modern Russian erotic and satirical folk-quatrains, one sample appearing in English translation in G. Legman, *The New Limerick* (*More Limericks*), 1977, p. xxiv. Being prepared for publication in *Maledicta: The International Journal of Verbal Aggression.* This has not yet appeared. Compare: Kabronsky; Spinkler; Stern-Szana; and *"Folklore de l'Ukraine,"* in *Kryptádia* (1898) vol. 5, presumably collected by Th. Volkov.

Rasmussen, I. *Den erotiske gådebog.* Kobenhavn, 1966. Compare: Klintberg; and *Skolan.*

The Raunchy Reader. "Fort Worth, Texas: SRI Publishing Co." (Arlington, Texas: John Newbern Co.), 1965. Off-color limericks and verse from the same publisher's humor magazine series, *Sex to Sexty,* q.v.

Ravenscroft, Thomas. *Pammelia* (1609); *Deuteromelia* (1609); and *Melismata* (1611). Facsimile reprint, edited by MacEdward Leach. Philadelphia: American Folklore Society, 1961. (Bibliographical Series, vol. 12.) Important early folksong and lyric collection, including rounds and catches, with the traditional music. Compare: Cutts.

Rawlinson, Thomas. *Poetic MSS.* Collection of English-language historical materials made by Thomas Rawlinson, d. 1725; repositoried in Bodleian Library, Oxford. Compare: Pepys; and Place.

Read, Allen Walker. "*Graffiti* as a Field of Folklore," in: *Maledicta* (1978) 2: 15–31. Compare:

————. *Lexical Evidence from Folk Epigraphy in western North America: A Glossarial study of the Low Element in the English Vocabulary.* Paris: Privately Printed, 1935. 84 pp. Limited to 75 copies. Introduction reprinted as "The Nature of Obscenity," in *Neurotica* (New York, 1949) No. 5: 23–30.

————. *Same* as: *Classic American Graffiti.* Waukesha, Wisc.: Maledicta Press, 1977. 89 pp., including the original reviews.

————. "An Obscenity Symbol," in: *American Speech* (1934) XI. 264–78. *Tour de force* on word "fuck," not using it a single time.

————. "Folk Criticism of Religiosity in the Graffiti of New York City," in: *Maledicta* (1990) X. 15–30.

Records of the Beggar's Benison. See: *Beggar's Benison.*

Recueil, dit de Maurepas. See: Maurepas.

Recueil de Vaudevilles gaillards. MS., 18th century. (In collection of M. Bottin, Librairie Niçoise, Nice,

France, 1959.) Valuable MS. collection of words and *music* to a large number of erotic songs of the period, importantly supplementing strictly textual contemporary works like *Les Muses en belle humeur,* q.v. Note: This *Recueil* is mentioned briefly in the Gay-Lemonnyer *Bibliographie,* 3: 971. Compare: *Anthologie de Cantiques.*

Reeves, James. *The Everlasting Circle: English Traditional Verse from the manuscripts of S. Baring-Gould, H. E. D. Hammond, and George B. Gardiner.* London: Heinemann, 1960. Omits the music collected with these formerly expurgated songs (note misleading "Verse" in title), later given by Purslow, q.v., with further texts. Important review of Reeves' work by A. L. Lloyd and Patrick Shuldham-Shaw, in: *Journal of the English Folk Dance and Song Society* (1958) p. 152, discussing the deficiencies of this approach, as to "The Foggy Dew."

———. *The Idiom of the People.* London: Heinemann, 1958. Song-texts only, without the music collected with the songs, from the MS. collection of Cecil Sharp, q.v. Pioneering, for its period, in Reeves' preface discussing the "lingua franca" of folksong. Compare: Pinto and Rodway.

Reeves, Nancy. *College Songs.* MS., Bloomington, Indiana, 1957. 55 or more items, typewritten. Includes students' bawdy songs. This MS. is repositoried in the Indiana University Folklore Archive, but divided up under the separate songs.

Reiskel, Karl. "Scatologische Inschriften," in: *Anthropophytéia* (1906) 3: 244–46. On graffiti.

———. "Schnadahüpfeln und Graseltänze," in: *Anthropophytéia* (1905) 2: 117–21. See also: Krauss and Reiskel.

———. "Spanisch Romanzen," in: *Anthropophytéia* (1905) 2: 122–24. German bawdy verses similar to limericks in their use of (Spanish!) geographical rhymes. Compare: "A Trip around the World" (by John Coulthard), in: Legman, *The New Limerick* (*More Limericks*), 1977, pp. 658–92.

Reisner, Robert. *Graffiti: Two Thousand Years of Wall Writing.* Chicago: Henry Regnery; and New York: Cowles Book Co., 1971. Expurgatory selection of "amusing" examples.

———. *Same (abridged).* New York: Parallax, 1967. 64 pp.

———, and L. Wechsler. *Encyclopedia of Graffiti.* New York: Macmillan, 1974. As the preceding. Compare: Newall.

Reno Wrecks. See: *The "Wrecks."*

Reuss, Richard A. *An Annotated Field Collection of Songs from the American college student oral tradition.* (Bloomington, Indiana: The Author, 1966.) 355 pp. Lithoprinted from typewriting. M.A, thesis, Indiana University, 1965. (Copies: Indiana University Folklore Archive; G. Legman.) Outstanding; the only unexpurgated published collection of the real folksongs of college students, both men and women. Compare: Goldstone.

Reymond, Carlos. *Douze Chansons de Route.* Paris: Typographie Fr. Bernouard, 1924. 58 pp. Limited to 186 copies. (Copy: Alain Kahn-Sriber, Paris.) Bawdy songs of the type of the *Chansons de Salles de Garde,* q.v. The first such signed and openly printed collection, though in a strictly limited edition.

Reynolds, Reginald. *Cleanliness and Godliness.* London: Allen and Unwin, 1943. With materials on graffiti.

Rhodi, Ibykos de (*pseud.?*). *The Imitation of Sappho.* "Bruxelles" (Translated from the French by Lupton Wilkinson. New York: "Guy D'Isère"/Joseph Gabors, for David Moss, 1930.) 63 pp. Translator or publisher given as "J. Sumner Radclyffe." Translation of *Les Tendres Epigrammes, de Cydno la Lesbienne* (Paris: Sansot, 1911), itself presumably translated from the Greek, in imitation of Pierre Louÿs' immortal literary Lesbian mystification, *Les Chansons de Bilitis;* but "Cydno" attributed to Nathalie Clifford Barney, and/or Renée Vivien ("Pauline Tarn"). The translator, L. Wilkinson (or Wylkinson), as "Seely Wilcox," has also privately issued erotic poems and parodies *in English* as: *Les Oraisons et Chansons de Marianne de Bon Coeur,* and *La Vierge Montagne,* about 1935. (MS. copies, Dr. C. Scheiner, Brooklyn, N.Y.)

———. *Same,* as: *The Golden Bed of Kydno the Lesbian.* (This is a different translation, issued as a British private pressbook about 1930.) For the *Calligrammes*-type typography of Gabors' New York edition, compare: Peignot.

The Rhyme of All Flesh. "Herein is presented for the reader's instruction and spiritual guidance a compilation of limericks, ancient, middle-aged and new, composed by the greatest poets as well as the humblest versifiers of English and American literature . . ." (Paris? ca. 1935.) viii, 69 pp.

8vo. Noted p. ii, as "First Edition." Anonymous continuation of Norman Douglas' *Some Limericks* (Florence, Italy, 1928), with witty mock-academic notes in his style. Dated by terminal reference to Thorne Smith's *Turnabout* transvestitist bagatelle, and Somerset Maugham's *Rain* (1932). Rare private publication by an American college professor abroad. (Copy: G. Legman.) Compare: Allen Walker Read, *Lexical Evidence* (Paris, 1935); also "Nosti," published in (Bern?) Switzerland, 1944.

———. "First revised edition." (U.S.A.? ca. 1948.) 75 pp. Facsimile reprint, adding a libel disclaimer, a final dating reference to the *Kinsey Report* of 1948, and an *"Ave atque Vale"* envoi signed "Don Bonmal." See also note at: *The Way of All Flesh* (1903) by Samuel Butler. (Copies: Dr. Clifford Scheiner, Brooklyn, N.Y.; Dr. Arthur Deex, Los Altos, Calif.) Author also apparently known as "Eric E. St. Aye Scott" (Davis?)

Richter, L. *"Mein Liebchen hat ein Etwas"*: *Der erotische Aspekt in den deutschen Volkslied-Sammlungen*. Leipzig, 1968. Compare: Röhrich.

Rickaby, Franz. *Ballads and Songs of the Shanty-Boy*. Cambridge: Harvard University Press, 1926.

Riddle, Almeda. *A Singer and her Songs: Almeda Riddle's Book of Ballads*. Edited by Roger D. Abrahams. Baton Rouge: Louisiana State University Press, 1970.

Rimbault, Edward F. *Nursery Rhymes, with Their Tunes*. London, (ca. 1860).

Ritchie, J. T. R. *The Singing Street*. Edinburgh, 1964. See also: MacColl.

Ritson, Joseph. *Pieces of Ancient Popular Poetry, from authentic manuscripts and old printed copies*. London, 1791. Reprinted, 1833. Compare: Fry.

Roberts, Roderick J. *Negro Folklore in a Southwestern "Industrial School."* (Bloomington, Indiana? 1964.) 200 pp. Reproduced from typewriting. M.A. thesis, Indiana University, 1963. An outstanding collection of Negro folkbrags, "toasts," and tales, from a reformatory for teen-agers.

Robinson, Capt. John. "Songs of the Chantey Man," in: *The Bellman* (Minneapolis, 14 July to 4 August 1917). Hugill observes that Robinson is the only person who "had a go" at titivating up for respectable publication the notably bawdy sea-chanteys.

Rochester, John Wilmot, Earl of. *Poems on Several Occasions*. "Antwerp" (London), 1680. Reprinted several times, some old editions including *The Cabinet of Venus,* an erotic miscellany. (Copies: British Museum Library, formerly in Private Case; Bodleian Library; Princeton University Library; and Huntington Library, San Marino, California.)

———. *Same: facsimile reprint* of 1680 edition. Princeton University Press, 1950. 12mo, printed on paper watermarked "Private Papers of Thomas Jefferson." The opening gun of the literary "New Freedom" in America. Edited by Prof. James Thorpe, who claims it was all written by someone other than Rochester, such as Capt. Radcliffe, the catch-composer Fishbourne, and so forth, thus leaving the purpose of this reprint somewhat obscure. Actually the bawdiest of the drollery collections, with verse by other hands.

Rochester Miscellany. MS., England, ca. 1680. (Copy: Harvard University, Houghton Library, MS. *Eng.* 636F.) Collection of erotic poetry by the Earl of Rochester (see preceding item) and others. Note: Other valuable Rochester MSS., including his famous bawdy play, *Sodom, or The Quintessence of Debauchery,* are in Princeton University Library, waiting for the definitive editor.

Röhrich, Lutz. *Adam und Eva: Das erste Menschenpaar in Volkskunst und Volksdichtung*. Stuttgart, 1968.

———. "Erotik/Sexualität," in: *Enzyklopädie des Märchens*, ed. K. Ranke (Berlin, 1982) 4: 234–78. Important conspectus and chronological bibliography on erotic elements in modern folklore and folksong. Note: that No. 101 refers to *unpublished* erotic folksongs collected in the Deutsche Volkslied Archive, at Freiburg.

———. "Liebesmetaphorik im Volkslied," in: *Folklore International: Wayland Hand Festschrift*, ed. Bruce Jackson (Hatboro, Pa.: Folklore Associates, 1967), pp. 187–200. See also: Wehse, "Erotic Metaphor."

Rolland, Eugene. See: *Gai Chansonnier,* and "Folklore de la France."

Rolland, Fred. "Street Songs of Children," in *New Masses* (New York, May 10, 1938). Expurgated but timely. Compare: Lowenstein; Mills; and McCosh.

Rollett, Hermann, et al. "Erotische und skatologische Volkslieder," in *Anthropophytéia* (1908) 5: 151–6. Erotic *Schnadehüpfel* and other songs.

Roll Me in Your Arms. See: Randolph and Legman.

Roll Me Over. See: *Songs of Roving and Raking*.

Ronsard, Pierre de. *Sonnets*. 1565; and modern scholarly editions. See: Putnam.

Rösch, Gisela. *Das deutsche Kiltlied*. Tübingen, 1957. Thesis; compare title to Sir Walter Scott's adjective "high-kilted," as to erotic Scottish folksongs.

———. "Kiltlied und Tagelied," in: R. W. Brednich and Lutz Röhrich, eds., *Handbuch des Volksliedes* (München, 1973) pp. 483–550.

Rosenberg, Bruce A. *The Folksongs of Virginia: A Checklist of the WPA Holdings, Alderman Library, University of Virginia*. Charlottesville, Virginia: University of Virginia Press, 1969.

Roth, Klaus. *Ehebruch-schwänke in Liedform: eine Untersuchung zur . . . Schwankballade*. München: Fink Verlag/Motive, 1977. 500 pp. Study of the humorous German and English "Child" ballads and tales concerning adultery.

Rowdy Rhymes. (Edited by Peter Beilenson.) Mount Vernon, New York: Peter Pauper Press, 1952. 62 pp. Reprinted by the same publisher-editor as: *Rowdy Rhymes and Bibulous Ballads,* "gathered from many gay minstrels"; Peter Pauper Press (1960). Expurgated semi-erotica for the gifte-book trade. Beilenson's treatment of "The Blue Velvet Band" is an object-lesson in folklore faking.

Roxburghe Ballads, A Book of. Edited by John Payne Collier. London: Longman, 1847. 340 pp. Excellent selection, not identical with Ebsworth's complete edition, following:

The Roxburghe Ballads, edited by William Chappell and J. Woodfall Ebsworth. Hertford and London: Ballad Society, 1879–99. 9 vols. Reprinted, New York: AMS (1968?) 8 vols. Compare: *Bagford Ballads; Pepys Ballads;* also Holloway.

———. (Selections:) *The Roxburghe Ballads,* edited by Charles Hindley. London, 1873–74. 2 vols. Disloyally undertaken after the complete Chappell-Ebsworth edition (above) had already announced publication. The most valuable item here is the anonymous article (by John Payne Collier) reprinted from his earlier edition of 1847, originally in: *The Athenæum* (August 23 and 30, 1845), ending with the only available discussion of the old "medleys," on which see further: Wardroper.

(Roy, Bernard.) *Cahier de Chansons de Jean Lapipe . . . et de Jean-Louis Postollec* (*pseud.;* Paris? *1939*. 40 folded double-sheet broadsides, with hand-colored illustrations and music. Limited to 100 sets. (Copies: Alain Kahn-Sriber, Paris; G. Legman.) Noted as "*Seconde édition,* réunissant en un seul volume, les deux cahiers précédemment publiés." Erotic sea songs, divided into "Chansons: Côté Hommes" for the 19 plainly bawdy songs. Compare: Hayet.

——— "Same," as: *Cahier de Chansons de Jean-Louis Postollec . . . et de Jean Lapipe* (*pseuds.;* Paris: Guy LePrat, ca. 1952). Note the reversal of the order of the pseudonyms in this partial reprint. Gives the editor-illustrator's real name on a pasted slip, but reprints only 24 of the songs, three being slipped from the Ladies' side over to the Gents', to help disguise the omission of all the bawdier songs.

Rudeck, Wilhelm. *Geschichte der öffentlichen Sittlichkeit in Deutschland*. Jena, 1897. Pages 96 ff. on erotic folksongs; on which a few sensible words are also said in Dr. Albert Moll's *The Sexual Life of the Child* (English translation, London, 1912) pp. 262–63.

Rugby Jokes. See: John A. Yates.

Rugby Songs, Why Was He Born So Beautiful and Other, (1967). See: Harry Morgan.

Rugby Songs. (Collected by Peg and Steve Chagnon; Philadelphia, 1980.) 13 pp., mimeographed, with MS. additions, pp. 12–13, by Martha Cornog. (Copy: G. Legman.) Mostly British bawdy songs, including several on homosexuality—very rare in original American songs—here seen in transmission to America, *via* rugby teams and clubs; as also in the following:

Rugger Hugger presents: Volume I. A Collection of the most Celebrated Bawdy Singing Verse, compiled full and by Persons of Quality, with intentions of Fitting Almost All Humors. (Denver, Colorado: Rugger Hugger, Inc., 1976.) 75 pp., offset from typewriting. No more published. (Copies: Jackie Martling, East Norwich, New York; G. Legman.) Cover-title: *Father Rugby Reveals*. Group-edited, as stated. Despite the American provenance of this booklet, it is largely composed of current bawdy British rugby songs.

Rühmkorf, Peter. *Über das Volksvermögen: Exkurse in den literarischen Untergrund*. Rheinbek-bei-Hamburg, 1974. Interesting study posing folk- vs. art-erotica.

Rymour Club, Miscellanea of the. Edinburgh, 1906–28. 4 vols.

Sagarin, Edward. *The Anatomy of Dirty Words.* Secaucus, N.J.: Lyle Stuart, 1966? Reprint, New York: Paperback Library, 1969.

Sailing Ship Shanties. See: Hugill.

(Sailland, Maurice Edmond, *pseud.* "Curnonsky") and J. Wladimir Bienstock. *Le Wagon des Fumeurs: Petites Histoires de tous et de personne.* Paris: G. Crès, 1925. Limited to 230 copies containing extra chapter, "Le Fourgon," pp. 335–50. (Copy: Ohio State University: Legman Jestbook Collection.) Bawdy jokes and verse; one of a series of 5 similar volumes.

Sala, George A. See: *Harlequin Prince Cherrytop;* Martial; *Cythera's Hymnal;* and *The Sods' Opera.*

La Salade Mythologique. Collection Mosaïque (Geneva: Sack, 1960). (Copy: A. Kahn-Sriber, Paris.) "Chansons de Salles de Garde" of French students; also obscœna, one punning fabulously on names.

Sandburg, Carl. *The American Songbag.* New York: Harcourt, 1927. Reprint: New York: B.M.I., 1950. Popular collection, on style of Lomax's; wholly expurgated folksong exploitation. Compare: *Immortalia,* intended as a bawdy supplement or reply to this work.

———. *New American Songbag.* New York: Broadcast Music, Inc., 1950.

———. *The People, Yes.* New York: Harcourt, 1936.

Sanders, Daniel. *Neugriechische Volks- und Freiheitslieder.* Leipzig, 1842. First publication of modern Greek erotic folksongs. Compare: Koukloulès; and Lelegos.

Santa-Cruz, Melchior de. *La Floresta Spagnola.* (1574?) French translation, also titled: *La Floresta Spagnola, ou Le Plaisant Bocage,* contenant plusieurs comptes, gosseries, brocards, cassades, and graves sentences de personnes de tous estats. Lyon, 1600. Valuable source on word-play of all kinds. Bk. 3, chap. 2, on insult in song-medleys. Compare: Belando; Peignot; and Tabourot; also *Roxburghe* (1873–74); and Wardroper.

Scarborough, Dorothy. *On the Trail of Negro Folk-Songs.* Cambridge, Mass., 1925. Reprint, Hatboro, Pa.: Folklore Associates, 1963.

———. *A Song Catcher in Southern Mountains: American Folk Songs of British Ancestry.* New York: Columbia University Press, 1937. Compare: Sharp.

(Schidrowitz, Leo.) *Der Lasterhafte Herr Biedermeyer: "Wollüstige Tändeleyen, unziemliche Reimereyen."* Wien (ca. 1930). Collection of "Frau Wirtin" quatrains. See: *Wirtshaus.*

———. *Das schamlose Volkslied: Eine Sammlung erotischer Volkslieder.* Wien: Privatdruck, 1921. Reprinted (1925?) (Copy: G. Legman.). Compare: Blümml; Ostwald; and especially Krauss; also the remarkable *Bilder-Lexikon der Erotik* (1928–31) which was edited by Schidrowitz.

Schlaffer, H. *Musa Jocosa:* Gattungspoetik und Gattungs-geschichte der erotischen Dichtung in Deutschland. Stuttgart, 1971.

Schloch, R., See: *Unexpurgated.*

Schnabel, Friedrich Erich, et al. "Kölner Nähbudenlieder," in: *Anthropophytéia* (1912) 9: 448–53 and 473–74. Erotic songs and children's rhymes from Köln, Hamburg, etc. Compare: Bornemann; and McCosh.

———. "Neue Parallelen zum 'Streit der Jungfrauen,'" in: *Anthropophytéia* (1911) 8: 365–69. On the vaginal bragging-song known in English as "Three Old Whores from Baltimore." See also: Lehmann-Nitzsche; and Schwaab.

Schrecker, H. *Die Erotik im Soldatenlied.* München, 1921. Dissertation on soldiers' songs. Compare: Maier; and Oppeln.

Schroeder, Rebecca B. "Unprintable Songs from the Ozarks: Forgotten Manuscripts," in: *Missouri Folklore Society Journal* (1982) 4: 43–50. Compare: Randolph.

———. "Vance Randolph and Ozark Folksongs," in: *Missouri Folklore Society Journal* (1980) 2: 57–67.

Schultz, F. *Die erotischen Motive* in den deutschen Dichtungen des 12 und 13 Jahrhunderts. Greifswald, 1907. Dissertation.

Schutte, P. *Die Liebe in den englischen und schottischen Volksballaden.* Halle, 1906. Dissertation.

Schwaab, Josef. "Beiträge zum erotischen Lexikon (und Lied) der Deutschen in Nordböhmen," in: *Anthropophytéia* (1905) 2: 14–16, and 110. On the "*Streit der Jungfrauen*" vaginal bragging-song.

Schwartz, Alvin. *A Twister of Twists: A Tangler of Tongues.* Philadelphia: Lippincott, 1972.

"*Schwedische Schwänke und Aberglauben* aus Norland," in: *Kryptádia* (1884) 2: 171–222. Outstanding article on Swedish erotic folklore. Compare: Klintberg; and Rasmussen.

Schweinickle, O. U. *pseud.* See: *The Book of a Thousand Laughs,* 1928.

Schwob, Marcel. *Le Parnasse Satyrique du Quinzième siècle.* Paris: Welter, 1905. (Forms vol. 9, pt. 1, of *Kryptádia.*) French erotic art-songs and folksongs from 15th-century manuscripts, as supplement to Anatole de Montaiglon, *Recueil de poésies françoises du XVe siècle* (Paris 1860–80); and the *Chansons du XVe siècle* of Gaston Pâris, whose own erotic supplement appeared as *Le Gai Chansonnier français,* q.v. See also: Poulaille.

Scodel, Alvin. "Changes in Song Lyrics, and Some Speculations on National Character," in: *Merrill Palmer Quarterly* (1961) 7: 39–47. See: sexual supplement by Lance and Berry.

Scotch Presbyterian Eloquence Display'd. (London, 1690?) Reprinted, Rotterdam, 1738. Anonymously edited by Gilbert Crockat and John Monroe; mocking-by-quoting the excesses of Protestant preaching, with reference to bawdy songs. Compare: Gabriel Peignot, *Prédicatoriana,* (ca. 1830), on bizarre and facetious French and Italian sermons similar.

The Scots Musical Museum. Edited by James Johnson (and Robert Burns). Edinburgh: James Johnson, 1787–1803. 6 vols. Reprinted as: *The Scottish Musical Museum,* edited by William Stenhouse (with additions by David Laing and Charles Kirkpatrick Sharpe), Edinburgh, 1839, and 1853, four vols. Reprint, Hatboro, Pa.: Folklore Associates, 1968, the printing of the music now rather unclear.

Scott, Harold. *The Early Doors.* London, 1946. On the British 19th-century music halls. Compare: Speaight.

Scroggins, Sterling. *Cowboy Songs.* Master's thesis, University of Colorado, 1976.

Sebeok, Thomas A., ed. *Sight, Sound and Sense.* Bloomington: Indiana University Press, 1978. Includes: Paul Bouissac and Ivan Karp, "A Sebiotic Approach to Nonsense: Clowns and Limericks," and "Smart Fishermen Take Care of Their Rods," pp. 244–263, reprinting a series of 28 erotic limericks (by Charles C. Walcutt), "The Misfortunes of Fyfe," with extravagant anti-Freudian demonstrations or reversals. A classic of unconscious humor.

Sechrest, Lee, and Luis Flores. "Homosexuality in the Philippines and the United States: The Handwriting on the Wall," in: *Journal of Social Psychology* (1969) 79: 3–12. On homosexual graffiti. See also: Humphreys.

———, and A. Kenneth Olson. "Graffiti in Four Types of Institutions of Higher Education," in: *Journal of Sex Research* (1971) pp. 62–71.

Secret Songs of Silence, by "Sir Oliver Orpheus." See: Peter Buchan.

Sedley, Stephen. *The Seeds of Love.* London? Essex Music, 1967. Reported as "unexpurgated but pretty mild."

Seeger, Peggy, and Ewan MacColl. *The Singing Island.* London: Mills Music, 1960. See also: MacColl.

Seeger, Peter. *The Incompleat Folksinger.* New York: Simon and Schuster, 1972.

(———.) *Notes of an Innocent Bystander.* (Saipan, 1945.) 19 pp. mimeographed. (Copies: Library of Congress, Folksong Archive; G. Legman.) Service songs of World War II, mostly bawdy, with musical notations in that unmistakable hand.

Select Reading, Profusely Illustrated for Gay Boys and Naughty Girls: An Interesting History of Diddle, Doodle, Dum! How done by those who Know How. Compiled by (mark of an anchor, Cleveland or Cincinnati? ca. 1915.) 432 pp., sm. 16mo. (Only known copy: Mr. David Barton-Jay, Brattleboro, Vt., who plans a facsimile reprint, according to Dr. Clifford Scheiner, Brooklyn, N.Y.) Rare erotic humor miscellany of verse and prose. Note: "Gay" in this title means high-living, not homosexual.

Sewall, Robert. See: *Songs of Sadism.*

Sex Songs. MS., Boulder, Colorado, 1978. Photocopied from typewriting. (Copy: G. Legman.) Collection of current American erotic folksongs made by a professional folklorist, with provenances marked. Compare: *Parker Folio Manuscript.*

Sex to Sexty. Edited by "Richard Rodman and Goose Reardon" (John Newbern and Peggy Rodebaugh). "Fort Worth, Texas: S.R.I. Pub. Co." (Arlington, Texas: John Newbern Co.) 1964–86? 4to., about 100 numbers published as companion publication to *Super Sex to Sexty,* issued above,

1967–76? folio, about 30 numbers published. Heavily illustrated sex-humor magazines; the materials "too-hot-to-handle" being included in Newbern's own *The World's Dirtiest Jokes,* 1969, (q.v.), of which the intended title was *The Cream of the Crap.*

Shakespeare, William. (*Plays.*) Written, 1592–1612; quarto editions, 1596–1616; folio, 1623.

———. *Sonnets.* London, 1609. Published surreptitiously.

Sharp, Cecil. *Collection of English Folk Songs.* Edited by Maud Karpeles. London: Oxford University Press, 1974. 2 vols., with the music. Note: Despite the misleading title, includes *less than half* of the unpublished Sharp MS. collection of English folksongs and ballads, made from about 1905 to 1922 in England and America; only 1,165 versions out of 2,470 collected being printed here.

———. *English Folksongs from the Southern Appalachians.* Edited by Maude Karpeles. London: Oxford University Press, 1932. 2 vols. Note: Only the first edition (New York, 1917) states on the title page the collaboration of Olive Dame Campbell, who planned the work and collected part of the materials.

———, and Charles L. Marson. *Folk Songs from Somerset.* 5 series. London, 1904–09.

(Sharpe, Charles Kirkpatrick.) *A Ballad Book* (Edinburgh, 1823). Limited to 20 (?) copies. Reprint, ed. David Laing and Sir Walter Scott, 1880; further reprinted by Edmund Goldsmid without the Laing-Scott materials, Edinburgh, 1883, and 1891. Unexpurgated Scottish folksongs.

Shaw, Susanna. *Women in the John: A Collection of Graffiti from women's "bathrooms"* (without bath-tubs). San Francisco: Carolyn Bean, 1978. 64 pp. Selected pro-feminist, anti-man graffiti. Compare: Martilla; and Newall, Venetia.

Shay, Frank. *American Sea Songs and Chanteys.* New York: Norton, 1948. First published under the infinitely better title of: *Iron Men and Wooden Ships* (New York: Doubleday, 1924). Expurgated and "selected" texts. Compare: Hugill; and "Dave E. Jones," which last is believed to be a pseudonym used by Shay to publish the sea-chanteys omitted and expurgated here.

———. *My Pious Friends and Drunken Companions.* New York: Macauley, 1927. Reprinted, New York: Dover Pubs., 1961, combined with:

———. *More Pious Friends and Drunken Companions.* New York: Macaulay, 1928. Reprinted, New York: Dover Pubs., 1961, with preceding item. Mostly mock-sentimental songs, replacing the real bawdry of drunken singing, as in Shay's similar *Drawn from the Wood.*

Shemel, Sidney, and William Krasilowsky. *The Business of Music.* New York, 1964. Insiders' view-point on the retooling of often bawdy authentic folksong into pop-culch. Compare: Oscar Brand, *The Ballad Mongers* (1962); Peter Seeger, *The Incompleat Folksinger* (1972); Charles Parker; and G. Legman, *The Horn Book* (1964), the two final essays.

Shepard, Leslie. *The Broadside Ballad: A Study in Origins and Meaning.* London, and Hatboro, Pa.: Folklore Associates, 1962. A deeply thought book on popular culture. Compare: Lloyd; and Nettel.

———. *The History of Street Literature: The Story of Broadside Ballads, Chapbooks, etc.* Newton Abbot, Devon: David and Charles, 1973. With many reproductions of old street ballads, including two erotic examples.

Sherwin, Sterling, and Harry A. Powell. *Bad Man Songs of the Wild and Woolly West.* New York: Sam Fox Publishing, 1933.

Shitty Songs of Sigma Nu. (Ca., 1970?) Mimeographed college collection. (Copy: Guy Logsdon:) Compare: Reuss.

Shoemaker, Henry W. *Mountain Minstrelsy of Pennsylvania.* Philadelphia, 1931. A revision of his *North Pennsylvania Minstrelsy* (1923). Note: A manuscript supplement of the erotic texts omitted from this work was supplied by Col. Shoemaker to G. Legman, for the present research.

Shoolbraid, Murray. "Burns and Bawdry," in: *Come All Ye, The Vancouver Folk Song Society Journal* (Jan. 1974) 3: 6–13.

———. *Musa Proterva.* MS., Vancouver, 1973. Collection of 50 modern Scottish and English bawdy songs, in part transcribed from tape-recordings. (Copies: M. Shoolbraid; G. Legman.)

Silber, Irwin. *Songs of the Civil War.* New York: Bonanza Books, Crown, 1960. Compare: *Rakish Rhymer;* and Williams, A.

Silverman, Jerry. *The Dirty Song Book.* New York: Scarborough House/Stein and Day, 1982. Reprint,

1986? Texts heavily revised into extra "dirtiness," to live up to the title. Compare the similar: Babad; Cray; Hart; and Logue.

———. *The Panic Is On.* New York: Oak Publications, 1966.

Simpson, Claude. *The British Broadside Ballad and Its Music.* New Brunswick, N.J.: Rutgers University Press, 1966. Important musical, historical, and index-work, largely revising, updating, and replacing Chappell, q.v.

Skolan skall sprängas. (Sweden, ca. 1970.) Pamphlet, 12mo. (Copy: Dr. Svante Kjellberg, Kalmar, Sweden.) Swedish children's songs and rhymes, mostly "obscene."

The Slime Sheet. Paris, 1930. Mimeographed (?) collection of bawdy songs cited by Godfrey Irwin, presumably its editor, in the Gordon "Inferno" MS. Not seen.

Smile and the World Smiles With You: My Contribution to the Mirth and Good Fellowship of My Friends, on Guam, 1948. (5th ed. 1952.) 21 pp. mimeographed. (Copy: Harry P. Johnson, Arlington, Va.) Army miscellany of bawdy jokes and poems.

Smith, Courtney Craig. *Restoration Drolleries and Jest Books.* Ph.D. thesis, Harvard, 1944. 620 pp. (Copy: Harvard Archival Laboratory, No. 3277.) Compare: Stokes.

Smith, Jane-Anne. *Poppety-Pet: A Pocket Full of Sexy Songs.* MS., Paris, 1954. 38 pp., typewritten. Danish, British, and American songs and rhymes. (Copy: G. Legman.)

Smith, Paul. *The Book of Nasty* (and *Nastier*) *Legends.* London: Routledge, 1983–86. 2 vols.

———. *The Complete Book of Office Mis-Practice.* (vol. I.) London: Routledge, 1984. Xeroxlore, with sequel:

———. *Reproduction Is Fun: A Book of Photocopy Joke Sheets.* (Vol. 2) London: Routledge, 1986. Compare: Dundes; and Orr.

Smith, Sydney Goodsir. "Burns and *The Merry Muses of Caledonia,*" in: *Arena* (London, 1950) No. 4. Reprinted with expurgations in *Hudson Review* (New York, 1954) vol. 7. Splendid essay intended as introduction to Smith's edition, with James Barke, of Burns' *Merry Muses of Caledonia* (Edinburgh, 1959), but unfortunately replaced there by an inferior introduction, by Barke.

Smith, Thomas R. *Poetica Erotica: A Collection of Rare and Curious Amatory Verse.* New York: Published for Subscribers Only by Boni and Liveright, 1921–22. 3 vols. "Enlarged" edition, 1927. 770 pp. Reprinted, New York: Crown Publishers (ca. 1933). Largely reprints material from Farmer's *Merry Songs and Ballads,* (1897) q.v., with modern poetry added. Compare: Smith's anonymous *Immortalia* (1927) and possibly *The (Reno) "Wrecks,"* the erotic folk supplements to this work. Compare: Cole; and Wentworth.

Smith, Vincent. See: *Anecdota Americana: Second Series.*

Smith-Hughes, Jack. *Eight Studies in Justice.* London: Cassell, 1953. On case in 1902, at Peasenhall, Suffolk, of a girl seduced and murdered by a Primitive Methodist elder. The murderer went scot-free owing to evidence that the girl "had been sufficiently intrigued by the pornographic ditties sung by the younger villagers of an evening to request the youth who lived next door to supply her with written copies of these edifying verses." They were made available to the jury in private.

Snatches and Lays: Songs Miss Lilywhite Should never have taught us. Edited by Sebastian Hogbotel and Simon ffuckes (*pseuds.:* Kenneth D. Gott and Stephen Murray-Smith. Melbourne, Australia,) 1962. 82 pp. mimeographed. Note: Not edited by Ian Turner, nor taken from Donald Laycock's similar MS. collection, *Obiter Dicta,* as complained of by him in "Digging up the Dirt," in *National Review* (Australia, Feb. 20, 1976).

———. *Snatches and Lays.* Hogbotel and ffuckes. Melbourne: Sun Books, 1973. 112 pp. Printed edition, publicly issued.

———. *Enlarged.* (Facsimile title of 1962 edition.) Hong Kong: Boozy Company, P.O. Box 20561, Causeway Bay (The Authors), 1975. 147 pp. The best edition, re-edited by K. D. Gott, with additions.

Snowdrops from a Curate's Garden. See: Aleister Crowley.

The Sods' Opera, "by Gilbert and Sullivan." See: *Harlequin Prince Cherrytop* (by G. A Sala).

69 Chansons. (Illustrations by Paul Claude. Paris?) 1947. French students' *Chansons de Salles de Garde.*

Sola Pinto, Vivian de. See: Pinto.

Soldatenkov. See: *Mejdu Druziami.*

Some Yarns! Love and Laugh. (Cover subtitle: *A Pocketfull of funny, nutty, risky, spicy, naughty . . . stories.*) Paris: Librairie des Editions Modernes (Charles Carrington), 1918. (Copy: Kinsey-ISR Library.)

Songs Compleat, Pleasant and Divertive. See: *Pills to Purge Melancholy.*

Songs for the Suds: A Collection of College Party Songs. MS. Fayetteville, Ark., 1957. Collection made by a girl student at the University of Arkansas, supplied to Vance Randolph; includes three rather mild off-color campus songs. (The "*Suds*" are beer, these being songs for student beer-busts.)

Songs My Mother Never Taught Me. (New York: Pershing Rifles, City College, 1944.) Mimeographed, with a short section of limericks titled "Shitty Ditties." (Copy: G. Legman.) Compare: *The Slime Sheet.* Note: This work, and the next are not to be confused with the mild, publicly issued collection of same title (1929) by John J. Niles.

Songs My Mother Never Taught Me. (At head: *Prudes Stay Out!*) (Bloomington, Indiana, 1963.) MS. 22 pp. photocopied from typewriting. (Copy: G. Legman.) College bawdy song collection made at Ohio Wesleyan University and Indiana University in men's fraternities, by Richard Reuss, q.v.

Songs of Raunch and Ill-Repute: A Collection of songs for beer parties, stags, and church youth groups. (Edited by David Singmaster and Larry Crissman.) Pasadena, Calif.: Sorair, Ricketts House, California Institute of Technology (1958). 31 pp., mimeographed. (Copy: G. Legman.) Note: Owing to the tactical error, at that date, of giving the student society's correct address on the title, this work was seized by the authorities and most of the edition destroyed.

Songs of Roving and Raking. (Edited by John Walsh. Champaign, Illinois: The Back Room Press, 1961.) 125 pp., with music, hektographed. (Copy: G. Legman.) An important and representative collection, competently edited and organized, with the musical notation.

(———.) *Enlarged,* as: *Roll Me Over.* Edited by Harry Babad, compiled and collected at the University of Illinois by the Illini Folk Arts Society. New York: Oak Publications, 1972. No changes made except small additions credited to Oscar Brand. Compare: Silverman.

Songs of Sadism, Lust, Rape, Brutality, and other goodies, that will make you g-nash your teeth. Composed, Caligraphed and Illuminated by G. Legman (*sic*), and the Rotten-Bastards Mariachi Band—Motherfuckers All!—MS., New Brunswick, New Jersey; and New York, 1942–44. 48 pp. Photostatted from typewriting. (Copy: G. Legman, *who is not the author.*) Edited and largely written by Robert Bragg ("Robert De Mexico") and Robert Sewall: an autograph album collection, group-written, of mock and parodied folksongs, and anti-gallant exercises, as the title indicates.

Songs of Silence. See: (Peter Buchan), *Secret Songs of Silence.*

Songs of the Airdales in the Pacific. (Australia: Air Forces, ca. 1944.) (*At head:* Restricted Material. Restricted to: Your Mother, Your Girlfriend(s), The Chaplain, Wonks, Polly Wogs and The W.C.T.U. Presenting, from a private collection, Anonymous:) 22 pp., mimeographed. (Copy: G. Legman.) Rather similar in contents, though texts are not identical, to the Canadian mimeographed folio, *North Atlantic Squadron* (1944).

The Songs You Hear No More. Privately Printed. (ca. 1937.) Songbook by a border radio performer. Cited by Logsdon.

Spaeth, Sigmund. *The Facts of Life in Popular Song.* New York: McGraw-Hill, 1934. Title-article first appeared in *American Spectator.* Supplement:

———. "*Salacious in Our Alley: The Sallies of our Tin Pan Alley Songwriters are Getting a Bit That Way.*" MS., New York, 1945. (Copy: G. Legman.) Unpublished article, written on assignment for Fulton Oursler, editor of *Liberty Magazine,* but never used. Compare: Urdang.

———. *A History of Popular Music in America.* New York: Random House, 1948.

———. *Read 'Em and Weep: The Songs You Forgot to Remember.* New York: Doubleday, 1926/27.

———. *Weep Some More, My Lady.* New York: Doubleday, 1927.

Spaeight, George. *Bawdy Songs of the Early Music Hall.* Newton Abbot, Devon: David and Charles, 1975. 96 pp. Reprints parodies from "smutty songsters" of the 1850s, with their tunes.

Spicy Breezes. (Vignette: two black cats *affrontés.* U.S., ca. 1930.) 52 pp. (Unique copy: Kinsey-ISR Library.) Erotic humor miscellany of prose and verse. Note: A typographically very similar pamphlet of close date also exists, giving all the purple passages from Petronius Arbiter's *Satyricon* in English translation, to accompany an expurgated 1920s edition. In this case the two title page animals are goats.

Spinkler, Edgar. "Gross-Russische erotische Volkdichtung," in: *Anthropophytéia* (1913) 10: 330–53. Discussion in German, and 67 untranslated examples in Russian only, owing to German government censorship case at that date against *Anthropophytéia,* of which this was therefore the final volume. See: Krauss.

Der Spittelberg und seine Lieder. See: Blümml.

Splinters from the Log-Book of "Our" Lodge: What I Saw and Heard, Through the Keyhole of Room Number (?) the First Night of the Marriage of a Young Couple. (England? ca. 1890.) Broadside, folio. (Unique copy: Leslie Shepard, Dublin.) Erotic broadside ballad, one of the latest in date ever recorded, possibly issued for a Masonic lodge.

Sportive Wit: The Muses Merriment. A new Spring of Lusty Drollery, Joviall Fancies, and *A la mode Lampounes . . .* Collected for the Public Good, by a Club of Sparkling Wits. London: Nathan Brook, 1656. (Unique copy: Oxford, Bodleian Library) Edited by John Phillips, the nephew of Milton. Original title was to have been *Love and Mirth, or Jovial Drollery.* All copies were ordered destroyed by Cromwell's authority on publication. The rarest of the drolleries, and one of the most interesting. Should urgently be reprinted.

Stag Bar Supplement to Songs of S.E.A. and other places, other things (Item 2). (Ubon, Thailand? "Wolfpack" 8th Tactical Fighter Wing, ca. 1967.) Supplement of bawdy songs to main collection, *Songs of S.E.A.* (provenance probably as above.) (Copy: C. Wm. Getz.)

The Stag Party. (This Book contains . . . The Chestnut Club Yarns . . . and thousands of other stories, full of pith and point.) (Chicago: Daily News Press, Eugene Field; or Boston: The Papyrus Club? 1888–89). (296) pp., unnumbered. (Only three copies known: Kinsey-ISR Library; Denver Public Library, Morse-Field Collection; and Yale University.) Very large repertory of humorous erotic poems, storiettes, and obscœna, including almost all the erotic output of Eugene Field, its editor. See: Harry J. Mooney, Jr.; "The *Sub Rosa* Writings of Eugene Field," in: *Papers of the Bibliographical Society of America* (1978) 72: 541–52.

Starr, Fred. *Pebbles from the Ozarks.* Siloam Springs, Arkansas, 1942.

Starr, William J. *The Fighter Pilots Hymn Book.* (Cannon Air Force Base, Cannon, New Mexico, 1958.) 121 pp., hektographed; with almost illegible *Smegmafax Addenda* (1959), comprising pp. 122–52, not present in most of the 100 copies issued. (Copy: G. Legman.) The best and most extensive of the American Air Force original bawdy song collections, and one of the few giving the compiler's name. Compare: Getz; and Hopkins.

Staub, Théo. *L'Enfer érotique de la chanson folklorique française.* Plan de la Tour (Var), France: Éditions d'Aujourd'hui, 1981. 2 vols. in 1, photoprint from typewriting, with the music. Ph.D. thesis (Université de Nice, May 1978), the author being in his seventies. Outstandingly the best, and only scholarly edition of the French students' erotic *Chansons de Salles de Garde,* q.v.

Stekert, Ellen. *'The Farmer's Curst Wife': A Modified Historical-Geographical Study,* M.A. thesis, Indiana University, 1961. Excellent Child-Ballad study. Author also published disabused critique of Bob Dylan.

Stern-Szana, Bernhard. *Geschichte der öffentlichen Sittlichkeit in Russland: Kultur, Aberglaube, Kirche, Klerus, Sekten, etc.* Berlin: Barsdorf, 1907–1919. 2 vols. Final chapter 10, "Folkloristische Dokumente," including erotic rhymes, proverbs, and songs, 2: 579–616. Compare: Raskin; Spinkler; and Krauss.

———. *Medizin, Aberglaube, und Geschlechtsleben in der Türkei.* Berlin, 1903. 2 vols. Similar to Stern's work on Russia, above. See also erotic folklore in Stern's private book collection catalogue, *Bibliotheca curiosa et erotica* (Privatdruck: Wien, 1921).

Stevenson, Burton. *The Home Book of Quotations.* 4th ed. New York: Dodd, Mead, 1944. Valuable sampling of ephemeral "popular" song refrains, pp. 1881–83, and appendix pp. 2273–98.

Stocker, Terrance, et al. "Social Analysis of *Graffiti,*" in: *Journal of American Folklore* (1972) 85: 356–66.

Stokes, Joseph. *Wit and Drollery, 1656.* MS., New Haven, Conn., 1935. Yale University dissertation, on the drolleries. (Copy: Yale Alumnus Society.) See also: Smith, C.

Stolz, Sandra. *Some Humorous Songs of Texas Young People*. MS., Austin, Texas, 1961. 26 pp. type-written. (Copies: Dr. Roger Abrahams; G. Legman.) College course paper, divided into "Children's Songs," mostly aggressive; and "College Songs," mostly bawdy.

Stone, Rosetta (*pseud.*). "Instructional *Graffiti*," in *Maledicta* (1980) X. 162.

Stone, Weldon. *Devil Take a Whittler*. New York, 1948.

The Story of a Dildoe, A Tale in five Tableaux. London: Privately Printed (W. Lazenby), 1880. 44 pp. Limited to 150 copies. (Copy: G. Legman.) Reprinted, Atlanta, Georgia: Pendulum Books, ca. 1968. A side-publication of *The Pearl*, q.v., interspersed with erotic poems.

Stovepipe Serenade. Edited by Ms. Logan Bently, q.v.

Straparola, Gian-Francesco. *Piacevoli Notti*. 1550–53. English translation as: *The Most Delectable Nights*. Paris: Carrington, 1906. 2 vols. The *locus classicus* on erotic riddling.

The Sugar of Life. (London: Dugdale?) 1854. (Copy: G. Legman.) Rare semi-erotic miscellany, includes verse.

Sullivan, Mark. *Our Times: 1900–25*. New York: Scribner, 1926–35. 6 vols.

Summers, Montague. *History of Witchcraft and Demonology*. London and New York, 1926. Compare: Michelet.

———. *Witchcraft and Black Magic*. London, 1945.

Super Sex to Sexty. See: *Sex to Sexty*.

Super Stag Treasury. (Edited by Edward B. Cray? Los Angeles:) Mada Co., 1963–64. 36 pp. Jokes and songs.

Susrata II, Dr. (*pseud.*). "Englische Soldatenlieder aus Zentral-Indien," in: *Anthropophytéia* (1911) 8: 374.

———. "Englische Volklieder (und Sprichwörter) aus Indien," in: *Anthropophytéia* (1910) 7: 375–82. Erotic songs, poems, and proverbs collected from British soldiers in India; with jokes and riddles, in *same,* 7: 238, 336–37. Compare: *Camp Fire Songs* (Madras, India, 1940). Note: With three short and mostly archaic English erotic glossaries, the above brief items are *the entirety of English-language erotic folklore* presented in the 19 massive volumes and "Beiwerke" of *Anthropophytéia,* and 12 volumes of *Kryptádia,* earlier. See: Legman; and *Symposium*.

Sutton-Smith, Brian, and David M. Abrams. *Psychosexual Material in the Stories told by Children: The Fucker*. (Paper presented at the First International Congress on Sexology, Montréal, Canada, 1976.) 31 pp. photoprinted.

Sweet Violets. MS., Cambridge, Mass., 1939. (Copy: Harry Brown, "college poet.") House-book or autograph album of erotic poetry, compiled by successive generations of students belonging to the Fox Club, Harvard College. Compare: Oxford University; *Lyra Ebriosa;* and Reuss.

Symposium on Obscenity in Folklore (edited by Tristram Coffin and Roger Abrahams), in: *Journal of American Folklore* (1962) 75: 189–265. An historic initiative in presenting erotic folklore study in English. Compare note on "Susruta," just above.

Tabler, Barbara, and James Angelo. *Bawdy-and-Soul Singing Limericks*. Berkeley, Calif.: Bar None Press (ca. 1980). (Copy: Dr. Arthur Deex, Los Altos, California.)

(Tabourot, Estienne.) *Les Bigarrures du Seigneur des Accords*. Lyon: Richer, 1615. Enlarged edition of important late-16th century anthology of forms of humor and obscœna. Compare: *Musarum Deliciæ;* and Peignot.

Talley, Thomas. *Negro Folk Rhymes*. New York: Macmillan, 1922. Compare: Perrow; and Northall.

Tate, Brad. *The Bastard from the Bush: Obscene Songs and Ballads of Australian Origin*. Part I. Kuranda, Queensland: Rams Skull Press, 1982. 74 pp. photoprint, limited to 200 copies. (Copy: G. Legman.) Compare: Edwards; Laycock; and Meredith.

Taylor, H. Hoyt. *The "Frankie and Johnnie" Variants*. MS. New York, 1924. Collection of 13 California texts.

The Tenth Muse Lately Hung Up in America: Being Lewd Lines and Vulgar Verses, Newly Inscribed by A Gentleman. (Dr. Jack Lowenherz. MS., New York, 1958.) (Copy: G. Legman.) Mostly limericks.

Texas Fraternity Songs: (Deep in the Heart of Texas). (Austin, Texas, 1961). 24 pp. hektographed. (Copies: Dr. Roger Abrahams; G. Legman.) Anonymous: includes "Bawdy and Sacrilegious Songs, and Song of Race" (i.e. anti-Negro).

Thomas, Dylan. "*A Kiss for Your Crotch, My Love.*" MS., New York, 1953. (Song transmitted by "his fellow alcoholic," Seámus Ennis, La Jolla, Calif., 1964.) Compare: Putnam; and Updike.

Thomas, Gates. *South Texas Negro Work Songs.* (Publications of the Texas Folklore Society, No. 5; 1926; and No. 7, 1928.) Collection made 1887–1905; expurgated as issued, but an important early record. Compare: Odum; and Perrow.

Thomason, John W., Jr. *Fix Bayonets!* New York: Scribner, 1926. Compare: Dolph; and Posselt.

Thompson, Harold W. *Body, Boots and Britches: Folktales, Ballads and Speech from Country New York.* Philadelphia: Lippincott, 1939–40. Reprint, ed. Thomas O'Donnell. Syracuse University Press, 1979. Compare: Goldstone.

————, and Edith Cutting. *A Pioneer Songster: Texts from the Stevens-Douglass Manuscript of Western New York, 1841–1856.* Ithaca: Cornell University Press, 1958. Compare: Jones, L.

Thompson, Stith. *Motif-Index of Folk Literature.* Enlarged ed. Bloomington, Indiana, 1955–58. 6 vols.

————, and Antti Aarne. *The Types of the Folktale.* Enlarged edition, Helsinki: (FF Communications, No. 184), 1964.

Thomson, William. *Orpheus Caledonius.* London, 1725. Enlarged 2nd ed., 1733, 2 vols. Reprinted, in facsimile, Hatboro, Pa.: Folklore Associates, 1965. Gives the music to Scottish songs from Ramsay's *Tea-Table Miscellany,* q.v. Compare: *Scots Musical Museum.*

Thorp, N. Howard. *Songs of the Cowboys* (1908), ed. Austin and Alta Fife. New York: Clarkson Potter, 1966. Reprinted, ed. Guy Logsdon. Lincoln: University of Nebraska Press, 1984.

Tillot, Émile. *Chansons médicales.* Paris: Husinger, 1874–1883. 28 and 46 pp. (Unique set: Bibliothèque de la Faculté de Médecine, Paris, Nos. 58509 and 76942.) First "medical" edition of French students' *Chansons de Salles de Garde,* q.v.

Tobiason, James. *Sexual Symbolism in the Popular Negro Blues.* Miami University, Oxford, Ohio, 1959–60. MS. in 5 pts., photoprinted. (Copies: Kinsey-ISR Library; Peter Tamony, San Francisco; G. Legman.) Compare: Oliver.

Toelken, J. Barre. "The Folklore of Academe," in: Jan Harold Brunvand, *The Study of American Folklore* (New York: Norton, 1968) pp. 317–37. On college folklore and songs.

Tolman, Albert H. "Some Songs Traditional in the United States," in: *Journal of American Folklore.* (1922) No. 29: 155–97.

————, and Mary O. Eddy. "Traditional Texts and Tunes," in: *Journal of American Folklore.* (1922) No. 35: 335–432. See: Perrow.

"*Tradiçáo (Da) oral Portuguesa,*" in: *Kryptádia* (1899) 6: 384–90. Portuguese erotic songs and rhyming-riddles.

A Treasury of Erotic and Facetious Memorabilia. (Compiled by Henry N. Cary.) MS. Chicago, ca. 1920. (Copy: Kinsey-ISR Library, formerly G. Legman.) Facetiæ collection, mostly jokes, but including Mark Twain's *The Mammoth Cod* and its covering letters, here disguised as by "Petroleum V. Nasby."

(Treldewehr, Alfred Klement von.) *Das Wirtshaus an der Lahn, hrsg. von Franz Graf Westenham* (*pseud.*) *1922.* See: P. Englisch, in: Hayn-Gotendorf, *Bibl. Germ.,* 9: 633.

————. *Same,* as: *Das Wirtshaus an der Lahn: Das unsterbliche Epos von der Frau Wirtin.* Hanau: Schustek, 1970. 38 pp.

Trimble, John. *5000 Adult Sex Words and Phrases.* North Hollywood, Calif.: Brandon House, 1966. Earlier issued as by "Roger Blake," 1964. Erotic slang dictionary with excellent synonymy lists. Compare: Chapman; Gillette; Farmer and Henley; and Morton.

Trois Orfèvres à la Saint-Éloi . . . du Quartier Latin à la Salle de Garde. "En Sorbonne, pour l'esbaud-issement des escholiers, 1430" (Paris: Guibal, for Edmond D. Bernard? 1930) 1 vol. in 2: 587 pp. (Copies: A. Kahn-Sriber, Paris; G. Legman.) Partial reprint of *Anthologie Hospitalière et Latinesque,* q.v., edited by Bernard.

————. *Same.* (Paris: Edmond D. Bernard, 1930.) 2 vols.: 258 and 295 pp. (Copies: British Museum Library, Private Case; and G. Legman.) In this 2-vol. edition new materials are added, vol. 2: pp. 226–95.

Tropicana. Kingston, Jamaica, ca. 1964. MS. typewritten. Small collection of bawdy West Indian "Calypso" songs in English. (Copy: G. Legman.)

"Tuft, Argus," (*pseud.,* pun!). See: *Argus Tuft's Compendium.*

Tune: My Bonny. See: *North Atlantic Squadron.*

Turner, Ian. *Cinderella Dressed in Yella.* Melbourne: Heinemann, 1969. The best collection of children's (mainly bawdy) rhymes in English. Compare: Gaignebet; and McCosh.

————. *Same.* Edited by Wendy Lowenstein and June Factor. Melbourne: Heinemann, 1978. Importantly enlarged. Compare: Lowenstein.

The Turquoise Book of Locker-Room Humor. Toronto: Peek-A-Boo Press (Rexdale, Ontario: Coles Pub. Co.) 1980. See: *Locker Room Humor.*

Tuso, Joseph F. "Folksongs of the American Fighter Pilot in Southeast Asia, 1967–1968," in: *Folklore Forum: Bibliographical and Special Series* (1971) No. 8: 1–39. Compare: Burke; and Getz.

Twain, Mark (*pseud.* of Samuel L. Clemens). *The Mammoth Cod, and Address to the Stomach Club,* ed. G. Legman. Milwaukee, Wisc.: Maledicta Press, 1976. 26 pp. First edition; written in 1902. See: *Treasury,* above.

————. *The Mysterious Stranger.* New York, 1916.

Unexpurgated. (Edited by Earl Eisinger, Edith Holden, and Ralph Brown). (Los Angeles, Calif.: Bidet Press, 1943.) 65 pp. Limited to 250 copies. (Copy: G. Legman.) Class-conscious erotic folksongs, including two political (Trotskyite) satirical pieces.

————. *Same,* as: *Unexpurgated,* "Edited by R. Schloch, Ph.D." (*pseud.*). The Open Box Press (California, *ante* 1951) 64 pp. Omits the two Trotskyite satires, the editors having now parted company.

The Unexpurgated Folk Songs of Men. Berkeley, Calif., 1964. Booklet of texts and discussion by Mack McCormick, q.v., accompanying an anonymously issued phonograph recording of same title.

Union Jack. Chelmsford, Essex, England, 1948–58. MS. collection of bawdy folk-poems, songs and jokes, (made by Robert Ash) in part from inmates at Chelmsford Prison.

Untermeyer, Louis. *A Treasury of Ribaldry.* London: Elek Books, 1957; and New York, 1959. Very mild; compare: *Rowdy Rhymes.*

Updike, John. *Tossing and Turning: Poems.* New York: Alfred A. Knopf, 1977. 87 pp. Includes "Cunts," "Pussy: A Preliminary Epithalamium," and other erotic poems first published as: *Six Poems,* New York: Frank Hallman, 1976. Compare: Auden; Eliot; Ficke; and especially Guthrie; Putnam; and Dylan Thomas.

Urdang, Laurence. "I Wanna Hot Dog for My Roll: Suggestive Song Titles," in: *Maledicta* (1981) 5: 69–75. Compare: Oliver; Johnson, G.; and Spaeth.

URNL: A Manuscript, Found in the Drawer of the Library Table of the Milwaukee Club. Edited and Annotated by the Perpetual Poet Laureate of the URNL Club. (Milwaukee, Wisc.) Done at the Pewaukee Press, 1901. 71 pp. Limited to 100 copies. (Copy: G. Legman.) In verse, turning on the "Urinal" title and name of the private club, with mock *apparatus criticus,* signed "Aquarius, the Waterman." Compare: *The Stag Party;* and *Select Reading.*

(Utterson, Edward V.) *Select Pieces of Early Popular Poetry: Re-published principally from early printed copies, in the black letter.* London: Longman, 1817. 2 vols. Compare: *Jyl of Brentford's Testament.*

Van Gennep, Arnold. "Remarques sur l'imagerie populaire," in: *Revue d'Ethnographie et de Sociologie* (1911) pp. 26–50.

"Verb, Edouard de," *pseud.* See: Ficke.

"Vicarrion, Count Palmiro," *pseud.* See: Logue.

"*Vierzeilen* aus den Oesterreichischen Alpen," in: *Kryptádia* (1888) 4: 79–133. The first published collection (by Gustav Meyer) of the erotic "Schnadahüpfeln" four-liners. See: Hand.

Viollet-le-Duc, Eugène. *La Bibliothèque poétique, ou Catalogue des livres* composant (sa) Bibliothèque. Avec des notes bibliographiques sur chacun des ouvrages. Paris, 1843. Reprinted, edited by A. Méray. Paris, 1859. Important private collection catalogue, forming a bibliography of French songbooks, from the beginning.

The Vocal Miscellany. Dublin, 1738.

"Voegelin, Beppo, Freiherr von" (*pseud.*). *Frau Wirtin in Klassikers Munde, oder "Die Wirtin an der*

Lahn" als literarisches Phänomen . . . Hrsg. und mit stilkritischen Kommentaren versehen. "Gräfelsing: Wissenschaftliche Verlagsanstalt zur Pflege deutscher Sinngutes" (München: Moos Verlag, 1969). 78 pp. The Germanic equivalant of English-language bawdy limericks, here jocularly attributed to Goethe, Kafka, etc.

(Volkov, Th.) "Folklore de l'Ukraine," in: *Kryptádia* (1898) 5: 1–182.

Volks-Erotik. Hanau: Verlag Karl Schustek, 1968. German students' and soldiers' bawdy songs and obscœna, taken from Krauss and Webinger, q.v.

Vorberg, Gaston, and W. Bähr. *Meisterstücke neuLateinischer Liebesdichtung.* München, G. Miller, 1920. 48 pp. (Copy: G. Legman.) Translations into German of medieval Latin erotic poetry, in preparation for Vorberg's great dictionary of Latin erotic speech, *Glossarium Eroticum* (Stuttgart, 1930), replacing that forming *Kryptádia,* vol. 12.

Vuk, Dr. (Note: One of the editors—G. Pâris, Gaidoz, or Rolland?—states concerning the article on Serbian erotic "*Poskochnika,*" in *Kryptádia,* 1884, II: 284–88, that he then possessed: "un cahier contenant une centaine, au moins, de strophes du *Lolo* et d'autres (*Poskochnika*) du même genre . . . des collections inédites de Vuk," author of the *Serbian Dictionary.* The later history of Vuk's unpublished collection is unknown.)

Wagner, Constance. *Sycamore.* New York, 1950.

Walker, Barbara. *A Folksong and Ballad Index to the Fife Mormon and Fife American Collections.* M.A. thesis, Utah State University, 1986.

Walker, William. (*Biography of Peter Buchan.*) See: Buchan, P.

Wallrich, William. *Air Force Airs.* Songs and Ballads of the United States Air Force. New York: Duell, Sloan and Pearce, 1957. Expurgated texts, in part taken from Posselt, q.v. Includes many non-folk parodies. Despite the title, no music is given. See: Getz.

Walsh, John. See: *Songs of Roving and Raking.* 1962.

(———.) As: *Roll Me Over.* Edited by Harry Babad. New York: Oak Pubs., 1972. Adds texts by Oscar Brand, q.v.

Walsh, William S. *Handy-Book of Literary Curiosities.* Philadelphia: Lippincott, 1892; repr. 1911. Art. "Pasquinade," pp. 874–77, on *graffiti* history. The best-researched and only reliable of the amateur "Treasuries of Serendipity." Compare: Peignot.

Walther, Th. *Die leichtgeschürtzte Muse: Galante und erotische Lieder, Volkweisen und Sprüchworte aus allen Zeiten. Leipzig, 1908.* Hardly lives up to the promise of its "high-kilted" title.

Wannan, Bill. *Fair Go, Spinner: A Treasury of Popular Australian Humor.* London: Argus and Robertson, 1965.

———. *Robust, Ribald and Rude Verse in Australia.* Melbourne: Lansdowne Press, 1972. Unexpurgated, but mostly light verse by named authors.

(Ward, Ned.) *A Dutch Riddle, or Parodoxical Character of An Hairy Monster, often found under Holland. London, ca. 1725.* Reprint, 1737.

Ward, Russel. *The Penguin Book of Australian Ballads.* London, 1964.

Ward-Jackson, C. H. *Airman's Song Book.* Edinburgh: William Blackwood, 1967. 200 songs sung by British airmen in World War II. Compare: Getz; Hopkins; and Page.

Wardroper, John. *Love and Drollery (:A Selection of Amatory, Merry and Satirical Verse of the 17th Century.)* London: Routledge, 1969. Outstanding collection of English drollery verse, mostly from MS sources, with valuable comparative notes on printed versions. Compare: Cutts; and Holloway; also *Roxburghe* (1873–74).

Warning! See: *Guam Air Force Songs.*

Watson, James. *A Choice Collection of Comic and Serious Scots Poems.* Edinburgh: James Watson, 1706–11. 3 vols. Reprint in 1 vol., Glasgow: Reprinted for Private Circulation (Maurice Ogle), 1869. Ltd. to 165 copies.

The Way of All Flesh. (Erroneously reported as title of work by "Don Bonmal," which see at: *The Rhyme of All Flesh.* The real "Way of All Flesh" is the anti-family autobiography of Samuel Butler, published only posthumously in 1903.)

Webinger, Alfred. See: Krauss: *Das Minnelied, 1929.*

Wedderburn, John and Robert. *A Compendious Book of The Gude and Godlie Ballatis, 1567.* Reprint, ed. Alex, Mitchell. Edinburgh: Scottish Text Soc. (Vol. 39), 1897. With 120-page introduction on "sacred contrefacts" of bawdy songs.

Wehse, R. "The Erotic Metaphor in Humorous Narrative Songs," in: Linda Dégh *Festschrift* (Bloomington, Indiana, 1980) pp. 223–32. See also: Röhrich, "Liebesmetaphorik."

———. *Schwanklied und Flugblatt in GrossBritannien.* Frankfurt/Bern/Las Vegas (!) 1979. On British broadsides; compare: Shepard.

Wells, Carolyn. *A Parody Anthology.* New York: Scribner, 1904.

Wells, F. L. "*Frau Wirtin* and associates: A Note on alien corn," in: *American Imago* (South Dennis, Mass., 1951) 8: 93–97. Parallels the German "Frau Wirtin" verses, quoting examples, with English-language bawdy limericks. See: *Wirtshaus an der Lahn,* below.

Welsh, Charles, and William Tillinghast. *Catalogue of English and American Chapbooks and Broadside Ballads in Harvard College Library.* Cambridge, Mass., 1905. Reprinted, with introduction by Leslie Shepard, Detroit: Singing Tree Press, 1968.

Wentworth, Harold. *American Dialect Dictionary.* New York, 1944.

———, and Stuart Flexner. *Dictionary of American Slang.* New York, 1960. Revised, 1971. Superseded by: Chapman, q.v.

Wepman, Dennis, Ronald B. Newman, and Murray Binderman. *The Life: The Lore and Folk Poetry of the Black Hustler.* Philadelphia: University of Pennsylvania Press, 1976. Excellent discussion and texts of Negro pimp and drug-addict bawdy "toast" recitations, collected in prison; with annotated bibliography. Compare: Jackson.

Westenham, Franz Graf von, *pseud.* See: Treldewehr.

Westermeier, Clifford P. "The Cowboy and Sex," in: Charles W. Harris and Buck Rainey, *The Cowboy: Six Shooters, Songs, and Sex.* (Norman, Oklahoma, 1976) pp. 85–105. Excellent, no-nonsense article, but damn few songs and less sex, despite the titles. Compare: Logsdon.

Western Kentucky Folklore Archive (WKFA), collected by D. K. Wilgus. Now repositoried at the University of California at Los Angeles. Compare: Dorson-Indiana.

Wheeler, Mary. *Steamboatin' Days.* Baton Rouge, La., 1944.

Wheeler, William. *Mother Goose Melodies.* Boston, 1878. Compare: Halliwell.

White, John I. *Git Along, Little Dogies: Songs and Songmakers of the American West.* Urbana: University of Illinois Press, 1975. Compare: Logsdon.

White, Newman I. *American Negro Folk-Songs.* Cambridge, Mass., 1928. Reprinted, Hatboro, Pa.: Folklore Associates, 1965. Compare: McAdams; Perrow; and Talley.

———, editor. *The Frank C. Brown Collection of North Carolina Folklore,* Vol. I: Durham, N.C., 1952.

Whitworth, John. *The Faber Book of Blue Verse.* London: Faber, 1990. Erotic art-poetry with some folk-verse. Compare: Cole, and Bold's similar anthologies; also Laycock, and T. R. Smith.

Why Was He Born So Beautiful? See: Harry Morgan.

Wickham, Littleton M. See: *Lyra Ebriosa.*

"*Wiegenlied* aus der Umgegend von Luxemburg," in: *Kryptádia* (1899) 6: 382–84. German erotic mock-lullaby.

Wiener Blut: Ein Bilderzyklus mit Liedern. Eingeleitet von Quirin Mark (*pseud.* of Zxel Matthes.) München: Rogner and Bernhard. 1970. 18 pp. and 50 colored pls. Illustrated reprint of Blümml and Gugitz's *Der Spittelberg und seine Lieder.*

Wier, Albert Ernest. *The Book of a Thousand Songs: The World's Largest Collection of the Songs of the People.* New York: C. Fischer, 1918. Best collection of old favorites. Compare: Chapple; and Morrison.

Wild Weasel Songbook. See: Anders.

Wilgus, D. K. *Anglo-American Folksong Scholarship Since 1898.* New Brunswick, N.J.: Rutgers University Press, 1959.

———. "The Josiah H. Combs Collection of Songs and Rhymes," in: *Kentucky Folklore Record,* vol. 6, no. 4. And see: *Western Kentucky Folklore Archive;* and Combs.

Wilkat, J. *Fresche Lieder.* München, 1967.

Wilkinson, Lupton. See: Rhodi.

Williams, Alfred. *Folk Songs of the Upper Thames*. London: Duckworth, 1923. Reprinted, Wakefield, Yorks.: S.R. Publishers, 1971. Expurgated texts, but with frank discussion.

———. "Folk-Songs of the Civil War," in: *Journal of American Folklore* (Dec. 1892) pp. 265–83. Compare: Silber.

Williams, Charles Hanbury. See: *Foundling Hospital for Wit*.

Williams, Cratis D. *Ballads and Songs*. Lexington, Kentucky, 1937. MS., typewritten. M.A. thesis, University of Kentucky. Courageously unexpurgated field collection of rural songs.

Williams, Oscar. *The Silver Treasury of Light Verse, from Geoffrey Chaucer to Ogden Nash*. New York: New American Library, 1957. The first relatively unexpurgated popular verse anthology in English since 1720. But compare: Smith, T. R.

(Williams, Tyrrell). "Missouri History Not Found in Textbooks: The Origin of 'Frankie and Johnnie.'" in: *Missouri Historical Review,* (Jan. 1940,) No. 34, 292–93.

Wilson, Edmund. "Shanty-boy Ballads and Blues," in: *New Republic* (1926) 47: 227–9. Compare: Abbe Niles.

Wilson, Robert Anton. Playboy's *Book of Forbidden Words: A Liberated Dictionary of Improper English*. Chicago: Playboy Press, 1972. Compare: Gillette; Morton; and Trimble; and especially Chapman.

Wilstach, Frank J. *Anecdota Erotica, or Stable Stories*. MS., New York, 1924. 44 pp., typewritten. (NYPL: 3*.) Jokes and verse: typewritten on stationery of the New York Lambs' Club. Compare: Abbott.

Winslow, David J. "Children's Derogatory Epithets," in: *Journal of American Folklore* (1969) 82: 255–63; and reply by Peter Opie, (1970) 83: 354–56.

Winterich, John T. *Mademoiselle from Armentières*. Mount Vernon, New York: Peter Pauper Press, 1953. 101 pre-selected and expurgated stanzas, still "too-hot-to-print" thirty-five years and another World War later.

"*Das Wirtshaus an der Lahn:* Die ungedruckten erotischen Strophen des Volkliedes," in: *Anthropophytéia* (1905) 2: 113–16. Edited by Friedrich S. Krauss and Karl Reiskel, this is the first publicly published collection of the German bawdy four-liners concerning the "Frau Wirtin" landlady, similar to bawdy limericks in British and American folklore. See further: Wells, F.

Wit and Drollery: Joviall poems. London, 1656. Same, corrected and much amended, with additions by Sir J. M(ennis), Ja: S(mith), Sir W. D., J. D., and the most refined Wits of the Age. London: N. Brooks, 1661.

———. With New Additions. London: Blagrave, 1682. (Copy: Harvard University Library) See: Joseph Stokes, *Wit and Drollery, 1656;* (Yale dissertation, 1935.) One of the most interesting of the drollery collections, for folksong inclusions. Compare: *New Academy of Complements*.

Wit and Mirth. See: *Pills to Purge Melancholy*.

Wit's Recreations refined. Augmented with Ingenious Conceites for thc wittie, and Merrie Medicines for the Melancholie. London, 1640. (5 editions by 1667.) Reprinted with *Musarum Deliciæ,* London: Pearson? 1873–74, in 2 vols., with other similar texts. Drollery and obscœna collection.

Wolf, Edwin, II. *American Song Sheets, Slip Ballads, and Poetical Broadsides, 1850–1870: A Catalogue of the Collection of the* (Rosenbach) *Library Company*. Philadelphia, Library Company, 1963.

Wolfenstein, Martha. *Children's Humor: A Psychological Analysis*. Glencoe, Ill.: Free Press/Ned Polsky, 1954. Reprinted, Bloomington, Indiana University Press, 1978. Outstanding study. Compare (including collections of materials): Borneman; Gaignebet; Lowenstein; McCosh; and Turner.

Wolford, Leah Jackson. *The Play-Party in Indiana*. Indianapolis: Indiana Historical Commission, 1916. Compare: Botkin.

Women' Songbook. (Editcd by Judy Busch?) Oral Herstory Library, 2325 Oak Street, Berkeley, Calif. (ca. 1970). Women's Liberation proposed folksongs: "We Don't Need the Men," "Male Supremacy," and 20 others.

Wood, Clement. *Lays for the Laity*. (Bozenkill, New York:) Privately Printed and Not for Sale, 1937. 32 pp. (Copy: G. Legman.) Bawdy art poems with obvious word-expurgations.

Wood, Ray. *Fun in American Folk Rhymes*. Philadelphia, 1952.

———. *Mother Goose in the Ozarks.* Raywood, Texas: The Author, 1938.

———. *What Happened to Mother Goose?* New York, 1946.

The World's Dirtiest Jokes. See: Newbern and Rodebaugh; and *Sex to Sexty.*

The "Wrecks": An Anthology of Ribald Verse. Collected at Reno. Privately Printed for Subscribers Only. (Reno, Nevada, ca. 1933.) (Copies: University of Nevada, Reno; Dr. Arthur Deex, Los Altos, Calif.; G. Legman.) Bawdy songs and poems divided into "mild" and "raw" sections, for unexplained purposes. Issued by the Reno "Wrecks," a sporting club. Largely derived from *Immortalia* (1927), and may have been edited for the club by Thomas R. Smith. Note: Two other editions (not seen) are reported; one entitled *Reno Wrecks* (ca. 1940?) which may be the present edition or a reprint; the other apparently an earlier, shorter collection, entitled in pig latin, *(The) X-Ray.*

(Wright, Nancy.) *Caution! Do Not Attempt to sing these ditties without at least three kegs of beer on hand.* (East Lansing, Michigan, 1951.) 17 or more sheets, 4to, typewritten. (Copies of these sheets now preserved in Indiana University Folklore Archive, but all separately filed by song-titles.) part 2 of a 3-part mimeographed (?) volume of "beer-bust" bawdy songs.

Wylie, Philip. See: *The Bedroom Companion.*

Wyman, Lorraine, and Howard Brockway. *Lonesome Tunes: Folk Songs from the Kentucky Mountains.* New York, 1916.

X-ray. (Pig latin for: *The "Wrecks,"* or *Reno Wrecks.*) Reported variant edition (Reno, Nevado, ca. 1930), giving the original bawdy song-and-poem repertory of the named western sporting club; presumably later enlarged with materials from *Immortalia*, q.v., as *The "Wrecks."*

Yale Tales. (Pittsfield, Mass., 1952.) 14 pp., mimeographed. (Edited by George Zuckerman.) 80 limericks, and ballad "The Good Ship Venus."

Yankah, Kwesi. "From Loose Abuse to Poetic Couplets: The Case of the Fante Tone Riddle," in: *Maledicta* (1984) 7: 167–77. Violently erotic and scatological contests in tone-rhymed abuse among the Fante (Akan) of Ghana. Compare the similar American Negro "dozens" rhymed recitations. S.v. Abrahams; Jackson; and Wepman.

(Yates, John.) *Rubgy Jokes.* London: Sphere Books Ltd., 1968. Bawdy jokes with obscœna and songs, pp. 153–73. Sequels:

(———.) *Son of Rugby Jokes.* London: Sphere Books Ltd., 1970.

(———.) *What Rugby Jokes Did Next.* London: Sphere Books Ltd. 1970. Songs and poems, pp. 94–103.

The Yellow Stream, by I. P. Standing (*pseud.,* U.S., ca. 1932). 38 pp. offset from typewriting. (Copy: G. Legman.) Made-up book, for private mail sales in response to classified magazine advertisements, composed of song texts copied from *Immortalia.* Also later offered as: *The Yellow River,* "Privately Printed" (ca. 1940).

Yumor Russkago naroda v skazkach. See: *Mejdu Druziami,* Second Series.

Zahrt, Lillian Fay. *College Songs.* Bloomington, Indiana, 1962. MS., 50 pp., typewritten. (Copy: Indiana University, Folklore Archive, the sheets being separately filed by song-titles.) Unexpurgated student collection. Compare: Goldstone; Nancy Reeves; Reuss; and Wright.

Zuckerman, George. See: *Yale Tales.*

INDEX

Note: For simplification, and to avoid confusion, all the Folk Songs and Rhymes are indexed by their item numbers (at the tops of the pages), and not by volume and page (at the bottom of the pages). Song Nos. 1 through 180 form Volume I, *Roll Me in Your Arms.* Song Nos. 181 through 244 form Section A of Volume II, *Blow the Candle Out;* followed by all the Rhymes, forming Section B of Volume II. Primary listings are given in bold.